Excel 2003 Power Programming with VBA

John Walkenbach

Wiley Publishing, Inc.

Excel 2003 Power Programming with VBA

Published by
Wiley Publishing, Inc.
10475 Crosspoint Boulevard
Indianapolis, IN 46256
www.wiley.com

Copyright © 2004 by Wiley Publishing, Inc., Indianapolis, Indiana

Published simultaneously in Canada

Library of Congress Catalog Card Number: 2003105685

ISBN: 0-7645-4072-6

Manufactured in the United States of America

10 9 8 7 6 5 4

1B/SZ/RS/QT/IN

Credits

SENIOR ACQUISITIONS EDITOR
Greg Croy

PROJECT EDITOR
Linda Morris

TECHNICAL EDITOR
Bill Manville

SENIOR COPY EDITOR
Teresa Artman

EDITORIAL MANAGER
Leah Cameron

VICE PRESIDENT & EXECUTIVE GROUP PUBLISHER
Richard Swadley

VICE PRESIDENT AND PUBLISHER
Andy Cummings

EDITORIAL DIRECTOR
Mary C. Corder

PROJECT COORDINATOR
Ryan Steffen

GRAPHICS AND PRODUCTION SPECIALISTS
Lauren Goddard
Michael Kruzil
Lynsey Osborn
Julie Trippetti
Melanie Wolven

PROOFREADERS
Carl William Pierce, TECHBOOKS Production Services

SENIOR PERMISSIONS EDITOR
Carmen Krikorian

MEDIA DEVELOPMENT SPECIALIST
Travis Silvers

INDEXER
TECHBOOKS Production Services

About the Author

John Walkenbach is a leading authority on spreadsheet software and is principal of JWalk and Associates Inc., a small San Diego-based consulting firm that specializes in spreadsheet application development. John is the author of more than 30 spreadsheet books and has written more than 300 articles and reviews for a variety of publications, including *PC World, InfoWorld, Windows,* and *PC/Computing.* He also maintains *The Spreadsheet Page,* a popular Internet Web site (www.j-walk.com/ss), and is the developer of Power Utility Pak, an award-winning add-in for Microsoft Excel. John graduated from the University of Missouri and earned a masters degree and a Ph.D. from the University of Montana.

In addition to computers and spreadsheet software, John's other interests include guitar, music, novels, digital photography, and puttering around in the garden.

Preface

Welcome to *Excel 2003 Power Programming with VBA*. If your job involves developing spreadsheets that others will use — or if you simply want to get the most out of Excel — you've come to the right place.

Why I Wrote This Book

Quite a few advanced Excel books are available, but this book is the only one that deals with spreadsheet application development from a larger perspective. Visual Basic for Applications (VBA) is just one component (albeit a fairly large component) of application development. Excel is an extremely deep software product: It has many interesting features that lurk in the background, unbeknownst to the typical user. And you can use some of the well-known features in novel ways.

Millions of people throughout the world use Excel. I monitor the spreadsheet-related newsgroups on the Internet, and it's very clear to me that people need (and want) help in the areas that this book covers. My guess is that only five percent of Excel users really understand what the product is capable of. In this book, I attempt to nudge you into that elite company. Are you up to it?

What You Need to Know

This is not a book for beginning Excel users. If you have no experience with Excel, a better choice might be my *Excel 2003 Bible,* which provides comprehensive coverage of all the features of Excel. It is meant for users of all levels.

To get the most out of this book, you should be a relatively experienced Excel user. I didn't spend much time writing basic how-to information. In fact, I assume that you know the following:

- ◆ How to create workbooks, insert sheets, save files, and so on
- ◆ How to navigate through a workbook
- ◆ How to use the menus and shortcut menus
- ◆ How to manage Excel's toolbars
- ◆ How to enter formulas
- ◆ How to use Excel's worksheet functions

◆ How to name cells and ranges

◆ How to use basic Windows features, such as file management techniques and the Clipboard

If you don't know how to perform the preceding tasks, you could find some of this material over your head, so consider yourself warned. If you're an experienced spreadsheet user who hasn't used Excel 2003, Chapter 2 presents a short overview of what this product offers.

What You Need to Have

To make the best use of this book, you need a copy of Excel. Although the book was written with Excel 2003 in mind, most of the material also applies to Excel 97 and later versions. If you use an earlier version (such as Excel 5 or Excel 95), you're reading the wrong book. Most of the material in this book also applies to Excel for Macintosh. However, I did no compatibility testing with the Mac version, so you're on your own.

Any computer system that can run Windows will suffice, but you'll be much better off with a fast machine with plenty of memory. Excel is a large program, and using it on a slower system or a system with minimal memory can be extremely frustrating.

I recommend using a high-resolution video driver (1024 x 768 is adequate, and 1600 x 1200 is even better). Using a lower resolution display will do in a pinch, but it just doesn't let you see enough onscreen.

To make use of the examples on the companion CD, you also need a CD-ROM drive.

Conventions in This Book

Take a minute to skim this section and learn some of the typographic conventions used throughout this book.

Keyboard conventions

You need to use the keyboard to enter data. In addition, you can work with menus and dialog boxes directly from the keyboard — a method that you might find easier if your hands are already positioned over the keys.

INPUT
Input that you type from the keyboard appears in boldface — for example, enter **=SUM(B2: B50)** into cell B51.

More lengthy input usually appears on a separate line in a monospace font. For example, I might instruct you to enter the following formula:

```
=VLOOKUP(STOCKNUMBER,PRICELIST,2)
```

VBA CODE

This book contains many snippets of VBA code as well as complete procedure listings. Each listing appears in a monospace font; each line of code occupies a separate line. (I copied these listings directly from the VBA module and pasted them into my word processor.) To make the code easier to read, I often use one or more tabs to create indentations. Indentation is optional, but it does help to delineate statements that go together.

If a line of code doesn't fit on a single line in this book, I use the standard VBA line continuation sequence: At the end of a line, a space followed by an underscore character indicates that the line of code extends to the next line. For example, the following two lines are a single line of code:

```
If Right(ActiveCell, 1) = "!" Then ActiveCell _
  = Left(ActiveCell, Len(ActiveCell) - 1)
```

You can enter this code either on two lines, exactly as shown, or on a single line without the underscore character.

FUNCTIONS, FILENAMES, AND NAMED RANGES

Excel's worksheet functions appear in uppercase font, like so: "Enter a SUM formula in cell C20." VBA procedure names, properties, methods, and objects appear in monospace font: "Execute the GetTotals procedure." I often use mixed upper- and lowercase to make these names easier to read.

Mouse conventions

If you're reading this book, you're well versed in mouse usage. The mouse terminology I use is all standard fare: pointing, clicking, right-clicking, dragging, and so on.

About the Figures

All the figures for this book were captured by using Windows XP classic mode — which I much prefer. If you use the default Windows XP display mode, the screen shots on the page will look a bit different from what you see on your screen. The content is exactly the same. The only differences are cosmetic.

What the Icons Mean

Throughout the book, I've used icons to call your attention to points that are particularly important.

I use this icon to indicate that the material discussed is new to Excel 2003. If you're developing an application that will be used for earlier versions of Excel, pay particular attention to these icons.

I use Note icons to tell you that something is important — perhaps a concept that could help you master the task at hand or something fundamental for understanding subsequent material.

Tip icons indicate a more efficient way of doing something or a technique that might not be obvious.

These icons indicate that an example file is on the companion CD-ROM. (See "About the Companion CD-ROM," later in the Introduction.) This CD holds many of the examples that I cover in the book as well as a trial copy of my popular Power Utility Pak software.

I use Caution icons when the operation that I'm describing can cause problems if you're not careful.

I use the Cross Reference icon to refer you to other chapters that have more to say on a subject.

How This Book Is Organized

The chapters of this book are grouped into eight main parts.

Part I: Some Essential Background

In this part, I set the stage for the rest of the book. Chapter 1 presents a brief history of spreadsheets so that you can see how Excel fits into the big picture. In Chapter 2, I offer a conceptual overview of Excel 2003 – quite useful for experienced spreadsheet users who are switching to Excel. In Chapter 3, I cover the essentials of formulas, including some clever techniques that might be new to you. Chapter 4 covers the ins and outs of the various files used and generated by Excel.

Part II: Excel Application Development

This part consists of just two chapters. In Chapter 5, I broadly discuss the concept of a spreadsheet application. Chapter 6 goes into more detail and covers the steps typically involved in a spreadsheet application development project.

Part III: Understanding Visual Basic for Applications

Chapters 7 through 11 make up Part III, and these chapters include everything that you need to know to learn VBA. In this part, I introduce you to VBA, provide programming fundamentals, and detail how to develop VBA subroutines and functions. Chapter 11 contains tons of useful VBA examples.

Part IV: Working with UserForms

The four chapters in this part cover custom dialog boxes (also known as *UserForms*). Chapter 12 presents some built-in alternatives to creating custom UserForms. Chapter 13 provides an introduction to UserForms and the various controls that you can use. Chapters 14 and 15 present many examples of custom dialog boxes, ranging from basic to advanced.

Part V: Advanced Programming Techniques

Part V covers additional techniques that are often considered advanced. The first three chapters discuss how to develop utilities and how to use VBA to work with pivot tables and charts. Chapter 19 covers *event handling,* which enables you to execute procedures automatically when certain events occur. Chapter 20 discusses various techniques that you can use to interact with other applications (such as Word). Chapter 21 concludes Part V with an in-depth discussion of creating add-ins.

Part VI: Developing Applications

The chapters in Part VI deal with important elements of creating user-oriented applications. Chapters 22 and 23 provide information on creating custom toolbars and menus. Chapter 24 presents several different ways to provide online help for your applications. In Chapter 25, I present some basic information about developing user-oriented applications, and I describe such an application in detail.

Part VII: Other Topics

The five chapters in Part VII cover additional topics. Chapter 26 presents information regarding compatibility. In Chapter 27, I discuss various ways to use VBA to work with files. In Chapter 28, I explain how to use VBA to manipulate Visual Basic components such as UserForms and modules. Chapter 29 covers the topic of class modules. I finish the part with a useful chapter that answers many common questions about Excel programming.

Part VIII: Appendixes

Four appendixes round out the book. Appendix A contains useful information about Excel resources online. Appendix B is a reference guide to all of VBA's keywords (statements and functions). I explain VBA error codes in Appendix C, and Appendix D describes the files available on the companion CD-ROM.

About the Companion CD-ROM

The inside back cover of this book contains a CD-ROM that holds many useful examples that I discuss in the text. When I write about computer-related material, I emphasize learning by example. I know that I learn more from a well-thought-out example than from reading a dozen pages in a book. I assume that this is true for many other people. Consequently, I spent more time developing the examples on the CD-ROM than I did writing chapters.

The files on the companion CD-ROM are not compressed, so you can access them directly from the CD.

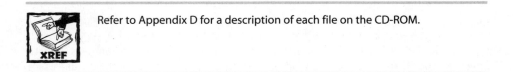

Refer to Appendix D for a description of each file on the CD-ROM.

About the Power Utility Pak Offer

Toward the back of the book, you'll find a coupon that you can redeem for a free copy of my popular Power Utility Pak software (normally $39.95). PUP is an award-winning collection of useful Excel utilities and many new worksheet functions. I developed this package exclusively with VBA.

I think you'll find this product useful in your day-to-day work with Excel, and I urge you to take advantage of this free offer. You can also purchase the complete VBA source code for a nominal fee. Studying the code is an excellent way to pick up some useful programming techniques.

You can take Power Utility Pak for a test drive by installing the 30-day trial version from the companion CD-ROM.

How to Use This Book

You can use this book any way that you please. If you choose to read it cover to cover, be my guest. But because I'm dealing with intermediate-to-advanced subject matter, the chapter order is often immaterial. I suspect that most readers will skip around, picking up useful tidbits here and there. If you're faced with a challenging task, you might try the index first to see whether the book specifically addresses your problem.

Reach Out

The publisher and I want your feedback. After you've had a chance to use this book, please take a moment to visit the Wiley Publishing, Inc. Web site to give us your comments. (Go to www. wiley.com and then click the Contact Us link.) Please be honest in your evaluation. If you thought a particular chapter didn't tell you enough, let us know. Of course, I would prefer to receive comments like, "This is the best book I've ever read," or "Thanks to this book, I was promoted and now make $105,000 a year."

I get at least a dozen questions every day, via e-mail, from people who have read my books. I appreciate the feedback. Unfortunately, I simply don't have the time to reply to questions. Appendix A provides a good list of sources that *can* answer your questions.

I also invite you to visit my Web site, which contains lots of Excel-related material. Despite the massive attempts to make this book completely accurate, a few errors have probably crept into its pages. My Web site includes a list of any such errors. The URL is

http://www.j-walk.com/ss/

Acknowledgments

First of all, thanks to everyone around the world who purchased the previous editions of this book. The daily positive feedback from readers continues to astound and encourage me.

Many of the ideas for the topics in this book came from postings to the Excel Internet newsgroups. Thanks to all who frequent these services; your problems and questions were the inspiration for many of the examples that I present in this book.

This book would not be in your hands if it weren't for the talented people at Wiley Publishing, Inc., including Linda Morris, my project editor, and Teresa Artman, my copy editor. Special thanks to Bill Manville, my technical editor. Bill provided lots of great feedback and suggestions and set me straight on more than a few issues.

John Walkenbach
La Jolla, California

Contents at a Glance

Contents

Part I

Some Essential Background

Chapter 1

Excel 2003: Where It Came From

IN THIS CHAPTER

To fully appreciate the application development features available in Excel 2003, it's important to understand where this product came from and how it fits into the overall scheme of things.

◆ A history of spreadsheets — where they came from, who makes them, and what differentiates them

◆ A discussion of Excel's evolution

◆ An analysis of why Excel is a good tool for developers

IF YOU'VE WORKED with personal computers and spreadsheets over the past decade, this information may be old hat. If you're a trivia buff, this chapter is a gold mine. Study this chapter, and you'll be a hit at the next computer geek party that you attend.

A Brief History of Spreadsheets

Most of us tend to take spreadsheet software for granted. In fact, it may be hard to fathom, but there really was a time when electronic spreadsheets were not available. Back then, people relied instead on clumsy mainframes or calculators and spent hours doing what now takes minutes.

It all started with VisiCalc

The world's first electronic spreadsheet, *VisiCalc,* was conjured up by Dan Bricklin and Bob Frankston back in 1978, when personal computers were pretty much unheard of in the office environment. VisiCalc was written for the Apple II computer, which was an interesting little machine that is something of a toy by today's standards. (But in its day, the Apple II kept me mesmerized for days at a time.) VisiCalc essentially laid the foundation for future spreadsheets, and its row-and-column-based layout and formula syntax are still found in modern spreadsheet products. VisiCalc caught on quickly, and many forward-looking companies purchased the Apple II for the sole purpose of developing their budgets with VisiCalc. Consequently, VisiCalc is often credited for much of the Apple II's initial success.

In the meantime, another class of personal computers was evolving; these PCs ran the CP/M operating system. A company called Sorcim developed SuperCalc, which was a spreadsheet that also attracted a legion of followers.

When the IBM PC arrived on the scene in 1981, legitimizing personal computers, VisiCorp wasted no time porting VisiCalc to this new hardware environment, and Sorcim soon followed with a PC version of SuperCalc.

By current standards, both VisiCalc and SuperCalc were extremely crude. For example, text entered into a cell could not extend beyond the cell — a lengthy title had to be entered into multiple cells. Nevertheless, the capability to automate the budgeting tedium was enough to lure thousands of accountants from paper ledger sheets to floppy disks.

Lotus 1-2-3

Envious of VisiCalc's success, a small group of computer freaks at a start-up company in Cambridge, Massachusetts, refined the spreadsheet concept. Headed by Mitch Kapor and Jonathan Sachs, the company designed a new product and launched the software industry's first full-fledged marketing blitz. I remember seeing a large display ad for 1-2-3 in *The Wall Street Journal*. It was the first time that I'd ever seen software advertised in a general interest publication. Released in January 1983, Lotus Development Corporation's 1-2-3 was an instant success. Despite its $495 price tag (yes, people really paid that much for software), it quickly outsold VisiCalc, rocketing to the top of the sales charts, where it remained for many years.

Lotus 1-2-3 not only improved on all the basics embodied in VisiCalc and SuperCalc but also was the first program to take advantage of the new and unique features found in the powerful 16-bit IBM PC AT. For example, 1-2-3 bypassed the slower DOS calls and wrote text directly to display memory, giving it a snappy and responsive feel that was unusual for the time. The online help system was a breakthrough, and the ingenious "moving bar" menu style set the standard for many years. One feature that really set 1-2-3 apart, though, was its macro capability — a powerful tool that enabled spreadsheet users to record their keystrokes to automate many procedures. When such a macro was "played back," the original keystrokes were sent to the application. Although this was a far cry from today's macro capability, 1-2-3 macros were definitely a step in the right direction.

1-2-3 was not the first integrated package, but it was the first successful one. It combined (1) a powerful electronic spreadsheet with (2) elementary graphics and (3) some limited but handy database features. Easy as 1, 2, 3 — get it?

Lotus followed up the original 1-2-3 Release 1 with Release 1A in April 1983. This product enjoyed tremendous success and put Lotus in the enviable position of virtually owning the spreadsheet market. In September 1985, Release 1A was replaced by Release 2, which was a major upgrade that was superseded by the bug-fixed Release 2.01 the following July. Release 2 introduced *add-ins,* which are special-purpose programs that can be attached to give an application new features and extend the application's useful life. Release 2 also had improved memory management, more @ functions (pronounced *at functions*), four times as many rows as its predecessor, and added support for a math coprocessor. It also enhanced the macro language, whose popularity exceeded the developers' wildest dreams.

Not surprisingly, the success of 1-2-3 spawned many *clones* — work-alike products that usually offered a few additional features and sold at a much lower price. Among the more notable were Paperback Software's VP Planner series and Mosaic Software's Twin. Lotus eventually took legal action against Paperback Software for copyright infringement (for copying the "look and feel" of 1-2-3); the successful suit essentially put Paperback out of business.

In the summer of 1989, Lotus shipped DOS and OS/2 versions of the long-delayed 1-2-3 Release 3. This product literally added a dimension to the familiar row-and-column-based spreadsheet: It extended the paradigm by adding multiple spreadsheet pages. The idea wasn't really new, however; a relatively obscure product called Boeing Calc originated the 3-D spreadsheet concept, and SuperCalc 5 and CubeCalc also incorporated it.

1-2-3 Release 3 offered features that users wanted — features that ultimately became standard fare: multilayered worksheets, the capability to work with multiple files simultaneously, file linking, improved graphics, and direct access to external database files. But it still lacked an important feature that users were begging for: a way to produce high-quality output.

Release 3 began life with a reduced market potential because it required an 80286-based PC and a minimum of 1MB of RAM — fairly hefty requirements in 1989. But Lotus had an ace up its corporate sleeve. Concurrent with the shipping of Release 3, the company surprised nearly everyone by announcing an upgrade of Release 2.01. (The product materialized a few months later as 1-2-3 Release 2.2.) Release 3 was *not* a replacement for Release 2, as most analysts had expected. Rather, Lotus made the brilliant move of splitting the spreadsheet market into two segments: those with high-end hardware and those with more mundane equipment.

1-2-3 Release 2.2 wasn't a panacea for spreadsheet buffs, but it was a significant improvement. The most important Release 2.2 feature was *Always,* an add-in that gave users the ability to churn out attractive reports, complete with multiple type-faces, borders, and shading. In addition, users could view the results onscreen in a WYSIWYG (What You See Is What You Get) manner. Always didn't, however, let users issue any worksheet commands while they viewed and formatted their work in WYSIWYG mode. Despite this rather severe limitation, most 1-2-3 users were overjoyed with this new capability because they could finally produce near-typeset-quality output.

In May 1990, Microsoft released Windows 3.0. As you probably know, Windows changed the way that people used personal computers. Apparently, the decision makers at Lotus weren't convinced that Windows was a significant product, and the company was slow getting out of the gate with its first Windows spreadsheet, 1-2-3 for Windows, which wasn't introduced until late 1991. Worse, this product was, in short, a dud. It didn't really capitalize on the Windows environment and disappointed many users. Consequently, Excel, which had already established itself as the premier Windows spreadsheet, became the overwhelming Windows spreadsheet market leader and has never left that position. Lotus came back with 1-2-3 Release 4 for Windows in June 1993, which was a vast improvement over the original. Release 5 for Windows appeared in mid-1994.

In mid-1994, Lotus unveiled 1-2-3 Release 4.0 for DOS. Many analysts (including myself) expected a product more compatible with the Windows product. But we were wrong; DOS Release 4.0 is simply an upgraded version of Release 3.4. Because of the widespread acceptance of Windows, this should be the last DOS version of 1-2-3 to see the light of day.

Over the years, spreadsheets became less important to Lotus (its flagship product turns out to be Notes). In mid-1995, IBM purchased Lotus Development Corporation. Two more versions of 1-2-3 became available, but it seems to be a case of too little, too late. Excel clearly dominates the spreadsheet market, and 1-2-3 continues to lose market share.

The most recent versions of 1-2-3 feature LotusScript, which is a scripting language similar to Visual Basic for Applications (VBA). Spreadsheet developers haven't exactly embraced this language with open arms. In retrospect, Lotus probably should have licensed VBA from Microsoft.

A Few Words about Copy Protection

In the early days of personal computing, copy-protected software was the rule rather than the exception. Most analysts agree that copy protection makes life more difficult for legitimate users and does very little to actually prevent software piracy.

As you may know, Microsoft Office incorporates *product activation* technology. This technology, which was introduced in Office XP, is targeted to consumers. Product activation technology is designed to prevent "casual copying," and it does not address the vastly more serious problem of real pirates who create and sell counterfeit software.

Ironically, one of the reasons why Microsoft Office initially gained prominence in the marketplace was because it was not copy protected. The competing products at the time (1-2-3 and WordPerfect) were. Other companies realized that copy protection doesn't work, and it soon became history.

Personally, I think the return to copy-protected software is a bad trend for the software industry; it will only make product installation more complex and frustrate legitimate customers when things go wrong.

Quattro Pro

The other significant player in the spreadsheet world is (or, I should say, *was*) Borland International. In 1994, Novell purchased both WordPerfect International and Borland's entire spreadsheet business. In 1996, WordPerfect and Quattro Pro were both purchased by Corel Corporation.

Borland started out in spreadsheets in 1987 with a product called *Quattro*. Essentially a clone of 1-2-3, Quattro offered a few additional features and an arguably better menu system at a much lower price. Importantly, users could opt for a 1-2-3-like menu system that let them use familiar commands and also ensured compatibility with 1-2-3 macros.

In the fall of 1989, Borland began shipping Quattro Pro, which was a more powerful product that built upon the original Quattro and trumped 1-2-3 in just about every area. For example, the first Quattro Pro let you work with multiple worksheets in movable and resizable windows — although it did *not* have a graphical user interface (GUI). More trivia: Quattro Pro was based on an obscure product called Surpass, which Borland acquired.

Released in late 1990, Quattro Pro Version 2.0 added 3-D graphs and a link to Borland's Paradox database. A mere six months later — much to the chagrin of Quattro Pro book authors — Version 3.0 appeared, featuring an optional graphical user interface and a slide show feature. In the spring of 1992, Version 4 appeared, having customizable SpeedBars and an innovative analytical graphics feature. Version 5, which came out in 1994, had only one significant new feature: worksheet notebooks (that is, 3-D worksheets).

Like Lotus, Borland was slow to jump on the Windows bandwagon. When Quattro Pro for Windows finally shipped in the fall of 1992, however, it provided some tough competition for the other two Windows spreadsheets, Excel 4.0 and 1-2-3 Release 1.1 for Windows. Importantly, Quattro Pro for Windows had an innovative feature, known as the *UI Builder,* that let developers and advanced users easily create custom user interfaces.

Also worth noting was a lawsuit between Lotus and Borland. Lotus won the suit, forcing Borland to remove the 1-2-3 macro compatibility and 1-2-3 menu option from Quattro Pro. This ruling was eventually overturned in late 1994, however, and Quattro Pro can now include 1-2-3 compatibility features (as if anyone really cares). Both sides spent millions of dollars on this lengthy legal fight, and when the dust cleared, no real winner emerged.

Borland followed up the original Quattro Pro for Windows with Version 5, which was upgraded to Version 6 after Novell took over Borland's spreadsheet business (see upcoming Figure 1-2). As I write this, the current version of Quattro Pro is Version 9, which is part of WordPerfect Office 2000. This product boasts some impressive specs, including support for 1 million rows and 18,278 columns (something many Excel users would kill for). In the spreadsheet market, Quattro Pro ranks a distant third.

For a while, Quattro Pro seemed the ultimate solution for spreadsheet developers. But then Excel 5 arrived.

Microsoft Excel

And now on to the good stuff.

Most people don't realize that Microsoft's experience with spreadsheets extends back to the early '80s. Over the years, Microsoft's spreadsheet offerings have come a long way, from the barely adequate MultiPlan to the powerful Excel 2003.

In 1982, Microsoft released its first spreadsheet, *MultiPlan*. Designed for computers running the CP/M operating system, the product was subsequently ported to several other platforms, including Apple II, Apple III, XENIX, and MS-DOS.

MultiPlan essentially ignored existing software user-interface standards. Difficult to learn and use, it never earned much of a following in the United States. Not surprisingly, Lotus 1-2-3 pretty much left MultiPlan in the dust.

Excel sort of evolved from MultiPlan, first surfacing in 1985 on the Macintosh. Like all Mac applications, Excel was a graphics-based program (unlike the character-based MultiPlan). In November 1987, Microsoft released the first version of Excel for Windows (labeled Excel 2.0 to correspond with the Macintosh version). Because Windows was not in widespread use at the time, this version included a runtime version of Windows — a special version that had just enough features to run Excel and nothing else. Less than a year later, Microsoft released Excel Version 2.1. In July 1990, Microsoft released a minor upgrade (2.1d) that was compatible with Windows 3.0. Although these 2.*x* versions were quite rudimentary by current standards (see Figure 1-1) and didn't have the attractive, sculpted look of later versions, they attracted a small but loyal group of supporters and provided an excellent foundation for future development. The macro language (XLM) consisted of functions that were evaluated in sequence. It was quite powerful, but very difficult to learn and use. As you'll see, the XLM macro language was replaced by VBA, which is the topic of this book.

Meanwhile, Microsoft developed a version of Excel (numbered 2.20) for OS/2 Presentation Manager, released in September 1989 and upgraded to Version 2.21 about ten months later. OS/2 never quite caught on, despite continued efforts by IBM.

In December 1990, Microsoft released Excel 3 for Windows, which was a significant improvement in both appearance and features (see Figure 1-2). The upgrade included a toolbar, drawing capabilities, a powerful optimization feature (Solver), add-in support, Object Linking and Embedding (OLE) support, 3-D charts, macro buttons, simplified file consolidation, workgroup editing, and wordwrap text in a cell. Excel 3 also had the capability to work with external databases (via the Q+E program). The OS/2 version upgrade appeared five months later.

Version 4, released in the spring of 1992, not only was easier to use but also had more power and sophistication for advanced users (see Figure 1-3). Excel 4 took top honors in virtually every spreadsheet product comparison published in the trade magazines. In the meantime, the relationship between Microsoft and IBM became increasingly strained; Excel 4 was never released for OS/2, and Microsoft has stopped making versions of Excel for OS/2.

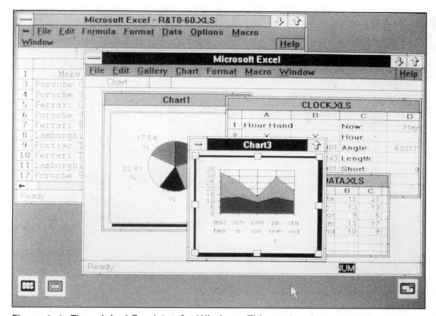

Figure 1-1: The original Excel 2.1 for Windows. This product has come a long way, no?
(Photo courtesy of Microsoft)

Revenues (in thousands)	1991	1992	1993	1994	1995
Canada	184,845	203,330	223,663	246,029	270,632
Mexico	49,292	49,785	50,283	50,786	51,294
United States	1,232,300	1,355,530	1,219,977	1,341,975	1,476,173
North America	1,466,437	1,608,645	1,493,923	1,638,790	1,798,099
France	184,845	194,087	203,791	213,981	224,680
Germany	308,075	369,690	373,387	410,726	414,833
Other European	61,615	92,423	184,846	258,784	362,298
United Kingdom	61,615	67,777	74,555	82,011	90,212
Europe	616,150	723,977		965,502	1,092,023
Australia	48,392	53,231		64,409	70,850
Japan	439,931	879,862		2,287,641	2,973,933
Korea	43,993	65,990		148,478	222,717
Taiwan	65,990	82,488	103,110	128,698	161,110
Far East	598,306	1,081,571	2,020,373	2,629,416	3,428,610
Total Revenue	2,680,893	3,414,193	4,350,875	5,233,708	6,318,732
Cost of Goods Sold	1,340,447	1,474,492	1,621,941	1,784,135	1,962,549

Figure 1-2: Excel 3 was a vast improvement over the original release.
(Photo courtesy of Microsoft)

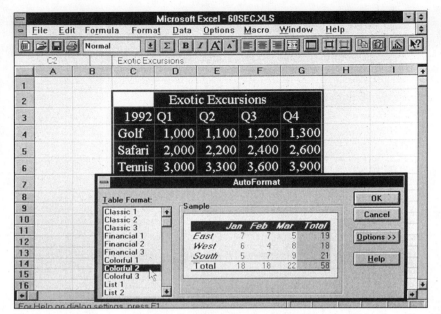

Figure 1-3: Excel 4 was another significant step forward, although still far from Excel 5.
(Photo courtesy of Microsoft)

Excel 5 hit the streets in early 1994 and immediately earned rave reviews. Like its predecessor, it finished at the top of every spreadsheet comparison published in the leading trade magazines. Despite stiff competition from 1-2-3 Release 5 for Windows and Quattro Pro for Windows 5 — both were fine products that could handle just about any spreadsheet task thrown their way — Excel 5 continued to rule the roost. This version, by the way, was the first to feature VBA.

Excel 95 (also known as Excel 7) was released concurrently with Microsoft Windows 95. (Microsoft skipped over Version 6 to make the version numbers consistent across its Office products.) On the surface, Excel 95 didn't appear to be much different from Excel 5. Much of the core code was rewritten, however, and speed improvements were apparent in many areas. Importantly, Excel 95 used the same file format as Excel 5, which is the first time that an Excel upgrade didn't use a new file format. This compatibility wasn't perfect, however, because Excel 95 included a few enhancements in the VBA language. Consequently, it was possible to develop an application using Excel 95 that would load but not run properly in Excel 5.

In early 1997, Microsoft released Office 97, which included Excel 97. Excel 97 is also known as Excel 8. This version included dozens of general enhancements plus a completely new interface for developing VBA-based applications. In addition, the product offered a new way of developing custom dialog boxes (called UserForms rather than dialog sheets). Microsoft tried to make Excel 97 compatible with previous versions, but the compatibility is far from perfect. Many applications that were developed using Excel 5 or Excel 95 require some tweaking before they will work with Excel 97 or later versions.

I discuss compatibility issues in Chapter 26.

Excel 2000 was released in early 1999 and was also sold as part of Office 2000. The enhancements in Excel 2000 dealt primarily with Internet capabilities, although a few significant changes were apparent in the area of programming.

Excel 2002 hit the market in mid-2001. Like its predecessor, it didn't offer a raft of significant new features. Rather, it had a number of minor new features and several refinements of existing features. Perhaps the most compelling new feature was the ability to repair damaged files and save your work when Excel crashed. Excel will continue its market dominance and will remain the standard for users of all levels.

The current version, Excel 2003, is easily the most disappointing upgrade yet. Excel 2003 (also known as Excel 11) was released in Fall, 2003. This version has very few new features, and most Excel 2002 users will not find it necessary to upgrade. A few users may like the ability to import and export eXtensible Markup Language (XML) files and map the data to specific cells in a worksheet. In addition, Microsoft introduced some "rights management" features that allow you to place restrictions on various parts of a workbook (for example, allow only certain users to view a particular worksheet). This version also has some new (but fairly insignificant) list-related features. You'll also find a new feature that lets you compare two sheets side-by-side with synchronized scrolling. The SUBTOTAL function has also been enhanced, and long-time problems with many of the statistical functions have been corrected. In addition, Excel 2003 has a new Help system (which now puts the Help contents in the task pane) and a new "research" feature that enables you to look up a variety of information in the task pane (some of these require a fee-based account).

For some reason, Microsoft chose to offer two sub-versions of Excel 2003. The XML and rights management features are available only in the stand-alone version of Excel and in the version of Excel that's included with the Professional version of Office 2003. Because of this, Excel developers may now need to deal with compatibility issues within a particular version!

Why Excel Is Great for Developers

Excel 2003 is a highly programmable product, and it is easily the best choice for developing spreadsheet-based applications. Excel uses the VBA language, which is now in widespread use.

For developers, Excel's key features include the following:

◆ *File structure:* The multisheet orientation makes it easy to organize elements of an application and store it in a single file. For example, a single workbook file can hold any number of worksheets and chart sheets. UserForms and VBA modules are stored with a workbook but are invisible to the end user.

◆ *Visual Basic for Applications:* This macro language lets you create structured programs directly in Excel. Excel isn't the only spreadsheet to include a structured scripting language (1-2-3 offers LotusScript, for example), but it's certainly the best implementation.

◆ *Easy access to controls:* Excel makes it very easy to add controls such as buttons, list boxes, and option buttons to a worksheet. Implementing these controls often requires little or no macro programming.

◆ *Custom dialog boxes:* You can easily create professional-looking dialog boxes. Excel's UserForm feature (introduced in Excel 97) is a vast improvement over the old dialog sheets.

◆ *Custom worksheet functions:* With VBA, you can create custom worksheet functions to simplify formulas and calculations.

◆ *Customizable menus:* You can change menu elements, add to existing menus, or create entirely new menus. Other products enable you to do this as well, but Excel makes it extremely easy.

◆ *Customizable shortcut menus:* Excel is the only spreadsheet that lets you customize the right-click, context-sensitive shortcut menus.

◆ *Customizable toolbars:* It's easy to create new toolbars as another user interface option. Again, other spreadsheets let you do this as well, but Excel outmuscles them all.

◆ *Powerful data analysis options:* Excel's pivot table feature makes it very easy to summarize large amounts of data with very little effort.

◆ *Microsoft Query:* You can access important data directly from the spreadsheet environment. Data sources include standard database file formats, text files, and Web pages.

◆ *Data Access Objects (DAO) and ActiveX Data Objects (ADO):* These features make it easy to work with external databases using VBA.

◆ *Extensive protection options:* Your applications can be kept confidential and protected from changes. Again, pretty standard fare, but Excel has some advantages.

◆ *Ability to create "compiled" add-ins:* With a single command, you can create XLA add-in files that install seamlessly.

◆ *Support for automation:* With VBA, you can control other applications that support automation. For example, you can generate a report in Microsoft Word.

◆ *Ability to create Web pages:* It's very easy to create a HyperText Markup Language (HTML) document from an Excel workbook.

◆ *Ability to import an XML* file and map the fields to spreadsheet cells.

Excel's Role in Microsoft's Strategy

Currently, most copies of Excel are sold as part of Microsoft Office – a suite of products that includes a variety of other programs. (The exact programs that you get depend on which version of Office you buy.) Obviously, it helps if the programs can communicate well with each other. Microsoft is at the forefront of this trend. All the Office products have extremely similar user interfaces, and all support VBA.

Therefore, after you hone your VBA skills in Excel, you'll be able to put them to good use in other applications – you just need to learn the object mode for the other applications.

Chapter 2

Excel in a Nutshell

IN THIS CHAPTER
In this chapter, I provide a broad overview of the major components of Excel 2003.

- ◆ An introduction to Excel's "object orientation"
- ◆ A conceptual overview of Excel 2003, including a description of its major features
- ◆ Some tips and techniques that even advanced users may find helpful

THIS CHAPTER WILL PROVE especially useful for readers who have experience with another spreadsheet and are moving up to Excel. Veteran 1-2-3 users, for example, usually need help thinking in Excel's terms. But even experienced Excel users still may learn a thing or two by skimming through this chapter.

Thinking in Terms of Objects

When you are developing applications with Excel (especially when you are dabbling with Visual Basic for Applications; VBA), it's helpful to think in terms of *objects*, or Excel elements that you can manipulate manually or via a macro. Some examples of Excel objects are

- ◆ The Excel application itself
- ◆ An Excel workbook
- ◆ A worksheet in a workbook
- ◆ A range in a worksheet
- ◆ A ListBox control on a UserForm (a custom dialog box)
- ◆ A chart sheet
- ◆ A chart on a chart sheet
- ◆ A chart series on a chart

Notice that something of an *object hierarchy* exists here: The Excel object contains workbook objects, which contain worksheet objects, which contain range objects. This hierarchy comprises Excel's *object model*. Excel has more than 200 classes of objects that you can control directly or by using VBA. Other Office 2003 products have their own object models.

 Controlling objects is fundamental to developing applications. Throughout this book, you learn how to automate tasks by controlling Excel's objects, and you do so by using VBA. This concept becomes clearer in subsequent chapters.

Workbooks

One of the most common Excel objects is a *workbook*. Everything that you do in Excel takes place in a workbook, which is stored in a file that, by default, has an XLS extension. An Excel workbook can hold any number of sheets (limited only by memory). There are four types of sheets:

◆ Worksheets

◆ Chart sheets

◆ XLM macro sheets (obsolete, but still supported)

◆ Dialog sheets (obsolete, but still supported)

You can open as many workbooks as you like (each in its own window), but at any given time, only one workbook is the *active workbook*. Similarly, only one sheet in a workbook is the *active sheet*. To activate a sheet, click its sheet tab, which is located at the bottom of the screen. To change a sheet's name, double-click the tab and enter the new text. Right-clicking a tab brings up a shortcut menu.

Beginning with Excel 2002, you can color-code the sheet tabs in a workbook. To do so, choose Format → Sheet → Tab Color. Color-coding sheet tabs may help identify a particular sheet, especially when the workbook has many sheets.

Where Are the VBA Module Sheets?

VBA first appeared in Excel 5. In this version (as well as in Excel 95), a VBA module appeared in a workbook as a separate sheet. A VBA module, as you may know, holds VBA code. Beginning with Excel 97, VBA modules no longer appear as separate sheets. Rather, you work with VBA modules in the Visual Basic Editor (VBE). To view or edit a VBA module, activate the VBE by pressing Alt+F11. Subsequent chapters discuss VBA modules in depth.

You can also hide the window that contains a workbook by using the Window → Hide command. A hidden workbook window remains open, but it is not visible.

Worksheets

The most common type of sheet is a worksheet, which is what people normally think of when they think of a spreadsheet. Worksheets contain cells, and the cells store data and formulas.

Every Excel worksheet has 256 columns and 65,536 rows. And, to answer a common question, the number of rows and columns cannot be changed. You can hide unneeded rows and columns to keep them out of view, but you cannot increase the number of rows or columns. The ability to increase the number of columns is probably among the top ten requests from Excel users, but Microsoft continues to ignore such requests. The reason is that it would require extensive rewriting of a large portion of the code.

 Versions prior to Excel 97 had only 16,384 rows.

The real value of using multiple worksheets in a workbook is not access to more cells. Rather, multiple worksheets enable you to organize your work better. Back in the old days, when a file comprised a single worksheet, developers wasted a lot of time trying to organize the worksheet to hold their information efficiently. Now you can store information on any number of worksheets and still access it instantly by clicking a sheet tab.

As you know, a worksheet cell can hold a constant value or the result of a formula. The value may be a number, a date, a Boolean value (True or False), or text. Every worksheet also has an invisible drawing layer, which lets you insert graphic objects, such as charts, diagrams, drawing objects, UserForm controls, pictures, and embedded objects.

You have complete control over the column widths and row heights — in fact, you can even hide rows and columns (as well as entire worksheets). Text in a cell can be displayed vertically (or at an angle) and even wrap around to occupy multiple lines.

Chart sheets

A chart sheet normally holds a single chart. Many users ignore chart sheets, preferring to store charts on the worksheet's drawing layer. Using chart sheets is optional, but they make it a bit easier to print a chart on a page by itself, and they are especially useful for presentations.

How Big Is a Worksheet?

It's interesting to stop and think about the actual size of a worksheet. Do the arithmetic (256 × 65,536), and you'll see that a worksheet has 16,777,216 cells. Remember that this is in just one worksheet. A single workbook can hold more than one worksheet.

If you're using an 800 x 600 video mode with the default row heights and column widths, you can see 12 columns and 28 rows (or 336 cells) at a time — which is about .002 percent of the entire worksheet. In other words, nearly 50,000 screens of information reside within a single worksheet.

If you entered a single digit into each cell at the relatively rapid clip of one cell per second, it would take you about 194 days, nonstop, to fill up a worksheet. To print the results of your efforts would require more than 36,000 sheets of paper — a stack about six feet high.

Filling an entire workbook with values is not recommended. Such a file would be huge and extremely slow to work with because Windows would be continually paging information to disk. As you may have surmised, Excel does not allocate memory for each cell; only cells that are actually used take up memory.

XLM macro sheets

An XLM macro sheet (also known as an *MS Excel 4 macro sheet*) is essentially a worksheet, but it has some different defaults. More specifically, an XLM macro sheet displays formulas rather than the results of formulas. In addition, the default column width is larger than in a normal worksheet.

As the name suggests, an XLM macro sheet is designed to hold XLM macros. As you may know, the XLM macro system is a holdover from previous versions of Excel (version 4.0 and earlier). Excel 2003 continues to support XLM macros for compatibility reasons — although it no longer provides the option of recording an XLM macro. This book does not cover the XLM macro system; instead, it focuses on the more powerful VBA macro system.

Excel 5/95 dialog sheets

In Excel 5 and Excel 95, you created a custom dialog box by inserting a special dialog sheet. Excel 97 and later versions still support these dialog sheets, but a much better alternative is available: UserForms. You work with UserForms in the VBE.

When you open a workbook that contains an Excel 5/95 dialog sheet, the dialog sheet appears as a sheet in the workbook.

TIP   If, for compatibility purposes, you need to insert an Excel 5/95 dialog sheet, you won't find the command to do so on the Insert menu. The only way to add an Excel 5/95 dialog sheet is to right-click any sheet tab and select Insert from the shortcut menu. Then, in the Insert dialog box, click the MS Excel 5.0 Dialog icon.

I do not discuss Excel 5/95 dialog sheets in this book.

Excel's User Interface

The *user interface* (UI) is the means by which an end user communicates with a computer program. A UI includes elements such as menus, toolbars, dialog boxes, keystroke combinations, and so on. For the most part, Excel uses the standard Windows UI to accept commands, but it deviates from the standard Windows UI in at least one area — Excel's menus are not "standard" Windows menus.

Menus

Beginning with Excel 97, the menus are actually toolbars in disguise. The icons that accompany some menu items are a dead giveaway.

Excel's menu system is relatively straightforward. Two different menu bars exist: one when a worksheet is active; the other when a chart sheet is active or when a chart object in a worksheet is selected. Consistent with Windows conventions, inappropriate menu commands are dimmed, and commands that open a dialog box are followed by an ellipsis. Where appropriate, the menus list any available short-cut key combinations (for example, the Edit menu lists Ctrl+Z as the shortcut key for Edit → Undo).

Several menu items are *cascading menus*. Clicking such a menu item leads to a submenu that has additional commands. (Edit → Fill is a cascading menu, for example.) Cascading menus are indicated by a small, right-pointing arrow.

The entire menu system can be customized by the end user or developer. To do so, choose the View → Toolbars → Customize command. It's important to understand that menu changes made by using this technique are permanent. In other words, the menu changes remain in effect even if you close Excel and restart it. You can, however, reset the menus at any time. Choose View → Toolbars → Customize. In the Customize dialog box, click the Toolbars tab. Select Worksheet Menu Bar (or Chart Menu Bar) from the Toolbars list, and then click Reset.

Excel 5 and Excel 95 included a menu editor feature, which is no longer supported. If you need to modify a menu created with the menu editor found in Excel 5 or Excel 95, you'll need to use Excel 5 or Excel 95 to make the change. Or, seek out a utility program that can do the job. If you need to convert an Excel 5/95 workbook that has menu edits incorporated in it, it is best to use the menu editor to remove those edits before converting the workbook to Excel 97 (or later) format.

Refer to Chapter 23 for more information about customizing menus.

Shortcut menus

Excel also features dozens of shortcut menus. These menus appear when the user right-clicks after selecting one or more objects. The shortcut menus are context-sensitive. In other words, the menu that appears depends on the location of the mouse pointer when you right-click. You can right-click just about anything – a cell, a row or column border, a workbook title bar, a toolbar, and so on.

With VBA, you can customize any of the shortcut menus.

Refer to Chapter 23 for more information about customizing shortcut menus.

Toolbars

Excel 2003 ships with dozens of predefined toolbars (including the two toolbars that function as menus), and you can create as many new toolbars as you like. Choose the View → Toolbars → Customize command to customize toolbars or create new ones. You can distribute customized toolbars by attaching them to workbooks.

You can *dock* toolbars (position them along any edge of the screen) or make them *float*. By default, Excel displays the Standard and Formatting toolbars directly below the menu bar.

The toolbar buttons can be displayed in either of two sizes – although the large size buttons are simply too large in my opinion. A crude but effective toolbar button editor is built into Excel (see Figure 2-1). Excel provides thousands of toolbar button images, however, so you probably won't need to use the button editor.

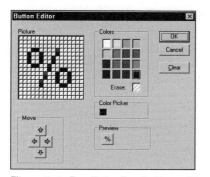

Figure 2-1: Excel's toolbar button editor is nothing to write home about, but it does the job.

 I discuss toolbars in detail in Chapter 22.

Dialog boxes

Most of the menu commands in Excel display a dialog box. These dialog boxes are quite consistent in terms of how they operate.

Most of Excel's dialog boxes are *modal* dialog boxes. This means that you must close the dialog box in order to access your worksheet. A few, however, are "stay on top" dialog boxes. For example, the Find and Replace dialog box (accessible with Edit → Find) can remain open while you're working in a workbook.

Some of Excel's dialog boxes use a notebook tab metaphor, which makes a single dialog box function as several different dialog boxes. The Options dialog box (choose Tools → Options) is an example of a tabbed dialog box (see Figure 2-2). This dialog box has 13 tabs.

Developers can create custom dialog boxes by using the UserForm feature (which debuted in Excel 97). As you'll see, it's possible to create more robust dialog boxes, including tabbed dialog boxes (using the MultiPage control).

Refer to Part IV for information about creating and working with UserForms.

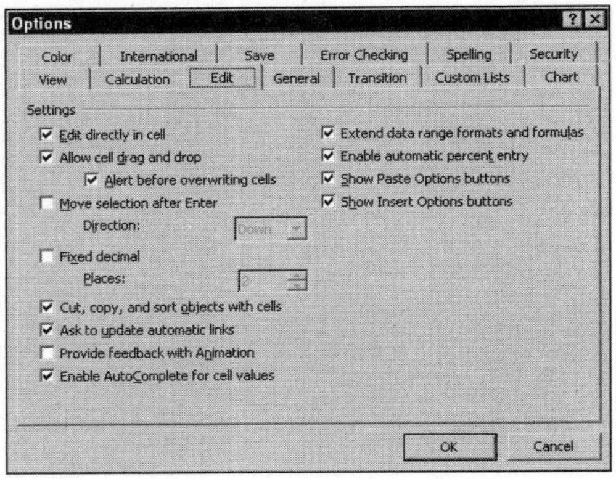

Figure 2-2: Tabbed dialog boxes make many options accessible without overwhelming the user.

Drag-and-drop

Excel's drag-and-drop UI feature enables you to freely drag objects that reside on the drawing layer to change their position. Pressing Ctrl while dragging duplicates the selected objects.

Excel also allows drag-and-drop actions on cells and ranges: You can easily drag a cell or range to a different position. Pressing Ctrl while dragging copies the selected range.

Drag-and-drop is optional; you can disable it in the Edit tab of the Options dialog box.

You can also drag a range to the Windows desktop, thus creating a "scrap" object. You can then drag this object to another workbook (or to another application) and insert it as an Object Linking and Embedding (OLE) object.

Keyboard shortcuts

Excel has many keyboard shortcuts. For example, you can press Ctrl+C to copy a selection. If you're a newcomer to Excel — or you just want to improve your efficiency — I urge you to check out the online help (access the *Keyboard Shortcuts* index and go from there). Learning these shortcuts is key to becoming proficient in Excel. The Help file has tables that summarize useful keyboard commands and shortcuts.

Smart Tags

A *Smart Tag* is a small icon that appears automatically in your worksheet. Clicking a Smart Tag reveals several clickable options. For example, if you copy and paste a range of cells, Excel generates a Smart Tag that appears below the pasted range (see Figure 2-3).

Excel features several other Smart Tags, and additional Smart Tags can be provided by third-party providers. Not everyone likes Smart Tags but fortunately, they can be turned off by using the Smart Tags tab in the AutoCorrect dialog box (choose Tools → AutoCorrect Options to display this dialog box).

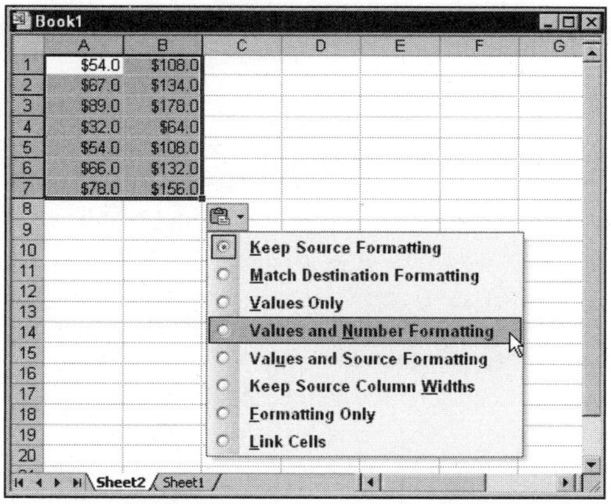

Figure 2-3: This Smart Tag appears when you paste a copied range.

Task pane

Excel 2002 introduced the task pane. This is a multipurpose, user interface element that is normally docked on the right side of Excel's window. The task pane is used for a variety of purposes, including displaying search results from Help, displaying the Office Clipboard, providing research assistance, and mapping eXtensible Markup Language (XML) data.

The task pane functionality has been enhanced quite a bit in Excel 2003.

Data Entry

Data entry in Excel is quite straightforward. Excel interprets each cell entry as one of the following:

- A numeric value (including date and time values)
- Text
- A Boolean value (True or False)
- A formula

Formulas always begin with an equal sign (=). Excel is accommodating to habitual 1-2-3 users, however, and accepts an each-at symbol (@), a plus sign (+), or a minus sign (−) as the first character in a formula. It automatically adjusts the entry after you press Enter.

Data Entry Tips

The following data entry tips are especially useful for those who are moving up to Excel from another spreadsheet:

- If you select a range of cells before entering data, you can press Enter to end a cell entry and move to the next cell in the selected range. Similarly, use Shift+Enter to move up, Tab to move to the right, and Shift+Tab to move to the left.

- To enter data without pressing the arrow keys, enable the Move Selection After Enter option in the Edit tab of the Options dialog box (which you access from the Tools → Options command). You can also choose the direction in which you want to go.

- To enter the same data into each cell of a range, select the range, type the information into the active cell, and then press Ctrl+Enter.

- To copy the contents of the active cell to all other cells in a selected range, press F2 and then press Ctrl+Enter.

- ◆ To fill a range with increments of a single value, press Ctrl while you drag the fill handle at the bottom-right corner of the selection.

- ◆ To create a custom AutoFill list, use the Custom Lists tab of the Options dialog box.

- ◆ To copy a cell without incrementing, drag the fill handle at the corner of the selection. Or press Ctrl+D to copy down or Ctrl+R to copy to the right.

- ◆ You can enter tabs and carriage returns in a cell to make the text easier to read. To enter a tab, press Ctrl+Alt+Tab. To enter a carriage return, press Alt+Enter. Carriage returns cause a cell's contents to wrap within the cell.

- ◆ To enter a fraction, press 0 (zero), a space, and then the fraction (using a forward slash). Excel formats the cell by using the Fraction number format.

- ◆ To automatically format a cell with the Currency format, type the currency symbol (for example, a dollar sign in the U.S.) before the value. To enter a value in Percent format, type a percent sign after the value. You can also include thousand separator symbols to separate thousands (for example, as commas are used in the U.S.: 4,123,434).

- ◆ Press Ctrl+; (semi-colon) to insert the current date and Ctrl+Shift+; to enter the current time into a cell.

- ◆ To set up a cell or range so it only accepts entries of a certain type (or within a certain value range), choose the Data → Validation command.

Formulas, Functions, and Names

Formulas are what make a spreadsheet a spreadsheet. Excel has some important formula-related features that are worth knowing. They enable you to write array formulas, use an intersection operator, include links, and create *megaformulas* (my term for a lengthy and incomprehensible – but very efficient – formula).

Chapter 3 covers formulas and presents lots of tricks and tips.

Excel also has some useful auditing capabilities that help you identify errors or track the logic in an unfamiliar spreadsheet. To access these features, select Tools → Formula Auditing.

Beginning with Excel 2002, the auditing features have been enhanced significantly. For example, you can now use these features to scan your worksheet and identify possibly erroneous formulas. In Figure 2-4, Excel identified a possibly inconsistent formula, and a Smart Tag provides you with some options.

Book1							
	A	B	C	D	E	F	G
1	$32.0	$64.0	$80.0	$96.0			
2	$15.0	$30.0	$37.5	$45.0			
3	$21.0	$42.0	$52.5	$63.0			
4	$65.0	$130.0	$90.0	$195.0			
5	$69.0	$138.0	$172.5	$207.0			
6	$75.0	$150.0	$187.5	$225.0			
7	$102.0	$204.0	$255.0	$306.0			
8	$	$694.0	$875.0	$1,137.0			

Inconsistent Formula
Copy Formula from Left
Help on this error
Ignore Error
Edit in Formula Bar
Error Checking Options...
Show Formula Auditing Toolbar

Sheet2 / Sheet1

Figure 2-4: Excel can monitor your formulas for possible errors.

Worksheet functions enable you to perform calculations or operations that would otherwise be impossible. Excel provides a huge number of built-in functions, and you can access even more functions (many of them quite esoteric) by attaching the Analysis ToolPak add-in.

The easiest way to locate the function that you need is to use the Insert Function dialog box, as shown in Figure 2-5. Access this dialog box by clicking the Insert Function button on the formula bar (or by choosing Insert → Function or pressing Shift+F3). If you're not familiar with this feature, I encourage you to check it out. It's very handy.

Beginning with Excel 2002, you can identify a function by searching for a keyword. This is useful if you can't remember the name of the function. (The *name* is an identifier that enables you to refer to a cell, range, value, formula, or graphic object.) For example, if you're looking for the function that converts text to its ASCII code, you can search for *code* and then click Go. Excel will propose five functions: CODE, CHAR, CELL, TODAY, and CLEAN.

Excel also lets you create your own worksheet functions by using VBA. For details about this powerful feature, see Chapter 10.

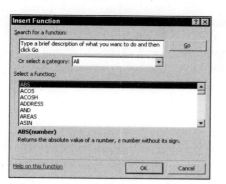

Figure 2-5: The Insert Function dialog box is the best way to insert a function into a formula.

A *name* is an identifier that enables you to refer to a cell, range, value, formula, or graphic object. Formulas that use names are much easier to read than formulas using cell references, and it's much easier to create formulas that use named references.

I discuss names in Chapter 3. As you can see there, Excel handles names in some unique ways.

Customizing the Display

Excel offers a great deal of flexibility regarding what is displayed onscreen (status bar, formula bar, toolbars, and so on). For example, by choosing View → Full Screen, you can get rid of everything except the menu bar, thereby maximizing the amount of information visible. In addition, you can choose Tools → Options to display the Options dialog box. From the View tab, you can customize what is displayed in a worksheet window. (You can even hide scroll bars and grid lines.)

In fact, Excel makes it possible to develop an application that doesn't even look like a spreadsheet.

Selecting Objects

Generally, selecting objects conforms to standard Windows practices. You can select a range of cells by clicking and dragging. Clicking an object that has been placed on the drawing layer selects the object. To select multiple objects or non-contiguous cells, press Ctrl while you select the objects or cells. To select a large range, click a cell at any corner of the range, scroll to the opposite corner of the range, and press Shift while you click the opposite corner cell.

If an object has a macro assigned to it, you'll find that clicking the object executes the macro. To actually select such an object, right-click it and press Esc to hide the shortcut menu.

 In versions prior to Excel 97, clicking an embedded chart selected the chart. In Excel 97 and later, clicking a chart selects a specific object within the chart. To select the chart object itself, press Ctrl while you click the chart.

Formatting

Excel provides two types of formatting: numeric formatting and stylistic formatting.

Numeric formatting

Numeric formatting refers to how a number appears in the cell. In addition to choosing from an extensive list of predefined formats, you can create your own formats (see Figure 2-6). The procedure is thoroughly explained in the online Help system.

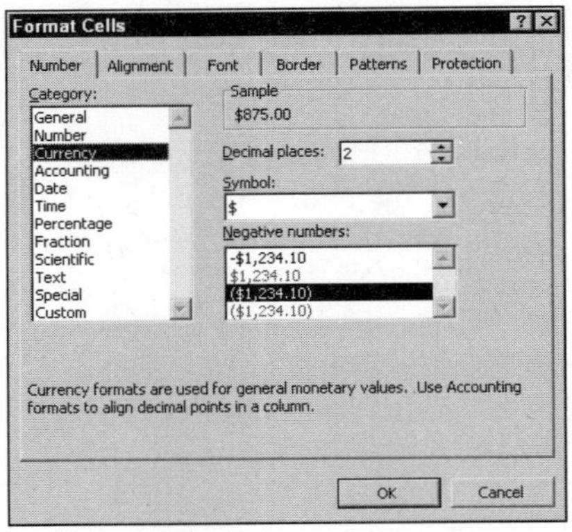

Figure 2-6: Excel's numeric formatting options are very flexible.

Excel applies some numeric formatting automatically, based on the entry. For example, if you precede a number with your currency symbol (a dollar sign in the U.S.), Excel applies Currency number formatting.

Stylistic formatting

Stylistic formatting refers to the formatting that you apply to make your work look good. Many toolbar buttons offer direct access to common formatting options, regardless of whether you're working with cells, drawn objects, or charts. For example, you can use the Fill Color toolbar button to change the background color of a cell, change the fill color of a drawn text box, or change the color of a bar in a chart. But you'll want to access the Format dialog box for the full range of formatting options.

The easiest way to get to the correct dialog box and format an object is to select the object and press Ctrl+1. Or, right-click the object and choose Format *xxx* (where *xxx* is the selected object) from the shortcut menu. This action brings up a tabbed dialog box that holds all the formatting options for the selected object.

Excel's conditional formatting feature is particularly useful. This feature, accessed by choosing Format → Conditional Formatting, allows you to specify formatting that will be applied only if certain conditions are met. For example, you can make cells that exceed a specified value appear in a different color.

Shapes

As I mention earlier in this chapter, each worksheet has an invisible drawing layer, which holds charts, maps, pictures, controls (such as buttons and list boxes), and shapes.

Excel enables you to easily draw a wide variety of geometric shapes directly on your worksheet, thanks to buttons on the Drawing toolbar. In addition, you should be aware that you can group objects into a single object, which is easier to size or position.

Several drawing objects are worthy of additional discussion:

- ◆ *AutoShapes:* You can insert AutoShapes from the Drawing toolbar. You can choose from a huge assortment of shapes. After a shape is placed on your worksheet, you can modify the shape by selecting it and dragging its handles. In addition, you can apply drop shadows, text, or 3-D effects to the shape. Figure 2-7 shows a few examples.

- ◆ *Text box:* The text box provides a way to display text that's independent of row and column boundaries.

- ◆ *Linked picture object:* For some reason, the designers of Excel made the linked picture object rather difficult to generate. Copy a range and then choose the Edit ' Paste Picture Link command (which appears on the Edit menu only when you press Shift). The Paste Picture Link command is useful for printing a noncontiguous selection of ranges. For example, you can "take pictures" of the ranges and then paste the pictures together in a single area, which can then be printed.

♦ *Control placement:* Many of the controls used in custom dialog boxes can be placed directly on a worksheet. Doing so can greatly enhance the usability of some worksheets and eliminate the need to create custom dialog boxes.

♦ *Diagram object type:* Beginning with Excel 2002, you can insert a new object type: Diagrams. Choose Insert → Diagram to select one of six diagram types. After the diagram is inserted, you can use the Diagram toolbar to make basic modifications to it.

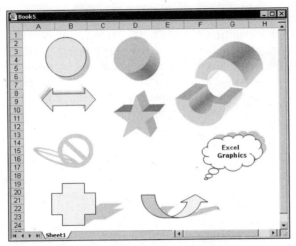

Figure 2-7: AutoShapes added to a worksheet.

Charts

Excel has decent charting capabilities, but this feature is definitely showing its age. As I mention earlier in this chapter, you can store charts on a chart sheet or float them on a worksheet.

The easiest way to create a chart is to select the data to be charted and then use the Chart Wizard. (You can choose the corresponding button on the Standard toolbar.) The Chart Wizard walks you through the steps to create a chart that meets your needs (see Figure 2-8).

You can also create pivot charts. A *pivot chart* is linked to a pivot table, and you can view various graphical summaries of your data by using the same techniques used in a pivot table.

Excel offers extensive chart customization options. If a chart is free-floating, just click a chart element to select it (or double-click it to display its formatting dialog box). Right-clicking a chart element displays a shortcut menu.

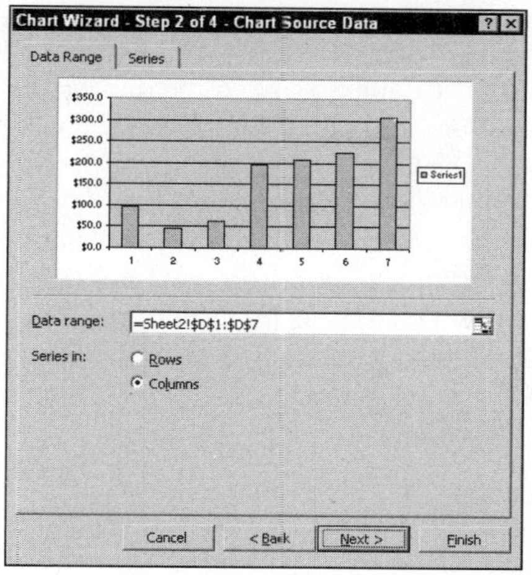

Figure 2-8: Use the Chart Wizard to create a chart.

Macros and Programming

Excel has two macro programming languages: XLM and VBA. The original XLM macro language is obsolete and has been replaced with VBA. Excel 2003 can still execute most XLM macros that you may run across, but you cannot record such macros. You'll want to use VBA to develop new macros.

 Part III of this book is devoted to the VBA language.

Database Access

Over the years, most spreadsheets have enabled users to work with simple flat database tables. (Even the original version of 1-2-3 contained this feature.) Excel has some slick tools.

Using databases from a spreadsheet falls into two categories:

◆ *Worksheet databases:* The entire database is stored in a worksheet, limiting the size of the database. In Excel, a worksheet database can have no more than 65,535 records (the top row holds the field names) and 256 fields.

◆ *External databases:* The data is stored in one or more disk files and accessed as needed.

Worksheet databases

Generally, when the cell pointer is located within a database, Excel recognizes it and displays the field names whenever possible. For example, if you move the cell pointer within a worksheet database and choose the Data → Sort command, Excel lets you select the sort keys by choosing field names from a drop-down list.

Particularly useful is Excel's *AutoFilter* feature, which enables you to display only the records that you want to see. When AutoFilter mode is on, you can filter the data by selecting values from pull-down lists (which appear in place of the field names when you choose the Data → Filter → AutoFilter command). Rows that don't qualify are temporarily hidden. See Figure 2-9 for an example.

	ListPrice	Date Listed	Area	Bedrooms	Baths	SquareFt	Type	Fe
6	ListPrice	Date Listed	Area	Bedrooms	Baths	SquareFt	Type	Fe
7	$350,000	January 12, 2003	N. County	Sort Ascending	2.5	1,991	Condo	FAL
8	$215,000	January 14, 2003	Central	Sort Descending	1.75	2,157	Single Family	TRl
9	$315,000	January 16, 2003	S. County	(All)	2	1,552	Condo	FAL
10	$379,000	January 20, 2003	N. County	(Top 10...)	3	3,000	Single Family	FAL
11	$248,500	January 30, 2003	?	(Custom...)	2.5	2,101	Single Family	TRl
12	$297,500	February 1, 2003	S. County	2 / 3	3.5	2,170	Single Family	FAL
13	$259,900	February 5, 2003	N. County	4	3	1,734	Condo	FAL
14	$325,000	February 9, 2003	S. County	5	3	2,800	Condo	TRl
15	$208,750	February 11, 2003	S. County	6 / 8	3	2,207	Single Family	TRl
16	$227,500	February 11, 2003	S. County	4	3	1,905	Condo	FAL
17	$259,900	February 11, 2003	N. County	3	2.5	2,122	Condo	FAL
18	$405,000	February 14, 2003	N. County	2	3	2,444	Single Family	TRl
19	$236,900	February 15, 2003	S. County	2	2	1,483	Condo	FAL
20	$240,000	February 15, 2003	S. County	3	2.5	1,595	Condo	FAL
21	$304,900	February 17, 2003	S. County	4	3	2,350	Single Family	FAL
22	$349,900	February 21, 2003	N. County	4	3	2,290	Single Family	TRl
23	$249,000	March 1, 2003	Central	4	3	1,940	Single Family	TRl
24	$229,500	March 4, 2003	Central	4	3	2,041	Single Family	FAL
25	$359,900	March 6, 2003	N. County	3	3	1,839	Condo	FAL

Figure 2-9: Excel's AutoFilter enables you to view database records that meet your criteria.

If you prefer to use the traditional spreadsheet database techniques that involve criteria ranges, choose the Data → Filter → Advanced Filter command.

Excel 2003 enables you to specifically designate a range as a list. You do this by choosing the Data → List → Create List command. After creating such a list, AutoFilter is turned on, and Excel displays a summary row at the end of the list (see Figure 2-10). You can pick a summary function from a list of functions (for example, SUM or AVERAGE). Most would agree that this is hardly a groundbreaking feature.

External databases

To work with external database tables, choose the Data → Import External Data → New Database Query command, which executes Microsoft Query and enables you to choose your databases and define queries. The results of a query can be directed back to your worksheet.

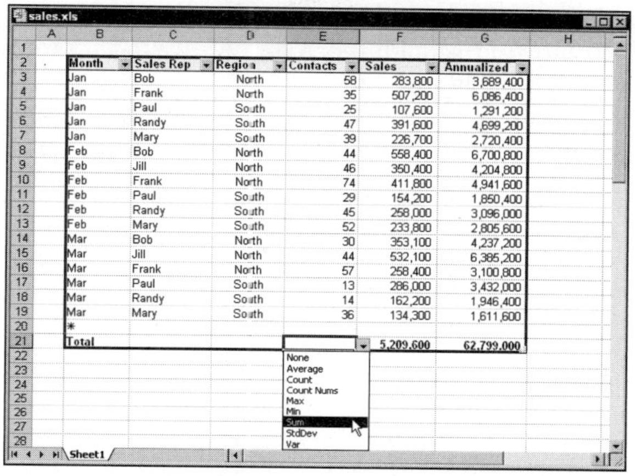

Figure 2-10: Excel 2003's new list feature makes it easy to identify a worksheet database.

Excel also lets you work with data objects independent of Excel through both Data Access Objects (DAO) and ActiveX Data Objects (ADO). Both systems allow you to access external databases from VBA and make changes to the database.

You can also create Web queries to bring in data stored in a corporate intranet or on the Internet. Figure 2-11 shows an example of a Web Query.

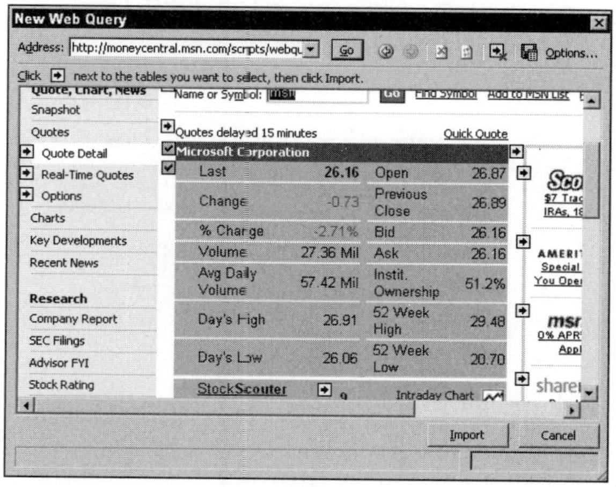

Figure 2-11: Create a Web Query to import data into a worksheet.

Internet Features

Excel includes a number of features that relate to the Internet. For example, you can save a worksheet or an entire workbook in HyperText Markup Language (HTML) format, accessible in a Web browser. In addition, you can insert clickable hyperlinks (including e-mail addresses) directly in cells.

Excel files can be saved as HTML files "with interactivity." This feature, which makes use of the Office Web Components, allows you to post interactive workbooks to a Web server and allow others (who have a license for the Office Web Components) to work with the workbook.

 Refer to Chapter 4 for more information about saving Excel files in HTML format.

XML Features

One of the few new features in Excel deals with XML files. (XML is an accepted standard that enables exchange of data between different applications.) You can import data from an XML file and then map the data to specific worksheet cells.

 This feature is available only in the Profession Edition of Excel 2003.

 Refer to Chapter 4 for more information about Excel 2003's XML features.

Analysis Tools

Excel is certainly no slouch when it comes to analysis. After all, that's what most people use a spreadsheet for. Most analysis tasks can be handled with formulas, but Excel offers many other options.

Outlines

A worksheet outline is often an excellent way to work with hierarchical data such as budgets. Excel can create an outline (horizontal, vertical, or both) automatically, or you can do so manually. After the outline is created, you can collapse or expand it to display various levels of detail.

Automatic subtotals

Excel can automatically insert or remove subtotal formulas in a table set up as a database. It also creates an outline from the data so that you can view only the subtotals or any level of detail that you desire. Figure 2-12 shows some automatic subtotals and the accompanying outline.

	Month	State	Region	Contacts	Sales
1	**Month**	**State**	**Region**	**Contacts**	**Sales**
2	Jan	New York	East	25	107,600
3	Jan	Washington	West	35	507,200
4	Jan	Oregon	West	39	226,700
5	Jan	New Jersey	East	47	391,600
6	Jan	California	West	58	283,800
7	**Jan Total**				1,516,900
8	Feb	New Jersey	East	29	154,200
9	Feb	California	West	44	558,400
10	Feb	Oregon	West	46	350,400
11	Feb	New York	East	52	233,800
12	Feb	Washington	West	74	411,800
13	**Feb Total**				1,708,600
14	Mar	New Jersey	East	14	162,200
15	Mar	California	West	30	353,100
16	Mar	New York	East	36	134,300
17	Mar	Oregon	West	44	532,100
18	Mar	Washington	West	57	258,400
19	**Mar Total**				1,440,100
20	**Grand Total**				4,665,600

Figure 2-12: Excel can automatically insert subtotal formulas and create outlines.

Analysis ToolPak

The Analysis ToolPak add-in provides 19 special-purpose analysis tools (primarily statistical in nature) and many specialized worksheet functions. These tools make Excel suitable for casual statistical analysis.

Many of the statistical functions in Excel have been found to be inaccurate in certain situations. Apparently, those errors have been corrected in Excel 2003.

Pivot tables

One of Excel's most powerful tools is its *pivot tables*. A pivot table is capable of summarizing data in a handy table, and this table can be arranged in many ways simply by dragging your mouse. In addition, a pivot table can be manipulated entirely by VBA. Data for a pivot table comes from a worksheet database or an external database and is stored in a special cache, which enables Excel to recalculate rapidly after a pivot table is altered. Figure 2-13 shows a pivot table.

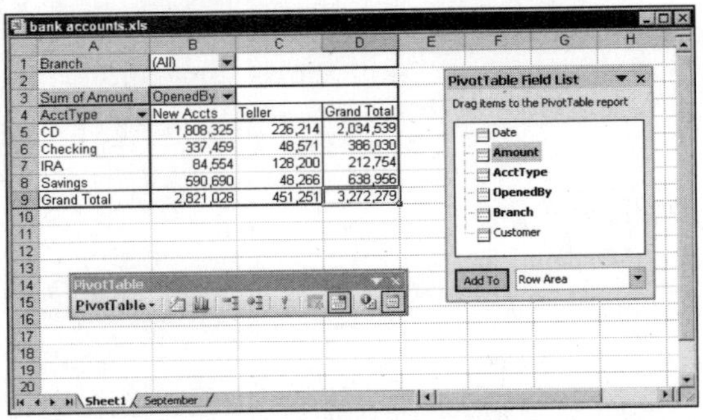

Figure 2-13: Excel's pivot table feature has many applications.

See Chapter 17 for information about manipulating pivot tables with VBA.

Solver

For specialized linear and nonlinear problems, Excel's Solver add-in calculates solutions to what-if scenarios based on adjustable cells, constraint cells, and, optionally, cells that must be maximized or minimized.

Add-Ins

An *add-in* is a program that's attached to an application to give it additional functionality. To attach an Excel add-in, choose the Tools → Add-Ins command.

In addition to the add-ins that ship with Excel, you can download additional add-ins from Microsoft's Web site. And there are many third-party add-ins that you can purchase or download from online services. You can use the coupon in the back of the book to acquire a free copy of the Power Utility Pak add-in. And, as I detail in Chapter 21, it's *very* easy to create your own add-ins.

Compatibility

Excel 97 through Excel 2003 all use the same file format, so file compatibility is not a problem for these four versions. But if you need your file to be compatible with earlier versions of Excel, you have the option of saving a workbook using an earlier file format.

It's important to understand the difference between file compatibility and feature compatibility. For example, even though Excel 97 can open files created with later versions, it cannot handle features that were introduced in later versions.

Excel can import a variety of files generated by other spreadsheet and database products (see Chapter 4 for details).

 Refer to Chapter 26 for more information about compatibility issues for developers.

Protection Options

Excel offers a number of different protection options. For example, you can protect formulas from being overwritten or modified, protect a workbook's structure, password-protect a workbook, and protect your VBA code.

Protecting formulas from being overwritten

In many cases, you might want to protect your formulas from being overwritten or modified. To do so, perform the following steps:

1. Select the cells that *may* be overwritten.

2. Choose Format → Cells and then click the Protection tab of the Format Cells dialog box.

3. In the Protection tab, clear the Locked check box.

4. Click OK to close the Format Cells dialog box.

5. Choose Tools → Protection → Protect Sheet to display the Protect Sheet dialog box, as shown in Figure 2-14. If you use a version prior to Excel 2002, this dialog box looks different.

Figure 2-14: The Protect Sheet dialog box.

6. In the Protect Sheet dialog box, specify a password if desired, and then click OK.

By default, all cells are locked. This has no effect, however, unless you have a protected worksheet.

Beginning with Excel 2002, Excel's protection options are much more flexible. When you protect a worksheet, the Protect Sheet dialog box lets you choose which elements won't be protected. For example, you can allow users to sort data or use AutoFilter on a protected sheet (tasks that weren't possible with earlier versions).

You can also hide your formulas so they won't appear in Excel's formula bar when the cell is activated. To do so, select the formula cells and make sure that the Hidden check box is marked in the Protection tab of the Format Cells dialog box.

Protecting a workbook's structure

When you protect a workbook's structure, you can't add or delete sheets. Choose the Tools→Protection→Protect Workbook command to display the Protect Workbook dialog box, as shown in Figure 2-15. Make sure that you enable the Structure check box. If you also mark the Windows check box, the window can't be moved or resized.

Applying password-protection to a workbook

In some cases, you might want to limit access to a workbook only to those who know the password. To save a workbook file with a password, choose File→Save As. Then, in the Save As dialog box, click the Tools button and select General Options. This displays the Save Options dialog box, as shown in Figure 2-16.

Specify a password and click OK. Or, click the Advanced button to specify the type of encryption to use.

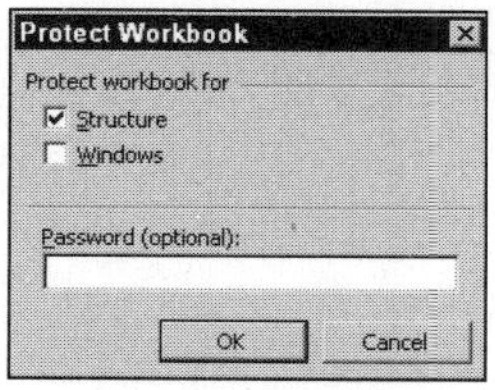

![Protect Workbook dialog box]

Figure 2–15: The Protect Workbook dialog box.

![Save Options dialog box]

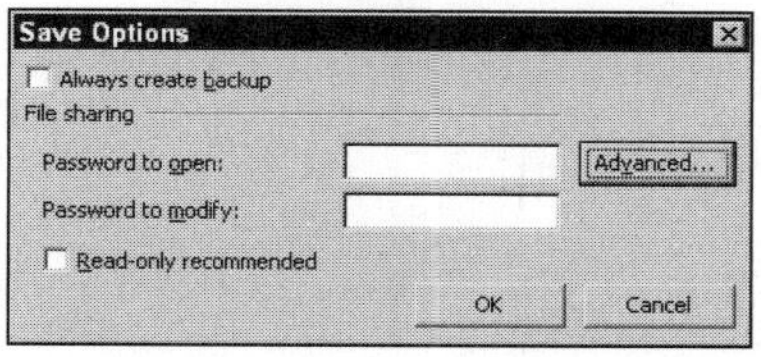

Figure 2–16: Use the Save Options dialog box to save a workbook with a password.

Protecting VBA code with a password

To apply a password to the VBA code in a workbook, activate the VBE and select your project in the Projects window. Then choose Tools → *xxxx* Properties (where *xxxx* corresponds to your Project name). This displays the Project Properties dialog box.

In the Project Properties dialog box, click the Protection tab (see Figure 2-17). Enable the Lock Project for Viewing check box and enter a password (twice). Click OK and then save your file. When the file is closed and then re-opened, a password will be required to view or modify the code.

It's important to keep in mind that Excel is not really a secure application. The protection features, even when used with a password, are intended to prevent casual users from accessing various components of your workbook. Anyone who really wants to defeat your protection can probably do so by using readily available password-cracking utilities (or by knowing a few "secrets").

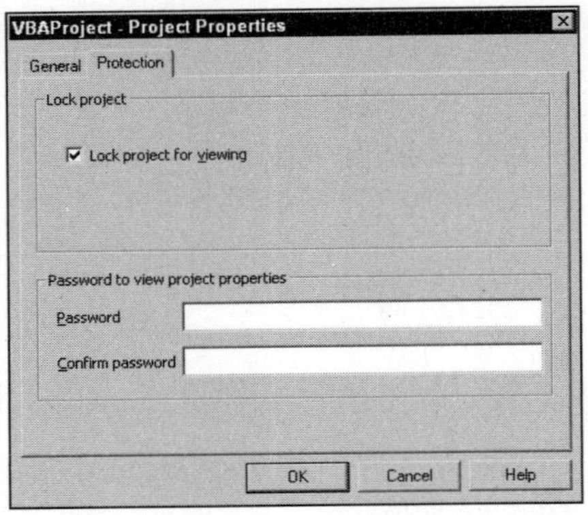

Figure 2-17: Protecting a VBA project with the Project Properties dialog box.

Excel's Help System

One of Excel's most important features is its Help system. When you get stuck, simply type some key words into the Type a Question for Help box, which is located to the right of Excel's menu bar (and also in the VBE). A list of Help topics is displayed in the task pane. Click a topic, and the help text appears in a separate window (see Figure 2-18). There's a good chance that you'll find the answer to your question. At the very least, the Help system will steer you in the right direction.

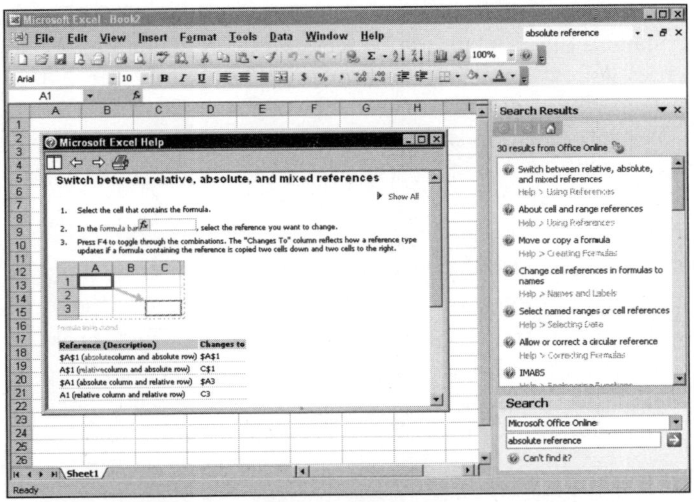

Figure 2-18: The task pane displays Help topics, and the Help text is displayed in a separate window.

Using the task pane to display help topics is new to Excel 2003. The Help information appears in a separate window. This means, of course, that using Help now requires two windows. My opinion is that the person who thought of this "new" method should be fired.

If your system is connected to the Internet, requests for help will search for updated help topics at the Microsoft Web site. To limit the help searches to your local system, select Offline Help from the Search box at the bottom of the task pane.

Chapter 3

Formula Tricks and Techniques

IN THIS CHAPTER

This chapter provides an overview of Excel's formula-related features and describes some techniques that might be new to you.

◆ An overview of Excel formulas

◆ Differentiating between absolute and relative references in formulas

◆ Understanding and using names

◆ Introducing array formulas

◆ Counting and summing cells

◆ Working with dates and times

◆ Creating megaformulas

VIRTUALLY EVERY SUCCESSFUL SPREADSHEET application uses formulas. In fact, constructing formulas can certainly be construed as a type of programming.

 For a much more comprehensive treatment of Excel formulas and functions, refer to my *Excel 2003 Formulas* book.

About Formulas

Formulas, of course, are what make a spreadsheet a spreadsheet. If it weren't for formulas, your worksheet would just be a static document — something that could be produced by a word processor with great support for tables.

Excel has a huge assortment of built-in functions, has excellent support for names, and even supports *array formulas* (a special type of formula that can perform otherwise impossible calculations).

A formula entered into a cell can consist of any of the following elements:

◆ Operators such as + (for addition) and * (for multiplication)

◆ Cell references (including named cells and ranges)

◆ Numbers or text strings

◆ Worksheet functions (such as SUM or AVERAGE)

A formula can consist of up to 1,024 characters. After you enter a formula into a cell, the cell displays the result of the formula. The formula itself appears in the formula bar when the cell is activated, however.

Calculating Formulas

You've probably noticed that the formulas in your worksheet get calculated immediately. If you change a cell that a formula uses, the formula displays a new result with no effort on your part. This is what happens when the Excel Calculation mode is set to Automatic. In this mode (which is the default mode), Excel uses the following rules when calculating your worksheet:

◆ When you make a change — enter or edit data or formulas, for example — Excel immediately calculates those formulas that depend on the new or edited data.

◆ If it's in the middle of a lengthy calculation, Excel temporarily suspends calculation when you need to perform other worksheet tasks; it resumes when you're finished.

◆ Formulas are evaluated in a natural sequence. In other words, if a formula in cell D12 depends on the result of a formula in cell D11, cell D11 is calculated before D12.

Sometimes, however, you might want to control when Excel calculates formulas. For example, if you create a worksheet with thousands of complex formulas, you'll find that operations can slow to a snail's pace while Excel does its thing. In such a case, you should set Excel's calculation mode to Manual. You can do this in the Calculation panel of the Options dialog box.

When you're working in Manual Calculation mode, Excel displays *Calculate* in the status bar when you have any uncalculated formulas. You can press the following shortcut keys to recalculate the formulas:

◆ *F9* calculates the formulas in all open workbooks.

◆ *Shift+F9* calculates only the formulas in the active worksheet. Other worksheets in the same workbook won't be calculated.

♦ *Ctrl+Alt+F9* forces a recalculation of everything. Use it if Excel (for some reason) doesn't seem to be calculating correctly, or if you want to force a recalculation of formulas that use custom functions created with Visual Basic for Applications (VBA).

 Excel's Calculation mode isn't specific to a particular worksheet. When you change Excel's Calculation mode, it affects all open workbooks, not just the active workbook.

Cell and Range References

Most formulas reference one or more cells. This reference can be made by using the cell's or range's address or name (if it has one). Cell references come in four styles:

♦ *Relative:* The reference is fully relative. When the formula is copied, the cell reference adjusts to its new location. Example: A1.

♦ *Absolute:* The reference is fully absolute. When the formula is copied, the cell reference does not change. Example: $A$1.

♦ *Row Absolute:* The reference is partially absolute. When the formula is copied, the column part adjusts, but the row part does not change. Example: A$1.

♦ *Column Absolute:* The reference is partially absolute. When the formula is copied, the row part adjusts, but the column part does not change. Example: $A1.

By default, all cell and range references are relative. To change a reference, you must manually add the dollar signs. Or, when editing a cell in the formula bar, move the cursor to a cell address and press F4 repeatedly to cycle through all four types of cell referencing.

Why use references that aren't relative?

If you think about it, you'll realize that the only reason why you would ever need to change a reference is if you plan to copy the formula. Figure 3-1 demonstrates why this is so. The formula in cell C4 is

=C$3*$B4

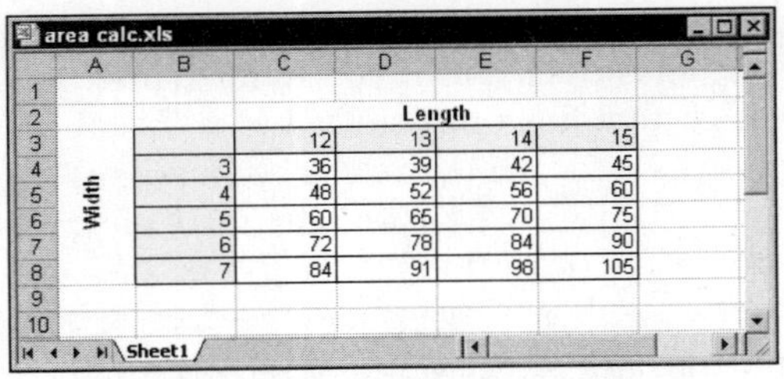

Figure 3-1: An example of using nonrelative references in a formula.

This formula calculates the area for various widths (listed in column B) and lengths (listed in row 3). After the formula is entered, it can then be copied down to C8 and across to F8. Because the formula uses absolute references to row 3 and column B and relative references for other rows and columns, each copied formula produces the correct result. If the formula used only relative references, copying the formula would cause all the references to adjust and thus produce incorrect results.

About R1C1 notation

Normally, Excel uses what's known as *A1 notation:* Each cell address consists of a column letter and a row number. However, Excel also supports *R1C1 notation.* In this system, cell A1 is referred to as cell R1C1, cell A2 as R2C1, and so on.

To change to R1C1 notation, choose Tools → Options, click the General tab, and place a check mark next to the R1C1 reference style. After you do so, you'll notice that the column letters all change to numbers. All the cell and range references in your formulas are also adjusted.

Table 3-1 presents some examples of formulas that use standard notation and R1C1 notation. The formula is assumed to be in cell B1 (also known as R1C2).

TABLE 3-1 COMPARING SIMPLE FORMULAS IN TWO NOTATIONS

Standard	R1C1
=A1+1	=RC[-1]+1
=$A$1+1	=R1C1+1
=$A1+1	=RC1+1
=A$1+1	=R1C[-1]+1
=SUM(A1:A10)	=SUM(RC[-1]:R[9]C[-1])
=SUM($A$1:$A$10)	=SUM(R1C1:R10C1)

If you find R1C1 notation confusing, you're not alone. R1C1 notation isn't too bad when you're dealing with absolute references. But when relative references are involved, the brackets can drive you nuts.

The numbers in brackets refer to the relative position of the references. For example, R[-5]C[-3] specifies the cell that's five rows above and three columns to the left. On the other hand, R[5]C[3] references the cell that's five rows below and three columns to the right. If the brackets are omitted, the notation specifies the same row or column. For example, R[5]C refers to the cell five rows below in the same column.

Although you probably won't use R1C1 notation as your standard system, it *does* have at least one good use. Using R1C1 notation makes it very easy to spot an erroneous formula. When you copy a formula, every copied formula is exactly the same in R1C1 notation. This is true regardless of the types of cell references that you use (relative, absolute, or mixed). Therefore, you can switch to R1C1 notation and check your copied formulas. If one looks different from its surrounding formulas, there's a good chance that it might be incorrect.

In addition, if you write VBA code to create worksheet formulas, you might find it easier to create the formulas by using R1C1 notation.

Referencing other sheets or workbooks

References to cells and ranges need not be in the same sheet as the formula. To refer to a cell in a different worksheet, precede the cell reference with the sheet name followed by an exclamation point. Here's an example of a formula that uses a cell reference in a different worksheet:

```
=Sheet2!A1+1
```

You can also create link formulas that refer to a cell in a different workbook. To do so, precede the cell reference with the workbook name (in square brackets), the worksheet name, and an exclamation point. Here's an example:

```
=[Budget.xls]Sheet1!A1+1
```

If the workbook name in the reference includes one or more spaces, you must enclose it (and the sheet name) in single quotation marks. For example:

```
='[Budget For 2003.xls]Sheet1'!A1+A1
```

If the linked workbook is closed, you must add the complete path to the workbook reference. Here's an example:

```
='C:\MSOffice\Excel\[Budget For 2003.xls]Sheet1'!A1+A1
```

Using Links to Recover Data in a Corrupt File

Excel 2002 and later versions has a detect-and-repair feature that attempts to fix damaged or corrupt files. If this feature doesn't work for you (or if you use an earlier version of Excel), you can try the technique described here.

If you are unable to load a corrupted Excel workbook, you can write a link formula to recover all or part of the data (but not the formulas). You can do so because the source file in a link formula does not need to be open. If your corrupt file is named `Badfile.xls`, for example, open a blank workbook and enter the following formula into cell A1 of `Sheet1` to attempt to recover the data from `Sheet1` of the corrupt workbook file:

```
=['C:\Files\[Badfile.xls]Sheet1,!A1
```

where `Badfile.xls` is the name of the corrupted workbook. In your new workbook, copy this formula down and to the right to recover as much information as you can. A better approach, however, is to maintain a backup of your important files.

Although you can enter link formulas directly, you can also create the reference by using normal pointing methods. To do so, the source file must be open. When you do so, Excel creates absolute cell references. (If you plan to copy the formula to other cells, make the references relative.)

Working with links can be tricky. For example, if you choose the File → Save As command to make a backup copy of the source worksheet, you automatically change the link formulas to refer to the new file (not usually what you want to do). Another way to mess up your links is to rename the source workbook when the dependent workbook is not open.

Using Names

One of the most useful features in Excel is its ability to provide meaningful names for various items. For example, you can name cells, ranges, rows, columns, charts, and other objects. An advantage unique to Excel is that you can name values or formulas that don't even appear in cells in your worksheet (see the "Naming constants" section later in this chapter).

Naming cells and ranges

You create names for cells or ranges by choosing the Insert → Name → Define command (or by pressing Ctrl+F3). An even faster way to create names is to use the Name Box (the drop-down list at the left side of the formula bar). When using the Name Box, just select the cell or range, type the name into the Name Box, and press Enter.

You can choose the Insert → Name → Create command to create names automatically for cells or ranges based on row or column titles on your worksheet. In Figure 3-2, for example, C3:F3 is named *North,* C4:F4 is named *South,* and so on. Vertically, C3:C6 is named *Qtr1,* D3:D6 is named *Qtr2,* and so on.

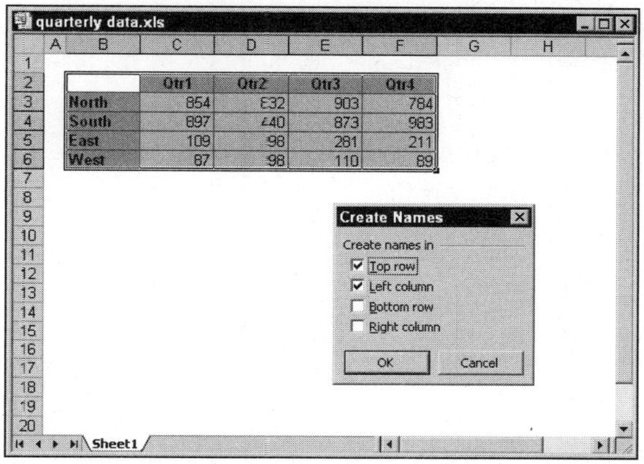

Figure 3-2: Excel makes it easy to create names that use descriptive text in your worksheet.

Using names is especially important if you write VBA code that uses cell or range references. The reason? VBA does not automatically update its references if you move a cell or range that's referred to in a VBA statement. For example, if your VBA code writes a value to Range("C4"), the data will be written to the wrong cell if the user inserts a new row above or a new column to the left of cell C4. Using a reference to a name cell such as Range("InterestRate") avoids these potential problems.

Applying names to existing references

When you create a new name for a cell or a range, Excel doesn't automatically use the name in place of existing references in your formulas. For example, assume that you have the following formula in cell F10:

```
=A1-A2
```

If you define the names *Income* for A1 and *Expenses* for A2, Excel won't automatically change your formula to =Income-Expenses. It's fairly easy to replace cell or range references with their corresponding names, however. Start by selecting the range that you want to modify. Then choose the Insert → Name → Apply command. In the Apply Names dialog box, select the names that you want to apply and then click OK. Excel replaces the range references with the names in the selected cells.

Hidden Names

Some Excel macros and add-ins create hidden names. These are names that exist in a workbook but don't appear in the Define Name dialog box. For example, the Solver add-in creates a number of hidden names. Normally, you can just ignore these hidden names. However, sometimes these hidden names create a problem. If you copy a sheet to another workbook, the hidden names are also copied, and they might create a link that is very difficult to track down.

You can use the following VBA procedure to delete all hidden names in a workbook:

```
Sub DeleteHiddenNames()
    Dim n As Name
    Dim Count As Integer
    For Each n In ActiveWorkbook.Names
        If Not n.Visible Then
            n.Delete
            Count = Count + 1
        End If
    Next n
    MsgBox Count & " hidden names were deleted."
End Sub
```

Unfortunately, there is no way to automatically unapply names. In other words, if a formula uses a name, you can't convert the name to an actual cell or range reference. Even worse, if you delete a name that is used in a formula, the formula does not revert to the cell or range address — it simply returns a #NAME? error.

My Power Utility Pak add-in (available on the companion CD-ROM) includes a utility that scans all formulas in a selection and automatically replaces names with their cell addresses.

Intersecting names

Excel has a special operator, called the *intersection operator,* that comes into play when you're dealing with ranges. This operator is a space character. Using names with the intersection operator makes it very easy to create meaningful formulas. For this example, refer to Figure 3-2. If you enter the following formula into a cell:

```
=Qtr2 South
```

the result is 440 — the intersection of the Qtr2 range and the South range. To get the total for the West region, you can use this formula:

```
=SUM(West)
```

Naming columns and rows

With Excel, you can also name complete rows and columns. In the preceding example, the name *Qtr1* is assigned to the range C3:C6. Alternatively, Qtr1 could be assigned to all of column C, Qtr2 to column D, and so on. You also can do the same horizontally so that *North* refers to row 3, *South* to row 4, and so on.

The intersection operator works exactly as before, but now you can add more regions or quarters without having to change the existing names.

When naming columns and rows, make sure that you don't store any extraneous information in named rows or columns. For example, remember that if you insert a value in cell C7, it is included in the Qtr1 range.

Scoping names

A named cell or range normally has a workbook-level *scope* — in other words, you can use the name in any worksheet in the workbook.

Another option is to create names that have a worksheet-level scope. To create a worksheet-level name, define the name by preceding it with the worksheet name followed by an exclamation point: for example, *Sheet1!Sales*. If the name is used on the sheet in which it is designed, you can omit the sheet qualifier when you reference the name. The Define Name dialog box lists worksheet-level names only if the sheet on which they are defined is active. You can, however, reference a worksheet-level on a different sheet if you precede the name with the sheet qualifier.

If you decide to use a combination of workbook-level and worksheet-level names, make sure that you understand how this works, or you may be in for some surprises when you figure out that your names don't refer to what you think they refer to.

Naming constants

Virtually every experienced Excel user knows how to create cell and range names (although not all Excel users actually do so). But most Excel users do not know that you can use names to refer to values that don't appear in your worksheet: that is, *constants*.

"Natural Language" References

Beginning with Excel 97, you can write "natural language" formulas that use row and column headers. It's not necessary to actually define these names — Excel figures them out automatically. You connect these pseudo-names by using the intersection operator (that is, a space character). For example, you might create a formula like this:

```
=January Sales
```

Excel would display the value at the intersection of the column header (Sales) and the row header (January).

Although this type of thing may be convenient, I suggest that you avoid this feature like the plague. Using these pseudo-names is unreliable and difficult to document, and you cannot use these names in your VBA code. When this feature first became available, Microsoft touted it as a significant ease-of-use feature. Microsoft now downplays this feature, and it is turned off by default. You can check the value of Accept Labels in Formulas setting in the Calculation panel of the Options dialog box.

Suppose that many formulas in your worksheet need to use a particular interest rate. Some people would type the interest rate into a cell and give it a name, such as *RATE,* so that they could use the name in their formulas. For example, the following formula uses the name RATE:

```
=RATE*A3
```

The other alternative is to call up the Define Name dialog box and enter the interest rate directly into the Refers To box (see Figure 3-3). Then you can use the name in your formulas just as if the value were stored in a cell. If the interest rate changes, just change the definition for RATE, and Excel updates all the cells that contain this name.

Figure 3-3: Excel lets you name constants that don't appear in worksheet cells.

TIP By the way, this technique also works for text. For example, you can define the name IWC to stand for *International Widget Corporation*. Then you can enter **=IWC** into a cell, and the cell displays the full name.

Naming formulas

In addition to naming cells, ranges, and constants, you can also enter a formula directly into the Refers To box in the Define Name dialog box to create a named formula. The formula that you enter uses cell references relative to the active cell — the cell that receives the formula. If you use the mouse to indicate related cells in the act of building a formula, however, the references will be absolute.

Figure 3-4 shows a formula (=A1^B1) entered directly in the Refers To box in the Define Name dialog box. In this case, the active cell is C1, so the formula refers to the two cells to its left. (Notice that the cell references are relative.) After this name is defined, entering **=Power** into a cell raises the value two cells to the left to the power represented by the cell directly to the left. For example, if B10 contains 3 and C10 contains 4, entering the following formula into cell D10 will return a value of 81 (3 to the 4th power):

```
=Power
```

```
Define Name                                          ×
Names in workbook:
Power                                            ┌──────┐
                                                 │  OK  │
                                                 └──────┘
                                                 ┌──────┐
                                                 │ Close│
                                                 └──────┘
                                                 ┌──────┐
                                                 │  Add │
                                                 └──────┘
                                                 ┌──────┐
                                                 │Delete│
                                                 └──────┘

Refers to:
=A1^B1│
```

Figure 3-4: You can name a formula that doesn't appear in any worksheet cell.

When you call up the Define Name dialog box after creating the named formula, you'll find that the Refers To box displays a formula that is relative to the active cell. For example, if cell D32 is active, the Refers To box displays

```
=Sheet1!B32^Sheet1!C32
```

Notice that Excel appends the worksheet name to the cells references used in your formula. This, of course, will cause the named formula to produce incorrect results if you use it on a worksheet other than the one in which it was defined. If you would like to use this named formula on a sheet other than Sheet1, you need to remove the sheet references from the formula (but keep the exclamation points). For example:

```
=!A1^!B1
```

After you understand the concept, you might discover some new uses for named formulas. One distinct advantage is apparent if you need to modify the formula. You can just change the definition in the Names in Workbook field rather than edit each occurrence of the formula.

 The companion CD-ROM contains a workbook with several examples of named formulas.

Naming objects

In addition to providing names for cells and ranges, you can give more meaningful names to objects such as charts and shapes. This can make it easier to refer to such objects, especially when you refer to them in your VBA code.

The Secret to Understanding Cell and Range Names

Excel users often refer to *named ranges* and *named cells*. In fact, I've used these terms frequently throughout this chapter. Actually, this terminology is not quite accurate.

Here's the secret to understanding names:

When you create a name for a cell or a range in Excel, you're actually creating a named formula — a formula that doesn't exist in a cell. Rather, these named formulas exist in Excel's memory.

When you work with the Define Name dialog box, the Refers To field contains the formula, and the Names in Workbook field contains the formula's name. You'll find that the contents of the Refers To field always begins with an equal sign — which makes it a formula.

This is not exactly an earthshaking revelation, but keeping this "secret" in mind could help you understand what's going on behind the scenes when you create and use names in your workbooks.

Contrary to what you might think, the Insert → Name → Define command doesn't enable you to name objects; it works only for cells and ranges. The only way to change the name of a nonrange object is to use the Name box, which is located to the left of the formula bar. Just select the item, type the new name in the Name box, and then press Enter.

If you simply click elsewhere in your workbook after typing the name in the Name box, the name won't stick. You *must* press Enter.

Formula Errors

It's not uncommon to enter a formula and receive an error in return. Formulas can return an error value if a cell that they refer to has an error value. This is known as the *ripple effect* – a single error value can make its way to lots of other cells that contain formulas that depend on the cell. The Excel Formula Auditing toolbar contains tools that can help you trace the source of formula errors.

Table 3-2 lists the types of error values that may appear in a cell that has a formula.

TABLE 3-2 EXCEL ERROR VALUES

Error Value	Explanation
#DIV/0!	The formula is trying to divide by 0 (zero) (an operation that's not allowed on this planet). This error also occurs when the formula attempts to divide by a cell that is empty.
#N/A	The formula is referring (directly or indirectly) to a cell that uses the NA worksheet function to signal the fact that data is not available. A LOOKUP function that can't locate a value also returns #NA.
#NAME?	The formula uses a name that Excel doesn't recognize. This can happen if you delete a name that's used in the formula or if you have unmatched quotes when using text. A formula will also display this error if it uses a function defined in an add-in and that add-in is not installed.
#NULL!	The formula uses an intersection of two ranges that don't intersect. (This concept is described earlier in the chapter.)

Continued

TABLE 3-2 EXCEL ERROR VALUES *(Continued)*

Error Value	Explanation
#NUM!	There is a problem with a function argument; for example, the SQRT function is attempting to calculate the square root of a negative number. This error also appears if a calculated value is too large or small. Excel does not support non-zero values which are less than 1E-307 or greater than 1E+308 in absolute value.
#REF!	The formula refers to a cell that isn't valid. This can happen if the cell has been deleted from the worksheet.
#VALUE!	The formula includes an argument or operand of the wrong type. An *operand* is a value or cell reference that a formula uses to calculate a result. This error also occurs if your formula uses a custom VBA worksheet function that contains an error.

Array Formulas

An *array* is simply a collection of cells or values that is operated on as a group. An *array formula* is a special type of formula that works with arrays. An array formula can produce a single result, or it can produce multiple results — with each result displayed in a separate cell (because Excel can fit only one value in a cell).

For example, when you multiply a 1 x 5 array by another 1 x 5 array, the result is a third 1 x 5 array. In other words, the result of this kind of operation occupies five cells; each element in the first array is multiplied by each corresponding element in the second array to create five new values, each getting its own cell. The array formula that follows multiplies the values in A1:A5 by the corresponding values in B1:B5. This array formula is entered into five cells simultaneously:

```
=A1:A5*B1:B5
```

 You enter an array formula by pressing Ctrl+Shift+Enter. To remind you that a formula is an array formula, Excel surrounds it with curly brackets ({}) in the formula bar. Don't enter the brackets yourself.

An array formula example

Excel's array formulas enable you to perform individual operations on each cell in a range in much the same way that a program language's looping feature enables you to work with elements of an array. If you've never used array formulas before, this section will get your feet wet with a hands-on example.

Figure 3-5 shows a worksheet with text in A1:A5. The goal of this exercise is to create a single formula that returns the sum of the total number of characters in the range. Without the single formula requirement, you would write a formula with the LEN function, copy it down the column, and then use the SUM function to add the results of the intermediate formulas.

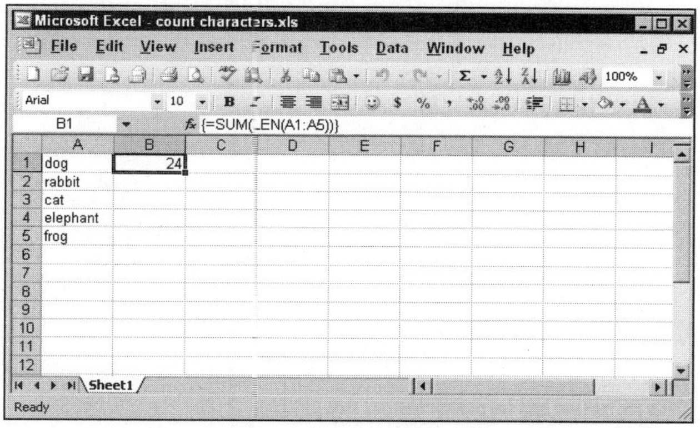

Figure 3-5: Cell B1 contains an array formula that returns the total number of characters contained in range A1:A5.

To demonstrate how an array formula can occupy more than one cell, create the worksheet shown in Figure 3-5, and then try this:

1. Select the range B1:B5.

2. Type the following formula:

   ```
   =LEN(A1:A5)
   ```

3. Press Ctrl+Shift+Enter.

The preceding steps enter a single array formula into five cells. Enter a SUM formula that adds the values in B1:B5, and you'll see that the total number of characters in A1:A5 is 24.

Here's the key point: It's not necessary to actually *display* those five array elements. Rather, Excel can store the array in memory. Knowing this, you can type the following single formula in any blank cell. **Remember:** Make sure that you enter it by pressing Ctrl+Shift+Enter:

```
=SUM(LEN(A1:A5))
```

This formula is displayed in the formula bar surrounded by brackets (refer to Figure 3-5):

```
{=SUM(LEN(A1:A5))}
```

This formula essentially creates a five-element array (in memory) that consists of the length of each string in A1:A5. The SUM function uses this array as its argument, and the formula returns 27.

An array formula calendar

Figure 3-6 shows a worksheet set up to display a calendar for any month. Believe it or not, the calendar is created with a single array formula that occupies 42 cells.

array examples.xls						
December ▼ ◄		► 2003					
December 2003							
Sun	Mon	Tue	Wed	Thu	Fri	Sat
	1	2	3	4	5	6
7	8	9	10	11	12	13
14	15	16	17	18	19	20
21	22	23	24	25	26	27
28	29	30	31			

Figure 3-6: One array formula is all it takes to make a calendar for any month in any year.

 The companion CD-ROM contains a workbook with the calendar example as well as several additional array formula examples.

Array formula pros and cons

The advantages of using array formulas rather than single-cell formulas include the following:

- ◆ They can sometimes use less memory.

- ◆ They can make your work much more efficient.

- ◆ They can eliminate the need for intermediate formulas.

- ◆ They can enable you to do things that would be difficult or impossible otherwise. For example, you can use an array formula to perform counts using multiple criteria (see the next section).

A few disadvantages of using array formulas are the following:

- ◆ Some can slow your spreadsheet recalculation time to a crawl.

- ◆ They can make your worksheet more difficult for others to understand.

- ◆ You must remember to enter an array formula with a special key sequence (by pressing Ctrl+Shift+Enter).

Counting and Summing Techniques

I spend quite a bit of time reading the Excel newsgroups on the Internet. Many of the questions posed in these groups deal with counting or summing various types of cells. In an attempt to answer most of these questions, I present a number of formula examples that deal with counting various things on a worksheet. You can probably adapt these formulas to your own needs.

Using the COUNTIF or SUMIF function

Excel's SUM, COUNT, COUNTA, and COUNTBLANK functions are very straightforward, so I'll skip them and get straight to the more useful COUNTIF and SUMIF functions.

- ◆ COUNTIF takes two arguments:
  - ■ The range that holds the data to be counted
  - ■ The criteria used to determine whether the cell is included in the count
- ◆ SUMIF takes three arguments:
  - ■ The range to be evaluated
  - ■ The criteria used to determine whether the cell is included in the count
  - ■ The range that holds the data to be summed

Table 3-3 demonstrates a variety of uses for the COUNTIF function. The formulas assume that you have a range named *data*. (You'll need to substitute the actual range name or address in these formulas.) Also, be aware that the second argument for the COUNTIF function can be a reference to a cell that contains the search criteria.

TABLE 3-3 EXAMPLES OF COMMON USES FOR THE COUNTIF FUNCTION

Formula	Return Value
=COUNTIF(data,12)	The number of cells that contain the value 12
=COUNTIF(data,1)+COUNTIF(data,12)	The number of cells that contain 1 or 12
=COUNTIF(data,"<0")	The number of cells that contain a negative number
=COUNTIF(data,"<>0")	The number of nonzero values
=COUNTIF(data,">=1")-COUNTIF(data,">10")	The number of cells that contain a value between 1 and 10
=COUNTIF(data,"yes")	The number of cells that contain the word *yes* (not case-sensitive)
=COUNTIF(data,"*")	The number of cells that contain any text
=COUNTIF(data,"*s*")	The number of cells that contain the letter *s* (not case-sensitive)
=COUNTIF(data,"???")	The number of three-letter words

Using array formulas to count and sum

If none of the standard counting techniques fits the bill, you may be able to construct an array formula (see "Array Formulas" earlier in this chapter). *Don't forget:* When you enter an array formula, press Ctrl+Shift+Enter.

To count the number of numerical values (skipping text and blanks), use this array formula:

```
=SUM(IF(ISNUMBER(data),1,0))
```

To count the number of cells that contain an error value, use this array formula:

```
=SUM(IF(ISERR(data),1,0))
```

To count the number of unique numeric values (skipping text, blanks not allowed), use this array formula:

```
=SUM(IF(FREQUENCY(data,data)>0,1,0))
```

Table 3-4 shows a number of array formula examples based on the worksheet shown in Figure 3-7.

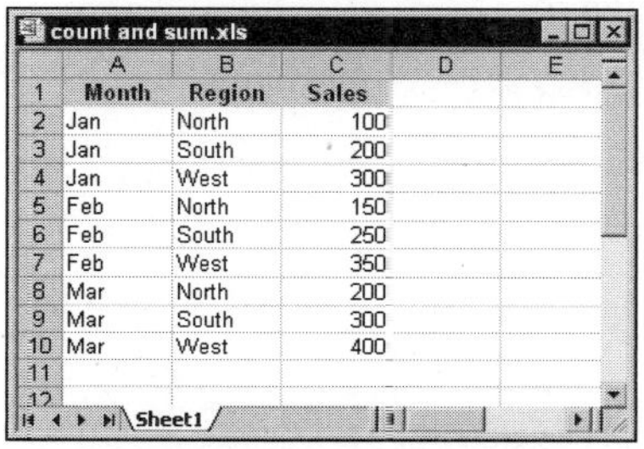

	A	B	C	D	E
1	Month	Region	Sales		
2	Jan	North	100		
3	Jan	South	200		
4	Jan	West	300		
5	Feb	North	150		
6	Feb	South	250		
7	Feb	West	350		
8	Mar	North	200		
9	Mar	South	300		
10	Mar	West	400		
11					
12					

Figure 3-7: This simple database demonstrates some useful array formulas for counting and summing.

ON THE CD

This workbook (including the formulas shown in Table 3-4) is available on the companion CD-ROM.

TABLE 3-4 COMPLEX ARRAY FORMULAS WITH THE SUM FUNCTION

Array Formula	Returns
=SUM((A2:A10="Jan")*(B2:B10="North")*C2:C10)	Sum of Sales where Month="Jan" AND Region="North"
=SUM((A2:A10="Jan")*(B2:B10<>"North")*C2:C10)	Sum of Sales where Month="Jan" AND Region<>"North"
=SUM((A2:A10="Jan")*(B2:B10="North"))	Count of Sales where Month="Jan" AND Region="North"
=SUM((A2:A10="Jan")*((B2:B10="North")+(B2:B10="South")))	Count of Sales where Region="North" or "South" and Month="Jan"

Continued

TABLE 3-4 COMPLEX ARRAY FORMULAS WITH THE SUM FUNCTION *(Continued)*

Array Formula	Returns
=SUM((A2:A10="Jan")*(C2:C10>=200) *(C2:C10))	Sum of Sales where Month="Jan" and Sales>=200
=SUM((C2:C10>=300)*(C2:C10<=400) *(C2:C10))	Sum of Sales between 300 and 400
=SUM((C2:C10>=300)*(C2:C10<=400))	Count of Sales between 300 and 400

Other counting tools

The COUNTIF function is useful when you have a single counting criterion. For more complex comparisons, you can use the DCOUNT function. To use the DCOUNT function, you must set your data up as a database (with field names in the first row), and you also need to create a separate criteria range to specify the counting criteria. The criteria range can also handle logical OR operations by using additional rows. Consult the online help for details.

Excel's SUBTOTAL function can be very useful when you need to get a count of rows that have been filtered by using the AutoFilter feature. The first argument for the subtotal function determines the type of subtotaling. An argument of 3 represents the COUNTA function, and it returns the number of visible cells in a range.

For the ultimate in counting, consider using a pivot table. If you're not familiar with pivot tables, you're missing out on one of the most powerful tools around.

Working with Dates and Times

Excel uses a serial number system to store dates. The earliest date that Excel can understand is January 1, 1900. This date has a serial number of 1. January 2, 1900, has a serial number of 2, and so on.

Most of the time, you don't have to be concerned with Excel's serial number date system. You simply enter a date in a familiar date format, and Excel takes care of the details behind the scenes. For example, if you need to enter June 1, 2004, you can simply enter the date by typing **June 1, 2004** (or use any of a number of different date formats). Excel interprets your entry and stores the value 38139, which is the serial number for that date.

In this chapter, I assume the U.S. date system. If your system uses a different date system, you'll need to adjust accordingly. For example, you might need to enter 1 June, 2004.

Entering dates and times

When working with times, you simply enter the time into a cell in a recognized format. Excel's system for representing dates as individual values is extended to include decimals that represent portions or fractions of days. In other words, Excel perceives all time with the same system whether that time is a particular day, a certain hour, or a specific second. For example, the date serial number for June 1, 2004, is 38139. Noon (halfway through the day) is represented internally as 38139.5. Again, you normally don't have to be concerned with these fractional serial numbers.

Because dates and times are stored as serial numbers, it stands to reason that you can add and subtract dates and times. For example, you can enter a formula to calculate the number of days between two dates. If cells A1 and A2 both contain dates, the following formula returns the number of intervening days:

```
=A2-A1
```

When performing calculations with time, things get a bit trickier. When you enter a time without an associated date, the date is assumed to be January 0, 1900. This is not a problem — unless your calculation produces a negative time value. When this happens, Excel displays an error (displayed as ########). The solution? Switch to the 1904 date system. Choose Tools → Options, click the Calculation tab, and then enable the 1904 Date System check box. Be aware that switching to the 1904 date system can cause problems with either dates already entered in your file or dates in workbooks that are linked to your file.

When you add time values, you'll find that you can't display more than 24 hours. For each 24-hour period, Excel simply adds another day to the total. The solution is to change the number formatting to use square brackets around the hour part of the format. The following number format, for example, displays more than 24 hours:

```
[hh]:mm
```

Using pre-1900 dates

The world, of course, didn't begin on January 1, 1900. People who work with historical information when using Excel often need to work with dates before January 1, 1900. Unfortunately, the only way to work with pre-1900 dates is to enter the date into a cell as text. For example, you can enter the following into a cell, and Excel won't complain:

```
July 4, 1776
```

You can't, however, perform any manipulation on dates that are actually text. For example, you can't change its formatting, you can't determine which day of the week this date occurred on, and you can't calculate the date that occurs seven days later.

The companion CD-ROM contains an add-in that I developed called *Extended Date Functions.* When this add-in is installed, you have access to eight new worksheet functions that let you work with any date in the years 0100 through 9999. Figure 3-8 shows a worksheet that uses these functions to calculate the number of days between various pre-1900 dates.

	A	B	C	D	E
1	President	Born	Died	Age	
2	William McKinley	1/29/1843	9/14/1901	58	
3	Franklin D. Roosevelt	1/30/1882	4/12/1945	63	
4	William Henry Harrison	2/9/1773	4/4/1841	68	
5	Abraham Lincoln	2/12/1809	4/15/1865	56	
6	Zachary Taylor	3/29/1790	7/9/1850	60	
7	Warren G. Harding	11/2/1865	8/2/1923	57	
8	James A. Garfield	11/19/1831	9/19/1881	49	
9					

Figure 3-8: The Extended Date Functions add-in lets you work with pre-1900 dates.

Creating Megaformulas

Often, spreadsheets require intermediate formulas to produce a desired result. In other words, a formula may depend on other formulas, which in turn depend on other formulas. After you get all these formulas working correctly, it's often possible to eliminate the intermediate formulas and use what I refer to as a single *megaformula* instead. The advantages? You use fewer cells (less clutter), and recalculation may be faster. Besides, people in the know will be impressed with your formula-building abilities. The disadvantages? The formula may be impossible to decipher or modify.

Here's an example: Imagine a worksheet with a column of people's names. And suppose that you've been asked to remove all the middle names and middle initials from the names – but not all the names have a middle name or initial. Editing the cells manually would take hours, so you opt for a formula-based solution. Although this is not a difficult task, it normally involves several intermediate formulas.

Figure 3-9 shows the results of the more conventional solution, which requires six intermediate formulas shown in Table 3-5. The names are in column A; the end result goes in column H. Columns B through G hold the intermediate formulas.

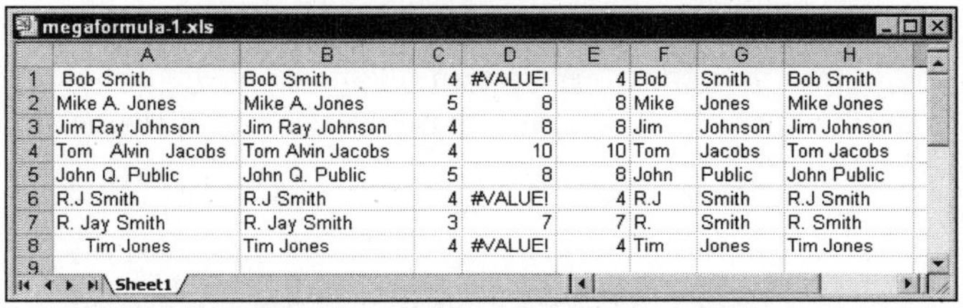
megaformula-1.xls

	A	B	C	D	E	F	G	H
1	Bob Smith	Bob Smith	4	#VALUE!	4	Bob	Smith	Bob Smith
2	Mike A. Jones	Mike A. Jones	5	8	8	Mike	Jones	Mike Jones
3	Jim Ray Johnson	Jim Ray Johnson	4	8	8	Jim	Johnson	Jim Johnson
4	Tom Alvin Jacobs	Tom Alvin Jacobs	4	10	10	Tom	Jacobs	Tom Jacobs
5	John Q. Public	John Q. Public	5	8	8	John	Public	John Public
6	R.J Smith	R.J Smith	4	#VALUE!	4	R.J	Smith	R.J Smith
7	R. Jay Smith	R. Jay Smith	3	7	7	R.	Smith	R. Smith
8	Tim Jones	Tim Jones	4	#VALUE!	4	Tim	Jones	Tim Jones
9								

Sheet1

Figure 3-9: Removing the middle names and initials requires six intermediate formulas.

TABLE 3-5 INTERMEDIATE FORMULAS WRITTEN IN THE FIRST ROW OF SHEET1 IN FIGURE 3-9

Cell	Intermediate Formula	What It Does
B1	=TRIM(A1)	Removes excess spaces.
C1	=FIND(" ",B1,1)	Locates the first space.
D1	=FIND(" ",B1,C1+1)	Locates the second space. Returns #VALUE! if there is no second space.
E1	=IF(ISERROR(D1),C1,D1)	Uses the first space if no second space exists.
F1	=LEFT(B1,C1)	Extracts the first name.
G1	=RIGHT(B1,LEN(B1)-E1)	Extracts the last name.
H1	=F1&G1	Concatenates the two names.

You can eliminate all the intermediate formulas by creating a megaformula. You do so by creating all the intermediate formulas and then going back into the final result formula and replacing each cell reference with a copy of the formula in the cell referred to (without the equal sign). Fortunately, you can use the Clipboard to copy and paste. Keep repeating this process until cell H1 contains nothing but references to cell A1. You end up with the following megaformula in one cell:

```
=LEFT(TRIM(A1),FIND
(" ",TRIM(A1),1))&RIGHT(TRIM(A1),LEN(TRIM(A1))-
IF(ISERROR(FIND(" ",TRIM(A1),FIND(" ",TRIM(A1),1)+1)),
FIND(" ",TRIM(A1),1),FIND(" ",TRIM(A1),FIND
(" ",TRIM(A1),1)+1)))
```

When you're satisfied that the megaformula is working, you can delete the columns that hold the intermediate formulas because they are no longer used.

The megaformula performs exactly the same tasks as all the intermediate formulas — although it's virtually impossible for anyone to figure out, even the author. If you decide to use megaformulas, make sure that the intermediate formulas are performing correctly before you start building a megaformula. Even better, keep a single copy of the intermediate formulas somewhere in case you discover an error or need to make a change.

The only limitation to the megaformula technique is that Excel formulas can contain no more than 1,024 characters. Another way to approach this problem is to create a custom worksheet function in VBA. Then you could replace the megaformula with a simple formula, such as

```
=NOMIDDLE(A1)
```

In fact, I wrote such a function to compare it with intermediate formulas and megaformulas.

Because a megaformula is so complex, you may think that using one would slow down recalculation. Actually, that's not the case. As a test, I created a worksheet that used a megaformula 65,536 times. Then I created another worksheet that used six intermediate formulas. I compared the results with the VBA function that I wrote. I recorded the statistics regarding the two methodologies; the results are shown in Table 3-6.

TABLE 3-6 INTERMEDIATE FORMULAS VERSUS MEGAFORMULA VERSUS VBA FUNCTION

Method	Recalculation Time (Seconds)	File Size
Intermediate formulas	10.8	24.4MB
Megaformula	6.2	8.9MB
VBA function	106.7	8.6MB

The actual results will vary significantly, depending on system speed and amount of memory installed.

As you can see, using the megaformula resulted in faster recalculations as well as a *much* smaller workbook. The VBA function was much slower — in fact, it wasn't even in the same ballpark. This is fairly typical of VBA functions; they are always slower than built-in Excel functions.

The three files used in this time test are available on the companion CD-ROM.

Chapter 4

Understanding Excel's Files

IN THIS CHAPTER
These topics are covered in this chapter.

- ◆ A description of the various ways to start Excel

- ◆ A discussion of the files used and produced by Excel – including the HTML file format

- ◆ An introduction to the new XML features in Excel 2003

- ◆ Details about how Excel uses the Windows Registry

IF YOU PLAN TO DO ANY ADVANCED WORK WITH EXCEL, it's critical that you become familiar with the various ways to start Excel as well as understand what happens when the application is launched. It's also a good idea to have an understanding of the various files used and generated by Excel.

Starting Excel

Excel can be started various ways (depending on how it's installed). All methods ultimately launch the Excel EXE (executable) file.

When Excel starts, it reads its settings from the Windows Registry and opens any add-ins that are installed (that is, those that are checked in the Add-Ins dialog box, which is displayed when you choose Tools → Add-Ins). It then displays an empty workbook; the number of sheets in the workbook is determined by a user-defined setting that is stored in the Windows Registry. You can change this number by editing the Sheets in the New Workbook setting located in the General tab of the Options dialog box (choose Tools → Options).

If your XLStart folder contains any workbooks, they are opened automatically – and a blank workbook does not appear. If your XLStart folder includes a workspace file, multiple workbooks are opened in a customized workspace. You can also define an alternate startup directory to hold other worksheet or workspace files that you want opened automatically. You can set up this alternate startup directory by specifying a path in the At Startup, Open All Files In setting located in the General tab of the Options dialog box. In previous versions of Excel, this field was labeled Alternate Startup File Location.

TIP If you want to change the default formats (or content) of blank workbooks that you create, create a default workbook and save it as a template with the name Book.xlt in your XLStart folder. For details on creating and using template files, refer to Excel's help.

Excel recognizes several command line switches. These are listed in Table 4-1.

TABLE 4-1 **EXCEL COMMAND LINE SWITCHES**

Switch	What It Does
/automation	Forces Excel to start without loading add-ins and templates or processing files in the XLStart directory or the alternate startup file location. Use this switch to perform a "clean boot" of Excel.
/e	Use this switch when you want to start Excel without creating a new workbook and without displaying its splash screen.
/embedded	Starts an invisible instance of Excel (not recommended).
/m	Forces Excel to create a new workbook that contains a single Microsoft Excel 4.0 macro sheet (obsolete).
/o	Causes Excel to register itself in the Windows Registry. It replaces missing Registry entries; it does not correct invalid entries (see /regserver, later in this table).
/p directory	Sets the active path to a directory other than the default directory.
/r filename	Forces Excel to open the specified file in read-only mode.
/regserver	Forces Excel to reregister itself in the Windows Registry and then quit. Use this switch when you want Excel to rewrite all its Registry keys and reassociate itself with Excel files, such as workbooks and charts.
/s	Forces Excel to start in Safe mode and does not load any add-ins or files in the XLStart or alternate startup file directories.
/unregserver	Forces Excel to unregister itself in the Windows Registry and then quit.

One way to specify any of these switches is to edit the properties of the shortcut that starts Excel. For example, if you want Excel to use a folder named Xlfiles as its default folder, you can use the /p switch and specify this in the Target field in the Properties dialog box for the Excel shortcut. To access the Properties dialog box, right-click the shortcut icon and click the Shortcut tab. For example, you can change the Target to

```
"C:\Program Files\Microsoft Office\Office11\EXCEL.EXE" /p C:\Xlfiles
```

Keep in mind that the path to Excel.exe can vary for different installations and for different versions.

You can run multiple instances of Excel on a single system. Each instance is treated as a separate task. Most people have pretty good success running multiple versions of Excel on a single system. For best results, install the versions in the order of their release dates.

Spreadsheet File Formats Supported

Although Excel's default file format is an XLS workbook file, it can also open and save a wide variety of files generated by several other applications.

An important consideration is whether a particular file type can survive a "round trip." In other words, do you lose any information if you save a file in a particular format and then reopen it in the same application? As you might expect, using Excel's native file format (XLS files) ensures that you'll lose absolutely nothing — as long as you use the latest version of XLS.

If you save and retrieve a file with a format other than the current XLS format, you run the risk of losing some types of information — typically formatting and macros, but sometimes formulas and charts.

In the sections that follow, I discuss the various types of files that you can and cannot use with Excel.

Lotus 1-2-3 spreadsheet files

Lotus spreadsheets come in several flavors:

◆ *WKS files* are single-sheet files used by 1-2-3 Release 1..*x* for DOS. Excel can read and write these files.

Excel can also open Microsoft Works 2.0 files, which also have a WKS extension.

◆ *WK1 files* are single-sheet files used by 1-2-3 Release 2..*x* for DOS. The formatting for these files is stored in `*.all` files (produced by the Allways add-in) or FM1 files (produced by the WYSIWYG add-in). Excel can read and write all these files. When you save a file to the `*.wk1` format, you can choose which (if any) type of formatting file to generate.

◆ *WK3 files* are generated by 1-2-3 Release 3.*x* for DOS, 1-2-3 Release 4.*x* for DOS, and 1-2-3 Release 1.*x* for Windows. These files may contain more than one sheet. The formatting for these files is stored in `*.fm3` files (produced by the WYSIWYG add-in). Excel can read and write WK3 files with or without the accompanying FM3 file.

◆ *WK4 files* are generated by 1-2-3 Release 4.*x* for Windows and 1-2-3 Release 5.*x* for Windows. (Lotus finally got its act together and eliminated the separate formatting file.) These files may contain more than one sheet. Excel can neither read nor write these files. If you need to read a WK4 file into Excel, your only option is to use 1-2-3 Release 4 for Windows (or later) and save the file in WK3 format, which Excel can read.

◆ *123 files* are generated by 1-2-3 97 and 1-2-3 Millennium Edition. These files may contain more than one sheet. Excel can neither read nor write these files. If you need to read a 1-2-3 file into Excel, your only option is to use 1-2-3 and save the file in WK3 format, which Excel can read.

Quattro Pro spreadsheet files

Quattro Pro files also exist in several versions:

◆ *WQ1 files* are the single-sheet files generated by Quattro Pro for DOS Versions 1, 2, 3, and 4. Excel can read and write these files.

◆ *WQ2 files* are generated by Quattro Pro for DOS Version 5. Excel can neither read nor write this file format.

◆ *WB1 files* are generated by Quattro Pro for Windows Versions 1 and 5. (Note: There are no Versions 2 through 4.) Excel can read, but not write, this file format.

◆ *WB2 files* are generated by Quattro Pro for Windows Version 6. Excel can neither read nor write this file format.

◆ *WB3 files* are generated by Quattro Pro for Windows Versions 7 and later. Excel can neither read nor write this file format.

You can download a Quattro Pro file converter from the Microsoft Web site. This converter enables you to import Quattro Pro 97 WB3 files. To locate this converter, search Microsoft's Web site because the URL changes frequently.

Database file formats

DBF files are single-table database files generated by dBASE and several other database programs. Excel can read and write DBF files up to and including dBASE 4.

Excel cannot read or write any other database file formats directly. You can, however, use Microsoft Query to access many other database file formats and then copy or link the data into an Excel worksheet. You can run Microsoft Query directly from Excel by choosing the Data → Import External Data → New Database Query command.

Text file formats

Text files simply contain data with no formatting. There are several relatively standard text file formats, but there are no standard file extensions.

◆ Each line in *tab-delimited files* consists of fields separated by tabs. Excel can read these files, converting each line to a row and each field to a column. Excel also can write these files, using TXT as the default extension.

◆ Each line in *comma-separated files* consists of fields usually separated by commas. (Countries that use a comma as a decimal symbol will use semicolons in CSV files.) Sometimes text appears in quotes. Excel can read these files, converting each line to a row and each field to a column. Excel can also write these files, using CSV as the default extension.

◆ Each line in *space-delimited files* consists of fields separated by spaces. Excel can read these files, converting each line to a row and each field to a column. Excel also can write these files, using PRN as the default extension.

When you attempt to load a text file into Excel, the Text Import Wizard might kick in to help you specify how you want the file retrieved.

To bypass the Text Import Wizard, press Shift when you click OK in the Open dialog box.

You can also perform queries using text files. Choose the Data → Import External Data → Import Data command.

Other file formats

Other spreadsheet file formats supported are the following:

◆ *DIF (Data Interchange Format):* This file format was used by VisiCalc. I haven't seen a DIF file in ages. Excel can read and write these files.

◆ *SYLK (SYmbolic LinK):* This file format was used by MultiPlan. SYLK files, too, are quite rare these days. Excel can read and write these files.

Files Written by Excel

Excel can write several types of files, which I discuss in this section.

XLS files

The XLS workbook files produced by Excel 2003 use the same file format as Excel 97, Excel 2000, Excel 2002, and Excel 2003. These files cannot be opened by any version of Excel prior to Excel 97. You can, however, save a workbook using any of the older Excel file formats. You might lose some information that is specific to the later file format.

 An Excel workbook or add-in file can have any extension that you like. In other words, these files don't need to be stored with an XLS (for workbooks) or XLA (for add-ins) extension.

Workspace files

A *workspace file* is a special file that contains information about an Excel workspace. For example, if you have a project that uses two workbooks and you like to have the workbook windows arranged in a particular way, you can save an XLW file (choose the File → Save Workspace command) to save this window configuration. Then, whenever you open the XLW file, Excel restores the desired workspace.

Which Version Created That XLS File?

Unfortunately, there is no direct way to determine which version of Excel created a particular XLS file. If you have an earlier version of Excel and attempt to open an XLS file that was created in a later version, you'll probably get an error message or a screenful of garbage characters. But if you can open the file successfully, you can use a simple Visual Basic for Applications (VBA) statement to determine the Excel version of the file.

Open the workbook, and make sure that it's the active workbook. Press Alt+F11 to activate the Visual Basic Editor (VBE) and then press Ctrl+G to activate the Immediate window. Type the following statement and then press Enter:

```
Print ActiveWorkbook.FileFormat
```

The Immediate window displays a value that corresponds to the version of the active workbook. This value is one of those shown in the following table:

Value	Excel Version
16	Excel 2
29	Excel 3
33	Excel 4
39	Excel 5, 95
−4143	Excel 97, 2000, 2002, 2003

It's important to understand that a workspace file does *not* include the workbooks — only the configuration information that makes those workbooks visible in your Excel workspace. So if you need to distribute a workspace to someone else, make sure that you include the workbook files as well as the XLW file. In addition, the File → Save Workspace command does not save the workbooks themselves.

Template files

You can save any workbook as a template file (XLT extension). Doing so is useful if you tend to create similar files on a regular basis. For example, you might need to generate a monthly sales report. You can save some time by creating a template that holds the necessary formulas and charts for your report. When you start new files based on the template, you need only plug in the values.

To create a new workbook that's based on an existing template, choose the File → New command and then select the template from the Templates dialog box.

Using Excel 2002 or 2003 requires an extra step because the preceding commands display the New Workbook task bar. From the task bar, you can choose a source for the template, including templates that you can download from the Microsoft Web site. If you click On My Computer for the source, you'll see the Templates dialog box, which lets you select a template file.

Clicking the New toolbar button or pressing Ctrl+N does not enable you to select a template. Rather, a default workbook is created.

If you create a template named `Book.xlt`, that template will be used as the basis for new workbooks. In addition, you can create a template named `Sheet.xlt`, which is used as the basis for new worksheets that you add to a workbook. Note that it is not possible to create a template for chart sheets because Excel handles chart templates differently.

Templates can be stored in two locations on your local computer:

◆ *Your XLStart folder:* This is where you store autotemplates named `Book.xlt` and `Sheet.xlt`. You can also put workbook templates in this folder.

◆ *Your Templates folder:* Workbook templates stored here appear in the New dialog box.

The location of the Templates folder varies, depending on the version of Excel. To find the location of your Templates folder, execute the following VBA statement:

`MsgBox Application.TemplatesPath`

Toolbar files

Excel stores toolbar and menu bar configurations in an XLB file. When you exit Excel 2003, the current toolbar configuration is saved in a file named `Excel11.xlb`. The exact location and name of this file varies with the version of Excel, so search your hard drive for *.xlb, and you'll find it. This file contains information regarding the position and visibility of all custom toolbars and custom menu bars, plus modifications that you've made to built-in toolbars or menu bars.

The Excel 2003 Help system lists the various names and locations of the XLB files for various versions of Excel. Do a search for *xlb* to find this information.

If the XLB file becomes corrupt, it can cause Excel to crash when it starts. If you experience a crash when you start Excel, try renaming your XLB file. Excel will create a new XLB file if it doesn't exist. However, you will lose any menu or toolbar customization — but that's probably better than not being able to run Excel at all.

Add-in files

An *add-in* is essentially a workbook file with a few important differences:

- ◆ The workbook's IsAddin property is True — which means that it can be loaded by choosing the Tools → Add-Ins command.

- ◆ The workbook is hidden and cannot be unhidden by the user. Consequently, an add-in is never the active workbook.

- ◆ When using VBA, the workbook is not part of the Workbooks collection.

Many add-ins provide new features or functions to Excel. You can access these new features as if they were built into the product.

You can create your own add-ins from XLS workbook files. In fact, creating add-ins is the preferred method of distributing some types of Excel applications. Add-ins have an XLA extension by default, but you can use any extension that you like.

Besides XLA add-ins, Excel supports XLL add-ins and (beginning with Excel 2000) COM add-ins. These types of add-ins are created using software other than Excel. This book discusses only XLA add-ins.

Chapter 21 covers the topic of add-ins in detail.

Excel and HTML

HyperText Markup Language (HTML) is the language of the World Wide Web. When you browse the Web, the documents that are retrieved and displayed by your browser are usually in HTML format. An HTML file consists of text information plus special tags that describe how the text is to be formatted. The browser interprets the tags, applies formatting, and displays the information.

Excel 2000 and later can use HTML as a native file format. In other words, you can save a workbook in HTML format, reopen the HTML file, and it will look exactly as it did before you first saved it. All the Excel-specific information (such as macros, charts, pivot tables, and worksheet settings) remains intact. HTML is a relatively simple file format. The fact that an Excel workbook can survive the round trip is just short of amazing.

Unfortunately, although using HTML as a native file format might be amazing, Microsoft may have overemphasized the importance of this feature. In real life, this simply isn't very useful except in a small number of situations.

How Excel uses HTML

The best way to understand how Excel can use HTML as a native file format is to perform some simple experiments. Start with a new workbook, and make sure it has only one worksheet. Enter a few values and a formula, do some simple formatting, and then save the workbook in HTML format. Choose the File → Save As Web Page command, and make sure you select the Entire Workbook option. Figure 4-1 shows a very simple workbook consisting of two values and a formula, with the formula cell formatted bold. This is a good candidate for learning about the HTML files saved by Excel.

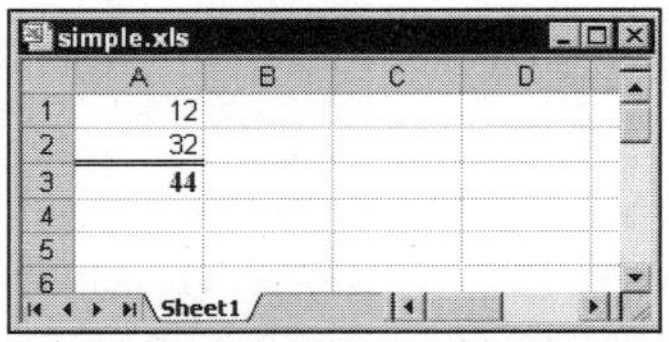

simple.xls				
	A	B	C	D
1	12			
2	32			
3	44			
4				
5				
6				
Sheet1				

Figure 4-1: Try saving a simple workbook like this in HTML format.

The remainder of the material in this section assumes that you're familiar with HTML.

Next, open the HTML file in your browser. It will, of course, look pretty much like the original workbook. However, it is a "dead" non-interactive document. Choose the browser's View → Source command to view the HTML code. You might be surprised by what you see. Even HTML gurus might be overwhelmed by the complexity of this so-called simple Web document.

Following are a few observations about the HTML file:

◆ The entire Excel workbook can usually be represented by a single HTML file. In other words, all the information needed to create an exact replica of the original workbook is contained in the HTML file. This isn't always the case, however. Keep reading to find out when a simple HTML file no longer suffices.

◆ Most of the document is contained within the <head> and </head> tags.

◆ A large portion consists of style definitions. This is the information between the <style> and </style> tags — which is embedded between the <head> and </head> tags.

◆ The actual text that's displayed in the browser is contained in a table (between the <table> and </table> tags).

◆ The formula is preserved by using a proprietary argument for the <td> tag. The proprietary argument is ignored by browsers, but Excel uses this information when the file is reopened.

The HTML file produced for the simple workbook is more than 4,000 bytes in size, which is quite large considering the simplicity of the displayed page. The extra information, of course, is what Excel uses to create a workbook when the HTML file is reopened.

Adding some complexity

The example workbook used in the preceding section is about as simple as it gets. Now add a small bit of complexity to the workbook and see what happens to the HTML file.

Using the simple example file, select A1:A3 and press F11 to create a new chart sheet. Save the file again and load it in your browser. You'll find that it closely resembles the Excel workbook, even down to the sheet tabs and navigation arrows at the bottom!

The HTML file has more than doubled in size; it's now up to about 10,000 bytes. More importantly, you'll find that the directory in which you saved the file has a new subdirectory that contains additional files (six extra files using my simple workbook). The files in this directory are necessary to display a replica of the workbook in a browser and to re-create the workbook when the HTML file is reopened in Excel.

If you examine the HTML file, you'll see that it's much more complicated than the original one and contains quite a bit of complex JavaScript code. (*JavaScript* is a scripting language supported by most Web browsers.) At this point, the HTML file has gotten well beyond the grasp of your average HTML author. And that's not even taking into account the other files dumped into the subdirectory. The files are

- ◆ Three HTML files (one for each sheet, plus a file that displays the tab strip).
- ◆ A GIF file (the chart).
- ◆ A CSS file (a cascading style sheet that holds formatting and display information).
- ◆ An XML file. This is an eXtensible Markup Language file. XML is well beyond the scope of this book. (Hey, I told you this stuff was getting complicated!)

You might want to open some other Excel workbooks and save them as HTML files. You'll soon discover another type of file that's created in the subdirectory, an MSO (Microsoft Office) file. This is a binary file that holds the information necessary to re-create Excel-specific features such as macros, pivot tables, conditional formatting, and so on.

 As you might have surmised by now, saving an Excel workbook in HTML format introduces lots of potential problems. For example, if you need to transfer your file to another location, it's imperative that you include all the supporting files as well. If any of the supporting files are damaged, Excel cannot re-create the workbook. To avoid this problem, you can save the workbook as a Single File Web Page with a `*.mht` extension. But this introduces another problem: Microsoft Internet Explorer is the only browser that can display these files.

Creating interactive HTML files

If you're still with me at this point, it's time to introduce yet another level of complexity. Excel can save HTML files that include spreadsheet interactivity. In other words, when the HTML file is displayed in a browser, the user can actually interact with the document as a spreadsheet — enter data, change formulas, adjust cell formatting, see "live" charts, and even drag data around in pivot tables.

In Excel 2003, you can create an HTML file with interactivity from a multi-sheet workbook. In previous versions, interactive HTML files were limited to a single sheet.

To get a feel for how this works, activate a sheet that contains formulas. Choose the File → Save as Web Page command. In the Save As dialog box, choose the Selection: Sheet option and then enable the Add Interactivity check box. Click the Publish button. You'll get another dialog box (Publish as Web Page). Accept the defaults and then click Publish.

 Spreadsheets that are saved with interactivity are readable only by Microsoft Internet Explorer.

When you open the HTML file in Internet Explorer, you'll find that it displays a spreadsheet-like object that is, in fact, interactive. You can change the values and even edit the formulas. Figure 4-2 shows an example.

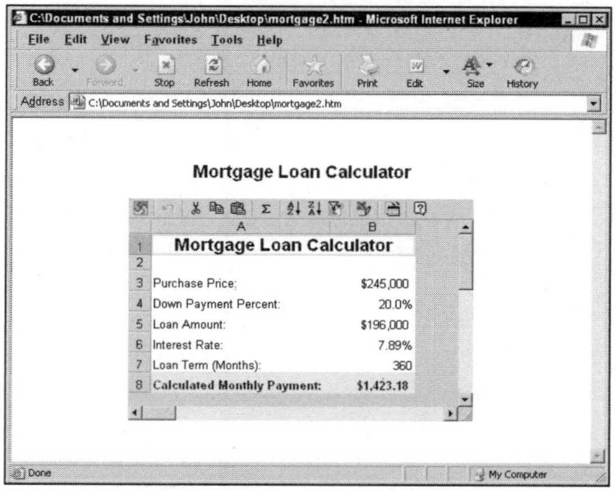

Figure 4-2: An example of an interactive Excel worksheet displayed in Internet Explorer.

What about the Script Editor?

You'll find that this book ignores one complete aspect of Excel: the Microsoft Script Editor, which you access by pressing Alt+Shift+F11. The Script Editor is used to edit the JavaScript (or VBScript) code in an HTML document. I consider this topic to be beyond the scope of this book as well as useful to only a very small number of readers. In fact, I have never been in contact with anyone who had any interest at all in this topic. Consequently, I focus on the real meat of Excel: non-Web-based application development by using VBA.

You might expect that the HTML file generated for an interactive worksheet would be much more complex than the example in the previous section. You'd be wrong. Such a worksheet occupies a single HTML file. The complexity is handled by an ActiveX control. Because of this, the end user must have Office 2000 or later installed (or have a license for the Microsoft Office Web Components ActiveX control) to view an interactive Excel file in Internet Explorer.

This section was intended to provide a brief overview of the HTML feature in Excel 2000 and later. This topic is definitely fodder for a complete book — one that I don't choose to write, thank you.

Importing and Exporting XML Files

One of the few new features in Excel 2003 is the ability to import and export data stored in XML files. This section provides a very brief introduction to this feature.

This section is relevant only to those who use Excel 2003. If you're using Excel 2000 or Excel 2002, you'll find that you can open some XML files in Excel (choose the File → Open command). The features described here, however, will not work.

What is XML?

XML is an accepted standard that enables exchange of data between different applications. XML is a markup language, just like HTML is a markup language.

XML uses tags to define elements within a document. XML *tags* define the document's structural elements and the meaning of those elements. Unlike HTML tags, which specify how a document looks or is formatted, XML can be used to define the document structure and content. Consequently, XML separates a document's content from its presentation.

Following is a very simple XML file that contains data from an e-mail message.

```
<?xml version="1.0" encoding="UTF-8"?>
<message>
<to>Bill Smith</to>
<from>Mark Jackson</from>
<subject>Meeting date</subject>
<body>The meeting will be at 8:00 a.m. on Tuesday</body>
</message>
```

When the file is viewed in Internet Explorer, the browser displays it as a structured document (as shown in Figure 4-3).

 All the files in this section are available on the companion CD-ROM.

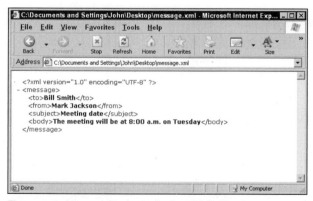

Figure 4–3: Internet Explorer displays XML files in a structured format.

Unlike HTML, the XML specification does not specify the tags themselves. Rather, it provides a standard way to define tags and relationships. Because there are no predefined tags, XML can be used to model virtually any type of document.

The information in this chapter is an admittedly cursory overview of XML. The fact is that XML can be extremely complex. Many books are devoted entirely to XML.

The three sections that follow consist of simplistic examples to give you a feel for how Excel handles XML.

Importing XML data by using a Map

This example uses the worksheet shown in Figure 4-4. This worksheet uses data in column B to generate a loan amortization schedule. Assume that a back-end system generates XML files and that each file contains data for a customer. An example of such a file is shown below:

```
<?xml version="1.0"?>
<Customer>
   <Name>Joe Smith</Name>
   <AcctNo>32374-94</AcctNo>
   <LoanAmt>$325,983</LoanAmt>
   <IntRate>6.25%</IntRate>
   <Term>30</Term>
</Customer>
```

	Loan Amortization Schedule			Payment Period	Payment Amount	Cumulative Payments	Interest	Cumulative Interest
1	Loan Amortization Schedule							
2								
3	Customer Name	Joe Smith		1	2,007	2,007	1,698	1,698
4	Prepared:	9/13/2003		2	2,007	4,014	1,696	3,394
5	Acct. Number	32374-94		3	2,007	6,021	1,695	5,089
6	Loan Amount:	$325,983		4	2,007	8,029	1,693	6,782
7	Annual Interest Rate:	6.25%		5	2,007	10,036	1,691	8,473
8	Term (years):	30		6	2,007	12,043	1,690	10,163
9	Number of Pmt Periods:	360		7	2,007	14,050	1,688	11,851
10				8	2,007	16,057	1,686	13,537
11				9	2,007	18,064	1,685	15,222
12				10	2,007	20,071	1,683	16,905
13				11	2,007	22,078	1,681	18,586

Figure 4–4: This worksheet uses imported XML data.

This file has five data elements: Name, AcctNo, LoanAmt, IntRate, and Term. Two of the fields (Prepared and Number of Pmt Periods) are calculated with formulas and are not considered data elements.

The trick here is to be able to import files, such as this, and have the data sent to the appropriate cells in the worksheet.

The first step is to add a Map to the workbook. Make sure that XML Source is displayed in the task pane (choose Data → XML → XML Source).

To add the Map, follow these steps:

1. Click the XML Maps button at the bottom of the task pane. The XML Maps dialog box appears.

2. Click Add to display the XML Source dialog box.

3. Select one of the customer XML files. The exact file doesn't matter. This will be used only to infer the schema.

4. Click OK to dismiss the XML Maps dialog box. The task pane displays the data elements from the file (as shown in Figure 4-5).

Figure 4-5: The task pane shows the XML data elements.

The next step is to map the data elements to the appropriate worksheet cells.

1. In the task pane, click the Name element and drag it to cell B3.

2. Drag the AcctNo element to cell B5.

3. Drag the LoanAmt element to cell B6.

4. Drag the IntRate element to cell B7.

5. Drag the Term element to cell B8.

Finally, you can import an XML file. Choose Data → XML → Import and then select a customer XML file. You'll find that the data is fed into the appropriate cells. To calculate another amortization schedule, just import another XML file.

Importing XML data to a list

The example in the preceding section used XML files that contained only a single record. XML files often contain multiple records, called *repeating elements*. Examples include a customer list or data for all employees in an organization.

You can use the Excel File → Open command to open an XML file that contains repeating elements. After you specify the filename, Excel presents the Open XML dialog box, as shown in Figure 4-6. This dialog box has three options:

♦ *As an XML List:* The file opens, and Excel converts the data to a List.

♦ *As a Read-Only Workbook:* The data is imported into the worksheet, but the workbook is read-only. This is to prevent you from accidentally over-writing the original file.

♦ *Use the XML Source Task Pane:* Excel infers the schema for the XML data and displays it in the task pane. (The data is not actually imported.) You can then map the elements to cells and import the actual data.

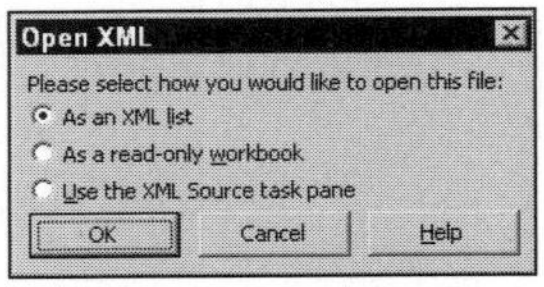

Figure 4-6: The Open XML dialog box.

Figure 4-7 shows an XML file that has been imported to a worksheet.

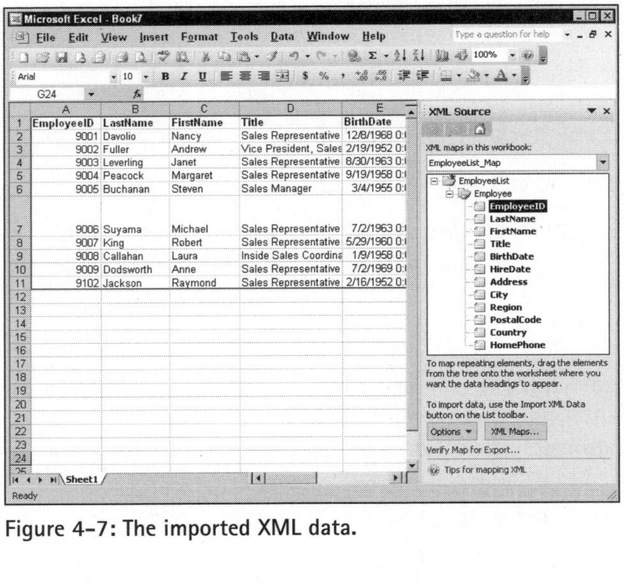

Figure 4-7: The imported XML data.

When displayed in the task pane, repeating elements use a different icon (a double folder). Non-repeating elements display a single folder icon.

Exporting XML data from Excel

In order to export data to an XML file, you must add a Map to the workbook, and the map must correspond to your data. Then you can use the Data → XML → Export command to create an XML file.

Contrary to what you might expect, you can't export an arbitrary range of data in XML format. For example, if you create a List Range on your worksheet, you can't export that List Range to an XML file unless you add an appropriate map to your worksheet first. And it's not possible to create (or modify) a map by using Excel.

Refer to Chapter 27 for an example of a VBA procedure to generate a simple XML file using the data in a range of cells.

If you choose the Excel File → Save As command, you'll notice that one of the options is XML Spreadsheet. This produces an XML file that uses the Microsoft XMLSS schema. It will not export the data to a normal XML file that is readable by other applications.

Excel Settings in the Registry

In this section, I provide some background information about the Windows Registry and discuss how Excel uses the Registry to store its settings.

About the Registry

Windows 3.1 used a Registration Database to store information about file association and Object Linking and Embedding (OLE) registration. The Windows 95 (or later) Registry extends this concept by storing configuration information for all types of applications as well as computer-specific information.

The *Registry* is essentially a hierarchical database that can be accessed by application software.

Before You Edit the Registry . . .

You can use the Regedit.exe program to change anything in the Registry, including information that is critical to your system's operation. In other words, if you change the wrong piece of information, Windows may no longer work properly.

Get into the habit of choosing the File → Export command in Regedit. This command enables you to save an ASCII version of the Registry or just a specific branch of the Registry. If you find that you messed up something, you can always import the ASCII file to restore the Registry to its previous condition (choose the Registry → Import Registry File command). Refer to the Help file for Regedit for details.

You can use the Registry Editor program (Regedit.exe, in the Windows folder) to browse the Registry – and even edit its contents if you know what you're doing. Before beginning your explorations, take a minute to read the sidebar titled "Before You Edit the Registry . . . ". Figure 4-8 shows what the Registry Editor looks like.

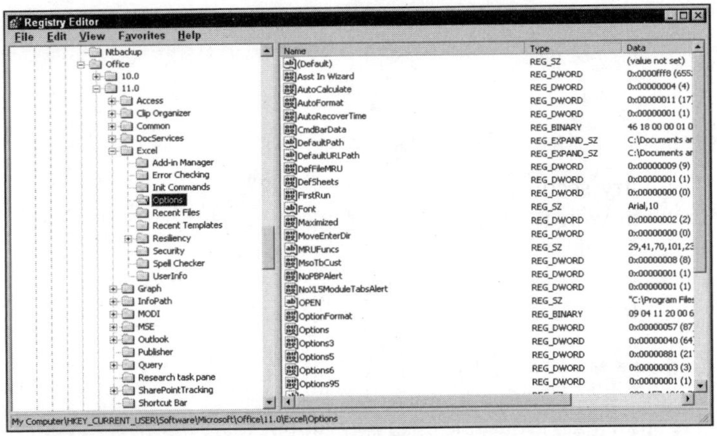

Figure 4-8: The Registry Editor lets you browse and make changes to the Registry.

As I mention, the Registry is hierarchical. It consists of keys and values:

◆ HKEY_CLASSES_ROOT

◆ HKEY_CURRENT_USER

◆ HKEY_LOCAL_MACHINE

◆ HKEY_USERS

◆ HKEY_CURRENT_CONFIG

◆ HKEY_DYN_DATA

Excel's settings

Information used by Excel 2003 is stored in this Registry section:

HKEY_CURRENT_USER\Software\Microsoft\Office\11.0\Excel

In this section of the Registry, you'll find a number of keys that contain specific values that determine how Excel operates.

The Registry settings are updated automatically by Excel when Excel closes.

 It's important to understand that Excel reads the Windows Registry only once — when it starts up. In addition, Excel updates the Registry settings only when Excel closes normally. If Excel crashes (unfortunately, not an uncommon occurrence), the Registry information is not updated. For example, if you change one of Excel's settings, such as the visibility of the status bar, this setting is not written to the Registry until Excel closes by normal means.

Table 4-2 lists the Registry sections that are relevant to Excel 2003. You might not find all these sections in your Registry database.

TABLE 4-2 EXCEL CONFIGURATION INFORMATION IN THE REGISTRY

Section	Description
Add-in Manager	Lists add-ins that appear in the list box when you choose the Tools → Add-Ins command. Add-ins that are included with Excel do not appear in this list. If you have an add-in entry in this list box that you no longer use, you can remove it by using the Registry Editor.
AutoSave	Holds the AutoSave option that you set.
Converters	Lists additional (external) file converters that are not built into Excel.
Delete Commands	Enables you to specify which menu commands you don't want to appear.

Continued

TABLE 4-2 EXCEL CONFIGURATION INFORMATION IN THE REGISTRY *(Continued)*

Section	Description
Error Checking	Holds the settings for formula error checking.
Init Commands	Holds information about custom commands.
Init Menus	Holds information about custom menus.
Line Print	Holds settings used in 1-2-3 macro printing. Excel updates this section whenever it executes a 1-2-3 macro that has /wgdu (Worksheet Global Default Update) in it.
Options	A catch-all section; holds a wide variety of settings, including the paths to files that are opened automatically when Excel starts (such as add-ins).
Recent Files	Stores the names of the last files saved (up to nine files).
Recent Templates	Stores the names of templates you've used recently.
Resiliency	Information used for recovering documents.
Security	Specifies the security level for opening files that contain macros.
Spell Checker	Stores information about your spelling checker options.
UserInfo	Information about the user.

Although you can change most of the settings via Excel's Options dialog box, several other useful settings cannot be changed directly from Excel (but you can use the Registry Editor to make changes).

One more warning is in order. Prior to making any changes to the Registry, refer to the sidebar "Before You Edit the Registry ...".

Part II

Excel Application Development

Chapter 5

What Is a Spreadsheet Application?

IN THIS CHAPTER

In this chapter, I attempt to clarify how people use spreadsheets in the real world. This is a topic that's germane to this entire book because it can help you determine how much effort you should devote to a particular development project. By the time you finish this chapter, you should have a pretty good idea of what I mean by a *spreadsheet application*. And after you've made it through the rest of the book, you'll be well on your way to developing your own spreadsheet applications with Excel. But first, let's get down to the basics.

- A working definition of a spreadsheet application

- The difference between a spreadsheet user and a spreadsheet developer

- A system for classifying spreadsheet users to help you conceptualize who the audience is for your applications

- A discussion of why people use spreadsheets

- A taxonomy of the basic types of spreadsheets

YOU'VE PROBABLY BEEN WORKING WITH SPREADSHEETS for several years, but chances are good that your primary focus has been on simply generating spreadsheets to get the job done. You probably never gave much thought to more global issues like those discussed in this chapter: the different types of spreadsheet users, how to classify various types of spreadsheets, and even basic questions such as why people use spreadsheets. If the title of this book attracted your attention, it's important for you to understand these issues so that you can become an effective power-programmer. I first discuss the concept of a *spreadsheet application*. This is, after all, the desired result of your power-programming efforts.

Spreadsheet Applications

Programming, as it relates to spreadsheet use, is essentially the process of building applications that use a spreadsheet rather than a traditional programming language such as C, Pascal, or BASIC. In both cases, however, these applications will be used by other people — not the developer of the application.

For purposes of this book, a spreadsheet application is a spreadsheet file (or group of related files) that is designed so that someone other than the developer can perform useful work without extensive training. According to this definition, most of the spreadsheet files that you've developed probably wouldn't qualify as spreadsheet applications. You may have dozens or hundreds of spreadsheet files on your hard drive, but it's a safe bet that most of them aren't really designed for others to use.

A good spreadsheet application has the following characteristics:

◆ It enables the end user to perform a task that he or she probably would not be able to do otherwise.

◆ It provides the appropriate solution to the problem. (A spreadsheet environment isn't always the optimal approach.)

◆ It accomplishes what it is supposed to do. This may be an obvious prerequisite, but it's not at all uncommon for applications to fail this test.

◆ It produces accurate results and is free of bugs.

◆ It uses appropriate and efficient methods and algorithms to accomplish its job.

◆ It traps errors before the user is forced to deal with them. Note that errors and bugs are not the same. Attempting to divide by zero is an *error*, whereas failure to identify that error before it occurs is a *bug*.

◆ It does not allow the user to delete or modify important components accidentally (or intentionally).

◆ Its user interface is clear and consistent so that the user always knows how to proceed.

◆ Its formulas, macros, and user interface elements are well documented, allowing for subsequent changes, if necessary.

◆ It is designed so that it can be modified in simple ways without making major changes. A basic fact of life is that a user's needs change over time.

◆ It has an easily accessible help system that provides useful information on at least the major procedures.

◆ It is designed so that it is portable and runs on any system that has the proper software (in this case, a copy of the appropriate version of Excel).

It should come as no surprise that it is possible to create spreadsheet applications for many different usage levels, ranging from simple fill-in-the-blank templates to extremely complex applications that use custom menus and dialog boxes and that may not even look like spreadsheets.

The Developer and the End User

I've already used the terms *developer* and *end user,* which are terms that you see frequently throughout this book. Because you've gotten this far, I think I can safely assume that you're either a spreadsheet application developer or a potential developer.

My definitions regarding developers and end users are simple. The person who creates the spreadsheet application is the *developer.* For joint projects, there are multiple developers: a development *team.* The person who uses the results of the developer's spreadsheet programming efforts is the *end user* (which I often shorten to simply *user*). In many cases, there will be multiple end users, and often the developer is one of the users.

Who are developers? What do they do?

I've spent about 15 years trading methodologies and basically hanging out with the motley crew of folks who call themselves spreadsheet developers. I divide them into two primary groups:

- ◆ *Insiders* are developers who are intimately involved with the users and thoroughly understand their needs. In many cases, these developers are also users of the application. Often, they developed the application in response to a particular problem.

- ◆ *Outsiders* are developers who are hired to produce a solution to a problem. In most cases, developers in this category are familiar with the business in general but not with the specifics of the application they are developing. In other cases, these developers are employed by the company that requests the application (but they normally work in a different department).

Some developers devote full time to development efforts. These developers may be either insiders or outsiders. A fair number of consultants (outsiders) make a decent living developing spreadsheet applications on a freelance basis.

Other spreadsheet developers don't work full time at the task and may not even realize they are developing spreadsheet applications. These developers are often office computer gurus who seem to know everything about computers and software. These folks often create spreadsheet applications as a way to make their lives easier — the time spent developing a well-designed application for others can often save hours of training time and can greatly reduce the time spent answering others' questions.

Spreadsheet developers are typically involved in the following activities, often performing most or all of each task on their own:

- ◆ Determining the needs of the user

- ◆ Planning an application that meets these needs

◆ Determining the most appropriate user interface

◆ Creating the spreadsheet, formulas, macros, and user interface

◆ Testing the application under all reasonable sets of conditions

◆ Making the application relatively bulletproof (often based on results from the testing)

◆ Making the application aesthetically appealing and intuitive

◆ Documenting the development effort

◆ Distributing the application to users

◆ Updating the application if and when it's necessary

 I discuss these developer activities in more detail in Chapter 6.

Developers must have a thorough understanding of their development environment (in this case, Excel). And there's certainly a lot to know when it comes to Excel. By any standard, Excel is easy to use, but defining what's easy to use depends on the user. Developing nontrivial spreadsheet applications with Excel requires an in-depth knowledge of formulas, functions, macros, custom dialog boxes, custom toolbars, menu modifications, and add-ins. Most Excel users, of course, don't meet these qualifications and have no intention of learning these details—which brings me to the next topic: classifying spreadsheet users.

Classifying spreadsheet users

Over the years, I've found that it's often useful to classify people who use spreadsheets (including both developers and end users) along two dimensions: their *degree of experience* with spreadsheets and their *interest in learning* about spreadsheets.

To keep things simple, each of these two dimensions has three levels. Combining them results in nine combinations, which are shown in Table 5-1. In reality, only seven segments are worth thinking about because both moderately experienced and very experienced spreadsheet users generally have at least *some* interest in spreadsheets. (After all, that's what motivated them to get their experience.) Users who have a lot of spreadsheet experience and a low level of interest would make very bad developers.

TABLE 5-1 CLASSIFICATION OF SPREADSHEET USERS
         BY EXPERIENCE AND INTEREST

	No Interest	Moderately Interested	Very Interested
Little Experience	User	User	User/Potential Developer
Moderately Experienced	N/A	User	Developer
Very Experienced	N/A	User	Developer

It should be clear that spreadsheet developers must have a great deal of experience with spreadsheets as well as a high interest in spreadsheets. Those with little spreadsheet experience, but with a great deal of interest, are potential developers. All they need is more experience. If you're reading this book, you probably fall into one of the boxes in the last column of the table.

The audience for spreadsheet applications

The remaining segments in the preceding table comprise spreadsheet end users, whom you can think of as the consumers of spreadsheet applications. When you develop a spreadsheet application for others to use, you need to know which of these groups of people will actually be using your application.

Users with little experience and no interest comprise a large percentage of all spreadsheet users, which is probably the largest segment of all. These are the people who need to use a spreadsheet for their jobs but who view the spreadsheet simply as a means to an end. Typically, they know very little about computers and software, and they usually have no interest in learning anything more than what's required to get their work done. They might even feel a bit intimidated by computers. Often, these users don't even know which version of their spreadsheet they use, and they are largely unfamiliar with what it can do. Obviously, applications developed for this group must be user-friendly. By that I mean straightforward, unintimidating, easy to use, and as bulletproof as possible.

From the developer's point of view, a more interesting group of users are those who have little or moderate spreadsheet experience but are interested in learning more. These users understand the concept of formulas, use built-in worksheet functions, and generally have a good idea of what the product is capable of doing. These users generally appreciate the work that you put into an application and are often impressed by your efforts. Even better, they'll often make excellent suggestions for improving your applications. Applications developed for this group should also be user-friendly (easy to use and bulletproof), but they can also be more complex and customizable than applications designed for the less experienced and less interested groups.

Solving Problems with a Spreadsheet

I've covered the basic concept of a spreadsheet application, discussed the end users and developers of such applications, and even attempted to figure out why people use spreadsheets at all. Now it's time to take a look at the types of tasks that are appropriate for spreadsheet applications.

You might already have a pretty good idea of the types of tasks for which you can use a spreadsheet. Traditionally, spreadsheet software has been used for numerical applications that are largely interactive in nature. Corporate budgets are an excellent example of this. After the model has been set up (that is, after formulas have been developed), working with a budget is simply a matter of plugging in amounts and observing the bottom-line totals. Often, budgeters simply need to allocate fixed resources among various activities and present the results in a reasonably attractive (or at least legible) format. A spreadsheet, of course, is ideal for this.

Budget-type problems, however, probably account for only a small percentage of your spreadsheet-development time. If you're like me, you've learned that uses for spreadsheet software (particularly in recent years) can often extend well beyond the types of tasks for which spreadsheets were originally designed.

Here are just a few examples of nontraditional ways that a spreadsheet such as Excel can be used:

◆ *As a presentation device:* For example, with minimal effort you can create an attractive, interactive on-screen slideshow with only Excel.

◆ *As a data-entry tool:* For repetitive data-entry tasks, a spreadsheet is often the most efficient route to take. The data can then be exported to a variety of formats for use in other programs.

◆ *As a forms generator:* For creating attractive printed forms, many find it easier to use Excel's formatting capabilities than to learn a desktop publishing package such as PageMaker.

◆ *As a text processor:* The text functions found in all spreadsheets enable you to manipulate text in ways that are impossible using a word processor.

◆ *As a platform for simple games:* Clearly, Excel was not designed with this in mind. However, I've downloaded (and written) some interesting strategy games by using the tools found in Excel and other spreadsheets.

You can probably think of many more examples for this list.

Ironically, the versatility of spreadsheets is a double-edged sword. On one hand, it's tempting to try to use a spreadsheet for every problem that crops up. On the other hand, you'll often be spinning your wheels by trying to use a spreadsheet for a problem that's better suited for a different solution.

Basic Spreadsheet Types

In this section, I classify spreadsheets into several basic types to provide a better perspective on how spreadsheet applications fit into the overall scheme of things. This is all quite arbitrary, of course, and is based solely on my own experience. Moreover, there is quite a bit of overlap between the categories, but they cover most of the spreadsheets that I've seen and developed.

My names for these categories are as follows:

◆ Quick-and-dirty

◆ For-your-eyes-only

◆ Single-user applications

◆ Spaghetti applications

◆ Utility applications

◆ Add-ins that contain worksheet functions

◆ Single-block budgets

◆ What-if models

◆ Data storage and access

◆ Database front ends

◆ Turnkey applications

I discuss each of these categories in the following sections.

Quick-and-dirty spreadsheets

This is probably the most common type of spreadsheet. Most of the spreadsheets in this category are fairly small and are developed to quickly solve a problem or answer a question. Here's an example: You're about to buy a new car, and you want to figure out your monthly payment for various loan amounts. Or perhaps you need to generate a chart that shows your company's sales by month, so you quickly enter 12 values and whip out a chart, which you paste into your word processor.

In both of the preceding cases, you can probably input the entire model in a few minutes, and you certainly won't take the time to document your work. You probably won't even think of developing any macros or custom dialog boxes. In fact, you might not even deem these simple spreadsheets worthy of saving to disk. Obviously, spreadsheets in this category are not applications.

For-your-eyes-only spreadsheets

As the name implies, no one except you – the creator – will ever see or use the spreadsheets that fall into this category. An example of this type might be a file in which you keep information relevant to your income taxes. You open the file whenever a check comes in the mail, you incur an expense that can be justified as business, you buy tax-deductible Girl Scout cookies, and so on. Another example is a spreadsheet that you use to keep track of your employees' time records (sick leave, vacation, and so on).

Spreadsheets in this category differ from quick-and-dirty spreadsheets in that you use them more than once, so you save these spreadsheets to files. But again, they're not worth spending a great deal of time on. You might apply some simple formatting, but that's about it. This type of spreadsheet also lacks any type of error detection because you understand how the formulas are set up; you know enough to avoid inputting data that will produce erroneous results. If an error does crop up, you immediately know what caused it.

Spreadsheets in this category don't qualify as applications although they sometimes increase in sophistication over time. For example, I have an Excel workbook that I use to track my income by source. This workbook was simple when I first set it up, but I tend to add accouterments to it on a regular basis – more summary formulas, better formatting, and even a chart that displays income by month. My latest modification was to add a best-fit line to the chart to project income based on past trends. I'll probably continue to add more to this file, and it may eventually qualify for the single-user application category.

Single-user applications

This is a spreadsheet application that only the developer uses, but its complexity extends beyond the spreadsheets in the for-your-eyes-only category. For example, I developed a workbook to keep track of registered users for my shareware applications. It started out as a simple worksheet database (for my eyes only), but then I realized that I could also use it to generate mailing labels and invoices. One day I spent an hour or so writing macros and then realized that I had converted this application from a for-your-eyes-only application to a single-user application.

No one else will ever use this spreadsheet, but it's a slick little application that's very easy to use. In this particular case, the time that I spent modifying the spreadsheet from a for-your-eyes-only spreadsheet to a single-user application was definitely time well spent because it has already saved me several hours of work. The application now has buttons that execute macros, and it has greatly reduced the amount of effort required to deal with the mechanics of tracking my customers and mailing products.

Creating single-user applications for yourself is an excellent way to get practice with Excel's developer's tools. For example, you can learn to create custom dialog boxes, modify menus, create a custom toolbar, write Visual Basic for Applications

(VBA) macros, and so on. You'll find that working on a meaningful project (even if it's meaningful only to you) is the best way to learn advanced features in Excel — or any other software, for that matter.

Spaghetti applications

An all-too-common type of spreadsheet is what I call a *spaghetti application*. The term stems from the fact that the parts of the application are difficult to follow, much like a plate of spaghetti. Most of these spreadsheets begin life as a reasonably focused, single-user application. But over time they are passed along to others who make their own modifications. As requirements change and employees come and go, new parts are added and others are ignored. Before too long, the original purpose of the workbook may have been forgotten. The result is a file that is used frequently, but no one really understands exactly how it all works.

Everyone who's involved with it knows that the spaghetti application should be completely reworked. But because nobody really understands it, the situation tends to worsen over time. Spreadsheet consultants make a lot of money untangling such applications. I've found that in most cases, the most efficient solution is to redefine the user needs and build a new application from scratch.

Utility applications

No one is ever completely satisfied with his or her spreadsheet product. Good as it is, I still find quite a bit lacking in Excel. This brings me to the next category of spreadsheets: *utility applications*. Utilities are special tools designed to perform a single recurring task. For example, if you often import text into Excel, you may want some additional text-handling commands, such as the ability to convert selected text to uppercase (without using formulas). The solution? Develop a text-handling utility that does exactly what you want.

The Power Utility Pak is a collection of utility applications for Excel. I developed these utilities to extend Excel's functionality. These utilities work just like normal Excel commands. You can find the shareware version of the Power Utility Pak on the companion CD-ROM, and you can get a free copy of the full version by using the coupon located at the back of the book. And if you're interested, the complete VBA source code is also available.

Utility applications are very general in nature. Most macros are designed to perform a specific operation on a specific type of data found in a specific type of workbook. A good utility application essentially works like a command normally found in Excel. In other words, the utility needs to recognize the context in which a command is executed and take appropriate action. This usually requires quite a bit of error-handling code so that the utility can handle any situation that comes up.

Utility applications always use macros and may or may not use custom dialog boxes. Fortunately, Excel makes it relatively easy to create such utilities, and they can be converted to add-ins and attached to Excel's user interface so that they appear to be part of Excel.

The topic of creating utilities is so important that I devote an entire chapter to it. Chapter 16 discusses how to create custom Excel utilities with VBA.

Add-ins that contain worksheet functions

As you know, Excel has many worksheet functions that you can use in formulas. Chances are that you've needed a particular function, only to find that it doesn't exist. The solution? Create your own by using VBA. Custom worksheet functions can often simplify your formulas and make your spreadsheet easier to maintain.

In Chapter 10, you'll find everything you need to know about creating custom worksheet functions, including lots of examples.

Single-block budgets

By a *single-block budget,* I mean a spreadsheet (not necessarily a budget model) that essentially consists of one block of cells. The top row might contain names that correspond to time (months, quarters, or years), and the left column usually contains categories of some type. Typically, the bottom row and right column contain formulas that add the numbers together. There may or may not be formulas that compute subtotals within the block.

This is a very common type of spreadsheet. In fact, VisiCalc (the world's first spreadsheet) was developed with this type of model in mind. In most cases, simple single-block budget models are not good candidates for applications because they are simple to begin with, but there *are* exceptions. For example, you might consider converting such a spreadsheet into an application if the model is an unwieldy 3-D spreadsheet, needs to include consolidations from other files, or will be used by departmental managers who might not understand spreadsheets.

What-if models

Many consider the what-if model category to be the epitome of spreadsheets at their best. The ability to instantly recalculate thousands of formulas makes spreadsheet software the ideal tool for financial modeling and other models that depend on the values of several variables. If you think about it, just about any spreadsheet that contains formulas is a what-if model (which are often distributed as templates). Changing the value of a cell used in a formula is akin to asking "what if . . .?" My view of this category, however, is a bit more sophisticated. It includes spreadsheets designed exclusively for systematically analyzing the effects of various inputs.

What-if models are often good candidates for user-oriented applications, especially if the model will be used for a lengthy period of time. Creating a good user interface on an application can make it very easy for anyone to use, including computer-illiterates. As an example, you might create an interface that lets the user provide names for various sets of assumptions and then lets you instantly view the results of a selected scenario and create a perfectly formatted summary chart with the click of a button.

Data storage and access spreadsheets

It's not surprising that spreadsheets are often used for keeping lists or modest database manipulations. Most people find that it's much easier to view and manipulate data in a spreadsheet than it is using normal database software. Beginning with Excel 97, each worksheet consists of 65,536 rows, which is a size increase that greatly extends the potential for database work.

Spreadsheets in this category are often candidates for applications, especially if end users need to perform moderately sophisticated operations. However, Excel's built-in Data Form dialog box and its AutoFilter feature make working with databases so easy that even beginning users can master simple database operations quickly.

For more sophisticated database applications, such as those that use multiple tables with relationships between them, you'll be better off using a real database program such as Access.

Database front ends

Increasingly, spreadsheet products are used to access external databases. Spreadsheet users can access data stored in external files, even if they come in a variety of formats, by using tools that Excel provides. When you create an application that does this, it's sometimes referred to as an *executive information system*, or *EIS*. This sort of system combines data from several sources and summarizes it for users.

Accessing external databases from a spreadsheet often strikes fear in the hearts of beginning users. Creating an executive information system is therefore an ideal sort of Excel application because its chief goal is usually ease of use.

Turnkey applications

The final category of spreadsheet types is the most complex. By *turnkey,* I mean ready to go, with little or no preparation by the end user. For example, the user loads the file and is presented with a user interface that makes user choices perfectly clear. Turnkey applications may not even look as if they are being powered by a spreadsheet; and often, the user interacts completely with dialog boxes rather than cells.

Actually, many of the categories just described can be converted into turnkey applications. The critical common elements, as I discuss throughout the remainder of the book, are good planning, error handling, and user interface design.

Chapter 6

Essentials of Spreadsheet Application Development

IN THIS CHAPTER
My goal in this chapter is to provide you with some *general* guidelines that you may find useful while you learn to create effective applications with Excel.

- ◆ A discussion of the basic steps involved in spreadsheet application development

- ◆ Determining end user needs and planning applications to meet those needs

- ◆ Guidelines for developing and testing your applications

- ◆ Documenting your development efforts and writing user documentation

THERE IS NO SIMPLE, SURE-FIRE RECIPE for developing an effective spreadsheet application. Everyone has his or her own style for creating such applications, and in my experience, I haven't discovered one best way that works for everyone. In addition, every project that you undertake will be different, and will therefore require its own approach. Finally, the demands and general attitudes of the people whom you'll be working with (or for) also play a role in how the development process will proceed.

As I mention in the preceding chapter, spreadsheet developers typically perform the following activities:

- ◆ Determine the needs of the user

- ◆ Plan an application that meets these needs

- ◆ Determine the most appropriate user interface

- ◆ Create the spreadsheet, formulas, macros, and user interface

- ◆ Test and debug the application

- ◆ Attempt to make the application bulletproof

- ◆ Make the application aesthetically appealing and intuitive

- ◆ Document the development effort

- ◆ Develop user documentation and help

- ◆ Distribute the application to the user

- ◆ Update the application when it's necessary

Not all these steps are required for each application, and the order in which these activities are performed may vary from project to project. Each of these activities is described in the pages that follow; and in most cases, the technical details are covered in subsequent chapters.

Determining User Needs

When you undertake a spreadsheet application development project, one of your first steps is to identify exactly what the end users require. Failure to thoroughly assess the end users' needs early on often results in additional work later when you have to adjust the application so that it does what it was supposed to do in the first place.

In some cases, you'll be intimately familiar with the end users — and you might even be an end user yourself. In other cases (for example, a consultant developing a project for a new client), you may know little or nothing about the users or their situation.

How do you determine the needs of the user? If you've been asked to develop a spreadsheet application, it's a good idea to meet with the end user and ask very specific questions. Better yet, get everything in writing, create flow diagrams, pay attention to minor details, and do anything else to ensure that the product you deliver is the product that is needed.

Following are some guidelines that may help to make this phase easier:

- ◆ Don't presume that you know what the user needs. Second-guessing at this stage almost always causes problems later on.

- ◆ If possible, talk directly to the end users of the application — not just their supervisor or manager.

- ◆ Learn what, if anything, is currently being done to meet the user's needs. You might be able to save some work by simply adapting an existing application. At the very least, looking at current solutions will familiarize you with the operation.

- ◆ Identify the resources available at the user's site. For example, try to determine whether there are any hardware or software limitations that you must work around.

- ◆ If possible, determine the specific hardware systems that will be used. If your application will be used on slower systems, you need to take that into account. See the later section "System speed."

◆ Identify which version(s) of Excel are in use. Although Microsoft does everything in its power to urge users to upgrade to the latest version of their software, I've read estimates that fewer than 50 percent of Microsoft Office users have the most recent version.

◆ Understand the skill levels of the end users. This information will help you design the application appropriately.

◆ Determine how long the application will be used and whether any changes are anticipated during the lifetime of the project. Knowing this may influence the amount of effort that you put into the project and help you plan for changes.

One final note: Don't be surprised if the project specifications change before you complete the application. This is quite common, and you'll be in a better position if you expect changes rather than are surprised by them. Just make sure that your contract (if you have one) addresses the issue of changing specifications.

Planning an Application That Meets User Needs

After you determined the end users' needs, it's very tempting to jump right in and start fiddling around in Excel — take it from someone who suffers from this problem. But try to restrain yourself. Builders don't construct a house without a set of blueprints, and you shouldn't develop a spreadsheet application without some type of plan. The formality of your plan depends on the scope of the project and your general style of working, but you should at least spend *some* time thinking about what you're going to do and coming up with a plan of action.

Before rolling up your sleeves and settling down at your keyboard, you'll benefit by taking some time to consider the various ways how you can approach the problem. Here is where a thorough knowledge of Excel pays off. Avoiding blind alleys before you stumble into them is always a good idea.

If you ask a dozen Excel experts to design an application based on very precise specifications, chances are that you'll get a dozen different implementations of the project that meet those specifications. And of those solutions, some will definitely be better than the others because Excel often provides several different options to accomplish a task. If you know Excel inside and out, you'll have a pretty good idea of the potential methods at your disposal, and you can choose the one most appropriate for the project at hand. Often, a bit of creative thinking yields an unusual approach that's vastly superior to other methods.

So at the beginning stage of this planning period, you'll be considering some general options, such as these:

◆ *File structure:* Think about whether you want to use one workbook with multiple sheets, several single-sheet workbooks, or a template file.

◆ *Data structure:* You should always consider how your data will be structured. This includes the use of external database files versus storing everything in worksheets.

◆ *Formulas versus VBA:* Should you use formulas or write Visual Basic for Applications (VBA) procedures to perform calculations? Both have advantages and disadvantages.

◆ *Add-in or XLS file:* In some cases, an add-in might be the best choice for your final product. Or, perhaps you might use an add-in in conjunction with a standard workbook.

◆ *Version of Excel:* Will your Excel application be used with Excel 2003 only? With Excel 2000 or Excel 2002? What about Excel 97, Excel 95, and Excel 5? Will it also be run on a Macintosh? These are very important considerations because each new version of Excel adds features that aren't available in previous versions.

◆ *Error handling:* Error handling is a major issue with applications. You need to determine how your application will detect and deal with errors. For example, if your application applies formatting to the active worksheet, you need to be able to handle a case in which a chart sheet is active.

◆ *Use of special features:* If your application needs to summarize a lot of data, you might want to consider using Excel's pivot table feature. Or, you might want to use Excel's data validation feature as a check for valid data entry.

◆ *Performance issues:* The time to start thinking about increasing the speed and efficiency of your application is at the development stage, not when the application is completed, and users are complaining.

◆ *Level of security:* As you may know, Excel provides several protection options to restrict access to particular elements of a workbook. For example, you can lock cells so that formulas cannot be changed, and you can assign a password to prevent unauthorized users from viewing or accessing specific files. Determining up front exactly what you need to protect — and what level of protection is necessary — will make your job easier.

 Be aware that Excel's protection features are not 100 percent effective. If you desire complete and absolute security for your application, Excel probably isn't the best platform.

You'll probably have to deal with many other project-specific considerations in this phase. The important thing is that you consider all options and don't settle on the first solution that comes to mind.

Another design consideration is remembering to plan for change. You'll do yourself a favor if you make your application as generic as possible. For example, don't write a procedure that works with only a specific range of cells. Rather, write a procedure that accepts any range as an argument. When the inevitable changes are requested, such a design makes it easier for you to carry out the revisions. Also, you might find that the work that you do for one project is similar to the work that you do for another. Keeping reusability in mind when you are planning a project is always a good idea.

One thing that I've learned from experience is to avoid letting the end user completely guide your approach to a problem. For example, suppose you meet with a manager who tells you that the department needs an application that writes text files, which will be imported into another application. Don't confuse the user's need with the solution. The user's real need is to share data. Using an intermediate text file to do it is one possible solution to the need. There might be other ways to approach the problem – such as direct transfer of information by using Dynamic Data Exchange (DDE) or Object Linking and Embedding (OLE). In other words, don't let the users define their problem by stating it in terms of a solution approach. Determining the best approach is *your* job.

Learning While You Develop

Now a few words about reality: Excel is a moving target. Excel's upgrade cycle is approximately 18–24 months, which means that you have fewer than two years to get up to speed with its current innovations before you have even more innovations to contend with.

Excel 5, which introduced VBA, represented a major paradigm shift for Excel developers. Thousands of people up until that point earned their living developing Excel applications that were largely based on the XLM macro language in Excel 2, 3, and 4. Beginning with Excel 5, dozens of new tools became available and developers, for the most part, eagerly embraced them.

When Excel 97 became available, developers faced yet another shift. This new version introduced a new file format, the Visual Basic Editor (VBE), and UserForms as a replacement for dialog sheets. Excel 2000, 2002, and 2003 introduced additional features, but these changes were not as radical as in previous upgrades.

VBA is not difficult to learn, but it definitely takes time to become comfortable with it – and even more time to master it. Consequently, it's not uncommon to be in the process of learning VBA while you're developing applications with it. In fact, I think it's impossible to learn VBA without developing applications. If you're like me, you'll find it much easier to learn VBA if you have a project that requires it. Learning VBA just for the sake of learning VBA usually doesn't work.

Determining the Most Appropriate User Interface

When you develop spreadsheets that others will use, you need to pay special attention to the user interface. By *user interface,* I mean the method by which the user interacts with the application – clicking buttons, using menus, pressing keys, accessing toolbars, and so on.

Again, it's important that you keep the end user in mind. It's likely that you have much more computer experience than the end users, and an interface that's intuitive to you might not be as intuitive to everyone else.

One way to approach the user interface issue is to rely on Excel's built-in features: its menus, toolbars, scroll bars, and so on. In other words, you can simply set up the workbook and then let the user work with it however he or she wants. This may be the perfect solution if the application will be used only by those who know Excel well. More often, however, you'll find that the audience for your application consists of relatively inexperienced (and often disinterested) users. This makes your job more difficult, and you'll need to pay particular attention to the user interface that drives your application.

Excel provides several features that are relevant to user interface design:

◆ Custom dialog boxes (UserForms)

◆ Controls (such as a ListBox or a CommandButton) placed directly on a worksheet

◆ Custom menus

◆ Custom toolbars

◆ Custom shortcut keys

I discuss these features briefly in the following sections and cover them more thoroughly in later chapters.

Creating custom dialog boxes

Anyone who has used a personal computer for any length of time is undoubtedly familiar with dialog boxes. Consequently, custom Excel dialog boxes play a major role in the user interfaces that you design for your applications.

 Excel 97 introduced a completely new way to create custom dialog boxes: UserForms. However, subsequent versions still support Excel 5/95 dialog sheets. This book focuses exclusively on UserForms.

You can use a custom dialog box to solicit user input, get a user's options or preferences, and direct the flow of your entire application. Custom dialog boxes are stored in UserForms (one dialog box per UserForm). You create and edit custom dialog boxes in the VBE, which you access by pressing Alt+F11. The elements that make up a dialog box (buttons, drop-down lists, check boxes, and so on) are called *controls* – more specifically, *ActiveX controls*. Excel provides a standard assortment of ActiveX controls, and you can also incorporate third-party controls.

After adding a control to a dialog box, you can link it to a worksheet cell so that it doesn't require any macros (except a simple macro to display the dialog box). Linking a control to a cell is easy, but it's not always the best way to get user input from a dialog box. Most of the time, you'll want to develop VBA macros that work with your custom dialog boxes.

I cover UserForms in detail in Part IV.

Using ActiveX controls on a worksheet

Excel also lets you add the UserForm ActiveX controls to a worksheet's *drawing layer* (an invisible layer on top of a sheet that holds pictures, charts, and other objects). Figure 6-1 shows a simple worksheet model with several UserForm controls inserted directly on the worksheet. This sheet contains some examples of an OptionButton, a ScrollBar, a CommandButton, and a CheckBox.

This workbook, which also includes a few simple macros, is available on the companion CD-ROM.

Perhaps the most common control is a CommandButton. By itself, a CommandButton doesn't do anything, so you have to attach a macro to each CommandButton.

Using dialog box controls directly in a worksheet often eliminates the need for custom dialog boxes. You can often greatly simplify the operation of a spreadsheet by adding a few ActiveX controls to a worksheet. This lets the user make choices by operating familiar controls rather than making entries into cells.

The ActiveX controls are found on the Control Toolbox toolbar. You can also use Excel 5/95 compatible controls on a worksheet. These controls, which are not ActiveX controls, are available on the Forms toolbar. These controls are not discussed in this book. Table 6-1 summarizes these two classes of controls.

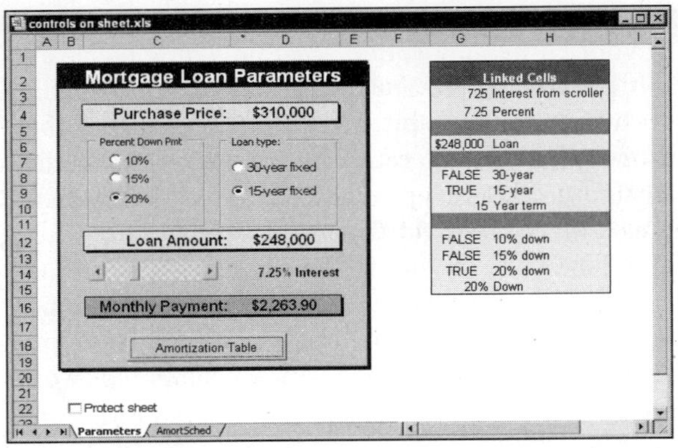

Figure 6-1: Directly adding UserForm controls may make a worksheet easier to use.

TABLE 6-1 ACTIVEX CONTROLS VERSUS EXCEL CONTROLS

	ActiveX Controls	Excel Controls
Excel versions	97, 2000, 2002, 2003	5, 95, 97, 2000, 2002, 2003
Which toolbar?	Control Toolbox	Forms
Controls available	CheckBox, TextBox, CommandButton, OptionButton, ListBox, ComboBox, ToggleButton, SpinButton, ScrollBar, Label, Image (and others can be added)	Label, GroupBox, Button, CheckBox, OptionButton, ListBox, DropDown (ComboBox), ScrollBar, Spinner
Macro code storage	In the code module for the Sheet	In any standard VBA module
Macro name	Corresponds to the control name (for example, CommandButton1_Click)	Any name you specify
Correspond to . . .	UserForm controls	Dialog Sheet controls
Customization	Extensive, using the Properties box	Minimal
Respond to events	Yes	Click or Change events only

Customizing menus

Another way to control the user interface in spreadsheet applications is to modify Excel's menus or to create your own menu system. Instead of creating buttons that execute macros, you can add one or more new menus or menu items to execute macros that you've already created. An advantage to custom menus is that the menu bar is always visible, whereas a button placed on a worksheet can easily scroll out of view.

Beginning with Excel 97, Microsoft implemented an entirely different way of dealing with menus. As you'll see in Chapter 22, a menu bar is actually a toolbar in disguise. Figure 6-2 shows an example of a new menu added to Excel. This menu was created by my Power Utility Pak add-in, which is included on the companion CD. Each menu item triggers a macro.

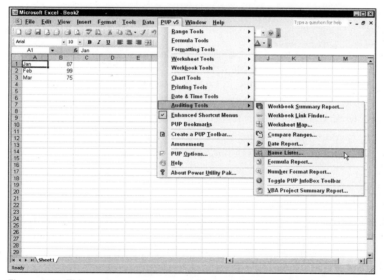

Figure 6-2: This new menu was created by an add-in.

There are two ways to customize Excel's menus. You can use VBA code to make the menu modifications, or you can edit the menu directly by choosing the View → Toolbars → Customize command.

As I explain in Chapter 23, the best approach is usually to use VBA commands to modify the menus. You have complete control over the menus, and you can even perform such operations as disabling the menu item or adding a checkmark to the item.

Menu modifications that you make by choosing the View → Toolbars → Customize command (see Figure 6-3) are permanent. In other words, if you make a menu change (such as the removal of a menu item), that change will remain in effect even if you restart Excel.

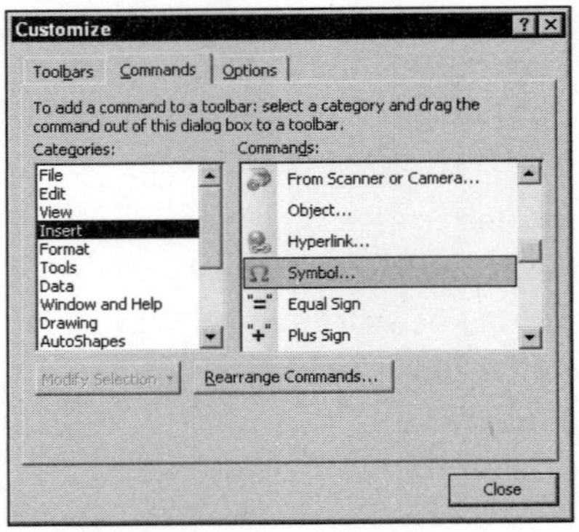

Figure 6-3: The Customize dialog box is where you make manual changes to the Excel menu system.

NOTE The Menu Editor (which debuted in Excel 5) was removed, beginning with Excel 97. Menus that were created by using the Menu Editor will continue to function when the workbook is loaded into Excel 97 or later. However, the only way to modify or delete menus created with the Menu Editor is to use Excel 5 or seek a utility that was designed for this purpose.

You'll find that you can customize every menu that Excel displays, even the shortcut menus that appear when you right-click an object. You must use VBA to customize the shortcut menus: You can't do so manually. Figure 6-4 shows a customized shortcut menu that appears when you right-click a chart. Notice that this shortcut menu has two new commands that aren't normally available (that is, the last two menu items).

I cover custom menus in detail in Chapter 23.

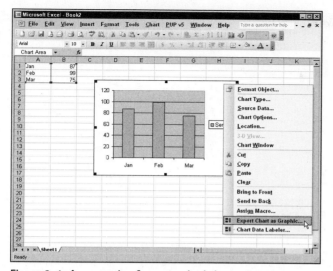

Figure 6-4: An example of a customized shortcut menu.

Customizing toolbars

Toolbars are very common in Windows applications, and Excel offers a huge assortment of built-in toolbars. Generally, toolbar buttons serve as shortcuts for commonly used menu commands to give users a quicker way to issue commands. Because a mouse is required to click a toolbar button, a toolbar button generally isn't the *only* way to execute a particular operation. Excel's toolbars, for example, make it possible to do most of the common spreadsheet operations without even using the menus.

You can create a custom toolbar that contains only the tools that you want users to be able to access. In fact, if you attach macros to these tools, a custom toolbar becomes the equivalent of a group of buttons placed on a worksheet. The advantage to using the toolbar in this way is that it is always visible and can be repositioned anywhere on the screen. Buttons inserted on a worksheet are fixed in place and can be scrolled off the screen.

Beginning with Excel 97, you can also add menus to a toolbar.

You can set up your application so that the toolbar appears whenever your application is loaded. You do this by attaching a toolbar to a workbook by using the Attach button in the Toolbars tab of the Customize dialog box (see Figure 6-5).

This lets you store individual toolbars with a workbook application so that you can distribute them to users of your application.

Attach Toolbars

Custom toolbars:
Chart Tools
Custom Formatting
My Shortcut Buttons

Toolbars in workbook:

Copy >>

OK   Cancel

Figure 6-5: You can attach a custom toolbar to a worksheet with the Attach Toolbars dialog box.

I discuss toolbars in detail in Chapter 22.

Creating shortcut keys

The final user interface option at your disposal is to create custom shortcut keys. If speed is essential, pressing a key combination is usually faster than issuing menu commands, using a toolbar, or working with a dialog box. Excel lets you assign a Ctrl key (or Shift+Ctrl key) combination (shortcut) to a macro. When the user presses the key combination, the macro executes.

Be cognizant, however, of these two caveats. One, obviously, you have to make it clear to the user which keys are active and what they do. Second, you need to be careful not to assign a key combination that's already in use for something else. In other words, a key combination that you assign to a macro takes precedence over the built-in shortcut keys. For example, Ctrl+S is a built-in Excel (and standard Microsoft) shortcut key used to save the current file. If you assign this key combination to a macro, you lose the ability to save the file with Ctrl+S. **Remember:** Shortcut keys are case-sensitive, so you can use a combination such as Ctrl+Shift+S.

Part III of this book is devoted to VBA, which is the language that you'll use to write your macros.

Executing the development effort

After you identify user needs, determine the approach that you'll take to meet those needs, and decide on the components that you'll use for the user interface, it's time to get down to the nitty-gritty and start creating the application. This step, of course, comprises a great deal of the total time that you spend on a particular project.

How you go about developing the application depends on your own personal style and the nature of the application. Except for simple fill-in-the-blanks template workbooks, your application will probably use macros. Developing the macros is the tough part. It's easy to create macros in Excel, but it's difficult to create *good* macros.

Concerning Yourself with the End User

In this section, I discuss the important development issues that surface as your application becomes more and more workable and as the time to package and distribute your work grows nearer.

Testing the application

How many times have you used a commercial software application, only to have it bomb out on you at a crucial moment? Most likely, the problem was caused by insufficient testing that didn't catch all the bugs. All nontrivial software has bugs, but in the best software, the bugs are simply more obscure. As you'll see, you sometimes have to work around the bugs in Excel to get your application to perform properly.

After you create your application, you need to test it. This is one of the most crucial steps; it's not uncommon to spend as much time testing and debugging an application as you did creating the application in the first place. Actually, you should be doing a great deal of testing during the development phase. After all, whether you're writing a VBA routine or creating formulas in a worksheet, you'll want to make sure that the application is working the way it's supposed to work.

Like standard compiled applications, spreadsheet applications that you develop are prone to bugs. A *bug* is usually defined as (1) something that does happen but shouldn't while a program (or application) is running, or (2) something that doesn't happen when it should happen. Both species of bugs are equally nasty, and you should plan on devoting a good portion of your development time to testing the application under all reasonable conditions and fixing any problems that you find. In some cases, unfortunately, the problems aren't entirely your fault. Excel, too, has its problems (see the "Bugs? In Excel?" sidebar).

Bugs? In Excel?

You might think that a product like Excel, which is used by millions of people throughout the world, would be relatively free of bugs. Think again. Excel is such a complex piece of software that it is only natural to expect some problems with it. And Excel *does* have some problems.

Getting a product like Excel out the door is not easy, even for a company like Microsoft with seemingly unlimited resources. Releasing a software product involves compromises and trade-offs. It's commonly known that most major software vendors release their products with full knowledge that they contain bugs. Most of the bugs are considered insignificant enough to ignore. Software companies could postpone their releases by a few months and fix many of them, but software, like everything else, is ruled by economics. The benefits of delaying a product often do not exceed the costs involved. Although Excel definitely has its share of bugs, my guess is that the majority of Excel users never encounter one.

In this book, I point out the problems with Excel that I know about. You'll surely discover some more on your own. Some problems occur only with a particular version of Excel — and under a specific configuration involving hardware and/or software. These are the worst of all bugs because they aren't easily reproducible.

So what's a developer to do? It's called a *workaround.* If something that you try to do doesn't work — and all indications say that it *should* work — it's time to move on to Plan B. Frustrating? Sure. A waste of your time? Absolutely. It's all part of being a developer.

I probably don't need to tell you to thoroughly test any spreadsheet development that you develop for others. And depending on its eventual audience, you might want to make your application bulletproof. In other words, try to anticipate all the errors and screw-ups that could possibly occur, making concerted efforts to avoid them — or at least, handle them gracefully. This not only helps the end user, but also makes it easier on you and your reputation. Also consider using beta testing; your end users are likely candidates because they are the ones who will be using your product. See the upcoming sidebar "What about Beta Testing?"

Although you cannot conceivably test for all possibilities, your macros should be able to handle common types of errors. For example, what if the user enters a text string instead of a numeric value? What if the user tries to run your macro when a workbook isn't open? What if he or she cancels a dialog box without making any selections? What happens if the user presses Ctrl+F6 and jumps to the next window? When you gain experience, issues like this become very familiar, and you'll account for them without even thinking.

Making the application bulletproof

If you think about it, it's fairly easy to destroy a spreadsheet. Erasing one critical formula or value often causes errors throughout the entire worksheet – and perhaps even other dependent worksheets. Even worse, if the damaged workbook is saved, it replaces the good copy on disk. Unless a backup procedure is in place, the user of your application could be in trouble, and *you'll* probably be blamed for it.

Obviously, it's easy to see why you need to add some protection when users – especially novices – will be using your worksheets. Excel provides several techniques for protecting worksheets and parts of worksheets:

◆ *Lock specific cells:* You can lock specific cells (by using the Protection tab in the Format Cells dialog box) so that they cannot be changed. This takes effect only when the document is protected with the Tools → Protection → Protect Sheet command.

◆ *Protect an entire workbook:* You can protect an entire workbook – the structure of the workbook, the window position and size, or both. Choose the Tools → Protection → Protect Workbook command for this purpose.

What about Beta Testing?

Software manufacturers typically have a rigorous testing cycle for new products. After extensive internal testing, the prerelease product is usually sent to a group of interested users for *beta testing.* This phase often uncovers additional problems that are usually corrected before the product's final release.

If you're developing an Excel application that more than a few people will use, you might want to consider a beta test. This enables your application to be used in its intended setting on different hardware (usually) and by the intended users.

The beta period should begin after you've completed all your own testing and you feel that the application is ready to distribute. You'll need to identify a group of users to help you. The process works best if you distribute everything that will ultimately be included in your application: user documentation, installation program, help, and so on. You can evaluate the beta test in a number of ways, including face-to-face discussions, questionnaires, and phone calls.

You will almost always become aware of problems that you need to correct or improvements that you need to make before you undertake a widespread distribution of the application. Of course, a beta testing phase takes additional time, and not all projects can afford that luxury.

How Secure Are Excel's Passwords?

As far as I know, Microsoft has never advertised Excel as a secure program. And for good reason: It's actually quite easy to thwart Excel's password system. Several commercial programs are available that can break passwords. Excel 2002 and later seem to have stronger security than previous versions. Bottom line? Don't think of password protection as foolproof. Sure, it will be effective for the casual user. But if someone *really* wants to break your password, it can probably be done.

◆ *Hide the formulas in specific cells:* You can hide the formulas in specific cells (by using the Protection tab in the Format Cells dialog box) so that others can't see them. Again, this takes effect only when the document is protected by choosing the Tools → Protection → Protect Sheet command.

◆ *Lock objects on the worksheet:* You can lock objects on the worksheet (by using the Protection tab in the Format Object dialog box). This takes effect only when the document is protected via the Tools → Protection → Protect Sheet command.

◆ *Hide rows, columns, sheets, and documents:* You can hide rows (choose Format → Row → Hide), columns (choose Format → Column → Hide), sheets (choose Format → Sheet → Hide), and documents (choose Window → Hide). This helps prevent the worksheet from looking cluttered and also provides some protection against prying eyes.

◆ *Designate an Excel workbook as read-only recommended:* You can designate an Excel workbook as read-only recommended (and use a password) to ensure that the file cannot be overwritten with any changes. You do this in the Save Options dialog box. Display this dialog box by choosing Tools → General Options in the Save As dialog box.

◆ *Assign a password:* You can assign a password to prevent unauthorized users from opening your file. You do this in the Save Options dialog box. Display this dialog box by choosing Tools → General Options in the Save As dialog box.

◆ *Use a password-protected add-in:* You can use a password-protected add-in, which doesn't allow the user to change *anything* on its worksheets.

Beginning with Excel 2002, you have several new options in the area of sheet protection. Choose Tools → Protection → Protect Sheet, and you'll see the Protect Sheet dialog box. This allows you to specify exactly which actions can be performed on a protected sheet. Also, the Save Options dialog box has an Advanced button. Clicking this button allows you to set the encryption level of the workbook.

Making the application aesthetically appealing and intuitive

If you've used many different software packages, you've undoubtedly seen examples of poorly designed user interfaces, difficult-to-use programs, and just plain ugly screens. If you're developing spreadsheets for other people, you should pay particular attention to how the application looks.

How a computer program looks can make all the difference in the world to users, and the same is true with the applications that you develop with Excel. Beauty, however, is in the eye of the beholder. If your skills lean more in the analytical direction, consider enlisting the assistance of someone with a more aesthetic sensibility to provide help with design.

The users of your applications will appreciate a good-looking user interface, and your applications will have a much more polished and professional look if you devote some additional time to design and aesthetic considerations. An application that looks good demonstrates that its developer cared enough about the product to invest some extra time and effort. Take the following suggestions into account:

◆ *Strive for consistency:* When designing dialog boxes, for example, try to emulate Excel's dialog box look and feel whenever possible. Be consistent with formatting, fonts, text size, and colors.

◆ *Keep it simple:* A common mistake that developers make is trying to cram too much information into a single screen or dialog box. A good rule is to present only one or two chunks of information at a time.

◆ *Break down input screens:* If you use an input screen to solicit information from the user, consider breaking it up into several, less crowded screens. If you use a complex dialog box, you might want to break it up by using a MultiPage control (which lets you create a familiar tabbed dialog box).

◆ *Don't overdo color:* Use color sparingly. It's very easy to overdo it and make the screen look gaudy.

◆ *Monitor typography and graphics:* Pay attention to numeric formats, and use consistent typefaces, font sizes, and borders.

Evaluating aesthetic qualities is very subjective. When in doubt, strive for simplicity and clarity.

Creating a user Help system

With regard to user documentation, you basically have two choices: paper-based documentation or electronic documentation. Providing electronic help is standard fare in Windows applications. Fortunately, your Excel applications can also provide help – even context-sensitive help. Developing help text takes quite a bit of additional effort, but for a large project, it may be worth it.

Another point to consider is support for your application. In other words, who gets the phone call if the user encounters a problem? If you aren't prepared to handle routine questions, you'll need to identify someone who is. In some cases, you'll want to arrange it so that only highly technical or bug-related issues escalate to the developer.

In Chapter 24, I discuss several alternatives for providing help for your applications.

Documenting the development effort

Putting a spreadsheet application together is one thing. Making it understandable for other people is another. As with traditional programming, it's important that you thoroughly document your work. Such documentation helps you if you need to go back to it (and you will), and it helps anyone else whom you might pass it on to.

You might want to consider a couple of things when you document your project. For example, if you were hired to develop an Excel application, you might not want to share all your hard-earned secrets by thoroughly documenting everything. If this is the case, you should maintain two versions: one thoroughly documented and the other partially documented.

How do you document a workbook application? You can either store the information in a worksheet or use another file. You can even use a paper document if you prefer. Perhaps the easiest way is to use a separate worksheet to store your comments and key information for the project. For VBA code, use comments liberally. (VBA text preceded with an apostrophe is ignored because it's a comment.) Although an elegant piece of VBA code can seem perfectly obvious to you today, when you come back to it in a few months, your reasoning might be completely obscured unless you use the VBA comment feature.

Distributing the application to the user

You've completed your project, and you're ready to release it to the end users. How do you go about doing this? You can choose from many ways to distribute your application, and the method that you choose depends on many factors.

You could just hand over a CD-ROM, scribble a few instructions, and be on your way. Or, you may want to install the application yourself — but this is not always feasible. Another option is to develop an official setup program that performs the task automatically. You can write such a program in a traditional programming language, purchase a generic setup program, or write your own in VBA.

Excel 2000 and later uses Microsoft Authenticode technology to enable developers to digitally "sign" their applications. This process is designed to help end users identify the author of an application, ensure that the project has not been altered, and help prevent the spread of macro viruses or other potentially destructive code. To digitally sign a project, you just first apply for a digital certificate from a formal certificate authority (or, you can self-sign your project by creating your own digital certificate). Refer to the Help system or the Microsoft Web site for additional information.

Why Is There No Runtime Version of Excel?

When you distribute your application, you need to be sure that each end user has a licensed copy of the appropriate version of Excel. It's illegal to distribute a copy of Excel along with your application. Why, you might ask, doesn't Microsoft provide a runtime version of Excel? A *runtime version* is an executable program that can load files but not create them. With a runtime version, the end user wouldn't need a copy of Excel to run your application. (This is common with database programs.)

I've never seen a clear or convincing reason why Microsoft does not have a runtime version of Excel, and no other spreadsheet manufacturer offers a runtime version of its product, either. The most likely reason is that spreadsheet vendors fear that doing so would reduce sales of the software. Or, it could be that developing a runtime version would require a tremendous amount of programming that would just never pay off.

On a related note . . . Microsoft does offer an Excel file *viewer.* This product lets you view Excel files if you don't own a copy of Excel. Macros, however, will not execute. You can get a copy of this free file viewer from the Microsoft Web site (http://office.microsoft.com/downloads).

Updating the application when necessary

After you distribute your application, you're finished with it, right? You can sit back, enjoy yourself, and try to forget about the problems that you encountered (and solved) during the course of developing your application. In rare cases, yes, you may be finished. More often, however, the users of your application will not be completely satisfied. Sure, your application adheres to all the *original* specifications, but things change. Seeing an application working frequently causes the user to think of other things that the application could be doing. We're talking *updates*.

When you need to update or revise your application, you'll appreciate that you designed it well in the first place and that you fully documented your efforts. If not, well . . . we learn from our experiences.

Other Development Issues

You need to keep several other issues in mind when developing an application — especially if you don't know exactly who will be using the application. If you're developing an application that will have widespread use (a shareware application, for example), you have no way of knowing how the application will be used, what type of system it will run on, or what other software will be running concurrently.

The user's installed version of Excel

With every new release of Excel, the issue of compatibility rears its head. As I write this, Excel 2003 is just about ready to be released — yet many large corporations are still using Excel 97, and some use even earlier versions.

Unfortunately, there is no guarantee that an application developed for, say Excel 97, will work perfectly with later versions of Excel. If you need your application to work with a variety of Excel versions, the best approach is to work with the lowest version — and then test it thoroughly with all other versions.

Things get even more complicated when you consider Excel's "sub-versions." Microsoft distributes service releases (SRs) to correct problems. For example, users might have the original Excel 2000, Excel 2000 with SR-1, or Excel 2000 with SR-2.

And it gets even more complicated with Excel 2003. Microsoft sells several different editions of Office. Many of the new features in Excel are available only in the Professional version.

I discuss compatibility issues in Chapter 26.

Language issues

Consider yourself very fortunate if all of your end users have the English language version of Excel. Non-English versions of Excel aren't always 100 percent compatible, so that means additional testing on your part. In addition, keep in mind that two users can both be using the English language version of Excel yet use different Windows regional settings. In some cases, you may need to be aware of potential problems.

I briefly discuss language issues in Chapter 26.

System speed

You're probably a fairly advanced computer user and tend to keep your hardware reasonably up to date. In other words, you have a fairly powerful system that is probably better than the average user's system. In some cases, you'll know exactly what hardware that the end users of your applications are using. If so, it's vitally important that you test your application on that system. A procedure that executes almost instantaneously on your system may take several seconds on another system. In the world of computers, several seconds may be unacceptable.

When you gain more experience with VBA, you'll discover that there are ways to get the job done, and there are ways to get the job done *fast*. It's a good idea to get into the habit of coding for speed. Other chapters in this book will certainly help you out in this area.

Video modes

As you probably know, users' video displays vary widely. A video resolution of 1024 x 768 is most common, but many systems are set up with an 800 x 600 display. And higher resolution displays are becoming increasingly common. Just because you have a super-high resolution monitor, you can't assume that everyone else does.

Video resolution can be a problem if your application relies on specific information being displayed on a single screen. For example, if you develop an input screen that uses 1024 x 768 mode, users with a 1024 x 768 display may not be able to see all the input screen without scrolling. Also, it's important to realize that a *restored* (that is, not maximized or minimized) workbook is displayed at its previous window size and position. In the extreme case, it's possible that a window saved by using a high-resolution display may be completely off the screen when opened on a system running in a lower resolution.

Unfortunately, there's no way to automatically scale things so that they look the same regardless of the display resolution. In some cases, you can zoom the worksheet (using View → Zoom), but doing so may be difficult to do reliably. Unless you're certain of the video resolution that the users of your application will be using, it's important that you design your application by using the lowest common denominator — 800 x 600 mode.

As you will learn later in the book (see Chapter 10), it's possible to determine the user's video resolution by using Windows API calls from VBA. In some cases, you may want to programmatically adjust things depending on the user's video resolution.

Part III

Understanding Visual Basic for Applications

Chapter 7

Introducing Visual Basic for Applications

IN THIS CHAPTER

This chapter introduces you to Visual Basic for Applications – VBA – and provides an introduction to the objects that make up Excel.

- ◆ An introduction to VBA – the programming language built into Excel
- ◆ How VBA differs from traditional spreadsheet macro languages, and how it differs from the Visual Basic language
- ◆ How to use the Visual Basic Editor (VBE)
- ◆ How to work in the Code windows in the VBE and customize the VBE environment
- ◆ Information on using Excel's macro recorder
- ◆ An overview of objects, collections, properties, and methods
- ◆ A case study of the Comment object
- ◆ Specific information and examples of working with Range objects
- ◆ How to access a lot of information about Excel objects, properties, and methods

PROGRAMMING EXCEL essentially boils down to manipulating objects, which you do by writing instructions in a language that Excel can understand: VBA.

Some BASIC Background

Many hard-core programmers scoff at the idea of programming in BASIC. The name itself (an acronym for Beginner's All-purpose Symbolic Instruction Code) suggests that it's not a professional language. In fact, BASIC was first developed in the early 1960s as a way to teach programming techniques to college students. BASIC caught on quickly and is available in hundreds of dialects for many types of computers.

BASIC has evolved and improved over the years. For example, in many early implementations, BASIC was an *interpreted* language. Each line was interpreted before it was executed, causing slow performance. Most modern dialects of BASIC allow the code to be compiled, resulting in much faster execution and improved program portability.

BASIC gained quite a bit of respectability in 1991 when Microsoft released Visual Basic for Windows. This product made it easy for the masses to develop standalone applications for Windows. Visual Basic has very little in common with early versions of BASIC, but BASIC is the foundation on which VBA was built.

About VBA

Excel 5 was the first application on the market to feature Visual Basic for Applications (VBA). VBA is best thought of as Microsoft's common application scripting language, and it's now included with all Office 2003 applications, and even applications from other vendors. Therefore, if you master VBA by using Excel, you'll be able to jump right in and write macros for other Microsoft (and non-Microsoft) products. Even better, you'll be able to create complete solutions that use features across various applications.

Object models

The secret to using VBA with other applications lies in understanding the *object model* for each application. VBA, after all, simply manipulates objects, and each product (Excel, Word, Access, PowerPoint, and so forth) has its own unique object model. You can program an application by using the objects that the application exposes.

Excel's object model, for example, exposes several very powerful data analysis objects, such as worksheets, charts, pivot tables, scenarios, and numerous mathematical, financial, engineering, and general business functions. With VBA, you can work with these objects and develop automated procedures. While you work with VBA in Excel, you'll gradually build an understanding of the object model. **Warning:** It will be very confusing at first. Eventually, however, the pieces will come together — and all of a sudden, you'll realize that you've mastered it!

VBA versus XLM

Before version 5, Excel used a powerful (but very cryptic) macro language called *XLM*. Later versions of Excel still execute XLM macros, but the ability to record macros in XLM was removed beginning with Excel 97. As a developer, you should be aware of XLM (in case you ever encounter macros written in that system), but you should use VBA for your development work.

Don't confuse the XLM macro language with eXtensible Markup Language (XML). Although these terms share the same letters, they have nothing in common. *XML* is a storage format for structured data. Excel 2003 contains some new XML-related features.

Figures 7-1 and 7-2 show a simple procedure coded in both XLM and VBA. This macro works on the selected cells. It changes the cell background color and adds a border around the cells. You probably agree that the VBA code is much easier to read. More importantly, however, the VBA code is also easier to modify when the need arises.

```
xlm vs vba.xls
        A              B          C
1  Macro1
2  =BORDER(2,0)
3  =PATTERNS(1,0,6,TRUE)
4  =RETURN()
5
6
7
8
H  ◀  ▶  H \Macro1 / Sheet1 /
```

Figure 7-1: A simple macro coded in Excel's XLM language, stored on a macro sheet.

```
xlm vs vba.xls - Module1 (Code)
(General)                          Macro2

Sub Macro2()
    With Selection
        .BorderAround Weight:=xlMedium, ColorIndex:=xlAutomatic
        .Interior.ColorIndex = 6
        .Interior.Pattern = xlSolid
    End With
End Sub
```

Figure 7-2: A simple macro coded in Excel's VBA language, stored in a VBA module.

The Basics of VBA

Before I get into the meat of things, I suggest that you read through the material in this section to get a broad overview of where I'm heading. These are the topics that I cover in the remainder of this chapter.

Following is a quick-and-dirty summary of what VBA is all about:

◆ *Code:* You perform actions in VBA by executing VBA code.

   You write (or record) VBA code, which is stored in a VBA module.

◆ *Module:* VBA modules are stored in an Excel workbook, but you view or edit a module by using the Visual Basic Editor (VBE).

A VBA module consists of procedures.

◆ *Procedures:* A procedure is basically a unit of computer code that performs some action.

■ Sub: Here's an example of a simple Sub procedure called Test: This procedure calculates a simple sum and then displays the result in a message box.

```
Sub Test()
    Sum = 1 + 1
    MsgBox "The answer is " & Sum
End Sub
```

■ Function: Besides Sub procedures, a VBA module can also have Function procedures.

A Function procedure returns a single value (or possibly an array). A Function can be called from another VBA procedure, or used in a worksheet formula. Here's an example of a Function named AddTwo:

```
Function AddTwo(arg1, arg2)
    AddTwo = arg1 + arg2
End Function
```

◆ *Objects:* VBA manipulates objects contained in its host application. (In this case, Excel is the host application.)

Excel provides you with more than 100 classes of objects to manipulate. Examples of objects include a workbook, a worksheet, a range on a worksheet, a chart, and a drawn rectangle. Many more objects are at your disposal, and you can manipulate them by using VBA code.

Object classes are arranged in a hierarchy.

Objects can act as containers for other objects. For example, Excel is an object called Application, and it contains other objects, such as Workbook and CommandBar objects. The Workbook object can contain other objects, such as Worksheet objects and Chart objects. A Worksheet object can contain objects such as Range objects, PivotTable objects, and so on. The arrangement of these objects is referred to as Excel's *object model.*

◆ *Collections:* Like objects form a *collection.*

For example, the Worksheets collection consists of all the worksheets in a particular workbook. The CommandBars collection consists of all CommandBar objects. Collections are objects in themselves.

◆ *Object hierarchy:* When you refer to a contained or member object, you specify its position in the object hierarchy by using a period (also known as a *dot*) as a separator between the container and the member.

For example, you can refer to a workbook named `Book1.xls` as

```
Application.Workbooks("Book1.xls")
```

This refers to the `Book1.xls` workbook in the `Workbooks` collection. The `Workbooks` collection is contained in the Excel `Application` object. Extending this to another level, you can refer to `Sheet1` in `Book1` as

```
Application.Workbooks("Book1.xls").Worksheets("Sheet1")
```

You can take it to still another level and refer to a specific cell as follows:

```
Application.Workbooks("Book1.xls").Worksheets("Sheet1").Range("A1")
```

◆ *Active objects:* If you omit a specific reference to an object, Excel uses the active objects.

If `Book1` is the active workbook, the preceding reference can be simplified as

```
Worksheets("Sheet1").Range("A1")
```

If you know that `Sheet1` is the active sheet, you can simplify the reference even more:

```
Range("A1")
```

◆ *Objects properties:* Objects have *properties.*

A property can be thought of as a *setting* for an object. For example, a range object has properties such as `Value` and `Name`. A chart object has properties such as `HasTitle` and `Type`. You can use VBA to determine object properties and also to change them.

You refer to properties by combining the object with the property, separated by a period.

For example, you can refer to the value in cell A1 on `Sheet1` as

```
Worksheets("Sheet1").Range("A1").Value
```

◆ *VBA variables:* You can assign values to VBA variables. Think of a variable as a name that you can use to store a particular value.

To assign the value in cell A1 on `Sheet1` to a variable called `Interest`, use the following VBA statement:

```
Interest = Worksheets("Sheet1").Range("A1").Value
```

◆ *Object methods:* Objects have methods.

A *method* is an action that is performed with the object. For example, one of the methods for a `Range` object is `ClearContents`. This method clears the contents of the range.

You specify methods by combining the object with the method, separated by a period.

For example, to clear the contents of cell A1 on the active worksheet, use this:

```
Range("A1").ClearContents
```

◆ *Standard programming constructs:* VBA also includes all the constructs of modern programming languages, including arrays, looping, and so on.

Believe it or not, the preceding section pretty much describes VBA. Now it's just a matter of learning the details, which is what I cover in the rest of this chapter.

An Analogy

If you like analogies, here's one for you. It might help you understand the relationships between objects, properties, and methods in VBA. In this analogy, I compare Excel with a fast-food restaurant chain.

The basic unit of Excel is a `Workbook` object. In a fast-food chain, the basic unit is an individual restaurant. With Excel, you can add workbooks and close workbooks, and all the open workbooks are known as `Workbooks` (a collection of `Workbook` objects). Similarly, the management of a fast-food chain can add restaurants and close restaurants — and all the restaurants in the chain can be viewed as the `Restaurants` collection — a collection of `Restaurant` objects.

An Excel workbook is an object, but it also contains other objects such as worksheets, charts, VBA modules, and so on. Furthermore, each object in a workbook can contain its own objects. For example, a `Worksheet` object can contain `Range` objects, `PivotTable` objects, `Shape` objects, and so on.

Continuing with the analogy, a fast-food restaurant (like a workbook) contains objects such as the `Kitchen`, `DiningArea`, and `Tables` (a collection). Furthermore, management can add or remove objects from the `Restaurant` object. For example, management can add more tables to the `Tables` collection. Each of these objects can contain other objects. For example, the `Kitchen` object has a `Stove` object, `VentilationFan` object, a `Chef` object, `Sink` object, and so on.

So far, so good. This analogy seems to work. Let's see whether I can take it further.

Excel objects have properties. For example, a `Range` object has properties such as `Value` and `Name`, and a `Shape` object has properties such as `Width`, `Height`, and so on. Not surprisingly, objects in a fast-food restaurant also have properties. The `Stove` object, for example, has properties such as `Temperature` and `NumberofBurners`. The `VentilationFan` has its own set of properties (`TurnedOn`, `RPM`, and so forth).

Besides properties, Excel's objects also have methods, which perform an operation on an object. For example, the `ClearContents` method erases the contents of a `Range` object. An object in a fast-food restaurant also has methods. You can easily envision a `ChangeThermostat` method for a `Stove` object, or a `SwitchOn` method for a `VentilationFan` object.

With Excel, methods sometimes change an object's properties. The `ClearContents` method for a `Range` changes the `Range Value` property. Similarly, the `ChangeThermostat` method on a `Stove` object affects its `Temperature` property.

With VBA, you can write procedures to manipulate Excel's objects. In a fast-food restaurant, the management can give orders to manipulate the objects in the restaurants. ("Turn on the stove, and switch the ventilation fan to high.") Now is it clear?

Introducing the Visual Basic Editor

All your VBA work is done in the Visual Basic Editor (VBE). The VBE is a separate application that works seamlessly with Excel. By seamlessly, I mean that Excel takes care of the details of opening the VBE when you need it. You can't run VBE separately; Excel must be running in order for the VBE to run.

 VBA modules are stored with workbook files; they just aren't visible unless you activate the VBE.

Activating the VBE

When you're working in Excel, you can switch to the VBE by using any of the following techniques:

◆ Press Alt+F11.

◆ Choose Tools → Macro → Visual Basic Editor.

◆ Click the Visual Basic Editor button, which is located on the Visual Basic toolbar.

In addition, you can access two special modules as follows. (These special VBA modules are used for event handler procedures, which I describe in Chapter 19.)

◆ Right-click a sheet tab and then select View Code to access the code module for the active sheet.

◆ Right-click the Excel icon (to the left of Excel's menu bar) and select View Code to access the code module for the `ThisWorkbook` object of the active workbook.

Don't confuse the Visual Basic Editor with the Microsoft Script Editor. These are two entirely different animals. The Script Editor is used to edit HyperText Markup Language (HTML) scripts written in VBScript or JavaScript. The Script Editor is not covered in this book.

Figure 7-3 shows the VBE. Chances are that your VBE window won't look exactly like the window shown in the figure. This window is highly customizable — you can hide windows, change their sizes, dock them, rearrange them, and so on.

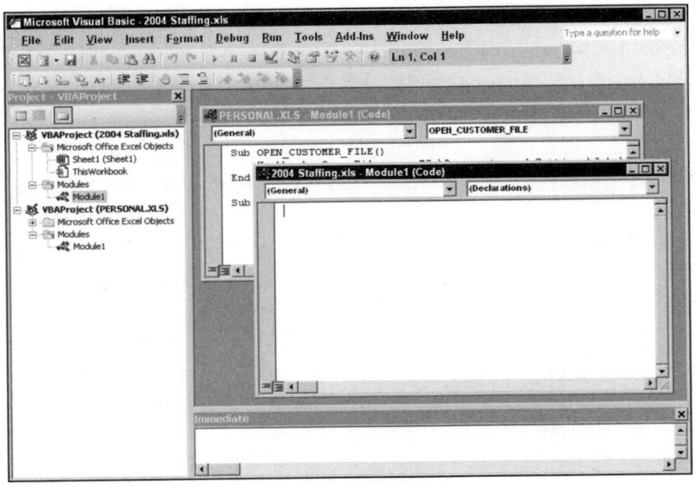

Figure 7-3: The Visual Basic Editor window.

The VBE windows

The VBE consists of a number of parts. I briefly describe some of the key components in the sections that follow.

VBE MENU BAR

The VBE menu bar, of course, works like every other menu bar that you've encountered. It contains commands that you use to work with the various components in the VBE. Also, you'll find that many of the menu commands have shortcut keys associated with them. For example, the View → Immediate Window command has a shortcut key of Ctrl+G.

 TIP The VBE also features shortcut menus. As you'll discover, you can right-click virtually anything in a VBE window, and you'll get a shortcut menu of common commands.

VBE TOOLBARS

The Standard toolbar, which is directly under the menu bar by default, is one of six VBE toolbars available; the menu bar is also considered a toolbar. VBE toolbars work just like those in Excel: You can customize toolbars, move them around, display other toolbars, and so forth. Choose the View → Toolbars → Customize command to work with VBE toolbars.

VBE PROJECT EXPLORER WINDOW

The Project Explorer window displays a tree diagram that consists of every workbook that is currently open in Excel (including add-ins and hidden workbooks). Each workbook is known as a *project*. I discuss the Project Explorer window in more detail in the next section ("Working with the Project Explorer").

If the Project Explorer window is not visible, press Ctrl+R. To hide the Project Explorer window, click the Close button in its title bar (or right-click anywhere in the Project Explorer window and select Hide from the shortcut menu).

CODE WINDOW

A Code window (sometimes known as a Module window) contains VBA code. Every item in a project has an associated code window. To view a code window for an object, double-click the object in the Project Explorer window. For example, to view the code window for the Sheet1 object, double-click Sheet1 in the Project Explorer window. Unless you've added some VBA code, the Code window will be empty.

Another way to view the Code window for an object is to select the object in the Project Explorer window and then click the View Code button in the toolbar at the top of the Project Explorer window.

I discuss Code windows later on in this chapter (see "Working with Code Windows").

IMMEDIATE WINDOW

The Immediate window is most useful for executing VBA statements directly, testing statements, and debugging your code. This window might or might not be visible. If the Immediate window isn't visible, press Ctrl+G. To close the Immediate window, click the Close button in its title bar (or right-click anywhere in the Immediate window and select Hide from the shortcut menu).

Working with the Project Explorer

When you're working in the VBE, each Excel workbook and add-in that's currently open is considered a *project*. You can think of a project as a collection of objects arranged as an outline. You can expand a project by clicking the plus sign (+) at the left of the project's name in the Project Explorer window. You contract a project by clicking the minus sign (–) to the left of a project's name. If you try to expand a project that's protected with a password, you'll be prompted to enter the password.

The top of the Project Explorer window contains three buttons. The third button, named *Toggle Folder,* controls whether the objects in a project are displayed in a hierarchy or are shown in a single non-hierarchical list.

Figure 7-4 shows a Project Explorer window with three projects listed (one add-in and two workbooks).

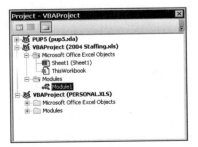

Figure 7-4: A Project Explorer window with three projects listed.

When you activate the VBE, you cannot assume that the code module that's displayed corresponds to the highlighted object in the Project Explorer window. To make sure that you're working in the correct code module, always double-click the object in the Project Explorer window.

If you have many workbooks and add-ins loaded, the Project Explorer window can be a bit overwhelming. Unfortunately, you can't hide projects in the Project Explorer window. However, you'll probably want to keep the project outlines contracted if you're not working on them.

Every project expands to show at least one node called Microsoft Excel Objects. This node expands to show an item for each worksheet and chart sheet in the workbook (each sheet is considered an object), and another object called ThisWorkbook (which represents the ActiveWorkbook object). If the project has any VBA modules, the project listing also shows a Modules node, and the modules are listed there. A project can also contain a node called Forms that contains UserForm objects (also known as custom dialog boxes). If your project has any class modules, it will display another node called Class Modules.

Adding a new VBA module

To add a new VBA module to a project, select the project's name in the Project Explorer window and choose Insert → Module. Or you can just right-click the project's name and choose Insert → Module from the shortcut menu.

When you record a macro, Excel automatically inserts a VBA module to hold the recorded code.

Removing a VBA module

If you need to remove a VBA module or a class module from a project, select the module's name in the Project Explorer window and choose File → Remove *xxx* (where *xxx* is the name of the module). Or you can right-click the module's name and choose Remove *xxx* from the shortcut menu. You'll be asked whether you want to export the module before removing it. See the next section for details. *Remember:* You cannot remove code modules associated with the workbook (the ThisWorkbook code module) or with a sheet (for example, the Sheet1 code module).

Exporting and importing objects

Except for those listed under the References node, every object in a project can be saved to a separate file. Saving an individual object in a project is *exporting*. And it stands to reason that you can also *import* objects into a project. Exporting and importing objects might be useful if you want to use a particular object (such as a VBA module or a UserForm) in a different project.

To export an object, select it in the Project Explorer window and choose File→ Export File (or press Ctrl+E). You'll get a dialog box that asks for a filename. Note that the object remains in the project (only a copy of it is exported). If you export a UserForm object, any code associated with the UserForm is also exported.

To import a file into a project, select the project's name in the Project Explorer window and choose File→ Import File. You'll get a dialog box that asks for a file. You can import only a file that has been exported by choosing the File→ Export File command.

TIP

If you would like to copy a module or UserForm object to another project, it's not really necessary to export and then import the object. Make sure that both projects are open; then simply activate the Project Explorer and drag the object from one project to the other.

Working with Code Windows

When you become proficient with VBA, you'll be spending *lots* of time working in code windows. Each object in a project has an associated code window. To summarize, these objects can be

◆ The workbook itself (ThisWorkbook in the Project Explorer window)

◆ A worksheet or chart sheet in a workbook (for example, Sheet1 or Chart1 in the Project Explorer window)

◆ A VBA module

◆ A *class module* (a special type of module that lets you create new object classes)

◆ A UserForm

Minimizing and maximizing windows

At any given time, the VBE can have lots of code windows, and things can get a bit confusing. Code windows are much like worksheet windows in Excel. You can minimize them, maximize them, hide them, rearrange them, and so on. Many people find it most efficient to maximize the Code window that they're working in. Doing so enables you to see more code and keeps you from getting distracted. To maximize a Code window, click the maximize button in its title bar or just double-click its title bar. To restore a Code window (making it nonmaximized), click the Restore button in its title bar.

Sometimes, you might want to have two or more Code windows visible. For example, you might want to compare the code in two modules or perhaps copy code from one module to another.

Minimizing a code window gets it out of the way. You can also click the Close button in a Code window's title bar to close the window completely. To open it again, just double-click the appropriate object in the Project Explorer window.

The VBE doesn't let you close a workbook. You must reactivate Excel and close it from there. You can, however, use the Immediate window to close a workbook or an add-in. Just activate the Immediate window, type a VBA statement like the one that follows, and press Enter:

```
Workbooks("myaddin.xla").Close
```

As you'll see, this statement executes the Close method of the Workbook object, which closes a workbook. In this case, the workbook happens to be an add-in.

Storing VBA code

In general, a code window can hold four types of code:

- ◆ Sub procedures: A *procedure* is a set of instructions that performs some action.

- ◆ Function procedures: A *function* is a set of instructions that returns a single value or an array (similar in concept to a worksheet function such as SUM).

- ◆ Property procedures: These are special procedures used in class modules.

- ◆ Declarations: A *declaration* is information about a variable that you provide to VBA. For example, you can declare the data type for variables you plan to use.

A single VBA module can store any number of Sub procedures, Function procedures, and declarations. How you organize a VBA module is completely up to you. Some people prefer to keep all their VBA code for an application in a single VBA module; others like to split up the code into several different modules.

Although you have lots of flexibility regarding where to store your VBA code, there are some restrictions. Event handler procedures must be located in the Code window for the object that responds to the event. For example, if you write a procedure that executes when the workbook is opened, that procedure must be located in the Code window for the ThisWorkbook object, and the procedure must have a special name. This concept will become clearer when I discuss events (Chapter 19) and UserForms (Part IV).

Entering VBA code

Before you can do anything meaningful, you must have some VBA code in a Code window. And the VBA code must be within a procedure. A procedure consists of VBA statements. For now, I focus on one type of Code window: a VBA module.

You can add code to a VBA module in three ways:

◆ *The old-fashioned way:* Enter the code the old-fashioned way: Type it from your keyboard.

◆ *The macro-recorder feature:* Use Excel's macro-recorder feature to record your actions and convert them into VBA code.

◆ *Copy and paste:* Copy the code from another module and paste it into the module that you are working in.

ENTERING CODE MANUALLY

Sometimes, the most direct route is the best one. Entering code directly involves . . . well, entering the code directly. In other words, you type the code by using your keyboard. You can use the Tab key to indent the lines that logically belong together — for example, the conditional statements between an If and an End If statement. This isn't really necessary, but it makes the code easier to read, so it's a good habit to acquire.

Pause for a Terminology Break

Throughout this book, I use the terms *routine*, *procedure*, and *macro*. Programming people typically use the word *procedure* to describe an automated task. In Excel, a procedure is also known as a *macro*. Technically, a procedure can be a Sub procedure or a Function procedure, both of which are sometimes called *routines*. I use all these terms pretty much interchangeably. There is, however, an important difference between Sub procedures and Function procedures. This distinction will become apparent in Chapters 9 and 10.

Entering and editing text in a VBA module works just as you would expect. You can select text, copy it or cut it, and then paste it to another location.

A single instruction in VBA can be as long as you need it to be. For readability's sake, however, you might want to break a lengthy instruction into two or more lines. To do so, end the line with a space followed by an underscore character; then press Enter and continue the instruction on the following line. The following code, for example, is a single VBA statement split over four lines.

```
MsgBox "Can't find " & UCase(SHORTCUTMENUFILE) _
    & vbCrLf & vbCrLf & "The file should be located in " _
    & ThisWorkbook.Path & vbCrLf & vbCrLf _
    & "You may need to reinstall BudgetMan", vbCritical, APPNAME
```

Notice that I indented the last three lines of this statement. Doing so is optional, but it helps clarify the fact that these four lines are, in fact, a single statement.

TIP Like Excel, the VBE has multiple levels of Undo and Redo. Therefore, if you find that you deleted an instruction that you shouldn't have, you can click the Undo button (or press Ctrl+Z) repeatedly until the instruction comes back. After undoing, you can click the Redo button to redo changes that were previously undone. This feature can be a lifesaver, so I recommend that you play around with it until you understand how it works.

Try this: Insert a VBA module into a project, and then enter the following procedure into the Code window of the module:

```
Sub SayHello()
    Msg = "Is your name " & Application.UserName & "?"
    Ans = MsgBox(Msg, vbYesNo)
    If Ans = vbNo Then
        MsgBox "Oh, never mind."
    Else
        MsgBox "I must be clairvoyant!"
    End If
End Sub
```

Figure 7-5 shows how this looks in a VBA module.

```
Microsoft Visual Basic - Hello World.xls - [Module1 (Code)]
File  Edit  View  Insert  Format  Debug  Run  Tools  Add-Ins  Window  Help              Ln 6, Col 1

Project - VBAProject          (General)                    SayHello

VBAProject (Hello World.xls)      Sub SayHello()
  Microsoft Office Excel Objects       Msg = "Is your name " & Application.UserName & "?"
    Sheet1 (Sheet1)                    Ans = MsgBox(Msg, vbYesNo)
    ThisWorkbook                       If Ans = vbNo Then
  Modules                                  MsgBox "Oh, never mind."
    Module1                            Else
                                           MsgBox "I must be clairvoyant!"
                                       End If
                                   End Sub
```

Figure 7-5: Your first VBA procedure.

While you enter the code, you might notice that the VBE makes some adjust-ments to the text that you enter. For example, if you omit the space before or after an equal sign (=), VBE inserts the space for you. Also, the color of some of the text is changed. This is all perfectly normal, and you'll appreciate it later.

To execute the SayHello procedure, make sure that the cursor is located any-where within the text that you typed. Then do any of the following:

◆ Press F5.

◆ Choose Run → Run Sub/UserForm.

◆ Click the Run Sub/UserForm button on the Standard toolbar.

If you entered the code correctly, the procedure will execute, and you can respond to a simple dialog box (see Figure 7-6) that displays the user name, as listed in Excel's Options dialog box. Notice that Excel is activated when the macro executes. At this point, it's not important that you understand how the code works; that becomes clear later in this chapter and in subsequent chapters.

```
Microsoft Excel                    [X]

    Is your name John Walkenbach?

       Yes            No
```

Figure 7-6: The result of running
the procedure in Figure 7-5.

Most of the time, you'll be executing your macros from Excel. However, it's often more efficient to test your macro by running it directly from the VBE.

What you did was write a VBA Sub procedure (also known as a *macro*). When you issued the command to execute the macro, the VBE quickly compiled the code and executed it. In other words, each instruction was evaluated, and Excel simply did what it was told to do. You can execute this macro any number of times, although it tends to lose its appeal after a while.

For the record, this simple procedure uses the following concepts (all of which I cover later in the book):

◆ Declaring a procedure (the first line)

◆ Assigning a value to variables (Msg and Ans)

◆ Concatenating strings (using the & operator)

◆ Using a built-in VBA function (MsgBox)

◆ Using built-in VBA constants (vbYesNo and vbNo)

◆ Using an If-Then-Else construct

◆ Ending a procedure (the last line)

Not bad for a first effort, eh?

USING THE MACRO RECORDER

Another way to get code into a VBA module is to record your actions by using the Excel macro recorder.

No matter how hard you try, there is absolutely no way to record the SayHello procedure shown previously. As you'll see, recording macros is very useful, but it has some limitations. In fact, when you record a macro, you almost always need to make some adjustments or enter some code manually.

This next example shows how to record a macro that simply changes the page setup to landscape orientation. If you want to try this, start with a blank workbook and follow these steps:

1. Activate a worksheet in the workbook (any worksheet will do).

2. Choose the Tools → Macro → Record New Macro command.

   Excel displays its Record Macro dialog box.

3. Just click OK to accept the defaults.

Excel automatically inserts a new VBA module into the project. From this point on, Excel converts your actions into VBA code. While recording, Excel displays the word `Recording` in the status bar and also displays a miniature floating toolbar that contains two toolbar buttons (Stop Recording and Relative Reference).

4. Choose the File → Page Setup command.

   Excel displays its Page Setup dialog box.

5. Select the Landscape option and click OK to close the dialog box.

6. Click the Stop Recording button on the miniature toolbar (or choose Tools → Macro → Stop Recording).

   Excel stops recording your actions.

To take a look at the macro, activate the VBE (pressing Alt+F11 is the easiest way) and locate the project in the Project Explorer window. Click the `Modules` node to expand it. Then click the `Module1` item to display the code window. (**Hint:** If the project already had a `Module1`, the new macro will be in `Module2`.) The code generated by this single command is shown in Listing 7-1. Remember that code lines preceded by an apostrophe are comments, and they are not executed.

Listing 7-1: Macro for Changing Page Setup to Landscape Orientation

```
Sub Macro1()
'
' Macro1 Macro
' Macro recorded by John Walkenbach
'
    With ActiveSheet.PageSetup
        .PrintTitleRows = ""
        .PrintTitleColumns = ""
    End With
    ActiveSheet.PageSetup.PrintArea = ""
    With ActiveSheet.PageSetup
        .LeftHeader = ""
        .CenterHeader = ""
        .RightHeader = ""
        .LeftFooter = ""
        .CenterFooter = ""
        .RightFooter = ""
        .LeftMargin = Application.InchesToPoints(0.75)
        .RightMargin = Application.InchesToPoints(0.75)
        .TopMargin = Application.InchesToPoints(1)
        .BottomMargin = Application.InchesToPoints(1)
        .HeaderMargin = Application.InchesToPoints(0.5)
```

```
        .FooterMargin = Application.InchesToPoints(0.5)
        .PrintHeadings = False
        .PrintGridlines = False
        .PrintComments = xlPrintNoComments
        .PrintQuality = 600
        .CenterHorizontally = False
        .CenterVertically = False
        .Orientation = xlLandscape
        .Draft = False
        .PaperSize = xlPaperLetter
        .FirstPageNumber = xlAutomatic
        .Order = xlDownThenOver
        .BlackAndWhite = False
        .Zoom = 100
        .PrintErrors = xlPrintErrorsDisplayed
    End With
End Sub
```

You might be surprised by the amount of code generated by this single command. (I know I was the first time when I tried something like this.) Although you changed only one simple setting in the Page Setup dialog box, Excel generates code that reproduces *all* the settings in the dialog box.

This brings up an important concept. Often, the code produced when you record a macro is overkill. For example, if you want your macro only to switch to landscape mode, you can simplify this macro considerably by deleting the extraneous code. This makes the macro easier to read, and the macro also runs faster because it doesn't do things that are not necessary. In fact, this macro can be simplified to the following:

```
Sub Macro1()
    With ActiveSheet.PageSetup
        .Orientation = xlLandscape
    End With
End Sub
```

I deleted all the code except for the line that sets the Orientation property. Actually, this macro can be simplified even more because the With-End With construct isn't necessary when you're changing only one property:

```
Sub Macro1()
    ActiveSheet.PageSetup.Orientation = xlLandscape
End Sub
```

In this example, the macro changes the Orientation property of the PageSetup object on the active sheet. By the way, xlLandscape is a built-in constant that's provided to make things easier for you. Variable `xlLandscape` has a value of 2, and `xlPortrait` has a value of 1. The following macro works the same as the preceding Macro1.

```
Sub Macro1a()
    ActiveSheet.PageSetup.Orientation = 2
End Sub
```

Most would agree that it's easier to remember the name of the constant than the arbitrary numbers. You can use the Help system to learn the relevant constants for a particular command.

You could have entered this procedure directly into a VBA module. To do so, you would have to know which objects, properties, and methods to use. Obviously, it's much faster to record the macro, and this example has a built-in bonus: You also learned that the `PageSetup` object has an `Orientation` property.

A point that I make clear throughout this book is that recording your actions is perhaps the *best* way to learn VBA. When in doubt, try recording. Although the result might not be exactly what you want, chances are that it will steer you in the right direction. You can use the Help system to check out the objects, properties, and methods that appear in the recorded code.

I discuss the macro recorder in more detail later in this chapter. See the section, "The Macro Recorder."

COPYING VBA CODE

So far, I've covered entering code directly and recording your actions to generate VBA code. The final method of getting code into a VBA module is to copy it from another module. For example, you may have written a procedure for one project that would also be useful in your current project. Rather than re-enter the code, you can simply open the workbook, activate the module, and use the normal Clipboard copy-and-paste procedures to copy it into your current VBA module. After you've finished pasting, you can modify the code as necessary.

TIP   As I note previously in this chapter, you can also import to a file an entire module that has been exported.

Customizing the VBE Environment

If you're serious about becoming an Excel programmer, you'll be spending a lot of time with the VBE window on your screen. To help make things as comfortable as possible, the VBE provides quite a few customization options.

When the VBE is active, choose Tools → Options. You'll see a dialog box with four tabs: Editor, Editor Format, General, and Docking. I discuss some of the most useful options on these tabs in the sections that follow. By the way, don't confuse this with the Excel Options dialog box, which you bring up by choosing Tools → Options in Excel. Although they have the same name, these two dialog boxes set different options.

Using the Editor tab

Figure 7-7 shows the options that you access by clicking the Editor tab of the Options dialog box.

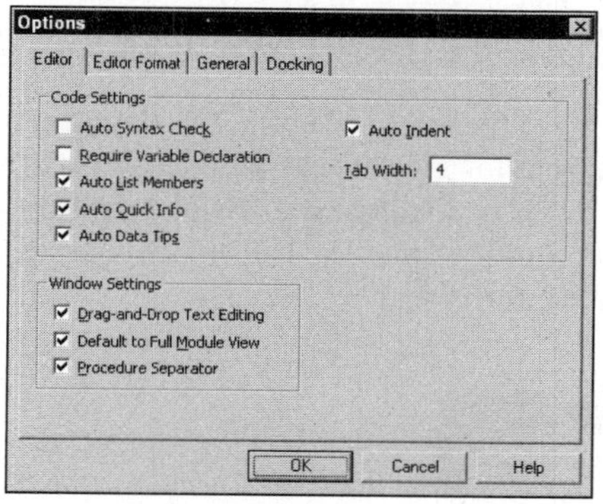

Figure 7-7: The Editor tab of the Options dialog box.

AUTO SYNTAX CHECK OPTION

The Auto Syntax Check setting determines whether the VBE pops up a dialog box if it discovers a syntax error while you're entering your VBA code. The dialog box tells you roughly what the problem is. If you don't choose this setting, VBE flags syntax errors by displaying them in a different color from the rest of the code, and you don't have to deal with any dialog boxes popping up on your screen.

I usually keep this setting turned off because I find the dialog boxes annoying, and I can usually figure out what's wrong with an instruction. But if you're new to VBA, you might find this assistance helpful.

REQUIRE VARIABLE DECLARATION OPTION

If the Require Variable Declaration option is set, VBE inserts the following statement at the beginning of each new VBA module that you insert:

```
Option Explicit
```

If this statement appears in your module, you must explicitly define each variable that you use. This is an excellent habit to get into although it does require some additional effort on your part. If you don't declare your variables, they will all be of the Variant data type, which is flexible but not efficient in terms of storage or speed. I discuss this in more depth in Chapter 8.

 Changing the Require Variable Declaration option affects only new modules, not existing modules.

AUTO LIST MEMBERS OPTION

If the Auto List Members option is set, VBE provides some help when you're entering your VBA code by displaying a list of member items for an object. These items include methods and properties for the object that you typed.

This option is very helpful, and I always keep it turned on. Figure 7-8 shows an example of Auto List Members (which will make a lot more sense when you actually start writing VBA code). In this example, VBE is displaying a list of members for the Application object. You can just select an item from the list, thus avoiding typing it. (*Hint:* This also ensures that it's spelled correctly.)

```
Book4 - Module1 (Code)                                      _ □ ×
(General)                           ▼   Test                     ▼
   Sub Test()
       Username=application.us
   End Sub               ☞ UsableHeight                  ▲
                         ☞ UsableWidth
                         ☞ UsedObjects
                         ☞ UserControl
                         ☞ UserLibraryPath
                         ☞ UserName
                         ☞ UseSystemSeparators            ▼
```

Figure 7-8: An example of Auto List Members.

AUTO QUICK INFO OPTION

If the Auto Quick Info option is set, the VBE displays information about the arguments available for functions, properties, and methods while you type. This can be very helpful, and I always leave this setting on. Figure 7-9 shows this feature in action. It's displaying the syntax for the Range property.

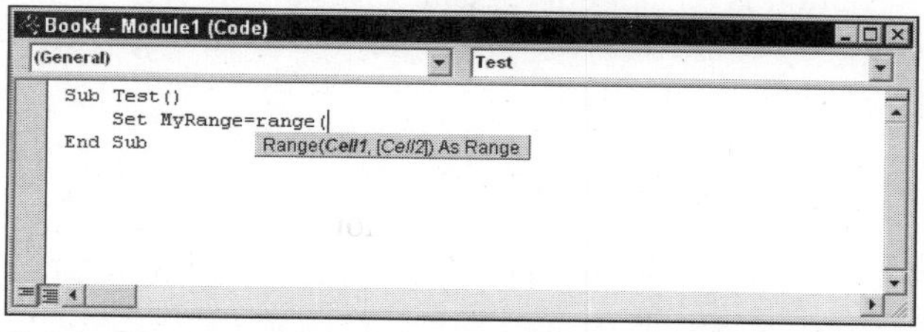

Figure 7-9: An example of Auto Quick Info offering help about the Range property.

AUTO DATA TIPS OPTION

If the Auto Data Tips option is set, VBE displays the value of the variable over which your cursor is placed when you're debugging code. When you enter the wonderful world of debugging, you'll definitely appreciate this option. I always keep this option turned on.

AUTO INDENT OPTION

The Auto Indent setting determines whether VBE automatically indents each new line of code by the same amount as the previous line. I'm a big fan of using indentations in my code, so I keep this option on. You can also specify the number of characters to indent; the default is four.

> **TIP** Use the Tab key to indent your code and not the space bar. Using the Tab key results in more consistent spacing. In addition, you can use Shift+Tab to unindent a line of code. These keys also work if you select more than one statement.

DRAG–AND–DROP TEXT EDITING OPTION

The Drag-and-Drop Text Editing option, when enabled, lets you copy and move text by dragging and dropping. I keep this option turned on, but I never use drag-and-drop editing. I just prefer to use keyboard shortcuts for copying and pasting.

DEFAULT TO FULL MODULE VIEW OPTION

The Default to Full Module View option specifies how procedures are viewed. If set, procedures in the code window appear as a single scrollable window. If this option is turned off, you can see only one procedure at a time. I keep this setting turned on.

PROCEDURE SEPARATOR OPTION

When the Procedure Separator option is turned on, it displays separator bars at the end of each procedure in a code window. I like the visual cues of knowing where my procedures end, so I keep this option turned on.

Using the Editor Format tab

Figure 7-10 shows the Editor Format tab of the Options dialog box.

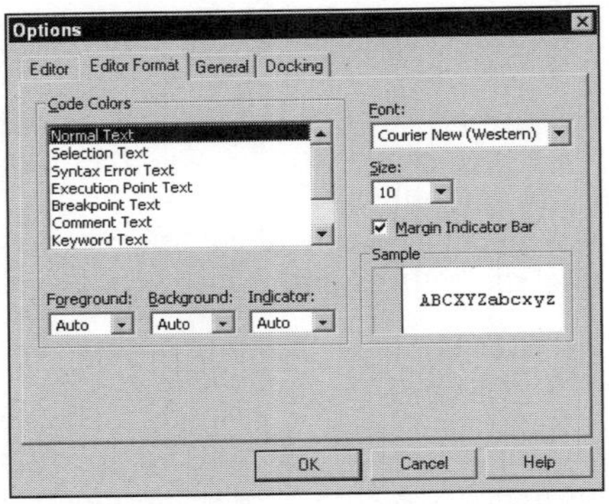

Figure 7-10: The Editor Format tab of the Options dialog box.

CODE COLORS OPTION

The Code Colors option lets you set the text color (foreground and background) and indicator color displayed for various elements of VBA code. This is largely a matter of individual preference. Personally, I find the default colors to be just fine. But for a change of scenery, I occasionally play around with these settings.

FONT OPTION

The Font option lets you select the font that's used in your VBA modules. For best results, stick with a fixed-width font (monofont) such as Courier New. In a *fixed-width font,* all characters are exactly the same width. This makes your code much more readable because the characters are nicely aligned vertically and you can easily distinguish multiple spaces.

SIZE SETTING

The Size setting specifies the size of the font in the VBA modules. This setting is a matter of personal preference determined by your video display resolution and your eyesight. The default size of 10 (point) works for me.

MARGIN INDICATOR BAR OPTION

The Margin Indicator Bar option controls the display of the vertical margin indicator bar in your modules. You should keep this turned on; otherwise, you won't be able to see the helpful graphical indicators when you're debugging your code.

Using the General tab

Figure 7-11 shows the options available under the General tab in the Options dialog box. In almost every case, the default settings are just fine.

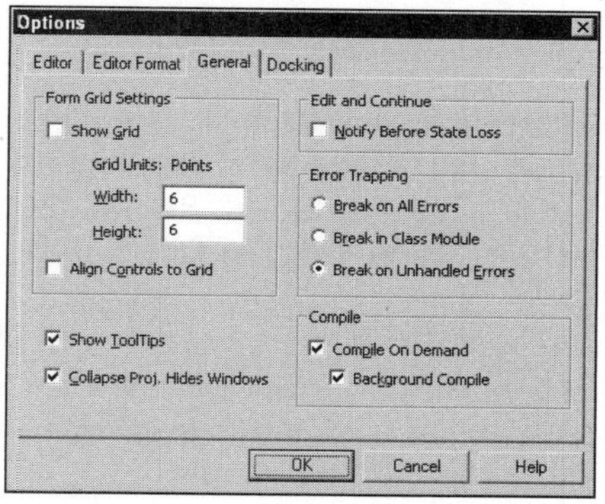

Figure 7-11: The General tab of the Options dialog box.

The Error Trapping setting determines what happens when an error is encountered. If you write any error-handling code, make sure that the Break on Unhandled Errors option is set. If the Break on All Errors option is set, error-handling code is ignored (which is hardly ever what you want). I discuss error-handling techniques in Chapter 9.

Using the Docking tab

Figure 7-12 shows the Docking tab of the Options dialog box. These options determine how the various windows in the VBE behave. When a window is docked, it is fixed in place along one of the edges of the VBE window. This makes it much easier to identify and locate a particular window. If you turn off all docking, you'll have a big mess of windows that will be very confusing. Generally, you'll find that the default settings work fine.

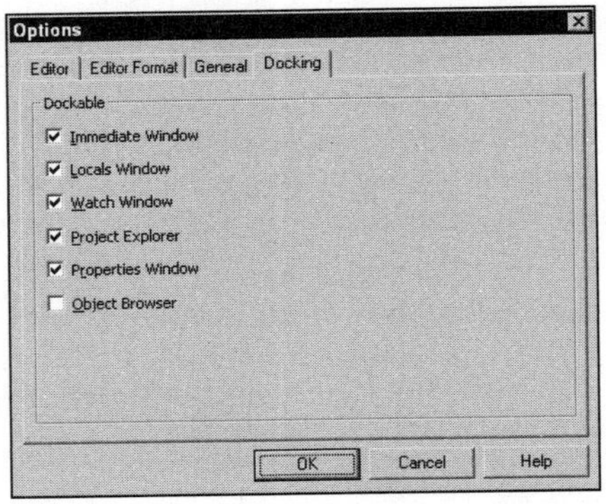

Figure 7-12: The Docking tab of the Options dialog box.

To dock a window, just drag it to the desired location. For example, you might want to dock the Project Explorer window to the left side of the screen. Just drag its title bar to the left, and you'll see an outline that shows it docked. Release the mouse, and it will be docked.

Docking windows in the VBE has always been a bit problematic. Often, you'll find that some windows simply refuse to be docked. I've found that if you persist long enough, it will eventually work. Unfortunately, I don't have any secret window docking techniques.

The Macro Recorder

Earlier in this chapter, I discuss the *macro recorder,* which is a tool that converts your Excel actions into VBA code. This section covers the macro recorder in more detail.

Excel's Visual Basic toolbar has several useful buttons for you. On this toolbar, you'll find the Run Macro, Record Macro, Stop Macro, and Visual Basic Editor buttons useful.

The macro recorder is an *extremely* useful tool, but it's important to remember the following points:

♦ The macro recorder is appropriate only for simple macros or for recording a small part of a more complex macro.

♦ The macro recorder cannot generate code that performs *looping* (that is, repeating statements), assigns variables, executes statements conditionally, displays dialog boxes, and so on.

♦ The code that is generated depends on certain settings that you specify.

♦ You'll often want to clean up the recorded code to remove extraneous commands.

What the macro recorder actually records

The Excel macro recorder translates your mouse and keyboard actions into VBA code. I could probably write several pages describing how this is done, but the best way to show you is by example. Follow these steps:

1. Start with a blank workbook.

2. Make sure that the Excel window is not maximized. You don't want it to fill the entire screen.

3. Press Alt+F11 to activate the VBE window.

   Note: Make sure that this window is not maximized. Otherwise, you won't be able to see the VBE window and Excel's window at the same time.

4. Resize and arrange Excel's window and the VBE window so both are visible. (For best results, minimize any other applications that are running.)

5. Activate Excel, choose Tools → Macro → Record New Macro, and then click OK to start the macro recorder.

   Excel inserts a new module (named `Module1`) and starts recording on that sheet.

6. Activate the VBE window.

7. In the Project Explorer window, double-click `Module1` to display that module in the code window.

8. Close the Project Explorer window in the VBE to maximize the view of the code window.

Your screen should look something like the example in Figure 7-13. The size of the windows will depend on your video resolution.

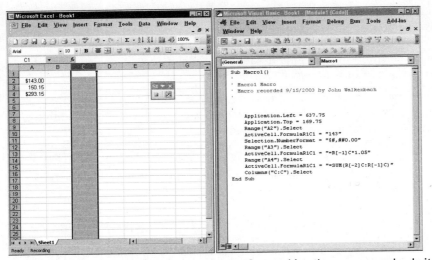

Figure 7-13: A convenient window arrangement for watching the macro recorder do its thing.

Now move around in the worksheet and select various Excel commands. Watch while the code is generated in the window that displays the VBA module. Select cells, enter data, format cells, use the menus and toolbars, create a chart, manipulate graphic objects, and so on. I guarantee that you'll be enlightened while you watch the code being spit out before your very eyes.

Relative or absolute?

When recording your actions, Excel normally records *absolute references* to cells. In other words, when you select a cell, it will remember that exact cell (not the cell relative to the current active cell). To demonstrate how this works, perform these steps and examine the code:

1. Activate a worksheet and start the macro recorder.

2. Activate cell B1.

3. Enter **Jan** into cell B1.

4. Move to cell C1 and enter **Feb**.

5. Continue this process until you've entered the first six months of the year in B1:G1.

6. Click cell B1 to activate it again.

7. Stop the macro recorder.

Excel generates the following code:

```
Sub Macro1()
    Range("B1").Select
    ActiveCell.FormulaR1C1 = "Jan"
    Range("C1").Select
    ActiveCell.FormulaR1C1 = "Feb"
    Range("D1").Select
    ActiveCell.FormulaR1C1 = "Mar"
    Range("E1").Select
    ActiveCell.FormulaR1C1 = "Apr"
    Range("F1").Select
    ActiveCell.FormulaR1C1 = "May"
    Range("G1").Select
    ActiveCell.FormulaR1C1 = "Jun"
    Range("B1").Select
End Sub
```

To execute this macro, choose the Tools → Macro → Macros command (or press Alt+F8) and select Macro1 (or whatever the macro is named) and click the Run button.

The macro, when executed, re-creates the actions that you performed when you recorded it. These same actions occur regardless of which cell is active when you execute the macro. Recording a macro using absolute references always produces the exact same results.

In some cases, however, you'll want your recorded macro to work with cell locations in a *relative* manner. For example, you'd probably want such a macro to start entering the month names in the active cell. In such a case, you'll want to use relative recording to record the macro.

The Stop Recording toolbar, which consists of only two buttons, is displayed when you are recording a macro. You can change the manner in which Excel records your actions by clicking the Relative Reference button on the Stop Recording toolbar. This button is a toggle. When the button appears in a pressed state, the recording mode is relative. When the button appears normally, you are recording in absolute mode. You can change the recording method at any time, even in the middle of recording.

To see how this works, erase the cells in B1:D1 and then perform the following steps:

1. Activate cell B1.

2. Choose Tools → Macro → Record New Macro.

3. Click OK to begin recording.

4. Click the Relative Reference button (on the Stop Recording toolbar) to change the recording mode to relative.

   When you click this button, it appears pressed.

5. Enter the first six months' names in B1:G1, as in the previous example.

6. Select cell B1.

7. Stop the macro recorder.

With the recording mode set to relative, the code that Excel generates is quite different:

```
Sub Macro2()
    ActiveCell.FormulaR1C1 = "Jan"
    ActiveCell.Offset(0, 1).Range("A1").Select
    ActiveCell.FormulaR1C1 = "Feb"
    ActiveCell.Offset(0, 1).Range("A1").Select
    ActiveCell.FormulaR1C1 = "Mar"
    ActiveCell.Offset(0, 1).Range("A1").Select
    ActiveCell.FormulaR1C1 = "Apr"
    ActiveCell.Offset(0, 1).Range("A1").Select
    ActiveCell.FormulaR1C1 = "May"
    ActiveCell.Offset(0, 1).Range("A1").Select
    ActiveCell.FormulaR1C1 = "Jun"
    ActiveCell.Offset(0, -5).Range("A1").Select
End Sub
```

You can execute this macro by activating a worksheet and then choosing the Tools → Macro command. Select the macro name and then click the Run button.

You'll also notice that I varied the procedure slightly in this example: I activated the beginning cell *before* I started recording. This is an important step when you record macros that use the active cell as a base.

Although it looks rather complicated, this macro is actually quite simple. The first statement simply enters Jan into the active cell. (It uses the active cell because it's not preceded by a statement that selects a cell.) The next statement uses the Offset property to move the selection one cell to the right. The next statement inserts more text, and so on. Finally, the original cell is selected by calculating a relative offset rather than an absolute cell. Unlike the preceding macro, this one always starts entering text in the active cell.

You'll notice that this macro generates code that appears to reference cell A1 — which might seem strange because cell A1 was not even involved in the macro. This is simply a by-product of how the macro recorder works. (I discuss the Offset property later in this chapter.) At this point, all you need to know is that the macro works as it should.

By the way, the code generated by Excel is much more complex than it need be, and it's not the most efficient way to code the operation. The macro that follows, which I entered manually, is a simpler and faster way to perform this same operation. This example demonstrates that VBA doesn't have to select a cell before it puts information into it — an important concept that can also speed things up considerably.

```
Sub Macro3()
    ActiveCell.Offset(0, 0) = "Jan"
    ActiveCell.Offset(0, 1) = "Feb"
    ActiveCell.Offset(0, 2) = "Mar"
    ActiveCell.Offset(0, 3) = "Apr"
    ActiveCell.Offset(0, 4) = "May"
    ActiveCell.Offset(0, 5) = "Jun"
End Sub
```

In fact, this macro can be made even more efficient by using the With-End With construct:

```
Sub Macro4()
    With ActiveCell
        .Offset(0, 0) = "Jan"
        .Offset(0, 1) = "Feb"
        .Offset(0, 2) = "Mar"
        .Offset(0, 3) = "Apr"
        .Offset(0, 4) = "May"
        .Offset(0, 5) = "Jun"
    End With
End Sub
```

Or, if you're a VBA guru (like the technical editor for this book), you can impress your colleagues, and do it in one statement:

```
Sub Macro54()
    ActiveCell.Resize(,6)=Array("Jan","Feb","Mar","Apr","May","Jun")
End Sub
```

The point here is that the recorder has two distinct modes, and you need to be aware of which mode you're recording in. Otherwise, the result will not be what you expected.

Recording options

When you record your actions to create VBA code, you have several options. Recall that the Tools → Macro → Record New Macro command displays the Record Macro dialog box before recording begins. This dialog box gives you quite a bit of control over your macro. The following paragraphs describe your options.

MACRO NAME

You can enter a name for the procedure that you are recording. By default, Excel uses the names Macro1, Macro2, and so on for each macro that you record. I usually just accept the default name and change the name of the procedure later. You, however, might prefer to name the macro before you record it. The choice is yours.

SHORTCUT KEY

The Shortcut key option lets you execute the macro by pressing a shortcut key combination. For example, if you enter w (lowercase), you can execute the macro by pressing Ctrl+W. If you enter W (uppercase), the macro comes alive when you press Ctrl+Shift+W.

You can add or change a shortcut key at any time, so you don't need to set this option while recording a macro.

STORE MACRO IN

The Store Macro In option tells Excel where to store the macro that it records. By default, Excel puts the recorded macro in a module in the active workbook. If you prefer, you can record it in a new workbook (Excel opens a blank workbook) or in your Personal Macro Workbook. (Read more about this in the upcoming sidebar, "The Personal Macro Workbook.")

DESCRIPTION

By default, Excel inserts five lines of comments (three of them blank) that list the macro name, the user's name, and the date. You can put anything you like here – or nothing at all. As far as I'm concerned, typing anything in is a waste of time because I always end up deleting this in the module.

In versions of Excel prior to Excel 97, the Record Macro dialog box provided an option that let you assign the macro to a new menu item on the Tools menu. This

---

The Personal Macro Workbook

If you create some VBA macros that you find particularly useful, you might want to store these routines on your Personal Macro Workbook. This is a workbook, named Personal.xls, that is stored in your XLStart directory. Whenever you start Excel, this workbook is loaded. It's a hidden workbook, so it's out of your way. When you record a macro, one of your options is to record it to your Personal Macro Workbook. The Personal.xls file doesn't exist until you record a macro to it.

option was removed, beginning with Excel 97. If you want to be able to execute a macro from a menu, you need to set this up yourself. See Chapter 23 for more details.

Cleaning up recorded macros

Earlier in this section, you saw how recording your actions while you issued a single command (the File→Page Setup command) can produce an enormous amount of VBA code. In many cases, the recorded code includes extraneous commands that you can delete.

It's also important to understand that the macro recorder doesn't always generate the most efficient code. If you examine the generated code, you'll see that Excel generally records what is selected (that is, an object) and then uses the Selection object in subsequent statements. For example, here's what is recorded if you select a range of cells and then use the buttons on the Formatting toolbar to change the numeric formatting, and apply bold and italic:

```
Range("A1:C5").Select
Selection.NumberFormat = "#,##0.00"
Selection.Font.Bold = True
Selection.Font.Italic = True
```

 TIP If you use the Formatting dialog box to record this macro, you'll find that Excel records quite a bit of extraneous code. Recording toolbar button clicks often produces more efficient code.

Remember: This is just one way to perform these actions. You can also use the more efficient With-End With construct, as follows:

```
Range("A1:C5").Select
With Selection
    .NumberFormat = "#,##0.00"
    .Font.Bold = True
    .Font.Italic = True
End With
```

Or you can avoid the Select method altogether and write the code even more efficiently, like this:

```
With Range("A1:C5")
    .NumberFormat = "#,##0.00"
    .Font.Bold = True
    .Font.Italic = True
End With
```

If speed is essential in your application, you'll always want to examine any recorded VBA code closely to make sure that it's as efficient as possible.

You will, of course, need to understand VBA thoroughly before you start cleaning up your recorded macros. But for now, just be aware that recorded VBA code isn't always the best, most efficient code.

About the Code Examples

Throughout this book, I present many small snippets of VBA code to make a point or to provide an example. Often, this code might consist of just a single statement. In some cases, the example consists of only an *expression*, which isn't a valid instruction by itself.

For example, the following is an expression:

```
Range("A1").Value
```

To test an expression, you must evaluate it. The MsgBox function is a handy tool for this:

```
MsgBox Range("A1").Value
```

To try out these examples, you need to put the statement within a procedure in a VBA module, like this:

```
Sub Test()
' statement goes here

End Sub
```

Then put the cursor anywhere within the procedure and press F5 to execute it. Also, make sure that the code is being executed within the proper context. For example, if a statement refers to Sheet1, make sure that the active workbook actually has a sheet named Sheet1.

If the code is just a single statement, you can use the VBE Immediate window. The Immediate window is very useful for executing a statement "immediately" — without having to create a procedure. If the Immediate window is not displayed, press Ctrl+G in the VBE.

Just type the VBA statement and press Enter. To evaluate an expression in the Immediate window, precede the expression with a question mark (?). The question mark is a shortcut for Print. For example, you can type the following into the Immediate window:

```
? Range("A1").Value
```

The result of this expression is displayed in the next line of the Immediate window.

About Objects and Collections

If you've worked through the first part of this chapter, you have an overview of VBA and you know the basics of working with VBA modules in the VBE. You've also seen some VBA code and were exposed to concepts such as objects and properties. This section gives you some additional details about objects and collections of objects.

When you work with VBA, you must understand the concept of objects and Excel's object model. It helps to think of objects in terms of a *hierarchy*. At the top of this model is the Application object — in this case, Excel itself. But if you're programming in VBA with Microsoft Word, the Application object is Word.

The object hierarchy

The Application object (that is, Excel) contains other objects. Here are a few examples of objects contained in the Application object:

◆ Workbooks (a collection of all Workbook objects)

◆ Windows (a collection of all Window objects)

◆ AddIns (a collection of all AddIn objects)

Some objects can contain other objects. For example, the Workbooks collection consists of all open Workbook objects, and a Workbook object contains other objects, a few of which are as follows:

◆ Worksheets (a collection of Worksheet objects)

◆ Charts (a collection of Chart objects)

◆ Names (a collection of Name objects)

Each of these objects, in turn, can contain other objects. The Worksheets collection consists of all Worksheet objects in a Workbook. A Worksheet object contains many other objects, which include the following:

◆ ChartObjects (a collection of ChartObject objects)

◆ Range

◆ PageSetup

◆ PivotTables (a collection of PivotTable objects)

If this seems confusing, trust me, it *will* make sense, and you'll eventually realize that this whole object hierarchy thing is quite logical and well structured. By the way, the complete Excel object model is diagrammed in the Help system.

About collections

Another key concept in VBA programming is collections. A *collection* is a group of objects of the same class, and a collection is itself an object. As I note earlier, `Workbooks` is a collection of all `Workbook` objects currently open. `Worksheets` is a collection of all `Worksheet` objects contained in a particular `Workbook` object. You can work with an entire collection of objects or with an individual object in a collection. To reference a single object from a collection, you put the object's name or index number in parentheses after the name of the collection, like this:

```
Worksheets("Sheet1")
```

If `Sheet1` is the first worksheet in the collection, you could also use the following reference:

```
Worksheets(1)
```

You refer to the second worksheet in a `Workbook` as `Worksheets(2)`, and so on. There is also a collection called `Sheets`, which is made up of all sheets in a workbook, whether they're worksheets or chart sheets. If `Sheet1` is the first sheet in the workbook, you can reference it as follows:

```
Sheets(1)
```

Referring to objects

When you refer to an object using VBA, you often must qualify the object by connecting object names with a period (also known as a *dot operator*). What if you had two workbooks open and they both had a worksheet named `Sheet1`? The solution is to qualify the reference by adding the object's container, like this:

```
Workbooks("Book1").Worksheets("Sheet1")
```

Without the workbook qualifier, VBA would look for `Sheet1` in the active workbook.

To refer to a specific range (such as cell A1) on a worksheet named `Sheet1` in a workbook named `Book1`, you can use the following expression:

```
Workbooks("Book1").Worksheets("Sheet1").Range("A1")
```

The fully qualified reference for the preceding example also includes the `Application` object, as follows:

```
Application.Workbooks("Book1").Worksheets("Sheet1").Range("A1")
```

Most of the time, however, you can omit the `Application` object in your references; it is assumed. If the `Book1` object is the active workbook, you can even omit that object reference and use this:

```
Worksheets("Sheet1").Range("A1")
```

And — I think you know where I'm going with this — if `Sheet1` is the active worksheet, you can use an even simpler expression:

```
Range("A1")
```

 Contrary to what you might expect, Excel does not have an object that refers to an individual cell that is called `Cell`. A single cell is simply a `Range` object that happens to consist of just one element.

Simply referring to objects (as in these examples) doesn't do anything. To perform anything meaningful, you must read or modify an object's properties or else specify a method to be used with an object.

Properties and Methods

It's easy to be overwhelmed with properties and methods; there are literally thousands available. In this section, I describe how to access properties and methods of objects.

Object properties

Every object has properties. For example, a `Range` object has a property called `Value`. You can write VBA code to display the `Value` property or write VBA code to set the `Value` property to a specific value. Here's a procedure that uses the VBA `MsgBox` function to pop up a box that displays the value in cell A1 on `Sheet1` of the active workbook:

```
Sub ShowValue()
    Msgbox Worksheets("Sheet1").Range("A1").Value
End Sub
```

MsgBox is a useful function that you'll use often to display results while your VBA code is executing. I use it extensively throughout this book.

The code in the preceding example displays the current setting of the Value property of a specific cell: cell A1 on a worksheet named Sheet1 in the active workbook. Note that if the active workbook does not have a sheet named Sheet1, the macro will generate an error.

Now, what if you want to change the Value property? The following procedure changes the value displayed in cell A1 by changing the cell's Value property:

```
Sub ChangeValue()
    Worksheets("Sheet1").Range("A1").Value = 123
End Sub
```

After executing this routine, cell A1 on Sheet1 has the value 123. You might want to enter these procedures into a module and experiment with them.

Most objects have a default property. For a Range object, the default property is the Value property. Therefore, you can omit the .Value part from the above code, and it will have the same effect. However, it's usually considered good programming practice to include the property, even if it is the default property.

Object methods

In addition to properties, objects also have methods. A *method* is an action that you perform with an object. Here's a simple example that uses the Clear method on a Range object. After you execute this procedure, A1:C3 on Sheet1 will be empty, and all cell formatting will be removed.

```
Sub ZapRange()
    Worksheets("Sheet1").Range("A1:C3").Clear
End Sub
```

If you'd like to delete the values in a range but keep the formatting, use the `ClearContents` method of the `Range` object.

Most methods also take arguments to define the action further. Here's an example that copies cell A1 to cell B1 by using the `Copy` method of the `Range` object. In this example, the `Copy` method has one argument (the destination of the copy). Notice that I use the line continuation character sequence (a space, followed by an underscore) in this example. You can omit the line continuation sequence and type the statement on a single line.

```
Sub CopyOne()
    Worksheets("Sheet1").Range("A1").Copy _
        Worksheets("Sheet1").Range("B1")
End Sub
```

Specifying Arguments for Methods and Properties

An issue that often leads to confusion among VBA programmers concerns arguments for methods and properties. Some methods use arguments to further clarify the action to be taken, and some properties use arguments to further specify the property value. In some cases, one or more of the arguments is optional.

If a method uses arguments, place the arguments after the name of the method, separated by commas. If the method uses optional arguments, you can insert blank placeholders for the optional arguments. Read on to discover how to insert these placeholders.

Consider the `Protect` method for a workbook object. Check the Help system, and you'll find that the `Protect` method takes three arguments: password, structure, and windows. These arguments correspond to the options in the Protect Workbook dialog box.

If you want to protect a workbook named `MyBook.xls`, for example, you might use a statement like this:

```
Workbooks("MyBook.xls").Protect "xyzzy", True, False
```

In this case, the workbook is protected with a password (argument 1). Its structure is protected (argument 2) but not its windows (argument 3).

Continued

Specifying Arguments for Methods and Properties
(Continued)

If you don't want to assign a password, you can use a statement like this:

```
Workbooks("MyBook.xls").Protect , True, False
```

Notice that the first argument is omitted and that I specified the placeholder by using a comma.

Another approach, which makes your code more readable, is to use named arguments. Here's an example of how you use named arguments for the preceding example:

```
Workbooks("MyBook.xls").Protect Structure:=True, Windows:=False
```

Using named arguments is a good idea, especially for methods that have lots of optional arguments, and also when you need to use only a few of them. When you use named arguments, there is no need to use a placeholder for missing arguments.

For properties (and methods) that return a value, you must use parentheses around the arguments. For example, the Address property of a Range object takes five arguments, all of which are optional. Because the Address property returns a value, the following statement is not valid because the parentheses are omitted:

```
MsgBox Range("A1").Address False    ' invalid
```

The proper syntax for such a statement requires parentheses, as follows:

```
MsgBox Range("A1").Address(False)
```

Or the statement could also be written by using a named argument:

```
MsgBox Range("A1").Address(rowAbsolute:=False)
```

These nuances will become clearer when you gain more experience with VBA.

The Comment Object: A Case Study

To help you better understand the properties and methods available for an object, I focus on a particular object: the Comment object. You create a Comment object when you choose the Excel Insert → Comment command to enter a cell comment. In the sections that follow, you'll get a feel for working with objects. If you're a bit overwhelmed by the material in this section, don't fret. These concepts will become much clearer over time.

Viewing Help for the Comment object

One way to learn about a particular object is to look it up in the Help system. Figure 7-14 shows the main help screen for the Comment object. I found this Help screen by typing **comment** in the VBE Type a Question for Help box. Additional help topics are listed in the VBE task bar.

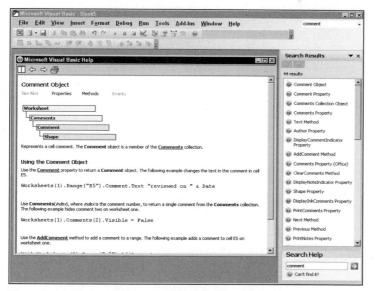

Figure 7–14: The main help screen for the Comment object.

Using the Help System

The easiest way to get specific help about a particular object, property, or method is to type the word in a code window and press F1. If there is any ambiguity about the word that you typed, you get a dialog box like the one shown in the Figure 7-14.

Unfortunately, the items listed in the dialog box are not always clear, so it may require some trial and error to locate the correct help topic. The dialog box in Figure 7-14 appears when you type **Comment** and then press F1. In this case, although Comment is an object, it may behave like a property. Clicking the first item displays the help topic for the Comment object; clicking the second item displays the help topic for the Comment property.

Notice that the colored or underlined words are hyperlinks that display additional information. For example, you can click the <u>Properties</u> hyperlink to get a list of all properties for the Comment object. Or click the <u>Methods</u> hyperlink to get a list of the object's methods.

Properties of a Comment object

The Comment object has six properties. Table 7-1 contains a list of these properties, along with a brief description of each. If a property is *read-only*, your VBA code can read the property but cannot change it.

TABLE 7-1 PROPERTIES OF A COMMENT OBJECT

Property	Read–Only	Description
Application	Yes	Returns an object that represents the application that created the comment (that is, Excel).
Author	Yes	Returns the name of the person who created the comment.
Creator	Yes	Returns a number that specifies the application that created the object. Not used in Excel for Windows (relevant only for Excel for Macintosh).
Parent	Yes	Returns the parent object for the comment. (It is always a Range object.)
Shape	Yes	Returns a Shape object that represents the shape attached to the comment.
Visible	No	Is True if the comment is visible.

Methods of a Comment object

Table 7-2 shows the methods that you can use with a Comment object. Again, these methods perform common operations that you may have performed manually with a comment at some point . . . but you probably never thought of these operations as methods.

TABLE 7-2 METHODS OF A COMMENT OBJECT

Method	Description
Delete	Deletes a comment
Next	Returns a Comment object that represents the next comment
Previous	Returns a Comment object that represents the previous comment
Text	Returns or sets the text in a comment (takes three arguments)

You might be surprised to see that Text is a method rather than a property. This leads to an important point: The distinction between properties and methods isn't always clear-cut, and the object model isn't perfectly consistent. In fact, it's not really important that you distinguish between properties and methods. As long as you get the syntax correct, it doesn't matter whether a word in your code is a property or a method.

The Comments collection

Recall that a collection is a group of like objects. Every worksheet has a Comments collection, which consists of all Comment objects on the worksheet. If the worksheet has no comments, this collection is empty.

For example, the following code refers to the first comment on Sheet1 of the active workbook:

```
Worksheets("Sheet1").Comments(1)
```

The following statement displays the text contained in the first comment on Sheet1:

```
MsgBox Worksheets("Sheet1").Comments(1).Text
```

Unlike most objects, a Comment object does not have a Name property. Therefore, to refer to a specific comment, you must either use an index number or use the Comment property of a Range object to return a specific comment. (Keep reading, and this will make sense.) The Comments collection is also an object and has its own set of properties and methods. For example, the following example shows the total number of comments:

```
MsgBox ActiveSheet.Comments.Count
```

The `Comments` collection here has a `Count` property that stores the number of `Comment` objects in the active worksheet. The next example shows the address of the cell that has the first comment:

```
MsgBox ActiveSheet.Comments(1).Parent.Address
```

Here, `Comments(1)` returns the first `Comment` object in the `Comments` collection. The `Parent` property of the `Comment` object returns its container, which is a `Range` object. The message box displays the `Address` property of the Range. The net effect is that the statement displays the address of the cell that contains the first comment.

You can also loop through all the comments on a sheet by using the `For Each-Next` construct. (This is explained in Chapter 8.) Here's an example that displays a separate message box for each comment on the active worksheet:

```
For Each cmt in ActiveSheet.Comments
    MsgBox cmt.Text
Next cmt
```

If you'd rather not deal with a series of message boxes, use this procedure to print the comments to the Intermediate window in the VBE:

```
For Each cmt in ActiveSheet.Comments
    Debug.Print cmt.Text
Next cmt
```

About the Comment property

In this section I've been discussing the `Comment` object. If you dig through the Help system, you'll find that a `Range` object has a property named `Comment`. If the cell contains a comment, the `Comment` property returns an object: a `Comment` object. For example, the following statement refers to the `Comment` object in cell A1:

```
Range("A1").Comment
```

If this were the first comment on the sheet, you could refer to the same `Comment` object as follows:

```
ActiveSheet.Comments(1)
```

To display the comment in cell A1 in a message box, use a statement like this:

```
MsgBox Range("A1").Comment.Text
```

If cell A1 does not contain a comment, this statement will generate an error.

The fact that a property can return an object is a very important concept — a difficult one to grasp, perhaps, but critical to mastering VBA.

Objects within a Comment object

Working with properties is confusing at first because some properties actually return objects. Suppose that you want to determine the background color of a particular comment on Sheet1. If you look through the list of properties for a Comment object, you won't find anything that relates to color. Rather, you must do this:

1. Use the Comment object's Shape property to return the Shape object that's contained in the comment.

2. Use the Shape object's Fill property to return a FillFormat object.

3. Use the FillFormat object's ForeColor property to return a ColorFormat object.

4. Use the ColorFormat object's RGB property (or SchemeColor property) to get the color.

Put another way, getting at the interior color for a Comment object involves accessing other objects contained in the Comment object. Here's a look at the object hierarchy that's involved.

Application (Excel)
   Workbook object
     Worksheet object
      Comment object
       Shape object
        FillFormat object
        ColorFormat object

I'll be the first to admit it: This can get very confusing! But, as an example of the "elegance" of VBA, code to change the color of a comment can be written with a single statement:

```
Worksheets("Sheet1").Comments(1).Shape.Fill.ForeColor _
    .RGB = RGB(0, 255, 0)
```

Or, if you use the `SchemeColor` property (which ranges from 0 to 80):

```
Worksheets("Sheet1").Comments(1).Shape.Fill.ForeColor _
    .SchemeColor = 12
```

Confused by Colors?

When you gain experience with VBA and start working with setting colors for various objects, you will probably reach a head-scratching point and wonder what's going on. Keep this in mind: Excel uses a 56-color palette, and the specific colors are saved with each workbook. These are the colors that you see when you use the Fill Color button on the Excel Formatting toolbar (the same colors that are displayed in the Color tab of the Options dialog box). So what does this mean for a VBA programmer? The color that you specify in your VBA code might or might not be the color that actually appears.

Things get even more confusing. Depending on the object that you're manipulating, you'll need to deal with several different color-related objects and properties.

You can set the color of a `Shape` object by using either the `RGB` property or the `SchemeColor` property. The `RGB` property lets you specify a color in terms of its red, green, and blue components. This is used in conjunction with VBA's `RGB` function, which takes three arguments, each of which ranges from 0 to 255. The `RGB` function returns a value between 0 and 16,777,215. But, as I mention, Excel can only handle 56 different colors. Therefore, the actual color that results when you use the `RGB` function will be the closest color match in the workbook's 56-color palette. The `SchemeColor` property accepts values between 0 and 80. The Help system says virtually nothing about what these colors actually represent. They are, however, limited to the workbook's color palette.

When you're dealing with colors in a `Range` object, you need to access the `Interior` object, contained in the `Range` object. You have a choice of setting the color by using either the `Color` property or the `ColorIndex` property. Valid values for the `ColorIndex` property are 0 through 56 (0 represents no fill). These values correspond to the workbook's color palette. Unfortunately, the order of the colors displayed bears no relationship to the numbering system for the `ColorIndex` property, so you'll need to record a macro to determine the `ColorIndex` value for a particular color. Even then, there's no guarantee that the user hasn't changed the color palette for the workbook. If so, the `ColorIndex` could result in a color completely different from the one that you had in mind.

If you use the `Color` property, you can specify a color value by using the VBA `RGB` function. But, again, the actual color that you get will be the one closest to a color in the workbook's color palette.

This type of referencing is certainly not intuitive at first, but it will eventually make sense. Fortunately, recording your actions in Excel almost always yields some insights regarding the hierarchy of the objects involved.

By the way, to change the color of the text in a comment, you need to access the `Comment` object's `TextFrame` object, which contains the `Characters` object, which contains the `Font` object. Then you have access to the `Font` object's `Color` or `ColorIndex` properties. Here's an example that sets `ColorIndex` property to 5:

```
Worksheets("Sheet1").Comments(1) _
   .Shape.TextFrame.Characters.Font.ColorIndex = 5
```

Determining whether a cell has a comment

The following statement will display the comment in cell A1 of the active sheet:

```
MsgBox Range("A1").Comment.Text
```

If cell A1 does not have a comment, executing this statement will generate a cryptic error message: `Object variable or With block variable not set`.

To determine whether a particular cell has a comment, you can write code to see whether the `Comment` object is `Nothing`. (Yes, `Nothing` is a valid keyword.) The following statement displays `True` if cell A1 does not have a comment:

```
MsgBox Range("A1").Comment Is Nothing
```

Note that I use the `Is` keyword and not an equal sign.

You can take this one step further, and write a statement that displays the cell comment only if the cell actually has a comment (and does not generate an error if the cell lacks a comment). The statement below accomplishes this task:

```
If Not Range("A1").Comment Is Nothing Then _
   MsgBox Range("A1").Comment.Text
```

Adding a new Comment object

You might have noticed that the list of methods for the `Comment` object doesn't include a method to add a new comment. This is because the `AddComment` method belongs to the `Range` object. The following statement adds a comment (an empty comment) to cell A1 on the active worksheet:

```
Range("A1").AddComment
```

If you consult the Help system, you'll discover that the `AddComment` method takes an argument that represents the text for the comment. Therefore, you can add a comment and then add text to the comment with a single statement, like this:

```
Range("A1").AddComment "Formula developed by JW."
```

The `AddComment` method generates an error if the cell already contains a comment.

If you'd like to see these `Comment` object properties and methods in action, check out the example workbook on the companion CD-ROM. This workbook contains several examples that manipulate `Comment` objects with VBA code. You probably won't understand all the code, but you will get a feel for how you can use VBA to manipulate an object.

Some useful application properties

When you're working with Excel, only one workbook at a time can be active. And if the sheet is a worksheet, one cell is the active cell (even if a multicell range is selected).

VBA knows this and lets you refer to these active objects in a simplified manner. This is often useful because you won't always know the exact workbook, worksheet, or range that you want to operate on. VBA handles this by providing properties of the `Application` object. For example, the `Application` object has an `ActiveCell` property that returns a reference to the active cell. The following instruction assigns the value 1 to the active cell:

```
ActiveCell.Value = 1
```

Notice that I omitted the reference to the `Application` object in the preceding example because it is assumed. It's important to understand that this instruction will fail if the active sheet is not a worksheet. For example, if VBA executes this statement when a chart sheet is active, the procedure halts, and you'll get an error message.

If a range is selected in a worksheet, the active cell will be in a cell within the selected range. In other words, the active cell is always a single cell (never a multicell range).

The `Application` object also has a `Selection` property that returns a reference to whatever is selected, which could be a single cell (the active cell), a range of cells, or an object such as `ChartObject`, `TextBox`, or `Shape`.

Table 7-3 lists the other `Application` properties that are useful when working with cells and ranges.

TABLE 7-3 SOME USEFUL PROPERTIES OF THE APPLICATION OBJECT

Property	Object Returned
ActiveCell	The active cell.
ActiveChart	The active chart sheet or chart contained in a `ChartObject` on a worksheet. This property will be `Nothing` if a chart is not active.
ActiveSheet	The active sheet (worksheet or chart).
ActiveWindow	The active window.
ActiveWorkbook	The active workbook.
RangeSelection	The selected cells on the worksheet in the specified window, even when a graphic object is selected.
Selection	The object selected. (It could be a `Range` object, `Shape`, `ChartObject`, and so on.)
ThisWorkbook	The workbook that contains the procedure being executed.

The advantage of using these properties to return an object is that you don't need to know which cell, worksheet, or workbook is active; nor do you have to provide a specific reference to it. This allows you to write VBA code that is not specific to a particular workbook, sheet, or range. For example, the following instruction clears the contents of the active cell, even though the address of the active cell is not known:

```
ActiveCell.ClearContents
```

The example that follows displays a message that tells you the name of the active sheet:

```
MsgBox ActiveSheet.Name
```

If you want to know the name of the active workbook, use a statement like this:

```
MsgBox ActiveWorkbook.Name
```

If a range on a worksheet is selected, you can fill the entire range with a value by executing a single statement. In the following example, the Selection property of the Application object returns a Range object that corresponds to the selected cells. The instruction simply modifies the Value property of this Range object, and the result is a range filled with a single value:

```
Selection.Value = 12
```

Note that if something other than a range is selected (such as a ChartObject or a Shape), the preceding statement will generate an error because ChartObject and Shape objects do not have a Value property.

The following statement, however, enters a value of 12 into the Range object that was selected before a non-Range object was selected. If you look up the RangeSelection property in the Help system, you'll find that this property applies only to a Window object.

```
ActiveWindow.RangeSelection.Value = 12
```

To find out how many cells are selected in the active window, access the Count property. Here's an example:

```
MsgBox ActiveWindow.RangeSelection.Count
```

Working with Range Objects

Much of the work that you will do in VBA involves cells and ranges in worksheets. After all, that's what spreadsheets are designed to do. The earlier discussion on relative versus absolute macro recording (see "Relative or absolute?") exposed you to working with cells in VBA, but you need to know a lot more.

A Range object is contained in a Worksheet object and consists of a single cell or range of cells on a single worksheet. In the sections that follow, I discuss three ways of referring to Range objects in your VBA code:

- The Range property of a Worksheet or Range class object
- The Cells property of a Worksheet object
- The Offset property of a Range object

The Range property

The `Range` property returns a `Range` object. If you consult the Help system for the `Range` property, you'll learn that this property has two syntaxes:

```
object.Range(cell1)
object.Range(cell1, cell2)
```

The `Range` property applies to two types of objects: a `Worksheet` object or a `Range` object. Here, `cell1` and `cell2` refer to placeholders for terms that Excel will recognize as identifying the range (in the first instance) and delineating the range (in the second instance). Following are a few examples of using the `Range` method.

You've already seen examples like the following one earlier in the chapter. The instruction that follows simply enters a value into the specified cell. In this case, it puts a 1 into cell A1 on `Sheet1` of the active workbook:

```
Worksheets("Sheet1").Range("A1").Value = 1
```

The `Range` property also recognizes defined names in workbooks. Therefore, if a cell is named `Input`, you can use the following statement to enter a value into that named cell:

```
Worksheets("Sheet1").Range("Input").Value = 1
```

The example that follows enters the same value into a range of 20 cells on the active sheet. If the active sheet is not a worksheet, this causes an error message:

```
ActiveSheet.Range("A1:B10").Value = 2
```

The next example produces exactly the same result as the preceding example:

```
Range("A1", "B10") = 2
```

The sheet reference is omitted, however, so the active sheet is assumed. Also, the value property is omitted, so the default property (which is `Value`, for a `Range` object) is assumed. This example also uses the second syntax of the `Range` property. With this syntax, the first argument is the cell at the top left of the range, and the second argument is the cell at the lower right of the range.

The following example uses the Excel range intersection operator (a space) to return the intersection of two ranges. In this case, the intersection is a single cell, C6. Therefore, this statement enters 3 into cell C6:

```
Range("C1:C10 A6:E6") = 3
```

And finally, this next example enters the value 4 into five cells: that is, a non-contiguous range. The comma serves as the union operator:

```
Range("A1,A3,A5,A7,A9") = 4
```

So far, all the examples have used the `Range` property on a `Worksheet` object. As I mentioned, you can also use the `Range` property on a `Range` object. This can be rather confusing, but bear with me.

Following is an example of using the `Range` property on a `Range` object. (In this case, the `Range` object is the active cell.) This example treats the `Range` object as if it were the upper-left cell in the worksheet, and then it enters a value of 5 into the cell that *would be* B2. In other words, the reference returned is relative to the upper-left corner of the `Range` object. Therefore, the statement that follows enters a value of 5 into the cell directly to the right and one row below the active cell:

```
ActiveCell.Range("B2") = 5
```

I *said* this is confusing. Fortunately, there is a much clearer way to access a cell relative to a range, called the `Offset` property. I discuss this property after the next section.

The Cells property

Another way to reference a range is to use the `Cells` property. Like the `Range` property, you can use the `Cells` property on `Worksheet` objects and `Range` objects. Check the Help system, and you'll see that the `Cells` property has three syntaxes:

```
object.Cells(rowIndex, columnIndex)
object.Cells(rowIndex)
object.Cells
```

I'll give you some examples that demonstrate how to use the `Cells` property. The first example enters the value 9 into cell A1 on `Sheet1`. In this case, I'm using the first syntax, which accepts the index number of the row (from 1–65536) and the index number of the column (from 1–256):

```
Worksheets("Sheet1").Cells(1, 1) = 9
```

Here's an example that enters the value 7 into cell D3 (that is, row 3, column 4) in the active worksheet:

```
ActiveSheet.Cells(3, 4) = 7
```

You can also use the `Cells` property on a `Range` object. When you do so, the `Range` object returned by the `Cells` property is relative to the upper-left cell of the referenced Range. Confusing? Probably. An example might help clear this up. The following instruction enters the value 5 into the active cell. Remember, in this case, the active cell is treated as if it were cell A1 in the worksheet:

```
ActiveCell.Cells(1, 1) = 5
```

 The real advantage of this type of cell referencing will be apparent when I discuss variables and looping (see Chapter 8). In most cases, you will not use actual values for the arguments. Rather, you use variables.

To enter a value of 5 into the cell directly below the active cell, you can use the following instruction:

```
ActiveCell.Cells(2, 1) = 5
```

Think of the preceding example as though it said this: "Start with the active cell and consider this cell as cell A1. Return the cell in the second row and the first column."

The second syntax of the Cells method uses a single argument that can range from 1–16,777,216. This number is equal to the number of cells in a worksheet (65,536 rows × 256 columns). The cells are numbered starting from A1 and continuing right and then down to the next row. The 256th cell is IV1; the 257th is A2.

The next example enters the value 2 into cell H3 (which is the 520th cell in the worksheet) of the active worksheet:

```
ActiveSheet.Cells(520) = 2
```

To display the value in the last cell in a worksheet (IV65536), use this statement:

```
MsgBox ActiveSheet.Cells(16777216)
```

This syntax can also be used with a Range object. In this case, the cell returned is relative to the Range object referenced. For example, if the Range object is A1:D10 (40 cells), the Cells property can have an argument from 1 to 40 and return one of the cells in the Range object. In the following example, a value of 2000 is entered into cell A2 because A2 is the fifth cell (counting from the top and to the right, then down) in the referenced range:

```
Range("A1:D10").Cells(5) = 2000
```

In the preceding example, the argument for the Cells property is not limited to values between 1 and 40. If the argument exceeds the number of cells in the range, the counting continues as if the range were larger than it actually is. Therefore, a statement like the preceding one could change the value in a cell that's outside of the range A1:D10.

The third syntax for the Cells property simply returns all cells on the referenced worksheet. Unlike the other two syntaxes, in this one, the return data is not a single cell. This example uses the ClearContents method on the range returned by using the Cells property on the active worksheet. The result is that the contents of every cell on the worksheet are cleared:

```
ActiveSheet.Cells.ClearContents
```

The Offset property

The Offset property (like the Range and Cells properties) also returns a Range object. But unlike the other two methods that I discussed, the Offset property applies only to a Range object and no other class. Its syntax is as follows:

```
object.Offset(rowOffset, columnOffset)
```

The Offset property takes two arguments that correspond to the relative position from the upper-left cell of the specified Range object. The arguments can be positive (down or right), negative (up or left), or zero. The example that follows enters a value of 12 into the cell directly below the active cell:

```
ActiveCell.Offset(1,0).Value = 12
```

The next example enters a value of 15 into the cell directly above the active cell:

```
ActiveCell.Offset(-1,0).Value = 15
```

By the way, if the active cell is in row 1, the Offset property in the preceding example generates an error because it cannot return a Range object that doesn't exist.

The Offset property is quite useful, especially when you use variables within looping procedures. I discuss these topics in the next chapter.

When you record a macro using the relative reference mode, Excel uses the `Offset` property to reference cells relative to the starting position (that is, the active cell when macro recording begins). For example, I used the macro recorder to generate the following code. I started with the cell pointer in cell B1, entered values into B1:B3, and then returned to B1.

```
Sub Macro1()
    ActiveCell.FormulaR1C1 = "1"
    ActiveCell.Offset(1, 0).Range("A1").Select
    ActiveCell.FormulaR1C1 = "2"
    ActiveCell.Offset(1, 0).Range("A1").Select
    ActiveCell.FormulaR1C1 = "3"
    ActiveCell.Offset(-2, 0).Range("A1").Select
End Sub
```

Notice that the macro recorder uses the `FormulaR1C1` property. Normally, you'll want to use the `Value` property to enter a value into a cell. However, using `FormulaR1C1` or even `Formula` produces the same result.

Also notice that the generated code references cell A1, which might seem a bit odd, because that cell was not even involved in the macro. This is a quirk in the macro recording procedure that makes the code more complex than necessary. You can delete all references to `Range("A1")`, and the macro still works perfectly:

```
Sub Modified Macro1()
    ActiveCell.FormulaR1C1 = "1"
    ActiveCell.Offset(1, 0).Select
    ActiveCell.FormulaR1C1 = "2"
    ActiveCell.Offset(1, 0).Select
    ActiveCell.FormulaR1C1 = "3"
    ActiveCell.Offset(-2, 0).Select
End Sub
```

In fact, here's a much more efficient version of the macro (which I wrote myself) that doesn't do any selecting:

```
Sub Macro1()
    ActiveCell = 1
    ActiveCell.Offset(1, 0) = 2
    ActiveCell.Offset(2, 0) = 3
End Sub
```

Things to Know about Objects

The preceding sections introduced you to objects (including collections), properties, and methods. But I've barely scratched the surface.

Essential concepts to remember

In this section, I add some more concepts that are essential for would-be VBA gurus. These concepts become clearer when you work with VBA and read subsequent chapters:

◆ *Objects have unique properties and methods.*

   Each object has its own set of properties and methods. Some objects, however, share some properties (for example, `Name`) and some methods (such as `Delete`).

◆ *You can manipulate objects without selecting them.*

   This might be contrary to how you normally think about manipulating objects in Excel, especially if you've programmed XLM macros. The fact is that it's usually more efficient to perform actions on objects without selecting them first. When you record a macro, Excel generally selects the object first. This is not necessary and may actually make your macro run slower.

◆ *It's important that you understand the concept of collections.*

   Most of the time, you refer to an object indirectly by referring to the collection that it's in. For example, to access a `Workbook` object named Myfile, reference the `Workbooks` collection as follows:

   ```
   Workbooks("Myfile.xls")
   ```

   This reference returns an object, which is the workbook with which you are concerned.

◆ *Properties can return a reference to another object.*

   For example, in the following statement, the `Font` property returns a `Font` object contained in a `Range` object:

   ```
   Range("A1").Font.Bold = True
   ```

◆ *There can be many different ways to refer to the same object.*

   Assume that you have a workbook named Sales, and it's the only workbook open. Then assume that this workbook has one worksheet, named Summary. You can refer to the sheet in any of the following ways:

```
Workbooks("Sales.xls").Worksheets("Summary")
Workbooks(1).Worksheets(1)
Workbooks(1).Sheets(1)
Application.ActiveWorkbook.ActiveSheet
ActiveWorkbook.ActiveSheet
ActiveSheet
```

The method that you use is usually determined by how much you know about the workspace. For example, more than one workbook is open, the second or third method is not reliable. If you want to work with the active sheet (whatever it may be), any of the last three methods would work. To be absolutely sure that you're referring to a specific sheet on a specific workbook, the first method is your best choice.

Learn more about objects and properties

If this is your first exposure to VBA, you're probably a bit overwhelmed about objects, properties, and methods. I don't blame you. If you try to access a property that an object doesn't have, you'll get a runtime error, and your VBA code will grind to a screeching halt until you correct the problem.

Fortunately, there are several good ways to learn about objects, properties, and methods.

READ THE REST OF THE BOOK

Don't forget, the name of this chapter is "Introducing Visual Basic for Applications." The remainder of this book covers a lot of additional details and provides many useful and informative examples.

RECORD YOUR ACTIONS

The absolute best way to become familiar with VBA, without question, is to simply turn on the macro recorder and record some actions that you make in Excel. This is a quick way to learn the relevant objects, properties, and methods for a task. It's even better if the VBA module in which the code is being recorded is visible while you're recording.

USE THE HELP SYSTEM

The main source of detailed information about Excel's objects, methods, and procedures is the Help system.

Figure 7-15 shows the help topic for the Value property. This particular property applies to a number of different objects, and the help topic contains hyperlinks labeled See Also, Applies To, and Example. If you click See Also, you get a list of related topics (if any). Clicking Applies To displays a window that lists all objects that use this property. If you click Example, you'll be able to view one or more examples. (You can copy the example text and paste it into a VBA module to try it out.)

The Help screen shown in Figure 7-15 shows the unexpanded topics. Click the Show All hyperlink to expand all of the topics in the screen.

```
Microsoft Visual Basic Help                          _ □ ✕
□ ⇦ ⇨ 🖨
                                          ▼ Show All

Value Property
See Also     Applies To     Example

▶ Value property as it applies to the Application, CubeField, and Style objects.
▶ Value property as it applies to the Borders and CustomProperty objects.
▶ Value property as it applies to the ControlFormat object.
▶ Value property as it applies to the Error and Validation objects.
▶ Value property as it applies to the Name, PivotField, PivotFormula, PivotItem, and PivotTable objects.
▶ Value property as it applies to the Parameter object.
▶ Value property as it applies to the Range object.
▶ Value property as it applies to the XmlNamespaces object.
▶ Value property as it applies to the XPath object.

Example
▶ As it applies to the Range object.
```

Figure 7–15: A typical VBA Help screen.

USE THE OBJECT BROWSER

The *Object Browser* is a handy tool that lists every property and method for every object available. When the VBE is active, you can bring up the Object Browser in any of the following three ways:

◆ Press F2.

◆ Choose the View → Object Browser command from the menu.

◆ Click the Object Browser tool on the Standard toolbar.

The Object Browser is shown in Figure 7-16.

The drop-down list in the upper-left corner of the Object Browser includes a list of all object libraries that you have access to:

◆ Excel itself

◆ MSForms (used to create custom dialog boxes)

◆ Office (objects common to all Microsoft Office applications)

◆ Stdole (OLE automation objects)

◆ VBA

◆ The current project (the project that's selected in the Project Explorer) and any workbooks referenced by that project

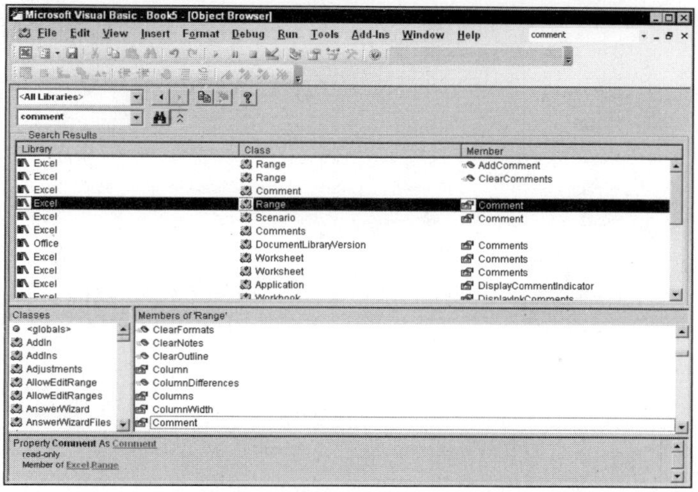

Figure 7-16: The Object Browser is a great reference source.

Your selection in this upper-left drop-down list determines what is displayed in the Classes window, and your selection in the Classes window determines what is visible in the members of window.

After you select a library, you can search for a particular text string to get a list of properties and methods that contain the text. You do so by entering the text in the second drop-down list and then clicking the binoculars (Search) icon. For example, assume that you're working on a project that manipulates cell comments:

1. Select the library of interest. If you're not sure which object library is appropriate, you can select <All Libraries>.

2. Enter **Comment** in the drop-down list below the library list.

3. Click the binoculars icon to begin the text search.

The Search Results window displays the matching text. Select an object to display its classes in the Classes window. Select a class to display its members (properties, methods, and constants). Pay attention to the bottom pane, which shows more information about the object. You can press F1 to go directly to the appropriate help topic.

The Object Browser might seem complex at first, but its usefulness to you will increase over time.

EXPERIMENT WITH THE IMMEDIATE WINDOW

As I describe in the sidebar earlier in this chapter (see "About the Code Examples"), the Immediate window of the VBE is very useful for testing statements and trying out various VBA expressions. I generally keep the Immediate window visible at all times, and I use it frequently to test various expressions and to help in debugging code.

Chapter 8

VBA Programming Fundamentals

IN THIS CHAPTER

In the preceding chapter, I introduce you to Visual Basic for Applications (VBA); now it's time to get better acquainted. This chapter discusses some of the key language elements and programming concepts in VBA.

- ◆ Understanding VBA language elements, including variables, data types, constants, and arrays

- ◆ Using VBA built-in functions

- ◆ Manipulating objects and collections

- ◆ Controlling the execution of your procedures

IF YOU'VE USED OTHER PROGRAMMING LANGUAGES, much of this information may sound familiar. VBA has a few unique wrinkles, however, so even experienced programmers may find some new information.

VBA Language Elements: An Overview

In Chapter 7, I present an overview of objects, properties, and methods. But I didn't tell you much about how to manipulate objects so that they do meaningful things. This chapter gently nudges you in that direction by exploring the VBA *language elements,* which are the keywords and control structures that you use to write VBA routines.

To get the ball rolling, I'll start by presenting a simple VBA Sub procedure. The following code, which is stored in a VBA module, calculates the sum of the first 100 integers. When the code finishes executing, the procedure displays a message with the result.

```
Sub VBA_Demo()
'    This is a simple VBA Example
    Dim Total As Integer, i As Integer
    Total = 0
    For i = 1 To 100
        Total = Total + i
    Next i
    MsgBox Total
End Sub
```

This procedure uses some common VBA language elements, including a comment (the line preceded by the apostrophe), two variables (`Total` and `i`), two assignment statements (`Total = 0` and `Total = Total + i`), a looping structure (`For-Next`), and a VBA statement (`MsgBox`). All these are discussed in subsequent sections of this chapter.

 VBA procedures need not manipulate any objects. The preceding procedure, for example, doesn't do anything with objects. It simply works with numbers.

Entering VBA Code

VBA code, which resides in a VBA module, consists of instructions. The accepted practice is to use one instruction per line. This standard is not a requirement, however; you can use a colon to separate multiple instructions on a single line. The following example combines four instructions on one line:

```
Sub OneLine()
    x= 1: y= 2: z= 3: MsgBox x + y + z
End Sub
```

Most programmers agree that code is easier to read if you use one instruction per line:

```
Sub OneLine()
    x = 1
    y = 2
    z = 3
    MsgBox x + y + z
End Sub
```

Each line can be as long as you like; the VBA module window scrolls to the left when you reach the right side. For lengthy lines, you may want to use VBA's line continuation sequence: an underscore (_) preceded by a space. For example:

```
Sub LongLine()
    SummedValue = _
        Worksheets("Sheet1").Range("A1").Value + _
        Worksheets("Sheet2").Range("A1").Value
End Sub
```

When you record macros, Excel often uses underscores to break long statements into multiple lines.

After you enter an instruction, VBA performs the following actions to improve readability:

◆ *It inserts spaces between operators.* If you enter `Ans=1+2` (without spaces), for example, VBA converts it to

```
Ans = 1 + 2
```

◆ *VBA adjusts the case of the letters for keywords, properties, and methods.* If you enter the following text:

```
Result=activesheet.range("a1").value=12
```

VBA converts it to

```
Result = ActiveSheet.Range("a1").Value = 12
```

Notice that text within quotation marks (in this case, `"a1"`) is not changed.

◆ *Because VBA variable names are not case-sensitive, the interpreter by default adjusts the names of all variables with the same letters so that their case matches the case of letters that you most recently typed.* For example, if you first specify a variable as `myvalue` (all lowercase) and then enter the variable as `MyValue` (mixed case), VBA changes all other occurrences of the variable to `MyValue`. An exception occurs if you declare the variable with `Dim` or a similar statement; in this case, the variable name always appears as it was declared.

◆ *VBA scans the instruction for syntax errors.* If VBA finds an error, it changes the color of the line and might display a message describing the problem. Choose the Visual Basic Editor Tools → Options command to display the Options dialog box, where you control the error color (use the Editor Format tab) and whether the error message is displayed (use the Auto Syntax Check option in the Editor tab).

Comments

A *comment* is descriptive text embedded within your code. The text of a comment is completely ignored by VBA. It's a good idea to use comments liberally to describe what you're doing because an instruction's purpose is not always obvious.

You can use a complete line for your comment, or you can insert a comment *after* an instruction on the same line. A comment is indicated by an apostrophe. VBA ignores any text that follows an apostrophe — except when the apostrophe is contained within quotation marks — up until the end of the line. For example, the following statement does not contain a comment, even though it has an apostrophe:

```
Msg = "Can't continue"
```

The following example shows a VBA procedure with three comments:

```
Sub Comments()
'   This procedure does nothing of value
    x = 0   'x represents nothingness
'   Display the result
    MsgBox x
End Sub
```

Although the apostrophe is the preferred comment indicator, you can also use the Rem keyword to mark a line as a comment. For example:

```
Rem -- The next statement prompts the user for a filename
```

The Rem keyword is essentially a holdover from old versions of BASIC; it is included in VBA for the sake of compatibility. Unlike the apostrophe, Rem can be written only at the beginning of a line — not on the same line as another instruction.

Using comments is definitely a good idea, but not all comments are equally beneficial. To be useful, comments should convey information that's not immediately obvious from reading the code. Otherwise, you're just chewing up valuable bytes. The following procedure, for example, contains many comments, none of which really adds anything of value:

```
Sub BadComments()
'   Declare variables
    Dim x As Integer
    Dim y As Integer
    Dim z As Integer
'   Start the routine
    x = 100 ' Assign 100 to x
    y = 200 ' Assign 200 to y
```

```
'   Add x and y and store in z
    z = x + y
'   Show the result
    MsgBox z
End Sub
```

Following are a few general tips on making the best use of comments:

◆ Use comments to describe briefly the purpose of each procedure that you write.

◆ Use comments to describe changes that you make to a procedure.

◆ Use comments to indicate that you're using functions or constructs in an unusual or nonstandard manner.

◆ Use comments to describe the purpose of variables so that you and other people can decipher otherwise cryptic names.

◆ Use comments to describe workarounds that you develop to overcome Excel bugs.

◆ Write comments *while* you code rather than after.

 TIP You might want to test a procedure without including a particular instruction or group of instructions. Instead of deleting the instruction, simply turn it into a comment by inserting an apostrophe at the beginning. VBA then ignores the instruction(s) when the routine is executed. To convert the comment back to an instruction, delete the apostrophe.

The Visual Basic Editor (VBE) Edit toolbar contains two very useful buttons. Select a group of instructions and then use the Comment Block button to convert the instructions to comments. The Uncomment Block button converts a group of comments back to instructions. These buttons are very useful, so you might want to copy them to your Standard toolbar.

Variables, Data Types, and Constants

VBA's main purpose in life is to manipulate data. Some data resides in objects, such as worksheet ranges. Other data is stored in variables that you create.

A *variable* is simply a named storage location in your computer's memory. Variables can accommodate a wide variety of *data types* — from simple Boolean values (True or False) to large, double-precision values (see the following section).

You assign a value to a variable by using the equal sign operator (more about this in the upcoming section, "Assignment Statements").

You'll make your life easier if you get into the habit of making your variable names as descriptive as possible. VBA does, however, have a few rules regarding variable names:

◆ You can use alphabetic characters, numbers, and some punctuation characters, but the first character must be alphabetic.

◆ VBA does not distinguish between case. To make variable names more readable, programmers often use mixed case (for example, `InterestRate` rather than `interestrate`).

◆ You cannot use spaces or periods. To make variable names more readable, programmers often use the underscore character (`Interest_Rate`).

◆ Special type declaration characters (#, $, %, &, or !) cannot be embedded in a variable name.

◆ Variable names can comprise as many as 254 characters — but no one in his right mind would create a variable name that long!

The following list contains some examples of assignment expressions that use various types of variables. The variable names are to the left of the equal sign. Each statement assigns the value to the right of the equal sign to the variable on the left.

```
x = 1
InterestRate = 0.075
LoanPayoffAmount = 243089
DataEntered = False
x = x + 1
MyNum = YourNum * 1.25
UserName = "Bob Johnson"
DateStarted = #3/14/98#
```

VBA has many *reserved words,* which are words that you cannot use for variable or procedure names. If you attempt to use one of these words, you get an error message. For example, although the reserved word `Next` might make a very descriptive variable name, the following instruction generates a syntax error:

```
Next = 132
```

Unfortunately, syntax error messages aren't always very descriptive. The preceding instruction generates this error message: `Compile error: Expected variable`. It would be nice if the error message were something like `Reserved word used as a variable`. So if an instruction produces a strange error message, check the VBA Help system to ensure that your variable name doesn't have a special use in VBA.

Defining data types

VBA makes life easy for programmers because it can automatically handle all the details involved in dealing with data. Not all programming languages make it so easy. For example, some languages are *strictly typed,* which means that the programmer must explicitly define the data type for every variable used.

Data type refers to how data is stored in memory — as integers, real numbers, strings, and so on. Although VBA can take care of data typing automatically, it does so at a cost: slower execution and less efficient use of memory. (There's no such thing as a free lunch.) As a result, letting VBA handle data typing may present problems when you're running large or complex applications. If you need to conserve every last byte of memory, you need to be on familiar terms with data types. Another advantage to explicitly declaring your variables as a particular data type is that VBA can perform some additional error checking at the compile stage. These errors might otherwise be difficult to locate.

Table 8-1 lists VBA's assortment of built-in data types. (Note that you can also define custom data types, which I describe later in this chapter in "User-Defined Data Types.")

TABLE 8-1 VBA BUILT-IN DATA TYPES

Data Type	Bytes Used	Range of Values
Byte	1 byte	0 to 255
Boolean	2 bytes	True or False
Integer	2 bytes	-32,768 to 32,767
Long	4 bytes	-2,147,483,648 to 2,147,483,647
Single	4 bytes	-3.402823E38 to -1.401298E-45 (for negative values); 1.401298E-45 to 3.402823E38 (for positive values)
Double	8 bytes	-1.79769313486232E308 to -4.94065645841247E-324 (negative values); 4.94065645841247E-324 to 1.79769313486232E308 (for positive values)
Currency	8 bytes	-922,337,203,685,477.5808 to 922,337,203,685,477.5807
Decimal	14 bytes	+/-79,228,162,514,264,337,593,543,950,335 with no decimal point; +/-7.9228162514264337593543950335 with 28 places to the right of the decimal

Continued

TABLE 8-1 VBA BUILT-IN DATA TYPES *(Continued)*

Data Type	Bytes Used	Range of Values
Date	8 bytes	January 1, 0100 to December 31, 9999
Object	4 bytes	Any object reference
String (variable length)	10 bytes + string length	0 to approximately 2 billion
String (fixed length)	Length of string	1 to approximately 65,400
Variant (with numbers)	16 bytes	Any numeric value up to the range of a double data type
Variant (with characters)	22 bytes + string length	0 to approximately 2 billion
User-defined	Varies	Varies by element

The Decimal data type was introduced in Excel 2000, and it cannot be used in previous versions. This is a rather unusual data type because you cannot actually declare it. In fact, it is a subtype of a variant. You need to use the VBA CDec function to convert a variant to the decimal data type.

Generally, it's best to use the data type that uses the smallest number of bytes yet still can handle all the data assigned to it. When VBA works with data, execution speed is a function of the number of bytes that VBA has at its disposal. In other words, the fewer bytes used by data, the faster VBA can access and manipulate the data.

Benchmarking Variant Data Types

To test whether data typing is important, I developed the following routine, which performs some meaningless calculations in a loop and then displays the procedure's total execution time:

```
Sub TimeTest()
    Dim x As Integer, y As Integer
    Dim A As Integer, B As Integer, C As Integer
    Dim i As Integer, j As Integer
    Dim StartTime As Date, EndTime As Date
```

```
'    Store the starting time
     StartTime = Timer
'    Perform some calculations
     x = 0
     y = 0
     For i = 1 To 5000
         For j = 1 To 5000
             A = x + y + i
             B = y - x - i
             C = x - y - i
         Next j
     Next i
'    Get ending time
     EndTime = Timer
'    Display total time in seconds
     MsgBox Format(EndTime - StartTime, "0.0")

End Sub
```

On my system, this routine took 5.2 seconds to run (the time will vary, depending on your system's processor speed). I then commented out the Dim statements, which declare the data types. That is, I turned the Dim statements into comments by adding an apostrophe at the beginning of the lines. As a result, VBA used the default data type, Variant. I ran the procedure again. It took 14.7 seconds, nearly three times as long as before.

The moral is simple: If you want your VBA applications to run as fast as possible, declare your variables!

A workbook that contains this code is available on the companion CD-ROM.

For worksheet calculation, Excel uses the Double data type, so that's a good choice for processing numbers in VBA when you don't want to lose any precision. For integer calculations, you can use the Integer type if you're sure that the values will not exceed 32,767. Otherwise, use the Long data type. When dealing with Excel worksheet row numbers, you'll want to use the Long data type because the number of rows in a worksheet exceeds the maximum value for the Integer data type.

Declaring variables

If you don't declare the data type for a variable that you use in a VBA routine, VBA uses the default data type, Variant. Data stored as a Variant acts like a chameleon: It changes type, depending on what you do with it. The following procedure demonstrates how a variable can assume different data types:

```
Sub VariantDemo()
    MyVar = "123"
    MyVar = MyVar / 2
    MyVar = "Answer: " & MyVar
    MsgBox MyVar
End Sub
```

In the `VariantDemo` procedure, `MyVar` starts out as a three-character string. Then this string is divided by two and becomes a numeric data type. Next, `MyVar` is appended to a string, converting `MyVar` back to a string. The `MsgBox` statement displays the final string: `Answer: 61.5`.

To further demonstrate the potential problems in dealing with `Variant` data types, try executing this procedure:

```
Sub VariantDemo2()
    MyVar = "123"
    MyVar = MyVar + MyVar
    MyVar = "Answer: " & MyVar
    MsgBox MyVar
End Sub
```

The message box will display `Answer: 123123`. This is probably *not* what you wanted. When dealing with variants that contain text string, the + operator performs string concatenation.

DETERMINING A DATA TYPE

You can use the VBA `TypeName` function to determine the data type of a variable. Here's a modified version of the previous procedure. This version displays the data type of `MyVar` at each step. You'll see that it starts out as a string, is then converted to a double, and finally ends up as a string again.

```
Sub VariantDemo2()
    MyVar = "123"
    MsgBox TypeName(MyVar)
    MyVar = MyVar / 2
    MsgBox TypeName(MyVar)
    MyVar = "Answer: " & MyVar
    MsgBox TypeName(MyVar)
    MsgBox MyVar
End Sub
```

Thanks to VBA, the data type conversion of undeclared variables is automatic. This process might seem like an easy way out, but remember that you sacrifice speed and memory.

It's an excellent habit to declare each variable in a procedure before you use it. Declaring a variable tells VBA its name and data type. Declaring variables provides two main benefits:

♦ *Your programs run faster and use memory more efficiently.* The default data type, `Variant`, causes VBA to repeatedly perform time-consuming checks and reserve more memory than necessary. If VBA knows the data type, it doesn't have to investigate, and it can reserve just enough memory to store the data.

♦ *You avoid problems involving misspelled variable names.* This assumes that you use `Option Explicit` to force yourself to declare all variables (see the next section). Say that you use an undeclared variable named `CurrentRate`. At some point in your routine, however, you insert the statement `CurentRate = .075`. This misspelled variable name, which is very difficult to spot, will likely cause your routine to give incorrect results.

FORCING YOURSELF TO DECLARE ALL VARIABLES
To force yourself to declare all the variables that you use, include the following as the first instruction in your VBA module:

```
Option Explicit
```

This statement causes your program to stop whenever VBA encounters a variable name that has not been declared. VBA issues an error message, and you must declare the variable before you can proceed.

TIP   To ensure that the `Option Explicit` statement is automatically inserted whenever you insert a new VBA module, enable the Require Variable Declaration option in the Editor tab of the VBE Options dialog box. I highly recommend doing so.

A Note about the Examples in This Chapter

This chapter contains many examples of VBA code, usually presented in the form of simple procedures. These examples demonstrate various concepts as simply as possible. Most of these examples do not perform any particularly useful task; in fact, the task can often be performed in a different way. In other words, don't use these examples in your own work. Subsequent chapters provide many more code examples that *are* useful.

Scoping variables

A variable's *scope* determines which modules and procedures the variable can be used in. As you can read in Table 8-2, a variable's scope can be any of the following:

TABLE 8-2 VARIABLE SCOPE

Scope	How a Variable with This Scope Is Declared
Single procedure	Include a Dim or Static statement within the procedure.
Single module	Include a Dim or Private statement before the first procedure in a module.
All modules	Include a Public statement before the first procedure in a module.

I discuss each scope further in the following sections.

LOCAL VARIABLES

A *local variable* is a variable declared within a procedure. Local variables can be used only in the procedure in which they are declared. When the procedure ends, the variable no longer exists, and Excel frees up its memory.

 If you need the variable to retain its value, declare it as a Static variable. (See "Static variables" later in this section.)

The most common way to declare a local variable is to place a Dim statement between a Sub statement and an End Sub statement. Dim statements usually are placed right after the Sub statement, before the procedure's code.

If you're curious about this word, Dim is a shortened form of *Dimension*. In old versions of BASIC, this statement was used exclusively to declare the dimensions for an array. In VBA, the Dim keyword is used to declare any variable and not just arrays.

The following procedure uses six local variables declared by using Dim statements:

```
Sub MySub()
    Dim x As Integer
    Dim First As Long
    Dim InterestRate As Single
    Dim TodaysDate As Date
```

```
    Dim UserName As String * 20
    Dim MyValue
'     - [The procedure's code goes here] -
End Sub
```

Notice that the last `Dim` statement in the preceding example doesn't declare a data type; it simply names the variable. As a result, that variable becomes a variant.

By the way, you also can declare several variables with a single `Dim` statement. For example:

```
Dim x As Integer, y As Integer, z As Integer
Dim First As Long, Last As Double
```

Another Way of Data-Typing Variables

Like most other dialects of BASIC, VBA lets you append a character to a variable's name to indicate the data type. For example, you can declare the `MyVar` variable as an integer by tacking % onto the name:

```
Dim MyVar%
```

Type-declaration characters exist for most of VBA data types. (Data types not listed don't have type-declaration characters.)

Data Type	Type-Declaration Character
Integer	%
Long	&
Single	!
Double	#
Currency	@
String	$

This method of data typing is essentially a holdover from BASIC; it's better to declare your variables using the techniques described in this chapter. I list these type declaration characters here just in case you encounter them in an older program.

Unlike some languages, VBA does not let you declare a group of variables to be a particular data type by separating the variables with commas. For example, the following statement, although valid, does *not* declare all the variables as integers:

```
Dim i, j, k As Integer
```

In VBA, only k is declared to be an integer; the other variables are declared variants. To declare i, j, and k as integers, use this statement:

```
Dim i As Integer, j As Integer, k As Integer
```

If a variable is declared with a local scope, other procedures in the same module can use the same variable name, but each instance of the variable is unique to its own procedure.

In general, local variables are the most efficient because VBA frees up the memory that they use when the procedure ends.

MODULEWIDE VARIABLES

Sometimes, you'll want a variable to be available to all procedures in a module. If so, just declare the variable *before* the module's first procedure (outside of any procedures or functions).

In the following example, the Dim statement is the first instruction in the module. Both MySub and YourSub have access to the CurrentValue variable.

```
Dim CurrentValue as Integer

Sub MySub()
'   - [Code goes here] -
End Sub

Sub YourSub()
'   - [Code goes here] -
End Sub
```

The value of a module-wide variable does not change when a procedure ends. An exception to this occurs if the procedure is halted with an End statement. When VBA encounters an End statement, all module-wide variables lose their values.

PUBLIC VARIABLES

To make a variable available to all the procedures in all the VBA modules in a project, declare the variable at the module level by using the Public keyword rather than Dim. Here's an example:

```
Public CurrentRate as Long
```

Variable Naming Conventions

Some programmers name variables so that their data types can be identified just by looking at their names. Personally, I usually don't use this technique very often because I think it makes the code more difficult to read, but you might find it helpful.

The naming convention involves using a standard lowercase prefix for the variable's name. For example, if you have a Boolean variable that tracks whether a workbook has been saved, you might name the variable bWasSaved. That way, it is clear that the variable is a Boolean variable. The following table lists some standard prefixes for data types:

Data Type	Prefix
Boolean	b
Integer	i
Long	l
Single	s
Double	d
Currency	c
Date/Time	dt
String	str
Object	obj
Variant	v
User-defined	u

The Public keyword makes the CurrentRate variable available to any procedure in the project, even those in other modules within the project. You must insert this statement before the first procedure in a module. This type of declaration must also appear in a standard VBA module, not in a code module for a sheet or a UserForm.

STATIC VARIABLES

Static variables are a special case. They are declared at the procedure level, and they retain their value when the procedure ends (unless the procedure is halted with an End statement).

You declare static variables by using the Static keyword:

```
Sub MySub()
    Static Counter as Integer
    - [Code goes here] -
End Sub
```

Working with constants

A variable's value may, and often does, change while a procedure is executing: That's why it's called a *variable*. Sometimes, you need to refer to a named value or string that never changes: a *constant*.

DECLARING CONSTANTS
You declare constants with the `Const` statement. Here are some examples:

```
Const NumQuarters as Integer = 4
Const Rate = .0725, Period = 12
Const ModName as String = "Budget Macros"
Public Const AppName as String = "Budget Application"
```

The second example doesn't declare a data type. Consequently, VBA determines the data type from the value. The `Rate` variable is a `Double`, and the `Period` variable is an `Integer`. Because a constant never changes its value, you'll normally want to declare your constants as a specific data type.

Like variables, constants also have a scope. If you want a constant to be available within a single procedure only, declare it after the `Sub` or `Function` statement to make it a local constant. To make a constant available to all procedures in a module, declare it before the first procedure in the module. To make a constant available to all modules in the workbook, use the `Public` keyword, and declare the constant before the first procedure in a module. For example:

```
Public Const InterestRate As Double = 0.0725
```

If you attempt to change the value of a constant in a VBA procedure, you get an error — which is what you would expect. A constant is a constant, not a variable.

Using constants throughout your code in place of hard-coded values or strings is an excellent programming practice. For example, if your procedure needs to refer to a specific value (such as an interest rate) several times, it's better to declare the value as a constant and use the constant's name rather than its value in your expressions. This technique not only makes your code more readable, it also makes it easier to change should the need arise — you have to change only one instruction rather than several.

USING PREDEFINED CONSTANTS

Excel and VBA provide many predefined constants, which you can use without declaring. In fact, you don't even need to know the value of these constants to use them. The macro recorder generally uses constants rather than actual values. The following procedure uses a built-in constant (xlLandscape) to set the page orientation to landscape for the active sheet:

```
Sub SetToLandscape()
    ActiveSheet.PageSetup.Orientation = xlLandscape
End Sub
```

I discovered the xlLandscape constant by recording a macro. I also could have found this information in the Help system. And, if you have the AutoList Members option turned on, you can often get some assistance while you enter your code. In many cases, VBA lists all the constants that can be assigned to a property.

The actual value for xlLandscape is 2. The other built-in constant for changing paper orientation is xlPortrait, which has a value of 1. Obviously, if you use the built-in constants, there is really no need to know their values.

The Object Browser, which I discuss briefly in Chapter 7, can display a list of all Excel and VBA constants. In the VBE, press F2 to bring up the Object Browser.

Working with strings

Like Excel, VBA can manipulate both numbers and text (strings). There are two types of strings in VBA:

◆ *Fixed-length strings* are declared with a specified number of characters. The maximum length is 65,535 characters.

◆ *Variable-length strings* theoretically can hold up to 2 billion characters.

Each character in a string requires 1 byte of storage, and a small additional amount of storage is used for the header of each string. When you declare a string variable with a Dim statement, you can specify the length if you know it (that is, a fixed-length string), or you can let VBA handle it dynamically (a variable-length string).

In the following example, the MyString variable is declared to be a string with a maximum length of 50 characters. YourString is also declared as a string, but its length is unfixed.

```
Dim MyString As String * 50
Dim YourString As String
```

Working with dates

You can use a string variable to store a date, of course, but you can't perform date calculations on one. Using the Date data type is a better way to work with dates.

A variable defined as a date uses 8 bytes of storage and can hold dates ranging from January 1, A.D 100 to December 31, 9999. That's a span of nearly 10,000 years — more than enough for even the most aggressive financial forecast! The Date data type is also useful for storing time-related data. In VBA, you specify dates and times by enclosing them between two hash marks (#), as shown next.

The range of dates that VBA can handle is much larger than Excel's own date range, which begins with January 1, 1900. Therefore, be careful that you don't attempt to use a date in a worksheet that is outside of Excel's acceptable date range.

Here are some examples of declaring variables and constants as Date data types:

```
Dim Today As Date
Dim StartTime As Date
Const FirstDay As Date = #1/1/2001#
Const Noon = #12:00:00#
```

Date constants are always defined using month/day/year format, even if your system is set up to display dates in a different format (for example, day/month/year).

If you use a message box to display a date, it will be displayed according to your system's short date format. Similarly, a time is displayed according to your system's time format (either 12- or 24-hour). You can modify these system settings by using the Regional Settings option in the Windows Control Panel.

About Excel's Date Bug

It is commonly known that Excel has a date bug: It incorrectly assumes that the year 1900 is a leap year. Even though there was no February 29, 1900, Excel accepts the following formula and displays the result as the 29th day of February, 1900:

=Date(1900,2,29)

VBA does not have this date bug. The VBA equivalent of Excel's DATE function is DateSerial. The following expression (correctly) returns March 1, 1900:

DateSerial(1900,2,29)

Therefore, Excel's date serial number system does not correspond exactly to the VBA date serial number system. These two systems return different values for dates between January 1, 1900 and February 28, 1900.

The companion CD-ROM contains an Excel add-in that I created called *Extended Date Functions*. This add-in, which was created with VBA, adds new worksheet functions to Excel. These new functions enable you to create formulas that work with dates prior to January 1, 1900.

Assignment Statements

An *assignment statement* is a VBA instruction that makes a mathematical evaluation and assigns the result to a variable or an object. Excel's Help system defines *expression* as "a combination of keywords, operators, variables, and constants that yields a string, number, or object. An expression can perform a calculation, manipulate characters, or test data."

I couldn't have said it better myself. Much of the work done in VBA involves developing (and debugging) expressions.

If you know how to create formulas in Excel, you'll have no trouble creating expressions in VBA. With a worksheet formula, Excel displays the result in a cell. A VBA expression, on the other hand, can be assigned to a variable or used as a property value.

VBA uses the equal sign (=) as its assignment operator. The following are examples of assignment statements (the expressions are to the right of the equal sign):

```
x = 1
x = x + 1
x = (y * 2) / (z * 2)
FileOpen = True
FileOpen = Not FileOpen
Range("TheYear").Value = 2004
```

 TIP Expressions can be very complex. You might want to use the continuation sequence (space followed by an underscore) to make lengthy expressions easier to read.

Often, expressions use functions. These functions can be built-in VBA functions, Excel's worksheet functions, or custom functions that you develop in VBA. I discuss built-in VBA functions later in this chapter (see "Built-in Functions").

Operators play a major role in VBA. Familiar operators describe mathematical operations, including addition (+), multiplication (*), division (/), subtraction (-), exponentiation (^), and string concatenation (&). Less-familiar operators are the backslash (\) (used in integer division) and the Mod operator (used in modulo arithmetic). The Mod operator returns the remainder of one number divided by another. For example, the following expression returns 2:

```
17 Mod 3
```

VBA also supports the same comparative operators used in Excel formulas: equal to (=), greater than (>), less than (<), greater than or equal to (>=), less than or equal to (<=), and not equal to (<>).

In addition, VBA provides a full set of logical operators, shown in Table 8-3. For complete details on these operators (including examples), use the VBA Help system.

TABLE 8-3 VBA LOGICAL OPERATORS

Operator	What It Does
Not	Performs a logical negation on an expression
And	Performs a logical conjunction on two expressions

Operator	What It Does
Or	Performs a logical disjunction on two expressions
Xor	Performs a logical exclusion on two expressions
Eqv	Performs a logical equivalence on two expressions
Imp	Performs a logical implication on two expressions

The order of precedence for operators in VBA is exactly the same as in Excel. Of course, you can add parentheses to change the natural order of precedence.

The following instruction uses the Not operator to toggle the grid-line display in the active window. The DisplayGridlines property takes a value of either True or False. Therefore, using the Not operator changes False to True and True to False.

```
ActiveWindow.DisplayGridlines = _
    Not ActiveWindow.DisplayGridlines
```

The following expression performs a logical And operation. The MsgBox statement displays True only when Sheet1 is the active sheet *and* the active cell is in row 1. If either or both of these conditions are not true, the MsgBox statement displays False.

```
MsgBox ActiveSheet.Name = "Sheet1" And ActiveCell.Row = 1
```

The following expression performs a logical Or operation. The MsgBox statement displays True when either Sheet1 *or* Sheet2 is the active sheet.

```
MsgBox ActiveSheet.Name = "Sheet1" _
    Or ActiveSheet.Name = "Sheet2"
```

Arrays

An *array* is a group of elements of the same type that have a common name; you refer to a specific element in the array by using the array name and an index number. For example, you can define an array of 12 string variables so that each variable corresponds to the name of a month. If you name the array MonthNames, you can refer to the first element of the array as MonthNames(0), the second element as MonthNames(1), and so on, up to MonthNames(11).

Declaring arrays

You declare an array with a `Dim` or `Public` statement, just as you declare a regular variable. You can also specify the number of elements in the array. You do so by specifying the first index number, the keyword `To`, and the last index number — all inside parentheses. For example, here's how to declare an array comprising exactly 100 integers:

```
Dim MyArray(1 To 100) As Integer
```

> When you declare an array, you need specify only the upper index, in which case VBA assumes that 0 is the lower index. Therefore, the two statements that follow have the same effect:
>
> ```
> Dim MyArray(0 to 100) As Integer
> Dim MyArray(100) As Integer
> ```
>
> In both these cases, the array consists of 101 elements.

If you would like VBA to assume that 1 is the lower index for all arrays that declare only the upper index, include the following statement before any procedures in your module:

```
Option Base 1
```

Declaring multidimensional arrays

The arrays examples in the preceding section were one-dimensional arrays. VBA arrays can have up to 60 dimensions, although it's rare to need more than 3 dimensions (a 3-D array). The following statement declares a 100-integer array with two dimensions (2-D):

```
Dim MyArray(1 To 10, 1 To 10) As Integer
```

You can think of the preceding array as occupying a 10 x 10 matrix. To refer to a specific element in a 2-D array, you need to specify two index numbers. For example, here's how you can assign a value to an element in the preceding array:

```
MyArray(3, 4) = 125
```

You can think of a 3-D array as a cube, but I can't tell you how to visualize the data layout of an array of more than three dimensions.

A *dynamic array* doesn't have a preset number of elements. You declare a dynamic array with a blank set of parentheses:

```
Dim MyArray() As Integer
```

Before you can use a dynamic array in your code, however, you must use the `ReDim` statement to tell VBA how many elements are in the array (or `ReDim Preserve` if you want to keep the existing values in the array). You can use the `ReDim` statement any number of times, changing the array's size as often as you need to.

Arrays crop up later in this chapter when I discuss looping ("Looping blocks of instructions").

Object Variables

An *object variable* is a variable that represents an entire object, such as a range or a worksheet. Object variables are important for two reasons:

◆ They can simplify your code significantly.

◆ They can make your code execute more quickly.

Object variables, like normal variables, are declared with the `Dim` or `Public` statement. For example, the following statement declares `InputArea` as a `Range` object:

```
Public InputArea As Range
```

To see how object variables simplify your code, examine the following procedure, which was written without using object variables:

```
Sub NoObjVar()
    Worksheets("Sheet1").Range("A1").Value = 124
    Worksheets("Sheet1").Range("A1").Font.Bold = True
    Worksheets("Sheet1").Range("A1").Font.Italic = True
End Sub
```

This routine enters a value into cell A1 of Sheet1 on the active workbook and then boldfaces and italicizes the cell's contents. That's a lot of typing. To reduce wear and tear on your fingers, you can condense the routine with an object variable:

```
Sub ObjVar()
    Dim MyCell As Range
    Set MyCell = Worksheets("Sheet1").Range("A1")
    MyCell.Value = 124
```

```
        MyCell.Font.Bold = True
        MyCell.Font.Italic = True
End Sub
```

After the variable `MyCell` is declared as a `Range` object, the `Set` statement assigns an object to it. Subsequent statements can then use the simpler `MyCell` reference in place of the lengthy `Worksheets("Sheet1").Range("A1")` reference.

After an object is assigned to a variable, VBA can access it more quickly than it can a normal lengthy reference that has to be resolved. So when speed is critical, use object variables. One way to think about this is in terms of *dot processing*. Every time VBA encounters a dot, as in `Sheets(1).Range("A1")`, it takes time to resolve the reference. Using an object variable reduces the number of dots to be processed. The fewer the dots, the faster the processing time. Another way to improve the speed of your code is by using the `With-End With` construct, which also reduces the number of dots to be processed. I discuss this construct later in this chapter.

The true value of object variables will become apparent when I discuss looping later in this chapter.

User-Defined Data Types

VBA lets you create custom, or *user-defined*, data types (a concept much like Pascal records or C structures). A user-defined data type can ease your work with some types of data. For example, if your application deals with customer information, you might want to create a user-defined data type named `CustomerInfo`, as follows:

```
Type CustomerInfo
    Company As String * 25
    Contact As String * 15
    RegionCode As Integer
    Sales As Long
End Type
```

You define custom data types at the top of your module, before any procedures.

After you create a user-defined data type, you use a `Dim` statement to declare a variable as that type. Usually, you define an array. For example:

```
Dim Customers(1 To 100) As CustomerInfo
```

Each of the 100 elements in this array consists of four components (as specified by the user-defined data type, `CustomerInfo`). You can refer to a particular component of the record as follows:

```
Customers(1).Company = "Acme Tools"
Customers(1).Contact = "Tim Robertson"
Customers(1).RegionCode = 3
Customers(1).Sales = 150677
```

You can also work with an element in the array as a whole. For example, to copy the information from `Customers(1)` to `Customers(2)`, use this instruction:

```
Customers(2) = Customers(1)
```

The preceding example is equivalent to the following instruction block:

```
Customers(2).Company = Customers(1).Company
Customers(2).Contact = Customers(1).Contact
Customers(2).RegionCode = Customers(1).RegionCode
Customers(2).Sales = Customers(1).Sales
```

Built-in Functions

Like most programming languages, VBA has a variety of built-in functions that simplify calculations and operations. Often, the functions enable you to perform operations that are otherwise difficult or even impossible. Many VBA functions are similar (or identical) to Excel worksheet functions. For example, the VBA function `UCase`, which converts a string argument to uppercase, is equivalent to the Excel worksheet function UPPER.

Appendix B contains a complete list of VBA functions, with a brief description of each. All are thoroughly described in the VBA Help system.

TIP

To get a list of VBA functions while you're writing your code, type **VBA** followed by a period (**.**). The VBE displays a list of all its members, including functions (see Figure 8-1). The functions are preceded by a green icon. If this technique doesn't work for you, make sure that the Auto List Members option is selected. Choose Tools → Options and then click the Editor tab.

```
Book3 - Module1 (Code)
(General)                        Test
  Sub Test()
    x=VBA.|
  End Sub    DateAdd
             DateDiff
             DatePart
             DateSerial
             DateTime
             DateValue
             Day
```

Figure 8-1: Displaying a list of VBA functions in the VBE.

You use functions in VBA expressions in much the same way that you use functions in worksheet formulas. For instance, you can nest VBA functions.

Here's a simple procedure that calculates the square root of a variable using the VBA Sqr function, stores the result in another variable, and then displays the result:

```
Sub ShowRoot()
    MyValue = 25
    SquareRoot = Sqr(MyValue)
    MsgBox SquareRoot
End Sub
```

The VBA Sqr function is equivalent to the Excel SQRT worksheet function.

You can use many (but not all) of Excel's worksheet functions in your VBA code. The WorksheetFunction object, which is contained in the Application object, holds all the worksheet functions that you can call from your VBA procedures.

To use a worksheet function in a VBA statement, just precede the function name with

```
Application.WorksheetFunction
```

The following example demonstrates how to use an Excel worksheet function in a VBA procedure. Excel's infrequently used ROMAN function converts a decimal number into a Roman numeral.

```
Sub ShowRoman()
    DecValue = 2001
    RomanValue = Application.WorksheetFunction.Roman(DecValue)
    MsgBox RomanValue
End Sub
```

When you execute this procedure, the MsgBox function displays the string MMI. Fans of old movies are often dismayed when they learn that Excel doesn't have a function to convert a Roman numeral to its decimal equivalent.

It's important to understand that you cannot use worksheet functions that have an equivalent VBA function. For example, VBA cannot access the Excel SQRT worksheet function because VBA has its own version of that function: Sqr. Therefore, the following statement generates an error:

```
MsgBox Application.WorksheetFunction.Sqrt(123)    'error
```

 As I describe in Chapter 10, you can use VBA to create custom worksheet functions that work just like Excel's built-in worksheet functions.

The MsgBox Function

The MsgBox function is one of the most useful VBA functions. Many of the examples in this chapter use this function to display the value of a variable.

This function often is a good substitute for a simple custom dialog box. It's also an excellent debugging tool because you can insert MsgBox functions at any time to pause your code and display the result of a calculation or assignment.

Most functions return a single value, which you assign to a variable. The MsgBox function not only returns a value, but also displays a dialog box that the user can respond to. The value returned by the MsgBox function represents the user's response to the dialog. You can use the MsgBox function even when you have no interest in the user's response but want to take advantage of the message display.

The official syntax of the MsgBox function has five arguments (those in square brackets are optional):

```
MsgBox(prompt[, buttons][, title][, helpfile][, context])
```

◆ prompt: (Required) The message displayed in the pop-up display.

Continued

The MsgBox Function *(Continued)*

◆ buttons: (Optional) A value that specifies which buttons and which icons, if any, appear in the message box. Use built-in constants — for example, vbYesNo.

◆ title: (Optional) The text that appears in the message box's title bar. The default is Microsoft Excel.

◆ helpfile: (Optional) The name of the help file associated with the message box.

◆ context: (Optional) The context ID of the help topic. This represents a specific help topic to display.

You can assign the value returned to a variable, or you can use the function by itself without an assignment statement. The next example assigns the result to the variable Ans.

```
Ans = MsgBox("Continue?", vbYesNo + vbQuestion, "Tell me")

If Ans = vbNo Then Exit Sub
```

Notice that I used the sum of two built-in constants (vbYesNo + vbQuestion) for the buttons argument. Using vbYesNo displays two buttons in the message box: one labeled Yes and one labeled No. (See the results in the accompanying figure.) Adding vbQuestion to the argument also displays a question mark icon (see the accompanying figure). When the first statement is executed, Ans contains one of two values, represented by the constants vbYes or vbNo. In this example, if the user clicks the No button, the procedure ends.

For more information, refer to the VBA Help system, which lists all the constants you can use.

Manipulating Objects and Collections

As an Excel programmer, you'll spend a lot of time working with objects and collections. Therefore, you'll want to know the most efficient ways to write your code to manipulate these objects and collections. VBA offers two important constructs that can simplify working with objects and collections:

◆ With-End With constructs

◆ For Each-Next constructs

With-End With constructs

The With-End With instruction construct enables you to perform multiple operations on a single object. To start understanding how the With-End With construct works, examine the following procedure, which modifies five properties of a selection's formatting (the selection is assumed to be a Range object):

```
Sub ChangeFont1()
    Selection.Font.Name = "Times New Roman"
    Selection.Font.FontStyle = "Bold Italic"
    Selection.Font.Size = 12
    Selection.Font.Underline = xlUnderlineStyleSingle
    Selection.Font.ColorIndex = 5
End Sub
```

This procedure can be rewritten using the With-End With construct. The following procedure performs exactly like the preceding one:

```
Sub ChangeFont2()
    With Selection.Font
        .Name = "Times New Roman"
        .FontStyle = "Bold Italic"
        .Size = 12
        .Underline = xlUnderlineStyleSingle
        .ColorIndex = 5
    End With
End Sub
```

Some people think that the second incarnation of the procedure is actually more difficult to read. Remember, though, that the objective is increased speed. Although the first version may be more straightforward and easier to understand, a procedure that uses the With-End With construct when changing several properties of an object can be significantly faster than the equivalent procedure that explicitly references the object in each statement.

When you record a VBA macro, Excel uses the With-End With construct every chance it gets. To see a good example of this construct, try recording your actions while you change the page setup by choosing the File → Page Setup command.

For Each-Next constructs

Recall from the preceding chapter that a *collection* is a group of related objects. For example, the Workbooks collection is a collection of all open Workbook objects. There are many other collections that you can work with. You don't have to know how many elements are in a collection to use the For Each-Next construct.

Suppose that you want to perform some action on all objects in a collection. Or suppose that you want to evaluate all objects in a collection and take action under certain conditions. These are perfect occasions for the For Each-Next construct.

The syntax of the For Each-Next construct is

```
For Each element In group
    [instructions]
    [Exit For]
    [instructions]
Next [element]
```

The following procedure uses the For Each-Next construct to refer to each of the six members of a fixed-length array one at a time:

```
Sub Macro1()
    Dim MyArray(5) As Double
    For i = 0 To 5
        MyArray(i) = Rnd
    Next i
    For Each n In MyArray
        Debug.Print n
    Next n
End Sub
```

The next procedure uses the For Each-Next construct with the Sheets collection in the active workbook. When you execute the procedure, the MsgBox function displays each worksheet's Name property. (If there are five worksheets in the active workbook, the MsgBox function is called five times.)

```
Sub CountSheets()
    Dim Item as WorkSheet
    For Each Item In ActiveWorkbook.WorkSheets
        MsgBox Item.Name
    Next Item
End Sub
```

In the preceding example, Item is an object variable (more specifically, a Worksheet object). There's nothing special about the name *Item;* you can use any valid variable name in its place.

The next example uses For Each-Next to cycle through all objects in the Windows collection:

```
Sub HiddenWindows()
    Dim AllVisible As Boolean
    Dim Item As Window
    AllVisible = True
    For Each Item In Windows
        If Item.Visible = False Then
            AllVisible = False
            Exit For
        End If
    Next Item
    MsgBox AllVisible
End Sub
```

If a window is hidden, the value of AllVisible is changed to False, and the For Each-Next loop is exited. The message box displays True if all windows are visible and False if at least one window is hidden. The Exit For statement is optional. It provides a way to exit the For Each-Next loop early. This is generally used in conjunction with an If-Then statement (which I describe later in this chapter).

Here's an example that closes all workbooks except the active workbook. This procedure uses the If-Then construct to evaluate each workbook in the Workbooks collection.

```
Sub CloseInActive()
    Dim Book as Workbook
    For Each Book In Workbooks
        If Book.Name <> ActiveWorkbook.Name Then Book.Close
    Next Book
End Sub
```

My final example of For Each-Next is designed to be executed after the user selects a range of cells. Here, the Selection object acts as a collection that consists of Range objects because each cell in the selection is a Range object. The procedure evaluates each cell and uses the VBA UCase function to convert its contents to uppercase. (Numeric cells are not affected.)

```
Sub MakeUpperCase()
    Dim Cell as Range
    For Each Cell In Selection
        Cell.Value = UCase(Cell.Value)
    Next Cell
End Sub
```

Controlling Execution

Some VBA procedures start at the top and progress line by line to the bottom. Macros that you record, for example, always work in this fashion. Often, however, you need to control the flow of your routines by skipping over some statements, executing some statements multiple times, and testing conditions to determine what the routine does next.

The preceding section described the For Each-Next construct, which is a type of loop. This section discusses the additional ways of controlling the execution of your VBA procedures:

◆ GoTo statements

◆ If-Then constructs

◆ Select Case constructs

◆ For-Next loops

◆ Do While loops

◆ Do Until loops

GoTo statements

The most straightforward way to change the flow of a program is to use a GoTo statement. This statement simply transfers program execution to a new instruction, which must be preceded by a label (a text string followed by a colon, or a number with no colon). VBA procedures can contain any number of labels, and a GoTo statement cannot branch outside of a procedure.

The following procedure uses the VBA InputBox function to get the user's name. If the name is not Howard, the procedure branches to the WrongName label and ends. Otherwise, the procedure executes some additional code. The Exit Sub statement causes the procedure to end.

```
Sub GoToDemo()
    UserName = InputBox("Enter Your Name:")
    If UserName <> "Howard" Then GoTo WrongName
    MsgBox ("Welcome Howard...")
'   -[More code here] -
```

```
    Exit Sub
WrongName:
    MsgBox "Sorry. Only Howard can run this."
End Sub
```

This simple procedure works, but in general you should use the GoTo statement only when there is no other way to perform an action. In fact, the only time you *really* need to use a GoTo statement in VBA is for error trapping (refer to Chapter 9).

By the way, the preceding example is not intended to demonstrate a useful security technique!

If-Then constructs

Perhaps the most commonly used instruction grouping in VBA is the If-Then construct. This common instruction is one way to endow your applications with decision-making capability. Good decision making is the key to writing successful programs. A successful Excel application essentially boils down to making decisions and acting on them.

The basic syntax of the If-Then construct is

```
If condition Then true_instructions [Else false_instructions]
```

The If-Then construct is used to execute one or more statements conditionally. The Else clause is optional. If included, it lets you execute one or more instructions when the condition that you're testing is not True.

The following procedure demonstrates an If-Then structure without an Else clause. The example deals with time. VBA uses a similar date-and-time serial number system as Excel. The time of day is expressed as a fractional value — for example, noon is represented as .5. The VBA Time function returns a value that represents the time of day, as reported by the system clock. In the following example, a message is displayed if the time is before noon. If the current system time is greater than or equal to .5, the procedure ends, and nothing happens.

```
Sub GreetMe1()
    If Time < 0.5 Then MsgBox "Good Morning"
End Sub
```

If you want to display a different greeting when the time of day is after noon, add another If-Then statement, like so:

```
Sub GreetMe2()
    If Time < 0.5 Then MsgBox "Good Morning"
    If Time >= 0.5 Then MsgBox "Good Afternoon"
End Sub
```

Notice that I used >= (greater than or equal to) for the second If-Then statement. This covers the extremely remote chance that the time is precisely 12 noon.

Another approach is to use the Else clause of the If-Then construct. For example,

```
Sub GreetMe3()
    If Time < 0.5 Then MsgBox "Good Morning" Else _
        MsgBox "Good Afternoon"
End Sub
```

Notice that I used the line continuation sequence; If-Then-Else is actually a single statement.

If you need to expand a routine to handle three conditions (for example, morning, afternoon, and evening), you can use either three If-Then statements or a nested If-Then-Else structure. The first approach is the simpler:

```
Sub GreetMe4()
    If Time < 0.5 Then MsgBox "Good Morning"
    If Time >= 0.5 And Time < 0.75 Then MsgBox "Good Afternoon"
    If Time >= 0.75 Then MsgBox "Good Evening"
End Sub
```

The value 0.75 represents 6 p.m. — three-quarters of the way through the day and a good point at which to call it an evening.

In the preceding examples, every instruction in the procedure gets executed, even in the morning. A more efficient procedure would include a structure that ends the routine when a condition is found to be True. For example, it might display the Good Morning message in the morning and then exit without evaluating the other, superfluous conditions. True, the difference in speed is inconsequential when you design a procedure as small as this routine. But for more complex applications, you need another syntax:

```
If condition Then
    [true_instructions]
[ElseIf condition-n Then
    [alternate_instructions]]
[Else
    [default_instructions]]
End If
```

Here's how you can use this syntax to rewrite the GreetMe procedure:

```
Sub GreetMe5()
    If Time < 0.5 Then
        MsgBox "Good Morning"
```

```
    ElseIf Time >= 0.5 And Time < 0.75 Then
        MsgBox "Good Afternoon"
    Else
        MsgBox "Good Evening"
    End If
End Sub
```

With this syntax, when a condition is True, the conditional statements are executed and the If-Then construct ends. In other words, the extraneous conditions are not evaluated. Although this syntax makes for greater efficiency, some may find the code to be more difficult to understand.

The following procedure demonstrates yet another way to code this example. It uses nested If-Then-Else constructs (without using ElseIf). This procedure is efficient and also easy to understand. Note that each If statement has a corresponding End If statement.

```
Sub GreetMe6()
    If Time < 0.5 Then
        MsgBox "Good Morning"
    Else
        If Time >= 0.5 And Time < 0.75 Then
            MsgBox "Good Afternoon"
        Else
            If Time >= 0.75 Then
                MsgBox "Good Evening"
            End If
        End If
    End If
End Sub
```

The following is another example that uses the simple form of the If-Then construct. This procedure prompts the user for a value for Quantity and then displays the appropriate discount based on that value. Note that Quantity is declared as a Variant data type. This is because Quantity will contain an empty string (not a numeric value) if the InputBox is cancelled. To keep it simple, this procedure does not perform any other error checking. For example, it does not ensure that the quantity entered is a non-negative numeric value.

```
Sub Discount1()
    Dim Quantity As Variant
    Dim Discount As Double
    Quantity = InputBox("Enter Quantity: ")
    If Quantity = "" Then Exit Sub
    If Quantity >= 0 Then Discount = 0.1
    If Quantity >= 25 Then Discount = 0.15
```

```
    If Quantity >= 50 Then Discount = 0.2
    If Quantity >= 75 Then Discount = 0.25
    MsgBox "Discount: " & Discount
End Sub
```

Notice that each If-Then statement in this procedure is always executed, and the value for Discount can change. The final value, however, is the desired value.

The following procedure is the previous one rewritten to use the alternate syntax. In this case, the procedure ends after executing the True instruction block.

```
Sub Discount2()
    Dim Quantity As Variant
    Dim Discount As Double
    Quantity = InputBox("Enter Quantity: ")
    If Quantity = "" Then Exit Sub
    If Quantity >= 0 And Quantity < 25 Then
        Discount = 0.1
    ElseIf Quantity < 50 Then
        Discount = 0.15
    ElseIf Quantity < 75 Then
        Discount = 0.2
    ElseIf Quantity >= 75 Then
        Discount = 0.25
    End If
    MsgBox "Discount: " & Discount
End Sub
```

I find nested If-Then structures rather cumbersome. As a result, I usually use the If-Then structure only for simple binary decisions. When you need to choose among three or more alternatives, the Select Case structure is often a better construct to use.

Select Case constructs

The Select Case construct is useful for choosing among three or more options. This construct also works with two options and is a good alternative to If-Then-Else. The syntax for Select Case is as follows:

```
Select Case testexpression
    [Case expressionlist-n
        [instructions-n]]
    [Case Else
        [default_instructions]]
End Select
```

VBA's IIf Function

VBA offers an alternative to the If-Then construct: the IIf function. This function takes three arguments and works much like Excel's IF worksheet function. The syntax is

```
IIf(expr, truepart, falsepart)
```

expr: (Required) Expression you want to evaluate.

truepart: (Required) Value or expression returned if expr is True.

falsepart: (Required) Value or expression returned if expr is False.

The following instruction demonstrates the use of the IIf function. The message box displays Zero if cell A1 contains a zero or is empty and displays Nonzero if cell A1 contains anything else.

```
MsgBox IIf(Range("A1") = 0, "Zero", "Nonzero")
```

It's important to understand that the third argument (falsepart) is always evaluated, even if the first argument (expr) is True. Therefore, the following statement will generate an error if the value of n is 0 (zero):

```
MsgBox IIf(n = 0, 0, 1 / n)
```

The following example of a Select Case construct shows another way to code the GreetMe examples that I presented in the preceding section:

```
Sub GreetMe()
    Dim Msg As String
    Select Case Time
        Case Is < 0.5
            Msg = "Good Morning"
        Case 0.5 To 0.75
            Msg = "Good Afternoon"
        Case Else
            Msg = "Good Evening"
    End Select
    MsgBox Msg
End Sub
```

And here's a rewritten version of the Discount example, using a Select Case construct. This procedure assumes that Quantity will always be an integer value. For simplicity, the procedure performs no error checking.

```
Sub Discount3()
    Dim Quantity As Variant
    Dim Discount As Double
    Quantity = InputBox("Enter Quantity: ")
    Select Case Quantity
        Case ""
            Exit Sub
        Case 0 To 24
            Discount = 0.1
        Case 25 To 49
            Discount = 0.15
        Case 50 To 74
            Discount = 0.2
        Case Is >= 75
            Discount = 0.25
    End Select
    MsgBox "Discount: " & Discount
End Sub
```

The Case statement also can use a comma to separate multiple values for a single case. The following procedure uses the VBA WeekDay function to determine whether the current day is a weekend (that is, the Weekday function returns 1 or 7). The procedure then displays an appropriate message.

```
Sub GreetUser()
    Select Case Weekday(Now)
        Case 1, 7
            MsgBox "This is the weekend"
        Case Else
            MsgBox "This is not the weekend"
    End Select
End Sub
```

The following example shows another way to code the previous procedure:

```
Sub GreetUser()
    Select Case Weekday(Now)
        Case 2, 3, 4, 5, 6
            MsgBox "This is not the weekend"
        Case Else
            MsgBox "This is the weekend"
    End Select
End Sub
```

Any number of instructions can be written below each `Case` statement, and they all are executed if that case evaluates to `True`. If you use only one instruction per case, as in the preceding example, you might want to put the instruction on the same line as the `Case` keyword (but don't forget the VBA statement-separator character, the colon). This technique makes the code more compact. For example:

```
Sub Discount3()
    Dim Quantity As Variant
    Dim Discount As Double
    Quantity = InputBox("Enter Quantity: ")
    Select Case Quantity
        Case "": Exit Sub
        Case  0 To 24: Discount = 0.1
        Case 25 To 49: Discount = 0.15
        Case 50 To 74: Discount = 0.2
        Case Is >= 75: Discount = 0.25
    End Select
    MsgBox "Discount: " & Discount
End Sub
```

 TIP　VBA exits a `Select  Case` construct as soon as a `True` case is found. Therefore, for maximum efficiency, you might want to check the most likely case first.

`Select Case` structures can also be nested. The following procedure, for example, tests for Excel's window state (maximized, minimized, or normal) and then displays a message describing the window state. If Excel's window state is normal, the procedure tests for the window state of the active window and then displays another message.

```
Sub AppWindow()
    Select Case Application.WindowState
        Case xlMaximized: MsgBox "App Maximized"
        Case xlMinimized: MsgBox "App Minimized"
        Case xlNormal: MsgBox "App Normal"
            Select Case ActiveWindow.WindowState
                Case xlMaximized: MsgBox "Book Maximized"
                Case xlMinimized: MsgBox "Book Minimized"
                Case xlNormal: MsgBox "Book Normal"
            End Select
    End Select
End Sub
```

You can nest Select Case constructs as deeply as you need, but make sure that each Select Case statement has a corresponding End Select statement.

This procedure demonstrates the value of using indentation in your code to clarify the structure. For example, take a look at the same procedure without the indentations:

```
Sub AppWindow()
Select Case Application.WindowState
Case xlMaximized: MsgBox "App Maximized"
Case xlMinimized: MsgBox "App Minimized"
Case xlNormal: MsgBox "App Normal"
Select Case ActiveWindow.WindowState
Case xlMaximized: MsgBox "Book Maximized"
Case xlMinimized: MsgBox "Book Minimized"
Case xlNormal: MsgBox "Book Normal"
End Select
End Select
End Sub
```

Fairly incomprehensible, eh?

Looping blocks of instructions

Looping is the process of repeating a block of instructions. You might know the number of times to loop, or it could be determined by the values of variables in your program.

The following code, which enters consecutive numbers into a range, demonstrates what I call a *bad loop*. The procedure uses two variables to store a starting value (StartVal) and the total number of cells to fill (NumToFill). This loop uses the GoTo statement to control the flow. If the Cnt variable, which keeps track of how many cells are filled, is less than the number requested by the user, program control loops back to DoAnother.

```
Sub BadLoop()
    Dim StartVal As Integer
    Dim NumToFill As Integer
    Dim Cnt As Integer
    StartVal = 1
    NumToFill = 100
    ActiveCell.Value = StartVal
    Cnt = 1
DoAnother:
    ActiveCell.Offset(Cnt, 0).Value = StartVal + Cnt
    Cnt = Cnt + 1
    If Cnt < NumToFill Then GoTo DoAnother Else Exit Sub
End Sub
```

This procedure works as intended, so why is it an example of bad looping? Programmers generally frown on using a GoTo statement when not absolutely necessary. Using GoTo statements to loop is contrary to the concept of structured coding (see the "What Is Structured Programming?" sidebar). In fact, a GoTo statement makes the code much more difficult to read because it's almost impossible to represent a loop using line indentations. In addition, this type of unstructured loop makes the procedure more susceptible to error. Furthermore, using lots of labels results in *spaghetti code* — code that appears to have little or no structure and flows haphazardly.

Because VBA has several structured looping commands, you almost never have to rely on GoTo statements for your decision making.

FOR-NEXT LOOPS
The simplest type of a good loop is a For-Next loop. Its syntax is

```
For counter = start To end [Step stepval]
    [instructions]
    [Exit For]
    [instructions]
Next [counter]
```

What Is Structured Programming?

Hang around with programmers, and sooner or later you'll hear the term *structured programming*. You'll also discover that structured programs are considered superior to unstructured programs.

So what is structured programming? And can you do it with VBA?

The basic premise is that a routine or code segment should have only one entry point and one exit point. In other words, a body of code should be a standalone unit, and program control should not jump into or exit from the middle of this unit. As a result, structured programming rules out the GoTo statement. When you write structured code, your program progresses in an orderly manner and is easy to follow — as opposed to spaghetti code, where a program jumps around.

A structured program is easier to read and understand than an unstructured one. More important, it's also easier to modify.

VBA is a structured language. It offers standard structured constructs, such as If-Then-Else and Select Case, and the For-Next, Do Until, and Do While loops. Furthermore, VBA fully supports modular code construction.

If you're new to programming, it's a good idea to form good structured programming habits early.

Following is an example of a For-Next loop that doesn't use the optional Step value or the optional Exit For statement. This routine executes the Sum = Sum + Sqr(Count) statement 100 times and displays the result — that is, the sum of the square roots of the first 100 integers.

```
Sub SumSquareRoots()
    Dim Sum As Double
    Dim Count As Integer
    Sum = 0
    For Count = 1 To 100
        Sum = Sum + Sqr(Count)
    Next Count
    MsgBox Sum
End Sub
```

In this example, Count (the loop counter variable) started out as 1 and increased by 1 each time the loop repeated. The Sum variable simply accumulates the square roots of each value of Count.

When you use For-Next loops, it's important to understand that the loop counter is a normal variable — nothing special. As a result, it's possible to change the value of the loop counter within the block of code executed between the For and Next statements. This is, however, a bad practice and can cause unpredictable results. In fact, you should take special precautions to ensure that your code does not change the loop counter.

You can also use a Step value to skip some values in the loop. Here's the same procedure rewritten to sum the square roots of the odd numbers between 1 and 100:

```
Sub SumOddSquareRoots()
    Dim Sum As Double
    Dim Count As Integer
    Sum = 0
    For Count = 1 To 100 Step 2
        Sum = Sum + Sqr(Count)
    Next Count
    MsgBox Sum
End Sub
```

In this procedure, Count starts out as 1 and then takes on values of 3, 5, 7, and so on. The final value of Count used within the loop is 99. When the loop ends, the value of Count is 101.

The following procedure performs the same task as the BadLoop example found at the beginning of the "Looping blocks of instructions" section. I eliminated the GoTo statement, however, converting a bad loop into a good loop that uses the For-Next structure.

```
Sub GoodLoop()
    Dim StartVal As Integer
    Dim NumToFill As Integer
    Dim Cnt As Integer
    StartVal = 1
    NumToFill = 100
    For Cnt = 0 To NumToFill - 1
      ActiveCell.Offset(Cnt, 0).Value = StartVal + Cnt
    Next Cnt
End Sub
```

For-Next loops can also include one or more Exit For statements within the loop. When this statement is encountered, the loop terminates immediately and control passes to the statement following the Next statement of the current For-Next loop. The following example demonstrates use of the Exit For statement. This procedure determines which cell has the largest value in column A of the active worksheet:

```
Sub ExitForDemo()
    Dim MaxVal As Double
    Dim Row As Long
    Dim TheCell As Range
    MaxVal = Application.WorksheetFunction.Max(Range("A:A"))
    For Row = 1 To 65536
        Set TheCell = Range("A1").Offset(Row - 1, 0)
        If TheCell.Value = MaxVal Then
            MsgBox "Max value is in Row " & Row
            TheCell.Activate
            Exit For
        End If
    Next Row
End Sub
```

The maximum value in the column is calculated by using the Excel MAX function. This value is then assigned to the MaxVal variable. The For-Next loop checks each cell in the column. If the cell being checked is equal to MaxVal, the Exit For statement ends the procedure. Before terminating the loop, though, the procedure informs the user of the row location and then activates the cell.

The `ExitForDemo` is presented to demonstrate how to use exit from a `For-Next` loop. However, it is not the most efficient way to activate the largest value in a range. In fact, a single statement will do the job:

```
Range("A:A").Find(Application.WorksheetFunction.Max _
    (Range("A:A"))).Activate
```

The previous examples use relatively simple loops. But you can have any number of statements in the loop, and you can even nest `For-Next` loops inside other `For-Next` loops. Here's an example that uses nested `For-Next` loops to initialize a 10 x 10 x 10 array with the value -1. When the procedure is finished, each of the 1,000 elements in `MyArray` will contain -1.

```
Sub NestedLoops()
    Dim MyArray(1 to 10, 1 to 10, 1 to 10)
    Dim i As Integer, j As Integer, k As Integer
    For i = 1 To 10
        For j = 1 To 10
            For k = 1 To 10
                MyArray(i, j, k) = -1
            Next k
        Next j
    Next i
End Sub
```

DO WHILE LOOPS

A `Do While` loop is another type of looping structure available in VBA. Unlike a `For-Next` loop, a `Do While` loop executes while a specified condition is met. A `Do While` loop can have either of two syntaxes:

```
Do [While condition]
    [instructions]
    [Exit Do]
    [instructions]
Loop
```

  or

```
Do
    [instructions]
    [Exit Do]
    [instructions]
Loop [While condition]
```

As you can see, VBA lets you put the While condition at the beginning or the end of the loop. The difference between these two syntaxes involves the point in time when the condition is evaluated. In the first syntax, the contents of the loop may never be executed. In the second syntax, the contents of the loop are always executed at least one time.

The following example uses a Do While loop with the first syntax.

```
Sub DoWhileDemo()
    Do While Not IsEmpty(ActiveCell)
        ActiveCell.Value = 0
        ActiveCell.Offset(1, 0).Select
    Loop
End Sub
```

This procedure uses the active cell as a starting point and then travels down the column, inserting a zero into the active cell. Each time the loop repeats, the next cell in the column becomes the active cell. The loop continues until VBA's IsEmpty function determines that the active cell is empty.

The following procedure uses the second Do While loop syntax. The loop will always be executed at least one time, even if the initial active cell is empty.

```
Sub DoWhileDemo2()
    Do
        ActiveCell.Value = 0
        ActiveCell.Offset(1, 0).Select
    Loop While Not IsEmpty(ActiveCell)
End Sub
```

The following is another Do While loop example. This procedure opens a text file, reads each line, converts the text to uppercase, and then stores it in the active sheet, beginning with cell A1 and continuing down the column. The procedure uses the VBA EOF function, which returns True when the end of the file has been reached. The final statement closes the text file.

```
Sub DoWhileDemo1()
    Dim LineCt As Long
    Open "c:\data\textfile.txt" For Input As #1
    LineCt = 0
    Do While Not EOF(1)
        Line Input #1, LineOfText
        Range("A1").Offset(LineCt, 0) = UCase(LineOfText)
        LineCt = LineCt + 1
```

```
      Loop
      Close #1
End Sub
```

 For additional information about reading and writing text files using VBA, see Chapter 27.

Do While loops can also contain one or more Exit Do statements. When an Exit Do statement is encountered, the loop ends immediately and control passes to the statement following the Loop statement.

DO UNTIL LOOPS

The Do Until loop structure is very similar to the Do While structure. The difference is evident only when the condition is tested. In a Do While loop, the loop executes *while* the condition is True. In a Do Until loop, the loop executes *until* the condition is True.

Do Until also has two syntaxes:

```
Do [Until condition]
    [instructions]
    [Exit Do]
    [instructions]
Loop
```

or

```
Do
    [instructions]
    [Exit Do]
    [instructions]
Loop [Until condition]
```

The following example was originally presented for the Do While loop but has been rewritten to use a Do Until loop. The only difference is the line with the Do statement. This example makes the code a bit clearer because it avoids the negative required in the Do While example.

```
Sub DoUntilDemo1()
    Dim LineCt As Long
    Open "c:\data\textfile.txt" For Input As #1
    LineCt = 0
    Do Until EOF(1)
        Line Input #1, LineOfText
        Range("A1").Offset(LineCt, 0) = UCase(LineOfText)
        LineCt = LineCt + 1
    Loop
    Close #1
End Sub
```

Chapter 9

Working with VBA Sub Procedures

IN THIS CHAPTER

A *procedure* holds a group of Visual Basic for Applications (VBA) statements that accomplishes a desired task. Most VBA code is contained in procedures. This chapter focuses on Sub procedures, which perform tasks but do not return discrete values.

◆ Declaring and creating VBA Sub procedures

◆ Executing procedures

◆ Passing arguments to a procedure

◆ Using error-handling techniques

◆ An example of developing a useful procedure

VBA ALSO SUPPORTS Function PROCEDURES, which I discuss in Chapter 10.

Chapter 11 has many additional examples of procedures that you can incorporate into your work.

About Procedures

A *procedure* is a series of VBA statements that resides in a VBA module, which you access in the Visual Basic Editor (VBE). A module can hold any number of procedures.

You have a number of ways to *call,* or execute, procedures. A procedure is executed from beginning to end, but it can also be ended prematurely.

A procedure can be any length, but many people prefer to avoid creating extremely long procedures that perform many different operations. You may find it easier to write several smaller procedures, each with a single purpose. Then, design a main procedure that calls those other procedures. This approach can make your code easier to maintain.

Some procedures are written to receive arguments. An *argument* is simply information that is used by the procedure that is passed to the procedure when it is executed. Procedure arguments work much like the arguments that you use in Excel worksheet functions. Instructions within the procedure generally perform logical operations on these arguments, and the results of the procedure are usually based on those arguments.

Declaring a Sub procedure

A procedure declared with the Sub keyword must adhere to the following syntax:

```
[Private | Public][Static] Sub name ([arglist])
    [instructions]
    [Exit Sub]
    [instructions]
End Sub
```

- ◆ Private: (Optional) Indicates that the procedure is accessible only to other procedures in the same module.

- ◆ Public: (Optional) Indicates that the procedure is accessible to all other procedures in all other modules in the workbook. If used in a module that contains an Option Private Module statement, the procedure is not available outside the project.

- ◆ Static: (Optional) Indicates that the procedure's variables are preserved when the procedure ends.

- ◆ Sub: (Required) The keyword that indicates the beginning of a procedure.

- ◆ name: (Required) Any valid procedure name.

- ◆ arglist: (Optional) Represents a list of variables, enclosed in parentheses, that receive arguments passed to the procedure. Use a comma to separate arguments. If the procedure uses no arguments, a set of empty parentheses is required.

- ◆ instructions: (Optional) Represents valid VBA instructions.

◆ `Exit Sub`: (Optional) A statement that forces an immediate exit from the procedure prior to its formal completion.

◆ `End Sub`: (Required) Indicates the end of the procedure.

 With a few exceptions, all VBA instructions in a module must be contained within procedures. Exceptions include module-level variable declarations, user-defined data type definitions, and a few other instructions that specify module-level options (for example, `Option Explicit`).

Scoping a procedure

In the preceding chapter, I note that a variable's *scope* determines the modules and procedures in which the variable can be used. Similarly, a procedure's scope determines which other procedures can call it.

PUBLIC PROCEDURES

By default, procedures are *public* — that is, they can be called by other procedures in any module in the workbook. It's not necessary to use the `Public` keyword, but programmers often include it for clarity. The following two procedures are both public:

```
Sub First()
'    ... [code goes here] ...
End Sub

Public Sub Second()
'    ... [code goes here] ...
End Sub
```

Naming Procedures

Every procedure must have a name. The rules governing procedure names are generally the same as for variable names. Ideally, a procedure's name should describe what its contained processes do. A good rule is to use a name that includes a verb and a noun (for example, `ProcessDate`, `PrintReport`, `Sort_Array`, or `CheckFilename`). Avoid meaningless names such as `DoIt`, `Update`, and `Fix`.

Some programmers use sentence-like names that describe the procedure (for example, `WriteReportToTextFile` and `Get_Print_Options_ and_Print_Report`). Although long names are very descriptive and unambiguous, they are also more difficult to type.

PRIVATE PROCEDURES

Private procedures can be called by other procedures in the same module but not by procedures in other modules.

When you choose the Excel Tools → Macro → Macros command, the Macro dialog box displays only the public procedures. Therefore, if you have procedures that are designed to be called only by other procedures in the same module, you should make sure that the procedure is declared as `Private`. This prevents the user from running the procedure from the Macro dialog box.

The following example declares a private procedure, named `MySub`:

```
Private Sub MySub()
'    ... [code goes here] ...
End Sub
```

You can force all procedures in a module to be private — even those declared with the `Public` keyword — by including the following statement before your first `Sub` statement:

`Option Private Module`

If you write this statement in a module, you can omit the `Private` keyword from your `Sub` declarations.

Excel's macro recorder normally creates new `Sub` procedures called `Macro1`, `Macro2`, and so on. These procedures are all public procedures, and they will never use any arguments.

Executing Sub Procedures

In this section, I describe the many ways to *execute,* or call, a VBA `Sub` procedure:

◆ With the Run Sub/UserForm command (in the Visual Basic Editor; VBE). Or you can press the F5 shortcut key. Excel executes the procedure at the cursor position. This method doesn't work if the procedure requires one or more arguments.

◆ From Excel's Macro dialog box, which you open by choosing Tools →
   Macro → Macros. Or you can press the Alt+F8 shortcut key to access the
   Macro dialog box.

◆ By using the Ctrl key shortcut assigned to the procedure (assuming that
   you assigned one).

◆ By clicking a button or a shape on a worksheet. The button or shape must
   have the procedure assigned to it.

◆ From another procedure that you write. Sub and Function procedures can
   execute (or "call") other procedures.

◆ From a toolbar button.

◆ From a custom menu that you develop.

◆ When an event occurs. These events include opening the workbook, saving the workbook, closing the workbook, making a change to a cell, activating a sheet, and many other things.

◆ From the Immediate window in the VBE. Just type the name of the procedure, including any arguments that may apply, and press Enter.

I discuss these methods of executing procedures in the following sections.

In many cases, a procedure will not work properly unless it is in the appropriate context. For example, if a procedure is designed to work with the
active worksheet, it will fail if a chart sheet is active. A good procedure incorporates code that checks for the appropriate context and exits gracefully if it
can't proceed.

Executing a procedure with the Run Sub/UserForm command

The VBE Run Sub/UserForm menu command is used primarily to test a procedure
while you are developing it. You would never expect a user to have to activate the
VBE to execute a procedure. Choose Run → Run Sub/UserForm (or press F5) in the
VBE to execute the current procedure (in other words, the procedure that contains
the cursor).

   If the cursor is not located within a procedure when you issue the Run
Sub/UserForm command, VBE displays its Macro dialog box so that you can select
a procedure to execute.

Executing a procedure from the Macro dialog box

Choosing Excel's Tools → Macro → Macros command displays the Macro dialog box, as shown in Figure 9-1. (You can also press Alt+F8 to access this dialog box.) The Macro dialog box lists all available Sub procedures. Use the Macros In drop-down box to limit the scope of the macros displayed (for example, show only the macros in the active workbook). The Macro dialog box does not display Function procedures. In addition, it does not display Sub procedures declared with the Private keyword, Sub procedures that require one or more arguments, or Sub procedures contained in add-ins.

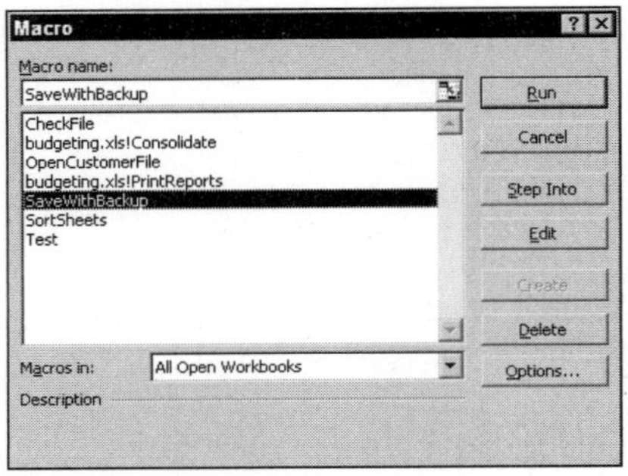

Figure 9-1: The Macro dialog box lists all available procedures.

 Procedures stored in an add-in are not listed in the Macro dialog box, but you still can execute such a procedure if you know the name. Simply type the procedure name into the Macro Name field in the Macro dialog box and then click Run.

Executing a procedure with a Ctrl+shortcut key combination

You can assign a Ctrl+shortcut key combination to any procedure that doesn't use any arguments. If you assign the Ctrl+U key combo to a procedure named Update, for example, pressing Ctrl+U executes the Update procedure.

When you begin recording a macro, the Record Macro dialog box gives you the opportunity to assign a shortcut key. However, you can assign a shortcut key at any time. To assign a Ctrl shortcut key to a procedure (or change a procedure's shortcut key), follow these steps:

1. Activate Excel and choose the Tools → Macro → Macros command.

2. Select the appropriate procedure from the list box in the Macro dialog box.

3. Click the Options button to display the Macro Options dialog box (see Figure 9-2).

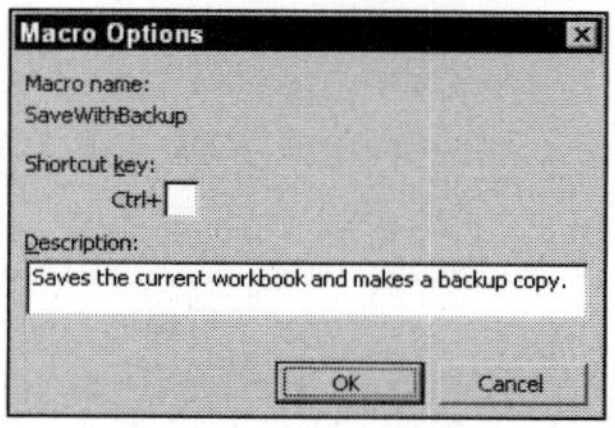

Figure 9-2: The Macro Options dialog box lets you assign a Ctrl key shortcut and an optional description to a procedure.

4. Enter a character into the Ctrl+ text box.

   Note: The character that you enter into the Ctrl+ text box is case-sensitive. If you enter a lowercase *s*, the shortcut key combo is Ctrl+S. If you enter an uppercase *S*, the shortcut key combo is Ctrl+Shift+S.

5. Enter a description (optional). If you enter a description for a macro, it is displayed at the bottom of the Macro dialog box when the procedure is selected in the list box.

6. Click OK to close the Macro Options dialog box, and then click Close to close the Macro dialog box.

If you assign one of Excel's predefined shortcut key combinations to a procedure, your key assignment takes precedence over the predefined key assignment. For example, Ctrl+S is the Excel predefined shortcut key for saving the active workbook. But if you assign Ctrl+S to a procedure, pressing Ctrl+S no longer saves the active workbook.

TIP

The following keyboard keys are *not* used by Excel for Ctrl+key combinations: E, J, L, M, Q, and T. Excel doesn't use too many Ctrl+Shift+key combinations. In fact, you can safely use any of them *except* F, O, and P (which are reserved for Find and Replace, Open, and Print, respectively).

Executing a procedure from a custom menu

As I describe in Chapter 23, Excel provides two ways for you to customize its menus: choosing the View → Toolbars → Customize command or writing VBA code. The latter method is preferable if you create applications, but you can use either technique to assign a macro to a new menu item.

Following are the steps required to display a new menu item on a menu and to assign a macro to the menu item. It assumes that the new menu item is on the Data menu, that the menu item text is Open Customer File, and that the procedure is named `OpenCustomerFile`.

1. Choose the View → Toolbars → Customize command. Excel displays the Customize dialog box.

   When the Customize dialog box is displayed, Excel is in a special "customization" mode. The menus and toolbars are not active, but they can be customized.

2. Click the Commands tab in the Customize dialog box.

3. Scroll down and click Macros in the Categories list.

4. In the Commands list, drag the first item (Custom Menu Item) to the bottom of the Data menu (after the Refresh Data menu item). The Data menu drops down when you click it.

5. Right-click the new menu item (Custom Menu Item) to display a shortcut menu.

6. Enter a new name for the menu item – &Open Customer File – in the Name text box (see Figure 9-3).

7. Click Assign Macro on the shortcut menu.

8. In the Assign Macro dialog box, select the `OpenCustomerFile` procedure from the list of macros.

9. Click OK to close the Assign Macro dialog box, and click Close to close the Customize dialog box.

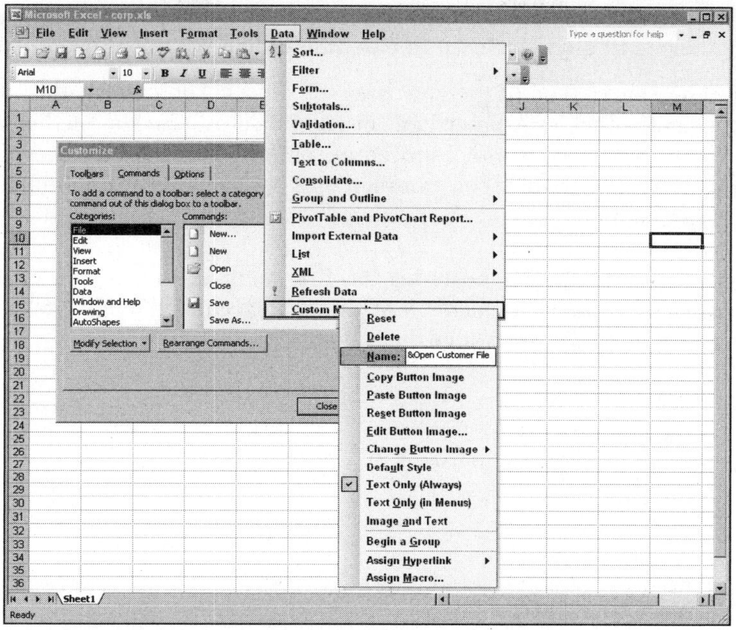

Figure 9-3: Changing the text for a menu item.

After you follow the process mentioned above, the new menu item always appears on the menu, even when the workbook that contains the macro is not open. In other words, changes that you make via the View → Toolbars → Customize command are permanent. Selecting the new menu item opens the workbook if it's not already open.

Refer to Chapter 23 to learn how to use VBA to create menu items that are displayed only when a particular workbook is open.

Executing a procedure from another procedure

One of the most common ways to execute a procedure is from another procedure. You have three ways to do this:

◆ Enter the procedure's name, followed by its arguments (if any), separated by commas.

◆ Use the `Call` keyword followed by the procedure's name and then its arguments (if any), enclosed in parentheses and separated by commas.

◆ Use the `Run` method of the `Application` object. You can use this method to execute other VBA procedures or XLM macros. The `Run` method is useful when you need to run a procedure, and the procedure's name is assigned to a variable. You can then pass the variable as an argument to the `Run` method.

The following example demonstrates the first method. In this case, the `MySub` procedure processes some statements (not shown), executes the `UpdateSheet` procedure, and then executes the rest of the statements.

```
Sub MySub()
'   ... [code goes here] ...
    UpdateSheet
'   ... [code goes here] ...
End Sub

Sub UpdateSheet()
'   ... [code goes here] ...
End Sub
```

The following example demonstrates the second method. The `Call` keyword executes the `Update` procedure, which requires one argument; the calling procedure passes the argument to the called procedure. I discuss procedure arguments later in this chapter (see "Passing Arguments to Procedures").

```
Sub MySub()
    MonthNum = InputBox("Enter the month number: ")
    Call UpdateSheet(MonthNum)
'   ... [code goes here] ...
End Sub

Sub UpdateSheet(MonthSeq)
'   ... [code goes here] ...
End Sub
```

TIP Even though it's optional, some programmers always use the `Call` keyword just to make it perfectly clear that another procedure is being called.

The next example uses the Run method to execute the UpdateSheet procedure and then pass MonthNum as the argument:

```
Sub MySub()
    MonthNum = InputBox("Enter the month number: ")
    Application.Run "UpdateSheet", MonthNum
'    ... [code goes here] ...
End Sub

Sub UpdateSheet(MonthSeq)
'    ... [code goes here] ...
End Sub
```

Perhaps the best reason to use the Run method is when the procedure name is assigned to a variable. In fact, it's the only way to execute a procedure in such a way. The following example demonstrates this. The Main procedure uses the VBA WeekDay function to determine the day of the week (an integer between 1 and 7, beginning with Sunday). The SubToCall variable is assigned a string that represents a procedure name. The Run method then calls the appropriate procedure (either WeekEnd or Daily).

```
Sub Main()
    Dim SubToCall As String
    Select Case WeekDay(Now)
        Case 1: SubToCall = "WeekEnd"
        Case 7: SubToCall = "WeekEnd"
        Case Else: SubToCall = "Daily"
    End Select
        Application.Run SubToCall
End Sub

Sub WeekEnd()
    MsgBox "Today is a weekend"
'   Code to execute on the weekend
'   goes here
End Sub

Sub Daily()
    MsgBox "Today is not a weekend"
'   Code to execute on the weekdays
'   goes here
End Sub
```

CALLING A PROCEDURE IN A DIFFERENT MODULE

If VBA can't locate a called procedure in the current module, it looks for public procedures in other modules in the same project.

If you need to call a private procedure from another procedure, both procedures must reside in the same module.

You can't have two procedures with the same name in the same module, but you can have identically named procedures in different modules. You can force VBA to execute an *ambiguously named* procedure – that is, another procedure in a different module that has the same name. To do so, precede the procedure name with the module name and a dot. For example, say that you define procedures named MySub in Module1 and Module2. If you want a procedure in Module2 to call the MySub in Module1, you can use either of the following statements:

```
Module1.MySub
Call Module1.MySub
```

If you do not differentiate between procedures that have the same name, you get an Ambiguous name detected error message.

CALLING A PROCEDURE IN A DIFFERENT WORKBOOK

In some cases, you may need your procedure to execute another procedure defined in a different workbook. To do so, you have two options: Either establish a reference to the other workbook, or use the Run method and specify the workbook name explicitly.

To add a reference to another workbook, choose the VBE's Tools → References command. Excel displays the References dialog box (see Figure 9-4), which lists all available references, including all open workbooks. Simply check the box that corresponds to the workbook that you want to add as a reference and then click OK. After you establish a reference, you can call procedures in the workbook as if they were in the same workbook as the calling procedure.

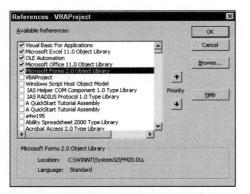

Figure 9-4: The References dialog box lets you establish a reference to another workbook.

A referenced workbook does not have to be open; it is treated like a separate object library. Use the Browse button in the References dialog box to establish a reference to a workbook that isn't open. The workbook names that appear in the list of references are listed by their VBE project names. By default, every project is initially named *VBAProject*. Therefore, the list may contain several identically named items. To distinguish a project, change its name in the Properties window of the VBE. The list of references displayed in the References dialog box also includes object libraries and ActiveX controls that are registered on your system. Your Excel 2003 workbooks always include references to the following object libraries:

◆ Visual Basic for Applications

◆ Microsoft Excel 11.0 Object Library

◆ OLE Automation

◆ Microsoft Office 11.0 Object Library

◆ Microsoft Forms 2.0 Object Library (optional, included only if your project includes a UserForm)

 Any additional references to other workbooks that you add are also listed in your project outline in the Project Explorer window in the VBE. These references are listed under a node called References.

If you've established a reference to a workbook that contains the procedure YourSub, for example, you can use either of the following statements to call YourSub:

```
YourSub
Call YourSub
```

To precisely identify a procedure in a different workbook, specify the project name, module name, and procedure name by using the following syntax:

```
MyProject.MyModule.MySub
```

Alternatively, you can use the Call keyword:

```
Call MyProject.MyModule.MySub
```

Another way to call a procedure in a different open workbook is to use the Run method of the Application object. This technique does not require that you establish a reference. The following statement executes the `Consolidate` procedure located in a workbook named `budget macros.xls`:

```
Application.Run "'budget macros.xls'!Consolidate"
```

Executing a procedure from a toolbar button

You can customize Excel's toolbars to include buttons that execute procedures when clicked. The procedure for assigning a macro to a toolbar button is virtually identical to the procedure for assigning a macro to a menu item.

Why Call Other Procedures?

If you're new to programming, you may wonder why anyone would ever want to call a procedure from another procedure. You may ask, "Why not just put the code from the called procedure into the calling procedure and keep things simple?"

One reason is to clarify your code. The simpler your code, the easier it is to maintain and modify. Smaller routines are easier to decipher and then debug. Examine the accompanying procedure, which does nothing but call other procedures. This procedure is very easy to follow.

```
Sub Main()
    Call GetUserOptions
    Call ProcessData
    Call CleanUp
    Call CloseItDown

End Sub
```

Calling other procedures also eliminates redundancy. Suppose that you need to perform an operation at ten different places in your routine. Rather than enter the code ten times, you can write a procedure to perform the operation and then simply call the procedure ten times.

Also, you may have a series of general-purpose procedures that you use frequently. If you store these in a separate module, you can import the module to your current project and then call these procedures as needed — which is much easier than copying and pasting the code into your new procedures.

Creating several small procedures rather than a single large one is often considered good programming practice. A modular approach not only makes your job easier but also makes life easier for the people who wind up working with your code.

Assume that you want to assign a procedure to a toolbar button on a toolbar. Here are the steps required to do so:

1. Choose the View → Toolbars → Customize command. Excel displays the Customize dialog box.

   When the Customize dialog box is displayed, Excel is in a special "customization" mode. The menus and toolbars are not active, but they can be customized.

2. Click the Commands tab in the Customize dialog box.

3. Scroll down and click Macros in the Categories list.

4. In the Commands list, drag the second item (Custom Button) to the desired toolbar.

5. Right-click the new button to display a shortcut menu.

6. Enter a new name for the button in the Name text box. This is the ToolTip text that appears when the mouse pointer moves over the button. This step is optional; if you omit it, the ToolTip displays `Custom`.

7. Right-click the new button and select Assign Macro from the shortcut menu.

   Excel displays its Assign Macro dialog box.

8. Select the procedure from the list of macros.

9. Click OK to close the Assign Macro dialog box.

10. Click Close to close the Customize dialog box.

After you follow the process above, the new toolbar button always appears on the assigned toolbar — even when the workbook that contains the macro is not open. In other words, changes that you make when choosing the View → Toolbars → Customize command are permanent. Clicking the new toolbar button item opens the workbook if it's not already open.

I cover custom toolbars in Chapter 22.

Executing a procedure by clicking an object

Excel provides a variety of objects that you can place on a worksheet or chart sheet, and you can attach a macro to any of these objects. These objects are available from three toolbars:

- ◆ The Drawing toolbar
- ◆ The Forms toolbar
- ◆ The Control Toolbox toolbar

In addition, you can assign a macro to pictures that you place on the worksheet by choosing the Insert → Picture command. Right-click the picture and then choose Assign Macro.

The Control Toolbox toolbar contains ActiveX controls, which are similar to the controls that you use in a UserForm. The Forms toolbar, which is included for compatibility purposes, contains similar controls (which are not ActiveX controls). The controls on the Forms toolbar were designed for Excel 5 and Excel 95. However, they can still be used in later versions (and may be preferable in some cases). The discussion that follows applies to the Button control from the Forms toolbar. Refer to Chapter 13 for information about using ActiveX controls on worksheets.

To assign a procedure to a Button object (which is on the Forms toolbar), follow these steps:

1. Make sure that the Forms toolbar is displayed.

2. Click the Button tool on the Forms toolbar.

3. Drag in the worksheet to create the button.

If you press Alt while dragging, the button will conform to the sheet's gridlines. Or, press Shift while dragging to force a perfectly square button.

Excel jumps right in and displays the Assign Macro dialog box. Select the macro that you want to assign to the button and then click OK.

To assign a macro to a shape, create a shape from the Drawing toolbar. Right-click the shape and then choose Assign Macro from the shortcut menu.

Executing a procedure when an event occurs

You might want a procedure to be executed when a particular event occurs. Examples of events include opening a workbook, entering data into a worksheet, saving a workbook, clicking a `CommandButton` control, and many others. A procedure that is executed when an event occurs is an *event handler* procedure. Event handler procedures are characterized by the following:

♦ They have special names that are made up of an object, an underscore, and the event name. For example, the procedure that is executed when a workbook is opened is `Workbook_Open`.

♦ They are stored in the Code module for the particular object.

Chapter 19 is devoted to event handler procedures.

Executing a procedure from the Immediate window

You also can execute a procedure by entering its name in the Immediate window of the VBE. If the Immediate window is not visible, press Ctrl+G. The Immediate window executes VBA statements while you enter them. To execute a procedure, simply enter the name of the procedure in the Immediate window and then press Enter.

This method can be quite useful when you're developing a procedure because you can insert commands to display results in the Immediate window. The following procedure demonstrates this technique:

```
Sub ChangeCase()
    Dim MyString As String
    MyString = "This is a test"
    MyString = UCase(MyString)
    Debug.Print MyString
End Sub
```

Figure 9-5 shows what happens when you enter **ChangeCase** in the Immediate window: The Debug.Print statement displays the result immediately.

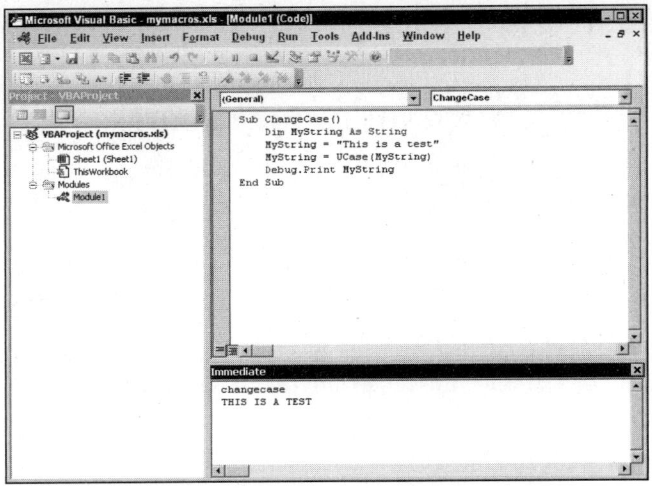

Figure 9-5: Executing a procedure by entering its name in the Immediate window.

Passing Arguments to Procedures

A procedure's *arguments* provide it with data that it uses in its instructions. The data that's passed by an argument can be any of the following:

- A variable
- A constant
- An array
- An object

With regard to arguments, procedures are very similar to worksheet functions in the following respects:

- A procedure may not require any arguments.
- A procedure may require a fixed number of arguments.
- A procedure may accept an indefinite number of arguments.
- A procedure may require some arguments, leaving others optional.
- A procedure may have all optional arguments.

For example, a few of Excel's worksheet functions, such as RAND, use no arguments. Others, such as COUNTIF, require two arguments. Others still, such as SUM, can use an indefinite number of arguments (up to 30). Still other worksheet functions have optional arguments. The PMT function, for example, can have five arguments (three are required; two are optional).

Most of the procedures that you've seen so far in this book have been declared without any arguments. They were declared with just the Sub keyword, the procedure's name, and a set of empty parentheses. Empty parentheses indicate that the procedure does not accept arguments.

The following example shows two procedures. The Main procedure calls the ProcessFile procedure three times (the Call statement is in a For-Next loop). Before calling ProcessFile, however, a three-element array is created. Inside the loop, each element of the array becomes the argument for the procedure call. The ProcessFile procedure takes one argument (named TheFile). Notice that the argument goes inside parentheses in the Sub statement. When ProcessFile finishes, program control continues with the statement after the Call statement.

```
Sub Main()
    Dim File(1 To 3) As String
    File(1) = "dept1.xls"
    File(2) = "dept2.xls"
    File(3) = "dept3.xls"
    For i = 1 To 3
        Call ProcessFile(File(i))
    Next i
End Sub

Sub ProcessFile(TheFile)
    Workbooks.Open FileName:=TheFile
'   ...[more code here]...
End Sub
```

You can also, of course, pass *literals* (that is, not variables) to a procedure. For example:

```
Sub Main()
    Call ProcessFile("budget.xls")
End Sub
```

You can pass an argument to a procedure in two ways: by reference and by value. Passing an argument by reference (the default method) simply passes the memory address of the variable. Passing an argument by value, on the other hand, passes a copy of the original variable. Consequently, changes to the argument within the procedure are not reflected in the original variable.

The following example demonstrates this concept. The argument for the Process procedure is passed by reference (the default method). After the Main procedure assigns a value of 10 to MyValue, it calls the Process procedure and passes

MyValue as the argument. The Process procedure multiplies the value of its argument (named YourValue) by 10. When Process ends and program control passes back to Main, the MsgBox function displays MyValue: 100.

```
Sub Main()
    Dim MyValue As Integer
    MyValue = 10
    Call Process(MyValue)
    MsgBox MyValue
End Sub

Sub Process(YourValue)
    YourValue = YourValue * 10
End Sub
```

If you don't want the called procedure to modify any variables passed as arguments, you can modify the called procedure's argument list so that arguments are passed to it by *value* rather than by *reference*. To do so, precede the argument with the ByVal keyword. This technique causes the called routine to work with a copy of the passed variable's data — not the data itself. In the following procedure, for example, the changes made to YourValue in the Process procedure do not affect the MyValue variable in Main. As a result, the MsgBox function displays 10 and not 100.

```
Sub Process(ByVal YourValue)
    YourValue = YourValue * 10
End Sub
```

In most cases, you'll be content to use the default reference method of passing arguments. However, if your procedure needs to use data passed to it in an argument — and you absolutely must keep the original data intact — you'll want to pass the data by value.

A procedure's arguments can mix and match by value and by reference. Arguments preceded with ByVal are passed by value; all others are passed by reference.

 If you pass a variable defined as a user-defined data type to a procedure, it must be passed by reference. Attempting to pass it by value generates an error.

Because I didn't declare a data type for any of the arguments in the preceding examples, all the arguments have been of the Variant data type. But a procedure that uses arguments can define the data types directly in the argument list. The following is a Sub statement for a procedure with two arguments of different data types. The first is declared as an integer, and the second is declared as a string.

```
Sub Process(Iterations As Integer, TheFile As String)
```

When you pass arguments to a procedure, it's important that the data that is passed as the argument matches the argument's data type. For example, if you call Process in the preceding example and pass a string variable for the first argument, you get an error: ByRef argument type mismatch.

Public Variables versus Passing Arguments to a Procedure

In Chapter 8, I point out how a variable declared as Public (at the top of the module) is available to all procedures in the module. In some cases, you might want to access a Public variable rather than pass the variable as an argument when calling another procedure.

For example, the procedure that follows passes the value of MonthVal to the ProcessMonth procedure:

```
Sub MySub()
    Dim MonthVal as Integer
'   ... [code goes here]
    MonthVal = 4
    Call ProcessMonth(MonthVal)
'   ... [code goes here]

End Sub
```

An alternative approach is

```
Public MonthVal as Integer

Sub MySub()
'   ... [code goes here]
    MonthVal = 4
    Call ProcessMonth
'   ... [code goes here]

End Sub
```

In the revised code, because MonthVal is a public variable, the ProcessMonth procedure can access it, thus eliminating the need for an argument for the ProcessMonth procedure.

Arguments are relevant to both Sub procedures and Function procedures. In fact, arguments are more often used in Function procedures. In Chapter 10, where I focus on Function procedures, I provide additional examples of using arguments with your routines, including how to handle optional arguments.

Error-Handling Techniques

When a VBA procedure is running, errors can occur, as you undoubtedly know. These include either *syntax errors* (which you must correct before you can execute a procedure) or *runtime errors* (which occur while the procedure is running). This section deals with runtime errors.

For error-handling procedures to work, the Break on All Errors setting *must* be turned off. In the VBE, choose Tools → Options and click the General tab in the Options dialog box. If Break on All Errors is selected, VBA ignores your error-handling code. You'll usually want to use the Break on Unhandled Errors option.

Normally, a runtime error causes VBA to stop, and the user sees a dialog box that displays the error number and a description of the error. A good application doesn't make the user deal with these messages. Rather, it incorporates error-handling code to trap errors and take appropriate actions. At the very least, your error-handling code can display a more meaningful error message than the one popped up by VBA.

Appendix C lists all the VBA error codes and descriptions.

Trapping errors

You can use the On Error statement to specify what happens when an error occurs. Basically, you have two choices:

◆ *Ignore the error and let VBA continue.* You can later examine the Err object to determine what the error was and then take action if necessary.

◆ *Jump to a special error-handling section of your code to take action.* This section is placed at the end of the procedure and is also marked by a label.

To cause your VBA code to continue when an error occurs, insert the following statement in your code:

```
On Error Resume Next
```

Some errors are inconsequential and can simply be ignored. But you may want to determine what the error was. When an error occurs, you can use the `Err` object to determine the error number. The VBA `Error` function can be used to display the text for `Err.ValueNumber`, which defaults to just `Err`. For example, the following statement displays the same information as the normal Visual Basic error dialog box (the error number and the error description):

```
MsgBox "Error " & Err & ": " & Error(Err)
```

Figure 9-6 shows a VBA error message, and Figure 9-7 shows the same error displayed in a message box. You can, of course, make the error message a bit more meaningful to your end users by using more descriptive text.

Referencing `Err` is equivalent to accessing the `Number` property of the `Err` object. Therefore, the following two statements have the same effect:

```
MsgBox Err
MsgBox Err.Number
```

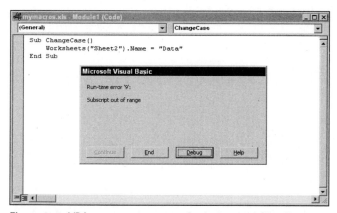

Figure 9-6: VBA error messages aren't always user-friendly.

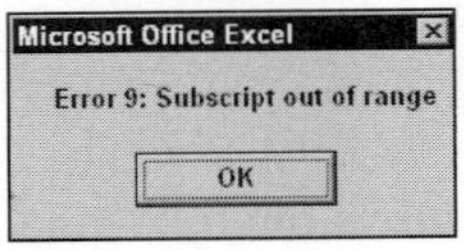

Figure 9-7: You can create
a message box to display the
error code and description.

You also use the On Error statement to specify a location in your procedure to jump to when an error occurs. You use a label to mark the location. For example:

```
On Error GoTo ErrorHandler
```

Error-handling examples

The first example demonstrates an error that can safely be ignored. The SpecialCells method selects cells that meet a certain criteria. (This method is equivalent to choosing the Edit → Go To command and then clicking the Special button to select, for example, all cells that contain formulas.)

In the example that follows, the SpecialCells method selects all the cells in the current range selection that contain a formula that returns a number. Normally, if no cells in the selection qualify, VBA generates an error message. Using the On Error Resume Next statement simply prevents the error message from appearing.

```
Sub SelectFormulas()
    On Error Resume Next
    Selection.SpecialCells(xlFormulas, xlNumbers).Select
    On Error GoTo 0
'    ...[more code goes here]
End Sub
```

Notice that the On Error GoTo 0 statement restores normal error handling for the remaining statements in the procedure.

The following procedure uses an additional statement to determine whether an error did occur:

```
Sub SelectFormulas2()
    On Error Resume Next
    Selection.SpecialCells(xlFormulas, xlNumbers).Select
    If Err <> 0 Then MsgBox "No formula cells were found."
    On Error GoTo 0
'    ...[more code goes here]
End Sub
```

If the value of Err is not equal to 0, an error occurred, and a message box displays a notice to the user.

The next example demonstrates error handling by jumping to a label.

```
Sub ErrorDemo()
    On Error GoTo Handler
    Selection.Value = 123
    Exit Sub
Handler:
    MsgBox "Cannot assign a value to the selection."
End Sub
```

The procedure attempts to assign a value to the current selection. If an error occurs (for example, a range is not selected or the sheet is protected), the assignment statement results in an error. The On Error statement specifies a jump to the Handler label if an error occurs. Notice the use of the Exit Sub statement before the label. This prevents the error-handling code from being executed if no error occurs. If this statement is omitted, the error message would be displayed even if an error did not occur.

Sometimes, you can take advantage of an error to get information. The example that follows simply checks whether a particular workbook is open. It does not use any error handling.

```
Sub CheckForFile1()
    Dim FileName As String
    Dim FileExists As Boolean
    Dim book As Workbook
    FileName = "BUDGET.XLS"
    FileExists = False

'   Cycle through all workbooks
    For Each book In Workbooks
        If UCase(book.Name) = FileName Then
            FileExists = True
        End If
    Next book

'   Display appropriate message
    If FileExists Then _
        MsgBox FileName & " is open." Else _
            MsgBox FileName & " is not open."
End Sub
```

Here, a `For Each-Next` loop cycles through all objects in the `Workbooks` collection. If the workbook is open, the `FileExists` variable is set to `True`. Finally, a message is displayed that tells the user whether the workbook is open.

The preceding routine can be rewritten to use error handling to determine whether the file is open. In the example that follows, the `On Error Resume Next` statement causes VBA to ignore any errors. The next instruction attempts to reference the workbook by assigning the workbook to an object variable (by using the `Set` keyword). If the workbook is not open, an error occurs. The `If-Then-Else` structure checks the value property of `Err` and displays the appropriate message.

```
Sub CheckForFile()
    Dim FileName As String
    Dim x As Workbook
    FileName = "BUDGET.XLS"
    On Error Resume Next
    Set x = Workbooks(FileName)
    If Err = 0 Then
        MsgBox FileName & " is open."
    Else
        MsgBox FileName & " is not open."
    End If
    On Error GoTo 0
End Sub
```

Chapter 11 presents several additional examples that use error handling.

A Realistic Example That Uses Sub Procedures

In this chapter, I have provided you with the basic foundation for creating `Sub` procedures. Most of the previous examples, I will admit, have been rather wimpy. The remainder of this chapter is a real-life exercise that demonstrates many of the concepts covered in this and the preceding two chapters.

This section describes the development of a useful utility that qualifies as an application as defined in Chapter 5. More important, I demonstrate the *process* of analyzing a problem and then solving it with VBA. A word of warning to the more experienced users in the audience: I wrote this section with VBA newcomers in mind. As a result, I don't simply present the code, but I also show how to find out what you need to know to develop the code.

The completed application can be found on the companion CD-ROM.

The goal

The goal of this exercise is to develop a utility that rearranges a workbook by alphabetizing its sheets (something that Excel cannot do on its own). If you tend to create workbooks that consist of many sheets, you know that it can be difficult to locate a particular sheet. If the sheets are ordered alphabetically, though, it's much easier to find a desired sheet.

Project requirements

Where to begin? One way to get started is to list the requirements for your application. When you develop your application, you can check your list to ensure that you're covering all the bases.

Here's the list of requirements that I compiled for this example application:

1. It should sort the sheets (that is, worksheets and chart sheets) in the active workbook in ascending order of their names.

2. It should be easy to execute.

3. It should always be available. In other words, the user shouldn't have to open a workbook to use this utility.

4. It should work properly for any open workbook.

5. It should not display any VBA error messages.

What you know

Often, the most difficult part of a project is figuring out where to start. In this case, I started by listing things that I know about Excel that may be relevant to the project requirements:

- ◆ Excel doesn't have a command that sorts sheets. Therefore, recording a macro to alphabetize the sheets is not an option.

- ◆ I can move a sheet easily by dragging its sheet tab.

  Mental note: Turn on the macro recorder and drag a sheet to a new location to find out what kind of code this action generates.

◆ Excel also has an Edit → Move or Copy Sheet command. Would recording a macro of this command generate different code than moving a sheet manually?

◆ I'll need to know how many sheets are in the active workbook. I can get this information with VBA.

◆ I'll need to know the names of all the sheets. Again, I can get this information with VBA.

◆ Excel has a command that sorts data in worksheet cells.

Mental note: Maybe I can transfer the sheet names to a range and use this feature. Or, maybe VBA has a sorting method that I can take advantage of.

◆ Thanks to the Macro Options dialog box, it's easy to assign a shortcut key to a macro.

◆ If a macro is stored in the Personal Macro Workbook, it will always be available.

◆ I need a way to test the application while I develop it. For certain, I don't want to be testing it using the same workbook in which I'm developing the code.

Mental note: Create a dummy workbook for testing purposes.

◆ If I develop the code properly, VBA won't display any errors.

Mental note: Wishful thinking. . . .

The approach

Although I still didn't know exactly how to proceed, I could devise a preliminary, skeleton plan that describes the general tasks required:

1. Identify the active workbook.

2. Get a list of all the sheet names in the workbook.

3. Count the sheets.

4. Sort them (somehow).

5. Rearrange the sheets in the sorted order.

What you need to know

I saw a few holes in the plan. I knew that I had to determine the following:

◆ How to identify the active workbook

◆ How to count the sheets in the active workbook

- ◆ How to get a list of the sheet names

- ◆ How to sort the list

- ◆ How to rearrange the sheets according to the sorted list

TIP

When you lack critical information about specific methods or properties, you can consult this book or the VBA Help system. You may eventually discover what you need to know. Your best bet, however, is to turn on the macro recorder and examine the code that it generates when you perform some relevant actions.

Some preliminary recording

Here's an example of using the macro recorder to learn about VBA. I started with a workbook that contained three worksheets. Then I turned on the macro recorder and specified my Personal Macro Workbook as the destination for the macro. With the macro recorder running, I dragged the third worksheet to the first sheet position. Here's the code that was generated by the macro recorder:

```
Sub Macro1()
    Sheets("Sheet3").Select
    Sheets("Sheet3").Move Before:=Sheets(1)
End Sub
```

I searched the VBA Help for *Move,* and discovered that it's a method that moves a sheet to a new location in the workbook. It also takes an argument that specifies the location for the sheet. Very relevant to the task at hand. Curious, I then turned on the macro recorder to see whether the Edit → Move or Copy Sheet command would generate different code. It didn't.

Next I needed to find out how many sheets were in the active workbook. I searched Help for the word *Count* and found out that it's a property of a collection. I activated the Immediate window in the VBE and typed the following statement:

```
? ActiveWorkbook.Count
```

Error! After a little more thought, I realized that I needed to get a count of the sheets within a workbook. So I tried this:

```
? ActiveWorkbook.Sheets.Count
```

Success. Figure 9-8 shows the result. More useful information.

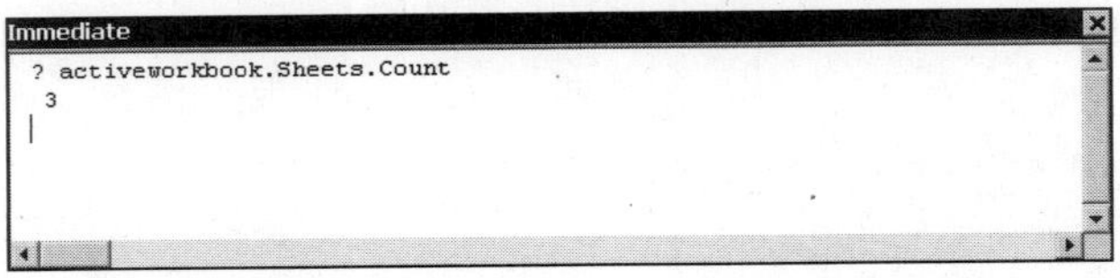

Figure 9-8: Use the VBE Immediate window to test a statement.

What about the sheet names? Time for another test. I entered the following statement in the Immediate window:

```
? ActiveWorkbook.Sheets(1).Name
```

This told me that the name of the first sheet is Sheet3, which is correct. More good information to keep in mind.

Then I remembered something about the For Each-Next construct: It is useful for cycling through each member of a collection. After consulting the Help system, I created a short procedure to test it:

```
Sub Test()
    For Each Sht In ActiveWorkbook.Sheets
        MsgBox Sht.Name
    Next Sht
End Sub
```

Another success. This macro displayed three message boxes, each showing a different sheet name.

Finally, it was time to think about sorting options. From the Help system, I learned that the Sort method applies to a Range object. So one option was to transfer the sheet names to a range and then sort the range, but that seemed like overkill for this application. I thought that a better option was to dump the sheet names into an array of strings and then sort the array by using VBA code.

Initial setup

Now I knew enough to get started writing some serious code. Before doing so, however, I needed to do some initial setup work. To re-create my steps, follow these instructions:

1. Create an empty workbook with five worksheets, named Sheet1, Sheet2, Sheet3, Sheet4, and Sheet5.

2. Move the sheets around randomly so that they aren't in any particular order.

3. Save the workbook as Test.xls.

4. Activate the VBE and select the `Personal.xls` project in the Project Window.

   If `Personal.xls` doesn't appear in the Project window in the VBE, this means that you've never used the Personal Macro Workbook. To have Excel create this workbook for you, simply record a macro (any macro) and specify the Personal Macro Workbook as the destination for the macro.

5. Insert a new VBA module (choose the Insert → Module command).

6. Create an empty procedure called `SortSheets` (see Figure 9-9).

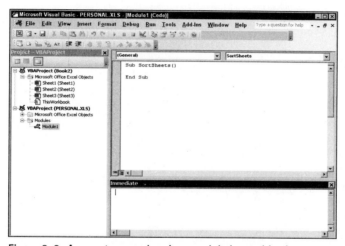

Figure 9-9: An empty procedure in a module located in the Personal Macro Workbook.

Actually, you can store this macro in any module in the Personal Macro Workbook. However, it's a good idea to keep each macro in a separate module. That way, you can easily export the module and import it into a different project later on.

7. Activate Excel. Choose the Tools → Macro → Macros command (Options button) to assign a shortcut key to this macro. The Ctrl+Shift+S key combination is a good choice.

Code writing

Now it's time to write some code. I knew that I needed to put the sheet names into an array of strings. Because I won't know yet how many sheets are in the active workbook, I used a `Dim` statement with empty parentheses to declare the array. I knew that I could use `ReDim` afterward to redimension the array for the proper number of elements.

I entered the following code, which inserts the sheet names into the SheetNames array. I also added a MsgBox function within the loop just to assure me that the sheets' names were indeed being entered into the array.

```
Sub SortSheets()
    Dim SheetNames() as String
    Dim i as Integer
    Dim SheetCount as Integer
    SheetCount = ActiveWorkbook.Sheets.Count
    ReDim SheetNames(1 To SheetCount)
    For i = 1 To SheetCount
        SheetNames(i) = ActiveWorkbook.Sheets(i).Name
        MsgBox SheetNames(i)
    Next i
End Sub
```

To test the preceding code, I activated the Test.xls workbook and pressed Ctrl+Shift+S. Five message boxes appeared, each displaying the name of a sheet in the active workbook.

I'm a major proponent of testing your work as you go. When you're convinced that your code is working correctly, remove the MsgBox statement. (These message boxes become annoying after a while.)

TIP

Rather than use the MsgBox function to test your work, you can use the Print method of the Debug object to display information in the Immediate window. For this example, use the following statement in place of the MsgBox statement:

```
Debug.Print SheetNames(i)
```

This technique is much less intrusive than using MsgBox statements.

At this point, the SortSheets procedure simply creates an array of sheet names, corresponding to the sheets in the active workbook. Two steps remain: Sort the values in the SheetNames array, and then rearrange the sheets to correspond to the sorted array.

Sort procedure writing

It was time to sort the SheetNames array. One option was to insert the sorting code in the SortSheets procedure, but I thought a better approach was to write a general-purpose sorting procedure that I could reuse with other projects (sorting arrays is a common operation).

You might be a bit daunted by the thought of writing a sorting procedure. The good news is that it's relatively easy to find commonly used routines that you can use or adapt. The Internet, of course, is a great source for such information.

You can sort an array in many ways. I chose the *bubble sort* method; although it's not a particularly fast technique, it's easy to code. Blazing speed is not really a requirement in this particular application.

The bubble sort method uses a nested For-Next loop to evaluate each array element. If the array element is greater than the next element, the two elements swap positions. This evaluation is repeated for every pair of items (that is, n–1 times).

In Chapter 11, I present some other sorting routines and compare them in terms of speed.

Here's the sorting procedure I developed (after consulting a few Web sites to get some ideas):

```
Sub BubbleSort(List() As String)
'    Sorts the List array in ascending order
     Dim First As Integer, Last As Integer
     Dim i As Integer, j As Integer
     Dim Temp As String
     First = LBound(List)
     Last = UBound(List)
     For i = First To Last - 1
         For j = i + 1 To Last
             If List(i) > List(j) Then
                 Temp = List(j)
                 List(j) = List(i)
                 List(i) = Temp
             End If
         Next j
     Next i
End Sub
```

This procedure accepts one argument: a one-dimensional array named List. An array passed to a procedure can be of any length. I used the LBound and UBound functions to define the lower bound and upper bound of the array to the variables First and Last, respectively.

After I was satisfied that this procedure worked reliably, I modified SortSheets by adding a call to the BubbleSort procedure, passing the SheetNames array as an argument. At this point, my module looked like this:

```
Sub SortSheets()
    Dim SheetNames() As String
    Dim SheetCount as Integer
    Dim i as Integer
    SheetCount = ActiveWorkbook.Sheets.Count
    ReDim SheetNames(1 To SheetCount)
    For i = 1 To SheetCount
        SheetNames(i) = ActiveWorkbook.Sheets(i).Name
    Next i
    Call BubbleSort(SheetNames)
End Sub

Sub BubbleSort(List() As String)
    Dim First As Integer, Last As Integer
    Dim i As Integer, j As Integer
    Dim Temp As String
    First = LBound(List)
    Last = UBound(List)
    For i = First To Last - 1
        For j = i + 1 To Last
            If List(i) > List(j) Then
                Temp = List(j)
                List(j) = List(i)
                List(i) = Temp
            End If
        Next j
    Next i
End Sub
```

When the `SheetSort` procedure ends, it contains an array that consists of the sorted sheet names in the active workbook. To verify this, you can display the array contents in the VBE Immediate window by adding the following code at the end of the `SortSheets` procedure (if the Immediate window is not visible, press Ctrl+G):

```
For i = 1 To SheetCount
    Debug.Print SheetNames(i)
Next i
```

So far, so good. Now I merely had to write some code to rearrange the sheets to correspond to the sorted items in the `SheetNames` array.

The code that I recorded earlier proved useful. Remember the instruction that was recorded when I moved a sheet to the first position in the workbook?

```
Sheets("Sheet3").Move Before:=Sheets(1)
```

After a little thought, I was able to write a For-Next loop that would go through each sheet and move it to its corresponding sheet location, specified in the SheetNames array:

```
For i = 1 To SheetCount
    Sheets(SheetNames(i)).Move Before:=Sheets(i)
Next i
```

For example, the first time through the loop, the loop counter (i) is 1. The first element in the SheetNames array is (in this example) Sheet1. Therefore, the expression for the Move method within the loop evaluates to

```
Sheets("Sheet1").Move Sheets(1)
```

The second time through the loop, the expression evaluates to

```
Sheets("Sheet2").Move Sheets(2)
```

I then added the new code to the SortSheets procedure:

```
Sub SortSheets()
    Dim SheetNames() As String
    Dim SheetCount as Integer
    Dim i as Integer
    SheetCount = ActiveWorkbook.Sheets.Count
    ReDim SheetNames(1 To SheetCount)
    For i = 1 To SheetCount
        SheetNames(i) = ActiveWorkbook.Sheets(i).Name
    Next i
    Call BubbleSort(SheetNames)
    For i = 1 To SheetCount
        ActiveWorkbook.Sheets(SheetNames(i)).Move _
            Before:=ActiveWorkbook.Sheets(i)
    Next i
End Sub
```

I did some testing, and it seemed to work just fine for the Test.xls workbook.

Time to clean things up. I made sure that all the variables used in the procedures were declared, and then I added a few comments and blank lines to make the code easier to read. The SortSheets procedure now looked like the following:

```
Sub SortSheets()
'   This routine sorts the sheets of the
'   active workbook in ascending order.
```

```
    Dim SheetNames() As String
    Dim SheetCount As Integer
    Dim i As Integer

'   Determine the number of sheets & ReDim array
    SheetCount = ActiveWorkbook.Sheets.Count
    ReDim SheetNames(1 To SheetCount)

'   Fill array with sheet names
    For i = 1 To SheetCount
        SheetNames(i) = ActiveWorkbook.Sheets(i).Name
    Next i

'   Sort the array in ascending order
    Call BubbleSort(SheetNames)

'   Move the sheets
    For i = 1 To SheetCount
        ActiveWorkbook.Sheets(SheetNames(i)).Move _
            ActiveWorkbook.Sheets(i)
    Next i
End Sub
```

Everything seemed to be working. To test the code further, I added a few more sheets to Test.xls and changed some of the sheet names. It worked like a charm!

More testing

I was tempted to call it a day. However, just because the procedure worked with the Test.xls workbook didn't mean that it would work with all workbooks. To test it further, I loaded a few other workbooks and retried the routine. I soon discovered that the application was not perfect. In fact, it was far from perfect. I identified the following problems:

◆ Workbooks with many sheets took a long time to sort because the screen was continually updated during the move operations.

◆ The sorting didn't always work. For example, in one of my tests, a sheet named SUMMARY (all uppercase) appeared before a sheet named Sheet1. This problem was caused by the BubbleSort procedure — an uppercase *U* is "greater than" a lowercase *h*.

◆ If Excel had no visible workbook windows, pressing the Ctrl+Shift+S shortcut key combo caused the macro to fail.

◆ If the workbook's structure was protected, the Move method failed.

◆ After sorting, the last sheet in the workbook became the active sheet. Changing the user's active sheet is not a good practice; it's better to keep the user's original sheet active.

◆ If I interrupted the macro by pressing Ctrl+Break, VBA displayed an error message.

Fixing the problems

Fixing the screen-updating problem was a breeze. I inserted the following instruction at the beginning of `SortSheets` to turn off screen updating:

```
Application.ScreenUpdating = False
```

This statement causes Excel's windows to freeze while the macro is running. A beneficial side effect is that it also speeds up the macro considerably.

It was also easy to fix the problem with the `BubbleSort` procedure: I used VBA's `UCase` function to convert the sheet names to uppercase. That way, all the comparisons were made by using uppercase versions of the sheet names. The corrected line read as follows:

```
If UCase(List(i)) > UCase(List(j)) Then
```

TIP

Another way to solve the "case" problem is to add the following statement to the top of your module:

```
Option Compare Text
```

This statement causes VBA to perform string comparisons based on a case-insensitive text sort order. In other words, *A* is considered the same as *a*.

To prevent the error message that appears when no workbooks are visible, I added some error checking. If no active workbook exists, an error occurred. I used `On Error Resume Next` to ignore the error and then checked the value of `Err`. If `Err` is not equal to 0, it means that an error occurred. Therefore, the procedure ends. The error-checking code is

```
On Error Resume Next
SheetCount = ActiveWorkbook.Sheets.Count
If Err <> 0 Then Exit Sub ' No active workbook
```

It occurred to me that I could avoid using `On Error Resume Next`. The following statement is a more direct approach to determining whether a workbook is not visible and doesn't require any error handling:

```
If ActiveWorkbook Is Nothing Then Exit Sub
```

There's usually a good reason that a workbook's structure is protected. I decided that the best approach was to not attempt to unprotect the workbook. Rather, the code should display a message box warning and let the user unprotect the workbook and re-execute the macro. Testing for a protected workbook structure was easy — the `ProtectStructure` property of a `Workbook` object returns `True` if a workbook is protected. I added the following block of code:

```
'   Check for protected workbook structure
    If ActiveWorkbook.ProtectStructure Then
        MsgBox ActiveWorkbook.Name & " is protected.", _
            vbCritical, "Cannot Sort Sheets."
        Exit Sub
    End If
```

To reactivate the original active sheet after the sorting was performed, I wrote code that assigned the original sheet to an object variable (`OldActive`) and then activated that sheet when the routine was finished.

Pressing Ctrl+Break normally halts a macro, and VBA usually displays an error message. But because one of my goals was to avoid VBA error messages, I needed to insert a command to prevent this situation. From the online help, I discovered that the `Application` object has an `EnableCancelKey` property that can disable Ctrl+Break. So I added the following statement at the top of the routine:

```
Application.EnableCancelKey = xlDisabled
```

 Be very careful when you disable the Cancel key. If your code gets caught in an infinite loop, there is no way to break out of it. For best results, insert this statement *only after you're sure* that everything is working properly.

After I made all these corrections, the `SortSheets` procedure looked like Listing 9-1.

Listing 9-1: The Final Build for the SortSheets Procedure

```
Option Explicit
Sub SortSheets()
'   This routine sorts the sheets of the
'   active workbook in ascending order.
```

```vba
    Dim SheetNames() As String
    Dim i As Integer
    Dim SheetCount As Integer
    Dim Item As Object
    Dim OldActive As Object

    If ActiveWorkbook Is Nothing Then Exit Sub ' No active workbook
    SheetCount = ActiveWorkbook.Sheets.Count

'   Check for protected workbook structure
    If ActiveWorkbook.ProtectStructure Then
        MsgBox ActiveWorkbook.Name & " is protected.", _
            vbCritical, "Cannot Sort Sheets."
        Exit Sub
    End If

'   Disable Ctrl+Break
    Application.EnableCancelKey = xlDisabled

'   Get the number of sheets
    SheetCount = ActiveWorkbook.Sheets.Count

'   Redimension the array
    ReDim SheetNames(1 To SheetCount)

'   Store a reference to the active sheet
    Set OldActive = ActiveSheet

'   Fill array with sheet names
    For i = 1 To SheetCount
        SheetNames(i) = ActiveWorkbook.Sheets(i).Name
    Next i

'   Sort the array in ascending order
    Call BubbleSort(SheetNames)

'   Turn off screen updating
    Application.ScreenUpdating = False

'   Move the sheets
    For i = 1 To SheetCount
        ActiveWorkbook.Sheets(SheetNames(i)).Move _
            Before:=ActiveWorkbook.Sheets(i)
    Next i
```

Continued

Listing 9-1: The Final Build for the SortSheets Procedure *(Continued)*

```
'   Reactivate the original active sheet
    OldActive.Activate
End Sub
```

Utility availability

Because the `SortSheets` macro is stored in the Personal Macro Workbook, it is available whenever Excel is running. At this point, the macro can be executed by selecting the macro's name from the Macro dialog box (Alt+F8 displays this dialog box) or by pressing Ctrl+Shift+F8.

If you like, you can also assign this macro to a new toolbar button or to a new menu item. Procedures for doing this are described earlier in this chapter.

Evaluating the project

So there you have it. The utility meets all the original project requirements: It sorts all sheets in the active workbook, it can be executed easily, it's always available, it seems to work for any workbook, and I have yet to see it display a VBA error message.

The procedure still has one slight problem: The sorting is strict and may not always be "logical." For example, after sorting, `Sheet11` is placed before `Sheet2`. Most would want `Sheet2` to be listed before `Sheet11`.

My Power Utility Pak add-in includes a much more sophisticated sheet sorting utility that handles the potential problem described in the preceding Note.

Chapter 10

Creating Function Procedures

IN THIS CHAPTER

A function is a VBA procedure that returns a value. You can use these functions in your Visual Basic for Applications (VBA) code or in formulas.

- ◆ The difference between Sub procedures and Function procedures

- ◆ How to create custom functions

- ◆ About Function procedures and function arguments

- ◆ How to create a function that emulates Excel SUM function

- ◆ How to debug functions, deal with the Paste Function dialog box, and use add-ins to store custom functions

- ◆ How to call the Windows Application Programming Interface (API) to perform otherwise impossible feats

VBA ENABLES YOU TO CREATE SUB PROCEDURES AND FUNCTION PROCEDURES. I cover Sub procedures in the preceding chapter, and in this chapter I discuss Function procedures.

Chapter 11 has many useful and practical examples of Function procedures. You can incorporate many of those techniques into your work.

Sub Procedures versus Function Procedures

You can think of a Sub procedure as a command that can be executed either by the user or by another procedure. Function procedures, on the other hand, usually return a single value (or an array), just like Excel worksheet functions and VBA built-in functions do. Like with built-in functions, your Function procedures can use arguments.

`Function` procedures are quite versatile and can be used in two situations:

◆ As part of an expression in a VBA procedure

◆ In formulas that you create in a worksheet

In fact, you can use a `Function` procedure anywhere that you can use an Excel worksheet function or a VBA built-in function.

Why Create Custom Functions?

You are undoubtedly familiar with Excel worksheet functions; even novices know how to use the most common worksheet functions, such as SUM, AVERAGE, and IF. By my count, Excel contains more than 300 predefined worksheet functions, plus additional functions available through the Analysis ToolPak add-in. If that's not enough, however, you can create custom functions by using VBA.

With all the functions available in Excel and VBA, you might wonder why you would ever need to create new functions. The answer: to simplify your work. With a bit of planning, custom functions are very useful in worksheet formulas and VBA procedures.

Often, for example, you can create a custom function that can significantly shorten your formulas. And shorter formulas are more readable and easier to work with. I should also point out, however, that custom functions used in your formulas are usually much slower than built-in functions.

When you create applications, you may notice that some procedures repeat certain calculations. In such a case, consider creating a custom function that performs the calculation. Then you can simply call the function from your procedure. A custom function can eliminate the need for duplicated code, thus reducing errors.

Also, co-workers often can benefit from your specialized functions. And some may be willing to pay you to create custom functions that save them time and work.

Although many cringe at the thought of creating custom worksheet functions, the process is not difficult. In fact, I *enjoy* creating custom functions. I especially like how my custom functions appear in the Paste Function dialog box along with Excel built-in functions, as if I'm re-engineering the software in some way.

In this chapter, I tell you what you need to know to start creating custom functions, and I provide lots of examples.

An Introductory Function Example

Without further ado, this section presents an example of a VBA `Function` procedure.

A custom function

The following is a custom function defined in a VBA module. This function, named Reverse, uses a single argument. The function reverses the characters in its argument (so that it reads backwards) and returns the result as a string.

If you use Excel 2000 or later, there is no real reason to create this function. You can just use the VBA StrReverse function.

```
Function Reverse(InString) As String
'    Returns its argument, reversed
     Dim StringLength as Integer , i as Integer
     Reverse = ""
     StringLength = Len(InString)
     For i = StringLength To 1 Step -1
         Reverse = Reverse & Mid(InString, i, 1)
     Next i
End Function
```

I explain how this function works later, in the "Analyzing the custom function" section.

When you create custom functions that will be used in a worksheet formula, make sure that the code resides in a normal VBA module. If you place your custom functions in a code module for a Sheet or ThisWorkbook, they will not work in your formulas.

Using the function in a worksheet

When you enter a formula that uses the Reverse function, Excel executes the code to get the value. Here's an example of how you would use the function in a formula:

```
=Reverse(A1)
```

See Figure 10-1 for examples of this function in action. The formulas are in column B, and they use the text in column A as their argument. As you can see, it returns its single argument, but its characters are in reverse order.

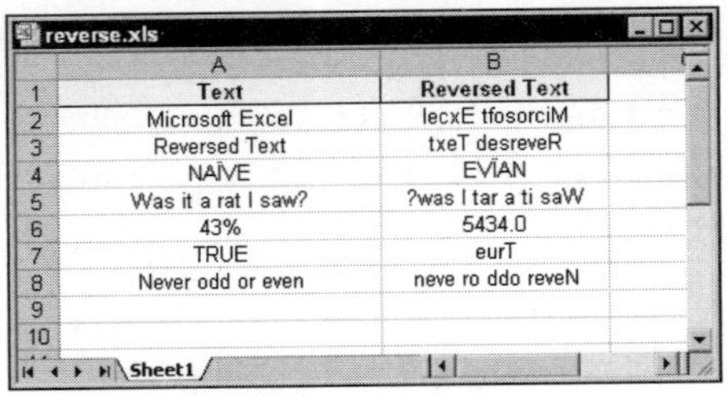

Figure 10-1: Using a custom function in a worksheet formula.

Actually, the function works pretty much like any built-in worksheet function. You can insert it in a formula by choosing the Insert → Function command or by clicking the Insert Function button (to the left of the formula bar). Either of these actions displays the Insert Function dialog box. In the Insert Function dialog box, your custom functions are located, by default, in the User Defined category.

Notice that in a few cases, the result of using the Reverse function leads to surprising results. If the function is applied to a value, the result is the unformatted value. And when used with a Boolean value (TRUE or FALSE), the function does not maintain the case of the text.

You can also nest custom functions and combine them with other elements in your formulas. For example, the following (useless) formula uses the Reverse function twice. The result is the original string:

```
=Reverse(Reverse(A1))
```

Using the function in a VBA procedure

In addition to using custom functions in worksheet formulas, you can also use them in other VBA procedures. The following VBA procedure, which is defined in the same module as the custom Reverse function, first displays an input box to solicit some text from the user. Then the procedure uses the VBA built-in MsgBox function to display the user input after it's processed by the Reverse function (see Figure 10-2). The original input appears as the caption in the message box.

```
Sub ReverseIt()
    Dim UserInput as String
    UserInput = InputBox("Enter some text:")
    MsgBox Reverse(UserInput), , UserInput
End Sub
```

In the example shown in Figure 10-2, the string entered in response to the InputBox function was Excel Power Programming With VBA. The MsgBox function displays the reversed text.

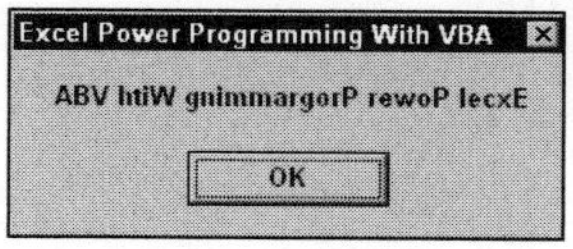

Figure 10-2: Using a custom function in a VBA procedure.

Analyzing the custom function

Function procedures can be as complex as you need. Most of the time, they are more complex and much more useful than this sample procedure. Nonetheless, an analysis of this example may help you understand what is happening.

Here's the code, again:

```
Function Reverse(InString) As String
'    Returns its argument, reversed
     Dim StringLength as Integer, i as Integer
     Reverse = ""
     StringLength = Len(InString)
     For i = StringLength To 1 Step -1
          Reverse = Reverse & Mid(InString, i, 1)
     Next i
End Function
```

Notice that the procedure starts with the keyword Function, rather than Sub, followed by the name of the function (Reverse). This custom function uses only one argument (InString), enclosed in parentheses. As String defines the data type of the function's return value. (Excel uses the Variant data type if no data type is specified.)

The second line is simply a comment (optional) that describes what the function does. This is followed by a Dim statement for the two variables (StringLength and i) used in the procedure.

The procedure initializes the result as an empty string. Note that I use the function name as a variable here. When a function ends, it always returns the current value of the variable that corresponds to the function's name.

Next, VBA's Len function determines the length of the input string and assigns this value to the StringLength variable.

The next three instructions make up a For-Next loop. The procedure loops through each character in the input (backwards) and builds the string. Notice that the Step value in the For-Next loop is a negative number, causing the looping to proceed in reverse. The instruction within the loop uses VBA's Mid function to return a single character from the input string. When the loop is finished, Reverse consists of the input string, with the characters rearranged in reverse order. This string is the value that the function returns.

The procedure ends with an End Function statement.

What Custom Worksheet Functions Can't Do

When you develop custom functions, it's important to understand a key distinction between functions that you call from other VBA procedures and functions that you use in worksheet formulas. Function procedures used in worksheet formulas must be passive. For example, code within a Function procedure cannot manipulate ranges or change things on the worksheet. An example can help make this clear.

You might be tempted to write a custom worksheet function that changes a cell's formatting. For example, it could be useful to have a formula that uses a custom function to change the color of text in a cell based on the cell's value. Try as you might, however, such a function is impossible to write. No matter what you do, the function will always return an error. Remember, a function simply returns a value. It cannot perform actions with objects.

Function Procedures

A custom Function procedure has a lot in common with a Sub procedure. (For more information on Sub procedures, see Chapter 9.)

Declaring a function

The syntax for declaring a function is as follows:

```
[Public | Private][Static] Function name ([arglist])[As type]
    [instructions]
    [name = expression]
    [Exit Function]
    [instructions]
    [name = expression]
End Function
```

In which:

◆ Public: (Optional) Indicates that the Function procedure is accessible to all other procedures in all other modules in all active Excel VBA projects.

◆ Private: (Optional) Indicates that the Function procedure is accessible only to other procedures in the same module.

◆ Static: (Optional) Indicates that the values of variables declared in the Function procedure are preserved between calls.

◆ Function: (Required) Is the keyword that indicates the beginning of a procedure that returns a value or other data.

◆ *name:* (Required) Represents any valid Function procedure name, which must follow the same rules as a variable name.

◆ *arglist:* (Optional) Represents a list of one or more variables that represent arguments passed to the Function procedure. The arguments are enclosed in parentheses. Use a comma to separate pairs of arguments.

◆ *type:* (Optional) Is the data type returned by the Function procedure.

◆ *instructions:* (Optional) Are any number of valid VBA instructions.

◆ Exit Function: (Optional) Is a statement that forces an immediate exit from the Function procedure prior to its completion.

◆ End Function: (Required) Is a keyword that indicates the end of the Function procedure.

The main thing to remember about a custom function written in VBA is that a value is always assigned to its name a minimum of one time, generally when it has completed execution.

To create a custom function, start by inserting a VBA module. (Or you can use an existing module.) Enter the keyword Function, followed by the function name and a list of its arguments (if any) in parentheses. You can also declare the data type of the return value by using the As keyword (this is optional, but recommended). Insert the VBA code that performs the work, making sure that the appropriate value is assigned to the term corresponding to the function name at least once within the body of the Function procedure. End the function with an End Function statement.

Function names must adhere to the same rules for variable names. If you plan to use your custom function in a worksheet formula, make sure that the name is not in the form of a cell address: For example, a function named J21 won't work in a formula. And, avoid using function names that correspond to Excel's built-in function names. If there is a function name conflict, Excel will always use its built-in function.

A function's scope

In Chapter 9, I discuss the concept of a procedure's scope (public or private). The same discussion applies to functions: A function's scope determines whether it can be called by procedures in other modules or in worksheets.

Here are a few things to keep in mind about a function's scope:

◆ If you don't declare a function's scope, its default is Public.

◆ Functions declared As Private do not appear in Excel's Paste Function dialog box. Therefore, when you create a function that should be used only in a VBA procedure, you should declare it Private so that users don't try to use it in a formula.

◆ If your VBA code needs to call a function that's defined in another work-book, set up a reference to the other workbook by choosing the Visual Basic Editor (VBE) Tools → References command.

Executing function procedures

Although you can execute a `Sub` procedure in many ways, you can execute a `Function` procedure in only two ways:

◆ Call it from another procedure

◆ Use it in a worksheet formula

FROM A PROCEDURE

You can call custom functions from a procedure the same way that you call built-in functions. For example, after you define a function called `SumArray`, you can enter a statement like the following:

```
Total = SumArray(MyArray)
```

This statement executes the `SumArray` function with `MyArray` as its argument, returns the function's result, and assigns it to the `Total` variable.

You also can use the `Run` method of the `Application` object. Here's an example:

```
Total = Application.Run ("SumArray", "MyArray")
```

The first argument for the `Run` method is the function name. Subsequent arguments represent the argument(s) for the function. The arguments for the `Run` method can be literal strings (as shown above), numbers, or variables.

IN A WORKSHEET FORMULA

Using custom functions in a worksheet formula is like using built-in functions except that you must ensure that Excel can locate the `Function` procedure. If the `Function` procedure is in the same workbook, you don't have to do anything special. If it's in a different workbook, you may have to tell Excel where to find it.

You can do so in three ways:

◆ *Precede the function name with a file reference.* For example, if you want to use a function called `CountNames` that's defined in an open workbook named `Myfuncs.xls`, you can use the following reference:

```
=Myfuncs.xls!CountNames(A1:A1000)
```

If you insert the function with the Paste Function dialog box, the workbook reference is inserted automatically.

◆ *Set up a reference to the workbook.* You do so by choosing the VBE Tools →
References command. If the function is defined in a referenced workbook,
you don't need to use the worksheet name. Even when the dependent
workbook is assigned as a reference, the Paste Function dialog box continues to insert the workbook reference (although it's not necessary).

◆ *Create an add-in.* When you create an add-in from a workbook that has
Function procedures, you don't need to use the file reference when you
use one of the functions in a formula. The add-in must be installed, however. I discuss add-ins in Chapter 21.

You'll notice that unlike Sub procedures, your Function procedures do not appear
in the Macro dialog box when you issue the Tools → Macro → Macros command. In
addition, you can't choose a function when you issue the VBE Run → Sub/UserForm
command (or press F5) if the cursor is located in a Function procedure. (You get
the Macro dialog box that lets you choose a macro to run.) As a result, you need to
do a bit of extra up-front work to test your functions while you're developing them.
One approach is to set up a simple procedure that calls the function. If the function
is designed to be used in worksheet formulas, you'll want to enter a simple formula
to test it.

Function Arguments

Keep in mind the following points about Function procedure arguments:

◆ Arguments can be variables (including arrays), constants, literals, or
expressions.

◆ Some functions do not have arguments.

◆ Some functions have a fixed number of required arguments (from 1 to 60).

◆ Some functions have a combination of required and optional arguments.

If your formula uses a custom worksheet function and it returns #VALUE!,
there is an error in your function. The error could be caused by logical errors
in your code, by passing incorrect arguments to the function, or by performing an illegal action (such as attempting to change the formatting of a cell).
See "Debugging Functions" later in this chapter.

Reinventing the Wheel

Just for fun, I wrote my own version of Excel's UPPER function (which converts a string to all uppercase) and named it UpCase:

```
Function UpCase(InString As String) As String
'     Converts its argument to all uppercase.
     Dim StringLength As Integer
     Dim i As Integer
     Dim ASCIIVal As Integer
     Dim CharVal As Integer

     StringLength = Len(InString)
     UpCase = InString
     For i = 1 To StringLength
         ASCIIVal = Asc(Mid(InString, i, 1))
         CharVal = 0
         If ASCIIVal >= 97 And ASCIIVal <= 122 Then
             CharVal = -32
             Mid(UpCase, i, 1) = Chr(ASCIIVal + CharVal)
         End If
     Next i

End Function
```

Notice that I resisted the urge to take the easy route — using the VBA UCase function.

I was curious to see how the custom function differed from the built-in function, so I created a worksheet that called the function 20,000 times, using an argument that was 26 characters long. The worksheet took about nine seconds to calculate. I then substituted Excel's UPPER function and ran the test again. The recalculation time was virtually instantaneous.

I don't claim that my UpCase function is the optimal algorithm for this task, but it's safe to say that a custom function will never match the speed of Excel's built-in functions.

Function Examples

In this section, I present a series of examples, demonstrating how to use arguments effectively with functions. By the way, this discussion also applies to Sub procedures.

All the function examples in this section are available on the companion CD-ROM.

A function with no argument

Like Sub procedures, Function procedures need not have arguments. Excel, for example, has a few built-in functions that don't use arguments, including RAND( ), TODAY( ), and NOW( ). You can create similar functions.

Here's a simple example of a function that doesn't use an argument. The following function returns the UserName property of the Application object. This name appears in the Options dialog box (General tab) and is stored in the Windows Registry.

```
Function User()
'    Returns the name of the current user
     User = Application.UserName
End Function
```

When you enter the following formula, the cell returns the name of the current user (assuming that it's listed properly in the Registry):

```
=User()
```

 When you use a function with no arguments in a worksheet formula, you must include a set of empty parentheses. This requirement is not necessary if you call the function in a VBA procedure, although including the empty parentheses does make it clear that you're calling a function.

To use this function in another procedure, you must assign it to a variable, use it in an expression, or use it as an argument for another function.

The following example calls the User function and uses the return value as an argument for the MsgBox statement. The concatenation operator (&) joins the literal string with the result of the User function.

```
Sub ShowUser()
    MsgBox "Your name is " & User()
End Sub
```

Another function with no argument

I used to use Excel's RAND( ) function to quickly fill a range of cells with values. But I didn't like the fact that the random numbers change whenever the worksheet is recalculated. So I usually had to convert the formulas to values by choosing the Edit → Paste Special command (with the Values option).

Then I realized that I could create a custom function that returned random numbers that didn't change. I used the VBA built-in Rnd function, which returns a random number between 0 and 1. The custom function is as follows:

```
Function StaticRand()
'    Returns a random number that doesn't
'    change when recalculated
     StaticRand = Rnd()
End Function
```

If you want to generate a series of random integers between 0 and 1,000, you can use a formula such as this:

```
=INT(StaticRand()*1000)
```

The values produced by this formula never change, unlike those created by the built-in RAND( ) function.

Controlling Function Recalculation

When you use a custom function in a worksheet formula, when is it recalculated?

Custom functions behave like Excel's built-in worksheet functions. Normally, a custom function is recalculated only when it needs to be — which is only when any of the function's arguments are modified. You can, however, force functions to recalculate more frequently. Adding the following statement to a Function procedure makes the function recalculate whenever the sheet is recalculated. If you're using automatic calculation mode, a calculation occurs whenever any cell is changed.

```
Application.Volatile True
```

The Volatile method of the Application object has one argument (either True or False). Marking a Function procedure as volatile forces the function to be calculated whenever recalculation occurs for any cell in the worksheet.

For example, the custom StaticRand function can be changed to emulate Excel's RAND() function using the Volatile method, as follows:

```
Function NonStaticRand()
'    Returns a random number that
'    changes with each calculation
     Application.Volatile True
     NonStaticRand = Rnd()

End Function
```

Using the False argument of the Volatile method causes the function to be recalculated only when one or more of its arguments change as a result of a recalculation. (If a function has no arguments, this method has no effect.)

To force an entire recalculation, including nonvolatile custom functions, press Ctrl+Alt+F9. This key combination, for example, will generate new random numbers for the StaticRand function presented in this chapter.

A function with one argument

This section describes a function for sales managers who need to calculate the commissions earned by their sales forces. The calculations in this example are based on the following table:

Monthly Sales	Commission Rate
0–$9,999	8.0%
$10,000–$19,999	10.5%
$20,000–$39,999	12.0%
$40,000+	14.0%

Note that the commission rate is nonlinear and also depends on the month's total sales. Employees who sell more earn a higher commission rate.

There are several ways to calculate commissions for various sales amounts entered into a worksheet. If you're not thinking too clearly, you might waste lots of time and come up with a lengthy formula such as this:

```
=IF(AND(A1>=0,A1<=9999.99),A1*0.08,
 IF(AND(A1>=10000,A1<=19999.99),A1*0.105,
 IF(AND(A1>=20000,A1<=39999.99),A1*0.12,
 IF(A1>=40000,A1*0.14,0))))
```

This is a bad approach for a couple of reasons. First, the formula is overly complex, making it difficult to understand. Second, the values are hard-coded into the formula, making the formula difficult to modify.

A better (non-VBA) approach is to use a lookup table function to compute the commissions. For example, the following formula uses VLOOKUP to retrieve the commission value from a range named Table, and multiplies that value by the value in cell A1.

```
=VLOOKUP(A1,Table,2)*A1
```

Yet another approach (which eliminates the need to use a lookup table) is to create a custom function such as the following:

```
Function Commission(Sales)
    Const Tier1 = 0.08
    Const Tier2 = 0.105
    Const Tier3 = 0.12
    Const Tier4 = 0.14
'   Calculates sales commissions
    Select Case Sales
        Case 0 To 9999.99: Commission = Sales * Tier1
        Case 10000 To 19999.99: Commission = Sales * Tier2
        Case 20000 To 39999.99: Commission = Sales * Tier3
        Case Is >= 40000: Commission = Sales * Tier4
    End Select
End Function
```

After you enter this function in a VBA module, you can use it in a worksheet formula or call the function from other VBA procedures.

Entering the following formula into a cell produces a result of 3,000; the amount — 25,000 — qualifies for a commission rate of 12 percent:

```
=Commission(25000)
```

Even if you don't need custom functions in a worksheet, creating Function procedures can make your VBA coding much simpler. For example, if your VBA procedure calculates sales commissions, you can use the exact same function and call it from a VBA procedure. Here's a tiny procedure that asks the user for a sales amount and then uses the Commission function to calculate the commission due:

```
Sub CalcComm()
    Dim Sales as Long
    Sales = InputBox("Enter Sales:")
    MsgBox "The commission is " & Commission(Sales)
End Sub
```

The `CalcComm` procedure starts by displaying an input box that asks for the sales amount. Then it displays a message box with the calculated sales commission for that amount.

This `Sub` procedure works, but it is rather crude. Following is an enhanced version that displays formatted values and keeps looping until the user clicks No (see Figure 10-3).

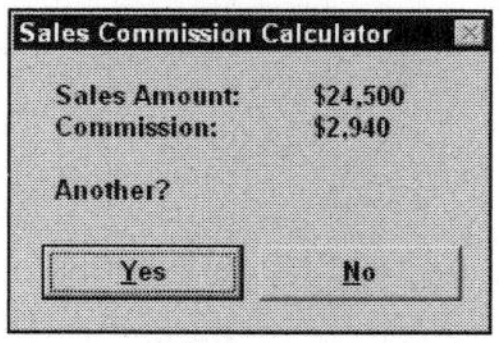

Figure 10-3: Using a function to display the result of a calculation.

```
Sub CalcComm()
    Dim Sales As Long
    Dim Msg As String, Ans As String

'   Prompt for sales amount
    Sales = Val(InputBox("Enter Sales:", _
     "Sales Commission Calculator"))

'   Build the Message
    Msg = "Sales Amount:" & vbTab & Format(Sales, "$#,##0.00")
    Msg = Msg & vbCrLf & "Commission:" & vbTab
    Msg = Msg & Format(Commission(Sales), "$#,##0.00")
    Msg = Msg & vbCrLf & vbCrLf & "Another?"

'   Display the result and prompt for another
    Ans = MsgBox(Msg, vbYesNo, "Sales Commission Calculator")
    If Ans = vbYes Then CalcComm
End Sub
```

This function uses two VBA built-in constants: `vbTab` represents a tab (to space the output), and `vbCrLf` specifies a carriage return and line feed (to skip to the next line). VBA's `Format` function displays a value in a specified format (in this case, with a dollar sign, comma, and two decimal places).

In both of these examples, the `Commission` function must be available in the active workbook; otherwise, Excel displays an error message saying that the function is not defined.

A function with two arguments

Imagine that the aforementioned hypothetical sales managers implement a new policy to help reduce turnover: The total commission paid is increased by 1 percent for every year that the salesperson has been with the company.

I modified the custom `Commission` function (defined in the preceding section) so that it takes two arguments. The new argument represents the number of years. Call this new function `Commission2`:

```
Function Commission2(Sales, Years)
'    Calculates sales commissions based on
'    years in service
     Const Tier1 = 0.08
     Const Tier2 = 0.105
     Const Tier3 = 0.12
     Const Tier4 = 0.14
     Select Case Sales
        Case 0 To 9999.99: Commission2 = Sales * Tier1
        Case 10000 To 19999.99: Commission2 = Sales * Tier2
        Case 20000 To 39999.99: Commission2 = Sales * Tier3
        Case Is >= 40000: Commission2 = Sales * Tier4
     End Select
     Commission2 = Commission2 + (Commission2 * Years / 100)
End Function
```

Pretty simple, eh? I just added the second argument (`Years`) to the `Function` statement and included an additional computation that adjusts the commission.

Here's an example of how you can write a formula using this function (it assumes that the sales amount is in cell A1 and the number of years the salesperson has worked is in cell B1):

```
=Commission2(A1,B1)
```

A function with an array argument

A `Function` procedure also can accept one or more arrays as arguments, process the array(s), and return a single value. The array can also consist of a range of cells.

The following function accepts an array as its argument and returns the sum of its elements:

```
Function SumArray(List) As Double
    Dim Item As Variant
    SumArray = 0
```

```
    For Each Item In List
        If WorksheetFunction.IsNumber(Item) Then _
            SumArray = SumArray + Item
    Next Item
End Function
```

Excel's IsNumber function checks to see whether each element is a number before adding it to the total. Adding this simple error-checking statement eliminates the type-mismatch error that occurs when you try to perform arithmetic with a string.

The following procedure demonstrates how to call this function from a `Sub` procedure. The `MakeList` procedure creates a 100-element array and assigns a random number to each element. Then the `MsgBox` function displays the sum of the values in the array by calling the `SumArray` function.

```
Sub MakeList()
    Dim Nums(1 To 100) As Double
    Dim i as Integer
    For i = 1 To 100
        Nums(i) = Rnd * 1000
    Next i
    MsgBox SumArray(Nums)
End Sub
```

Because the `SumArray` function doesn't declare the data type of its argument (it's a variant), the function also works in your worksheet formulas. For example, the following formula returns the sum of the values in A1:C10:

```
=SumArray(A1:C10)
```

You might notice that, when used in a worksheet formula, the `SumArray` function works very much like Excel's SUM function. One difference, however, is that `SumArray` does not accept multiple arguments. (SUM accepts up to 30 arguments.) Be aware that this example is for educational purposes only. Using the `SumArray` function in a formula offers absolutely no advantages over the Excel SUM function.

A function with optional arguments

Many of Excel's built-in worksheet functions use optional arguments. An example is the LEFT function, which returns characters from the left side of a string. Its syntax is

```
LEFT(text,num_chars)
```

The first argument is required, but the second is optional. If the optional argument is omitted, Excel assumes a value of 1. Therefore, the following two formulas return the same result:

```
=LEFT(A1,1)
=LEFT(A1)
```

The custom functions that you develop in VBA also can have optional arguments. You specify an optional argument by preceding the argument's name with the keyword Optional. In the argument list, optional arguments must appear after any required arguments.

Following is a simple function example that returns the user's name. The function's argument is optional.

```
Function User(Optional UpperCase As Variant)
    If IsMissing(UpperCase) Then UpperCase = False
    If UpperCase = True Then
        User = Ucase(Application.UserName)
    Else
        User = Application.UserName
    End If
End Function
```

If the argument is False or omitted, the user's name is returned without any changes. If the argument is True, the user's name converts to uppercase (using the VBA Ucase function) before it is returned. Notice that the first statement in the procedure uses the VBA IsMissing function to determine whether the argument was supplied. If the argument is missing, the statement sets the UpperCase variable to False (the default value).

All the following formulas are valid (and the first two have the same effect):

```
=User()
=User(False)
=User(True)
```

 If you need to determine whether an optional argument was passed to a function, you must declare the optional argument as a Variant data type. Then you can use the IsMissing function within the procedure, as demonstrated in this example.

The following is another example of a custom function that uses an optional argument. This function randomly chooses one cell from an input range and returns that cell's contents. If the second argument is True, the selected value changes whenever the worksheet is recalculated (that is, the function is made volatile). If the second argument is False (or omitted), the function is not recalculated unless one of the cells in the input range is modified.

```
Function DrawOne(RngAs Variant, Optional Recalc As Variant = False)
'    Chooses one cell at random from a range

'    Make function volatile if Recalc is True
     Application.Volatile Recalc

'    Determine a random cell
     DrawOne = Rng(Int((Rng.Count) * Rnd + 1))
End Function
```

Notice that the second argument for DrawOne includes the Optional keyword, along with a default value.

All the following formulas are valid, and the first two have the same effect:

```
=Draw(A1:A100)
=Draw(A1:A100,False)
=Draw(A1:A100,True)
```

This function might be useful for choosing lottery numbers, picking a winner from a list of names, and so on.

A function that returns a VBA array

VBA includes a useful function called Array. The Array function returns a variant that contains an array (that is, multiple values). If you're familiar with array formulas in Excel, you'll have a head start understanding VBA's Array function. You enter an array formula into a cell by pressing Ctrl+Shift+Enter. Excel inserts brackets around the formula to indicate that it's an array formula. See Chapter 3 for more details on array formulas.

 It's important to understand that the array returned by the Array function is not the same as a normal array that's made up of elements of the Variant data type. In other words, a variant array is not the same as an array of variants.

The MonthNames function, which follows, is a simple example that uses VBA's Array function in a custom function:

```
Function MonthNames()
    MonthNames = Array("Jan", "Feb", "Mar", "Apr","May", "Jun", _
        "Jul", "Aug", "Sep", "Oct", "Nov", "Dec")
End Function
```

The `MonthNames` function returns a horizontal array of month names. You can create a multicell array formula that uses the `MonthNames` function. Here's how to use it: Make sure that the function code is present in a VBA module. Then in a worksheet, select multiple cells in a row (start by selecting 12 cells). Then enter the formula that follows, followed by pressing Ctrl+Shift+Enter:

```
=MonthNames()
```

What if you'd like to generate a vertical list of month names? No problem; just select a vertical range, enter the following formula, and then press Ctrl+Shift+ Enter:

```
=TRANSPOSE(MonthNames())
```

This formula uses the Excel TRANSPOSE function to convert the horizontal array to a vertical array.

The following example is a variation on the `MonthNames` function:

```
Function MonthNames(Optional MIndex)
    Dim AllNames As Variant
    AllNames = Array("Jan", "Feb", "Mar", "Apr", _
      "May", "Jun", "Jul", "Aug", "Sep", "Oct", _
      "Nov", "Dec")
    If IsMissing(MIndex) Then
        MonthNames = AllNames
    Else
        Select Case MIndex
            Case Is >= 1
              'Determine month value (for example, 13=1)
              MonthVal = ((MIndex - 1) Mod 12)
              MonthNames = AllNames(MonthVal)
            Case Is <= 0 ' Vertical array
              MonthNames = Application.Transpose(AllNames)
        End Select
    End If
End Function
```

Notice that I use the VBA `IsMissing` function to test for a missing argument. In this situation, it is not possible to specify the default value for the missing argument in the argument list of the function because the default value is defined within the function. You can use the IsMissing function only if the optional argument is a variant.

This enhanced function uses an optional argument that works as follows:

◆ *If the argument is missing*, the function returns a horizontal array of month names.

◆ *If the argument is less than or equal to 0*, the function returns a vertical array of month names. It uses Excel's TRANSPOSE function to convert the array.

◆ *If the argument is greater than or equal to 1*, it returns the month name that corresponds to the argument value.

This procedure uses the Mod operator to determine the month value. The Mod operator returns the remainder after dividing the first operand by the second. An argument of 13, for example, returns 1. An argument of 24 returns 12, and so on. Keep in mind that the AllNames array is zero-based and that indices range from 0–11. In the statement that uses the Mod operator, 1 is subtracted from the function's argument. Therefore, an argument of 13 returns 0 (corresponding to Jan), and an argument of 24 returns 11 (corresponding to Dec).

You can use this function in a number of ways, as illustrated in Figure 10-4.

	A	B	C	D	E	F	G	H	I	J	K	L	M
1	Jan	Feb	Mar	Apr	May	Jun	Jul	Aug	Sep	Oct	Nov	Dec	
2													
3	1	Jan		Jan									
4	2	Feb		Feb									
5	3	Mar		Mar									
6	4	Apr		Apr									
7	5	May		May									
8	6	Jun		Jun									
9	7	Jul		Jul									
10	8	Aug		Aug									
11	9	Sep		Sep									
12	10	Oct		Oct									
13	11	Nov		Nov									
14	12	Dec		Dec									
15													
16													

month names.xls

Figure 10-4: Different ways of passing an array or a single value to a worksheet.

Range A1:L1 contains the following formula entered as an array. Start by selecting A1:L1, enter the formula, and then press Ctrl+Shift+Enter.

```
=MonthNames()
```

Range A3:A14 contains integers from 1 to 12. Cell B3 contains the following (nonarray) formula, which was copied to the 11 cells below it:

```
=MonthNames(A3)
```

Range D3:D14 contains the following formula entered as an array:

```
=MonthNames(-1)
```

Remember: To enter an array formula, you must press Ctrl+Shift+Enter.

 The lower bound of an array created using the Array function is determined by the lower bound specified with the Option Base statement at the top of the module. If there is no Option Base statement, the default lower bound is 0.

A function that returns an error value

In some cases, you might want your custom function to return a particular error value. Consider the Reverse function, which I presented earlier in this chapter:

```
Function Reverse(InString) As String
'    Returns its argument, reversed
    Dim i as Integer, StringLength as Integer
    Reverse = ""
    StringLength = Len(InString)
    For i = StringLength To 1 Step -1
        Reverse = Reverse & Mid(InString, i, 1)
    Next i
End Function
```

When used in a worksheet formula, this function reverses the contents of its single-cell argument (which can be text or a value). Assume that you want this function to work only with text strings. If the argument doesn't contain a string, you want the function to return an error value (#N/A).

You might be tempted simply to assign a string that looks like an Excel formula error value. For example:

```
Reverse = "#N/A"
```

Although the string *looks* like an error value, it is not treated as such by other formulas that may reference it. To return a *real* error value from a function, use the VBA CVErr function, which converts an error number to a real error.

Fortunately, VBA has built-in constants for the errors that you would want to return from a custom function. These errors are Excel formula error values and not VBA runtime error values. These constants are as follows:

- xlErrDiv0 (for #DIV/0!)
- xlErrNA (for #N/A)
- xlErrName (for #NAME?)
- xlErrNull (for #NULL!)
- xlErrNum (for #NUM!)
- xlErrRef (for #REF!)
- xlErrValue (for #VALUE!)

To return a #N/A error from a custom function, you can use a statement like this:

```
Reverse = CVErr(xlErrNA)
```

The revised Reverse function follows. This function uses Excel's IsText function to determine whether the argument contains text. If it does, the function proceeds normally. If the cell doesn't contain text (or is empty), the function returns the #N/A error.

```
Function Reverse(InString) as Variant
'   If a string, returns its argument, reversed
'   Otherwise returns #N/A error
    Dim i as Integer, StringLength as Integer
    If Application.WorksheetFunction.IsText(InString) Then
        Reverse = ""
        StringLength = Len(InString)
        For i = StringLength To 1 Step -1
            Reverse = Reverse & Mid(InString, i, 1)
        Next i
```

```
    Else
        Reverse = CVErr(xlErrNA)
    End If
End Function
```

Notice that I also changed the data type for the function's return value. Because the function can now return something other than a string, I changed the data type to Variant.

A function with an indefinite number of arguments

Some Excel worksheet functions take an indefinite number of arguments. A familiar example is the SUM function, which has the following syntax:

```
SUM(number1,number2...)
```

The first argument is required, but you can have as many as 29 additional arguments. Here's an example of a SUM function with four range arguments:

```
=SUM(A1:A5,C1:C5,E1:E5,G1:G5)
```

You can even mix and match the argument types. For example, the following example uses three arguments: the first is a range, the second is a value, and the third is an expression.

```
=SUM(A1:A5,12,24*3)
```

You can create Function procedures that have an indefinite number of arguments. The trick is to use an array as the last (or only) argument, preceded by the keyword ParamArray.

ParamArray can apply only to the *last* argument in the procedure's argument list. It is always a Variant data type, and it is always an optional argument (although you don't use the Optional keyword).

Following is a function that can have any number of single-value arguments. (It doesn't work with multicell range arguments.) It simply returns the sum of the arguments.

```
Function SimpleSum(ParamArray arglist() As Variant) As Double
    For Each arg In arglist
        SimpleSum = SimpleSum + arg
    Next arg
End Function
```

The `SimpleSum` function is not nearly as flexible as Excel's SUM function. Try it out by using various types of arguments, and you'll see that it fails unless each argument is either a value or a reference to a single cell that contains a value.

Emulating Excel's SUM Function

In this section, I present a custom function called `MySum`. Unlike the `SimpleSum` function listed in the previous section, the `MySum` function emulates Excel's SUM function perfectly.

Before you look at the code for `MySum`, take a minute to think about the Excel SUM function. It is, in fact, very versatile. It can have as many as 30 arguments (even "missing" arguments), and the arguments can be numerical values, cells, ranges, text representations of numbers, logical values, and even embedded functions. For example, consider the following formula:

```
=SUM(B1,5,"6",,TRUE,SQRT(4),A1:A5)
```

This formula, which is a perfectly valid formula, contains all the following types of arguments, listed here in the order of their presentation:

- A single cell reference
- A literal value
- A string that looks like a value
- A missing argument
- A logical TRUE value
- An expression that uses another function
- A range reference

The `MySum` function (see Listing 10-1) handles all these argument types.

A workbook containing the `MySum` function is available on the companion CD-ROM.

Listing 10-1: MySum Function

```
Function MySum(ParamArray args() As Variant) As Variant
' Emulates Excel's SUM function

' Variable declarations
Dim i As Variant
Dim TempRange As Range, cell As Range
Dim ECode As String
MySum = 0

' Process each argument
For i = LBound(args) To UBound(args)
'  Skip missing arguments
  If Not IsMissing(args(i)) Then
'    What type of argument is it?
    Select Case TypeName(args(i))
      Case "Range"
'        Create temp range to handle full row or column ranges
        Set TempRange = Intersect(args(i).Parent.UsedRange, args(i))
        For Each cell In TempRange
          Select Case TypeName(cell.Value)
            Case "Double"
              MySum = MySum + cell.Value
            Case "String"
              'MySum = MySum + Evaluate(cell.Value)
            Case "Error"
              Select Case cell.Text
                Case "#DIV/0!"
                  MySum = CVErr(xlErrDiv0)
                Case "#N/A"
                  MySum = CVErr(xlErrNA)
                Case "#NAME?"
                  MySum = CVErr(xlErrName)
                Case "#NULL!"
                  MySum = CVErr(xlErrNull)
                Case "#NUM!"
                  MySum = CVErr(xlErrNum)
                Case "#REF!"
                  MySum = CVErr(xlErrRef)
                Case "#VALUE!"
                  MySum = CVErr(xlErrValue)
              End Select
              Exit Function
            Case "Date"
              MySum = MySum + cell.Value
```

```
          Case "Empty"
          Case "Boolean"
             MySum = MySum + 0
        End Select
      Next cell
    Case "Null" 'ignore it
    Case "Error" 'return the error
      MySum = args(i)
      Exit Function
    Case "Boolean"
'      Check for literal TRUE and compensate
      If args(i) = "True" Then MySum = MySum + 1
    Case "Date"
      MySum = MySum + args(i)
    Case Else
       MySum = MySum + args(i)
    End Select
  End If
 Next i
End Function
```

As you study the code for MySum, keep the following points in mind:

◆ Missing arguments (determined by the IsMissing function) are simply ignored.

◆ The procedure uses VBA's TypeName function to determine the type of argument (Range, Error, and so on). Each argument type is handled differently.

◆ For a range argument, the function loops through each cell in the range, determines the type of data in the cell, and (if appropriate) adds its value to a running total.

◆ The data type for the function is Variant because the function needs to return an error if any of its arguments is an error value.

◆ If an argument contains an error (for example, #DIV/0!), the MySum function simply returns the error — just like Excel's SUM function.

◆ Excel's SUM function considers a text string to have a value of 0 unless it appears as a literal argument (that is, as an actual value, not a variable). Therefore, MySum adds the cell's value only if it can be evaluated as a number. (VBA's IsNumeric function is used for this.)

◆ For range arguments, the function uses the Intersect method to create a temporary range that consists of the intersection of the range and the sheet's used range. This handles cases in which a range argument consists of a complete row or column, which would take forever to evaluate.

You might be curious about the relative speeds of SUM and `MySum`. `MySum`, of course, is much slower, but just how much slower depends on the speed of your system and the formulas themselves. On my system, a worksheet with 1,000 SUM formulas recalculated instantly. After I replaced the SUM functions with `MySum` functions, it took about eight seconds. `MySum` may be improved a bit, but it can never come close to SUM's speed.

By the way, I hope you understand that the point of this example is *not* to create a new SUM function. Rather, it demonstrates how to create custom worksheet functions that look and work like those built into Excel.

Debugging Functions

When you're using a formula in a worksheet to test a `Function` procedure, runtime errors do not appear in the all-too-familiar, pop-up error box. If an error occurs, the formula simply returns an error value (#VALUE!). Luckily, this does not present a problem for debugging functions because you have several possible workarounds:

◆ *Place `MsgBox` functions at strategic locations to monitor the value of specific variables.* Message boxes in `Function` procedures do pop up when the procedure is executed. But make sure that you have only one formula in the worksheet that uses your function, or message boxes will appear for each formula that is evaluated, which is a repetition that will quickly become annoying.

◆ *Test the procedure by calling it from a `Sub` procedure, not from a worksheet formula.* Runtime errors are displayed in the usual manner, and you can either fix the problem (if you know it) or jump right into the Debugger.

◆ *Set a breakpoint in the function and then step through the function.* You then can access all the standard debugging tools. To set a breakpoint, move the cursor to the statement at which you want to pause execution and then choose Debug → Toggle Breakpoint (or press F9).

◆ *Use one or more temporary `Debug.Print` statements in your code to write values to the VBE Immediate window.* For example, if you want to monitor a value inside of a loop, use something like the following routine:

```
Function VowelCount(r)
    Count = 0
    For i = 1 To Len(r)
        Ch = UCase(Mid(r, i, 1))
        If Ch Like "[AEIOU]" Then
            Count = Count + 1
            Debug.Print Ch, i
        End If
```

```
      Next i
      VowelCount = Count
End Function
```

In this case, the values of two variables, Ch and i, are printed to the Immediate window whenever the Debug.Print statement is encountered. Figure 10-5 shows the result when the function has an argument of Mississippi.

Figure 10-5: Use the Immediate window to display results while a function is running.

Dealing with the Insert Function Dialog Box

Excel's Insert Function dialog box is a handy tool. When creating a worksheet formula, this tool lets you select a particular worksheet function from a list of functions (see Figure 10-6). These functions are grouped into various categories to make it easier to locate a particular function. The Insert Function dialog box also displays your custom worksheet functions and prompts you for a function's arguments.

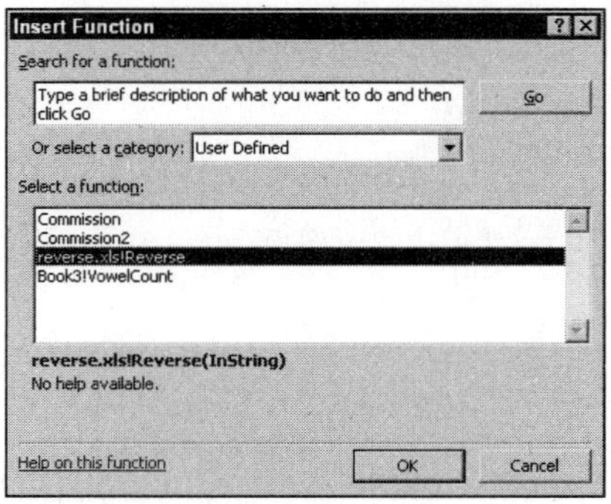

Figure 10-6: Inserting a custom function into a formula.

Custom `Function` procedures defined with the `Private` keyword do not appear in the Paste Function dialog box (although they can still be entered into formulas manually). If you develop a function for exclusive use of your other VBA procedures, you should declare it by using the `Private` keyword.

By default, custom functions are listed under the User Defined category, but you can have them appear under a different category if you like. You also can add some text to describe the function. (I highly recommend this step.)

In the Insert Function dialog box, notice that the workbook name is also displayed for functions that are defined in a workbook other than the active workbook.

In versions prior to Excel 2002, the Insert Function dialog box was known as the Paste Function dialog box. This dialog box was enhanced in Excel 2002 and now offers the ability to search for a function by keyword. Unfortunately, this search feature cannot be used to locate custom functions created in VBA.

Specifying a function category

Oddly, Excel does not provide a direct way to assign a custom function to a category. If you would like your custom function to appear in a function category other than User Defined, you need to do so by writing and executing some VBA code.

The following statement assigns the function named `Commission` to the Financial category (category number 1):

```
Application.MacroOptions Macro:="Commission", Category:=1
```

You only need to execute this statement one time (not each time the workbook is opened). From then on, every time the workbook is opened, the function will appear in the category that you specified.

Table 10-1 lists the category numbers that you can use. Notice that a few of these categories (10 through 13) are normally not displayed in the Insert Function dialog box. If you assign your function to one of these categories, the category will appear in the dialog box.

TABLE 10-1 FUNCTION CATEGORIES

Category Number	Category Name
0	All (no specific category)
1	Financial
2	Date & Time
3	Math & Trig
4	Statistical
5	Lookup & Reference
6	Database
7	Text
8	Logical
9	Information
10	Commands
11	Customizing
12	Macro Control
13	DDE/External
14	User Defined
15	Engineering

Adding a function description

When you select a function in the Insert Function dialog box, a brief description of the function appears (see Figure 10-7). You can specify a description for your custom function in two ways: Either use the Macro dialog box or write VBA code.

If you don't provide a description for your custom function, the Insert Function dialog box displays the following text: `No help available.`

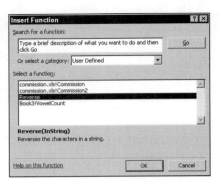

Figure 10-7: Excel's Insert Function dialog
box displays brief descriptions of functions.

DESCRIBING YOUR FUNCTION IN THE MACRO DIALOG BOX

Follow these steps to provide a description for a custom function:

1. Create your function in the VBE.

2. Activate Excel, making sure that the workbook that contains the function is the active workbook.

3. Choose Tools → Macro → Macros (or press Alt+F8).

   The Macro dialog box lists available procedures, but your functions will not be in the list.

4. Type the name of your function in the Macro Name box.

5. Click the Options button to display the Macro Options dialog box.

6. Enter the function description in the Description box (see Figure 10-8). The Shortcut Key field is irrelevant for functions.

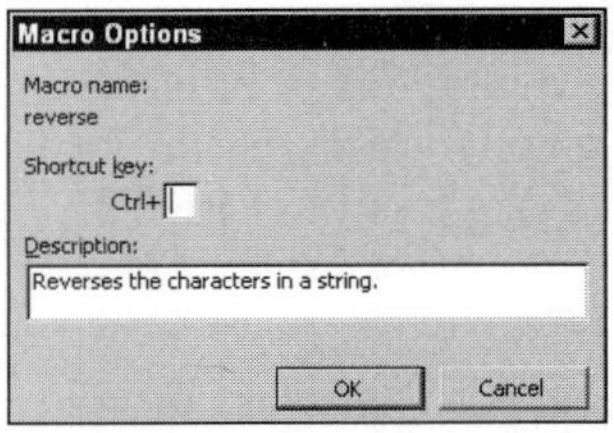

Figure 10-8: Provide a function
description in the Macro Options
dialog box.

7. Click OK and then click Cancel.

After you perform the preceding steps, the Insert Function dialog box displays the description that you entered in Step 6 when the function is selected.

For information on creating a custom help topic accessible from the Insert Function dialog box, refer to Chapter 24.

When you use the Insert Function dialog box to enter a function, the Function Arguments dialog box is displayed after you click OK. For built-in functions, the Function Arguments dialog box displays a description for each of the function's arguments. Unfortunately, you cannot provide such descriptions for custom function arguments.

DESCRIBING YOUR FUNCTION WITH VBA CODE

Another way to provide a description for a custom function is to write VBA code. The following statement assigns a description for the function named Commission:

```
Application.MacroOptions _
    Macro:= "Commission", _
    Description:= "Calculates sales commissions"
```

You need to execute this statement only one time (not each time the workbook is opened).

Using Add-ins to Store Custom Functions

You might prefer to store frequently used custom functions in an add-in file. A primary advantage of doing this is that the functions can be used in formulas without a filename qualifier.

Assume that you have a custom function named ZapSpaces and that it's stored in Myfuncs.xls. To use this function in a formula in a workbook other than Myfuncs.xls, you need to enter the following formula:

```
=Myfuncs.xls!ZapSpaces(A1:C12)
```

If you create an add-in from Myfuncs.xls and the add-in is loaded, you can omit the file reference and enter a formula such as the following:

```
=ZapSpaces(A1:C12)
```

I discuss add-ins in Chapter 21.

Using the Windows API

VBA can borrow methods from other files that have nothing to do with Excel or VBA – for example, the Dynamic Link Library (DLL) files that Windows and other software use. As a result, you can do things with VBA that would otherwise be outside the language's scope.

The Windows *Application Programming Interface* (API) is a set of functions available to Windows programmers. When you call a Windows function from VBA, you're accessing the Windows API. Many of the Windows resources used by Windows programmers are available in *DLLs,* which store programs and functions and are linked at runtime rather than at compile time.

Excel itself uses several DLLs, for example. The code in many of these DLLs could have been compiled right into the `excel.exe` executable file, but the designers chose to store it in DLLs, which are loaded only when needed. This technique makes Excel's main executable file smaller. In addition, it is a more efficient use of memory because the library is loaded only when it's needed.

DLLs are also used to share code. For example, most Windows programs use dialog boxes to open and save files. Windows comes with a DLL that has the code to generate several standard dialog boxes. Programmers thus can call this DLL rather than write their own routines.

If you're a C programmer, you can produce your own DLLs and use them from VBA. Microsoft's Visual Basic language also has the capability to create DLL files that can be called from Excel.

Windows API examples

Before you can use a Windows API function, you must declare the function at the top of your code module. If the code module is not a standard VBA module (that is, it's a code module for a UserForm, Sheet, or ThisWorkbook), you must declare the API function as `Private`.

Declaring an API function is a bit tricky; it must be declared precisely. The declaration statement tells VBA:

♦ Which API function you're using

♦ In which library the API function is located

♦ The API function's arguments

After you declare an API function, you can use it in your VBA code.

Determining the Windows directory

Following is an example of an API function declaration:

```
Declare Function GetWindowsDirectoryA Lib "kernel32" _
  (ByVal lpBuffer As String, ByVal nSize As Long) As Long
```

This function, which has two arguments, returns the name of the directory in which Windows is installed (something that is not normally possible using VBA). After calling the function, the Windows directory is contained in lpBuffer, and the length of the directory string is contained in nSize.

After inserting the Declare statement at the top of your module, you can access the function by calling the GetWindowsDirectoryA function. The following is an example of calling the function and displaying the result in a message box:

```
Sub ShowWindowsDir()
    Dim WinPath As String * 255
    Dim WinDir As String
    WinPath = Space(255)
    WinDir = Left(WinPath, GetWindowsDirectoryA _
        (WinPath, Len(WinPath)))
    MsgBox WinDir, vbInformation, "Windows Directory"
End Sub
```

Executing the ShowWindowsDir procedure displays a message box with the Windows directory.

Often, you'll want to create a *wrapper* for API functions. In other words, you'll create your own function that uses the API function. This greatly simplifies using the API function. Here's an example of a wrapper VBA function:

```
Function WindowsDir() As String
'   Returns the Windows directory
    Dim WinPath As String * 255
    WinPath = Space(255)
    WindowsDir = Left(WinPath, GetWindowsDirectoryA _
        (WinPath, Len(WinPath)))
End Function
```

After declaring this function, you can call it from another procedure:

```
Msgbox WindowsDir()
```

You can even use the function in a worksheet formula:

```
=WindowsDir()
```

The reason for using API calls is to perform an action that would otherwise be impossible (or at least very difficult). If your application needs to find the path of the Windows directory, you could search all day and not find a function in Excel or VBA to do the trick. But knowing how to access the Windows API may solve your problem.

When you work with API calls, system crashes during testing are not uncommon, so save your work often.

Detecting the Shift key

Here's another example: Suppose you've written a VBA macro that will be executed from a toolbar button. Furthermore, suppose you want the macro to perform differently if the user presses the Shift key when the button is clicked. Normally, there is no way to detect whether the Shift key is pressed. But you can use the GetKeyState API function to find out. The GetKeyState function tells you whether a particular key is pressed. It takes a single argument, nVirtKey, which represents the code for the key that you are interested in.

Chapter 11 has several additional examples of using Windows API functions.

The following code demonstrates how to detect whether the Shift key is pressed when the Button_Click event handler procedure is executed. Notice that I define a constant for the Shift key (using a hexadecimal value) and then use this constant as the argument for GetKeyState. If GetKeyState returns a value less than zero, it means that the Shift key was pressed; otherwise, the Shift key was not pressed.

```
Declare Function GetKeyState Lib "user32" _
  (ByVal nVirtKey As Long) As Integer

Sub Button_Click()
    Const VK_SHIFT As Integer = &H10
    If GetKeyState(VK_SHIFT) < 0 Then
        MsgBox "Shift is pressed"
    Else
        MsgBox "Shift is not pressed"
    End If
End Sub
```

A workbook on the companion CD-ROM demonstrates how to detect the following keys (as well as any combinations): Ctrl, Shift, and Alt.

Learning more about API functions

Working with the Windows API functions can be tricky. Many programming reference books list the declarations for common API calls and often provide examples. Usually, you can simply copy the declarations and use the functions without really understanding the details. In reality (at least the reality that I've seen), most Excel programmers take a cookbook approach to API functions. The Internet has hundreds of examples that can be copied and pasted and that work quite reliably.

The companion CD-ROM includes a file named `win32api.txt`, which is a text file that contains Windows API declarations and constants. You can open this file with a text editor and copy the appropriate declarations to a VBA module.

If you develop applications that need to work in all versions of Excel, be aware of some potentially serious compatibility issues that arise when you use API calls. For example, if you develop an application using Excel 97, or later, that uses API calls, the application will not run with Excel 5 — even if you save the workbook in the Excel 5 format — because Excel 5 is a 16-bit application. Excel 97 and later versions are 32-bit applications. Refer to Chapter 26 for additional information and tips on how to circumvent this problem.

Chapter 11

VBA Programming Examples and Techniques

IN THIS CHAPTER

I believe that learning programming concepts is accelerated by a heavy emphasis on examples. And based on the feedback that I've received from readers of previous editions of this book, I have plenty of company. Visual Basic for Applications (VBA) programmers especially benefit from a hands-on approach. A well-thought-out example usually communicates a concept much better than a description of the underlying theory. I decided, therefore, not to write a reference book that painstakingly describes every nuance of VBA. Rather, I prepared numerous examples to demonstrate useful Excel programming techniques.

- ◆ Examples of using VBA to work with ranges

- ◆ Examples of using VBA to work with workbooks and sheets

- ◆ Custom functions for use in your VBA procedures and in worksheet formulas

- ◆ Examples of miscellaneous VBA tricks and techniques

- ◆ Examples of using Windows Application Programming Interface (API) functions

THE PREVIOUS CHAPTERS IN THIS SECTION PROVIDE enough information to get you started. The Help system provides all the details that I left out. In this chapter, I pick up the pace and present examples that solve practical problems while furthering your knowledge of VBA.

I've categorized this chapter's examples into six groups:

- ◆ Working with ranges

- ◆ Working with workbooks and sheets

- ◆ VBA techniques

- ◆ Functions that are useful in your VBA procedures

- ◆ Functions that you can use in worksheet formulas

- ◆ Windows API calls

Using the Examples in this Chapter

Not all the examples in this chapter are intended to be standalone programs. They are, however, set up as executable procedures that you can adapt for your own applications.

I urge you to follow along on your computer as you read this chapter. Better yet, modify the examples and see what happens. I guarantee that this hands-on experience will help you more than reading a reference book.

Subsequent chapters in this book present additional feature-specific examples: charts, pivot tables, events, UserForms, and so on.

Working with Ranges

The examples in this section demonstrate how to manipulate worksheet ranges with VBA.

The examples in this section are available on the companion CD-ROM.

Copying a range

Excel's macro recorder is useful not so much for generating usable code as for discovering the names of relevant objects, methods, and properties. The code that's generated by the macro recorder isn't always the most efficient, but it can usually provide you lots of useful insights.

For example, recording a simple copy-and-paste operation generates five lines of VBA code:

```
Sub Macro1()
    Range("A1").Select
    Selection.Copy
    Range("B1").Select
```

```
        ActiveSheet.Paste
        Application.CutCopyMode = False
End Sub
```

Notice that the generated code selects cell A1, copies it, and then selects cell B1 and performs the paste operation. But in VBA, it's not necessary to select an object to work with it. You would never learn this important point by mimicking the preceding recorded macro code, where two statements incorporate the Select method. This procedure can be replaced with the following much simpler routine, which doesn't select any cells. It also takes advantage of the fact that the Copy method can use an argument that represents the destination for the copied range:

```
Sub CopyRange()
        Range("A1").Copy Range("B1")
End Sub
```

Both of these macros assume that a worksheet is active and that the operation takes place on the active worksheet. To copy a range to a different worksheet or workbook, simply qualify the range reference for the destination. The following example copies a range from Sheet1 in File1.xls to Sheet2 in File2.xls. Because the references are fully qualified, this example works regardless of which workbook is active.

```
Sub CopyRange2()
        Workbooks("File1.xls").Sheets("Sheet1").Range("A1").Copy _
            Workbooks("File2.xls").Sheets("Sheet2").Range("A1")
End Sub
```

Another way to approach this task is to use object variables to represent the ranges, as the following example demonstrates:

```
Sub CopyRange3()
        Dim Rng1 As Range, Rng2 As Range
        Set Rng1 = Workbooks("File1.xls").Sheets("Sheet1").Range("A1")
        Set Rng2 = Workbooks("File2.xls").Sheets("Sheet2").Range("A1")
        Rng1.Copy Rng2
End Sub
```

As you might expect, copying is not limited to one single cell at a time. The following procedure, for example, copies a large range. Notice that the destination consists of only a single cell (which represents the upper-left cell for the destination).

```
Sub CopyRange4()
        Range("A1:C800").Copy Range("D1")
End Sub
```

Moving a range

The VBA instructions for moving a range are very similar to those for copying a range, as the following example demonstrates. The difference is that you use the `Cut` method instead of the `Copy` method. Note that you need to specify only the upper-left cell for the destination range.

The following example moves 18 cells (in A1:C6) to a new location, beginning at cell H1:

```
Sub MoveRange1()
   Range("A1:C6").Cut Range("H1")
End Sub
```

Copying a variably sized range

In many cases, you need to copy a range of cells, but you don't know the exact row and column dimensions of the range. For example, you might have a workbook that tracks weekly sales, and the number of rows changes weekly when you add new data.

Figure 11-1 shows a very common type of worksheet. This range consists of several rows, and the number of rows changes each week. Because you don't know the exact range address at any given time, writing a macro to copy the range requires some additional coding.

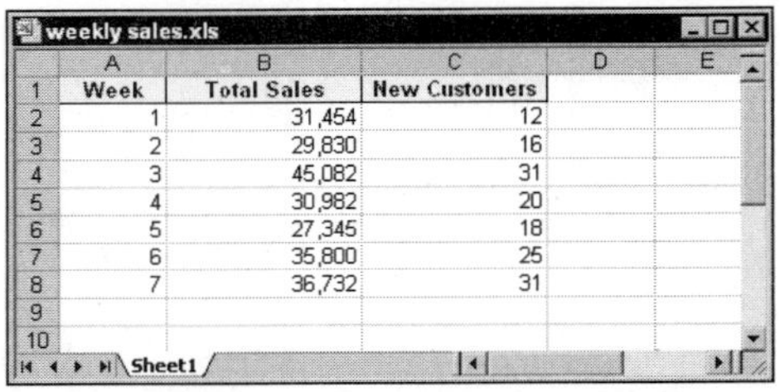

Week	Total Sales	New Customers
1	31,454	12
2	29,830	16
3	45,082	31
4	30,982	20
5	27,345	18
6	35,800	25
7	36,732	31

Figure 11-1: The number of rows in the data range changes every week.

The following macro demonstrates how to copy this range from `Sheet1` to `Sheet2` (beginning at cell A1). It uses the `CurrentRegion` property, which returns a `Range` object that corresponds to the block of cells around a particular cell (in this case, A1).

```
Sub CopyCurrentRegion2()
    Range("A1").CurrentRegion.Copy Sheets("Sheet2").Range("A1")
End Sub
```

Using the `CurrentRegion` property is equivalent to choosing the Edit →
Go To command, clicking the Special button, and selecting the Current
Region option (or by using the Ctrl+* shortcut). To see how this works, record
your actions while you issue that command. Generally, the `CurrentRegion`
property setting consists of a rectangular block of cells surrounded by one
or more blank rows or columns.

Tips for Working with Ranges

When you work with ranges, keep the following points in mind:

◆ Your code doesn't need to select a range in order to work with it.

◆ If your code does select a range, its worksheet must be active. You can use
the `Activate` method of the `Worksheets` collection to activate a particular sheet.

◆ The macro recorder doesn't always generate the most efficient code. Often,
you can create your macro by using the recorder and then edit the code to
make it more efficient.

◆ It's a good idea to use named ranges in your VBA code. For example, referring
to `Range("Total")` is better than `Range("D45")`. In the latter case, if
you add a row above row 45, the cell address will change. You would then
need to modify the macro so that it uses the correct range address (D46).

◆ If you rely on the macro recorder when selecting ranges by using shortcut
keys (for example, pressing Ctrl+Shift+→ to select to the end of a row),
examine your code carefully. Excel sometimes records hard-coded references
to the actual cells that you selected.

◆ When running a macro that works on each cell in the current range selection, the user might select entire columns or rows. In most cases, you don't
want to loop through every cell in the selection. Your macro should create a
subset of the selection consisting of only the nonblank cells. See "Looping
through a selected range efficiently," later in this chapter.

◆ Excel allows multiple selections. For example, you can select a range, press
Ctrl, and select another range. You can test for this in your macro and take
appropriate action. See "Determining the type of selected range," later in this
chapter.

Selecting or otherwise identifying various types of ranges

Much of the work that you will do in VBA will involve working with ranges — either selecting a range or identifying a range so that you can do something with the cells.

In earlier versions of Excel, recording a macro that selects cells (such as pressing Ctrl+Shift+→) was a hit or miss proposition. Beginning with Excel 2002, the macro recorder seems to handle these types of selections much better than in previous versions. However, it's always a good idea to check your recorded code very carefully to make sure that the selection code works as you intended.

In addition to the `CurrentRegion` property (which I discussed earlier), you should also be aware of the `End` method of the `Range` object. The `End` method takes one argument, which determines the direction in which the selection is extended. The following statement selects a range from the active cell to the last nonempty cell:

```
Range(ActiveCell, ActiveCell.End(xlDown)).Select
```

As you might expect, three other constants simulate key combinations in the other directions: `xlUp`, `xlToLeft`, and `xlToRight`.

Be careful when using the `End` method. If the active cell is at the perimeter of a range or if the range contains one or more empty cells, the `End` method may not produce the desired results.

The companion CD-ROM includes a workbook that demonstrates several common types of range selections. When you open this workbook, you'll see a new menu command: `Selection Demo`. This menu contains commands that enable the user to make various types of selections, as shown in Figure 11-2.

The following macro is in the example workbook. The `SelectCurrentRegion` macro simulates pressing Ctrl+Shift+*.

```
Sub SelectCurrentRegion()
    ActiveCell.CurrentRegion.Select
End Sub
```

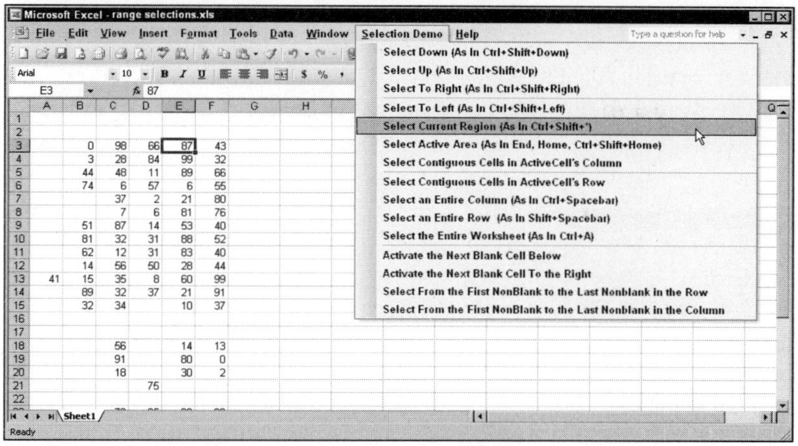

Figure 11-2: This workbook demonstrates how to select variably sized ranges by using VBA.

Often, you won't want to actually select the cells. Rather, you'll want to work with them in some way (for example, format them). The cell-selecting procedures can easily be adapted. The following procedure was adapted from SelectCurrentRegion. This procedure doesn't select cells; it applies formatting to the range that's defined as the current region around the active cell. The other procedures in the example workbook can also be adapted in this manner.

```
Sub FormatCurrentRegion()
    ActiveCell.CurrentRegion.Font.Bold = True
End Sub
```

Prompting for a cell value

The following procedure demonstrates how to ask the user for a value and then insert it into cell A1 of the active worksheet:

```
Sub GetValue1()
    Range("A1").Value = InputBox("Enter the value")
End Sub
```

Figure 11-3 shows how the input box looks.

This procedure has a problem, however. If the user clicks the Cancel button in the input box, the procedure deletes any data already in the cell. The following modification checks for the Cancel button clicks but takes no action:

```
Sub GetValue2()
    Dim UserEntry As String
     UserEntry = InputBox("Enter the value")
     If UserEntry <> "" Then Range("A1").Value = UserEntry
End Sub
```

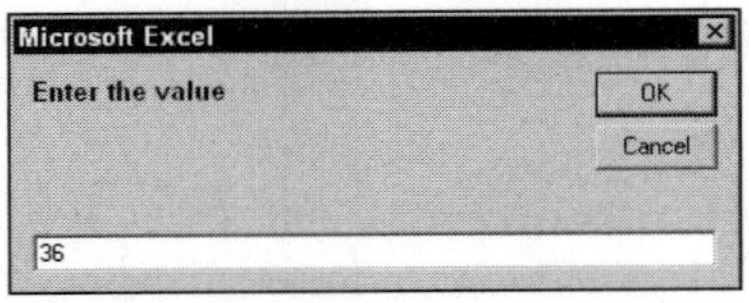

Figure 11-3: The InputBox function gets a value from
the user to be inserted into a cell.

In many cases, you'll need to validate the user's entry in the input box. For example, you may require a number between 1 and 12. The following example demonstrates one way to validate the user's entry. In this example, an invalid entry is ignored, and the input box is displayed again. This cycle keeps repeating until the user enters a valid number or clicks Cancel.

```
Sub GetValue3()
    Dim MinVal As Integer, MaxVal As Integer
    Dim UserEntry As String
    Dim Msg As String
    Dim DblEntry As Double
    MinVal = 1
    MaxVal = 12
    Msg = "Enter a value between " & MinVal & " and " & MaxVal
    Do
        UserEntry = InputBox(Msg)
        If UserEntry = "" Then Exit Sub
        If IsNumeric(UserEntry) Then
            DblEntry = Val(UserEntry)
            If DblEntry >= MinVal And DblEntry <= MaxVal Then Exit Do
        End If
        Msg = "Your previous entry was INVALID."
        Msg = Msg & vbNewLine
        Msg = Msg & "Enter a value between " & MinVal & " and " & MaxVal
    Loop
    ActiveSheet.Range("A1").Value = UserEntryEnd Sub
```

As you can see in Figure 11-4, the code also changes the message displayed if the user makes an invalid entry.

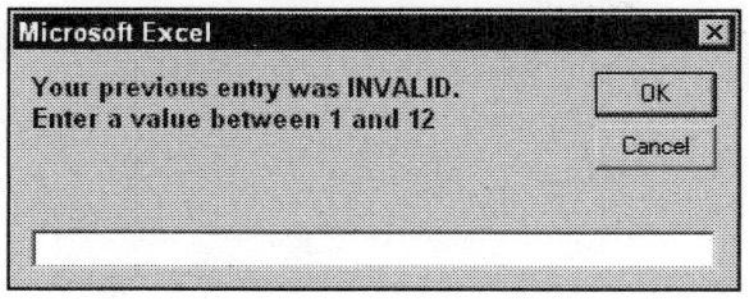

Microsoft Excel

Your previous entry was INVALID.
Enter a value between 1 and 12

OK

Cancel

Figure 11-4: Validate a user's entry with the VBA
`InputBox` function.

The `InputBox` function returns a string, so I use VBA's `Val` function to convert the string to a value prior to using the `If` statement to perform the
numerical comparisons.

Entering a value in the next empty cell

A common requirement is to enter a value into the next empty cell in a column or
row. The following example prompts the user for a name and a value and then
enters the data into the next empty row (see Figure 11-5).

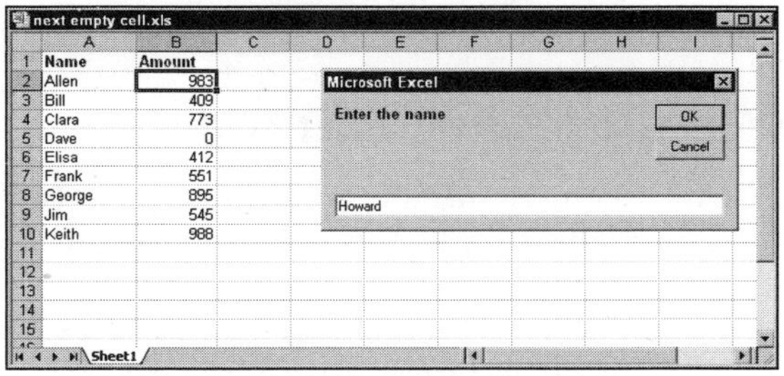

next empty cell.xls

	A	B	C	D	E	F	G	H	I
1	Name	Amount							
2	Allen	983							
3	Bill	409							
4	Clara	773							
5	Dave	0							
6	Elisa	412							
7	Frank	551							
8	George	895							
9	Jim	545							
10	Keith	988							
11									
12									
13									
14									
15									

Microsoft Excel

Enter the name

OK

Cancel

Howard

Sheet1

Figure 11-5: A macro for inserting data into the next
empty row in a worksheet.

```
Sub GetData()
    Dim NextRow As Long
    Dim Entry1 As String, Entry2 As String
  Do
    NextRow = Range("A65536").End(xlUp).Row + 1
    Entry1 = InputBox("Enter the name")
    If Entry1 = "" Then Exit Sub
    Entry2 = InputBox("Enter the amount")
    If Entry2 = "" Then Exit Sub
```

```
        Cells(NextRow, 1) = Entry1
        Cells(NextRow, 2) = Entry2
    Loop
End Sub
```

Notice that the loop continues indefinitely. I use `Exit Sub` statements to get out of the loop when the user clicks Cancel in the input box.

 To keep things simple, this procedure doesn't perform any validation.

Notice the statement that determines the value of the `NextRow` variable. If you don't understand how this works, try the manual equivalent: Activate cell A65536 (the last cell in column A). Press End and then press the up-arrow key. At this point, the last nonblank cell in column A will be selected. The `Row` property returns this row number, and it is incremented by 1 in order to get the row of the cell below it (the next empty row).

Note that this technique of selecting the next empty cell has a slight glitch. If the column is completely empty, it will calculate row 2 as the next empty row.

Pausing a macro to get a user-selected range

You can create a macro that pauses while the user specifies a range of cells. The procedure in this section describes how to do this with Excel's InputBox method.

 Do not confuse Excel's InputBox method with VBA's `InputBox` function. Although these two functions have the same name, they are not the same.

The `Sub` procedure that follows demonstrates how to pause a macro and let the user select a cell:

```
Sub GetUserRange()
    Dim UserRange As Range

    Output = 565
    Prompt = "Select a cell for the output."
    Title = "Select a cell"
```

```
'    Display the Input Box
     On Error Resume Next
     Set UserRange = Application.InputBox( _
         Prompt:=Prompt, _
         Title:=Title, _
         Default:=ActiveCell.Address, _
         Type:=8) 'Range selection
     On Error GoTo 0

'    Was the Input Box canceled?
     If UserRange Is Nothing Then
         MsgBox "Canceled."
     Else
         UserRange.Range("A1") = Output
     End If
End Sub
```

The input box is shown in Figure 11-6.

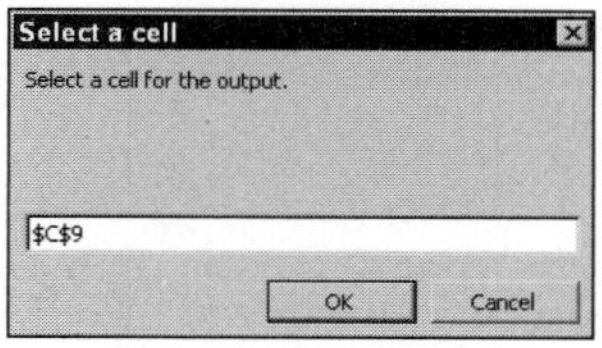

Figure 11-6: Use an input box to pause a macro.

Specifying a Type argument of 8 is the key to this procedure. Also, note the use of On Error Resume Next. This statement ignores the error that occurs if the user clicks the Cancel button. If so, the UserRange object variable is not defined. This example displays a message box with the text Canceled. If the user clicks OK, the macro continues. Using On Error GoTo 0 resumes normal error handling.

By the way, it's not necessary to check for a valid range selection. Excel takes care of this for you.

Make sure that screen updating is not turned off. Otherwise, you won't be able to select a cell. Use the ScreenUpdating property of the Application object to control screen updating while a macro is running.

Counting selected cells

You can create a macro that works with the selected range of cells. Use the `Count` property of the `Range` object to determine how many cells are contained in a range selection (or any range, for that matter). For example, the following statement displays a message box that contains the number of cells in the current selection:

```
MsgBox Selection.Count
```

If the active sheet contains a range named `data`, the following statement assigns the number of cells in the `data` range to a variable named `CellCount`:

```
CellCount = Range("data").Count
```

You can also determine how many rows or columns are contained in a range. The following expression calculates the number of columns in the currently selected range:

```
Selection.Columns.Count
```

And, of course, you can also use the `Rows` property to determine the number of rows in a range. The following statement counts the number of rows in a range named `data` and assigns the number to a variable named `RowCount`:

```
RowCount = Range("data").Rows.Count
```

Determining the type of selected range

Excel supports several types of range selections:

- A single cell
- A contiguous range of cells
- One or more entire columns
- One or more entire rows
- The entire worksheet
- Any combination of the above (that is, a multiple selection)

As a result, when your VBA procedure processes a selected range, you can't make any presumptions about what that range might be.

In the case of a multiple range selection, the `Range` object comprises separate areas. To determine whether a selection is a multiple selection, use the `Areas` method, which returns an `Areas` collection. This collection represents all the ranges within a multiple range selection.

You can use an expression like the following to determine whether a selected range has multiple areas:

```
NumAreas = Selection.Areas.Count
```

If the `NumAreas` variable contains a value greater than 1, the selection is a multiple selection.

The `AboutRangeSelection` procedure uses the `AreaType` custom function listed here:

```
Function AreaType(RangeArea As Range) As String
'    Returns the type of a range in an area
    Select Case True
        Case RangeArea.Cells.Count = 1
            AreaType = "Cell"
        Case RangeArea.Count = Cells.Count
            AreaType = "Worksheet"
        Case RangeArea.Rows.Count = Cells.Rows.Count
            AreaType = "Column"
        Case RangeArea.Columns.Count = Cells.Columns.Count
            AreaType = "Row"
        Case Else
            AreaType = "Block"
    End Select
End Function
```

This function accepts a `Range` object as its argument and returns one of five strings that describe the area: `Cell`, `Worksheet`, `Column`, `Row`, or `Block`. The function uses a `Select Case` construct to determine which of five comparison expressions is `True`. For example, if the range consists of a single cell, the function returns `Cell`. If the number of cells in the range is equal to the number of cells in the worksheet, it returns `Worksheet`. If the number of rows in the range equals the number of rows in the worksheet, it returns `Column`. If the number of columns in the range equals the number of columns in the worksheet, the function returns `Row`. If none of the `Case` expressions is `True`, the function returns `Block`.

 Notice that the comparison doesn't involve absolute numbers. For example, rather than use 65,536 to determine whether the range is a column, it uses `Cells.Rows.Count`. Because of this, the function works properly even with Excel 5 and Excel 97 (which contain only 16,384 rows). And it will continue to work if Microsoft ever increases the number of rows in a worksheet.

A workbook on the companion CD-ROM contains a procedure (named `AboutRangeSelection`) that uses the `AreaType` function to display a message box that describes the current range selection. Figure 11-7 shows an example. Understanding how this routine works will give you a good foundation for working with `Range` objects.

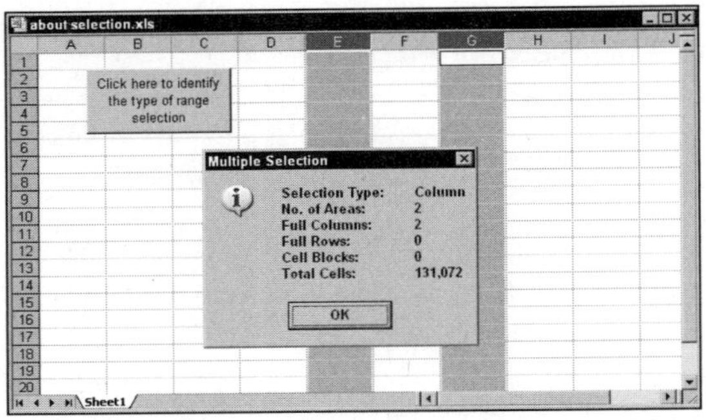

Figure 11-7: The `AboutRangeSelection` procedure analyzes the currently selected range.

You might be surprised to discover that Excel allows multiple selections to be identical. For example, if you hold down Ctrl and click five times in cell A1, the selection will have five identical areas. The `AboutRangeSelection` procedure takes this into account.

Looping through a selected range efficiently

A common task is to create a macro that evaluates each cell in a range and performs an operation if the cell meets a certain criterion. Listing 11-1 provides an example of such a macro. In this example, the `SelectiveColor1` procedure applies a red background to all cells in the selection that have a negative value. The background of other cells is reset.

Listing 11-1: Coloring All Negative Cells' Backgrounds Red

```
Sub SelectiveColor1()
'   Makes cell background red if the value is negative
    Dim cell As Range
    If TypeName(Selection) <> "Range" Then Exit Sub
    Const REDINDEX = 3
```

```
       Application.ScreenUpdating = False
       For Each cell In Selection
           If cell.Value < 0 Then
               cell.Interior.ColorIndex = REDINDEX
           Else
               cell.Interior.ColorIndex = xlNone
           End If
       Next cell
End Sub
```

The SelectiveColor1 procedure certainly works, but it has a serious flaw. For example, what if the selection consists of an entire column? Or ten columns? Or the entire worksheet? The user would probably give up before all the cells were evaluated. A better solution (SelectiveColor2) is shown in Listing 11-2.

Listing 11-2: Improving This Procedure to Include Wider, Multiple-column Ranges

```
Sub SelectiveColor2()
'   Makes cell background red if the value is negative

    Dim cell As Range
    Dim FormulaCells As Range
    Dim ConstantCells As Range
    Const REDINDEX = 3

'   Ignore errors
    On Error Resume Next

    Application.ScreenUpdating = False

'   Create subsets of original selection
    Set FormulaCells = Selection.SpecialCells (xlFormulas, xlNumbers)
    Set ConstantCells = Selection.SpecialCells (xlConstants, xlNumbers)
    On Error GoTo 0

'   Process the formula cells
    If Not FormulaCells Is Nothing Then
        For Each cell In FormulaCells
            If cell.Value < 0 Then
                cell.Interior.ColorIndex = REDINDEX
            Else
                cell.Interior.ColorIndex = xlNone
            End If
        Next cell
    End If
```

Continued

Listing 11-2 *(Continued)*

```
'    Process the constant cells
    If Not ConstantCells Is Nothing Then
        For Each cell In ConstantCells
            If cell.Value < 0 Then
                cell.Interior.ColorIndex = REDINDEX
            Else
                cell.Interior.ColorIndex = xlNone
            End If
        Next cell
    End If
End Sub
```

This procedure performs some extra steps that make it very efficient. I use the `SpecialCells` method to generate two subsets of the selection: One subset includes only the cells with numeric constants; the other subset includes only the cells with numeric formulas. Then I process the cells in these subsets by using two `For Each-Next` constructs. The net effect: Only nonblank cells are evaluated, thus speeding up the macro considerably.

The `On Error` statement is necessary because the `SpecialCells` method generates an error if no cells qualify. This statement also handles situations in which a range is not selected when the procedure is executed.

Deleting all empty rows

The following procedure deletes all empty rows in the active worksheet. This routine is fast and efficient because it doesn't check all rows. It checks only the rows in the used range, which is determined by using the `UsedRange` property of the `Worksheet` object.

```
Sub DeleteEmptyRows()
    Dim LastRow As Long, r As Long
    LastRow = ActiveSheet.UsedRange.Rows.Count
    LastRow = LastRow + ActiveSheet.UsedRange.Row - 1
    Application.ScreenUpdating = False
    For r = LastRow To 1 Step -1
        If WorksheetFunction.CountA(Rows(r)) = 0 Then Rows(r).Delete
    Next r
End Sub
```

The first step is to determine the last used row and then assign this row number to the `LastRow` variable. This is not as simple as you might think because the used range may or may not begin in row 1. Therefore, LastRow is calculated by determining the number of rows in the used range, adding the first row number in the used range, and subtracting 1.

The procedure uses Excel's COUNTA worksheet function to determine whether a row is empty. If this function returns 0 for a particular row, the row is empty. Notice that the procedure works on the rows from bottom to top and also uses a negative step value in the For-Next loop. This is necessary because deleting rows causes all subsequent rows to move up in the worksheet. If the looping occurred from top to bottom, the counter within the loop would not be accurate after a row is deleted.

Determining whether a range is contained in another range

The following InRange function accepts two arguments, both Range objects. The function returns True if the first range is contained in the second range.

```
Function InRange(rng1, rng2) As Boolean
'     Returns True if rng1 is a subset of rng2
      InRange = False
      If rng1.Parent.Parent.Name = rng2.Parent.Parent.Name Then
          If rng1.Parent.Name = rng2.Parent.Name Then
              If Union(rng1, rng2).Address = rng2.Address Then
                  InRange = True
              End If
          End If
      End If
End Function
```

The InRange function may appear a bit more complex than it needs to be because the code needs to ensure that the two ranges are in the same worksheet and workbook. Notice that the procedure uses the Parent property, which returns an object's container object. For example, the following expression returns the name of the worksheet for the rng1 object reference:

```
rng1.Parent.Name
```

The following expression returns the name of the workbook for rng1:

```
rng1.Parent.Parent.Name
```

VBA's Union function returns a Range object that represents the union of two Range objects. The union is the cells that the two ranges have in common. If the address of the union of the two ranges is the same as the address of the second range, the first range is contained within the second range.

Determining a cell's data type

Excel provides a number of built-in functions that can help determine the type of data contained in a cell. These include ISTEXT, ISLOGICAL, and ISERROR. In addition, VBA includes functions such as IsEmpty, IsDate, and IsNumeric.

The following CellType function accepts a range argument and returns a string (Blank, Text, Logical, Error, Date, Time, or Number) that describes the data type of the upper-left cell in the range. You can use this function in a worksheet formula or from another VBA procedure.

```
Function CellType(Rng)
'    Returns the cell type of the upper left
'    cell in a range
    Dim TheCell As Range
    Set TheCell = Rng.Range("A1")
    Select Case True
        Case IsEmpty(TheCell)
            CellType = "Blank"
        Case Application.IsText(TheCell)
            CellType = "Text"
        Case Application.IsLogical(TheCell)
            CellType = "Logical"
        Case Application.IsErr(TheCell)
            CellType = "Error"
        Case IsDate(TheCell)
            CellType = "Date"
        Case InStr(1, TheCell.Text, ":") <> 0
            CellType = "Time"
        Case IsNumeric(TheCell)
            CellType = "Number"
    End Select
End Function
```

Notice the use of the Set Rng statement. The CellType function accepts a range argument of any size, but this statement causes it to operate on only the upper-left cell in the range (which is represented by the TheCell variable).

Reading and writing ranges

Many spreadsheet tasks involve transferring the values either from an array to a range or from a range to an array. For some reason, Excel reads from ranges much faster than it writes to ranges. The WriteReadRange procedure shown in Listing 11-3 demonstrates the relative speeds of writing and reading a range.

This procedure creates an array and then uses For-Next loops to write the array to a range and then read the range back into the array. It calculates the time required for each operation by using the Excel Timer function.

Listing 11-3: Benchmarking Read and Write Operations Involving Ranges

```
Sub WriteReadRange()
    Dim MyArray()
    Dim Time1 As Double
    Dim NumElements As Long, i As Long
    Dim WriteTime As String, ReadTime As String
    Dim Msg As String

    NumElements = 60000
    ReDim MyArray(1 To NumElements)

'   Fill the array
    For i = 1 To NumElements
        MyArray(i) = i
    Next i

'   Write the array to a range
    Time1 = Timer
    For i = 1 To NumElements
        Cells(i, 1) = MyArray(i)
    Next i
    WriteTime = Format(Timer - Time1, "00:00")

'   Read the range into the array
    Time1 = Timer
    For i = 1 To NumElements
        MyArray(i) = Cells(i, 1)
    Next i
    ReadTime = Format(Timer - Time1, "00:00")

'   Show results
    Msg = "Write: " & WriteTime
    Msg = Msg & vbCrLf
    Msg = Msg & "Read: " & ReadTime
    MsgBox Msg, vbOKOnly, NumElements & " Elements"
End Sub
```

On my system, it took 8 seconds to write a 60,000-element array to a range but only 1 second to read the range into an array.

A better way to write to a range

The example in the previous section uses a For-Next loop to transfer the contents of an array to a worksheet range. In this section, I demonstrate a more efficient way to accomplish this.

Start with the example in Listing 11-4, which illustrates the most obvious (but not the most efficient) way to fill a range. This example uses a For-Loop to insert its values in a range.

Listing 11–4: Filling a Range by Brute Force

```
Sub LoopFillRange()
'    Fill a range by looping through cells

     Dim CellsDown As Long, CellsAcross As Integer
     Dim CurrRow As Long, CurrCol As Integer
     Dim StartTime As Double
     Dim CurrVal As Long

'    Get the dimensions
     CellsDown = Val(InputBox("How many cells down?"))
     CellsAcross = Val(InputBox("How many cells across?"))

'    Record starting time
     StartTime = Timer

'    Loop through cells and insert values
     CurrVal = 1
     Application.ScreenUpdating = False
     For CurrRow = 1 To CellsDown
         For CurrCol = 1 To CellsAcross
             ActiveCell.Offset(CurrRow - 1, _
             CurrCol - 1).Value = CurrVal
             CurrVal = CurrVal + 1
         Next CurrCol
     Next CurrRow

'    Display elapsed time
     Application.ScreenUpdating = True
     MsgBox Format(Timer - StartTime, "00.00") & " seconds"
End Sub
```

The example in Listing 11-5 demonstrates a faster way to produce the same result. This code inserts the values into an array and then uses a single statement to transfer the contents of an array to the range.

Listing 11–5: Borrowing Arrays to Fill Ranges Faster

```
Sub ArrayFillRange()
'    Fill a range by transferring an array
```

```
        Dim CellsDown As Long, CellsAcross As Integer
        Dim i As Long, j As Integer
        Dim StartTime As Double
        Dim TempArray() As Long
        Dim TheRange As Range
        Dim CurrVal As Long

    '   Get the dimensions
        CellsDown = Val(InputBox("How many cells down?"))
        CellsAcross = Val(InputBox("How many cells across?"))

    '   Record starting time
        StartTime = Timer

    '   Redimension temporary array
        ReDim TempArray(1 To CellsDown, 1 To CellsAcross)

    '   Set worksheet range
        Set TheRange = ActiveCell.Range(Cells(1, 1), _
            Cells(CellsDown, CellsAcross))

    '   Fill the temporary array
        CurrVal = 0
        Application.ScreenUpdating = False
        For i = 1 To CellsDown
            For j = 1 To CellsAcross
                TempArray(i, j) = CurrVal + 1
                CurrVal = CurrVal + 1
            Next j
        Next i

    '   Transfer temporary array to worksheet
        TheRange.Value = TempArray

    '   Display elapsed time
        Application.ScreenUpdating = True
        MsgBox Format(Timer - StartTime, "00.00") & " seconds"
    End Sub
```

On my system, using the loop method to fill a 500 x 256 cell range (128,000 cells) took 24.12 seconds. The array transfer method took only 0.24 seconds to generate the same results — about 100 times faster! The moral of this story? If you need to transfer large amounts of data to a worksheet, avoid looping whenever possible.

Transferring one-dimensional arrays

The example in the preceding section involves a two-dimensional array, which works out nicely for row-and-column-based worksheets.

When transferring a one-dimensional array to a range, the range must be horizontal — that is, one row with multiple *columns*. If you have to use a vertical range instead, you must first transpose the array to make it vertical. You can use Excel's TRANSPOSE function to do this. The following example transfers a 100-element array to a vertical worksheet range (A1:A100):

```
Range(A1:A100).Value = Application.WorksheetFunction.Transpose(MyArray)
```

Transferring a range to a variant array

This section discusses yet another way to work with worksheet data in VBA. The following example transfers a range of cells to a two-dimensional variant array. Then message boxes display the upper bounds for each dimension of the variant array.

```
Sub RangeToVariant()
    Dim x As Variant
    x = Range("A1:L600").Value
    MsgBox UBound(x, 1)
    MsgBox UBound(x, 2)
End Sub
```

In this example, the first message box displays 600 (the number of rows in the original range), and the second message box displays 12 (the number of columns). You'll find that transferring the range data to a variant array is virtually instantaneous.

The following example reads a range into a variant array, performs a simple multiplication operation on each element in the array, and then transfers the variant array back to the range: Notice that it uses the VBA function IsNumeric to ensure that the data is numeric.

```
Sub RangeToVariant2()
    Dim x As Variant
    Dim r As Long, c As Integer

'   Read the data into the variant
    x = Range("A1:L50").Value

'   Loop through the variant array
    For r = 1 To UBound(x, 1)
        For c = 1 To UBound(x, 2)
'           Multiply by 2
```

```
      If IsNumeric(x(r, c)) And IsNumeric(x(r, c)) _
          Then x(r, c) = x(r, c) * 2
    Next c
  Next r

'   Transfer the variant back to the sheet
    Range("A1:L50") = x
End Sub
```

Again, you'll find that this procedure runs amazingly fast.

Selecting the maximum value in a range

The GoToMax procedure in Listing 11-6 activates the worksheet cell that contains the maximum value. The procedure determines the maximum value in the selected range; but if a single cell is selected, it determines the maximum value for the entire worksheet. Next, it uses the Find method to locate the value and select the cell.

Listing 11-6: Moving the Pointer to the Cell Containing the Greatest Value

```
Sub GoToMax()
'   Activates the cell with the largest value
    Dim WorkRange as Range
    Dim MaxVal as Double

'   Exit if a range is not selected
    If TypeName(Selection) <> "Range" Then Exit Sub

'   If one cell is selected, search entire worksheet;
'   Otherwise, search the selected range
    If Selection.Count = 1 Then
        Set Workrange = Cells
    Else
        Set Workrange = Selection
    End If

'   Determine the maximum value
    MaxVal = Application.Max(Workrange)

'   Find it and select it
    On Error Resume Next
    Workrange.Find(What:=MaxVal, _
        After:=Workrange.Range("A1"), _
        LookIn:=xlValues, _
        LookAt:=xlWhole, _
```

Continued

Listing 11-6 *(Continued)*

```
        SearchOrder:=xlByRows, _
        SearchDirection:=xlNext, MatchCase:=False _
        ).Select
    If Err <> 0 Then MsgBox "Max value was not found: " _
    & MaxVal
End Sub
```

You'll notice that the arguments for the Find method correspond to the controls in Excel's Find and Replace dialog box.

Selecting all cells with a particular format

The example in this section demonstrates how to use the FindFormat method to locate and select all cells in a worksheet that contain a particular format. When these cells are selected, you can then do what you want with them — change the formatting, delete them, and so on. Figure 11-8 shows an example.

	A	B	C	D	E	F	G	H	I	J	
1	262	305	60	442	174	120	85	58	361	81	
2	58	83	460	385	496	145	171	390	429	391	
3	404		Select Bold	251	272	354	9	439	299	189	
4	470	1	Yellow Cells	249	153	222	114	456	390	20	
5	173	67	105	418	338	260	276	352	138	113	
6	138	253	326	75	111	274	436	259	109	348	
7	343	230	189	256				66	10	186	
8	471	204	421	250	Microsoft Excel			280	32	48	
9	2319	1323	2050	2326				2300	1768	1376	
10	391	160	298	172	Matching cells found: 20			402	134	455	
11	292	246	272	270				430	296	222	
12	144	480	400	453	OK			493	317	31	
13	53	203	441	359				50	367	332	
14	35	257	410	354	455	441	367	210	429	236	
15	256	480	214	31	118	91	252	201	288	273	
16	45	70	257	315	235	102	240	456	418	99	
17	325	495	107	181	97	289	78	388	139	310	
18	135	369	254	55	31	49	199	382	307	113	
19	280	219	327	183	378	38	241	360	182	353	
20	19	260	111	109	480	463	260	62	146	8	
21	1975	3239	3091	2482	3410	2548	2484	3434	3023	2432	
22											

Figure 11-8: Selecting all cells with a particular format.

The FindFormat property was introduced in Excel 2002. Consequently, this procedure will not work with earlier versions of Excel.

For reasons known only to Microsoft, recording a macro that uses the Format feature in the Find and Replace dialog box does not work. Therefore, you need to code these types of macros manually.

The SelectByFormat procedure is as follows:

```vba
Sub SelectByFormat()
'   Selects cells based on their formatting

'   Make sure version is Excel 2002 or later
    If Val(Application.Version) < 10 Then
        MsgBox "This requires Excel 2002 or later."
        Exit Sub
    End If

    Dim FirstCell As Range, FoundCell As Range
    Dim AllCells As Range

'   Specify the formatting to look for
    With Application.FindFormat
        .Clear
        .Interior.ColorIndex = 6 'yellow
        .Font.Bold = True
    End With

'   Look for the first matching cell
    Set FirstCell = ActiveSheet.UsedRange.Find(what:="", searchformat:=True)

'   If nothing was found, then exit
    If FirstCell Is Nothing Then
        MsgBox "No matching cells were found."
        Exit Sub
    End If

'   Initialize AllCells
    Set AllCells = FirstCell
    Set FoundCell = FirstCell

'   Loop until the FirstCell is found again
    Do
        Set FoundCell = ActiveSheet.UsedRange.Find _
          (After:=FoundCell, what:="", searchformat:=True)
        If FoundCell Is Nothing Then Exit Do
        Set AllCells = Union(FoundCell, AllCells)
        If FoundCell.Address = FirstCell.Address Then Exit Do
    Loop

'   Select the found cells and inform the user
    AllCells.Select
    MsgBox " Matching cells found: " & AllCells.Count
End Sub
```

The procedure starts by setting properties of the FindFormat object. In this example, the formatting to be searched for consists of two components: a yellow interior and bold text. You can, of course, change this to any formatting that you like.

The Find method is used to locate the first qualifying cell. The Find method's What argument is set to an empty string because the search involves only formatting — not cell contents. Also, the SearchFormat argument is True because we are, in fact, searching for formatting.

If the formatting is not found, the user is informed, and the code ends. Otherwise, the found cell is assigned to the AllCells object variable (which stores all the found cells). A loop uses the Find method to continue searching but after the most recently found cell. The search continues until the cell found first is found again. Finally, all the found cells are selected in the worksheet, and the user is given the count.

This procedure will not locate cells that have a particular formatting as a result of Excel's conditional formatting feature.

Working with Workbooks and Sheets

The examples in this section demonstrate various ways to use VBA to work with workbooks and worksheets.

The examples in this section are available on the companion CD-ROM.

Saving all workbooks

The following procedure loops through all workbooks in the Workbooks collection and saves each file that has been saved previously:

```
Public Sub SaveAllWorkbooks()
    Dim Book As Workbook
    For Each Book In Workbooks
        If Book.Path <> "" Then Book.Save
    Next Book
End Sub
```

Notice the use of the Path property. If a workbook's Path property is empty, the file has never been saved (it's a new workbook). This procedure ignores such workbooks and only saves the workbooks that have a nonempty Path property.

Saving and closing all workbooks

The following procedure loops through the Workbooks collection. The code saves and closes all workbooks.

```
Sub CloseAllWorkbooks()
    Dim Book As Workbook
    For Each Book In Workbooks
        If Book.Name <> ThisWorkbook.Name Then
            Book.Close savechanges:=True
        End If
    Next Book
    ThisWorkbook.Close savechanges:=True
End Sub
```

Notice that the procedure uses an If statement to determine whether the workbook is the workbook that contains the code. This is necessary because closing the workbook that contains the procedure would end the code, and subsequent workbooks would not be affected.

Accessing workbook properties

Excel's File → Properties command displays a dialog box that contains information about the active workbook. You can access the properties from VBA. The following procedure, for example, displays the date and time when the active workbook was saved:

```
Sub LastSaved()
    Dim SaveTime As String
    On Error Resume Next
    SaveTime = ActiveWorkbook. _
      BuiltinDocumentProperties("Last Save Time").Value
    If SaveTime = "" Then
        MsgBox ActiveWorkbook.Name & " has not been saved."
    Else
        MsgBox "Saved: " & SaveTime, , ActiveWorkbook.Name
    End If
End Sub
```

If the workbook has not been saved, attempting to access the Last Save Time property will generate an error. The On Error statement causes this error to be ignored. The `If-Then-Else` structure checks the value of the `SaveTime` variable and displays the appropriate message. If this variable is empty, the file was not saved. Figure 11-9 shows an example of this procedure's result.

Figure 11-9: Displaying the date and time when a workbook was saved.

Quite a few other built-in properties are available, but they're not all relevant to Excel. Consult the Help system for a complete list of built-in properties.

Synchronizing worksheets

If you use multisheet workbooks, you probably know that Excel cannot synchronize the sheets in a workbook. In other words, there is no automatic way to force all sheets to have the same selected range and upper-left cell. The VBA macro that follows uses the active worksheet as a base and then performs the following on all other worksheets in the workbook:

◆ Selects the same range as the active sheet

◆ Makes the upper-left cell the same as the active sheet

Following is the listing for the subroutine:

```
Sub SynchSheets()
'   Duplicates the active sheet's active cell upperleft cell
'   Across all worksheets
    If TypeName(ActiveSheet) <> "Worksheet" Then Exit Sub
    Dim UserSheet As Worksheet, sht As Worksheet
    Dim TopRow As Long, LeftCol As Integer
    Dim UserSel As String

    Application.ScreenUpdating = False

'   Remember the current sheet
    Set UserSheet = ActiveSheet
```

```
'   Store info from the active sheet
    TopRow = ActiveWindow.ScrollRow
    LeftCol = ActiveWindow.ScrollColumn
    UserSel = ActiveWindow.RangeSelection.Address

'   Loop through the worksheets
    For Each sht In ActiveWorkbook.Worksheets
        If sht.Visible Then 'skip hidden sheets
            sht.Activate
            Range(UserSel).Select
            ActiveWindow.ScrollRow = TopRow
            ActiveWindow.ScrollColumn = LeftCol
        End If
    Next sht

'   Restore the original position
    UserSheet.Activate
    Application.ScreenUpdating = True
End Sub
```

VBA Techniques

The examples in this section illustrate common VBA techniques that you might be able to adapt to your own projects.

 The examples in this section are available on the companion CD-ROM.

Toggling a Boolean property

A *Boolean property* is one that is either `True` or `False`. The easiest way to toggle a Boolean property is to use the `Not` operator, as shown in the following example, which toggles the `WrapText` property of a selection.

```
Sub ToggleWrapText()
'   Toggles text wrap alignment for selected cells
    If TypeName(Selection) = "Range" Then
        Selection.WrapText = Not ActiveCell.WrapText
    End If
End Sub
```

Note that the active cell is used as the basis for toggling. When a range is selected and the property values in the cells are inconsistent (for example, some cells are bold, and others are not), it is considered *mixed,* and Excel uses the active cell to determine how to toggle. If the active cell is bold, for example, all cells in the selection are made not bold when you click the Bold toolbar button. This simple procedure mimics the way Excel works, which is usually the best practice.

Note also that this procedure uses the TypeName function to check whether the selection is a range. If it isn't, nothing happens.

You can use the Not operator to toggle many other properties. For example, to toggle the display of row and column borders in a worksheet, use the following code:

```
ActiveWindow.DisplayHeadings = Not _
    ActiveWindow.DisplayHeadings
```

To toggle the display of grid lines in the active worksheet, use the following code:

```
ActiveWindow.DisplayGridlines = Not _
    ActiveWindow.DisplayGridlines
```

Determining the number of printed pages

If you need to determine the number of printed pages for a worksheet printout, you can use Excel's Print Preview feature and view the page count displayed at the bottom of the screen. The VBA procedure that follows calculates the number of printed pages for the active sheet by counting the number of horizontal and vertical page breaks:

```
Sub PageCount()
    MsgBox (ActiveSheet.HPageBreaks.Count + 1) * _
      (ActiveSheet.VPageBreaks.Count + 1)
End Sub
```

The following VBA procedure loops through all worksheets in the active workbook and displays the total number of printed pages:

```
Sub ShowPageCount()
    Dim PageCount As Integer
    Dim sht As Worksheet
    PageCount = 0
    For Each sht In Worksheets
        PageCount = PageCount + (sht.HPageBreaks.Count + 1) * _
          (sht.VPageBreaks.Count + 1)
    Next sht
    MsgBox "Total Pages = " & PageCount
End Sub
```

Displaying the date and time

If you understand the serial number system that Excel uses to store dates and times, you won't have any problems using dates and times in your VBA procedures.

The `DateAndTime` procedure displays a message box with the current date and time, as depicted in Figure 11-10. This example also displays a personalized message in the message box title bar.

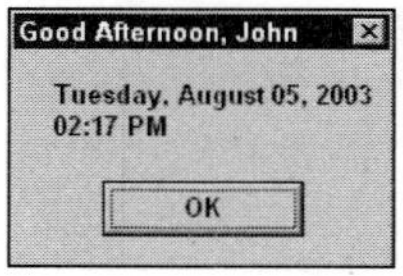

Figure 11-10: A message box displaying the date and time.

The procedure shown in Listing 11-7 uses the `Date` function as an argument for the `Format` function. The result is a string with a nicely formatted date. I used the same technique to get a nicely formatted time.

Listing 11-7: Displaying the Current Date and Time

```
Sub DateAndTime()
    Dim TheDate As String, TheTime As String
    Dim Greeting As String
    Dim FullName As String, FirstName As String
    Dim SpaceInName As Integer

    TheDate = Format(Date, "Long Date")
    TheTime = Format(Time, "Medium Time")

'   Determine greeting based on time
    Select Case Time
        Case Is < TimeValue("12:00"): Greeting = "Good Morning, "
        Case Is >= TimeValue("17:00"): Greeting = "Good Evening, "
        Case Else: Greeting = "Good Afternoon, "
    End Select

'   Append user's first name to greeting
    FullName = Application.UserName
    SpaceInName = InStr(1, FullName, " ", 1)

'   Handle situation when name has no space
    If SpaceInName = 0 Then SpaceInName = Len(FullName)
```

Continued

Listing 11-7 *(Continued)*

```
    FirstName = Left(FullName, SpaceInName)
    Greeting = Greeting & FirstName

'   Show the message
    MsgBox TheDate & vbCrLf & TheTime, vbOKOnly, Greeting
End Sub
```

In the preceding example, I used named formats (Long Date and Medium Time) to ensure that the macro will work properly regardless of the user's international settings. You can, however, use other formats. For example, to display the date in mm/dd/yy format, you can use a statement like the following:

```
TheDate = Format(Date, "mm/dd/yy")
```

I used a Select Case construct to base the greeting displayed in the message box's title bar on the time of day. VBA time values work just as they do in Excel. If the time is less than .5 (noon), it's morning. If it's greater than .7083 (5 p.m.), it's evening. Otherwise, it's afternoon. I took the easy way out and used VBA's TimeValue function, which returns a time value from a string.

The next series of statements determines the user's first name, as recorded in the General tab in the Options dialog box. I used VBA's InStr function to locate the first space in the user's name. When I first wrote this procedure, I didn't consider a user name that has no space. So when I ran this procedure on a machine with a user's name of *Nobody,* the code failed — which goes to show you that I can't think of everything, and even the simplest procedures can run aground. (By the way, if the user's name is left blank, Excel always substitutes the name *User.*) The solution to this problem was to use the length of the full name for the SpaceInName variable so that the Left function extracts the full name.

The MsgBox function concatenates the date and time but uses the built-in vbCrLf constant to insert a line break between them. vbOKOnly is a predefined constant that returns 0, causing the message box to appear with only an OK button. The final argument is the Greeting, constructed earlier in the procedure.

Getting a list of fonts

If you need to get a list of all installed fonts, you'll find that Excel does not provide a direct way to retrieve that information. One approach is to read the font names from the Font control on the Formatting toolbar.

The following procedure displays a list of the installed fonts in column A of the active worksheet. It uses the FindControl method to locate the Font control on the Formatting toolbar. If this control is not found (for example, it was removed by the user), a temporary CommandBar is created, and the Font control is added to it.

Refer to Chapter 22 for more information about working with `CommandBar` controls.

```
Sub ShowInstalledFonts()
    Dim FontList As CommandBarControl
    Dim TempBar As CommandBar
    Dim i As Integer

    Set FontList = Application.CommandBars("Formatting"). _
        FindControl(ID:=1728)

'   If Font control is missing, create a temp CommandBar
    If FontList Is Nothing Then
        Set TempBar = Application.CommandBars.Add
        Set FontList = TempBar.Controls.Add(ID:=1728)
    End If

'   Put the fonts into column A
    Range("A:A").ClearContents
    For i = 0 To FontList.ListCount - 1
        Cells(i + 1, 1) = FontList.List(i + 1)
    Next i

'   Delete temp CommandBar if it exists
    On Error Resume Next
    TempBar.Delete
End Sub
```

As an option, you can display each font name using the actual font. To do so, add this statement inside of the `For-Next` loop:

`Cells(i+1,1).Font.Name = FontList.List(i+1)`

Be aware, however, that using many fonts in a workbook can eat up lots of system resources, and it could even crash your system.

Sorting an array

Although Excel has a built-in command to sort worksheet ranges, VBA doesn't offer a method to sort arrays. One viable (but cumbersome) workaround is to transfer your array to a worksheet range, sort it by using Excel's commands, and then return the result to your array. But if speed is essential, it's better to write a sorting routine in VBA.

In this section, I describe four different sorting techniques:

◆ *Worksheet sort* transfers an array to a worksheet range, sorts it, and transfers it back to the array. This procedure accepts an array as its only argument and is limited to arrays with no more than 65,536 elements – the number of rows in a worksheet.

◆ *Bubble sort* is a simple sorting technique (also used in the Chapter 9 sheet-sorting example). Although easy to program, the bubble-sorting algorithm tends to be rather slow, especially when the number of elements is large.

◆ *Quick sort* is a much faster sorting routine than Bubble Sort, but it is also more difficult to understand. This technique only works with `Integer` or `Long` data types.

◆ *Counting sort* is lightning fast but also difficult to understand.

 The companion CD-ROM includes a workbook application that demonstrates these sorting methods. This workbook is useful for comparing the techniques with arrays of varying sizes.

Figure 11-11 shows the dialog box for this project. I tested the sorting procedures with seven different array sizes, ranging from 100 to 100,000 elements (random numbers). The arrays contained random numbers (of type `Long`).

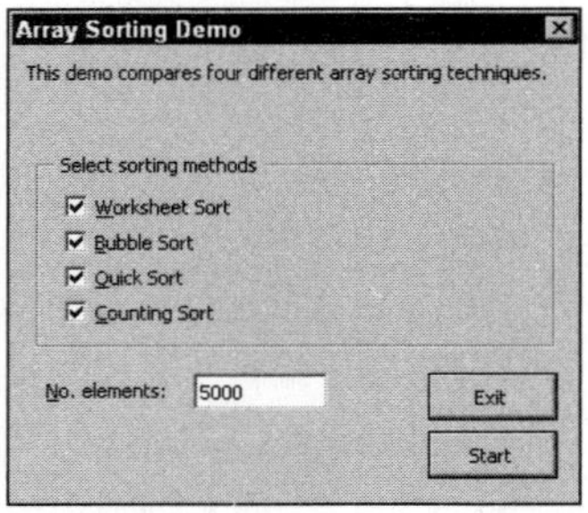

Figure 11-11: Comparing the time required to perform sorts of various array sizes.

Table 11-1 shows the results of my tests. A 0.00 entry means that the sort was virtually instantaneous (less than .01 second). Note that the worksheet sort is limited to 65,536 items.

TABLE 11-1 SORTING TIMES IN SECONDS FOR FOUR SORT ALGORITHMS USING RANDOMLY FILLED ARRAYS

Array Elements	Excel Worksheet Sort	VBA Bubble Sort	VBA Quick Sort	VBA Counting Sort
100	0.03	0.01	0.00	0.02
500	0.04	0.03	0.01	0.02
1,000	0.04	0.15	0.01	0.03
5,000	0.10	0.50	0.02	0.03
10,000	0.19	14.55	0.05	0.09
50,000	0.95	329.24	0.27	0.09
100,000	N/A	1,199.70	0.54	0.17

The worksheet sort algorithm is amazingly fast, especially when you consider that the array is transferred to the sheet, sorted, and then transferred back to the array. If the array is almost sorted, the worksheet sort technique is even faster.

The bubble sort algorithm is reasonably fast with small arrays, but for larger arrays (more than 5,000 elements), forget it. The quick sort algorithm is a winner, but the counting sort wins by a long shot.

Processing a series of files

One common use for macros, of course, is to repeat an operation a number of times. The example in Listing 11-8 demonstrates how to execute a macro on several different files stored on disk. This example — which may help you set up your own routine for this type of task — prompts the user for a file specification and then processes all matching files. In this case, processing consists of importing the file and entering a series of summary formulas that describe the data in the file.

Listing 11-8: A Macro That Processes Multiple Stored Files

```
Sub BatchProcess()
    Dim FS As FileSearch
    Dim FilePath As String, FileSpec As String
    Dim i As Integer
```

Continued

Listing 11-8 *(Continued)*

```
'    Specify path and file spec
     FilePath = ThisWorkbook.Path & "\"
     FileSpec = "text??.txt"

'    Create a FileSearch object
     Set FS = Application.FileSearch
     With FS
         .LookIn = FilePath
         .FileName = FileSpec
         .Execute
'        Exit if no files are found
         If .FoundFiles.Count = 0 Then
             MsgBox "No files were found"
             Exit Sub
         End If
     End With

'    Loop through the files and process them
     For i = 1 To FS.FoundFiles.Count
         Call ProcessFiles(FS.FoundFiles(i))
     Next i
End Sub
```

 This example uses three additional files, which are also provided on the CD-ROM: `Text01.txt`, `Text02.txt`, and `Text03.txt`. You'll need to modify the routine to import other text files. This procedure uses the `FileSearch` object, so it will work in Excel 2000 or later.

The matching files are retrieved by the `FileSearch` object, and the procedure uses a `For-Next` loop to process the files. Within the loop, the processing is done by calling the `ProcessFiles` procedure, which follows. This simple procedure uses the `OpenText` method to import the file and then inserts five formulas. You may, of course, substitute your own routine in place of this one:

```
Sub ProcessFiles(FileName As String)
'    Import the file
     Workbooks.OpenText FileName:=FileName, _
         Origin:=xlWindows, _
         StartRow:=1, _
         DataType:=xlFixedWidth, _
```

```
        FieldInfo:= _
        Array(Array(0, 1), Array(3, 1), Array(12, 1))
'   Enter summary formulas
    Range("D1").Value = "A"
    Range("D2").Value = "B"
    Range("D3").Value = "C"
    Range("E1:E3").Formula = "=COUNTIF(B:B,D1)"
    Range("F1:F3").Formula = "=SUMIF(B:B,D1,C:C)"
End Sub
```

Some Useful Functions for Use in Your Code

In this section, I present some custom utility functions that you may find useful in your own applications and that may provide inspiration for creating similar functions. These functions are most useful when called from another VBA procedure. Therefore, they are declared by using the `Private` keyword and thus will not appear in Excel's Insert Function dialog box.

The examples in this section are available on the companion CD-ROM.

The FileExists function

This function takes one argument (a path with filename) and returns `True` if the file exists:

```
Private Function FileExists(fname) As Boolean
'   Returns TRUE if the file exists
    FileExists = (Dir(fname) <> "")
End Function
```

The FileNameOnly function

This function accepts one argument (a path with filename) and returns only the filename. In other words, it strips out the path.

```
Private Function FileNameOnly(pname) As String
'    Returns the filename from a path/filename string
    Dim i As Integer, length As Integer, temp As String
    length = Len(pname)
    temp = ""
    For i = length To 1 Step -1
        If Mid(pname, i, 1) = Application.PathSeparator Then
            FileNameOnly = temp
            Exit Function
        End If
        temp = Mid(pname, i, 1) & temp
    Next i
    FileNameOnly = pname
End Function
```

The `FileNameOnly` function works with any path and filename (even if the file does not exist). If the file exists, the following function is a simpler way to strip off the path and return only the filename.

```
Private Function FileNameOnly2(pname) As String
    FileNameOnly2 = Dir(pname)
End Function
```

The PathExists function

This function accepts one argument (a path) and returns `True` if the path exists:

```
Private Function PathExists(pname) As Boolean
'   Returns TRUE if the path exists
  If Dir(pname, vbDirectory) = "" Then
    PathExists = False
  Else
    PathExists = (GetAttr(pname) And vbDirectory) = vbDirectory
  End If
End Function
```

The RangeNameExists function

This function accepts a single argument (a range name) and returns `True` if the range name exists in the active workbook:

```
Private Function RangeNameExists(nname) As Boolean
'    Returns TRUE if the range name exists
    Dim n As Name
    RangeNameExists = False
```

```
      For Each n In ActiveWorkbook.Names
          If UCase(n.Name) = UCase(nname) Then
              RangeNameExists = True
              Exit Function
          End If
      Next n
End Function
```

The SheetExists function

This function accepts one argument (a worksheet name) and returns `True` if the worksheet exists in the active workbook:

```
Private Function SheetExists(sname) As Boolean
'    Returns TRUE if sheet exists in the active workbook
     Dim x As Object
     On Error Resume Next
     Set x = ActiveWorkbook.Sheets(sname)
     If Err = 0 Then SheetExists = True _
         Else SheetExists = False
End Function
```

The WorkbookIsOpen function

This function accepts one argument (a workbook name) and returns `True` if the workbook is open:

```
Private Function WorkbookIsOpen(wbname) As Boolean
'    Returns TRUE if the workbook is open
     Dim x As Workbook
     On Error Resume Next
     Set x = Workbooks(wbname)
     If Err = 0 Then WorkbookIsOpen = True _
         Else WorkbookIsOpen = False
End Function
```

Retrieving a value from a closed workbook

VBA does not include a method to retrieve a value from a closed workbook file. You can, however, take advantage of Excel's ability to work with linked files. This section contains a VBA function (`GetValue`, which follows) that retrieves a value from a closed workbook. It does so by calling an *XLM macro,* which is an old-style macro used in versions prior to Excel 5.

Testing for Membership in a Collection

The following function procedure is a generic function that you can use to determine whether an object is a member of a collection:

```
Private Function IsInCollection(Coln As Object, _
   Item As String) As Boolean
     Dim Obj As Object
     On Error Resume Next
     Set Obj = Coln(Item)
     IsInCollection = Not Obj Is Nothing

End Function
```

This function accepts two arguments: the collection (an object) and the item (a string) that might or might not be a member of the collection. The function attempts to create an object variable that represents the item in the collection. If the attempt is successful, the function returns True; otherwise, it returns False.

You can use the IsInCollection function in place of three other functions listed in this chapter: RangeNameExists, SheetExists, and WorkbookIsOpen. To determine whether a range named Data exists in the active workbook, call the IsInCollection function with this statement:

```
MsgBox IsInCollection(ActiveWorkbook.Names, "Data")
```

To determine whether a workbook named Budget is open, use this statement:

```
MsgBox IsInCollection(Workbooks, "budget.xls")
```

To determine whether the active workbook contains a sheet named Sheet1, use this statement.

```
MsgBox IsInCollection(ActiveWorkbook.Worksheets, "Sheet1")
```

```
Private Function GetValue(path, file, sheet, ref)
'    Retrieves a value from a closed workbook
     Dim arg As String

'    Make sure the file exists
     If Right(path, 1) <> "\" Then path = path & "\"
     If Dir(path & file) = "" Then
         GetValue = "File Not Found"
         Exit Function
     End If
```

```
'   Create the argument
    arg = "'" & path & "[" & file & "]" & sheet & "'!" & _
      Range(ref).Range("A1").Address(, , xlR1C1)

'   Execute an XLM macro
    GetValue = ExecuteExcel4Macro(arg)
End Function
```

The `GetValue` function takes four arguments:

◆ `path`: The drive and path to the closed file (for example, "d:\files")

◆ `file`: The workbook name (for example, "budget.xls")

◆ `sheet`: The worksheet name (for example, "Sheet1")

◆ `ref`: The cell reference (for example, "C4")

The following `Sub` procedure demonstrates how to use the `GetValue` function. It simply displays the value in cell A1 in `Sheet1` of a file named `99Budget.xls`, located in the `XLFiles\Budget` directory on drive C.

```
Sub TestGetValue()
    p = "c:\XLFiles\Budget"
    f = "99Budget.xls"
    s = "Sheet1"
    a = "A1"
    MsgBox GetValue(p, f, s, a)
End Sub
```

Another example follows. This procedure reads 1,200 values (100 rows and 12 columns) from a closed file and then places the values into the active worksheet.

```
Sub TestGetValue2()
    p = "c:\XLFiles\Budget"
    f = "99Budget.xls"
    s = "Sheet1"
    Application.ScreenUpdating = False
    For r = 1 To 100
        For c = 1 To 12
            a = Cells(r, c).Address
            Cells(r, c) = GetValue(p, f, s, a)
        Next c
    Next r
    Application.ScreenUpdating = True
End Sub
```

The GetValue function does not work if used in a worksheet formula. Actually, there is no need to use this function in a formula. You can simply create a link formula to retrieve a value from a closed file.

Some Useful Worksheet Functions

The examples in this section are custom functions that can be used in worksheet formulas. Remember, these Function procedures must be defined in a VBA module (not a code module associated with ThisWorkbook, a sheet, or a UserForm).

The examples in this section are available on the companion CD-ROM.

Returning cell formatting information

This section contains a number of custom functions that return information about a cell's formatting. These functions are useful if you need to sort data based on formatting (for example, sort such that all bold cells are together).

You'll find that these functions aren't always updated automatically. This is because changing formatting, for example, doesn't trigger Excel's recalculation engine. To force a global recalculation (and update all the custom functions), press Ctrl+Alt+F9.

Alternatively, you can add the following statement to your function:

Application.Volatile

When this statement is present, then pressing F9 will recalculate the function.

The following function returns TRUE if its single-cell argument has bold formatting:

```
Function ISBOLD(cell) As Boolean
'   Returns TRUE if cell is bold
    ISBOLD = cell.Range("A1").Font.Bold
End Function
```

The following function returns TRUE if its single-cell argument has italic formatting:

```
Function ISITALIC(cell) As Boolean
'    Returns TRUE if cell is italic
     ISITALIC = cell.Range("A1").Font.Italic
End Function
```

Both of the preceding functions will return an error if the cell has mixed formatting — for example, only some characters are bold. The following function returns TRUE only if all characters in the cell are bold.

```
Function ALLBOLD(cell) As Boolean
'    Returns TRUE if all characters in cell
'    are bold
     If IsNull(cell.Font.Bold) Then
         ALLBOLD = False
     Else
         ALLBOLD = cell.Font.Bold
     End If
End Function
```

The FILLCOLOR function, which follows, returns an integer that corresponds to the color index of the cell's interior (the cell's fill color). If the cell's interior is not filled, the function returns -4142.

```
Function FILLCOLOR(cell) As Integer
'    Returns an integer corresponding to
'    cell's interior color
     FILLCOLOR = cell.Range("A1").Interior.ColorIndex
End Function
```

Displaying the date when a file was saved or printed

An Excel workbook contains several built-in document properties, accessible from the BuiltinDocumentProperties property of the Workbook object. The following function returns the date and time that the workbook was last saved:

```
Function LASTSAVED()
     Application.Volatile
     LASTSAVED = ThisWorkbook. _
       BuiltinDocumentProperties("Last Save Time")
End Function
```

The following function is similar, but it returns the date and time when the workbook was last printed or previewed.

```
Function LASTPRINTED()
    Application.Volatile
    LASTPRINTED = ThisWorkbook. _
        BuiltinDocumentProperties("Last Print Date")
End Function
```

If you use these functions in a formula, you might need to force a recalculation (by pressing F9) to get the current values of these properties.

 Quite a few additional built-in properties are available, but Excel does not use all of them. For example, attempting to access the Number of Bytes property will generate an error.

The LASTSAVED and LASTPRINTED functions listed here are designed to be stored in the workbook in which they are used. In some cases, you might want to store the function in a different workbook (for example, personal.xls) or in an add-in. Because these functions reference ThisWorkbook, they will not work correctly. Following are more general-purpose versions of these functions. These functions use Application.Caller, which returns a Range object that represents the cell that calls the function. The use of Parent.Parent returns the workbook (that is, the parent of the parent of the Range object — a Workbook object). This topic is explained further in the next section.

```
Function LastSaved2()
    Application.Volatile
    LastSaved2 = Application.Caller.Parent.Parent. _
        BuiltinDocumentProperties("Last Save Time")
End Function

Function LASTPRINTED2()
    Application.Volatile
    LASTPRINTED2 = Application.Caller.Parent.Parent. _
        BuiltinDocumentProperties("Last Print Date")
End Function
```

Understanding object parents

As you know, Excel's object model is a hierarchy: Objects are contained in other objects. At the top of the hierarchy is the Application object. Excel contains other objects, and these objects contain other objects, and so on. The following hierarchy depicts how a Range object fits into this scheme:

Application object

   Workbook object

      Worksheet object

         Range object

In the lingo of object-oriented programming, a Range object's parent is the Worksheet object that contains it. A Worksheet object's parent is the Workbook object that contains the worksheet, and a Workbook object's parent is the Application object.

How can this information be put to use? Examine the SheetName VBA function that follows. This function accepts a single argument (a range) and returns the name of the worksheet that contains the range. It uses the Parent property of the Range object. The Parent property returns an object: the object that contains the Range object.

```
Function SheetName(ref) As String
    SheetName = ref.Parent.Name
End Function
```

The next function, WorkbookName, returns the name of the workbook for a particular cell. Notice that it uses the Parent property twice. The first Parent property returns a Worksheet object, and the second Parent property returns a Workbook object.

```
Function WorkbookName(ref) As String
    WorkbookName = ref.Parent.Parent.Name
End Function
```

The AppName function, which follows, carries this exercise to the next logical level, accessing the Parent property three times. This function returns the name of the Application object for a particular cell. It will, of course, always return Microsoft Excel.

```
Function AppName(ref) As String
    AppName = ref.Parent.Parent.Parent.Name
End Function
```

Counting cells between two values

The following function, named COUNTBETWEEN, returns the number of values in a range (first argument) that fall between values represented by the second and third arguments:

```
Function COUNTBETWEEN(InRange, num1, num2) As Long
'    Counts number of values between num1 and num2
     With Application.WorksheetFunction
         If num1 <= num2 Then
             COUNTBETWEEN = .CountIf(InRange, ">=" & num1) - _
                 .CountIf(InRange, ">" & num2)
         Else
             COUNTBETWEEN = .CountIf(InRange, ">=" & num2) - _
                 .CountIf(InRange, ">" & num1)
         End If
     End With
End Function
```

Note that this function uses Excel's COUNTIF function. In fact, the COUNTBETWEEN function is essentially a wrapper that can simplify your formulas.

Following is an example formula that uses the COUNTBETWEEN function. The formula returns the number of cells in A1:A100 that are greater than or equal to 10 and less than or equal to 20.

```
=COUNTBETWEEN(A1:A100,10,20)
```

Using this VBA function is simpler than entering the following lengthy formula:

```
=COUNTIF(A1:A100,">=10")-COUNTIF(A1:A100,">20")
```

Counting visible cells in a range

The COUNTVISIBLE function, which follows, accepts a range argument and returns the number of non-empty visible cells in the range. A cell is not visible if it's in a hidden row or a hidden column.

```
Function COUNTVISIBLE(rng)
'    Counts visible cells
     Dim CellCount As Long
     Dim cell As Range
     Application.Volatile
     CellCount = 0
     Set rng = Intersect(rng.Parent.UsedRange, rng)
     For Each cell In rng
        If Not IsEmpty(cell) Then
           If Not cell.EntireRow.Hidden And _
              Not cell.EntireColumn.Hidden Then _
              CellCount = CellCount + 1
        End If
```

```
    Next cell
    COUNTVISIBLE = CellCount
End Function
```

This function loops through each cell in the range, first checking whether the cell is empty. If it's not empty, it checks the hidden properties of the cell's row and column. If either the row or column is hidden, the `CellCount` variable is incremented.

The `COUNTVISIBLE` function is useful when you're working with AutoFilters or outlines. Both of these features make use of hidden rows.

Excel's SUBTOTAL function (with a first argument of 2 or 3) is also useful for counting visible cells in an AutoFiltered list.

In Excel 2003, you can add 100 to the first argument of the SUBTOTAL function. Doing so causes the function to use only visible cells in its calculation. For example, to count the visible numeric cells in a range, use a first argument of 102. This new feature works even if rows or columns are hidden manually. In previous versions, the SUBTOTAL function worked correctly only if the cells were hidden by using AutoFilters or outlines.

Determining the last nonempty cell in a column or row

In this section, I present two useful functions: `LASTINCOLUMN` returns the contents of the last nonempty cell in a column; `LASTINROW` returns the contents of the last nonempty cell in a row. Each function accepts a range as its single argument. The range argument can be a complete column (for `LASTINCOLUMN`) or a complete row (for `LASTINROW`). If the supplied argument is not a complete column or row, the function uses the column or row of the upper-left cell in the range. For example, the following formula returns the last value in column B:

```
=LASTINCOLUMN(B5)
```

The following formula returns the last value in row 7:

```
=LASTINROW(C7:D9)
```

THE LASTINCOLUMN FUNCTION

The LASTINCOLUMN function follows:

```
Function LASTINCOLUMN(rng As Range)
'   Returns the contents of the last non-empty cell in a column
    Dim LastCell As Range
    Application.Volatile
    With rng.Parent
        With .Cells(.Rows.Count, rng.Column)
            If Not IsEmpty(.Value) Then
                LASTINCOLUMN = .Value
            ElseIf IsEmpty(.End(xlUp)) Then
                LASTINCOLUMN = ""
            Else
                LASTINCOLUMN = .End(xlUp).Value
            End If
        End With
    End With
End Function
```

This function is rather complicated, so here are a few points that may help you understand it:

- ◆ Application.Volatile causes the function to be executed whenever the sheet is calculated.

- ◆ Rows.Count returns the number of rows in the worksheet. I used this, rather than hard-code the value 65536, for forward compatibility. (A future version of Excel may contain more rows.)

- ◆ rng.Column returns the column number of the upper-left cell in the rng argument.

- ◆ Using rng.Parent causes the function to work properly even if the rng argument refers to a different sheet or workbook.

- ◆ The End method (with the xlUp argument) is equivalent to activating the last cell in a column, pressing End, and then pressing the up-arrow key.

- ◆ The IsEmpty function checks whether the cell is empty. If so, it returns an empty string. Without this statement, an empty cell would be returned as 0.

THE LASTINROW FUNCTION

The LASTINROW function follows. This is very similar to the LASTINCOLUMN function.

```
Function LASTINROW(rng As Range)
'   Returns the contents of the last non-empty cell in a row
    Application.Volatile
```

```
   With rng.Parent
      With .Cells(rng.Row, .Columns.Count)
         If Not IsEmpty(.Value) Then
            LASTINROW = .Value
         ElseIf IsEmpty(.End(xlToLeft)) Then
            LASTINROW = ""
         Else
            LASTINROW = .End(xlToLeft).Value
         End If
      End With
   End With
End Function
```

Does a string match a pattern?

The ISLIKE function is very simple (but also very useful). This function returns True if a text string matches a specified pattern.

This function, which follows, is remarkably simple. As you can see, the function is essentially a wrapper that lets you take advantage of VBA's powerful Like operator in your formulas.

```
Function ISLIKE(text As String, pattern As String) As Boolean
'   Returns true if the first argument is like the second
    ISLIKE = text Like pattern
End Function
```

This ISLIKE function takes two arguments:

◆ text: A text string or a reference to a cell that contains a text string

◆ pattern: A string that contains wildcard characters according to the following list:

Character(s) in pattern	Matches in text
?	Any single character
*	Zero or more characters
#	Any single digit (0–9)
[charlist]	Any single character in charlist
[!charlist]	Any single character not in charlist

The following formula returns TRUE because * matches any number of characters. It returns TRUE if the first argument is any text that begins with "g".

```
=ISLIKE("guitar","g*")
```

The following formula returns TRUE because ? matches any single character. If the first argument were "Unit12", the function would return FALSE.

```
=ISLIKE("Unit1","Unit?")
```

The next formula returns TRUE because the first argument is a single character in the second argument.

```
=ISLIKE("a","[aeiou]")
```

The following formula returns TRUE if cell A1 contains a, e, i, o, u, A, E, I, O, or U. Using the UPPER function for the arguments makes the formula not case-sensitive.

```
=ISLIKE(UPPER(A1),UPPER ("[aeiou]"))
```

The following formula returns TRUE if cell A1 contains a value that begins with 1 and has exactly three digits (that is, any integer between 100 and 199).

```
=ISLIKE(A1,"1##")
```

Extracting the nth element from a string

ExtractElement is a custom worksheet function (which can also be called from a VBA procedure) that extracts an element from a text string. For example, if a cell contains the following text, you can use the ExtractElement function to extract any of the substrings between the hyphens.

```
123-456-789-0133-8844
```

The following formula, for example, returns 0133, which is the fourth element in the string. The string uses a hyphen (-) as the separator.

```
=ExtractElement("123-456-789-0133-8844",4,"-")
```

The ExtractElement function uses three arguments:

- ◆ Txt: The text string from which you're extracting. This can be a literal string or a cell reference.
- ◆ n: An integer that represents the element to extract.
- ◆ Separator: A single character used as the separator.

If you specify a space as the Separator character, multiple spaces are treated as a single space, which is almost always what you want. If n exceeds the number of elements in the string, the function returns an empty string.

The VBA code for the EXTRACTELEMENT function follows:

```
Function EXTRACTELEMENT(Txt, n, Separator) As String
'   Returns the nth element of a text string, where the
'   elements are separated by a specified separator character
    Dim AllElements As Variant
    AllElements = Split(Txt, Separator)
    EXTRACTELEMENT = AllElements(n - 1)
End Function
```

This function uses VBA's Split function, which returns a variant array that contains each element of the text string. This array begins with 0 (not 1), so using n-1 references the desired element.

The Split function was introduced in Excel 2000. If you're using an older version of Excel, you'll need to use the following function:

```
Function EXTRACTELEMENT2(Txt, n, Separator) As String
'   Returns the nth element of a text string, where the
'   elements are separated by a specified separator character

    Dim Txt1 As String, TempElement As String
    Dim ElementCount As Integer, i As Integer

    Txt1 = Txt
'   If space separator, remove excess spaces
    If Separator = Chr(32) Then Txt1 = Application.Trim(Txt1)

'   Add a separator to the end of the string
    If Right(Txt1, Len(Txt1)) <> Separator Then _
        Txt1 = Txt1 & Separator

'   Initialize
    ElementCount = 0
    TempElement = ""

'   Extract each element
    For i = 1 To Len(Txt1)
        If Mid(Txt1, i, 1) = Separator Then
            ElementCount = ElementCount + 1
```

```
            If ElementCount = n Then
                Found it, so exit
                EXTRACTELEMENT2 = TempElement
                Exit Function
            Else
                TempElement = ""
            End If
        Else
            TempElement = TempElement & Mid(Txt1, i, 1)
        End If
    Next i
    EXTRACTELEMENT2 = ""
End Function
```

A multifunctional function

This example describes a technique that may be helpful in some situations: making a single worksheet function act like multiple functions. For example, the following VBA listing is for a custom function called StatFunction. It takes two arguments: the range (rng) and the operation (op). Depending on the value of op, the function returns a value computed using any of the following worksheet functions: AVERAGE, COUNT, MAX, MEDIAN, MIN, MODE, STDEV, SUM, or VAR.

For example, you can use this function in your worksheet as follows:

```
=STATFUNCTION(B1:B24,A24)
```

The result of the formula depends on the contents of cell A24, which should be a string such as Average, Count, Max, and so on. You can adapt this technique for other types of functions.

```
Function STATFUNCTION(rng, op)
    Select Case UCase(op)
        Case "SUM"
            STATFUNCTION = WorksheetFunction.Sum(rng)
        Case "AVERAGE"
            STATFUNCTION = WorksheetFunction.Average(rng)
        Case "MEDIAN"
            STATFUNCTION = WorksheetFunction.Median(rng)
        Case "MODE"
            STATFUNCTION = WorksheetFunction.Mode(rng)
        Case "COUNT"
            STATFUNCTION = WorksheetFunction.Count(rng)
        Case "MAX"
            STATFUNCTION = WorksheetFunction.Max(rng)
        Case "MIN"
            STATFUNCTION = WorksheetFunction.Min(rng)
```

```
        Case "VAR"
            STATFUNCTION = WorksheetFunction.Var(rng)
        Case "STDEV"
            STATFUNCTION = WorksheetFunction.StDev(rng)
        Case Else
            STATFUNCTION = CVErr(xlErrNA)
    End Select
End Function
```

The SHEETOFFSET function

You probably know that Excel's support for 3-D workbooks is limited. For example, if you need to refer to a different worksheet in a workbook, you must include the worksheet's name in your formula. This is not a big problem . . . until you attempt to copy the formula across other worksheets. The copied formulas continue to refer to the original worksheet name, and the sheet references are not adjusted as they would be in a true 3-D workbook.

The example discussed in this section is a VBA function (named SHEETOFFSET) that enables you to address worksheets in a relative manner. For example, you can refer to cell A1 on the previous worksheet by using this formula:

```
=SHEETOFFSET(-1,A1)
```

The first argument represents the relative sheet, and it can be positive, negative, or zero. The second argument must be a reference to a single cell. You can copy this formula to other sheets, and the relative referencing will be in effect in all the copied formulas.

The VBA code for the SHEETOFFSET function follows:

```
Function SHEETOFFSET(Offset As Long, Optional Cell As Variant)
'    Returns cell contents at Ref, in sheet offset
    Dim WksIndex As Long, WksNum As Long
    Dim wks As Worksheet
    Application.Volatile
    If IsMissing(Cell) Then Set Cell = Application.Caller
    WksNum = 1
    For Each wks In Application.Caller.Parent.Parent.Worksheets
        If Application.Caller.Parent.Name = wks.Name Then
            SHEETOFFSET = Worksheets(WksNum + Offset).Range(Cell(1).Address)
            Exit Function
        Else
            WksNum = WksNum + 1
        End If
    Next wks
End Function
```

Returning the maximum value across all worksheets

If you need to determine the maximum value in cell B1 across a number of worksheets, you would use a formula such as this:

```
=MAX(Sheet1:Sheet4!B1)
```

This formula returns the maximum value in cell B1 for Sheet1, Sheet4, and all the sheets in between.

But what if you add a new sheet (Sheet5) after Sheet4? Your formula won't adjust automatically, so you need to edit it to include the new sheet reference:

```
=MAX(Sheet1:Sheet5!B1)
```

The MAXALLSHEETS function, which follows, accepts a single-cell argument and returns the maximum value in that cell across all worksheets in the workbook. The formula that follows, for example, returns the maximum value in cell B1 for all sheets in the workbook:

```
=MAXALLSHEETS(B1)
```

If you add a new sheet, there's no need to edit the formula:

```
Function MAXALLSHEETS(cell)
    Dim MaxVal As Double
    Dim Addr As String
    Dim Wksht As Object
    Application.Volatile
    Addr = cell.Range("A1").Address
    MaxVal = -9.9E+307
    For Each Wksht In cell.Parent.Parent.Worksheets
        If Wksht.Name = cell.Parent.Name And _
          Addr = Application.Caller.Address Then
        ' avoid circular reference
        Else
            If IsNumeric(Wksht.Range(Addr)) Then
                If Wksht.Range(Addr) > MaxVal Then _
                MaxVal = Wksht.Range(Addr).Value
            End If
        End If
    Next Wksht
    If MaxVal = -9.9E+307 Then MaxVal = 0
    MAXALLSHEETS = MaxVal
End Function
```

The For Each statement uses the following expression to access the workbook:

```
cell.Parent.Parent.Worksheets
```

The parent of the cell is a worksheet, and the parent of the worksheet is the workbook. Therefore, the For Each-Next loop cycles among all worksheets in the workbook. The first If statement inside of the loop performs a check to see whether the cell being checked is the cell that contains the function. If so, that cell is ignored to avoid a circular reference error.

 This function can be modified easily to perform other cross-worksheet calculations: Minimum, Average, Sum, and so on.

Returning an array of nonduplicated random integers

The function in this section, RANDOMINTEGERS, returns an array of nonduplicated integers. The function is intended to be used in a multicell array formula.

```
{=RANDOMINTEGERS()}
```

Select a range and then enter the formula by using Ctrl+Shift+Enter. The formula returns an array of nonduplicated integers, arranged randomly. For example, if you enter the formula into a 50-cell range, the formulas will return nonduplicated integers from 1 to 50.

The code for RANDOMINTEGERS follows:

```
Function RANDOMINTEGERS()
    Dim FuncRange As Range
    Dim V() As Variant, ValArray() As Variant
    Dim CellCount As Double
    Dim i As Integer, j As Integer
    Dim r As Integer, c As Integer
    Dim Temp1 As Variant, Temp2 As Variant
    Dim RCount As Integer, CCount As Integer
    Randomize

'   Create Range object
    Set FuncRange = Application.Caller
```

```
'    Return an error if FuncRange is too large
     CellCount = FuncRange.Count
     If CellCount > 1000 Then
         RANDOMINTEGERS = CVErr(xlErrNA)
         Exit Function
     End If

'    Assign variables
     RCount = FuncRange.Rows.Count
     CCount = FuncRange.Columns.Count
     ReDim V(1 To RCount, 1 To CCount)
     ReDim ValArray(1 To 2, 1 To CellCount)

'    Fill array with random numbers
'    and consecutive integers
     For i = 1 To CellCount
         ValArray(1, i) = Rnd
         ValArray(2, i) = i
     Next i

'    Sort ValArray by the random number dimension
     For i = 1 To CellCount
         For j = i + 1 To CellCount
             If ValArray(1, i) > ValArray(1, j) Then
                 Temp1 = ValArray(1, j)
                 Temp2 = ValArray(2, j)
                 ValArray(1, j) = ValArray(1, i)
                 ValArray(2, j) = ValArray(2, i)
                 ValArray(1, i) = Temp1
                 ValArray(2, i) = Temp2
             End If
         Next j
     Next i

'    Put the randomized values into the V array
     i = 0
     For r = 1 To RCount
         For c = 1 To CCount
             i = i + 1
             V(r, c) = ValArray(2, i)
         Next c
     Next r
     RANDOMINTEGERS = V
End Function
```

Randomizing a range

The RANGERANDOMIZE function, which follows, accepts a range argument and returns an array that consists of the input range – in random order:

```
Function RANGERANDOMIZE(rng)
    Dim V() As Variant, ValArray() As Variant
    Dim CellCount As Double
    Dim i As Integer, j As Integer
    Dim r As Integer, c As Integer
    Dim Temp1 As Variant, Temp2 As Variant
    Dim RCount As Integer, CCount As Integer
    Randomize

'   Return an error if rng is too large
    CellCount = rng.Count
    If CellCount > 1000 Then
        RANGERANDOMIZE = CVErr(xlErrNA)
        Exit Function
    End If

'   Assign variables
    RCount = rng.Rows.Count
    CCount = rng.Columns.Count
    ReDim V(1 To RCount, 1 To CCount)
    ReDim ValArray(1 To 2, 1 To CellCount)

'   Fill ValArray with random numbers
'   and values from rng
    For i = 1 To CellCount
        ValArray(1, i) = Rnd
        ValArray(2, i) = rng(i)
    Next i

'   Sort ValArray by the random number dimension
    For i = 1 To CellCount
        For j = i + 1 To CellCount
            If ValArray(1, i) > ValArray(1, j) Then
                Temp1 = ValArray(1, j)
                Temp2 = ValArray(2, j)
                ValArray(1, j) = ValArray(1, i)
                ValArray(2, j) = ValArray(2, i)
                ValArray(1, i) = Temp1
                ValArray(2, i) = Temp2
            End If
```

```
        Next j
    Next i

'   Put the randomized values into the V array
    i = 0
    For r = 1 To RCount
        For c = 1 To CCount
            i = i + 1
            V(r, c) = ValArray(2, i)
        Next c
    Next r
    RANGERANDOMIZE = V
End Function
```

The code is very similar to that for the RANDOMINTEGERS function.
Figure 11-12 shows the function in use. The array formula in B2:B11 is:

```
{=RANGERANDOMIZE(A2:A11)}
```

This formula returns the contents of A2:A11, but in random order.

	A	B	C
1	Original	Randomized	
2	1	9	
3	2	10	
4	3	3	
5	4	2	
6	5	1	
7	6	6	
8	7	4	
9	8	8	
10	9	7	
11	10	5	
12			

Figure 11-12: The RANGERANDOMIZE function returns the contents of a range, in random order.

Windows API Calls

One of VBA's most important features is the capability to use functions that are stored in Dynamic Link Libraries (DLLs). The examples in this section use common Windows API calls.

The API declarations that you can use depend on your version of Excel. If you attempt to use a 32-bit API function with 16-bit Excel 5, you'll get an error.

Similarly, if you attempt to use a 16-bit API function with 32-bit Excel 95 or later, you'll get an error. The examples in this section are for 32-bit Excel.

I discuss this and other compatibility issues in detail in Chapter 25.

Determining file associations

In Windows, many file types are associated with a particular application. This association makes it possible to double-click the file to load it into its associated application.

The following function, named GetExecutable, uses a Windows API call to get the full path to the application associated with a particular file. For example, your system has many files with a .txt extension — one named Readme.txt is probably in your Windows directory right now. You can use the GetExecutable function to determine the full path of the application that opens when the file is double-clicked.

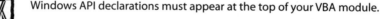

Windows API declarations must appear at the top of your VBA module.

```
Private Declare Function FindExecutableA Lib "shell32.dll" _
    (ByVal lpFile As String, ByVal lpDirectory As String, _
    ByVal lpResult As String) As Long

Function GetExecutable(strFile As String) As String
    Dim strPath As String
    Dim intLen As Integer
    strPath = Space(255)
    intLen = FindExecutableA(strFile, "\", strPath)
    GetExecutable = Trim(strPath)
End Function
```

Figure 11-13 shows the result of calling the GetExecutable function, with an argument of the filename for a Word file. The function returns the full path of the application that's associated with the file.

Figure 11-13: Determining the path of the application associated with a particular file.

Determining default printer information

The example in this section uses a Windows API function to return information about the active printer. The information is contained in a single text string. The example parses the string and displays the information in a more readable format.

```
Private Declare Function GetProfileStringA Lib "kernel32" _
   (ByVal lpAppName As String, ByVal lpKeyName As String, _
   ByVal lpDefault As String, ByVal lpReturnedString As _
   String, ByVal nSize As Long) As Long

Sub DefaultPrinterInfo()
    Dim strLPT As String * 255
    Dim Result As String
    Call GetProfileStringA _
      ("Windows", "Device", "", strLPT, 254)

    Result = Application.Trim(strLPT)
    ResultLength = Len(Result)

    Comma1 = InStr(1, Result, ",", 1)
    Comma2 = InStr(Comma1 + 1, Result, ",", 1)

'   Gets printer's name
    Printer = Left(Result, Comma1 - 1)

'   Gets driver
    Driver = Mid(Result, Comma1 + 1, Comma2 - Comma1 - 1)

'   Gets last part of device line
    Port = Right(Result, ResultLength - Comma2)

'   Build message
    Msg = "Printer:" & Chr(9) & Printer & Chr(13)
    Msg = Msg & "Driver:" & Chr(9) & Driver & Chr(13)
    Msg = Msg & "Port:" & Chr(9) & Port
```

```
'     Display message
      MsgBox Msg, vbInformation, "Default Printer Information"
End Sub
```

The `ActivePrinter` property of the `Application` object returns the name of the active printer (and lets you change it), but there's no direct way to determine what printer driver or port is being used. That's why this function is useful.

Figure 11-14 shows a sample message box returned by this procedure.

Figure 11-14: Getting information about the active printer by using a Windows API call.

Determining the current video mode

The example in this section uses Windows API calls to determine a system's current video mode. If your application needs to display a certain amount of information on one screen, knowing the display size helps you scale the text accordingly.

```
'32-bit API declaration
Declare Function GetSystemMetrics Lib "user32" _
  (ByVal nIndex As Long) As Long

Public Const SM_CXSCREEN = 0
Public Const SM_CYSCREEN = 1

Sub DisplayVideoInfo()
    vidWidth = GetSystemMetrics(SM_CXSCREEN)
    vidHeight = GetSystemMetrics(SM_CYSCREEN)

    Msg = "The current video mode is: "
    Msg = Msg & vidWidth & " X " & vidHeight
    MsgBox Msg
End Sub
```

Figure 11-15 shows the message box returned by this procedure when running on a system set to 1600 x 1024 resolution.

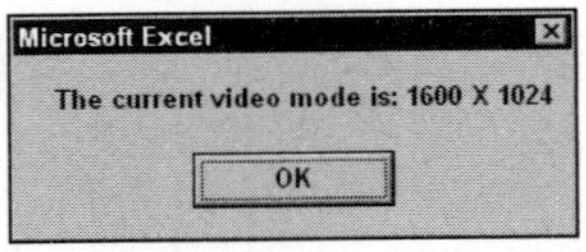

```
Microsoft Excel                    [X]
  The current video mode is: 1600 X 1024
         [    OK    ]
```

Figure 11-15: Using a Windows API call to determine the video display mode.

Adding sound to your applications

By itself, Excel doesn't have much to offer in the area of sound — VBA's Beep command is about as good as it gets. However, with a few simple API calls, your application can play WAV or MIDI files.

The text-to-speech feature, which debuted in Excel 2002, extends the sound capability quite a bit. In fact, Excel 2002 and later can "speak" text by using the Speak method of the Speech object. The examples in this section focus on playing sound files, not speech.

Not all systems support sound. To determine whether a system supports sound, use the CanPlaySounds method. Here's an example:

```
If Not Application.CanPlaySounds Then
    MsgBox "Sorry, sound is not supported on your system."
    Exit Sub
End If
```

PLAYING A WAV FILE

The following example contains the API function declaration plus a simple procedure to play a sound file called dogbark.wav, which is presumed to be in the same directory as the workbook:

```
Private Declare Function PlaySound Lib "winmm.dll" _
  Alias "PlaySoundA" (ByVal lpszName As String, _
  ByVal hModule As Long, ByVal dwFlags As Long) As Long

Const SND_SYNC = &H0
Const SND_ASYNC = &H1
Const SND_FILENAME = &H20000
```

```
Sub PlayWAV()
    WAVFile = "dogbark.wav"
    WAVFile = ThisWorkbook.Path & "\" & WAVFile
    Call PlaySound(WAVFile, 0&, SND_ASYNC Or SND_FILENAME)
End Sub
```

In the preceding example, the WAV file is played asynchronously. This means that execution continues while the sound is playing. To stop code execution while the sound is playing, use this statement instead:

```
Call PlaySound(WAVFile, 0&, SND_SYNC Or SND_FILENAME)
```

PLAYING A MIDI FILE

If the sound file is a MIDI file, you'll need to use a different API call. The `PlayMIDI` procedure starts playing a MIDI file. Executing the `StopMIDI` procedure stops playing the MIDI file. This example uses a file named `xfiles.mid`.

```
Private Declare Function mciExecute Lib "winmm.dll" _
  (ByVal lpstrCommand As String) As Long

Sub PlayMIDI()
    MIDIFile = "xfiles.mid"
    MIDIFile = ThisWorkbook.Path & "\" & MIDIFile
    mciExecute ("play " & MIDIFile)
End Sub

Sub StopMIDI()
    MIDIFile = "xfiles.mid"
    MIDIFile = ThisWorkbook.Path & "\" & MIDIFile
    mciExecute ("stop " & MIDIFile)
End Sub
```

PLAYING SOUND FROM A WORKSHEET FUNCTION

The `Alarm` function, which follows, is designed to be used in a worksheet formula. It uses a Windows API function to play a sound file when a cell meets a certain condition.

```
Declare Function PlaySound Lib "winmm.dll" _
  Alias "PlaySoundA" (ByVal lpszName As String, _
  ByVal hModule As Long, ByVal dwFlags As Long) As Long

Function ALARM(Cell, Condition)
    Dim WAVFile As String
    Const SND_ASYNC = &H1
    Const SND_FILENAME = &H20000
```

```
    If Evaluate(Cell.Value & Condition) Then
        WAVFile = ThisWorkbook.Path & "\sound.wav"
        Call PlaySound(WAVFile, O&, SND_ASYNC Or SND_FILENAME)
        ALARM = True
    Else
        ALARM = False
    End If
End Function
```

The `Alarm` function accepts two arguments: a cell reference and a condition (expressed as a string). The following formula, for example, uses the `Alarm` function to play a WAV file when the value in cell B13 is greater than or equal to 1000.

```
=ALARM(B13,">=1000")
```

The function uses VBA's `Evaluate` function to determine whether the cell's value matches the specified criterion. When the criterion is met (and the alarm has sounded), the function returns `True`; otherwise, it returns `False`.

Reading from and writing to the Registry

Most Windows applications use the Windows Registry database to store settings. (See Chapter 4 for some additional information about the Registry.) Your VBA procedures can read values from the Registry and write new values to the Registry. Doing so requires the following Windows API declarations:

```
Private Declare Function RegOpenKeyA Lib "ADVAPI32.DLL" _
    (ByVal hKey As Long, ByVal sSubKey As String, _
    ByRef hkeyResult As Long) As Long

Private Declare Function RegCloseKey Lib "ADVAPI32.DLL" _
    (ByVal hKey As Long) As Long

Private Declare Function RegSetValueExA Lib "ADVAPI32.DLL" _
    (ByVal hKey As Long, ByVal sValueName As String, _
    ByVal dwReserved As Long, ByVal dwType As Long, _
    ByVal sValue As String, ByVal dwSize As Long) As Long

Private Declare Function RegCreateKeyA Lib "ADVAPI32.DLL" _
    (ByVal hKey As Long, ByVal sSubKey As String, _
    ByRef hkeyResult As Long) As Long

Private Declare Function RegQueryValueExA Lib "ADVAPI32.DLL" _
    (ByVal hKey As Long, ByVal sValueName As String, _
    ByVal dwReserved As Long, ByRef lValueType As Long, _
    ByVal sValue As String, ByRef lResultLen As Long) As Long
```

I developed two wrapper functions that simplify the task of working with the Registry: GetRegistry and WriteRegistry. These functions are available on the companion CD-ROM. This workbook includes a procedure that demonstrates reading from the Registry and writing to the Registry.

READING FROM THE REGISTRY

The GetRegistry function returns a setting from the specified location in the Registry. It takes three arguments:

- ◆ RootKey: A string that represents the branch of the Registry to address. This string can be one of the following:

    HKEY_CLASSES_ROOT

    HKEY_CURRENT_USER

    HKEY_LOCAL_MACHINE

    HKEY_USERS

    HKEY_CURRENT_CONFIG

    HKEY_DYN_DATA

- ◆ Path: The full path of the Registry category being addressed.

- ◆ RegEntry: The name of the setting to retrieve.

Here's an example. If you'd like to find out the current setting for the active window title bar, you can call GetRegistry as follows. (Notice that the arguments are not case-sensitive.)

```
RootKey = "hkey_current_user"
Path = "Control Panel\Colors"
RegEntry = "ActiveTitle"
MsgBox GetRegistry(RootKey, Path, RegEntry), _
  vbInformation, Path & "\RegEntry"
```

The message box will display three values, representing the red/green/blue (RGB) value of the color.

WRITING TO THE REGISTRY

The WriteRegistry function writes a value to the Registry at a specified location. If the operation is successful, the function returns True; otherwise, it returns False. WriteRegistry takes the following arguments (all of which are strings):

◆ RootKey: A string that represents the branch of the Registry to address. This string may be one of the following:

HKEY_CLASSES_ROOT

HKEY_CURRENT_USER

HKEY_LOCAL_MACHINE

HKEY_USERS

HKEY_CURRENT_CONFIG

HKEY_DYN_DATA

◆ Path: The full path in the Registry. If the path doesn't exist, it is created.

◆ RegEntry: The name of the Registry category to which the value will be written. If it doesn't exist, it is added.

◆ RegVal: The value that you are writing.

Here's an example that writes a value representing the time and date Excel was started to the Registry. The information is written in the area that stores Excel's settings.

```
Sub Auto_Open()
    RootKey = "hkey_current_user"
    Path = "software\microsoft\office\11.0\excel\LastStarted"
    RegEntry = "DateTime"
    RegVal = Now()
```

An Easier Way to Access the Registry

If you want to use the Windows Registry to store and retrieve settings for your Excel applications, you don't have to bother with the Windows API calls. Rather, you can use VBA's GetSetting and SaveSetting functions.

These two functions are described in the online help, so I won't cover the details here. However, it's important to understand that these functions work only with the following key name:

HKEY_CURRENT_USER\Software\VB and VBA Program Settings

In other words, you can't use these functions to access *any* key in the Registry. Rather, these functions are most useful for storing information about your Excel application that you need to maintain between sessions.

```
    If WriteRegistry(RootKey, Path, RegEntry, RegVal) Then
        msg = RegVal & " has been stored in the registry."
          Else msg = "An error occurred"
    End If
    MsgBox msg
End Sub
```

If you store this routine in your personal macro workbook, the setting is automatically updated whenever you start Excel.

Part IV

Working with UserForms

Chapter 12

Custom Dialog Box Alternatives

IN THIS CHAPTER

Dialog boxes are, perhaps, the most important user interface element in Windows programs. Virtually every Windows program uses them, and most users have a good understanding of how they work. Excel developers implement custom dialog boxes by creating UserForms. To that end, I cover the following:

- ◆ Using an input box to get user input
- ◆ Using a message box to display messages or get a simple response
- ◆ Selecting a file from a dialog box
- ◆ Selecting a directory
- ◆ Displaying Excel's built-in dialog boxes

BEFORE I GET INTO THE NITTY-GRITTY OF CREATING USERFORMS, you might find it helpful to understand some of Excel's built-in tools that display dialog boxes. That's the focus of this chapter.

Before You Create That UserForm . . .

In some cases, you can save yourself the trouble of creating a custom dialog box by using one of several prebuilt dialog boxes:

- ◆ An input box
- ◆ A message box
- ◆ A dialog box for selecting a file to open
- ◆ A dialog box for specifying a filename and location for a save operation
- ◆ A dialog box for specifying a directory
- ◆ A dialog box for data entry

I describe these dialog boxes in the following sections.

Using an Input Box

An *input box* is a simple dialog box that allows the user to make a single entry. For example, you can use an input box to let the user enter text, a number, or even select a range. There are actually two `InputBox` functions: one from VBA and one from Excel.

The VBA InputBox function

The syntax for VBA's `InputBox` function is

```
InputBox(prompt[,title][,default][,xpos][,ypos][,helpfile, context])
```

- ◆ `prompt`: Required. The text displayed in the input box.

- ◆ `title`: Optional. The caption of the input box window.

- ◆ `default`: Optional. The default value to be displayed in the dialog box.

- ◆ `xpos, ypos`: Optional. The screen coordinates at the upper-left corner of the window.

- ◆ `helpfile, context`: Optional. The helpfile and help topic.

The `InputBox` function prompts the user for a single bit of information. The function always returns a string, so it may be necessary to convert the results to a value.

The prompt may consist of about 1,024 characters (more or less, depending on the width of the characters used). In addition, you can provide a title for the dialog box, a default value, and specify its position on the screen. And you can specify a custom help topic; if you do, the input box includes a Help button.

The following example, whose output is shown in Figure 12-1, uses the VBA `InputBox` function to ask the user for his or her full name. The code then extracts the first name and displays a greeting, using a message box.

Figure 12-1: VBA's `InputBox` function at work.

```
Sub GetName()
    Dim UserName As String
    Dim FirstSpace As Integer
```

```
    Do Until UserName <> ""
        UserName = InputBox("Enter your full name: ", _
            "Identify Yourself")
    Loop
    FirstSpace = InStr(UserName, " ")
    If FirstSpace <> 0 Then
        UserName = Left(UserName, FirstSpace - 1)
    End If
    MsgBox "Hello " & UserName
End Sub
```

 This example is available on the companion CD-ROM.

Notice that this InputBox function is written in a Do Until loop to ensure that something is entered when the input box appears. If the user clicks Cancel or doesn't enter any text, UserName contains an empty string, and the input box reappears. The procedure then attempts to extract the first name by searching for the first space character (by using the InStr function) and then using the Left function to extract all characters before the first space. If a space character is not found, the entire name is used as entered.

As I mentioned, the InputBox function always returns a string. If the string returned by the InputBox function looks like a number, you can convert it to a value by using VBA's Val function. Or, you can use Excel's InputBox method, which I describe next.

The Excel InputBox method

Using Excel's InputBox method (rather than VBA's InputBox function) offers three advantages:

◆ You can specify the data type returned.

◆ The user can specify a worksheet range by dragging in the worksheet.

◆ Input validation is performed automatically.

The syntax for the Excel InputBox method is

```
object.InputBox(prompt,title,default,left,top,helpFile,
helpContextID,type)
```

- ◆ `prompt`: Required. The text displayed in the input box.

- ◆ `title`: Optional. The caption in the input box window.

- ◆ `default`: Optional. The default value to be returned by the function if the user enters nothing.

- ◆ `left`, `top`: Optional. The screen coordinates at the upper-left corner of the window.

- ◆ `helpFile`, `helpContextID`: Optional. The help file and help topic.

- ◆ `type`: Optional. A code for the data type returned, as listed in Table 12-1.

TABLE 12-1   CODES TO DETERMINE THE DATA TYPE RETURNED BY EXCEL'S INPUTBOX METHOD

Code	Meaning
0	A formula
1	A number
2	A string (text)
4	A logical value (`True` or `False`)
8	A cell reference, as a range object
16	An error value, such as #N/A
64	An array of values

Excel's InputBox method is quite versatile. To allow more than one data type to be returned, use the sum of the pertinent codes. For example, to display an input box that can accept text or numbers, set `type` equal to 3 (that is, 1 + 2, or *number* plus *text*). If you use 8 for the `type` argument, the user can enter a cell or range address manually, or point to a range in the worksheet.

The `EraseRange` procedure, which follows, uses the InputBox method to allow the user to select a range to erase (see Figure 12-2). The user can either type the range address manually or use the mouse to select the range in the sheet.

The InputBox method with a `type` argument of 8 returns a `Range` object (note the `Set` keyword). This range is then erased (by using the `Clear` method). The default value displayed in the input box is the current selection's address. The `On Error` statement ends the procedure if the input box is cancelled.

```
Sub EraseRange()
    Dim UserRange As Range
```

```
    DefaultRange = Selection.Address
    On Error GoTo Canceled
    Set UserRange = Application.InputBox _
        (Prompt:="Range to erase:", _
        Title:="Range Erase", _
        Default:=DefaultRange, _
        Type:=8)
    UserRange.Clear
    UserRange.Select
Canceled:
End Sub
```

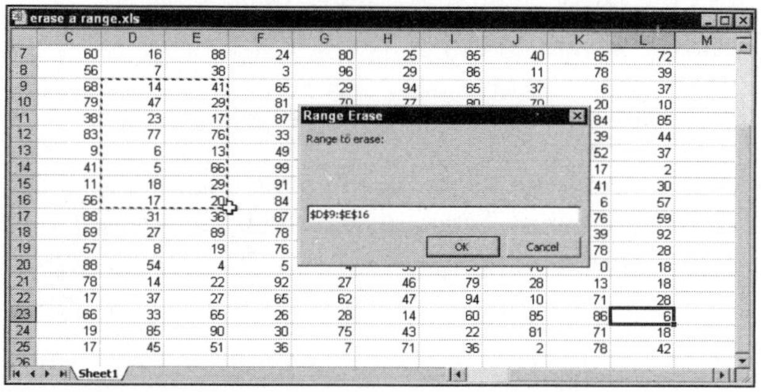

Figure 12-2: Using the InputBox method to specify a range.

This example is available on the companion CD-ROM.

Yet another advantage of using Excel's InputBox method is that Excel performs input validation automatically. In the `GetRange` example, if you enter something other than a range address, Excel displays an informative message and lets the user try again (see Figure 12-3).

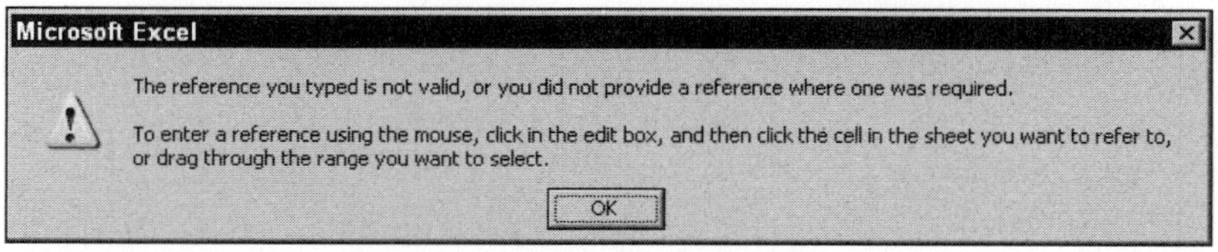

Figure 12-3: Excel's InputBox method performs validation automatically.

The VBA MsgBox Function

VBA's `MsgBox` function is an easy way to display a message to the user or to get a simple response (such as OK or Cancel). I use the `MsgBox` function in many of this book's examples as a way to display a variable's value.

The official syntax for `MsgBox` is as follows:

```
MsgBox(prompt[,buttons][,title][,helpfile, context])
```

 ◆ `prompt`: Required. The text displayed in the message box.

 ◆ `buttons`: Optional. A numeric expression that determines which buttons and icon are displayed in the message box. See Table 12-2.

 ◆ `title`: Optional. The caption in the message box window.

 ◆ `helpfile`, `context`: Optional. The helpfile and help topic.

You can easily customize your message boxes because of the flexibility of the `buttons` argument. (Table 12-2 lists the many constants that you can use for this argument.) You can specify which buttons to display, whether an icon appears, and which button is the default.

TABLE 12-2 CONSTANTS USED FOR BUTTONS IN THE MSGBOX FUNCTION

Constant	Value	Description
vbOKOnly	0	Display OK button only.
vbOKCancel	1	Display OK and Cancel buttons.
vbAbortRetryIgnore	2	Display Abort, Retry, and Ignore buttons.
vbYesNoCancel	3	Display Yes, No, and Cancel buttons.
vbYesNo	4	Display Yes and No buttons.
vbRetryCancel	5	Display Retry and Cancel buttons.
vbCritical	16	Display Critical Message icon.
vbQuestion	32	Display Warning Query icon.
vbExclamation	48	Display Warning Message icon.
vbInformation	64	Display Information Message icon.
vbDefaultButton1	0	First button is default.
vbDefaultButton2	256	Second button is default.

Constant	Value	Description
vbDefaultButton3	512	Third button is default.
vbDefaultButton4	768	Fourth button is default.
vbSystemModal	4096	All applications are suspended until the user responds to the message box (might not work under all conditions).

You can use the MsgBox function by itself (to simply display a message) or assign its result to a variable. When MsgBox does return a result, it represents the button clicked by the user. The following example displays a message and does not return a result:

```
Sub MsgBoxDemo()
    MsgBox "Click OK to continue"
End Sub
```

To get a response from a message box, you can assign the results of the MsgBox function to a variable. In the following code, I use some built-in constants (described in Table 12-3) to make it easier to work with the values returned by MsgBox:

```
Sub GetAnswer()
    Ans = MsgBox("Continue?", vbYesNo)
    Select Case Ans
        Case vbYes
'       ...[code if Ans is Yes]...
        Case vbNo
'       ...[code if Ans is No]...
    End Select
End Sub
```

TABLE 12-3 CONSTANTS USED FOR MSGBOX RETURN VALUE

Constant	Value	Button Clicked
vbOK	1	OK
vbCancel	2	Cancel

Continued

TABLE 12-3 CONSTANTS USED FOR MSGBOX RETURN VALUE *(Continued)*

Constant	Value	Button Clicked
vbAbort	3	Abort
vbRetry	4	Retry
vbIgnore	5	Ignore
vbYes	6	Yes
vbNo	7	No

Actually, it's not even necessary to use a variable to utilize the result of a message box. The following procedure displays a message box with Yes and No buttons. If the user doesn't click the Yes button, the procedure ends.

```
Sub GetAnswer2()
    If MsgBox("Continue?", vbYesNo) <> vbYes Then Exit Sub
'   ...[code if Yes button is not clicked]...
End Sub
```

The following function example uses a combination of constants to display a message box with a Yes button, a No button, and a question mark icon; the second button is designated as the default button (see Figure 12-4). For simplicity, I assigned these constants to the Config variable.

Figure 12-4: The buttons argument of the MsgBox function determines which buttons appear.

```
Private Function ContinueProcedure() As Boolean
    Dim Config As Integer
    Dim Ans As Integer
    Config = vbYesNo + vbQuestion + vbDefaultButton2
    Ans = MsgBox("An error occurred. Continue?", Config)
    If Ans = vbYes Then ContinueProcedure = True _
        Else ContinueProcedure = False
End Function
```

The `ContinueProcedure` function can be called from another procedure. For example, the following statement calls the `ContinueProcedure` function (which displays the message box). If the function returns `False` (that is, the user selects No), the procedure ends. Otherwise, the next statement would be executed.

```
If Not ContinueProcedure() Then Exit Sub
```

If you would like to force a line break in the message, use the `vbCrLf` (or `vbNewLine`) constant in the text. The following example displays the message in three lines:

```
Sub MultiLine()
    Dim Msg As String
    Msg = "This is the first line" & vbCrLf
    Msg = Msg & "Second line" & vbCrLf
    Msg = Msg & "Last line"
    MsgBox Msg
End Sub
```

You can also insert a tab character by using the `vbTab` constant. The following procedure uses a message box to display the values in a 20 x 8 range of cells (see Figure 12-5). It separates the columns by using a `vbTab` constant and inserts a new line by using the `vbCrLF` constant. The `MsgBox` function accepts a maximum string length of 1,023 characters, which will limit the number of cells that you can display.

```
Sub ShowRange()
    Dim Msg As String
    Dim r As Integer, c As Integer
    Msg = ""
    For r = 1 To 20
        For c = 1 To 8
            Msg = Msg & Cells(r, c) & vbTab
        Next c
        Msg = Msg & vbCrLf
    Next r
    MsgBox Msg
End Sub
```

Chapter 15 includes a UserForm example that emulates the `MsgBox` function.

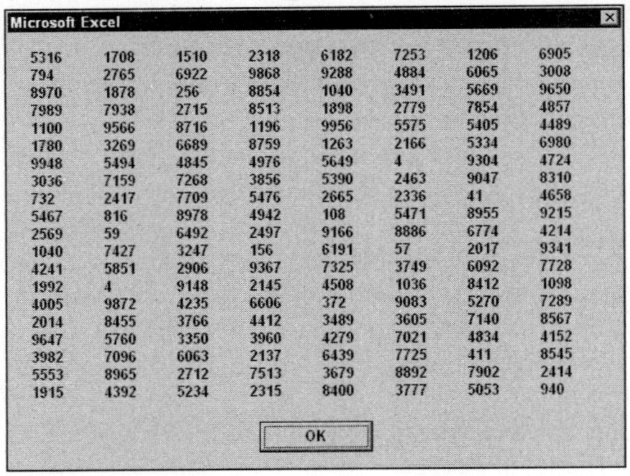

Microsoft Excel							
5316	1708	1510	2318	6182	7253	1206	6905
794	2765	6922	9868	9288	4884	6065	3008
8970	1878	256	8854	1040	3491	5669	9650
7989	7938	2715	8513	1898	2779	7854	4857
1100	9566	8716	1196	9956	5575	5405	4489
1780	3269	6689	8759	1263	2166	5334	6980
9948	5494	4845	4976	5649	4	9304	4724
3036	7159	7268	3856	5390	2463	9047	8310
732	2417	7709	5476	2665	2336	41	4658
5467	816	8978	4942	108	5471	8955	9215
2569	59	6492	2497	9166	8886	6774	4214
1040	7427	3247	156	6191	57	2017	9341
4241	5851	2906	9367	7325	3749	6092	7728
1992	4	9148	2145	4508	1036	8412	1098
4005	9872	4235	6606	372	9083	5270	7289
2014	8455	3766	4412	3489	3605	7140	8567
9647	5760	3350	3960	4279	7021	4834	4152
3982	7096	6063	2137	6439	7725	411	8545
5553	8965	2712	7513	3679	8892	7902	2414
1915	4392	5234	2315	8400	3777	5053	940

OK

Figure 12-5: This message box displays text with tabs and line breaks.

The Excel GetOpenFilename Method

If your application needs to ask the user for a filename, you can use the InputBox function. But this approach often leads to typographical errors. A better approach is to use the GetOpenFilename method of the Application object, which ensures that your application gets a valid filename (as well as its complete path).

This method displays the normal Open dialog box (displayed when you choose the File → Open command) but does not actually open the file specified. Rather, the method returns a string that contains the path and filename selected by the user. Then you can do whatever you want with the filename. The syntax for this method is as follows (all arguments are optional):

```
object.GetOpenFilename(FileFilter, FilterIndex, Title, ButtonText,
MultiSelect)
```

- ◆ FileFilter: Optional. A string specifying file-filtering criteria.

- ◆ FilterIndex: Optional. The index numbers of the default file-filtering criteria.

- ◆ Title: Optional. The title of the dialog box. If omitted, the title is Open.

- ◆ ButtonText: For Macintosh only.

- ◆ MultiSelect: Optional. If True, multiple filenames can be selected. The default value is False.

The FileFilter argument determines what appears in the dialog box's Files of Type drop-down list. The argument consists of pairs of file filter strings followed by the wildcard file filter specification, with each part and each pair separated by commas. If omitted, this argument defaults to

```
" All Files (*.*),*.*"
```

Notice that the first part of this string (All Files (*.*)) is the text displayed in the Files of Type drop-down list. The second part (*.*) actually determines which files are displayed.

The following instruction assigns a string to a variable named Filt. This string can then be used as a FileFilter argument for the GetOpenFilename method. In this case, the dialog box will allow the user to select from four different file types (plus an All Files option). Notice that I used VBA's line continuation sequence to set up the Filt variable; doing so makes it much easier to work with this rather complicated argument.

```
Filt = "Text Files (*.txt),*.txt," & _
       "Lotus Files (*.prn),*.prn," & _
       "Comma Separated Files (*.csv),*.csv," & _
       "ASCII Files (*.asc),*.asc," & _
       "All Files (*.*),*.*"
```

The FilterIndex argument specifies which FileFilter is the default, and the title argument is text that is displayed in the title bar. If the MultiSelect argument is True, the user can select multiple files, all of which are returned in an array.

The following example prompts the user for a filename. It defines five file filters.

```
Sub GetImportFileName()
    Dim Filt As String
    Dim FilterIndex As Integer
    Dim Title As String
    Dim FileName As Variant

'   Set up list of file filters
    Filt = "Text Files (*.txt),*.txt," & _
           "Lotus Files (*.prn),*.prn," & _
           "Comma Separated Files (*.csv),*.csv," & _
           "ASCII Files (*.asc),*.asc," & _
           "All Files (*.*),*.*"

'   Display *.* by default
    FilterIndex = 5

'   Set the dialog box caption
    Title = "Select a File to Import"
```

```
'   Get the file name
    FileName = Application.GetOpenFilename _
        (FileFilter:=Filt, _
         FilterIndex:=FilterIndex, _
         Title:=Title)

'   Exit if dialog box canceled
    If FileName = False Then
        MsgBox "No file was selected."
        Exit Sub
    End If

'   Display full path and name of the file
    MsgBox "You selected " & FileName
End Sub
```

Figure 12-6 shows the dialog box that appears when this procedure is executed.

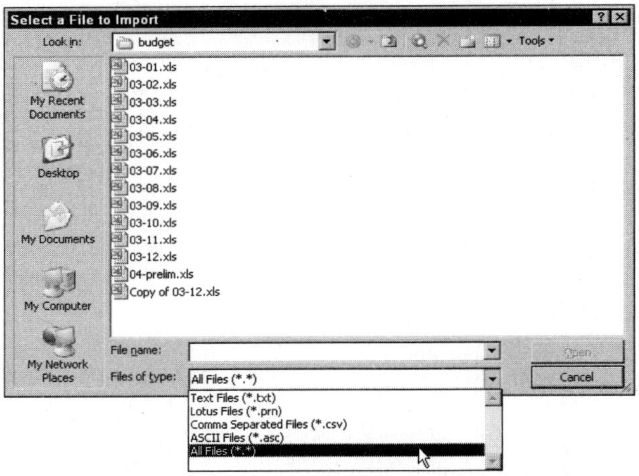

Figure 12-6: The GetOpenFilename method displays a customizable dialog box.

The following example is similar to the previous example. The difference is that the user can press Ctrl or Shift and select multiple files when the dialog box is displayed. Notice that I check for the Cancel button click by determining whether FileName is an array. If the user doesn't click Cancel, the result is an array that consists of at least one element. In this example, a list of the selected files is displayed in a message box.

```
Sub GetImportFileName2()
    Dim Filt As String
    Dim FilterIndex As Integer
    Dim FileName As Variant
    Dim Title As String
    Dim i As Integer
    Dim Msg As String
'   Set up list of file filters
    Filt  = "Text Files (*.txt),*.txt," & _
            "Lotus Files (*.prn),*.prn," & _
            "Comma Separated Files (*.csv),*.csv," & _
            "ASCII Files (*.asc),*.asc," & _
            "All Files (*.*),*.*"
'   Display *.* by default
    FilterIndex = 5

'   Set the dialog box caption
    Title = "Select a File to Import"

'   Get the file name
    FileName = Application.GetOpenFilename _
        (FileFilter:=Filt, _
        FilterIndex:=FilterIndex, _
        Title:=Title, _
        MultiSelect:=True)

'   Exit if dialog box canceled
    If Not IsArray(FileName) Then
        MsgBox "No file was selected."
        Exit Sub
    End If

'   Display full path and name of the files
    For i = LBound(FileName) To UBound(FileName)
        Msg = Msg & FileName(i) & vbCrLf
    Next i
    MsgBox "You selected:" & vbCrLf & Msg
End Sub
```

Notice that the FileName variable is defined as a variant (not a string, as in the previous examples). This is done because FileName can potentially hold an array rather than a single filename.

The Excel GetSaveAsFilename Method

The GetSaveAsFilename method is very similar to the GetOpenFilename method. It displays a Save As dialog box and lets the user select (or specify) a file. It returns a filename and path but doesn't take any action.

The syntax for this method is

```
object.GetSaveAsFilename(InitialFilename, FileFilter, FilterIndex,
Title, ButtonText)
```

The arguments are

- ◆ InitialFilename: Optional. Specifies the suggested filename.

- ◆ FileFilter: Optional. A string specifying file-filtering criteria.

- ◆ FilterIndex: Optional. The index number of the default file-filtering criteria.

- ◆ Title: Optional. The title of the dialog box.

- ◆ ButtonText: For Macintosh only.

Prompting for a Directory

If you need to get a filename, the simplest solution is to use the GetOpenFileName method, as I describe earlier. But if you only need to get a directory name, the solution will depend on which version of Excel you (and your users) have.

This section describes two ways to prompt for a directory. The first method is more complicated but works with Excel 97 and later. The second method is much easier but requires Excel 2002 or later.

Using a Windows API function to select a directory

In this section, I present a function named GetDirectory that displays the dialog box shown in Figure 12-7 and returns a string that represents the selected directory. If the user clicks Cancel, the function returns an empty string. This technique will work with Excel 97 and later versions.

The GetDirectory function takes one argument, which is optional. This argument is a string that will be displayed in the dialog box. If the argument is omitted, the dialog box displays Select a folder as the message.

Figure 12-7: Use an API function to display this dialog box.

 The companion CD-ROM contains a workbook that demonstrates this procedure.

Following are the API declarations required at the beginning of the workbook module. This function also uses a custom data type, called BROWSEINFO.

```
'32-bit API declarations
Declare Function SHGetPathFromIDList Lib "shell32.dll" _
  Alias "SHGetPathFromIDListA" (ByVal pidl As Long, ByVal _
  pszPath As String) As Long

Declare Function SHBrowseForFolder Lib "shell32.dll" _
  Alias "SHBrowseForFolderA" (lpBrowseInfo As BROWSEINFO) _
  As Long

Public Type BROWSEINFO
    hOwner As Long
    pidlRoot As Long
    pszDisplayName As String
    lpszTitle As String
    ulFlags As Long
    lpfn As Long
    lParam As Long
    iImage As Long
End Type
```

The GetDirectory function follows:

```
Function GetDirectory(Optional Msg) As String
    Dim bInfo As BROWSEINFO
    Dim path As String
    Dim r As Long, x As Long, pos As Integer

'   Root folder = Desktop
    bInfo.pidlRoot = 0&

'   Title in the dialog
    If IsMissing(Msg) Then
        bInfo.lpszTitle = "Select a folder."
    Else
        bInfo.lpszTitle = Msg
    End If

'   Type of directory to return
    bInfo.ulFlags = &H1

'   Display the dialog
    x = SHBrowseForFolder(bInfo)

'   Parse the result
    path = Space$(512)
    r = SHGetPathFromIDList(ByVal x, ByVal path)
    If r Then
        pos = InStr(path, Chr$(0))
        GetDirectory = Left(path, pos - 1)
    Else
        GetDirectory = ""
    End If
End Function
```

The simple procedure that follows demonstrates how to use the GetDirectory
function in your code. Executing this procedure displays the dialog box. When the
user clicks OK, the MsgBox function displays the full path of the selected directory.
If the user clicks Cancel, the message box displays Canceled.

```
Sub GetAFolder1()
    Dim Msg As String
    Dim UserFile As String
    Msg = "Please select a location for the backup."
    UserFile = GetDirectory(Msg)
    If UserFile = "" Then
        MsgBox "Canceled"
```

```
    Else
        MsgBox UserFile
    End If
End Sub
```

 Unfortunately, there is no easy way to specify a default or starting directory.

Using the FileDialog object to select a directory

If users of your application all use Excel 2002 or later, you might prefer to use a much simpler technique that makes use of the `FileDialog` object.

 The `FileDialog` object was introduced in Excel 2002. Therefore, this technique will not work with earlier versions of Excel.

The following procedure displays a dialog box, which allows the user to select a directory. The selected directory name (or `Canceled`) is then displayed by using the `MsgBox` function.

```
Sub GetAFolder2()
'    For Excel 2002 and later
    With Application.FileDialog(msoFileDialogFolderPicker)
        .InitialFileName = Application.DefaultFilePath & "\"
        .Title = "Please select a location for the backup"
        .Show
        If .SelectedItems.Count = 0 Then
            MsgBox "Canceled"
        Else
            MsgBox .SelectedItems(1)
        End If
    End With
End Sub
```

The `FileDialog` object lets you specify the starting directory by specifying a value for the `InitialFileName` property. In this case, the code uses Excel's default file path as the starting directory.

Displaying Excel's Built-In Dialog Boxes

Code that you write in VBA can execute Excel's menu commands. And, if the command leads to a dialog box, your code can "make choices" in the dialog box (although the dialog box itself isn't displayed). For example, the following VBA statement is equivalent to choosing the Edit → Go To command, specifying range A1:C3, and clicking OK. But the Go To dialog box never appears (which is what you want).

```
Application.Goto Reference:=Range("A1:C3")
```

In some cases, however, you may want to display one of Excel's built-in dialog boxes so that the end user can make the choices. There are two ways to do this:

◆ Access the Dialogs collection of the Application object.

◆ Execute a menu item directly.

I discuss each of these techniques in the sections that follow.

Using the Dialogs collection

The Dialogs collection of the Application object consists of more than 200 members that represent most of Excel's built-in dialog boxes. Each has a predefined constant to make it easy to specify the dialog box that you need. For example, Excel's Go To dialog box is represented by the constant xlDialogFormulaGoto.

Use the Show method to actually display the dialog box. Here's an example that displays the Go To dialog box (see Figure 12-8):

```
Application.Dialogs(xlDialogFormulaGoto).Show
```

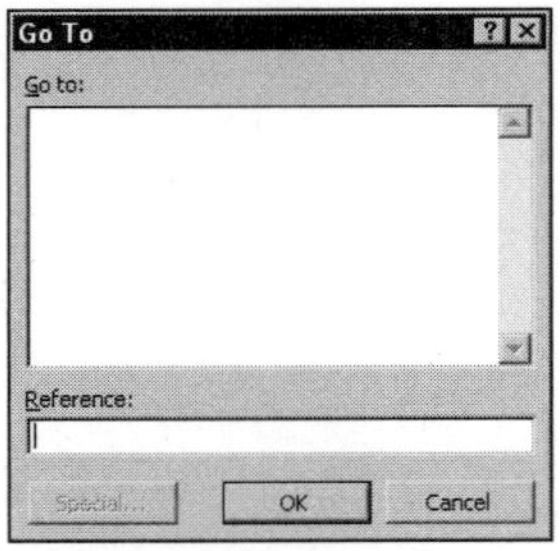

Figure 12-8: This dialog box was displayed with a VBA statement.

When the Go To dialog box is shown, the user can specify a named range or enter a cell address to go to. This dialog box is the one that appears when you choose the Edit → Go To command (or press F5).

You can also write code to determine how the user dismissed the dialog box. Do this by using a variable. In the following statement, the Result variable will be True if the user clicked OK and False if the user clicked Cancel or pressed Esc.

```
Result = Application.Dialogs(xlDialogFormulaGoto).Show
```

Contrary to what you might expect, the Result variable does *not* hold the range that was specified in the Go To dialog box.

This feature is not documented very well. The Help system is very sketchy, and it doesn't mention the fact that displaying one of Excel's dialog boxes via VBA code might not always work exactly the same as using a menu command to display the dialog box. Consequently, you might have to do some experimentation to make sure that your code performs as it should.

In the case of the Go To dialog box, you'll notice that the Special button is grayed out when the dialog is shown when using a VBA statement. Clicking this button normally displays the Go To Special dialog box. To display the Go To Special dialog box with VBA code, use this statement:

```
Application.Dialogs(xlDialogSelectSpecial).Show
```

Another potential problem is that you can't display some tabbed dialog boxes correctly. For example, there is no way to show the Format Cells dialog box with the tabs. Rather, you can only show one tab at a time. The following statement displays the Alignment tab of the Format Cells dialog box (see Figure 12-9):

```
Application.Dialogs(xlDialogAlignment).Show
```

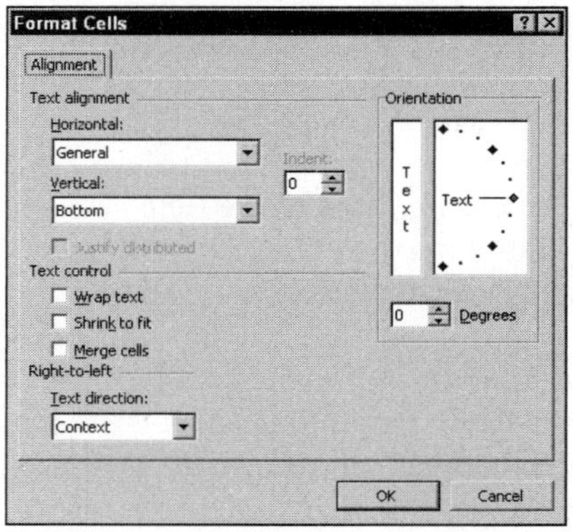

Figure 12-9: The Alignment tab of the Format Cells dialog box.

To show other tabs in the Format Cells dialog box, use any of these constants: `xlDialogFormatNumber`, `xlDialogBorder`, `xlDialogCellProtection`, `xlDialog Patterns`, or `xlDialogFontProperties`. Notice that there is no consistency in the naming of these constants.

Learning more about built-in dialog boxes

You can get a list of all the dialog box constants either by consulting the Help system or by using the Object Browser. Follow these steps to display the members of the `Dialogs` collection in the Object Browser:

1. In a VBA module, press F2 to bring up the Object Browser.

2. In the Object Browser dialog box, select Excel from the top list.

3. Type **xlDialog** in the second list.

4. Click the binoculars (Search) button.

 Attempting to display a built-in dialog box in an incorrect context will result in an error. For example, if you select a series in a chart and then attempt to display the `xlDialogFontProperties` dialog box, you'll get an error message because that dialog box is not appropriate for that selection.

Using arguments with built-in dialog boxes

Most of the built-in dialog boxes also accept arguments, which (usually) correspond to the controls on the dialog box. For example, the Cell Protection dialog box (invoked by using the `xlDialogCellProtection` constant) uses two arguments: `locked` and `hidden`. If you want to display that dialog box with both of these options checked, use the following statement:

```
Application.Dialogs(xlDialogCellProtection).Show True, True
```

The arguments for each of the built-in dialog boxes are listed in the Help system. To locate the help topic, search for *Built-In Dialog Box Argument Lists*. Unfortunately, the Help system provides no explanation of what the arguments are used for!

According to the Help system, the Go To dialog box (invoked by using the `xlDialogFormulaGoTo` constant) takes two arguments: `reference` and `corner`. The `reference` argument is used to provide a default range that appears in the Reference box. The `corner` argument is a logical value that specifies whether to display the reference so it appears in the upper-left corner of the window. Here's an example that uses both of these arguments:

```
Application.Dialogs(xlDialogFormulaGoto). _
  Show Range("Z100"), True
```

As you might have surmised, successfully using the `Dialogs` collection may require some trial and error.

Executing a menu item directly

The second technique to display a built-in dialog box requires some knowledge of toolbars (officially known as `CommandBar` objects). For now, be aware that you can execute a menu item. And you can take advantage of the fact that selecting a menu item displays a dialog box.

 I cover `CommandBars` extensively in Chapters 22 and 23.

The following statement, for example, is equivalent to selecting the Go To menu item on the Edit menu:

```
Application.CommandBars("Worksheet Menu Bar"). _
  Controls("Edit").Controls("Go To...").Execute
```

This statement, when executed, displays the Go To dialog box. Notice that the menu item captions must match exactly (including the ellipsis after "Go To").

Unlike using the `Dialogs` collection, this technique does not allow you to specify default values for the dialog boxes.

 The examples in this section use language-specific references to the `CommandBar` controls. Consequently, these statements will work only in English language versions of Excel. For applications that will be used with other language versions of Excel, you can use the `FindControl` method, along with the `Id` property for the command. See Chapter 22 for more information.

In the previous section, I point out a problem with accessing the `Dialogs` collection: It's not possible to display a tabbed dialog box. That problem doesn't exist when you execute a menu command. The following statement, for example, displays the Format Cells dialog box (with all its tabs):

```
Application.CommandBars("Worksheet Menu Bar"). _
    Controls("Format").Controls("Cells...").Execute
```

By the way, the `Execute` method also works with toolbar controls that don't display a dialog box. The following statement, for example, is equivalent to clicking the Bold button on the Formatting toolbar:

```
Application.CommandBars("Formatting").Controls("Bold").Execute
```

I can't think of any reason to do this, however. A more efficient way to toggle the Bold property of the selected cells is to use a statement like this:

```
Selection.Font.Bold = Not Selection.Font.Bold
```

Chapter 13

Introducing UserForms

IN THIS CHAPTER

Excel makes it relatively easy to create custom dialog boxes for your applications. In fact, you can duplicate the look and feel of almost all of Excel's dialog boxes. This chapter provides an introduction and overview of UserForms.

◆ Creating, showing, and unloading UserForms

◆ A discussion of the UserForm controls available to you

◆ Setting the properties of UserForm controls

◆ Controlling UserForms with VBA procedures

◆ A hands-on example of creating a UserForm

◆ An introduction to the types of events relevant to UserForms and controls

◆ Customizing your control Toolbox

◆ A handy checklist for creating UserForms

EXCEL DEVELOPERS HAVE ALWAYS HAD THE ABILITY TO CREATE custom dialog boxes for their applications. Beginning with Excel 97, things changed substantially – UserForms replaced the clunky old dialog sheets. However, for compatibility purposes, Excel 97 and later still support Excel 5/95 dialog sheets. The good news is that UserForms are *much* easier to work with, and they offer lots of additional capabilities.

How Excel Handles Custom Dialog Boxes

A custom dialog box is created on a UserForm, and you access UserForms in the Visual Basic Editor (VBE).

Following is the typical sequence that you will follow when you create a UserForm:

1. Insert a new UserForm into your workbook's VBProject.

2. Write a procedure that will display the UserForm. This procedure will be located in a VBA module (not in the code module for the UserForm).

3. Add controls to the UserForm.

4. Adjust some of the properties of the controls that you added.

5. Write event handler procedures for the controls. These procedures, which are located in the code window for the UserForm, are executed when various events (such as a button click) occur.

Inserting a New UserForm

To insert a new UserForm, activate the VBE (press Alt+F11), select your workbook's project from the Project window, and then choose Insert → UserForm. UserForms have names like `UserForm1`, `UserForm2`, and so on.

 You can change the name of a UserForm to make it easier to identify. Select the form and use the Properties window to change the Name property. (Press F4 if the Properties window is not displayed.) Figure 13-1 shows the Properties window when an empty UserForm is selected.

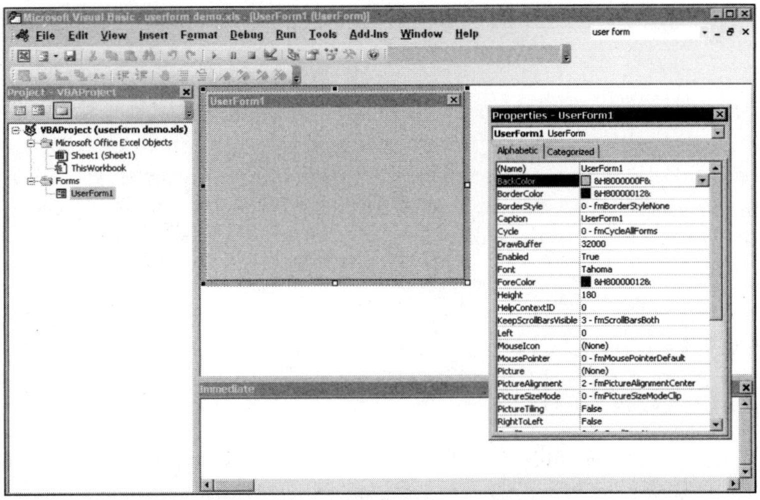

Figure 13-1: The Properties window for an empty UserForm.

A workbook can have any number of UserForms, and each UserForm holds a single custom dialog box.

Adding Controls to a UserForm

To add controls to a UserForm, use the Toolbox. (The VBE does not have menu commands that add controls.) If the Toolbox is not displayed, choose View → Toolbox. Figure 13-2 shows the Toolbox.

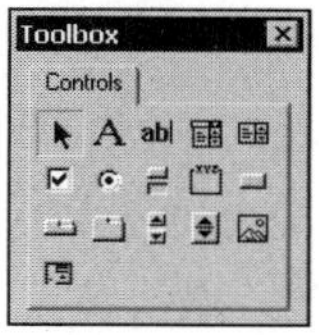

Figure 13-2: Use the Toolbox to add controls to a UserForm.

Just click the Toolbox button that corresponds to the control that you want to add, and then click inside the dialog box to create the control (using its default size). Or, you can click the control and then drag in the dialog box to specify the dimensions for the control.

When you add a new control, it is assigned a name that combines the control type with the numeric sequence for that type of control. For example, if you add a CommandButton control to an empty UserForm, it is named CommandButton1. If you then add a second CommandButton control, it is named CommandButton2.

It's a good idea to rename all the controls that you will be manipulating with your VBA code. Doing so lets you refer to meaningful names (such as ProductListBox) rather than generic names (such as ListBox1). To change the name of a control, use the Properties window in the VBA. Just select the object and enter a new name.

Toolbox Controls

In the sections that follow, I briefly describe the controls available to you in the Toolbox.

Your UserForms can also use other ActiveX controls. See "Customizing the Toolbox," later in this chapter.

CheckBox

A CheckBox control is useful for getting a binary choice: yes or no, true or false, on or off, and so on. When a CheckBox is checked, it has a value of True; when it's not checked, the CheckBox value is False.

ComboBox

A ComboBox control is similar to a ListBox control. (See the upcoming section, "ListBox.") A ComboBox, however, is a drop-down box, and it displays only one item at a time. Another difference is that the user could be allowed to enter a value that doesn't appear in the list of items.

CommandButton

Every dialog box that you create will probably have at least one CommandButton. Usually, you'll want to have a CommandButton labeled OK and another labeled Cancel.

Frame

A Frame control is used to enclose other controls. You do this either for aesthetic purposes or to logically group a set of controls. A frame is particularly useful when the dialog box contains more than one set of OptionButton controls.

Image

An Image control is used to display a graphic image, which can come from a file or pasted from the Clipboard. You might want to use an Image control to display your company's logo in a dialog box. The graphics image is stored in the workbook. That way, if you distribute your workbook to someone else, you don't have to include a copy of the graphics file.

 Some graphics files are very large, and using such images can make your workbook increase dramatically in size. For best results, use graphics sparingly or use small graphics files.

Label

A Label control simply displays text in your dialog box.

ListBox

The ListBox control presents a list of items, and the user can select an item (or multiple items). ListBox controls are very flexible. For example, you can specify a worksheet range that holds the ListBox items, and this range can consist of multiple columns. Or you can fill the ListBox with items by using VBA.

MultiPage

A MultiPage control lets you create tabbed dialog boxes, like the one that appears when you choose the Tools → Options command. By default, a MultiPage control has two pages. To add additional pages, right-click a tab and select New Page from the shortcut menu.

OptionButton

OptionButton controls are useful when the user needs to select one item from a small number of choices. OptionButtons are always used in groups of at least two. When an OptionButton is selected, the other OptionButtons in its group are unselected.

If your UserForm contains more than one set of OptionButtons, the OptionButtons in each set must share a unique GroupName property value. Otherwise, all OptionButtons become part of the same set. Alternatively, you can enclose the OptionButtons in a Frame control, which automatically groups the OptionButtons contained in the frame.

RefEdit

The RefEdit control is used when you need to let the user select a range in a worksheet.

ScrollBar

The ScrollBar control is similar to a SpinButton control. The difference is that the user can drag the ScrollBar button to change the control's value in larger increments. The ScrollBar control is most useful for selecting a value that extends across a wide range of possible values.

SpinButton

The SpinButton control lets the user select a value by clicking either of two arrows: one to increase the value and the other to decrease the value. A SpinButton is often used in conjunction with a TextBox control or Label control, which displays the current value of the SpinButton.

TabStrip

A `TabStrip` control is similar to a `MultiPage` control, but it's not as easy to use. A `TabStrip` control, unlike a `MultiPage` control, does not serve as a container for other objects. Generally, you'll find that the `MultiPage` control is much more versatile.

TextBox

A `TextBox` control lets the user input text.

ToggleButton

A `ToggleButton` control has two states: on or off. Clicking the button toggles between these two states, and the button changes its appearance. Its value is either `True` (pressed) or `False` (not pressed). This is not exactly a standard control, and using two OptionButtons or one CheckBox might be a better choice.

Using Controls on a Worksheet

Many of the UserForm controls can be embedded directly into a worksheet. These controls are accessible from the Control Toolbox toolbar (in Excel, not the VBE). Adding such controls to a worksheet requires much less effort than creating a dialog box. In addition, you may not have to create any macros because you can link a control to a worksheet cell. For example, if you insert a `CheckBox` control on a worksheet, you can link it to a particular cell by setting its `LinkedCell` property. When the CheckBox is checked, the linked cell displays `TRUE`. When the CheckBox is unchecked, the linked cell displays `FALSE`.

The accompanying figure shows a worksheet that contains some embedded controls.

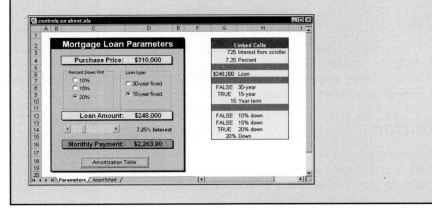

Adding controls to a worksheet can be a bit confusing because controls can come from either of two toolbars:

◆ *Forms toolbar:* These controls are insertable objects (and are compatible with Excel 5 and Excel 95).

◆ *Control Toolbox toolbar:* These are ActiveX controls. These controls are a subset of those that are available for use on UserForms. These controls work only with Excel 97 and later versions and are not compatible with Excel 5 and Excel 95.

You can use the controls from either of these toolbars, but it's important that you understand the distinctions between them. The controls from the Forms toolbar work much differently than the ActiveX controls.

When you use the Control Toolbox toolbar to add a control to a worksheet, Excel goes into *design mode*. In this mode, you can adjust the properties of any controls on your worksheet, add or edit event handler procedures for the control, or change its size or position. To display the Properties window for an ActiveX control, right-click the control and select Properties from the shortcut menu.

For simple buttons, I often use the `Button` control on the Forms toolbar because it lets me attach any macro to it. If I use a `CommandButton` control from the Control Toolbox, clicking it will execute its event handler procedure (for example, `CommandButton1_Click`) in the code module for the `Sheet` object — you can't attach just any macro to it.

When Excel is in design mode, you can't try out the controls. To test the controls, you must exit design mode by clicking the Exit Design Mode button on the Control Toolbox toolbar.

This workbook, plus another that demonstrates all worksheet controls, are available on the companion CD-ROM.

Adjusting UserForm Controls

After a control is placed in a dialog box, you can move and resize it with standard mouse techniques.

You can select multiple controls by Shift-clicking or by clicking and dragging to lasso a group of controls.

A UserForm can contain vertical and horizontal grid lines (displayed as dots) that help you align the controls that you add. When you add or move a control, it *snaps* to the grid to help you line up the controls. If you don't like to see these grid lines, you can turn them off by choosing Tools → Options in the VBE. In the Options dialog box, select the General tab and set your desired options in the Form Grid Settings section.

The Format menu in the VBE window provides several commands to help you precisely align and space the controls in a dialog box. Before you use these commands, select the controls that you want to work with. These commands work just as you would expect, so I don't explain them here. Figure 13-3 shows a dialog box with several `OptionButton` controls about to be aligned.

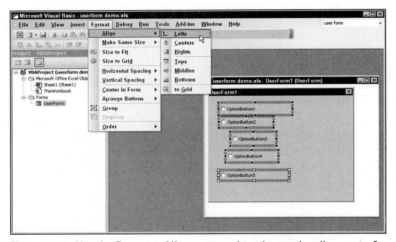

Figure 13-3: Use the Format → Align command to change the alignment of controls.

When you select multiple controls, the last control that you select appears with white handles rather than the normal black handles. The control with the white handles is used as the model against which the other black-handled controls are compared for size or position.

Adjusting a Control's Properties

Every control has a number of properties that determine how the control looks and behaves. You can change a control's properties

◆ *At design time* when you're developing the UserForm. You use the Properties window for this.

◆ *During runtime* when the UserForm is being displayed for the user. You use VBA instructions to change a control's properties at runtime.

Using the Properties window

In the VBE, the Properties window adjusts to display the properties of the selected item (which can be a control or the UserForm itself). In addition, you can select a control from the drop-down list at the top of the Properties window (see Figure 13-4).

Figure 13-4: Selecting a control (OptionButton3) from the drop-down list at the top of the Properties window.

 The Properties window has two tabs. The Alphabetic tab displays the properties for the selected object in alphabetical order. The Categorized tab displays them grouped into logical categories. Both tabs contain the same properties but in a different order.

To change a property, just click it and specify the new property. Some properties can take on a finite number of values, selectable from a list. If so, the Properties window will display a button with a downward-pointing arrow. Click the button, and you'll be able to select the property's value from the list. For example, the TextAlign property can have any of the following values: 1 - fmTextAlignLeft, 2 - fmTextAlignCenter, or 3 - fmTextAlignRight.

A few properties (for example, `Font` and `Picture`) display a small button with an ellipsis when selected. Click the button to display a dialog box associated with the property.

The `Image` control `Picture` property is worth mentioning because you can either select a graphic file that contains the image or paste an image from the Clipboard. When pasting an image, first copy it to the Clipboard; then select the `Picture` property for the `Image` control and press Ctrl+V to paste the Clipboard contents.

If you select two or more controls at once, the Properties window displays only the properties that are common to the selected controls.

The UserForm itself has many properties that you can adjust. These properties are then used as defaults for controls that you add to the UserForm. For example, if you change the UserForm `Font` property, all controls added to the UserForm will use that font.

Common properties

Although each control has its own unique set of properties, many controls have some common properties. For example, every control has a `Name` property and properties that determine its size and position (`Height`, `Width`, `Left`, and `Right`).

If you're going to manipulate a control by using VBA, it's an excellent idea to provide a meaningful name for the control. For example, the first OptionButton that you add to a UserForm has a default name of `OptionButton1`. You refer to this object in your code with a statement such as

```
OptionButton1.Value = True
```

But if you give the `OptionButton` a more meaningful name (such as `obLandscape`), you can use a statement such as

```
obLandscape.Value = True
```

Many people find it helpful to use a name that also identifies the type of object. In the preceding example, I use `ob` as the prefix to identify the fact that this control is an OptionButton.

You can adjust the properties of several controls at once. For example, you might have several OptionButtons that you want left-aligned. You can simply select all the OptionButtons and then change the `Left` property in the Properties box. All the selected controls will then take on that new `Left` property value.

Learning more about properties

The best way to learn about the various properties for a control is to use the Help system. Simply click on a property in the Property window and press F1. Figure 13-5 shows an example of the type of help provided for a property.

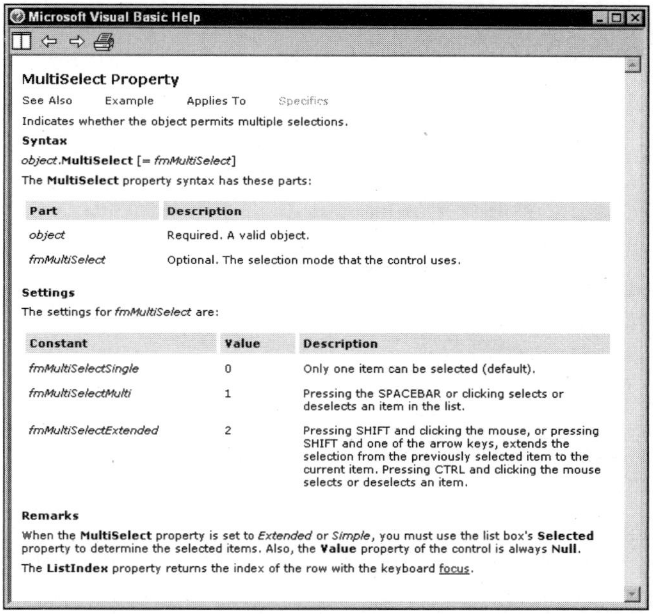

Microsoft Visual Basic Help

MultiSelect Property

See Also Example Applies To Specifics

Indicates whether the object permits multiple selections.

Syntax

object.**MultiSelect** [= *fmMultiSelect*]

The **MultiSelect** property syntax has these parts:

Part	Description
object	Required. A valid object.
fmMultiSelect	Optional. The selection mode that the control uses.

Settings

The settings for *fmMultiSelect* are:

Constant	Value	Description
fmMultiSelectSingle	0	Only one item can be selected (default).
fmMultiSelectMulti	1	Pressing the SPACEBAR or clicking selects or deselects an item in the list.
fmMultiSelectExtended	2	Pressing SHIFT and clicking the mouse, or pressing SHIFT and one of the arrow keys, extends the selection from the previously selected item to the current item. Pressing CTRL and clicking the mouse selects or deselects an item.

Remarks

When the **MultiSelect** property is set to *Extended* or *Simple*, you must use the list box's **Selected** property to determine the selected items. Also, the **Value** property of the control is always **Null**.

The **ListIndex** property returns the index of the row with the keyboard focus.

Figure 13-5: The Help system provides information about each property for every control.

Accommodating keyboard users

Many users prefer to navigate through a dialog box by using the keyboard: The Tab and Shift+Tab keystrokes cycle through the controls, and pressing a hot key operates the control. To make sure that your dialog box works properly for keyboard users, you must be mindful of two issues: tab order and accelerator keys.

CHANGING THE TAB ORDER OF CONTROLS

The *tab order* determines the sequence in which the controls are activated when the user presses Tab or Shift+Tab. It also determines which control has the initial *focus*.

If a user is entering text into a `TextBox` control, for example, the TextBox has the focus. If the user clicks an OptionButton, the OptionButton has the focus. The control that's first in the tab order has the focus when a dialog box is first displayed.

To set the tab order of your controls, choose View→Tab Order. You can also right-click the dialog box and choose Tab Order from the shortcut menu. In either case, Excel displays the Tab Order dialog box as shown in Figure 13-6. The Tab Order dialog box lists all the controls, the sequence of which corresponds to the order in which controls pass the focus between each other in the UserForm. To move a control, select it and click the arrow keys up or down. You can choose more than one control (click while pressing Shift or Ctrl) and move them all at once.

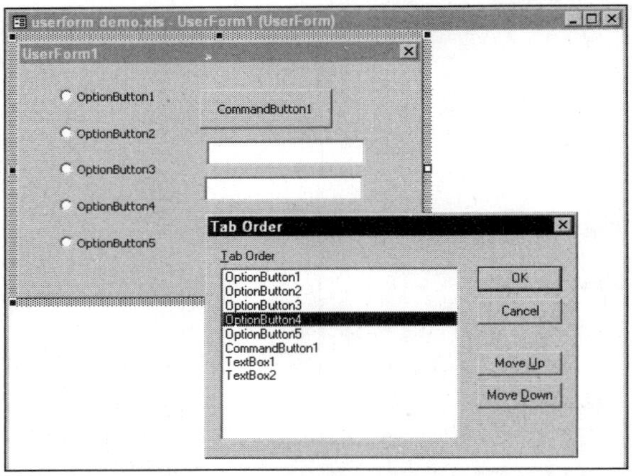

Figure 13-6: Use the Tab Order dialog box to specify the tab order of the controls.

Alternatively, you can set an individual control's position in the tab order via the Properties window. The first control in the tab order has a `TabIndex` property of 0. Changing the `TabIndex` property for a control may also affect the `TabIndex` property of other controls. These adjustments are made automatically to ensure that no control has a `TabIndex` greater than the number of controls. If you want to remove a control from the tab order, set its `TabStop` property to `False`.

Some controls, such as `Frame` and `MultiPage`, act as containers for other controls. The controls inside a container have their own tab order. To set the tab order for a group of OptionButtons inside a `Frame` control, select the `Frame` control before you choose the View → Tab Order command.

Testing a UserForm

You'll usually want to test your UserForm while you're developing it. There are three ways that you can test a UserForm without actually calling it from a VBA procedure:

◆ Choose the Run → Run Sub/UserForm command.

◆ Press F5.

◆ Click the Run Sub/UserForm button on the Standard toolbar.

These three techniques all trigger the UserForm's Initialize event. When a dialog box is displayed in this test mode, you can try out the tab order and the accelerator keys.

SETTING HOT KEYS

You can assign an accelerator key, or hot key, to most dialog box controls. This allows the user to access the control by pressing Alt+ the hot key. Use the Accelerator property in the Properties window for this purpose.

TIP   Some controls, such as a TextBox, don't have an Accelerator property because they don't display a caption. You still can allow direct keyboard access to these controls by using a Label control. Assign an accelerator key to the Label and put it ahead of the TextBox in the tab order.

Displaying and Closing UserForms

In this section, I provide an overview of using VBA to work with UserForms.

Displaying a UserForm

To display a UserForm from VBA, you create a procedure that uses the Show method of the UserForm object. You cannot display a UserForm without using at least one line of VBA code. If your UserForm is named UserForm1, the following procedure displays the dialog box on that form:

```
Sub ShowForm()
    UserForm1.Show
End Sub
```

This procedure must be located in a standard VBA module and not in the code module for the UserForm.

When the UserForm is displayed, it remains visible onscreen until it is dismissed. Usually, you'll add a CommandButton to the UserForm that executes a procedure that dismisses the UserForm. The procedure can either unload the UserForm (with the Unload command) or hide the UserForm (with the Hide method of the UserForm object). This concept will become clearer as you work through various examples in this and subsequent chapters.

In addition, you can display a modeless UserForm. When a modeless UserForm is displayed, you can continue working in Excel, and the UserForm remains visible. By default, UserForms are displayed modally. (You must dismiss the UserForm before you can do anything else.) To display a modeless UserForm, use the following syntax:

```
UserForm1.Show 0
```

 Excel versions prior to Excel 2000 do not support modeless UserForms.

If the name of the UserForm is stored as a string variable, you can use the Add method to add the UserForm to the UserForms collection and then use the Show method of the UserForms collection. Here's an example that assigns the name of a UserForm to the MyForm variable and then displays the UserForm.

```
MyForm = "UserForm1"
UserForms.Add(MyForm).Show
```

This technique might be useful if your project contains several UserForms and the UserForm to be shown is determined by your code.

VBA also has a Load statement. Loading a UserForm loads it into memory, but it is not visible until you use the Show method. To load a UserForm, use a statement like this:

```
Load UserForm1
```

If you have a complex UserForm, you might want to load it into memory before it is needed so that it will appear more quickly when you use the Show method. In the majority of situations, however, it's not necessary to use the Load statement.

Closing a UserForm

To close a UserForm, use the Unload command. For example:

```
Unload UserForm1
```

Or, if the code is located in the code module for the UserForm, you can use the following:

```
Unload Me
```

In this case, the keyword Me refers to the UserForm.

Normally, your VBA code should include the Unload command after the UserForm has performed its actions. For example, your UserForm may have a CommandButton that serves as an OK button. Clicking this button executes a macro. One of the statements in the macro will unload the UserForm. The UserForm remains visible on the screen until the macro that contains the Unload statement finishes.

When a UserForm is unloaded, its controls are reset to their original values. In other words, your code will not be able to access the user's choices after the UserForm is unloaded. If the user's choice must be used later on (after the UserForm is unloaded), you need to store the value in a Public variable, declared in a standard VBA module. Or, you could store the value in a worksheet cell.

 A UserForm is automatically unloaded when the user clicks the Close button (the X in the UserForm title bar). This action also triggers a UserForm QueryClose event, followed by a UserForm Terminate event.

UserForms also have a Hide method. When you invoke this method, the UserForm disappears, but it remains loaded in memory, so your code can still access the various properties of the controls. Here's an example of a statement that hides a UserForm:

```
UserForm1.Hide
```

Or, if the code is in the code module for the UserForm, you can use the following:

```
Me.Hide
```

If for some reason you would like your UserForm to disappear immediately while its macro is executing, use the Hide method at the top of the procedure and follow it with a DoEvents command. For example, in the following procedure, the UserForm disappears immediately when CommandButton1 is clicked. The last statement in the procedure unloads the UserForm.

```
Private Sub CommandButton1_Click()
    Me.Hide
    DoEvents
    For r = 1 To 10000
        Cells(r, 1) = r
```

```
    Next r
    Unload Me
End Sub
```

In Chapter 15, I describe how to display a progress indicator, which takes advantage of the fact that a UserForm remains visible while the macro executes.

About event handler procedures

After the UserForm is displayed, the user interacts with it—selecting an item from a ListBox, clicking a CommandButton, and so on. In official terminology, the user causes an *event* to occur. For example, clicking a CommandButton raises the `Click` event for the CommandButton. You will need to write procedures that are executed when these events occur. These procedures are sometimes known as *event handler* procedures.

Event handler procedures must be located in the Code window for the UserForm. However, your event handler procedure can call another procedure that's located in a standard VBA module.

Your VBA code can change the properties of the controls while the UserForm is displayed (that is, at runtime). For example, you could assign to a `ListBox` control a procedure that changes the text in a Label when an item is selected. This type of manipulation will become clearer later in this chapter.

Creating a UserForm: An Example

If you've never created a UserForm, you might want to walk through the example in this section. The example includes step-by-step instructions for creating a simple dialog box and developing a VBA procedure to support the dialog box.

This example uses a UserForm to get two pieces of information: a person's name and sex. The dialog box uses a `TextBox` control to get the name and three OptionButtons to get the sex (Male, Female, or Unknown). The information collected in the dialog box is then sent to the next blank row in a worksheet.

Creating the UserForm

Figure 13-7 shows the finished UserForm for this example. For best results, start with a new workbook with only one worksheet in it. Then follow these steps:

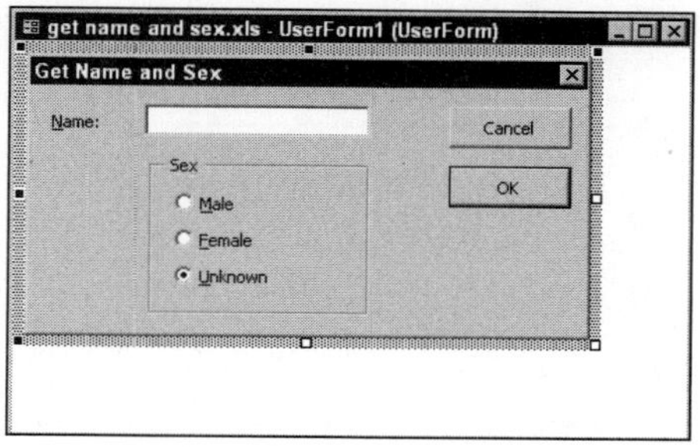

Figure 13-7: This dialog box asks the user to enter a name and a sex.

1. Press Alt+F11 to activate the VBE.

2. In the Project window, select the workbook's project and choose Insert → UserForm to add an empty UserForm.

3. The UserForm's Caption property will have its default value: UserForm1. Use the Properties window to change the UserForm's Caption property to Get Name and Sex. (If the Properties window isn't visible, press F4.)

4. Add a Label control and adjust the properties as follows:

Property	Value
Accelerator	N
Caption	Name:
TabIndex	0

5. Add a TextBox control and adjust the properties as follows:

Property	Value
Name	TextName
TabIndex	1

6. Add a `Frame` control and adjust the properties as follows:

Property	Value
Caption	Sex
TabIndex	2

7. Add an `OptionButton` control inside the `Frame` and adjust the properties as follows:

Property	Value
Accelerator	M
Caption	Male
Name	OptionMale
TabIndex	0

8. Add another `OptionButton` control inside the `Frame` and adjust the properties as follows:

Property	Value
Accelerator	F
Caption	Female
Name	OptionFemale
TabIndex	1

9. Add yet another OptionButton control inside the Frame and adjust the properties as follows:

Property	Value
Accelerator	U
Caption	Unknown
Name	OptionUnknown
TabIndex	2
Value	True

10. Add a CommandButton control outside the Frame and adjust the properties as follows:

Property	Value
Caption	OK
Default	True
Name	OKButton
TabIndex	3

11. Add another CommandButton control and adjust the properties as follows:

Property	Value
Caption	Cancel
Cancel	True
Name	CancelButton
TabIndex	4

When you are creating several controls that are similar, you may find it easier to copy an existing control rather than create a new one. To copy a control, press Ctrl while you drag the control to make a new copy of it. Then adjust the properties on the copied control.

Writing code to display the dialog box

Next, you add a CommandButton to the worksheet. This button will execute a procedure that displays the UserForm. Here's how:

1. Activate Excel. (Alt+F11 is the shortcut key combination.)

2. Right-click any toolbar and select Control Toolbox from the shortcut menu. Excel displays its Control Toolbox toolbar, which closely resembles the VBE Toolbox.

3. Use the Control Toolbox toolbar to add a CommandButton to the worksheet. Click the CommandButton tool; then drag in the worksheet to create the button.

   If you like, you can change the caption for the worksheet CommandButton. To do so, right-click the button and choose CommandButton Object → Edit from the shortcut menu. You can then edit the text that appears on the CommandButton.

4. Double-click the CommandButton.

   This activates the VBE. More specifically, the code module for the worksheet will be displayed, with an empty event handler procedure for the worksheet's CommandButton.

5. Enter a single statement in the CommandButton1_Click procedure (see Figure 13-8). This short procedure uses the Show method of an object (UserForm1) to display the UserForm.

Testing the dialog box

The next step is to try out the procedure that displays the dialog box.

When you click the CommandButton on the worksheet, you'll find that nothing happens. Rather, the button is selected. That's because Excel is still in design mode — which happens automatically when you insert a control using the Control Toolbox toolbar. To exit design mode, click the button on the Control Toolbox toolbar labeled Exit Design Mode. To make any changes to your CommandButton, you'll need to put Excel back into design mode.

Figure 13-8: The CommandButton1_Click procedure is executed when the button on the worksheet is clicked.

When you exit design mode, clicking the button will display the UserForm (see Figure 13-9).

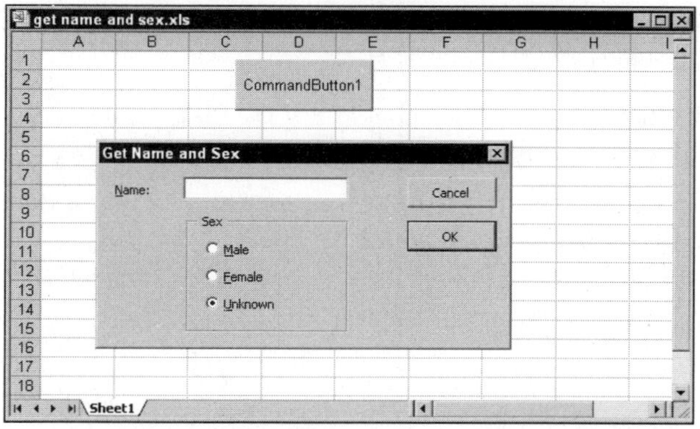

Figure 13-9: The CommandButton's Click event procedure displays the UserForm.

When the dialog box is displayed, enter some text into the text box and click OK. You'll find that nothing happens – which is understandable because you haven't yet created any event handler procedures for the UserForm.

Click the Close button in the UserForm title bar to get rid of the dialog box.

Adding event handler procedures

In this section, I explain how to write the procedures that will handle the events that occur when the UserForm is displayed. To continue the example, do the following:

1. Press Alt+F11 to activate the VBE.

2. Make sure the UserForm is displayed and double-click its Cancel button. This will activate the Code window for the UserForm and insert an empty procedure named `CancelButton_Click`. Notice that this procedure consists of the object's name, an underscore character, and the event that it handles.

3. Modify the procedure as follows. (This is the event handler for the CancelButton's `Click` event.)

```
Private Sub CancelButton_Click()
    Unload UserForm1
End Sub
```

This procedure, which is executed when the user clicks the Cancel button, simply unloads the UserForm.

4. Press Shift+F7 to redisplay `UserForm1` (or click the View Object icon at the top of the Project Explorer window).

5. Double-click the OK button and enter the following procedure. (This is the event handler for the OKButton's `Click` event.)

```
Private Sub OKButton_Click()
'   Make sure Sheet1 is active
    Sheets("Sheet1").Activate

'   Determine the next empty row
    NextRow = _
      Application.WorksheetFunction.CountA(Range("A:A")) + 1
'   Transfer the name
    Cells(NextRow, 1) = TextName.Text

'   Transfer the sex
    If OptionMale Then Cells(NextRow, 2) = "Male"
    If OptionFemale Then Cells(NextRow, 2) = "Female"
    If OptionUnknown Then Cells(NextRow, 2) = "Unknown"
```

```
'     Clear the controls for the next entry
      TextName.Text = ""
      OptionUnknown = True
      TextName.SetFocus
End Sub
```

6. Activate Excel and click the CommandButton again to display the UserForm. Run the procedure again.

You'll find that the UserForm controls now function correctly. Figure 13-10 shows how this looks in action.

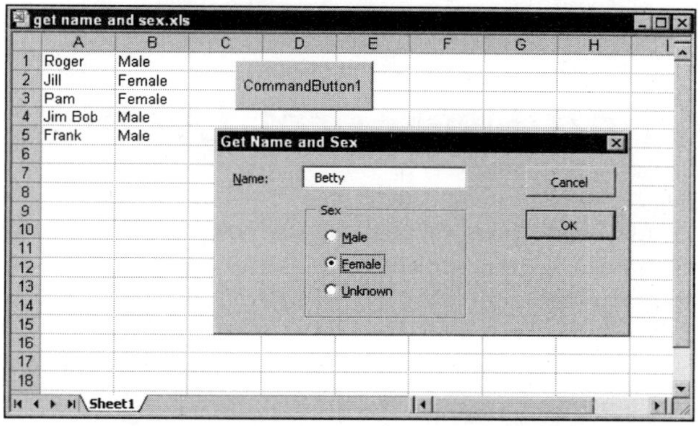

Figure 13-10: The information entered into the UserForm is added to the end of the data.

Here's how the OKButton_Click procedure works: First, the procedure makes sure that the proper worksheet (Sheet1) is active. It then uses Excel's COUNTA function to determine the next blank cell in column A. Next, it transfers the text from the TextBox to column A. It then uses a series of If statements to determine which OptionButton was selected and writes the appropriate text (Male, Female, or Unknown) to column B. Finally, the dialog box is reset to make it ready for the next entry. Notice that clicking OK doesn't close the dialog box. To end data entry (and unload the UserForm), click the Cancel button.

Validating the data

Play around with this example some more, and you'll find that it has a small problem: It doesn't ensure that the user actually enters a name into the text box. The following code is inserted in the OKButton_Click procedure before the text is transferred to the worksheet. It ensures that the user enters a name (well, at least some text) in the TextBox. If the TextBox is empty, a message appears, and the focus is set to the TextBox so that the user can try again. The Exit Sub statement ends the procedure with no further action.

```
'   Make sure a name is entered
    If TextName.Text = "" Then
        MsgBox "You must enter a name."
        TextName.SetFocus
        Exit Sub
    End If
```

The finished dialog box

After making all these modifications, you'll find that the dialog box works flaw-lessly. (Don't forget to test the hot keys.) In real life, you'd probably need to collect more information than just name and sex. However, the same basic principles apply. You just need to deal with more UserForm controls.

Understanding UserForm Events

Each UserForm control (as well as the UserForm itself) is designed to respond to certain types of events, and these events can be triggered by a user or by Excel. For example, clicking a CommandButton generates a Click event for the CommandButton. You can write code that is executed when a particular event occurs.

Some actions generate multiple events. For example, clicking the upward arrow of a SpinButton control generates a SpinUp event and also a Change event. When a UserForm is displayed by using the Show method, Excel generates an Initialize event and an Activate event for the UserForm. Actually, the Initialize event occurs when the UserForm is loaded into memory and before it is actually displayed.

Excel also supports events associated with a Sheet object, Chart objects, and the ThisWorkbook object. I discuss these types of events in Chapter 18.

Learning about events

To find out which events are supported by a particular control:

1. Add a control to a UserForm.

2. Double-click the control to activate the code module for the UserForm. The VBE will insert an empty event handler procedure for the default event for the control.

3. Click the drop-down list in the upper-right corner of the module window, and you'll see a complete list of events for the control (see Figure 13-11).

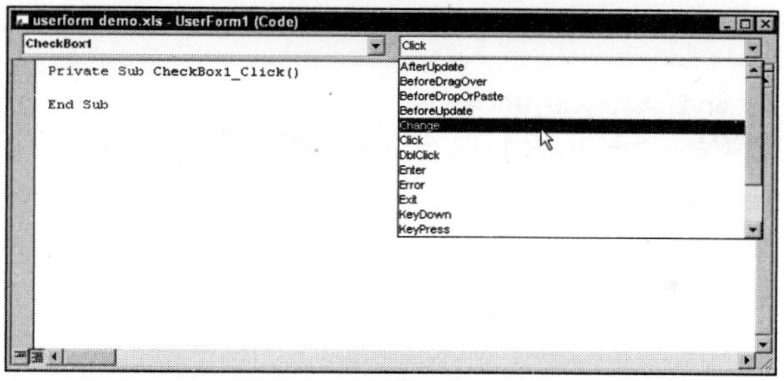

Figure 13-11: The event list for a CheckBox control.

4. Select an event from the list, and the VBE will create an empty event handler procedure for you.

> **NOTE**
> To find out specific details about an event, consult the Help system. The Help system also lists the events available for each control.

> **CAUTION**
> Event handler procedures incorporate the name of the object in the procedure's name. Therefore, if you change the name of a control, you'll also need to make the appropriate changes to the control's event handler procedure(s). The name changes are not performed automatically! To make things easy on yourself, it's a good idea to provide names for your controls before you begin creating event handler procedures.

UserForm events

Several events are associated with showing and unloading a UserForm:

◆ `Initialize`: Occurs before a UserForm is loaded or shown but does not occur if the UserForm was previously hidden

◆ `Activate`: Occurs when a UserForm is shown

◆ `Deactivate`: Occurs when a UserForm is deactivated but does not occur if the form is hidden

◆ `QueryClose`: Occurs before a UserForm is unloaded

◆ `Terminate`: Occurs after the UserForm is unloaded

Often, it's critical that you choose the appropriate event for your event handler procedure and that you understand the order in which the events occur. Using the Show method invokes the Initialize and Activate events (in that order). Using the Load command invokes only the Initialize event. Using the Unload command triggers the QueryClose and Terminate events (in that order). Using the Hide method doesn't trigger either of these events.

The companion CD-ROM contains a workbook that monitors all these events and displays a message box when an event occurs. If you're confused about UserForm events, studying the code in this example should clear things up.

SpinButton events

To help clarify the concept of events, this section takes a close look at the events associated with a SpinButton control.

The companion CD-ROM contains a workbook that demonstrates the sequence of events that occur for a SpinButton and the UserForm that contains it. The workbook contains a series of event-handler routines — one for each SpinButton and UserForm event. Each of these routines simply displays a message box that tells you the event that just fired.

Table 13-1 lists all the events for the SpinButton control.

TABLE 13-1 SPINBUTTON EVENTS

Event	Description
AfterUpdate	Occurs after the control is changed through the user interface
BeforeDragOver	Occurs when a drag-and-drop operation is in progress

Event	Description
BeforeDropOrPaste	Occurs when the user is about to drop or paste data onto the control
BeforeUpdate	Occurs before the control is changed
Change	Occurs when the Value property changes
Enter	Occurs before the control actually receives the focus from a control on the same UserForm
Error	Occurs when the control detects an error and cannot return the error information to a calling program
Exit	Occurs immediately before a control loses the focus to another control on the same form
KeyDown	Occurs when the user presses a key and the object has the focus
KeyPress	Occurs when the user presses any key that produces a typeable character
KeyUp	Occurs when the user releases a key and the object has the focus
SpinDown	Occurs when the user clicks the lower (or left) SpinButton arrow
SpinUp	Occurs when the user clicks the upper (or right) SpinButton arrow

A user can operate a SpinButton control by clicking it with the mouse or (if the control has the focus) using the up-arrow or down-arrow keys.

MOUSE-INITIATED EVENTS

When the user clicks the upper SpinButton arrow, the following events occur in this precise order:

1. Enter (triggered only if the SpinButton did not already have the focus)

2. Change

3. SpinUp

KEYBOARD-INITIATED EVENTS

The user can also press Tab to set the focus to the SpinButton and then use the arrow keys to increment or decrement the control. If so, the following events occur (in this order):

1. Enter

2. KeyDown (or KeyUp)

3. Change

4. SpinUp

WHAT ABOUT CHANGES VIA CODE?

The SpinButton control can also be changed by VBA code — which also triggers the appropriate event(s). For example, the following statement sets the SpinButton1 Value property to zero and also triggers the Change event for the SpinButton control — but only if the SpinButton value were not already 0:

```
SpinButton1.Value = 0
```

You might think that you could disable events by setting the EnableEvents property of the Application object to False. Unfortunately, this property only applies to events that involve true Excel objects: Workbooks, Worksheets, and Charts.

Pairing a SpinButton with a TextBox

A SpinButton has a Value property, but this control doesn't have a caption in which to display its value. In many cases, however, you will want the user to see the SpinButton value. And sometimes you'll want the user to be able to change the SpinButton value directly instead of clicking the SpinButton repeatedly.

The solution is to pair a SpinButton with a TextBox, which enables the user to specify a value either by typing it into the TextBox directly or by clicking the SpinButton to increment or decrement the value in the TextBox.

Figure 13-12 shows a simple example. The SpinButton's Min property is 1, and its Max property is 100. Therefore, clicking the SpinButton's arrows will change its value to an integer between 1 and 100.

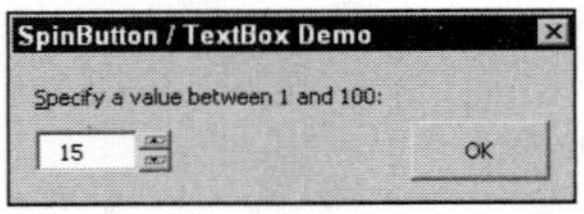

SpinButton / TextBox Demo	✕
Specify a value between 1 and 100:	
15 ▲▼	OK

Figure 13-12: This SpinButton is
paired with a TextBox.

This workbook is available on the companion CD-ROM.

The code required to link a SpinButton with a TextBox is relatively simple. It's basically a matter of writing event handler procedures to ensure that the SpinButton's Value property is in sync with the TextBox's Text property.

The following procedure is executed whenever the SpinButton's Change event is triggered. That is, the procedure is executed when the user clicks the SpinButton or changes its value by pressing the up arrow or down arrow.

```
Private Sub SpinButton1_Change()
    TextBox1.Text = SpinButton1.Value
End Sub
```

The procedure simply assigns the SpinButton's Value to the Text property of the TextBox control. Here, the controls have their default names (SpinButton1 and TextBox1). If the user enters a value directly into the TextBox, its Change event is triggered, and the following procedure is executed:

```
Private Sub TextBox1_Change()
    NewVal = Val(TextBox1.Text)
    If NewVal >= SpinButton1.Min And _
        NewVal <= SpinButton1.Max Then _
        SpinButton1.Value = NewVal
End Sub
```

This procedure starts by using VBA's Val function to convert the text in the TextBox to a value. (If the TextBox contains a string, the Val function returns 0.) The next statement determines whether the value is within the proper range for the SpinButton. If so, the SpinButton's Value property is set to the value entered in the TextBox.

The example is set up so that clicking the OK button (which is named OKButton) transfers the SpinButton's value to the active cell. The event handler for this CommandButton's Click event is as follows:

```
Private Sub OKButton_Click()
'   Enter the value into the active cell
    If CStr(SpinButton1.Value) = TextBox1.Text Then
        ActiveCell = SpinButton1.Value
        Unload Me
    Else
        MsgBox "Invalid entry.", vbCritical
        TextBox1.SetFocus
        TextBox1.SelStart = 0
        TextBox1.SelLength = Len(TextBox1.Text)
    End If
End Sub
```

This procedure does one final check: It makes sure that the text entered in the TextBox matches the SpinButton's value. This is necessary in the case of an invalid entry. For example, should the user enter **3r** into the TextBox, the SpinButton's value would not be changed, and the result placed in the active cell would not be what the user intended. Notice that the SpinButton's `Value` property is converted to a string that uses the `CStr` function. This ensures that the comparison will not generate an error if a value is compared with text. If the SpinButton's value does not match the TextBox's contents, a message box is displayed. Notice that the focus is set to the `TextBox` object, and the contents are selected (by using the `SelStart` and `SelLength` properties). This makes it very easy for the user to correct the entry.

About the Tag Property

Every UserForm and control has a `Tag` property. This property doesn't represent anything specific, and, by default, is empty. You can use the `Tag` property to store information for your own use.

For example, you might have a series of `TextBox` controls in a UserForm. The user may be required to enter text into some but not all of them. You can use the `Tag` property to identify (for your own use) which fields are required. In this case, you can set the `Tag` property to a string such as `Required`. Then when you write code to validate the user's entries, you can refer to the `Tag` property.

The following example is a function that examines all `TextBox` controls on `UserForm1` and returns the number of required `TextBox` controls that are empty:

```
Function EmptyCount()
  Dim ctl As Control
  EmptyCount= 0
  For Each ctl In UserForm1.Controls
    If TypeName(ctl) = "TextBox" Then
      If ctl.Tag = "Required" Then
        If ctl.Text = "" Then
          EmptyCount = EmptyCount + 1
        End If
      End If
    End If
  Next ctl

End Function
```

As you work with UserForms, you will probably think of other uses for the `Tag` property.

Referencing UserForm Controls

When working with controls on a UserForm, the VBA code is usually contained in the code window for the UserForm. You can also refer to UserForm controls from a general VBA module. To do so, you need to qualify the reference to the control by specifying the UserForm name. For example, consider the following procedure, which is located in a VBA module. It simply displays the UserForm named UserForm1.

```
Sub GetData()
    UserForm1.Show
End Sub
```

Assume that UserForm1 contains a text box (named TextBox1), and you want to provide a default value for the text box. You could modify the procedure as follows:

```
Sub GetData()
    UserForm1.TextBox1.Value = "John Doe"
    UserForm1.Show
End Sub
```

Understanding the Controls Collection

The controls on a UserForm comprise a collection. For example, the following statement displays the number of controls on UserForm1:

```
MsgBox UserForm1.Controls.Count
```

There is *not* a collection of each control type. For example, there is no collection of CommandButton controls. However, you can determine the type of control using the TypeName function. The following procedure uses a For Each structure to loop through the Controls collection and then displays the number of CommandButton controls on UserForm1:

```
Sub CountButtons()
    Dim cbCount As Integer
    Dim ctl as Control
    cbCount = 0
    For Each ctl In UserForm1.Controls
        If TypeName(ctl) = "CommandButton" Then _
            cbCount = cbCount + 1
    Next ctl
    MsgBox cbCount
End Sub
```

Another way to set the default value is to take advantage of the UserForm's Initialize event. You can write code in the UserForm_Initialize procedure, which is located in the code module for the UserForm. Here's an example:

```
Private Sub UserForm_Initialize()
    TextBox1.Value = "John Doe"
End Sub
```

Notice that, when the control is referenced in the code module for the UserForm, there is no need to qualify the references with the UserForm name. However, qualifying references to controls does have an advantage: You will then be able to take advantage of the Auto List Members feature, which lets you choose the control names from a drop-down list. Rather than use the actual name of the UserForm, it is preferable to use Me. Then, if you change the name of the UserForm, you will not need to replace the references in your code.

Customizing the Toolbox

When a UserForm is active in the VBE, the Toolbox displays the controls that you can add to the UserForm. This section describes ways to customize the Toolbox.

Changing icons or tip text

If you would prefer a different icon or different tip text for a particular tool, right-click the tool and select Customize *xxx* from the shortcut menu (where *xxx* is the control's name). This brings up a new dialog box that lets you change the ToolTip text, edit the icon, or load a new icon image from a file.

Adding new pages

The Toolbox initially contains a single tab. Right-click this tab and select New Page to add a new tab to the Toolbox. You can also change the text displayed on the tab by selecting Rename from the shortcut menu.

Customizing or combining controls

A very handy feature lets you customize a control and then save it for future use. You can, for instance, create a CommandButton control that's set up to serve as an OK button. For example, you can set the following properties: Width, Height, Caption, Default, and Name. Then drag the customized CommandButton to the Toolbox. This will create a new control. Right-click the new control to rename it or change its icon.

You can also create a new Toolbox entry that consists of multiple controls. For example, you can create two CommandButtons that represent a UserForm's OK and Cancel buttons. Customize them as you want and then select them both and drag them to the Toolbox. In this case, you can use this new Toolbox control to add two customized buttons in one fell swoop.

This also works with controls that act as containers. For example, create a `Frame` control and add four customized OptionButtons, neatly spaced and aligned. Then drag the Frame to the Toolbox to create a customized `Frame` control.

TIP You might want to place your customized controls on a separate page in the Toolbox. This lets you export the entire page so you can share it with other Excel users. To export a Toolbox page, right-click the tab and select Export Page.

ON THE CD The companion CD-ROM contains a PAG file that contains some customized controls. You can import this file as a new page in your Toolbox. Right-click a tab and select Import Page. Then locate the PAG file. Your Toolbox will resemble Figure 13-13.

Figure 13-13: The Toolbox, with a new page of controls.

Adding new ActiveX controls

UserForms can contain other ActiveX controls developed by Microsoft or other vendors. To add an additional ActiveX control to the toolbox, right-click the Toolbox and select Additional Controls. This will display the dialog box shown in Figure 13-14.

The Additional Controls dialog box lists all ActiveX controls that are installed on your system. Select the control(s) that you want to add; then click OK to add an icon for each selected control.

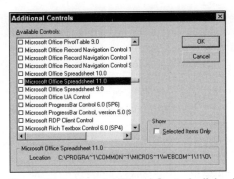

Figure 13-14: The Additional Controls dialog box
lets you add other ActiveX controls.

 Not all ActiveX controls that are installed on your system will work in Excel
UserForms. In fact, most of them probably won't work. Also, some controls
require a license in order to use them in an application. If you (or the users of
your application) aren't licensed to use a particular control, an error will
occur.

Creating UserForm Templates

You might find that when you design a new UserForm, you tend to add the same
controls each time. For example, every UserForm might have two CommandButtons
that serve as OK and Cancel buttons. In the previous section, I describe how to create a new control that combines these two (customized) buttons into a single control. Another option is to create your UserForm template and then export it so it
can be imported into other projects. An advantage is that the event handler code
for the controls is stored with the template.

Emulating Excel's Dialog Boxes

The look and feel of Windows dialog boxes differ from program to program. When
developing applications for Excel, it's best to try to mimic Excel's dialog box style
whenever possible.

In fact, a good way to learn how to create effective dialog boxes is to try to copy one
of Excel's dialog boxes down to the smallest detail. For example, make sure that you
get all the hot keys defined and be sure that the tab order is the same. To re-create
one of Excel's dialog boxes, you need to test it under various circumstances and see

> how it behaves. I guarantee that your analysis of Excel's dialog boxes will improve your own dialog boxes.
>
> You will find that it's impossible to duplicate some of Excel's dialog boxes. For example, when you choose the Find All option in Excel 2002's Find and Replace dialog box, the dialog box becomes resizable. It is not possible to create a resizable UserForm.

Start by creating a UserForm that contains all the controls and customizations that you would need to re-use in other projects. Then make sure the UserForm is selected and choose File → Export File (or press Ctrl+E). You'll be prompted for a filename. Then when you start your next project, choose File → Import File to load the saved UserForm.

A UserForm Checklist

Before you unleash a UserForm on end users, be sure that everything is working correctly. The following checklist should help you identify potential problems.

- ◆ Are similar controls the same size?
- ◆ Are the controls evenly spaced?
- ◆ Is the dialog box too overwhelming? If so, you may want to group the controls by using a `MultiPage` control.
- ◆ Can every control be accessed with a hot key?
- ◆ Are any of the hot keys duplicated?
- ◆ Is the tab order set correctly?
- ◆ Will your VBA code take appropriate action if the user presses Esc or clicks the Close button on the UserForm?
- ◆ Are there any misspellings in the text?
- ◆ Does the dialog box have an appropriate caption?
- ◆ Will the dialog box display properly at all video resolutions? Sometimes labels that display properly with a high-resolution display will appear cut-off in VGA display mode.
- ◆ Are the controls grouped logically (by function)?
- ◆ Do `ScrollBar` and `SpinButton` controls allow valid values only?
- ◆ Are ListBoxes set properly (Single, Multi, or Extended)?

Chapter 14

UserForm Examples

IN THIS CHAPTER

This chapter presents lots of useful and informative examples that introduce you to some additional techniques that involve UserForms.

♦ Using a UserForm for a simple menu

♦ Selecting ranges from a UserForm

♦ Using a UserForm as a splash screen

♦ Changing the size of a UserForm while it's displayed

♦ Zooming and scrolling a sheet from a UserForm

♦ Understanding various techniques that involve a `ListBox` control

♦ Using the `MultiPage` control

YOU MIGHT BE ABLE TO ADAPT THESE TECHNIQUES TO YOUR OWN WORK. All the examples are available on the CD-ROM that accompanies this book.

 Chapter 15 contains additional examples of more advanced UserForm techniques.

Creating a UserForm "Menu"

Sometimes, you might want to use a UserForm as a type of menu. In other words, the UserForm would present some options, and the user makes a choice. This section presents two ways to do this: using CommandButtons or using a ListBox.

Using CommandButtons in a UserForm

Figure 14-1 shows an example of a UserForm that uses `CommandButton` controls as a simple menu. Setting up this sort of thing is very easy, and the code behind the UserForm is very straightforward. Each CommandButton has its own event handler procedure. For example, the following procedure is executed when `CommandButton1` is clicked:

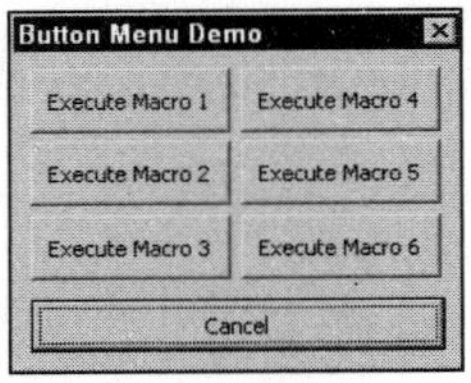

Figure 14-1: This dialog box uses CommandButtons as a menu.

```
Private Sub CommandButton1_Click()
    Call Macro1
    Unload Me
End Sub
```

This procedure simply calls `Macro1` and closes the UserForm. The other buttons have similar event handler procedures.

Using a ListBox in a UserForm

Figure 14-2 shows another example that uses a ListBox as a menu. Before the UserForm is displayed, its `Initialize` event handler procedure is called. This procedure, which follows, uses the `AddItem` method to add six items to the ListBox:

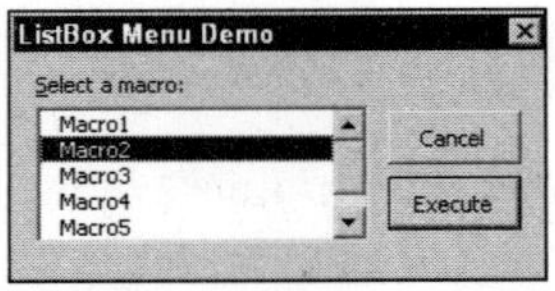

Figure 14-2: This dialog box uses a ListBox as a menu.

```
Private Sub UserForm_Initialize()
    With ListBox1
        .AddItem "Macro1"
        .AddItem "Macro2"
```

```
        .AddItem "Macro3"
        .AddItem "Macro4"
        .AddItem "Macro5"
        .AddItem "Macro6"
    End With
End Sub
```

The Execute button also has a procedure to handle its `Click` event:

```
Private Sub ExecuteButton_Click()
    Select Case ListBox1.ListIndex
        Case -1
            MsgBox "Select a macro from the list."
            Exit Sub
        Case 0: Call Macro1
        Case 1: Call Macro2
        Case 2: Call Macro3
        Case 3: Call Macro4
        Case 4: Call Macro5
        Case 5: Call Macro6
    End Select
    Unload Me
End Sub
```

This procedure accesses the `ListIndex` property of the ListBox to determine which item is selected. (If the `ListIndex` is -1, nothing is selected.) Then the appropriate macro is executed.

Excel, of course, also lets you create real menus and toolbars. Refer to Chapters 22 and 23 for details.

Selecting Ranges from a UserForm

Several of Excel's built-in dialog boxes allow the user to specify a range. For example, the Goal Seek dialog box asks the user to select two ranges. The user can either type the range name directly or use the mouse to point and click in a sheet to make a range selection.

Your UserForms can also provide this type of functionality, thanks to the `RefEdit` control. The `RefEdit` control doesn't look exactly like the range selection control used in Excel's built-in dialog boxes, but it works in a similar manner. If the user clicks the small button on the right side of the control, the dialog box disappears temporarily, and a small range selector is displayed – which is exactly what happens with Excel's built-in dialog boxes.

 Unfortunately, Excel's RefEdit control does not allow the user to use shortcut range selection keys. For example, pressing Shift+↓ will not select cells to the end of the column.

Figure 14-3 shows a UserForm that contains a RefEdit control. This dialog box performs a simple mathematical operation on all nonformula (and nonempty) cells in the selected range. The operation that's performed corresponds to the selected OptionButton.

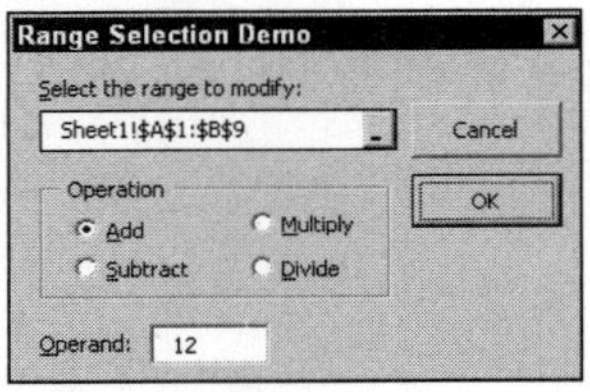

Figure 14-3: The RefEdit control
shown here allows the user to select a range.

Following are a few things to keep in mind when using a RefEdit control:

♦ The RefEdit control returns a text string that represents a range address. You can convert this string to a Range object by using a statement such as

```
Set UserRange = Range(RefEdit1.Text)
```

♦ It's a good practice to initialize the RefEdit control to display the current range selection. You can do so in the UserForm_Initialize procedure by using a statement such as

```
RefEdit1.Text = ActiveWindow.RangeSelection.Address
```

♦ Don't assume that RefEdit will always return a valid range address. Pointing to a range isn't the only way get text into this control. The user can type any text and also edit or delete the displayed text. Therefore, you need to make sure that the range is valid. The following code is an example of a way to check for a valid range. If an invalid range is detected, the user is given a message, and focus is set to the RefEdit control so the user can try again.

```
On Error Resume Next
Set UserRange = Range(RefEdit1.Text)
```

```
If Err <> 0 Then
    MsgBox "Invalid range selected"
    RefEdit1.SetFocus
    Exit Sub
End If
On Error GoTo 0
```

◆ The user can also click the worksheet tabs while selecting a range with the RefEdit control. Therefore, you can't assume that the selection will be on the active sheet. However, if a different sheet is selected, the range address will be preceded by a sheet name. For example:

```
Sheet2!$A$1:$C:4
```

◆ If you need to get a single cell selection from the user, you can pick out the upper-left cell of a selected range by using a statement such as

```
Set OneCell = Range(RefEdit1.Text).Range("A1")
```

As I discuss in Chapter 12, you can also use VBA's InputBox function to allow the user to select a range.

Creating a Splash Screen

Some developers like to display some introductory information when the application is opened. This is commonly known as a *splash screen.* You are undoubtedly familiar with Excel's splash screen, which appears for a few seconds when Excel is loading.

You can create a splash screen for your Excel application with a UserForm. This example is essentially a UserForm that displays automatically and then dismisses itself after five seconds. Follow these instructions to create a splash screen for your project:

1. Create your workbook.

2. Activate the Visual Basic Editor (VBE) and insert a new UserForm into the project. The code in this example assumes that this form is named UserForm1.

3. Place any controls that you like on UserForm1. For example, you may want to insert an Image control that has your company's logo. Figure 14-4 shows an example.

4. Insert the following procedure into the code module for the ThisWorkbook object:

```
Private Sub Workbook_Open()
    UserForm1.Show
End Sub
```

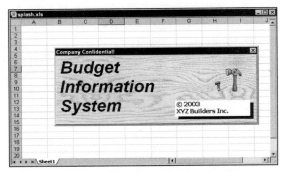

Figure 14-4: This splash screen is displayed briefly when the workbook is opened.

5. Insert the following procedure into the code module for UserForm1 (this assumes a five-second delay):

```
Private Sub UserForm_Activate()
    Application.OnTime Now + _
      TimeValue("00:00:05"), "KillTheForm"
End Sub
```

6. Insert the following procedure into a general VBA module:

```
Private Sub KillTheForm()
    Unload UserForm1
End Sub
```

When the workbook is opened, the Workbook_Open procedure is executed. This procedure displays the UserForm. At that time, its Activate event occurs, which triggers the UserForm_Activate procedure. This procedure uses the OnTime method of the Application object to execute a procedure named KillTheForm at a particular time. In this case, the time is five seconds after the activation event. The KillTheForm procedure simply unloads the UserForm.

7. As an option, you can add a small CommandButton named CancelButton, set its Cancel property to True, and insert the following event handler procedure in the UserForm's code module:

```
Private Sub CancelButton_Click()
    KillTheForm
End Sub
```

Doing so lets the user cancel the splash screen before the time has expired by pressing Esc. You can stash this small button behind another object so it won't be visible.

Keep in mind that the splash screen is not displayed until the workbook is entirely loaded. In other words, if you would like to display the splash screen to give the user something to look at while the workbook is loading, this technique won't fill the bill.

If your application needs to run some VBA procedures at startup, you can display the UserForm "modeless" so that the code will continue running while the UserForm is displayed. To do so, change the `Workbook_Open` procedure as follows:

```
Private Sub Workbook_Open()
    UserForm1.Show vbModeless
    ' other code goes here
End Sub
```

Disabling a UserForm's Close Button

When a UserForm is displayed, clicking the Close button (the X in the upper-right corner) will unload the form. You might have a situation in which you don't want this to happen. For example, you might require that the UserForm be closed only by clicking a particular CommandButton.

Although you can't actually disable the Close button, you can prevent the user from closing a UserForm by clicking it. You can do so by monitoring the UserForm's `QueryClose` event.

The following procedure, which is located in the code module for the UserForm, is executed before the form is closed (that is, when the `QueryClose` event occurs):

```
Private Sub UserForm_QueryClose _
  (Cancel As Integer, CloseMode As Integer)
    If CloseMode = vbFormControlMenu Then
        MsgBox "Click the OK button to close the form."
        Cancel = True
    End If
End Sub
```

The `UserForm_QueryClose` procedure uses two arguments. The `CloseMode` argument contains a value that indicates the cause of the `QueryClose` event. If `CloseMode` is equal to `vbFormControlMenu` (a built-in constant), that means that the user clicked the Close button. If a message is displayed, the `Cancel` argument is set to `True`, and the form is not actually closed.

Keep in mind that a user can press Ctrl+Break to break out of the macro. In this example, pressing Ctrl+Break while the UserForm is displayed will cause the UserForm to be dismissed. To prevent this from happening, execute the following statement prior to displaying the UserForm:

`Application.EnableCancelKey = xlDisabled`

Make sure that your application is debugged before you add this statement. Otherwise, you'll find that it's impossible to break out of an accidental endless loop.

Changing a UserForm's Size

Many applications use dialog boxes that change their own size. For example, Excel's AutoFormat dialog box (displayed when you choose Format → AutoFormat) increases its height when the user clicks the Options button.

This example demonstrates how to get a UserForm to change its size dynamically. Changing a dialog box's size is done by altering the `Width` or `Height` property of the UserForm object.

Figure 14-5 shows the dialog box as it is first displayed, and Figure 14-6 shows it after the user clicks the Options button. Notice that the button's caption changes, depending on the size of the UserForm.

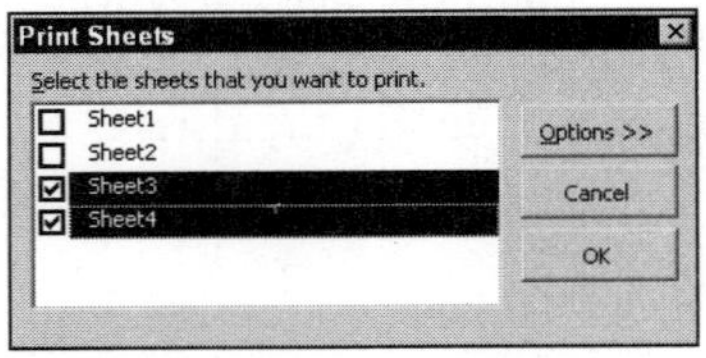

Figure 14-5: A sample dialog box in its standard mode.

While you're creating the UserForm, set it to its largest size to enable you to work with the controls. Then use the `UserForm_Initialize` procedure to set it to its default (smaller) size.

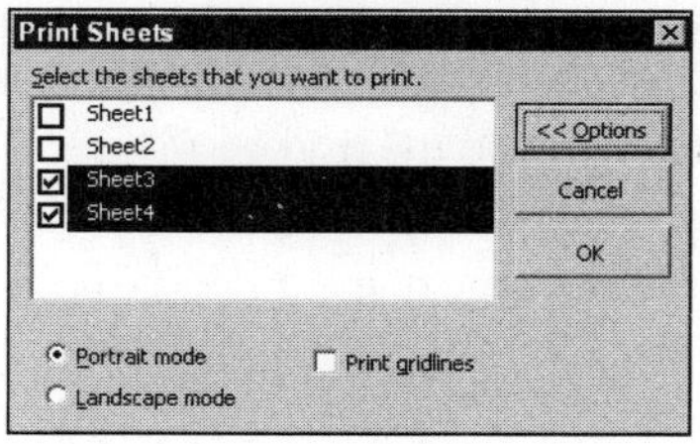

Figure 14-6: The same dialog box enlarged
to show some options.

This example displays a list of worksheets in the active workbook and lets the user select which sheets to print. Following is the event handler that's executed when the CommandButton named `OptionsButton` is clicked:

```
Private Sub OptionsButton_Click()
    If OptionsButton.Caption = "Options >>" Then
        Me.Height = 164
        OptionsButton.Caption = "<< Options"
    Else
        Me.Height = 128
        OptionsButton.Caption = "Options >>"
    End If
End Sub
```

This procedure examines the `Caption` of the CommandButton and sets the UserForm's `Height` property accordingly.

> **NOTE** When controls are not displayed because they are outside the visible portion of the UserForm, the accelerator keys for such controls continue to function. In this example, the user can press the Alt+L hot key (to select the Landscape mode option) even if that option is not visible. To block access to nondisplayed controls, you can write code to disable the controls when they are not displayed.

Zooming and Scrolling a Sheet from a UserForm

When you display a dialog box, it's often helpful if the user can scroll through the worksheet to examine various ranges. Normally, this is impossible while a dialog box is displayed.

Beginning with Excel 2000, a UserForm can be *modeless*. That is, the user doesn't have to dismiss the dialog box before activating the workbook and doing other work in Excel. The `Show` method of the UserForm object defaults to displaying the form modally. To display a modeless dialog box, use an instruction such as

```
UserForm1.Show vbModeless
```

The example in this section demonstrates how to use `ScrollBar` controls to allow sheet scrolling and zooming while a dialog box is displayed. Figure 14-7 shows how the example dialog box is set up. When the UserForm is displayed, the user can adjust the worksheet's zoom factor (from 10% to 400% by using the ScrollBar at the top). The two ScrollBars in the bottom section of the dialog box allow the user to scroll the worksheet horizontally or vertically.

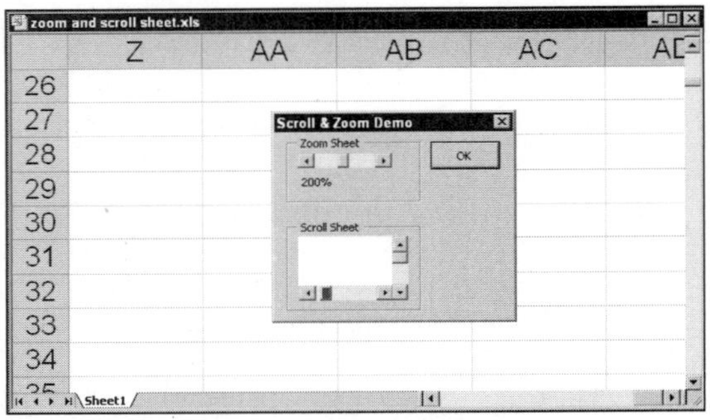

Figure 14-7: Here, ScrollBar controls allow zooming and scrolling of the worksheet.

If you look at the code for this example, you'll see that it's remarkably simple. The controls are initialized in the `UserForm_Initialize` procedure, which follows:

```
Private Sub UserForm_Initialize()
    LabelZoom.Caption = ActiveWindow.Zoom & "%"
'   Zoom
    With ScrollBarZoom
        .Min = 10
        .Max = 400
        .SmallChange = 1
        .LargeChange = 10
        .Value = ActiveWindow.Zoom
    End With
```

```
'   Horizontally scrolling
    With ScrollBarColumns
        .Min = 1
        .Max = 256
        .Value = ActiveWindow.ScrollColumn
        .LargeChange = 25
        .SmallChange = 1
    End With

'   Vertically scrolling
    With ScrollBarRows
        .Min = 1
        .Max = ActiveSheet.UsedRange.Rows.Count _
            + ActiveSheet.UsedRange.Row
        .Value = ActiveWindow.ScrollRow
        .LargeChange = 25
        .SmallChange = 1
    End With
End Sub
```

This procedure sets various properties of the ScrollBar controls by using values based on the active window.

When the ScrollBarZoom control is used, the ScrollBarZoom_Change procedure (which follows) is executed. This procedure sets the ScrollBar control's Value to the ActiveWindow's Zoom property value. It also changes a label to display the current zoom factor.

```
Private Sub ScrollBarZoom_Change()
    With ActiveWindow
        .Zoom = ScrollBarZoom.Value
        LabelZoom = .Zoom & "%"
    End With
End Sub
```

Worksheet scrolling is accomplished by the two procedures that follow. These procedures set the ScrollRow or ScrollColumns property of the ActiveWindow object equal to the appropriate ScrollBar control value.

```
Private Sub ScrollBarColumns_Change()
    ActiveWindow.ScrollColumn = ScrollBarColumns.Value
End Sub

Private Sub ScrollBarRows_Change()
    ActiveWindow.ScrollRow = ScrollBarRows.Value
End Sub
```

Rather than use the Change event in the preceding procedures, you can use the Scroll event. The difference is that the event is triggered when the ScrollBars are dragged — resulting in smooth zooming and scrolling. To use the Scroll event, just make the Change part of the procedure name Scroll.

ListBox Techniques

The ListBox control is extremely versatile, but it can be a bit tricky to work with. This section consists of a number of simple examples that demonstrate common techniques that involve the ListBox control.

In most cases, the techniques described in this section also work with a ComboBox control.

About the ListBox control

Following are a few points to keep in mind when working with ListBox controls. Examples in the sections that follow demonstrate many of these points.

◆ The items in a ListBox can be retrieved from a range of cells (specified by the RowSource property), or they can be added by using VBA code (using the AddItem method).

◆ A ListBox can be set up to allow a single selection or a multiple selection. This is determined by the MultiSelect property.

◆ If a ListBox is not set up for a multiple selection, the value of the ListBox can be linked to a worksheet cell by using the ControlSource property.

◆ It's possible to display a ListBox with no items selected (the ListIndex property will be -1). However, after an item is selected, the user cannot deselect all items. The exception to this is if the MultiSelect property is True.

◆ A ListBox can contain multiple columns (controlled by the ColumnCount property) and even a descriptive header (controlled by the ColumnHeads property).

◆ The vertical height of a ListBox displayed in a UserForm window isn't always the same as the vertical height when the UserForm is actually displayed.

◆ The items in a ListBox can be displayed either as check boxes (if multiple selection is allowed) or as option buttons (if a single selection is allowed). This is controlled by the ListStyle property.

For complete details on the properties and methods for a ListBox control, consult the online help.

Adding items to a ListBox control

Before displaying a UserForm that uses a ListBox control, you'll probably need to fill the ListBox with items. You can fill a ListBox at design time using items stored in a worksheet range or at runtime, using VBA to add the items to the ListBox.

The two examples in this section presume that

◆ You have a UserForm named UserForm1.

◆ This UserForm contains a ListBox control named ListBox1.

◆ The workbook contains a sheet named Sheet1, and range A1:A12 contains the items to be displayed in the ListBox.

ADDING ITEMS TO A LISTBOX AT DESIGN TIME

To add items to a ListBox at design time, the ListBox items must be stored in a worksheet range. Use the RowSource property to specify the range that contains the ListBox items. Figure 14-8 shows the Properties window for a ListBox control. The RowSource property is set to Sheet1!A1:A12. When the UserForm is displayed, the ListBox will contain the 12 items in this range. The items appear in the ListBox at design time as soon as you specify the range for the RowSource property.

Make sure that you include the worksheet name when you specify the RowSource property; otherwise, the ListBox will use the specified range on the active worksheet. In some cases, you might need to fully qualify the range by including the workbook name. For example:

[Book1.xls]Sheet1!A1:A12

A better practice is to define a name for the range and use that name in your code. This will ensure that the proper range is used even if rows above the range are added or deleted.

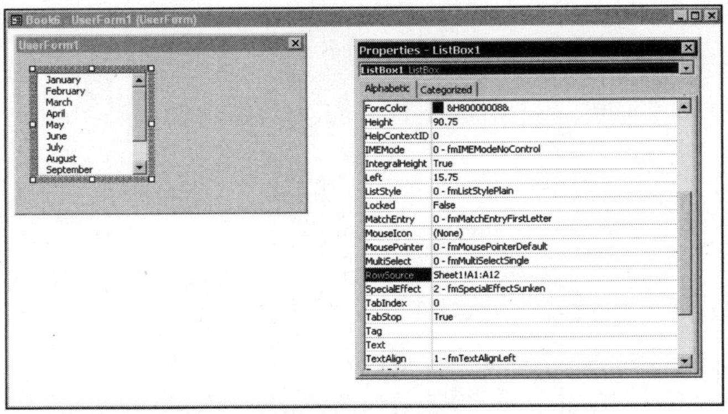

Figure 14-8: Setting the RowSource property at design time.

ADDING ITEMS TO A LISTBOX AT RUNTIME

To add ListBox items at runtime, you have two choices:

◆ Set the RowSource property to a range address by using code.

◆ Write code that uses the AddItem method to add the ListBox items.

As you might expect, you can set the RowSource property via code rather than with the Properties window. For example, the following procedure sets the RowSource property for a ListBox before displaying the UserForm. In this case, the items consist of the cell entries in a range named Categories on the Budget worksheet.

```
UserForm1.ListBox1.RowSource = "Budget!Categories"
UserForm1.Show
```

If the ListBox items are not contained in a worksheet range, you can write VBA code to fill the ListBox before the dialog box appears. The procedure fills the ListBox with the names of the months by using the AddItem method.

```
Sub ShowUserForm2()
'   Fill the list box
    With UserForm2.ListBox1
        .RowSource=""
        .AddItem "January"
```

```
            .AddItem "February"
            .AddItem "March"
            .AddItem "April"
            .AddItem "May"
            .AddItem "June"
            .AddItem "July"
            .AddItem "August"
            .AddItem "September"
            .AddItem "October"
            .AddItem "November"
            .AddItem "December"
        End With
        UserForm2.Show
End Sub
```

In the preceding code, notice that I set the RowSource property to an empty string. This is to avoid a potential error that occurs if the Properties window has a nonempty RowSource setting. If you try to add items to a ListBox that has a non-null RowSource setting, you'll get a "permission denied" error.

You can also use the AddItem method to retrieve ListBox items from a range. Here's an example that fills a ListBox with the contents of A1:A12 on Sheet1.

```
For Row = 1 To 12
  UserForm1.ListBox1.AddItem Sheets("Sheet1").Cells(Row, 1)
Next Row
```

If your data is stored in a one-dimensional array, you can assign the array to the ListBox with a single instruction. For example, assume that you have an array named dData that contains 50 elements. The following statement will create a 50-item list in ListBox1:

```
ListBox1.List = dData
```

ADDING ONLY UNIQUE ITEMS TO A LISTBOX

In some cases, you might need to fill a ListBox with *unique* (nonduplicated) items from a list. For example, assume you have a worksheet that contains customer data. One of the columns might contain the state (see Figure 14-9). You would like to fill a ListBox with the state name of your customers, but you don't want to include duplicate state names.

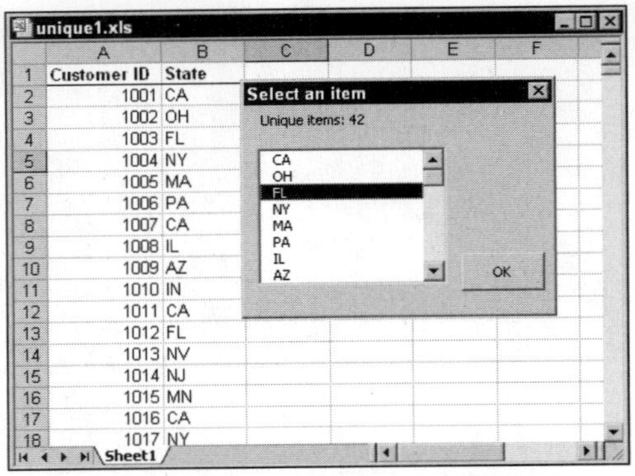

Figure 14-9: A Collection object is used to fill a
ListBox with the unique items from column B.

One technique involves using a Collection object. You can add items to a
Collection object with the following syntax:

```
object.Add item, key, before, after
```

The *key* argument, if used, must be a unique text string that specifies a separate
key that can be used to access a member of the collection. The important word here
is *unique*. If you attempt to add a nonunique key to a collection, an error occurs,
and the item is not added. You can take advantage of this situation and use it to
create a collection that consists only of unique items.

The following procedure demonstrates: It starts by declaring a new Collection
object named NoDupes. It assumes that a range named Data contains a list of items,
some of which may be duplicated.

The code loops through the cells in the range and attempts to add the cell's value
to the NoDupes collection. It also uses the cell's value (converted to a string) for the
key argument. Using the On Error Resume Next statement causes VBA to ignore
the error that occurs if the key is not unique. When an error occurs, the item is not
added to the collection – which is just what you want. The procedure then transfers
the items in the NoDupes collection to the ListBox. The UserForm also contains a
label that displays the number of unique items.

```
Sub RemoveDuplicates1()
    Dim AllCells As Range, Cell As Range
    Dim NoDupes As New Collection

    On Error Resume Next
    For Each Cell In Range("Data")
        NoDupes.Add Cell.Value, CStr(Cell.Value)
    Next Cell
    On Error GoTo 0
```

```
'    Add the non-duplicated items to a ListBox
     For Each Item In NoDupes
         UserForm1.ListBox1.AddItem Item
     Next Item

'    Display the count
     UserForm1.Label1.Caption = _
       "Unique items: " & NoDupes.Count

'    Show the UserForm
     UserForm1.Show
End Sub
```

This workbook, along with a slightly more sophisticated version of this example, is available on the CD-ROM.

Determining the selected item

The examples in preceding sections merely display a UserForm with a ListBox filled with various items. These procedures omit a key point: how to determine which item or items were selected by the user.

This discussion assumes a single-selection ListBox object — one whose MultiSelect property is set to 0.

To determine which item was selected, access the ListBox's Value property. The statement that follows, for example, displays the text of the selected item in ListBox1.

```
MsgBox ListBox1.Value
```

If no item is selected, this statement will generate an error.

If you need to know the position of the selected item in the list (rather than the content of that item), you can access the ListBox's ListIndex property. The following example uses a message box to display the item number of the selected ListBox item:

```
MsgBox "You selected item #" & ListBox1.ListIndex
```

If no item is selected, the ListIndex property will return -1.

NOTE

The numbering of items in a ListBox begins with 0 — not 1. Therefore, the ListIndex of the first item is 0, and the ListIndex of the last item is equivalent to the value of the ListCount property less 1.

Determining multiple selections in a ListBox

Normally, a ListBox's MultiSelect property is 0, which means that the user can select only one item in the ListBox.

If the ListBox allows multiple selections (that is, if its MultiSelect property is either 1 or 2), trying to access the ListIndex or Value properties will result in an error. Instead, you need to use the Selected property, which returns an array whose first item has an index of 0. For example, the following statement displays True if the first item in the ListBox list is selected:

```
MsgBox ListBox1.Selected(0)
```

ON THE CD

The companion CD-ROM contains a workbook that demonstrates how to identify the selected item(s) in a ListBox. It works for single-selection and multiple-selection ListBoxes.

The following code, from the example workbook on the CD-ROM, loops through each item in the ListBox. If the item was selected, it appends the item's text to a variable called Msg. Finally, the names of all the selected items are displayed in a message box.

```
Private Sub OKButton_Click()
    Msg = ""
    For i = 0 To ListBox1.ListCount - 1
        If ListBox1.Selected(i) Then _
            Msg = Msg & ListBox1.List(i) & vbCrLf
    Next i
    MsgBox "You selected: " & vbCrLf & Msg
    Unload Me
End Sub
```

Figure 14-10 shows the result when multiple ListBox items are selected.

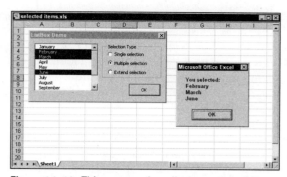

Figure 14-10: This message box displays a list of items selected in a ListBox.

Multiple lists in a single ListBox

This example demonstrates how to create a ListBox in which the contents change depending on the user's selection from a group of OptionButtons.

Figure 14-11 shows the sample UserForm. The ListBox gets its items from a worksheet range. The procedures that handle the Click event for the OptionButton controls simply set the ListBox's RowSource property to a different range. One of these procedures follows:

```
Private Sub obMonths_Click()
    ListBox1.RowSource = "Sheet1!Months"
End Sub
```

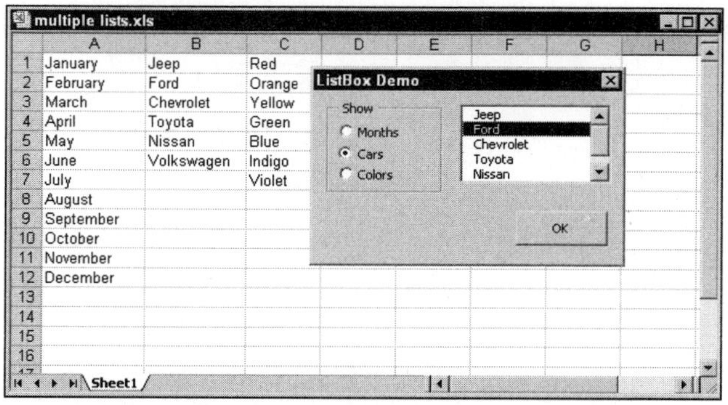

Figure 14-11: The contents of this ListBox depend on the OptionButton selected.

Clicking the OptionButton named obMonths changes the RowSource property of the ListBox to use a range named Months on Sheet1.

ListBox item transfer

Some applications require a user to select several items from a list. It's often useful to create a new list of the selected items. For an example of this situation, check out the Attach Toolbars dialog box that appears when you click the Attach button in the Customize dialog box (which appears when you choose View → Toolbars → Customize).

Figure 14-12 shows a dialog box with two ListBoxes. The Add button adds the item selected in the left ListBox to the right ListBox. The Delete button removes the selected item from the list on the right. A check box determines the behavior when a duplicate item is added to the list: Namely, if the Allow Duplicates check box is not marked, a message box appears if the user attempts to add an item that's already on the list.

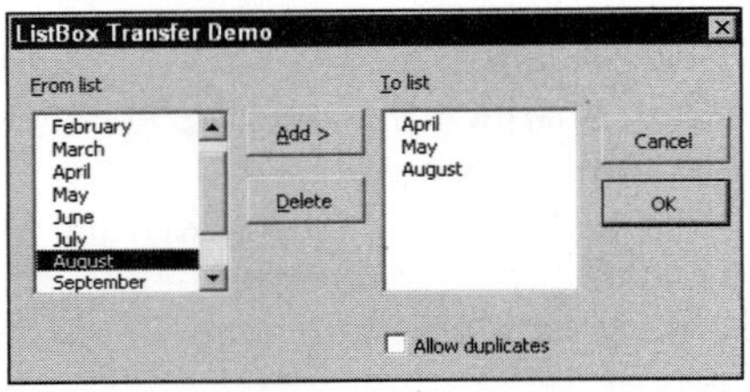

Figure 14-12: Building a list from another list.

The code for this example is relatively simple. Here's the procedure that is executed when the user clicks the Add button:

```
Private Sub AddButton_Click()
    If ListBox1.ListIndex = -1 Then Exit Sub
    If Not cbDuplicates Then
'       See if item already exists
        For i = 0 To ListBox2.ListCount - 1
            If ListBox1.Value = ListBox2.List(i) Then
                Beep
                Exit Sub
            End If
        Next i
    End If
    ListBox2.AddItem ListBox1.Value
End Sub
```

The code for the Delete button is even simpler:

```
Private Sub DeleteButton_Click()
    If ListBox2.ListIndex = -1 Then Exit Sub
```

```
      ListBox2.RemoveItem ListBox2.ListIndex
End Sub
```

Notice that both of these routines check to make sure that an item is actually selected. If the ListBox's ListIndex property is -1, no items are selected, and the procedure ends.

Moving items in a ListBox

The example in this section demonstrates how to allow the user to move items up or down in a ListBox. The VBE uses this type of technique to let you control the tab order of the items in a UserForm.

Figure 14-13 shows a dialog box that contains a ListBox and two Command Buttons. Clicking the Move Up button moves the selected item up in the ListBox; clicking the Move Down button moves the selected item down.

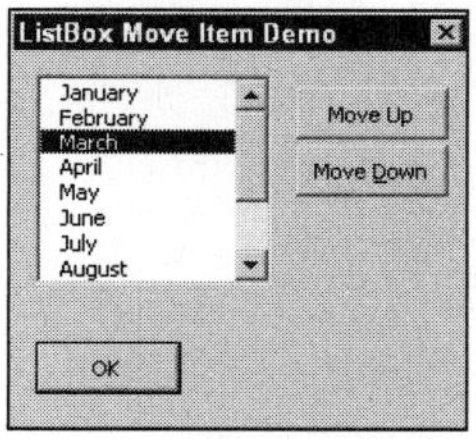

Figure 14-13: The buttons allow
the user to move items
up or down in the ListBox.

The event handler procedures for the two CommandButtons follow:

```
Private Sub MoveUpButton_Click()
    If ListBox1.ListIndex <= 0 Then Exit Sub
    NumItems = ListBox1.ListCount
    Dim TempList()
    ReDim TempList(0 To NumItems - 1)
'   Fill array with list box items
    For i = 0 To NumItems - 1
        TempList(i) = ListBox1.List(i)
    Next i
'   Selected item
    ItemNum = ListBox1.ListIndex
'   Exchange items
    TempItem = TempList(ItemNum)
    TempList(ItemNum) = TempList(ItemNum - 1)
    TempList(ItemNum - 1) = TempItem
    ListBox1.List = TempList
```

```
'   Change the list index
    ListBox1.ListIndex = ItemNum - 1
End Sub

Private Sub MoveDownButton_Click()
    If ListBox1.ListIndex = ListBox1.ListCount - 1 Then Exit Sub
    NumItems = ListBox1.ListCount
    Dim TempList()
    ReDim TempList(0 To NumItems - 1)
'   Fill array with list box items
    For i = 0 To NumItems - 1
        TempList(i) = ListBox1.List(i)
    Next i
'   Selected item
    ItemNum = ListBox1.ListIndex
'   Exchange items
    TempItem = TempList(ItemNum)
    TempList(ItemNum) = TempList(ItemNum + 1)
    TempList(ItemNum + 1) = TempItem
    ListBox1.List = TempList
'   Change the list index
    ListBox1.ListIndex = ItemNum + 1
End Sub
```

These procedures work fairly well, but you'll find that for some reason, relatively rapid clicking doesn't always register. For example, you may click the Move Down button three times in quick succession, but the item only moves one or two positions. The solution is to add a new DblClick event handler for each CommandButton. These procedures, which simply call the Click procedures, are as follows:

```
Private Sub MoveUpButton_DblClick _
  (ByVal Cancel As MSForms.ReturnBoolean)
    Call MoveUpButton_Click
End Sub

Private Sub MoveDownButton_DblClick _
  (ByVal Cancel As MSForms.ReturnBoolean)
    Call MoveDownButton_Click
End Sub
```

Working with multicolumn ListBox controls

A normal ListBox has a single column for its contained items. You can, however, create a ListBox that displays multiple columns and (optionally) column headers.

Figure 14-14 shows an example of a multicolumn ListBox that gets its data from a worksheet range.

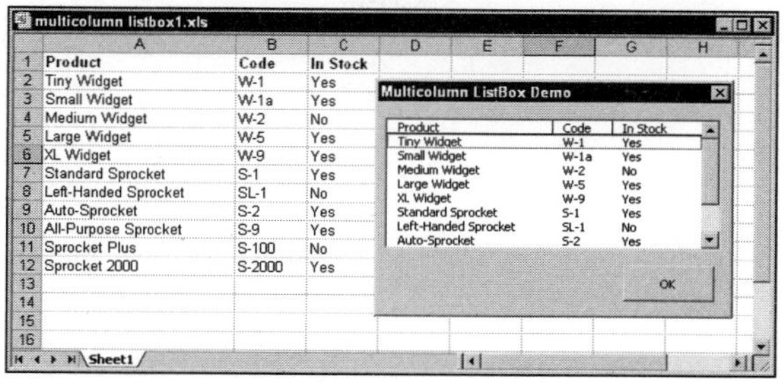

Figure 14-14: This ListBox displays a three-column list with column headers.

To set up a multicolumn ListBox that uses data stored in a worksheet range, follow these steps:

1. Make sure that the ListBox's `ColumnCount` property is set to the correct number of columns.

2. Specify the correct multicolumn range in the Excel worksheet as the ListBox's `RowSource` property.

3. If you want to display column heads like the ListBox in Figure 14-14, set the `ColumnHeads` property to `True`. Do not include the column headings on the worksheet in the range setting for the `RowSource` property. VBA will instead automatically use the row directly above the first row of the `RowSource` range.

4. Adjust the column widths by assigning a series of values, specified in *points* ($\frac{1}{72}$ of one inch) and separated by semicolons, to the `ColumnWidths` property. For example, for a three-column list box, the `ColumnWidths` property might be set to the following text string:

   `100;40;30`

5. Specify the appropriate column as the `BoundColumn` property. The bound column specifies which column is referenced when an instruction polls the ListBox's `Value` property.

To fill a ListBox with multicolumn data without using a range, you first create a two-dimensional array and then assign the array to the ListBox's `List` property. The following statements demonstrate, using a 12-row x 2-column array named `Data`. The two-column ListBox shows the month names in column 1 and the number of the days in the month in column 2 (see Figure 14-15). Notice that the procedure sets the `ColumnCount` property to `2`.

```
Private Sub UserForm_Initialize()
'    Fill the list box
    Dim Data(1 To 12, 1 To 2)
    For i = 1 To 12
        Data(i, 1) = Format(DateSerial(2001, i, 1), "mmmm")
    Next i
    For i = 1 To 12
        Data(i, 2) = Day(DateSerial(2001, i + 1, 1) - 1)
    Next i
    ListBox1.ColumnCount = 2
    ListBox1.List = Data
End Sub
```

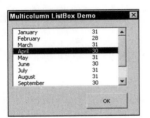

Figure 14-15: A two-column ListBox
filled with data
stored in an array.

 There appears to be no way to specify column headers for the `ColumnHeads`
property when the list source is a VBA array.

Using a ListBox to select worksheet rows

The example in this section is actually a useful utility. It displays a ListBox that consists of the entire used range of the active worksheet (see Figure 14-16). The user can select multiple items in the ListBox. Clicking the All button selects all items, and clicking the None button deselects all items. Clicking OK selects those corresponding rows in the worksheet. You can, of course, select multiple noncontiguous rows directly in the worksheet by pressing Ctrl while you click the row borders. However, you might find that selecting rows is easier when using this method.

Selecting multiple items is possible because the ListBox's `MultiSelect` property is set to `1 - fmMultiSelectMulti`. The check boxes on each item are displayed because the ListBox's `ListStyle` property is set to `1 - fmListStyleOption`.

The UserForm's `Initialize` procedure follows. This procedure creates a `Range` object named `rng` that consists of the active sheet's used range. Additional code sets the ListBox's `ColumnCount` and `RowSource` properties and adjusts the `ColumnWidths` property such that the ListBox columns are proportional to the column widths in the worksheet.

```
Private Sub UserForm_Initialize()
    ColCnt = ActiveSheet.UsedRange.Columns.Count
    Set rng = ActiveSheet.UsedRange
    With ListBox1
        .ColumnCount = ColCnt
        .RowSource = rng.Address
        cw = ""
        For c = 1 To .ColumnCount
            cw = cw & rng.Columns(c).Width & ";"
        Next c
        .ColumnWidths = cw
        .ListIndex = 0
    End With
End Sub
```

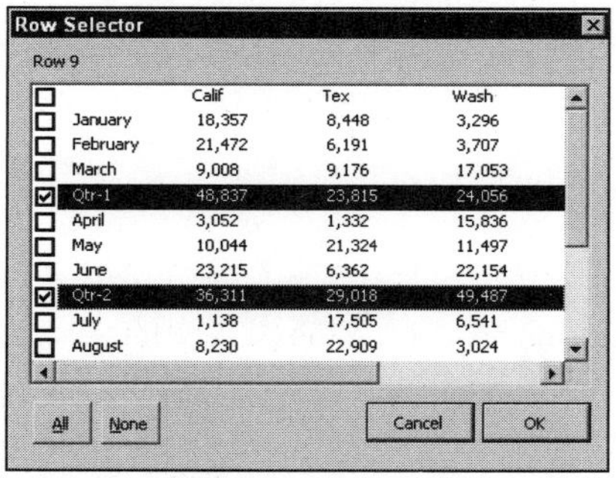

Figure 14–16: This ListBox makes it easy to select rows in a worksheet.

The All and None buttons (named `SelectAllButton` and `SelectNoneButton`, respectively) have simple event handler procedures and are as follows:

```
Private Sub SelectAllButton_Click()
    For r = 0 To ListBox1.ListCount - 1
        ListBox1.Selected(r) = True
    Next r
End Sub

Private Sub SelectNoneButton_Click()
    For r = 0 To ListBox1.ListCount - 1
        ListBox1.Selected(r) = False
```

```
        Next r
End Sub
```

The `OKButton_Click` procedure follows. This procedure creates a `Range` object named `RowRange` that consists of the rows that correspond to the selected items in the ListBox. To determine whether a row was selected, the code examines the `Selected` property of the ListBox control. Notice that it uses the `Union` function to add additional ranges to the `RowRange` object.

```
Private Sub OKButton_Click()
    Dim RowRange As Range
    RowCnt = 0
    For r = 0 To ListBox1.ListCount - 1
        If ListBox1.Selected(r) Then
            RowCnt = RowCnt + 1
            If RowCnt = 1 Then
                Set RowRange = ActiveSheet.Rows(r + 1)
            Else
                Set RowRange = _
                    Union(RowRange, ActiveSheet.Rows(r + 1))
            End If
        End If
    Next r
    If Not RowRange Is Nothing Then RowRange.Select
    Unload Me
End Sub
```

Using a ListBox to activate a sheet

The example in this section is just as useful as it is instructive. This example uses a multicolumn ListBox to display a list of sheets within the active workbook. The columns represent

◆ The sheet's name

◆ The type of sheet (worksheet, chart, or Excel 5/95 dialog sheet)

◆ The number of nonempty cells in the sheet

◆ Whether the sheet is visible

Figure 14-17 shows an example of the dialog box.

The code in the `UserForm_Initialize` procedure (which follows) creates a two-dimensional array and collects the information by looping through the sheets in the active workbook. It then transfers this array to the ListBox.

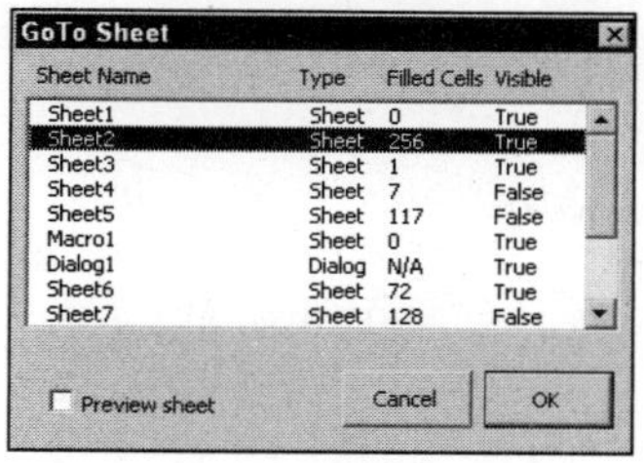

Figure 14-17: This dialog box lets
the user activate a sheet.

```
Public OriginalSheet As Object

Private Sub UserForm_Initialize()
    Dim SheetData() As String
    Set OriginalSheet = ActiveSheet
    ShtCnt = ActiveWorkbook.Sheets.Count
    ReDim SheetData(1 To ShtCnt, 1 To 4)
    ShtNum = 1
    For Each Sht In ActiveWorkbook.Sheets
        If Sht.Name = ActiveSheet.Name Then _
          ListPos = ShtNum - 1
        SheetData(ShtNum, 1) = Sht.Name
        Select Case TypeName(Sht)
            Case "Worksheet"
                SheetData(ShtNum, 2) = "Sheet"
                SheetData(ShtNum, 3) = _
                  Application.CountA(Sht.Cells)
            Case "Chart"
                SheetData(ShtNum, 2) = "Chart"
                SheetData(ShtNum, 3) = "N/A"
            Case "DialogSheet"
                SheetData(ShtNum, 2) = "Dialog"
                SheetData(ShtNum, 3) = "N/A"
        End Select
        If Sht.Visible Then
            SheetData(ShtNum, 4) = "True"
        Else
            SheetData(ShtNum, 4) = "False"
        End If
        ShtNum = ShtNum + 1
    Next Sht
    With ListBox1
        .ColumnWidths = "100 pt;30 pt;40 pt;50 pt"
        .List = SheetData
```

```
            .ListIndex = ListPos
       End With
End Sub
```

The `ListBox1_Click` procedure follows:

```
Private Sub ListBox1_Click()
    If cbPreview Then _
        Sheets(ListBox1.Value).Activate
End Sub
```

The value of the `CheckBox` control (named `cbPreview`) determines whether the selected sheet is previewed when the user clicks an item in the ListBox.

Clicking the OK button (named `OKButton`) executes the `OKButton_Click` procedure, which follows:

```
Private Sub OKButton_Click()
    Dim UserSheet As Object
    Set UserSheet = Sheets(ListBox1.Value)
    If UserSheet.Visible Then
        UserSheet.Activate
    Else
        If MsgBox("Unhide sheet?", _
          vbQuestion + vbYesNoCancel) = vbYes Then
            UserSheet.Visible = True
            UserSheet.Activate
        Else
            OriginalSheet.Activate
        End If
    End If
    Unload Me
End Sub
```

The `OKButton_Click` procedure creates an object variable that represents the selected sheet. If the sheet is visible, it is activated. If it's not visible, the user is presented with a message box asking whether it should be unhidden. If the user responds in the affirmative, the sheet is unhidden and activated. Otherwise, the original sheet (stored in a public object variable named `OriginalSheet`) is activated.

Double-clicking an item in the ListBox has the same result as clicking the OK button. The `ListBox1_DblClick` procedure, which follows, simply calls the `OKButton_Click` procedure.

```
Private Sub ListBox1_DblClick(ByVal Cancel As  MSForms.ReturnBoolean)
    Call OKButton_Click
End Sub
```

Using the MultiPage Control in a UserForm

The MultiPage control is very useful for UserForms that must display many controls. The MultiPage control lets you group the choices and place each group on a separate tab.

Figure 14-18 shows an example of a UserForm that contains a MultiPage control. In this case, the control has three pages, each with its own tab.

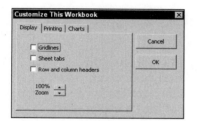

Figure 14–18: MultiPage groups your controls on pages, making them accessible from a tab.

The Toolbox also contains a control named TabStrip, which resembles a MultiPage control. However, unlike the MultiPage control, the TabStrip control is not a container for other objects. The MultiPage control is much more versatile, and I've never had a need to actually use the TabStrip control.

Using a MultiPage control can be a bit tricky. The following are some things to keep in mind when using this control:

◆ The tab (or page) that's displayed up front is determined by the control's Value function. A value of 0 displays the first tab, a value of 1 displays the second tab, and so on.

◆ By default, a MultiPage control has two pages. To add a new page in the VBE, right-click a tab and select New Page from the shortcut menu.

◆ When you're working with a MultiPage control, just click a tab to set the properties for that particular page. The Properties window will display the properties that you can adjust.

◆ You might find it difficult to select the actual `MultiPage` control because clicking the control selects a page within the control. To select the control itself, click its border. Or, you can use the Tab key to cycle among all the controls. Yet another option is to select the `MultiPage` control from the drop-down list in the Properties window.

◆ If your `MultiPage` control has lots of tabs, you can set its `MultiRow` property to `True` to display the tabs in more than one row.

◆ If you prefer, you can display buttons instead of tabs. Just change the `Style` property to 1. If the `Style` property value is 2, the `MultiPage` control won't display tabs or buttons.

◆ The `TabOrientation` property determines the location of the tabs on the `MultiPage` control.

◆ For each page, you can set a transition effect by changing the `TransitionEffect` property. For example, clicking a tab can cause the new page to push the former page out of the way. Use the `TransitionPeriod` property to set the speed of the transition effect.

The next chapter contains several examples that use the `MultiPage` control.

Chapter 15

Advanced UserForm Techniques

IN THIS CHAPTER

This chapter picks up where Chapter 13 left off. Here you'll find additional examples of UserForms.

- ◆ Displaying a progress indicator (three techniques)
- ◆ Creating a *wizard* — an interactive series of dialog boxes
- ◆ Creating a function that emulates VBA's `MsgBox` function
- ◆ Using modeless UserForms
- ◆ Handling multiple objects with a single event handler
- ◆ Using a dialog box to select a color
- ◆ Displaying cell information in a UserForm
- ◆ Displaying a chart in a UserForm (two techniques)
- ◆ Displaying a complete spreadsheet in a UserForm
- ◆ Using an enhanced data form

MOST OF THESE EXAMPLES ARE MORE ADVANCED, but you'll find that they all focus on practical applications.

Displaying a Progress Indicator

One of the most common requests among Excel developers involves progress indicators. A *progress indicator* is a graphical thermometer-type display that shows the progress of a task such as a lengthy macro.

Before Excel 97, creating a progress indicator was a difficult task. But now, it's relatively easy. In this section, I describe how to create three types of progress indicators for

♦ A macro that's not initiated by a UserForm (a standalone progress indicator).

♦ A macro that is initiated by a UserForm. In this case, the UserForm makes use of a `MultiPage` control that displays the progress indicator while the macro is running.

♦ A macro that is initiated by a UserForm. In this case, the UserForm increases in height, and the progress indicator appears at the bottom of the dialog box.

Using a progress indicator requires that you are (somehow) able to gauge how far along your macro might be in completing its given task. How you do this will vary, depending on the macro. For example, if your macro writes data to cells (and you know the number of cells that will be written to), it's a simple matter to write code that calculates the percent completed.

 A progress indicator will slow down your macro a bit because of the extra overhead of having to update it. If speed is absolutely critical, you might prefer to forgo using a progress indicator.

Displaying Progress in the Status Bar

A simple way to display the progress of a macro is to use Excel's status bar. The advantage is that it's very easy to program. However, the disadvantage is that most users aren't accustomed to watching the status bar and prefer a more visual display.

To write text to the status bar, use a statement such as

```
Application.StatusBar = "Please wait..."
```

You can, of course, update the status bar while your macro progresses. For example, if you have a variable named `Pct` that represents the percent completed, you can write code that periodically executes a statement such as this:

```
Application.StatusBar = "Processing... " & Pct & "% Completed"
```

When your macro finishes, reset the status bar to its normal state with the following statement:

```
Application.StatusBar = False
```

Creating a standalone progress indicator

This section describes how to set up a standalone progress indicator – that is, not initiated by displaying a UserForm – to display the progress of a macro.

 This example is available on the companion CD-ROM.

BUILDING THE STANDALONE PROGRESS INDICATOR USERFORM

Follow these steps to create the UserForm that will be used to display the progress of your task:

1. Insert a new UserForm and change its Caption property setting to Progress.

2. Add a Frame control and name it FrameProgress.

3. Add a Label control inside the Frame and name it LabelProgress. Remove the label's caption and make its background color (BackColor property) red. The label's size and placement don't matter for now.

4. Add another label above the frame to describe what's going on (optional).

5. Adjust the UserForm and controls so that they look something like Figure 15-1.

You can, of course, apply any other type of formatting to the controls. For example, I changed the SpecialEffect property for the Frame control shown in Figure 15-1.

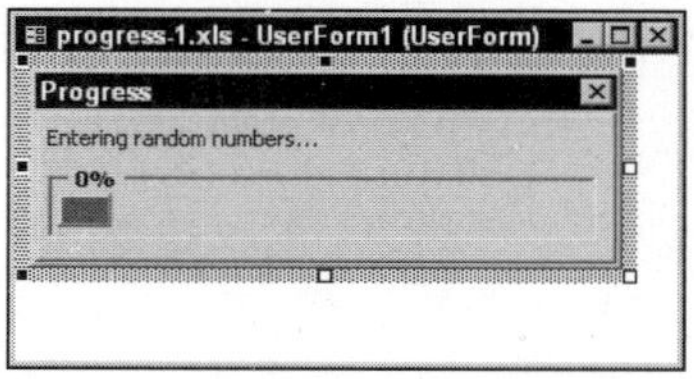

progress-1.xls - UserForm1 (UserForm)

Progress

Entering random numbers...

0%

Figure 15-1: This UserForm will serve as a progress indicator.

CREATING THE EVENT HANDLER PROCEDURES FOR THE STANDALONE PROGRESS INDICATOR

The trick here involves running a procedure automatically when the UserForm is displayed. One option is to use the Initialize event. However, this event occurs *before* the UserForm is actually displayed, so it's not appropriate. The Activate event, on the other hand, is triggered when the UserForm is displayed, so it's perfect for this application.

Insert the following procedure in the code window for the UserForm. This procedure simply calls a procedure named Main when the UserForm is displayed. The Main procedure, which is stored in a VBA module, is the actual macro that runs while the progress indicator is displayed.

```
Private Sub UserForm_Activate()
    Call Main
End Sub
```

The Main procedure follows. This demo routine simply inserts random numbers into the active worksheet. While it does so, it changes the width of the Label control and displays the percentage completed in the Frame's caption. This procedure is just for exercising the progress bar; you can, of course, substitute your own for more meaningful purposes.

```
Sub Main()
'    Inserts random numbers on the active worksheet
    Cells.Clear
    Counter = 1
    RowMax = 200
    ColMax = 25
    For r = 1 To RowMax
        For c = 1 To ColMax
            Cells(r, c) = Int(Rnd * 1000)
            Counter = Counter + 1
        Next c
        PctDone = Counter / (RowMax * ColMax)
        Call UpdateProgress(PctDone)
    Next r
    Unload UserForm1
End Sub
```

The Main procedure contains a loop (two loops, actually). Inside the loop is a call to the UpdateProgress procedure. This procedure, which follows, takes one argument: a value between 0 and 100 that represents the progress of the macro.

```
Sub UpdateProgress(Pct)
    With UserForm1
       .FrameProgress.Caption = Format(Pct, "0%")
       .LabelProgress.Width = Pct * (.FrameProgress.Width - 10)
       .Repaint
    End With
End Sub
```

CREATING THE START-UP PROCEDURE FOR A STANDALONE PROGRESS INDICATOR

All that's missing is a procedure to display the UserForm. Enter the following procedure in a VBA module:

```
Sub ShowDialog()
    UserForm1.LabelProgress.Width = 0
    UserForm1.Show
End Sub
```

HOW THE STANDALONE PROGRESS INDICATOR WORKS

When you execute the ShowDialog procedure, the Label object's width is set to 0. Then the Show method of the UserForm1 object displays the UserForm (which is the progress indicator). When the UserForm is displayed, its Activate event is triggered, which executes the Main procedure. The Main procedure periodically updates the width of the label. Notice that the procedure uses the Repaint method of the UserForm object. Without this statement, the changes to the label would not be updated. Before the procedure ends, the last statement unloads the UserForm.

To customize this technique, you need to figure out how to determine the percentage completed and assign it to the PctDone variable. This will vary, depending on your application. If your code runs in a loop (as in this example), determining the percentage completed is easy. If your code is not in a loop, you might need to estimate the progress completed at various points in your code.

Showing a progress indicator by using a MultiPage control

In the preceding example, the macro was not initiated by a UserForm. If your lengthy macro is kicked off when a UserForm is displayed, however, the technique that I describe in this section is a better solution. It assumes the following:

◆ Your project is completed and debugged.

◆ Your project uses a UserForm (without a MultiPage control) to initiate a lengthy macro.

◆ You have a way to gauge the progress of your macro.

The companion CD-ROM contains an example that demonstrates this technique.

MODIFYING YOUR USERFORM FOR A PROGRESS INDICATOR WITH A MULTIPAGE CONTROL

This step assumes that you have a UserForm all set up. You'll add a MultiPage control. The first page of the MultiPage control will contain all your original controls. The second page will contain the controls that display the progress indicator. When the macro begins executing, VBA code will change the Value property of the MultiPage control. This will effectively hide the original controls and display the progress indicator.

The first step is to add a MultiPage control to your UserForm. Then move all the existing controls on the UserForm and paste them to Page1 of the MultiPage control.

Next activate Page2 of the MultiPage control and set it up as in Figure 15-2. This is essentially the same combination of controls used in the example in the previous section.

1. Add a Frame control and name it FrameProgress.

2. Add a Label control inside the Frame and name it LabelProgress. Remove the label's caption and make its background color red.

3. Add another label to describe what's going on (optional).

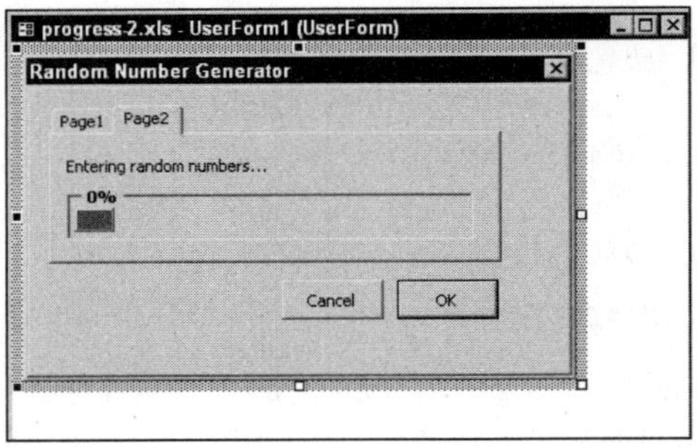

![Screenshot of a UserForm titled "progress-2.xls - UserForm1 (UserForm)" containing a dialog "Random Number Generator" with Page1 and Page2 tabs, text "Entering random numbers...", a progress bar showing 0%, and Cancel and OK buttons.]

Figure 15-2: Page2 of the MultiPage control will display the progress indicator.

4. Next, activate the MultiPage control itself (not a page on the control) and set its Style property to 2 - fmTabStyleNone. (This will hide the tabs.) The easiest way to select the MultiPage control is to use the drop-down list in the Properties window. You'll probably need to adjust the size of the MultiPage control to account for the fact that the tabs are not displayed.

INSERTING THE UPDATEPROGRESS PROCEDURE FOR A PROGRESS INDICATOR WITH A MULTIPAGE CONTROL

Insert the following procedure in the code module for the UserForm:

```
Sub UpdateProgress(Pct)
    With UserForm1
      .FrameProgress.Caption = Format(Pct, "0%")
      .LabelProgress.Width = Pct * (.FrameProgress.Width - 10)
      .Repaint
    End With
End Sub
```

This procedure will be called from the main macro and do the actual updating of the progress indicator.

MODIFYING YOUR PROCEDURE FOR A PROGRESS INDICATOR WITH A MULTIPAGE CONTROL

You need to modify the procedure that is executed when the user clicks the OK Button — the Click event handler procedure for the button, named OK_Click. First, insert the following statement at the top of your procedure:

```
MultiPage1.Value = 1
```

This statement activates Page2 of the MultiPage control (the page that displays the progress indicator).

In the next step, you're pretty much on your own. You need to write code to calculate the percent completed and assign this value to a variable named PctDone. Most likely, this calculation will be performed inside of a loop. Then insert the following statement, which will update the progress indicator:

```
Call UpdateProgress(PctDone)
```

HOW A PROGRESS INDICATOR WITH A MULTIPAGE CONTROL WORKS

This technique is very straightforward and, as you've seen, it involves only one UserForm. The code switches pages of the MultiPage control and converts your normal dialog box into a progress indicator.

Showing a progress indicator without using a MultiPage control

The example in this section is similar to the example in the previous section. However, this technique is simpler because it doesn't use a MultiPage control. Rather, the progress indicator is stored at the bottom of the UserForm — but the UserForm's height is reduced such that the progress indicator controls are not visible.

When it's time to display the progress indicator, the UserForm's height is increased, which makes the progress indicator visible.

The companion CD-ROM contains an example that demonstrates this technique.

Figure 15-3 shows the UserForm in the VBE. The Height property of the UserForm is 172. However, before the UserForm is displayed, the Height is changed to 124 (which means the progress indicator controls are not visible to the user). When the user clicks OK, VBA code changes the Height property to 172 with the following statement:

```
Me.Height = 172
```

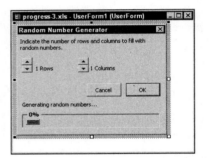

Figure 15-3: The progress indicator will be hidden by reducing the height of the UserForm.

Creating Wizards

Many applications incorporate wizards to guide users through an operation. Excel's Text Import Wizard is a good example. A *wizard* is essentially a series of dialog boxes that solicit information from the user. Often, the user's choices in earlier dialog boxes influence the contents of later dialog boxes. In most wizards, the user is free to go forward or backward through the dialog box sequence or to click the Finish button to accept all defaults.

You can, of course, create wizards by using VBA and a series of UserForms. However, I've found that the most efficient way to create a wizard is to use a single UserForm and a MultiPage control.

Figure 15-4 shows an example of a simple four-step wizard, which consists of a single UserForm that contains a `MultiPage` control. Each step of the wizard displays a different page in the `MultiPage` control.

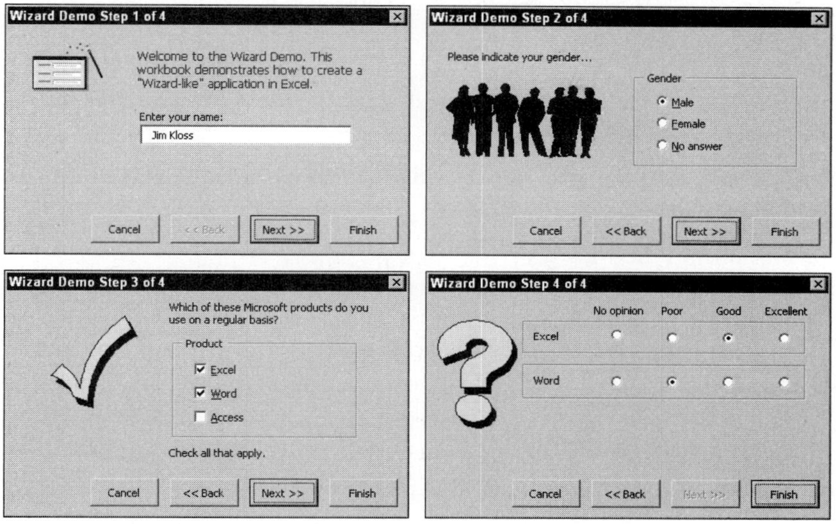

Figure 15-4: This four-step wizard uses a `MultiPage` control.

If you need to create a wizard, the example workbook on the CD-ROM will serve as a good starting point. This is a four-step wizard that collects information and inserts it into a worksheet.

The sections that follow describe how I created the sample wizard.

Setting up the MultiPage control for the wizard

Start with a new UserForm and add a `MultiPage` control. By default, this control contains two pages. Right-click the MultiPage tab and insert enough new pages to handle your wizard (one page for each wizard step). The example on the CD-ROM is a four-step wizard, so the `MultiPage` control has four pages. The names of the MultiPage tabs are irrelevant. The `MultiPage` control's `Style` property will eventually be set to `2 - fmTabStyleNone`. While working on the UserForm, you'll want to keep the tabs visible to make it easier to access various pages.

Next, add the desired controls to each page of the `MultiPage` control. This will, of course, vary depending on your application. You might need to resize the `MultiPage` control while you work in order to have room for the controls.

Adding the buttons to the wizard UserForm

Now add the buttons that control the progress of the wizard. These buttons are placed outside the `MultiPage` control because they are used while any of the pages are displayed. Most wizards have four buttons:

- ◆ *Cancel:* Cancels the wizard.
- ◆ *Back:* Returns to the previous step. During Step 1 of the wizard, this button should be disabled.
- ◆ *Next:* Advances to the next step. During the last wizard step, this button should be disabled.
- ◆ *Finish:* Finishes the wizard.

 In some cases, the user is allowed to click the Finish button at any time and accept the defaults for items that were skipped over. In other cases, the wizard requires a user response for some items. If this is the case, the Finish button is disabled until all required input is made. The example on the CD-ROM requires an entry in the TextBox in Step 1.

In the example, these CommandButtons are named `CancelButton`, `BackButton`, `NextButton`, and `FinishButton`.

Programming the wizard buttons

Each of the four wizard buttons requires a procedure to handle its `Click` event. The event handler for `CancelButton` follows. This procedure uses a `MsgBox` function (see Figure 15-5) to verify that the user really wants to exit. If the user clicks the Yes button, the UserForm is unloaded with no action taken. This type of verification, of course, is optional.

```
Private Sub CancelButton_Click()
    Msg = "Cancel the wizard?"
    Ans = MsgBox(Msg, vbQuestion + vbYesNo, APPNAME)
    If Ans = vbYes Then Unload Me
End Sub
```

The event handler procedures for the Back and Next buttons follow:

```
Private Sub BackButton_Click()
    MultiPage1.Value = MultiPage1.Value - 1
    UpdateControls
End Sub

Private Sub NextButton_Click()
    MultiPage1.Value = MultiPage1.Value + 1
    UpdateControls
End Sub
```

Figure 15-5: Clicking the Cancel button displays a message box.

These two procedures are very simple. They change the Value property of the MultiPage control and then call another procedure named UpdateControls (which follows).

The UpdateControls procedure in Listing 15-1 is responsible for enabling and disabling the BackButton and NextButton controls.

Listing 15-1: Procedures That Enable the Key Controls in the Wizard

```
Sub UpdateControls()
    Select Case MultiPage1.Value
        Case 0
            BackButton.Enabled = False
            NextButton.Enabled = True
        Case MultiPage1.Pages.Count - 1
            BackButton.Enabled = True
            NextButton.Enabled = False
        Case Else
            BackButton.Enabled = True
            NextButton.Enabled = True
    End Select

'   Update the caption
    Me.Caption = APPNAME & " Step " _
      & MultiPage1.Value + 1 & " of " _
      & MultiPage1.Pages.Count
```

Continued

Listing 15-1 *(Continued)*

```
'   The Name field is required
    If tbName.Text = "" Then
        FinishButton.Enabled = False
    Else
        FinishButton.Enabled = True
    End If
End Sub
```

The procedure changes the UserForm's caption to display the current step and the total number of steps (APPNAME is a public constant, defined in Module1). It then examines the name field on the first page (a TextBox named tbName). This is a required field, so the Finish button can't be clicked if it's empty. If the TextBox is empty, the FinishButton is disabled; otherwise, it's enabled.

Programming dependencies in a wizard

In most wizards, a user's response on a particular step can affect what's displayed in a subsequent step. In the CD-ROM example, the user indicates which products he or she uses in Step 3 and then rates those products in Step 4. The OptionButtons for a product's rating are visible only if the user has indicated a particular product.

Programmatically, this is accomplished by monitoring the MultiPage's Change event. Whenever the value of the MultiPage is changed (by clicking the Back or Next button), the MultiPage1_Change procedure is executed. If the MultiPage control is on the last tab (Step 4), the procedure examines the values of the CheckBox controls in Step 3 and makes the appropriate adjustments in Step 4.

In this example, the code uses two arrays of controls — one for the product CheckBox controls (Step 3) and one for the Frame controls (Step 4). The code uses a For-Next loop to hide the Frames for the products that are not used and then adjusts their vertical positioning. If none of the check boxes in Step 3 are checked, everything in Step 4 is hidden except a TextBox that displays Click Finish to exit (if a name is entered in Step 1) or A name is required in Step 1 (if a name is not entered in Step 1). The MultiPage1_Change procedure is shown in Listing 15-2.

Listing 15-2: Bringing Up the Page Corresponding to the User's Choice

```
Private Sub MultiPage1_Change()
'   Set up the Ratings page?
    If MultiPage1.Value = 3 Then
'       Create an array of CheckBox controls
        Dim ProdCB(1 To 3) As MSForms.CheckBox
        Set ProdCB(1) = cbExcel
        Set ProdCB(2) = cbWord
        Set ProdCB(3) = cbAccess
```

```
'       Create an array of Frame controls
        Dim ProdFrame(1 To 3) As MSForms.Frame
        Set ProdFrame(1) = FrameExcel
        Set ProdFrame(2) = FrameWord
        Set ProdFrame(3) = FrameAccess

        TopPos = 22
        FSpace = 8
        AtLeastOne = False

'       Loop through all products
        For i = 1 To 3
            If ProdCB(i) Then
                ProdFrame(i).Visible = True
                ProdFrame(i).Top = TopPos
                TopPos = TopPos + ProdFrame(i).Height + FSpace
                AtLeastOne = True
            Else
                ProdFrame(i).Visible = False
            End If
        Next i

'       Uses no products?
        If AtLeastOne Then
            lblHeadings.Visible = True
            Image4.Visible = True
            lblFinishMsg.Visible = False
        Else
            lblHeadings.Visible = False
            Image4.Visible = False
            lblFinishMsg.Visible = True
            If tbName = "" Then
                lblFinishMsg.Caption = _
                    "A name is required in Step 1."
            Else
                lblFinishMsg.Caption = _
                    "Click Finish to exit."
            End If
        End If
    End If
End Sub
```

Performing the task with the wizard

When the user clicks the Finish button, the wizard performs its task: transferring the information from the UserForm to the next empty row in the worksheet. This procedure, shown in Listing 15-3, is very straightforward. It starts by determining the next empty worksheet row and assigns this value to a variable (r). The remainder of the procedure simply translates the values of the controls and enters data into the worksheet.

Listing 15-3: Inserting the Acquired Data into the Worksheet

```
Private Sub FinishButton_Click()
    r = Application.WorksheetFunction. _
      CountA(Range("A:A")) + 1

'   Insert the name
    Cells(r, 1) = tbName.Text

'   Insert the gender
    Select Case True
        Case obMale: Cells(r, 2) = "Male"
        Case obFemale: Cells(r, 2) = "Female"
        Case obNoAnswer: Cells(r, 2) = "Unknown"
    End Select


'   Insert usage
    Cells(r, 3) = cbExcel
    Cells(r, 4) = cbWord
    Cells(r, 5) = cbAccess

'   Insert ratings
    If obExcel1 Then Cells(r, 6) = ""
    If obExcel2 Then Cells(r, 6) = 0
    If obExcel3 Then Cells(r, 6) = 1
    If obExcel4 Then Cells(r, 6) = 2
    If obWord1 Then Cells(r, 7) = ""
    If obWord2 Then Cells(r, 7) = 0
    If obWord3 Then Cells(r, 7) = 1
    If obWord4 Then Cells(r, 7) = 2
    If obAccess1 Then Cells(r, 8) = ""
    If obAccess2 Then Cells(r, 8) = 0
    If obAccess3 Then Cells(r, 8) = 1
    If obAccess4 Then Cells(r, 8) = 2

'   Unload the form
    Unload Me
End Sub
```

After you test your wizard, and everything seems to be working, you can set the MultiPage control's `Style` property to `2 - fmTabStyleNone`.

Emulating the MsgBox Function

VBA's `MsgBox` function is a bit unusual because unlike most functions, it displays a dialog box. But, like other functions, it also returns a value: namely, an integer that represents which button the user clicked.

This example discusses a custom function that I created that emulates VBA's `MsgBox` function. On first thought, creating such a function might seem rather easy. Think again! The `MsgBox` function is extraordinarily versatile because of the arguments that it accepts. Consequently, creating a function to emulate `MsgBox` is no small feat.

The point of this exercise is not to create an alternative messaging function. Rather, it's to demonstrate how to develop a relatively complex function that also incorporates a UserForm. However, some people might like the idea of being able to customize their messages. If so, you'll find that this function is very easy to customize. For example, you can change the font, colors, button text, and so on.

I named my pseudo `MsgBox` function `MyMsgBox`. The emulation is not perfect. `MyMsgBox` has the following limitations:

- It does not support the `Helpfile` argument (which adds a Help button that, when clicked, opens a Help file).

- It does not support the `Context` argument (which specifies the context ID for the Help file).

- It does not support the *system modal* option, which puts everything in Windows on hold until you respond to the dialog.

The syntax for `MyMsgBox` is

```
MyMsgBox(prompt[, buttons] [, title])
```

This syntax is exactly the same as the `MsgBox` syntax except that it doesn't use the last two optional arguments (`Helpfile` and `Context`). `MyMsgBox` also uses the same predefined constants as `MsgBox`: `vbOKOnly`, `vbQuestion`, `vbDefaultButton1`, and so on.

 You might want to examine the MsgBox listing in the Help system to become familiar with its arguments.

MsgBox emulation: MyMsgBox code

The MyMsgBox function makes use of a UserForm named MyMsgBoxForm. The function itself, which follows, is very short. The bulk of the work is done in the UserForm_Initialize procedure.

 The complete code for the MyMsgBox function is too lengthy to list here, but it's available in a workbook on the companion CD-ROM.

```
Public Prompt1 As String
Public Buttons1 As Integer
Public Title1 As String
Public UserClick As Integer

Function MyMsgBox(ByVal Prompt As String, _
  Optional ByVal Buttons As Integer, _
  Optional ByVal Title As String) As Integer
    Prompt1 = Prompt
    Buttons1 = Buttons
    Title1 = Title
    MyMsgBoxForm.Show
    MyMsgBox = UserClick
End Function
```

Figure 15-6 shows MyMsgBox in action. (I used a different font for the message text.)

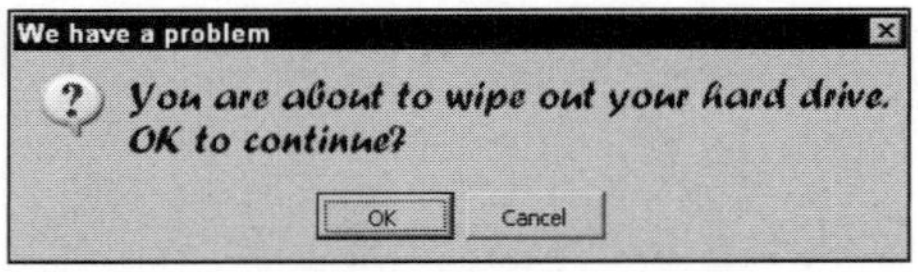

Figure 15-6: The result of the MsgBox emulation function (using a different font).

Here's the code that I used to execute the function:

```
Prompt = "You are about to wipe out your hard drive."
Prompt = Prompt & vbCrLf & vbCrLf & "OK to continue?"
Buttons = vbQuestion + vbYesNo
```

```
Title = "We have a problem"
Ans = MyMsgBox(Prompt, Buttons, Title)
```

How the MsgBox emulation works

Notice the use of four Public variables. The first three (Prompt1, Buttons1, and Title1) represent the arguments that are passed to the function. The other variable (UserClick) represents the values returned by the function. The UserForm_Initialize procedure needs a way to get this information and send it back to the function, and using Public variables is the only way to accomplish that.

The UserForm (shown in Figure 15-7) contains four Image controls (one for each of the four possible icons), three CommandButton controls, and a TextBox control.

Figure 15-7: The UserForm for the MyMsgBox function.

The code in the UserForm_Initialize procedure examines the arguments and does the following:

◆ Determines which, if any, image to display (and hides the others)

◆ Determines which button(s) to display (and hides the others)

◆ Determines which button is the default button

◆ Centers the buttons in the dialog box

◆ Determines the captions for the CommandButtons

◆ Determines the position of the text within the dialog box

◆ Determines how wide to make the dialog box (by using an Application Programming Interface [API] call to get the video resolution)

◆ Determines how tall to make the dialog box

◆ Displays the UserForm

Three additional event handler procedures are included (one for each CommandButton). These routines determine which button was clicked and return a value for the function by setting a value for the `UserClick` variable.

Interpreting the second argument *(buttons)* is a bit challenging. This argument can consist of a number of constants added together. For example, the second argument can be something like:

```
VbYesNoCancel + VbQuestion + VbDefaultButton3
```

This argument creates a three-button `MsgBox` (with Yes, No, and Cancel buttons), displays the Question icon, and makes the third button the default button. The actual argument is 547 (3 + 32 + 512). The challenge was pulling three pieces of information from a single number. The solution involves converting the argument to a binary number and then having the interpreter examine specific bits. For example, 547 in binary is 1000100011. Binary digits 4 through 6 determine the image displayed; digits 8 through 10 determine which buttons to display; and digits 1 and 2 determine which button is the default button.

Using the MyMsgBox function in the MsgBox emulation

To use this function in your own project, export the `MyMsgBoxMod` module and the `MyMsgBoxForm` UserForm. Then import these two files into your project.

A Modeless Dialog Box

Most dialog boxes that you encounter are *modal* dialog boxes, which must be dismissed from the screen before the user can do anything with the underlying application. Some dialogs, however, are *modeless,* which means the user can continue to work in the application while the dialog box is displayed.

 Excel 2000 was the first version of Excel to support modeless custom dialog boxes. Therefore, this feature will not work with earlier versions of Excel.

To display a modeless UserForm, use a statement such as

```
UserForm1.Show vbModeless
```

The word `vbModeless` is a built-in constant that has a value of 0. Therefore, the following statement works identically:

```
UserForm1.Show 0
```

Figure 15-8 shows a modeless dialog box that displays information about the active cell. When the dialog box is displayed, the user is free to move the cell cursor and activate other sheets.

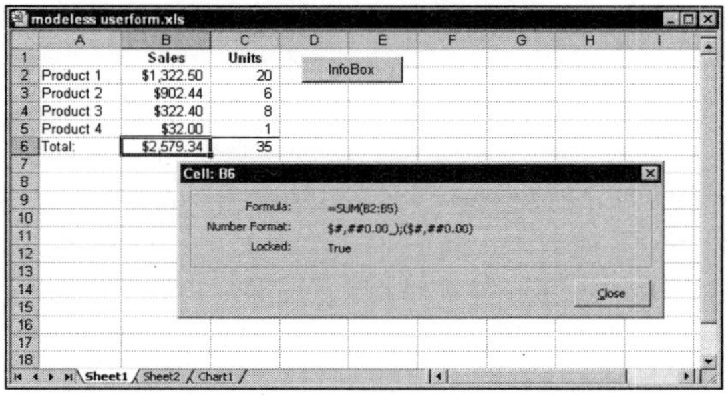

Figure 15-8: This modeless dialog box remains visible while the user continues working.

This example is available on the companion CD-ROM.

The trick here is determining when to update the information in the dialog box. To do so, the example monitors two workbook events: SheetSelectionChange and SheetActivate. These event handler procedures are located in the code module for the ThisWorkbook object.

Refer to Chapter 18 for additional information about events.

The event handler procedures follow:

```
Private Sub Workbook_SheetSelectionChange _
  (ByVal Sh As Object, ByVal Target As Range)
    Call UpdateBox
End Sub
```

```
Private Sub Workbook_SheetActivate(ByVal Sh As Object)
    Call UpdateBox
End Sub
```

These procedures call the `UpdateBox` procedure, which follows:

```
Sub UpdateBox()
    With UserForm1
'       Make sure a worksheet is active
        If TypeName(ActiveSheet) <> "Worksheet" Then
            .lblFormula.Caption = "N/A"
            .lblNumFormat.Caption = "N/A"
            .lblLocked.Caption = "N/A"
            Exit Sub
        End If

        .Caption = "Cell: " & ActiveCell.Address(False, False)
'       Formula
        If ActiveCell.HasFormula Then
            .lblFormula.Caption = ActiveCell.Formula
        Else
            .lblFormula.Caption = "(none)"
        End If
'       Number format
        .lblNumFormat.Caption = ActiveCell.NumberFormat
'       Locked
        .lblLocked.Caption = ActiveCell.Locked
    End With
End Sub
```

The `UpdateBox` procedure changes the UserForm's caption to show the active cell's address; then it updates the three `Label` controls (`lblFormula`, `lblNumFormat`, and `lblLocked`).

Following are a few points to help you understand how this example works:

◆ The UserForm is displayed modeless so that you can still access the worksheet while it's displayed. *Remember:* Modeless UserForms are not supported in Excel 97 or earlier versions.

◆ Code at the top of the procedure checks to make sure that the active sheet is a worksheet. If the sheet is not a worksheet, the `Label` controls are assigned the text `N/A`.

◆ The workbook monitors the active cell by using a `Selection_Change` event (which is located in the `ThisWorkbook` code module).

◆ The information is displayed in `Label` controls on the UserForm.

Figure 15-9 shows a much more sophisticated version of this example (it's also on the CD-ROM). This version displays quite a bit of additional information about the selected cell. Long-time Excel users might notice the similarity with the Info window – a feature that was removed from Excel several years ago. The code is too lengthy to display here, but you can view the well-commented code in the example workbook. Following are some key points about this more sophisticated version:

◆ The UserForm has a check box (Auto Update). When this check box is selected, the UserForm is updated automatically. When Auto Update is not turned on, the user can use the Update button to refresh the information.

◆ The workbook uses a class module to monitor two events for all open workbooks: the `SheetSelectionChange` event and the `SheetActivate` event. As a result, the code to display the information about the current cell is executed automatically whenever these events occur in any workbook (assuming that the Auto Update option is in effect). Some actions (such as changing a cell's number format) do not trigger either of these events. Therefore, the UserForm also contains an Update button.

Refer to Chapter 29 for more information about class modules.

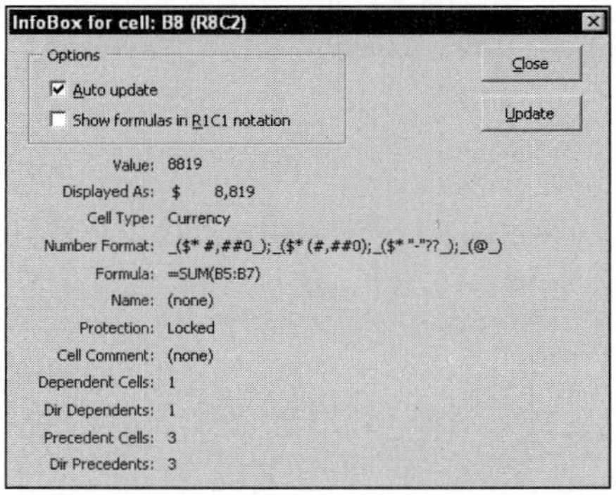

Figure 15-9: This UserForm displays information about the active cell.

◆ The counts displayed for the cell precedents and dependents field include cells in the active sheet only. This is a limitation of the Precedents and Dependents properties.

◆ Because the length of the information will vary, VBA code is used to size and vertically space the labels — and also change the height of the UserForm if necessary.

Handling Multiple UserForm Buttons With One Event Handler

Every CommandButton on a UserForm must have its own procedure to handle its Click event. For example, if you have two CommandButtons, you'll need at least two event handler procedures:

```
Private Sub CommandButton1_Click()
' Code goes here
End Sub

Private Sub CommandButton2_Click()
' Code goes here
End Sub
```

In other words, you cannot assign a macro to execute when *any* CommandButton is clicked. Each Click event handler is hard-wired to its CommandButton. You can, however, have each event handler call another all-inclusive macro in the event handler procedures, but you'll need to pass an argument to indicate which button was clicked. In the following examples, clicking either CommandButton1 or CommandButton2 both execute the ButtonClick procedure, and the single argument tells the ButtonClick procedure which button was clicked.

```
Private Sub CommandButton1_Click()
    Call ButtonClick(1)
End Sub

Private Sub CommandButton2_Click()
    Call ButtonClick(2)
End Sub
```

If your UserForm has many CommandButtons, setting up all these event handlers can get tedious. You might prefer to have a single procedure that can determine which button was clicked and take the appropriate action.

This section describes a way around this limitation by using a class module to define a new class.

This example is available on the companion CD-ROM.

The following steps describe how to re-create the example workbook:

1. Create your UserForm as usual and add several CommandButtons. (The example on the CD contains 16 CommandButtons.) This example assumes that the form is named UserForm1.

2. Insert a class module into your project (choose Insert → Class Module), give it the name BtnClass, and enter the following code. You will need to customize the ButtonGroup_Click procedure.

```
Public WithEvents ButtonGroup As MsForms.CommandButton

Private Sub ButtonGroup_Click()
    Msg = "You clicked " & ButtonGroup.Name & vbCrLf _
      & vbCrLf
    Msg = Msg & "Caption: " & ButtonGroup.Caption _
      & vbCrLf
    Msg = Msg & "Left Position: " & ButtonGroup.Left _
      & vbCrLf
    Msg = Msg & "Top Position: " & ButtonGroup.Top
    MsgBox Msg, vbInformation, ButtonGroup.Name
End Sub
```

3. Insert a normal VBA module and enter the following code. This routine simply displays the UserForm:

```
Sub ShowDialog()
    UserForm1.Show
End Sub
```

4. In the code module for the UserForm, enter the code in Listing 15-4. This procedure is kicked off by the UserForm's Initialize event. Notice that the code excludes a button named OKButton from the button group. Therefore, clicking the OKButton does not execute the ButtonGroup_Click procedure.

Listing 15-4: Establishing the Buttons() Object Array

```
Dim Buttons() As New BtnClass

Private Sub UserForm_Initialize()
```

Continued

Listing 15-4 *(Continued)*

```
    Dim ButtonCount As Integer
    Dim ctl As Control

'   Create the Button objects
    ButtonCount = 0
    For Each ctl In UserForm1.Controls
        If TypeName(ctl) = "CommandButton" Then
            If ctl.Name <> "OKButton" Then 'Skip the OKButton
                ButtonCount = ButtonCount + 1
                ReDim Preserve Buttons(1 To ButtonCount)
                Set Buttons(ButtonCount).ButtonGroup = ctl
            End If
        End If
    Next ctl
End Sub
```

After performing these steps, you can execute the ShowDialog procedure to display the UserForm. Clicking any of the CommandButtons (except the OKButton) executes the ButtonGroup_Click procedure. Figure 15-10 shows an example of the message displayed when a button is clicked.

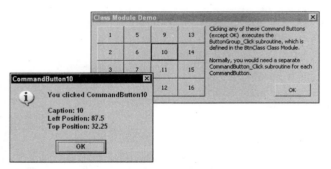

Figure 15-10: The ButtonGroup_Click procedure describes the button that was clicked.

You can adapt this technique to work with other types of controls. You need to change the type name in the Public WithEvents declaration. For example, if you have OptionButtons instead of CommandButtons, use a declaration statement like this:

```
Public WithEvents ButtonGroup As MsForms.OptionButton
```

Selecting a Color In a UserForm

This example is similar to the example in the previous section but a bit more complex. The example workbook demonstrates a technique to display a UserForm that allows the user to select a color from the workbook's color palette (which consists of 56 colors).

The example is actually a function (named `GetAColor`) that displays a UserForm and returns a color value.

 This example is available on the companion CD-ROM.

The `GetAColor` function follows:

```
Public ColorValue As Variant
Dim Buttons(1 To 56) As New ColorButtonClass

Function GetAColor() As Variant
'    Displays a UserForm and returns a
'    color value - or False if no color is selected
    Dim ctl As Control
    Dim ButtonCount As Integer
    ButtonCount = 0
    For Each ctl In UserForm1.Controls
'        The 56 color buttons have their '
'        Tag property set to "ColorButton"
        If ctl.Tag = "ColorButton" Then
            ButtonCount = ButtonCount + 1
            Set Buttons(ButtonCount).ColorButton = ctl
'            Get colors from the active workbook's palette
            Buttons(ButtonCount).ColorButton.BackColor = _
                ActiveWorkbook.Colors(ButtonCount)
        End If
    Next ctl
    UserForm1.Show
    GetAColor = ColorValue
End Function
```

The UserForm contains 56 `CommandButton` controls, which are colored by using the colors in the active workbook's palette.

You can access the GetAColor function with a statement such as the following:

```
UserColor = GetAColor()
```

Executing this statement displays the UserForm and assigns a color value to the UserColor variable. The color corresponds to the color selected by the user.

Figure 15-11 shows the UserForm (it looks better in color), which contains 56 CommandButton controls. The BackColor property of each button corresponds to one of the colors in the workbook's color palette. Clicking a button unloads the UserForm and provides a value for the function to return.

Figure 15-11: This dialog box lets the user select a color by clicking a button.

The example file on the accompanying CD-ROM contains the following:

◆ A UserForm (UserForm1) that contains a dialog box with 56 CommandButtons (plus a few other accouterments)

◆ A class module (ColorButtonClass) that defines a ColorButton class

◆ A VBA module (Module1) that contains a Function procedure (GetAColor)

◆ Two examples that demonstrate the GetAColor Function procedure

The GetAColor procedure sets up the UserForm and displays it. It later returns the color value of the selected button. If the user clicks Cancel, GetAColor returns False. When the user moves the mouse pointer over the color buttons, the Color Sample image displays the color.

The code behind this UserForm is rather lengthy, so it's not listed here. You can, however, open the workbook from the CD-ROM and examine the code.

Displaying a Chart in a UserForm

With Excel 5 or Excel 95, it was very easy to display a live chart in a custom dialog box (using a dialog sheet): Just copy a chart and paste it into your dialog sheet. Oddly, there is no direct way to display a chart in a UserForm. You can, of course, copy the chart and paste it to the `Picture` property of an `Image` control, but this creates a static image of the chart and thus won't display any changes to the chart. Although UserForms are vastly superior to the old dialog sheets, this is one area that Microsoft seems to have overlooked.

> You can still use dialog sheets in Excel 97 or later. Therefore, you are certainly free to use a dialog sheet to display a live chart in a dialog box.

This section describes two methods to display a chart in a UserForm: saving the chart as a file or using the Office Web Components (OWC) `ChartSpace` control.

Method 1: Save the chart as a file

Just because Microsoft doesn't allow a live chart to be displayed in a UserForm doesn't mean it can't be done! Figure 15-12 shows a UserForm with a chart displayed in an `Image` object. The chart actually resides on a worksheet, and the UserForm always displays the current chart. This technique works by copying the chart to a temporary graphics file and then setting the Image control's `Picture` property to the temporary file. Read on to discover how.

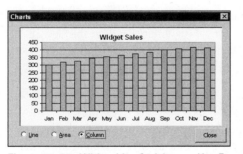

Figure 15-12: With a bit of trickery, a UserForm can display "live" charts.

GENERAL STEPS TO DISPLAY A CHART IN A USERFORM

To display a chart in a UserForm, follow these general steps:

1. Create your chart or charts as usual.

2. Insert a UserForm and then add an `Image` control.

3. Write VBA code to save the chart as a GIF file and then set the `Image` control's `Picture` property to the GIF file. You need to use VBA's `LoadPicture` function to do this.

4. Add other bells and whistles as desired. For example, the UserForm in the demo file contains controls that let you change the chart type. Alternatively, you could write code to display multiple charts.

SAVING A CHART AS A GIF FILE

The following code demonstrates how to create a GIF file (named `temp.gif`) from a chart (in this case, the first chart object on the sheet named `Data`):

```
Set CurrentChart = Sheets("Data").ChartObjects(1).Chart
Fname = ThisWorkbook.Path & "\temp.gif"
CurrentChart.Export FileName:=Fname, FilterName:="GIF"
```

When this code is executed, you'll see a pop-up window that displays the progress. (In response to a question that I'm frequently asked, I'm not aware of any way to suppress this progress display.)

CHANGING THE IMAGE CONTROL PICTURE PROPERTY

If the `Image` control on the UserForm is named `Image1`, the following statement loads the image (represented by the `Fname` variable) into the `Image` control:

```
Image1.Picture = LoadPicture(Fname)
```

This technique works fine, but you might notice a slight delay when the chart is saved and then retrieved. On a fast system, however, this delay is barely noticeable.

Method 2: Use the OWC ChartSpace control

As I mention in Chapter 13, a UserForm may contain other controls that aren't normally included in the Toolbox. Microsoft includes the Office Web Components (OWC) with Office 2003, and you can use the Web Component controls in your UserForms. Figure 15-13 shows an example of a UserForm that contains a `ChartSpace` control.

This technique does not allow you to display an existing Excel chart on a UserForm. Rather, you must write code that creates the chart in the `ChartSpace` control.

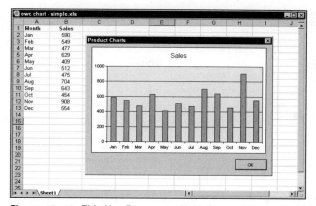

Figure 15-13: This UserForm contains a ChartSpace control.

MAKING THE CHARTSPACE CONTROL AVAILABLE

The first step is to add the ChartSpace control to your Toolbox. Right-click the toolbox to display the Additional Controls dialog box. Scroll down the list and place a check mark next to Microsoft Office Chart 11.0. If you're using Excel 2002, the item will be named Microsoft Office Chart 10.0. And if you're using Excel 2000, it will be named Microsoft Office Chart 9.0. Click OK, and your Toolbox will have a new icon.

ADDING THE CHARTSPACE CONTROL TO A USERFORM

Adding a ChartSpace control to your UserForm works just like any of the standard controls. When the control is added, you won't see a chart displayed. It is, after all, just an empty control. You'll need to write code that creates the actual chart.

CREATING THE CHART FOR AN OWC CHARTSPACE CONTROL

The following code, which is located in the UserForm code module, creates a chart using data stored on a worksheet. The category labels are in A2:A13, and the chart data is in B2:B13. It assumes that the ChartSpace object is named ChartSpace1.

```
Sub CreateChart()
    Dim Chart1 As ChChart 'WCChart
    Dim Series1 As ChSeries 'WCSeries
    Dim r As Integer
    Dim XValues(1 To 12)
    Dim DataValues(1 To 12)

'    Add a chart to the ChartSpace
    Set Chart1 = ChartSpace1.Charts.Add

'    Give it a title
    With Chart1
```

```
        .HasTitle = True
        .Title.Caption = Range("B1")
    End With

    For r = 2 To 13
        XValues(r - 1) = Cells(r, 1)
        DataValues(r - 1) = Cells(r, 2)
    Next r

'   Create a chart series
    Set Series1 = Chart1.SeriesCollection.Add

'   Specify chart type and data
    With Series1
        .Type = chChartTypeColumnClustered
        .SetData chDimCategories, chDataLiteral, XValues
        .SetData chDimValues, chDataLiteral, DataValues
    End With
End Sub
```

The code starts with variable declaration. Two arrays are declared: one to hold the category labels (XValues) and one to hold the data (DataValues).

The Set statement creates a Chart object within the ChartSpace. This Chart object is named Chart1. The next block of statements sets the chart's title, using the label in cell B1. A For-Next loop reads the worksheet data into the arrays.

The next Set statement adds a series to the chart, and the Series object is named Series1. The With-End With block of code specifies the chart type (a standard column chart) and specifies the data for the series.

You'll find documentation for the OWC objects on your hard drive. These Help files are installed when the OWC is installed. Or, you can use the Object Browser to learn more about the properties and methods of these controls.

 It's important to understand that the object model for creating a chart in the OWC does not correspond to the object model for creating a chart in Excel. Chapter 18 explains how to use VBA to manipulate "real" Excel charts.

Figure 15-14 shows a slightly more sophisticated version of this example. In this case, the user can choose which data will appear in the chart; this version also includes an option to export the chart as a GIF file.

Using the Office Web Components

The Office Web Components were designed to create interactive Web pages. The components include a Spreadsheet, a Chart, and a Pivot Table. When you create an application that uses the OWC, anyone who uses your application must have the OWC installed on his or her computer.

The OWC is included with Microsoft Office 2000 and later. Installation is not automatic. In other words, you can't assume that all Microsoft Office users have the OWC installed on their system because they might have chosen not to install it.

Therefore, you should use caution before deciding to include any OWC controls in your Excel application. If your application will have general distribution, you'll probably want to avoid using the OWC.

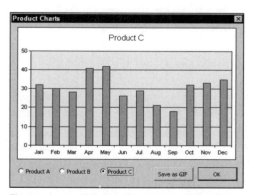

Figure 15-14: This UserForm contains a `ChartSpace` control (part of the Office Web Components).

 This application is available on the companion CD-ROM. It requires Excel 2002 or later.

Displaying a Spreadsheet in a UserForm

Not content to simply display a chart in a UserForm? How about an entire spreadsheet?

Figure 15-15 shows an example of a UserForm that contains a Microsoft Office Spreadsheet 11.0 control. This control can contain an entire interactive spreadsheet, complete with formulas and formatting. In fact, this Spreadsheet control has a significant advantage over a standard Excel sheet: Its dimensions are 18,278 columns x 262,144 rows. This is nearly 300 times as many cells as a standard Excel worksheet!

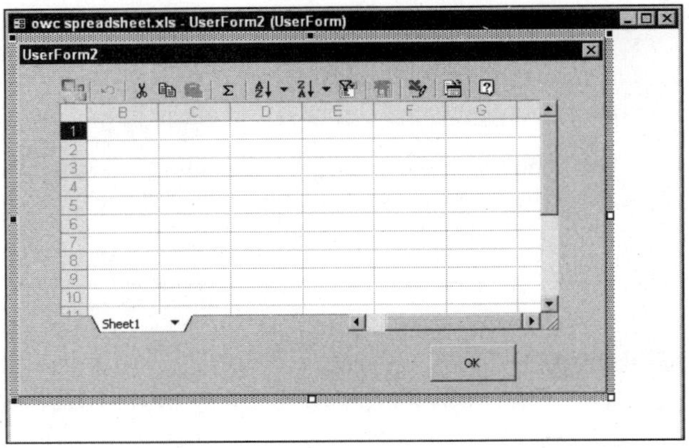

Figure 15-15: This UserForm contains a Spreadsheet control.

Making the Spreadsheet control available

First, you need to add the Spreadsheet control to your Toolbox. Right-click the Toolbox to display the Additional Controls dialog box. Scroll down the list and place a check mark next to Microsoft Office Spreadsheet 11.0. If you're using Excel 2002, the item will be named Microsoft Office Spreadsheet 10.0. And for Excel 2000, it will be named Microsoft Office Spreadsheet 9.0. Click OK to add the new icon to your Toolbox.

Adding the Spreadsheet control to a UserForm

Adding a Spreadsheet control to your UserForm works just like any of the standard controls. When the control is added to the UserForm, you'll see a three-sheet spreadsheet. As you'll see, this spreadsheet can be customized quite a bit.

A simple example using the OWC Spreadsheet control

This example uses a Spreadsheet control to create a simple loan payment calculator in a UserForm. The finished product is shown in Figure 15-16. The user can enter loan information into column B, and the monthly payment is calculated (by using a formula) and then displayed in the bottom-right cell.

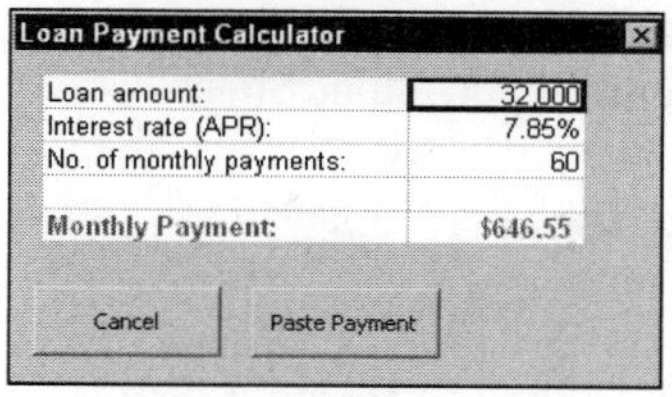

Loan Payment Calculator

Loan amount:	32,000
Interest rate (APR):	7.85%
No. of monthly payments:	60
Monthly Payment:	$646.55

Cancel   Paste Payment

Figure 15-16: This UserForm uses a Spreadsheet
control for a simple loan payment calculator.

This example is primarily for illustration only. Using a Spreadsheet control
is overkill. It is much more efficient to use EditBox controls to get the information and calculate the loan payment by using VBA code.

To create this UserForm, start with a new workbook and follow the steps presented next. *Remember:* Make sure to first add the Spreadsheet control to your
Toolbox. (See the earlier section, "Adding the Spreadsheet control to a UserForm.")

1. Insert a new UserForm and add a Spreadsheet control. Don't change its
   default name (Spreadsheet1).

   By default, the spreadsheet displays with a toolbar, row and column headings, scroll bars, and a sheet selector tab. To keep the interface as clean as
   possible, get rid of these items later.

2. Select any cell in the Spreadsheet control; then right-click and choose
   Commands and Options from the shortcut menu.

   You'll see the tabbed dialog box shown in Figure 15-17.

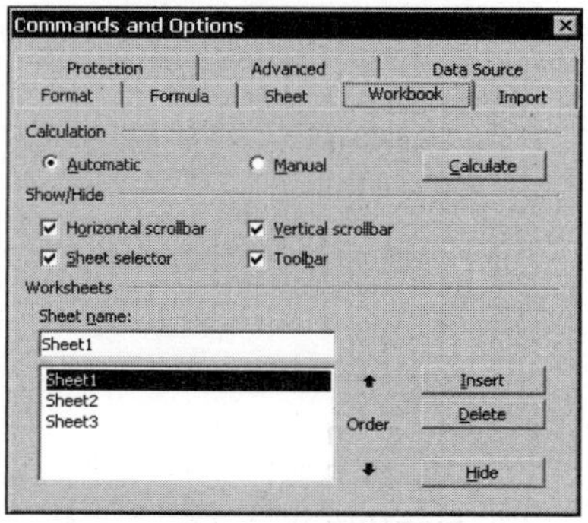

Commands and Options

| Protection | Advanced | Data Source |
| Format | Formula | Sheet | Workbook | Import |

Calculation
- (●) Automatic   ( ) Manual   Calculate

Show/Hide
- [✓] Horizontal scrollbar   [✓] Vertical scrollbar
- [✓] Sheet selector   [✓] Toolbar

Worksheets
Sheet name:
Sheet1

Sheet1
Sheet2
Sheet3

Order

Insert
Delete
Hide

Figure 15-17: Use this dialog box to customize the
Spreadsheet control.

3. Click the Workbook tab and delete Sheet2 and Sheet3. Then remove the check marks from the Horizontal Scrollbar, Vertical Scrollbar, Sheet Selector, and Toolbar check boxes.

4. In column A, enter the text shown in Figure 15-16. Then adjust the width of column A so that it's wide enough to handle the text.

5. Enter some number into B1:B3. Then enter the following formula into cell B5:

```
=PMT(B2/12,B3,-B1)
```

6. Select B1:B3 and then click the Format tab in the Commands and Options dialog box. Click the key icon to unlock the selected cells. (The other cells will remain locked, which is the default.)

7. Click the Sheet tab in the Commands and Options dialog box. In the Viewable Range box, enter **A1:B5**.

This essentially hides all the unused rows and columns.

8. Next, remove the check marks from the Row Headers and the Column Headers check boxes.

9. Finally, add two `CommandButton` controls. One, named `CancelButton`, will be the Cancel button. The other (named `PasteButton`) will execute code that pastes the calculated result to the active cell in the Excel worksheet.

Now it's time to add some VBA code. In the preceding steps, the three input cells were unlocked. Locking cells, however, has no effect unless the sheet is protected (just like Excel). Therefore, add some code to protect the sheet when the UserForm is initialized. You could protect the sheet at design time (from the Commands and Options dialog box), but that makes it impossible to edit the sheet — and it's easy to forget to protect it again after you make changes. Protecting the sheet at runtime ensures that the sheet will be protected, and the user can only change the input cells.

The simple code that follows does the job:

```
Private Sub UserForm_Initialize()
    Spreadsheet1.ActiveSheet.Protect
End Sub
```

The UserForm button labeled `Paste Payment`, when clicked, executes the following code:

```
Private Sub PasteButton_Click()
    ActiveCell.Value = Spreadsheet1.Range("B5")
    Unload Me
End Sub
```

This procedure simply puts the contents of cell B5 (from the Spreadsheet control) into the active cell on the Excel worksheet and then unloads the UserForm.

Finally, you need an event handler procedure for the Cancel button:

```
Private Sub CancelButton_Click()
    Unload Me
End Sub
```

I really can't think of too many good reasons to use a Spreadsheet control in a UserForm. However, it's nice to know that this feature is available should you need it.

UserForm Deluxe: An Enhanced Data Form

Next is one of the more complex UserForms that you'll encounter. I designed it as a replacement for Excel's Data Form, shown in Figure 15-18. You'll recall this is the dialog box that appears when you choose Data → Form.

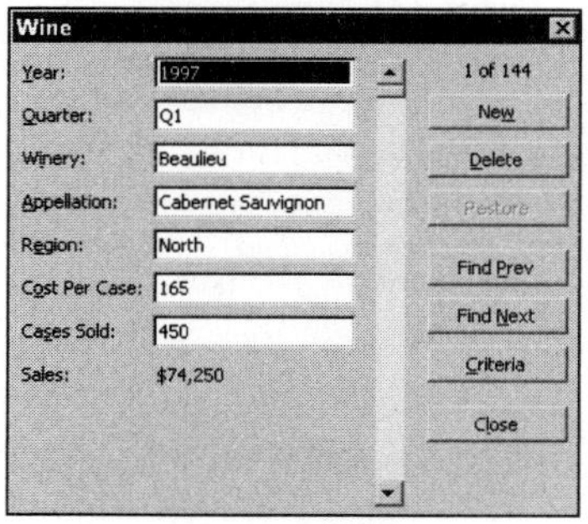

Figure 15-18: Excel's Data Form.

Like Excel's Data Form, my Enhanced Data Form works with a list in a worksheet. But as you can see in Figure 15-19, it has a dramatically different appearance and offers several advantages.

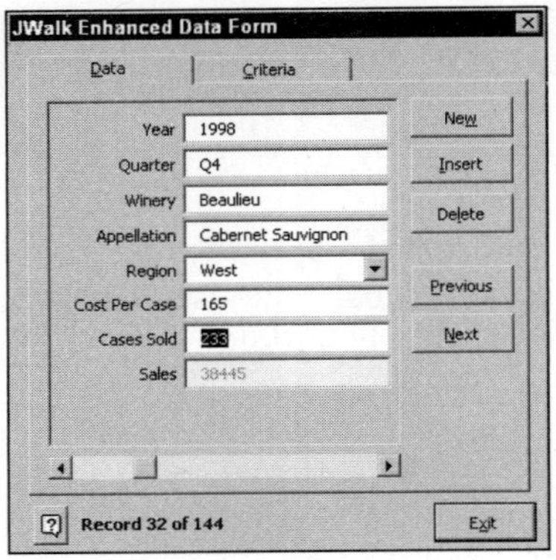

Figure 15-19: The author's Enhanced Data Form.

About the Enhanced Data Form

The Enhanced Data Form features the following enhancements, as listed in Table 15-1.

TABLE 15-1 COMPARING THE ENHANCED DATA FORM WITH THE EXCEL
             DATA FORM

Enhanced Data Form	Excel Data Form
Handles any number of records and fields.	Limited to 32 fields.
Dialog box can be displayed in any size that you like.	Dialog box adjusts its size based on the number of fields. In fact, it can take up the entire screen!
Fields can consist of either Text Box or ComboBox controls.	Dialog box uses only Text Boxes.
Record displayed in the dialog box is always visible onscreen and is highlighted so you know exactly where you are.	Doesn't scroll the screen for you and does not highlight the current record.
At startup, the dialog box always displays the record at the active cell.	Always starts with the first record in the database.
When you close the dialog, the current record is selected for you.	Doesn't change your selection when you exit.
Lets you insert a new record at any position in the database.	Adds new records only at the end of the database.

Enhanced Data Form	Excel Data Form
Includes an Undo button for Data Entry, Insert Record, Delete Record, and New Record.	Includes only a Restore button.
Search criteria are stored in a separate panel, so you always know exactly what you're searching for.	The search criteria are not always apparent.
Supports approximate matches while searching (*, ?, and #).	Excel's Data Form does not.
The complete VBA source code is available, so you can customize it to your needs.	Data Form is not written in VBA and cannot be customized.

 The Enhanced Data Form is a commercial product (sort of). It is available on the companion CD-ROM, and it can be used and distributed freely. Access to the complete VBA source is available for a modest fee.

Installing the Enhanced Data Form add-in

To try out the Enhanced Data Form, install the add-in:

1. Copy the `dataform2.xla` file from the CD-ROM to a directory on your hard drive.

2. In Excel, choose Tools → Add-Ins.

3. In the Add-Ins dialog box, click Browse and locate the `dataform.xla` in the directory from Step 1.

Using the Enhanced Data Form

When the Enhanced Data Form add-in is installed, a new menu command is available: Data → JWalk Enhanced Data Form. You can use the Enhanced Data Form to work with any worksheet database.

Part V

Advanced Programming Techniques

Chapter 16

Developing Excel Utilities with VBA

IN THIS CHAPTER

A *utility*, in general, is something that enhances software, adding useful features or making existing features more accessible. This chapter is about Excel utilities:

◆ About Excel utilities and utilities in general

◆ Why use VBA to develop utilities

◆ What you need to know to develop good utilities

◆ Step-by-step details for developing a useful Excel utility to manipulate text in cells

◆ Where to go for more Excel utilities

As YOU'LL SEE, creating utilities for Excel is an excellent way to make a great product even better.

About Excel Utilities

A utility isn't an end product, such as a quarterly report. Rather, it's a tool that helps you produce an end product, such as a quarterly report. An Excel utility is (almost always) an add-in that enhances Excel with new features or capabilities.

Excel is a decent product, but many users soon develop a wish-list of features that they would like to see added to the software. For example, some users who turn off the grid-line display want a feature that toggles this attribute so that they don't have to go through the tedious Tools → Options command. Users who work with dates might want a pop-up calendar feature to facilitate entering dates into cells. And some users desire an easier way to export a range of data to a separate file. These are all examples of features that will probably never find their way into Excel. You can, however, add these features by creating a utility.

Utilities don't need to be complicated. Some of the most useful ones are actually very simple. For example, the following Visual Basic for Applications (VBA) procedure is a utility that toggles the grid-line display in the active window:

```
Sub ToggleGridDisplay()
    ActiveWindow.DisplayGridlines = _
        Not ActiveWindow.DisplayGridlines
End Sub
```

You can store this macro in your Personal Macro Workbook so that it's always available. For quicker access, you can assign the macro to a toolbar button, a new menu item, a right-click shortcut menu, or a keystroke combination.

 Several of the examples in Part IV are actually utilities — or can easily be turned into utilities.

Using VBA to Develop Utilities

Excel 5, released in 1992, was the first version of Excel to include VBA. When I received the beta version of Excel 5, I was very impressed by VBA's potential. VBA was light-years ahead of Excel's powerful (but cryptic) XLM macro language, and I decided that I wanted to explore this new language and see what it was capable of.

In an effort to learn VBA, I wrote a collection of Excel utilities by using only VBA. I figured that I would learn the language more quickly if I gave myself a tangible goal. The result was a product that I call the *Power Utility Pak for Excel,* which is available to you at no charge as a benefit of buying this book. Use the coupon in the back of the book to order your copy.

I learned several things from my initial efforts on this project:

◆ VBA can be difficult to grasp at first, but it becomes much easier with practice.

◆ Experimentation is the key to mastering VBA. Every project that I undertake usually involves dozens of small coding experiments that eventually lead to a finished product.

◆ VBA enables you to extend Excel in a way that is entirely consistent with Excel's look and feel, including menus, toolbars, and dialog boxes.

◆ Excel can do almost anything. When you reach a dead end, chances are that another path leads to a solution. It helps if you're creative and know where to look for help.

Few other software packages include such an extensive set of tools that enable the end user to extend the software.

What Makes a Good Utility?

An Excel utility, of course, should ultimately make your job easier or more efficient. But if you're developing utilities for other users, what makes an Excel utility valuable? I've put together a list of elements that are common to good utilities:

◆ *It adds something to Excel.* This could be a new feature, a way to combine existing features, or just a way to make an existing feature easier to use.

◆ *It's general in nature.* Ideally, a utility should be useful under a wide variety of conditions. Of course, it's more difficult to write a general-purpose utility than it is to write one that works in a highly defined environment.

◆ *It's flexible.* The best utilities provide many options to handle various situations.

◆ *It looks, works, and feels like an Excel command.* Although adding your own special touch to utilities is tempting, other users will find them easier to use if they look and act like familiar Excel commands.

◆ *It provides help for the user when needed.* In other words, the utility requires documentation that's thorough and accessible.

◆ *It traps errors.* An end user should never see a VBA error message. Any error messages that appear should be ones that you write.

◆ *Its effects are undoable.* Users who don't like the result caused by your utility should be able to reverse their path.

Text Tools: The Anatomy of a Utility

In this section, I describe an Excel utility that I developed (and is part of my Power Utility Pak). The Text Tools utility enables the user to manipulate text in a selected range of cells. Specifically, this utility enables the user to do the following:

◆ Change the case of the text (uppercase, lowercase, proper case, sentence case, or toggle case).

◆ Add characters to the text (at the beginning, to the end, or at a specific character position).

◆ Remove characters from the text (from the beginning, from the end, or from a specific position within the string).

◆ Remove spaces from the text (either all spaces or excess spaces).

◆ Delete characters from text (non-printing characters, alphabetic characters, non-numeric characters, non-numeric and non-alphabetic characters, or numeric characters).

Figure 16-1 shows the Text Tools utility in action.

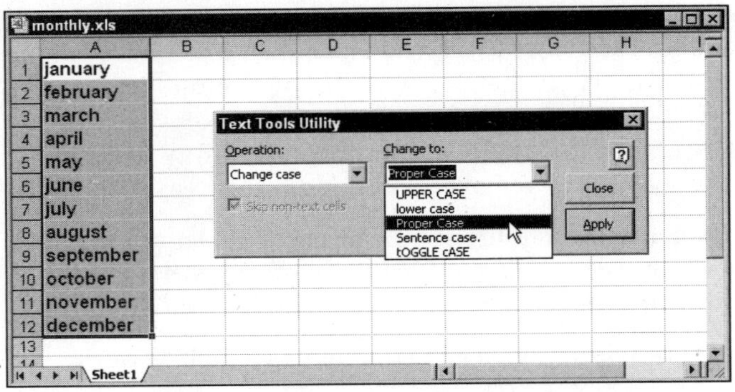

Figure 16–1: Use the Text Tools utility to change the case of selected text.

ON THE CD The Text Tools utility is available on the CD-ROM that accompanies this book. This is a standalone version of the tool that is included with the Power Utility Pak. It's an add-in file, and you can install it by choosing the Excel Tools → Add-Ins command (click the Browse button and locate the *.xla file). Or, you can simply open it by choosing the Excel File → Open command. Either way, you'll be able to view the complete VBA source code. (The VBA project is not protected with a password.)

Background for Text Tools

Excel has many text functions that can manipulate text strings in useful ways. For example, you can uppercase the text in a cell, delete characters from text, remove spaces, and so on. But to perform any of these operations, you need to write formulas, copy them, convert the formulas to values, and then paste the values over the original text. In other words, Excel doesn't make it particularly easy to modify text. Wouldn't it be nice if Excel had some text manipulation tools that didn't require formulas?

By the way, many good utility ideas come from statements that begin, "Wouldn't it be nice if . . .?"

Project goals for Text Tools

The first step in designing a utility is to envision exactly how you want the utility to work. Here's my original plan, stated in the form of ten goals:

- Its main features will be those listed at the beginning of this section.

- It will enable the user to request the preceding types of changes to non-text cells as well as to text cells.

- It will have the same look and feel of other Excel commands. In other words, it will have a dialog box that looks like Excel's dialog boxes.

- It will be in the form of an add-in and will also be accessible from the Tools menu.

- It will operate with the current selection of cells (including multiple selections), and it will enable the user to modify the range selection while the dialog box is displayed.

- It will remember the last operation used and display those settings the next time that the dialog box is invoked.

- It will have no effect on cells that contain formulas.

- It will be fast and efficient. For example, if the user selects an entire column, the utility should ignore the empty cells in the column.

- It will enable the user to undo the changes.

- Comprehensive help will be available.

How the Text Tools utility works

When the Text Tools add-in opens, it creates a new menu item on the Tools menu: Text Tools Utility. Selecting this item executes the RunTextTools procedure, which checks to make sure that Excel is in the proper context (a worksheet is active) and then displays the main Text Tools Utility dialog box.

The user can specify various modifications and click the Apply button to perform them. The changes are visible in the worksheet, and the dialog box remains displayed. Each operation can be undone, or the user can perform additional text modifications. Clicking the Help button displays a help window, and clicking the Close button dismisses the dialog box. Note that this is a *modeless* dialog box: In other words, you can keep working in Excel while the dialog box is displayed.

The Text Tools workbook

The Text Tools workbook consists of the following components:

- *One worksheet:* Every workbook must have at least one worksheet. I take advantage of this fact and use this worksheet to handle the undo procedure (see "Implementing Undo," later in this chapter).

◆ *One VBA module:* This module contains public variable and constant declaration, the code to display the UserForm, and the code to handle the undo procedure. The code that does the actual work is stored in the code modules for the UserForm.

◆ *One UserForm:* This contains the dialog box.

◆ *ThisWorkbook code module:* This contains the code to create (and remove) the menu item on the Tools menu.

The UserForm for the Text Tools utility

When I create a utility, I usually begin by designing the user interface. In this case, it's the dialog box that's displayed to the user. Creating the dialog box forces me to think through the project one more time.

Figure 16-2 shows the UserForm for the Text Tools utility. Notice that the configuration of the controls varies, depending on which option is selected.

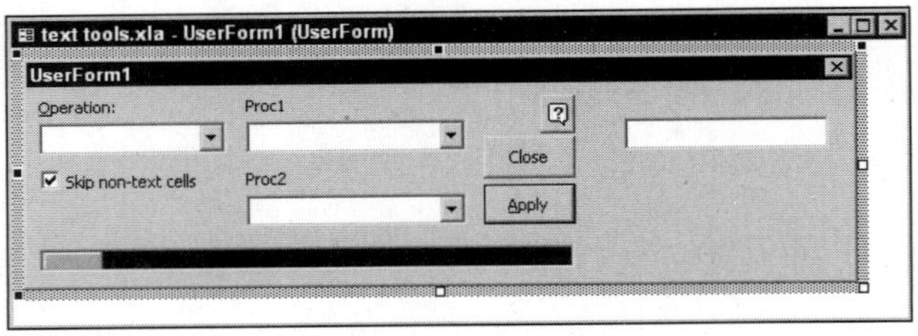

Figure 16-2: The UserForm for the Text Tools utility.

You'll notice that the controls on this UserForm are laid out differently from how they actually appear. That's because some options use different controls, and the positioning of the controls is handled dynamically in the code. The controls are listed and described below.

◆ *The Operation ComboBox:* This always appears on the left, and it is used to select the operation to be performed.

◆ *Proc1 ComboBox:* Most of the text manipulation options use this ComboBox to further specify the operation.

◆ *Proc2 ComboBox:* Two of the text manipulation options use this combo box to specify the operation even further. Specifically, this additional ComboBox is used by Add Text and Remove by Position.

◆ *Check box:* The Skip Non-Text Cells check box is an option relevant to some of the operations.

◆ *Help button:* Clicking this CommandButton displays help.

- *Close button:* Clicking this CommandButton unloads the UserForm.

- *Apply button:* Clicking this CommandButton applies the selected text manipulation option.

- *Progress bar:* This consists of a `Label` control inside of a `Frame` control.

- *Text box:* This text box is used for the Add Text option.

Figure 16-3 shows how the UserForm looks for each of the five operations. Notice that the configuration of the controls varies, depending on which option is selected.

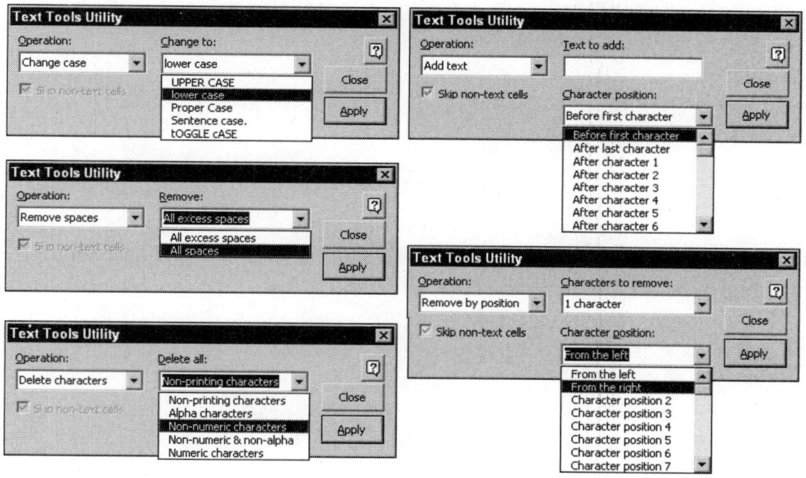

Figure 16-3: The UserForm layout changes for each operation.

You might notice that this utility violates one of my design rules that I outline earlier in this chapter (see "What Makes a Good Utility?"). Unlike most of Excel's built-in dialog boxes, the MainForm dialog box does not have an OK or a Cancel button, and clicking the Apply button does not dismiss the dialog box. The original version of Text Tools had an OK button and was designed so that clicking OK performed the task and closed the dialog box. User feedback, however, convinced me to change the design. Many people, it turns out, like to perform several different manipulations at one time. Therefore, I changed the utility to accommodate user preferences.

The ThisWorkbook code module

When the add-in is opened, the Workbook_Open procedure runs. This procedure, which is listed below, adds a menu item to the Tools menu. The menu item contains the text defined by the APPNAME constant, which is declared in Module1 (see the next section).

```
Private Sub Workbook_Open()
    Dim ToolsMenu As CommandBarPopup
    Dim NewMenuItem As CommandBarButton
    Set ToolsMenu = Application.CommandBars(1).FindControl(Type:=10,
ID:=30007)
    Set NewMenuItem = ToolsMenu.Controls.Add(Type:=1,
Temporary:=True)
    With NewMenuItem
        .Caption = APPNAME
        .OnAction = "RunTextTools"
    End With
End Sub
```

When the add-in is closed, the Workbook_BeforeClose procedure is executed. This procedure removes the menu item from the Tools menu.

```
Private Sub Workbook_BeforeClose(Cancel As Boolean)
    On Error Resume Next
    Application.CommandBars(1).FindControl(Type:=10,
ID:=30007).Controls(APPNAME).Delete
    On Error GoTo 0
End Sub
```

Figure 16-4 shows the Tools menu when the Text Tools utility is opened.

Refer to Chapter 23 for more information about adding a menu item to a menu.

The Module1 VBA module

The Module1 VBA module contains the declarations, a simple procedure that kicks off the utility, and a procedure that handles the undo operation.

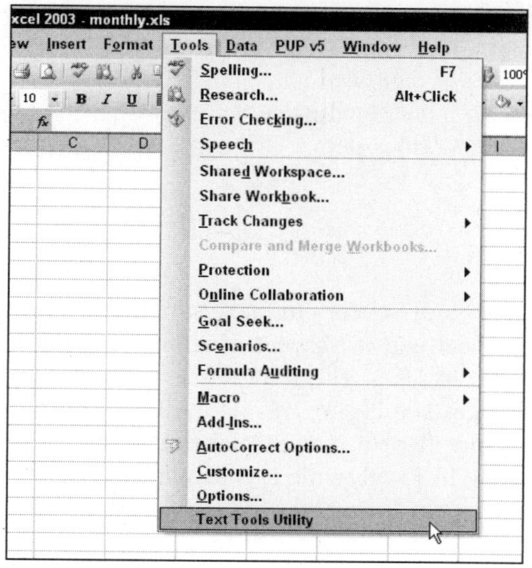

Figure 16-4: The Tools menu displays an additional menu item.

DECLARATIONS IN THE MODULE1 VBA MODULE

Following are the declarations at the top of the `Module1` module:

```
Public Const APPNAME As String = "Text Tools Utility"
Public Const PROGRESSTHRESHHOLD = 2000
Public UserChoices(1 To 8) As Variant 'stores user's last choices
Public UndoRange As Range ' For undoing
Public UserSelection As Range 'For Udoing
```

I declare a `Public` constant containing a string that stores the name of the application. This string is used in the UserForm caption and in various message boxes. It is also used as the caption for the menu item that's created. (See "The ThisWorkbook code module," earlier in this chapter.)

The `PROGRESSTHRESHHOLD` constant specifies the number of cells that will display the progress indicator. When this constant is `2,000`, the progress indicator will be shown only if the utility is working on 2,000 or more cells.

The `UserChoices` array holds the value of each control. This information is stored in the Windows Registry and is retrieved when the utility is executed.

Two other `Range` object variables are used to store information used for undoing.

THE RUNTEXTTOOLS PROCEDURE IN THE MODULE1 VBA MODULE

The `RunTextTools` procedure follows:

```
Sub RunTextTools()
    Dim InvalidContext As Boolean
```

```
    If ActiveSheet Is Nothing Then InvalidContext = True
    If TypeName(ActiveSheet) <> "Worksheet" Then InvalidContext = True
    If InvalidContext Then
        MsgBox "Select some cells in a range.", vbCritical, APPNAME
    Else
        UserForm1.Show 0
    End If
End Sub
```

As you can see, it's rather simple. The procedure checks to make sure that a sheet is active, and then it makes sure that the sheet is a worksheet. If either of these is not true, the `InvalidContext` variable is set to `True`. The `If-Then-Else` construct checks this variable and displays a message (see Figure 16-5) or the UserForm. Notice that the `Show` method uses an argument of 0, which makes it a *modeless* UserForm (that is, the user can keep working in Excel while it is displayed).

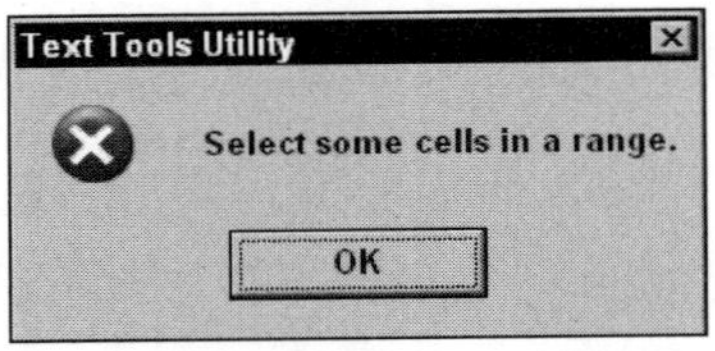

Text Tools Utility ✕

❌ **Select some cells in a range.**

OK

Figure 16-5: This message is displayed if no workbook is
active or if the active sheet is not a worksheet.

 The code does not ensure that a range is selected. This type of error handling is included in the code that's executed when the Apply button is clicked.

THE UNDOTEXTTOOLS PROCEDURE IN THE MODULE1 VBA MODULE

This `UndoTextTools` procedure is executed when the user chooses Edit → Undo (or clicks the Undo button in the Standard toolbar). This is explained later in this chapter (see "Implementing Undo").

The UserForm1 code module

All the real work is done by VBA code contained in the code module for UserForm1. Here, I briefly describe each of the procedures in this module. The code is too lengthy to list here, but you can view it by opening the `text tools.xla` file on the companion CD-ROM.

THE USERFORM_INITIALIZE PROCEDURE IN THE USERFORM1 CODE MODULE

This procedure is executed before the UserForm is displayed. It sizes the UserForm and retrieves (from the Windows Registry) the previously selected values for the controls. It also adds the list items to the ComboBox (named ComboBoxOperation) that determines which operation will be performed.

THE COMBOBOXOPERATION_CHANGE PROCEDURE IN THE USERFORM1 CODE MODULE

This procedure is executed whenever the user selects an item in the ComboBox Operation. It does the work of displaying or hiding the other controls.

THE APPLYBUTTON_CLICK PROCEDURE IN THE USERFORM1 CODE MODULE

This procedure is executed when the Apply button is clicked. It does some error checking and then calls the CreateWorkRange function to ensure that empty cells are not included in the cells to be processed. (See the upcoming section, "Making the Text Tools utility efficient.") The ApplyButton_Click procedure also calls the SaveForUndo procedure, which saves the current data in case the user needs to undo the operation. (See "Implementing Undo," later in this chapter.)

The procedure then uses a Select Case construct to call the appropriate procedure to perform the operation. It calls one of the following Sub procedures: ChangeCase, AddText, RemoveText, RemoveSpaces, or RemoveCharacters. Some of these procedures make calls to function procedures. For example, the ChangeCase procedure might call the ToggleCase or SentenceCase procedures.

THE CLOSEBUTTON_CLICK PROCEDURE IN THE USERFORM1 CODE MODULE

This procedure is executed when the Close button is clicked. It saves the current control settings to the Windows Registry and then unloads the UserForm.

THE HELPBUTTON_CLICK PROCEDURE IN THE USERFORM1 CODE MODULE

This procedure is executed when the Help button is clicked. It simply displays the Help file.

Making the Text Tools utility efficient

The procedures in the Text Tools utility work by looping through a range of cells. It makes no sense to loop through cells that will not be changed — for example, empty cells and cells that contain a formula.

As I mention earlier, the ApplyButton_Click procedure calls a Function procedure named CreateWorkRange. This function creates and returns a Range object that consists of all nonempty and nonformula cells in the user's select range. For example, assume that column A contains text in the range A1:A12. If the user selects the entire column, the CreateWorkRange function would convert that complete column range into a subset that consists of only the nonempty cells (that is, the range A:A would be converted to A1:A12). This makes the code much more efficient because empty cells and formula need not be included in the loop.

The CreateWorkRange function accepts two arguments:

◆ Rng: A Range object that represents the range selected by the user.

◆ TextOnly: A Boolean value. If True, the function returns only text cells. Otherwise it returns all non-empty cells.

The function is listed below.

```
Private Function CreateWorkRange(Rng, TextOnly)
'    Creates and returns a Range object
    Set CreateWorkRange = Nothing
'    Single cell, has a formula
    If Rng.Count = 1 And Rng.HasFormula Then
        Set CreateWorkRange = Nothing
        Exit Function
    End If
'    Single cell, or single merged cell
    If Rng.Count = 1 Or Rng.MergeCells = True Then
        If TextOnly Then
            If Not IsNumeric(Rng(1).Value) Then
                Set CreateWorkRange = Rng
                Exit Function
            Else
                Set CreateWorkRange = Nothing
                Exit Function
            End If
        Else
            If Not IsEmpty(Rng(1)) Then
                Set CreateWorkRange = Rng
                Exit Function
            End If
        End If
    End If
    On Error Resume Next
    Set Rng = Intersect(Rng, Rng.Parent.UsedRange)
    If TextOnly = True Then
        Set CreateWorkRange = Rng.SpecialCells(xlConstants, xlTextValues)
        If Err <> 0 Then
            Set CreateWorkRange = Nothing
```

```
            On Error GoTo 0
            Exit Function
        End If
    Else
        Set CreateWorkRange = Rng.SpecialCells _
          (xlConstants, xlTextValues + xlNumbers)
        If Err <> 0 Then
            Set CreateWorkRange = Nothing
            On Error GoTo 0
            Exit Function
        End If
    End If
End Function
```

 The CreateWorkRange function makes heavy use of the SpecialCells property. To learn more about the SpecialCells property, try recording a macro while making various selections in Excel's Go To Special dialog box. You can display this dialog box by pressing F5 and then clicking the Special button in the Go To dialog box.

You'll notice a quirk when you use the Go To Special dialog box. Normally it operates on the current range selection. For example, if an entire column is selected, the result is a subset of that column. But if a single cell is selected, it operates on the entire worksheet. Because of this, the CreateWorkRange function checks the number of cells in the range passed to it.

Saving the Text Tools utility settings

The Text Tools utility has a very useful feature: It remembers the last settings that you used. This is handy because most people tend to use the same option each time that they invoke it.

As I mentioned, the most recent settings are stored in the Windows Registry. When the user clicks the Close button, the code uses VBA's SaveSetting function to save the value of each control. When the Text Tools utility is started, it uses the GetSetting function to retrieve those values and set the controls accordingly.

In the Windows Registry, the settings are stored at the following location:

```
HKEY_CURRENT_USER\Software\VB and VBA Program Settings\
Text Tools Utility\Settings
```

Figure 16-6 shows these settings in the Windows Registry Editor program (regedit.exe).

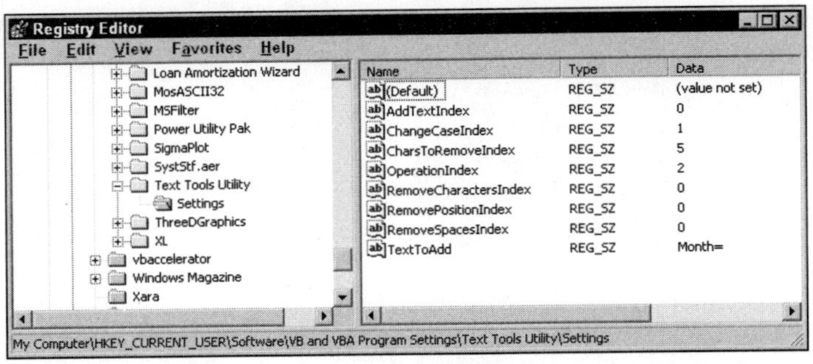

Figure 16-6: Use the Windows Registry Editor program to view the settings stored in the Registry.

If you examine the code for Text Editor, you'll find that I used an array (named UserChoices) to store the settings. I could have used separate variables for each setting, but using an array made the coding a bit easier.

Implementing Undo

Unlike Excel's Undo feature, the undo technique used in the Text Tools utility is a single level. In other words, the user can undo only the most recent operation. Refer to the sidebar "Undoing a VBA Procedure" for additional information about using Undo with your applications.

The Text Tools utility saves the original data in a worksheet. If the user undoes the operation, that data is then copied back to the user's workbook.

In the Text Tools utility, recall that the Module1 VBA module declared two public variables for handling undo:

```
Public UndoRange As Range
Public UserSelection As Range
```

Before modifying any data, the ApplyButton_Click procedure calls the SaveForUndo procedure. The procedure starts with three statements:

```
Set UserSelection = Selection
Set UndoRange = WorkRange
ThisWorkbook.Sheets(1).UsedRange.Clear
```

WorkRange, as you'll recall from the previous section, is a Range object that consists of the nonempty and nonformula cells in the user's selection. The third statement, above, erases any existing saved data from the worksheet.

Next, the following loop is executed:

```
For Each RngArea In WorkRange.Areas
    ThisWorkbook.Sheets(1).Range _
       (RngArea.Address).Formula = RngArea.Formula
Next RngArea
```

This code loops through each area of the WorkRange and stores the data in the worksheet. (If the WorkRange consists of a contiguous range of cells, it will contain only one area.)

After the specified operation is performed, the code then uses the OnUndo method to specify the procedure to execute if the user chooses Undo. For example, after performing a case change operation, this statement is executed:

```
Application.OnUndo "Undo Change Case", "UndoTextTools"
```

Excel's Edit menu will then contain a menu item: Undo Case Change. If the user selects the command, the UndoTextTools procedure, shown below, will be executed.

```
Private Sub UndoTextTools()
'    Undoes the last operation
    Dim a As Range
'     On Error GoTo ErrHandler
    Application.ScreenUpdating = False
    With UserSelection
        .Parent.Parent.Activate
        .Parent.Activate
        .Select
    End With
    For Each a In UndoRange.Areas
        a.Formula = ThisWorkbook.Sheets(1).Range(a.Address).Formula
    Next a
    Application.ScreenUpdating = True
    On Error GoTo 0
    Exit Sub
ErrHandler:
    Application.ScreenUpdating = True
    MsgBox "Can't undo", vbInformation, APPNAME
    On Error GoTo 0
End Sub
```

The UndoTextTools procedure first ensures that the correct workbook and worksheet is activated and then selects the original range selected by the user. Then it loops through each area of the stored data (which is available because of the UndoRange public variable) and puts the data back to its original location (overwriting the changes, of course).

Undoing a VBA Procedure

Computer users have become accustomed to the ability to undo an operation. Almost every operation that you perform in Excel can be undone. Even better, beginning with Excel 97, the program features multiple levels of undo.

If you program in VBA, you may have wondered whether it's possible to undo the effects of a procedure. Although the answer is *yes*, the qualified answer is *it's not always easy.*

Making the effects of your VBA procedures undoable isn't automatic. Your procedure needs to store the previous state so that it can be restored if the user chooses the Edit → Undo command. How you do this can vary depending on what the procedure does. In extreme cases, you might need to save an entire worksheet. If your procedure modifies a range, for example, you need to save only the contents of that range.

The `Application` object contains an `OnUndo` method, which lets the programmer specify text to appear on the Edit → Undo menu and a procedure to execute if the user chooses Edit → Undo. For example, the following statement causes the Undo menu item to display `Undo my cool macro`. If the user chooses Edit → Undo My Cool Macro, the `UndoMyMacro` procedure is executed:

```
Application.OnUndo "Undo my cool macro", "UndoMyMacro"
```

 The companion CD-ROM contains a simpler example that demonstrates how to enable the Edit → Undo command after a VBA procedure is executed.

Post-mortem of the project

The previous sections described each component of the Text Tools utility. At this point, it's useful to revisit the original project goals to see whether they were met. The original goals, along with my comments, are as follows:

◆ *Its main features will be those listed at the beginning of this section.* Accomplished.

◆ *It will enable the user to request the preceding types of changes on nontext cells as well as text cells.* Accomplished.

◆ *It will have the same look and feel of other Excel commands. In other words, it will have a dialog box that looks like Excel's dialog boxes.* As I noted earlier, the Text Tools utility deviates from Excel's normal look and feel by using an Apply button rather than an OK button. And, unlike most of Excel's dialog boxes, Text Tools uses a stay-on-top dialog box. In light of the enhanced usability, I think these deviations are quite reasonable.

◆ *It will be in the form of an add-in and will be accessible from the Tools menu.* Accomplished.

◆ *It will operate with the current selection of cells (including multiple selections), and it will enable the user to modify the range selection while the dialog box is displayed.* Accomplished. And because the dialog box need not be dismissed, it didn't require the use of a RefEdit control.

◆ *It will remember the last operation used and display those settings the next time that the dialog box is invoked.* Accomplished (thanks to the Windows Registry).

◆ *It will have no effect on cells that contain formulas.* Accomplished.

◆ *It will be fast and efficient. For example, if the user selects an entire range, the utility should ignore empty cells.* Accomplished.

◆ *It will enable the user to undo the changes.* Accomplished.

◆ *Comprehensive help will be available.* Accomplished.

Understand the Text Tools utility

If you don't fully understand how this utility works, I urge you to load the add-in and use the Debugger to step through the code. Try it out with different types of selections, including an entire worksheet. You will see that regardless of the size of the original selection, only appropriate cells are processed and empty cells are completely ignored. If a worksheet has only one cell with text in it, the utility operates just as quickly whether you select that cell or the entire worksheet.

If you convert the add-in to a standard workbook, you'll be able to see how the original data is stored in the worksheet for undo. To convert the add-in to a workbook, double-click the ThisWorkbook code module. Press F4 to display the Properties box and then change the IsAddin property to False.

More about Excel Utilities

You can use the coupon in the back of this book to order a free copy of my Power Utility Pak (PUP). Figure 16-7 shows the PUP menu, through which you access the utilities. This product includes several dozen useful utilities (plus many custom worksheet functions). The complete VBA source code also is available for a small fee. You can get a feel for how the product works by installing the trial version, available on the companion CD-ROM.

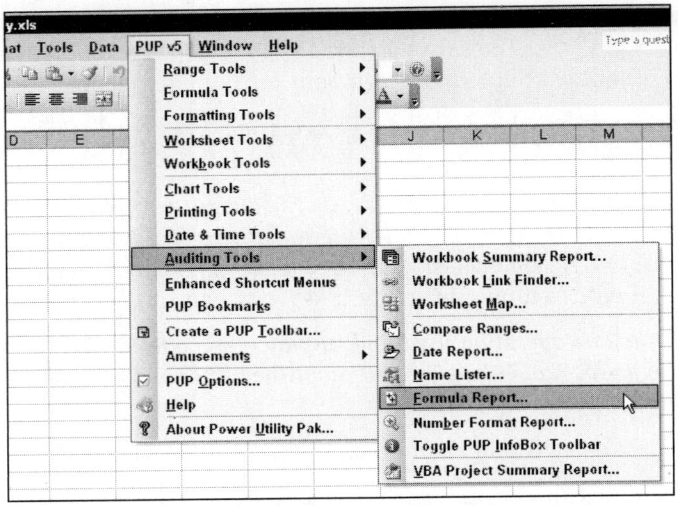

Figure 16-7: The author's Power Utility Pak contains many useful
Excel utilities.

In addition to the Power Utility Pak, several other utility packages exist, and
they can be downloaded from the Internet. A good starting point for locating additional Web utilities is my Web site. Visit The Spreadsheet Page at `http://www.`
`j-walk.com/ss`.

Chapter 17

Working with Pivot Tables

IN THIS CHAPTER

Excel's pivot table feature is, arguably, its most innovative and powerful feature. Pivot tables first appeared in Excel 5, and the feature remains unique to Excel. (No other spreadsheet has anything that comes close to it.) This chapter is not an introduction to pivot tables. I assume that you're familiar with this feature and understand how to create and modify pivot tables manually. In this chapter, I cover

◆ What you need to know to create pivot tables with VBA

◆ Examples of VBA procedures that create pivot tables

◆ An example of how to use VBA to modify an existing pivot table

AS YOU PROBABLY KNOW, creating a pivot table from a database or list enables you to summarize data in ways that otherwise would not be possible — and it's amazingly fast. You also can write Visual Basic for Applications (VBA) code to generate and modify pivot tables.

Excel's pivot table feature was enhanced significantly in Excel 2000. It uses more efficient data caching, and it also supports pivot charts. A *pivot chart* is a chart that's linked to a pivot table. Consequently, some of the material in this chapter does not apply to Excel 97 or earlier.

An Introductory Pivot Table Example

This section gets the ball rolling with a simple example of using VBA to create a pivot table.

Figure 17-1 shows a very simple worksheet database. It contains four fields: SalesRep, Region, Month, and Sales. Each record describes the sales for a particular sales representative in a particular month.

SalesRep	Region	Month	Sales
Amy	North	Jan	33,488
Amy	North	Feb	47,008
Amy	North	Mar	32,128
Bob	North	Jan	34,736
Bob	North	Feb	92,872
Bob	North	Mar	76,128
Chuck	South	Jan	41,536
Chuck	South	Feb	23,192
Chuck	South	Mar	21,736
Doug	South	Jan	44,834
Doug	South	Feb	32,002
Doug	South	Mar	23,932

Figure 17-1: This simple database is a good candidate for a pivot table.

Creating a pivot table

Figure 17-2 shows a pivot table created from the data. This pivot table summarizes the sales by sales representative and month. This pivot table is set up with the following fields:

- *Region:* A page field in the pivot table
- *SalesRep:* A row field in the pivot table
- *Month:* A column field in the pivot table
- *Sales:* A data field in the pivot table that uses the SUM function

Region	(All)			
Sum of Sales	Month			
SalesRep	Jan	Feb	Mar	Grand Total
Amy	33488	47008	32128	112624
Bob	34736	92872	76128	203736
Chuck	41536	23192	21736	86464
Doug	44834	32002	23932	100768
Grand Total	154594	195074	153924	503592

Figure 17-2: A pivot table created from the data in Figure 17-1.

I turned on the macro recorder before I created this pivot table. The code that was generated follows:

```
Sub Macro1()
'    Recorded macro
     Range("A1").Select
     ActiveWorkbook.PivotCaches.Add _
         (SourceType:=xlDatabase, _
         SourceData:="Sheet1!R1C1:R13C4"). _
         CreatePivotTable _
         TableDestination:="", _
         TableName:="PivotTable1", _
         DefaultVersion:=xlPivotTableVersion10

     ActiveSheet.PivotTableWizard _
         TableDestination:=ActiveSheet.Cells(3, 1)
     ActiveSheet.Cells(3, 1).Select

     With ActiveSheet.PivotTables("PivotTable1"). _
         PivotFields("Region")
         .Orientation = xlPageField
         .Position = 1
     End With

     With ActiveSheet.PivotTables("PivotTable1"). _
         PivotFields("SalesRep")
         .Orientation = xlRowField
         .Position = 1
     End With

     With ActiveSheet.PivotTables("PivotTable1"). _
         PivotFields("Month")
         .Orientation = xlColumnField
         .Position = 1
     End With
     ActiveSheet.PivotTables("PivotTable1"). _
         AddDataField ActiveSheet.PivotTables("PivotTable1"). _
         PivotFields("Sales"), "Sum of Sales", xlSum
End Sub
```

How the macro recorder generates code for you depends on how you built the pivot table. In the preceding example, I created a pivot table, which was empty until I dragged in the fields from the PivotTable toolbar. The alternative method is to click the Layout button in the second step of the PivotTable Wizard and lay out the pivot table before it's created.

You can, of course, execute the recorded macro to create another identical pivot table.

Examining the recorded code for the pivot table

VBA code that works with pivot tables can be confusing. To make any sense of the recorded macro, you need to know about a few relevant objects, all of which are thoroughly explained in the online help.

◆ `PivotCaches`: A collection of `PivotCache` objects in a `Workbook` object.

◆ `PivotTables`: A collection of `PivotTable` objects in a `Worksheet` object.

◆ `PivotFields`: A collection of fields in a `PivotTable` object.

◆ `PivotItems`: A collection of individual data items within a field category.

◆ `CreatePivotTable`: A `PivotCache` object method that creates a pivot table by using the data in a pivot cache.

◆ `PivotTableWizard`: A `Worksheet` object method that creates a pivot table. As you see in the next section, this method isn't necessary.

Cleaning up the recorded pivot table code

As with most recorded macros, the preceding example is not as efficient as it could be. It can be simplified to make it more understandable. Listing 17-1 generates the same pivot table as the procedure previously listed.

Listing 17-1: A More Efficient Way to Generate a Pivot Table in VBA

```vba
Sub CreatePivotTable()
    Dim PTCache As PivotCache
    Dim PT As PivotTable

    Set PTCache = ActiveWorkbook.PivotCaches.Add _
        (SourceType:=xlDatabase, _
        SourceData:=Range("A1").CurrentRegion.Address)

    Set PT = PTCache.CreatePivotTable _
        (TableDestination:="", _
        TableName:="PivotTable1")

    With PT
        .PivotFields("Region").Orientation = xlPageField
        .PivotFields("Month").Orientation = xlColumnField
        .PivotFields("SalesRep").Orientation = xlRowField
        .PivotFields("Sales").Orientation = xlDataField
    End With
End Sub
```

The `CreatePivotTable` procedure is simplified (and might be easier to understand) because it declares two object variables: `PTCache` and `PT`. These take the place of the indexed references to `ActiveSheet.PivotCaches` and `ActiveSheet.PivotTables`. A new `PivotCache` object is created by using the `Add` method. Then a new `PivotTable` object is created by using the `CreatePivotTable` method of the `PivotCaches` collection. The last section of the code adds the fields to the pivot table and specifies their location within it (page, column, row, or data field).

Notice that the original macro hard-coded the data range used to create the `PivotCache` object (that is, `'Sheet1!R1C1:R13C4'`). In the `CreatePivotTable` procedure, the pivot table is based on the current region surrounding Cell A1. This ensures that the macro will continue to work properly when more data is added.

The code also could be more general through the use of indices rather than literal strings for the `PivotFields` collections. This way, if the user changes the column headings, the code will still work. For example, more general code would use `PivotFields(1)` rather than `PivotFields('Region')`. This alternative is best suited for situations in which the the columns will never be rearranged.

As always, the best way to master this topic is to record your actions within a macro to find out its relevant objects, methods, and properties. Then study the online help topics to understand how everything fits together. In almost every case, you'll need to modify the recorded macros. Or, after you understand how to work with pivot tables, you can write code from scratch and avoid the macro recorder.

Creating a More Complex Pivot Table

In this section, I present VBA code to create a relatively complex pivot table.

Data for a more complex pivot table

Figure 17-3 shows part of a worksheet database. This table contains 15,840 rows containing hierarchical budget data for a corporation. There are 5 divisions, and each division contains 11 departments. Each department has four budget categories, and each budget category contains several budget items. Budgeted and actual amounts are included for each of the 12 months.

This workbook is available on the companion CD-ROM.

	A	B	C	D	E	F	G	H
1	DIVISION	DEPARTMENT	CATEGORY	ITEM	MONTH	BUDGET	ACTUAL	
2	N. America	Data Processing	Compensation	Salaries	Jan	2583	3165	
3	N. America	Data Processing	Compensation	Benefits	Jan	4496	2980	
4	N. America	Data Processing	Compensation	Bonuses	Jan	3768	3029	
5	N. America	Data Processing	Compensation	Commissions	Jan	3133	2815	
6	N. America	Data Processing	Compensation	Payroll Taxes	Jan	3559	3770	
7	N. America	Data Processing	Compensation	Training	Jan	3099	3559	
8	N. America	Data Processing	Compensation	Conferences	Jan	2931	3199	
9	N. America	Data Processing	Compensation	Entertainment	Jan	2632	2633	
10	N. America	Data Processing	Facility	Rent	Jan	2833	2508	
11	N. America	Data Processing	Facility	Lease	Jan	3450	2631	
12	N. America	Data Processing	Facility	Utilities	Jan	4111	3098	
13	N. America	Data Processing	Facility	Maintenance	Jan	3070	2870	
14	N. America	Data Processing	Facility	Telephone	Jan	3827	4329	
15	N. America	Data Processing	Facility	Other	Jan	3843	3322	
16	N. America	Data Processing	Supplies & Services	General Office	Jan	2642	3218	
17	N. America	Data Processing	Supplies & Services	Computer Supplies	Jan	3052	4098	
18	N. America	Data Processing	Supplies & Services	Books & Subs	Jan	4346	3361	
19	N. America	Data Processing	Supplies & Services	Outside Services	Jan	2869	3717	
20	N. America	Data Processing	Supplies & Services	Other	Jan	3328	3116	
21	N. America	Data Processing	Equipment	Computer Hardware	Jan	3088	2728	
22	N. America	Data Processing	Equipment	Software	Jan	4226	2675	
23	N. America	Data Processing	Equipment	Photocopiers	Jan	3780	3514	
24	N. America	Data Processing	Equipment	Telecommunications	Jan	3893	3664	
25	N. America	Data Processing	Equipment	Other	Jan	2851	4380	
26	N. America	Human Resources	Compensation	Salaries	Jan	3604	3501	
27	N. America	Human Resources	Compensation	Benefits	Jan	2859	4493	
28	N. America	Human Resources	Compensation	Bonuses	Jan	3020	2676	

Figure 17-3: The data in this workbook will be summarized in a pivot table.

Figure 17-4 shows a pivot table created from the data. Notice that the pivot table contains a calculated field named Variance, plus four calculated items (Q1, Q2, Q3, and Q4), which calculate quarterly totals.

The code that created the pivot table

The VBA code that created the pivot table is shown in Listing 17-2.

Listing 17-2: Creating a Compartmentalized Pivot Table

```
Sub CreatePivotTable()
    Dim PTCache As PivotCache
    Dim PT As PivotTable

    Application.ScreenUpdating = False

'   Delete PivotSheet if it exists
    On Error Resume Next
    Application.DisplayAlerts = False
```

```
    Sheets("PivotSheet").Delete
    On Error GoTo 0
    Application.DisplayAlerts = True

'   Create a Pivot Cache
    Set PTCache = ActiveWorkbook.PivotCaches.Add( _
      SourceType:=xlDatabase, _
      SourceData:=Range("A1").CurrentRegion.Address)

'   Add new worksheet
    Worksheets.Add
    ActiveSheet.Name = "PivotSheet"

'   Create the Pivot Table from the Cache
    Set PT = PTCache.CreatePivotTable( _
      TableDestination:=Sheets("PivotSheet").Range("A1"), _
      TableName:="BudgetPivot")

    With PT
'       Add fields
        .PivotFields("DEPARTMENT").Orientation = xlRowField
        .PivotFields("MONTH").Orientation = xlColumnField
        .PivotFields("DIVISION").Orientation = xlPageField
        .PivotFields("BUDGET").Orientation = xlDataField
        .PivotFields("ACTUAL").Orientation = xlDataField

'       Add a calculated field to compute variance
        .CalculatedFields.Add "Variance", "=BUDGET-ACTUAL"
        .PivotFields("Variance").Orientation = xlDataField

'       Add calculated items
        .PivotFields("MONTH").CalculatedItems.Add _
          "Q1", "= Jan+Feb+Mar"
        .PivotFields("MONTH").CalculatedItems.Add _
          "Q2", "= Apr+May+Jun"
        .PivotFields("MONTH").CalculatedItems.Add _
          "Q3", "= Jul+Aug+Sep"
        .PivotFields("MONTH").CalculatedItems.Add _
          "Q4", "= Oct+Nov+Dec"

'       Move the calculated items
        .PivotFields("MONTH").PivotItems("Q1").Position = 4
        .PivotFields("MONTH").PivotItems("Q2").Position = 8
```

Continued

Listing 17-2 *(Continued)*

```
            .PivotFields("MONTH").PivotItems("Q3").Position = 12
            .PivotFields("MONTH").PivotItems("Q4").Position = 16

'           Change the captions
            .PivotFields("Sum of BUDGET").Caption = "Budget ($)"
            .PivotFields("Sum of ACTUAL").Caption = "Actual ($)"
            .PivotFields("Sum of Variance").Caption ="Variance ($)"
    End With
    Application.ScreenUpdating = True
End Sub
```

		A	B	C	D	E	F	G	H	I	J	K
1	DIVISION	(All)										
2												
3				MONTH								
4	DEPARTMENT	Data	Jan	Feb	Mar	Q1	Apr	May	Jun	Q2	Jul	
5	Accounting	Budget ($)	422455	433317	420522	1276294	417964	411820	414012	1243796	427431	
6		Actual ($)	422662	413163	416522	1252347	420672	431303	429993	1281968	425879	
7		Variance ($)	-207	20154	4000	23947	-2708	-19483	-15981	-38172	1552	
8	Advertising	Budget ($)	424590	419331	417949	1261870	420324	427150	424169	1271643	421183	
9		Actual ($)	416008	420828	425437	1262273	417310	419996	428330	1265636	428958	
10		Variance ($)	8582	-1497	-7488	-403	3014	7154	-4161	6007	-7775	
11	Data Processing	Budget ($)	422197	422057	419659	1263913	417260	422848	421038	1261146	421676	
12		Actual ($)	414743	438990	430545	1284278	424214	411775	421909	1257898	420210	
13		Variance ($)	7454	-16933	-10886	-20365	-6954	11073	-871	3248	1466	
14	Human Resources	Budget ($)	422053	425313	418634	1266000	423038	423514	419602	1266154	415197	
15		Actual ($)	424934	429275	407053	1261262	429187	410258	421870	1261315	428551	
16		Variance ($)	-2881	-3962	11581	4738	-6149	13256	-2268	4839	-13354	
17	Operations	Budget ($)	413530	427975	419527	1261032	422299	415298	414805	1252402	413149	
18		Actual ($)	415819	406592	426827	1249238	418223	431307	413201	1262731	416350	
19		Variance ($)	-2289	21383	-7300	11794	4076	-16009	1604	-10329	-3201	
20	Public Relations	Budget ($)	424896	414507	415179	1254582	417100	426223	408425	1251748	422138	
21		Actual ($)	413526	414084	415476	1243086	414040	396652	416201	1226893	423826	
22		Variance ($)	11370	423	-297	11496	3060	29571	-7776	24855	-1686	
23	R&D	Budget ($)	417771	429880	424066	1271717	421539	417440	421174	1260153	417151	
24		Actual ($)	432019	426644	419595	1278258	427567	412038	425932	1265537	426686	
25		Variance ($)	-14248	3236	4471	-6541	-6028	5402	-4758	-5384	-9535	
26	Sales	Budget ($)	420659	421962	417814	1260435	420302	422409	426802	1269513	428460	
27		Actual ($)	431565	421251	408661	1261477	408912	425620	428596	1263128	424737	
28		Variance ($)	-10906	711	9153	-1042	11390	-3211	-1794	6385	3723	
29	Security	Budget ($)	419195	419294	413258	1251747	421700	421875	421231	1264806	417392	
30		Actual ($)	409486	418697	427401	1255584	419221	421266	420388	1260875	423826	
31		Variance ($)	9709	597	-14143	-3837	2479	609	843	3931	-6436	

Figure 17-4: A pivot table created from the data in Figure 17-3.

How the more complex pivot table works

The second `CreatePivotTable` procedure in Listing 17-2 starts by deleting the `PivotSheet` worksheet if it already exists. It then creates a `PivotCache` object, inserts a new worksheet named `PivotSheet`, and creates the pivot table. The code then adds the following fields to the pivot table:

- ◆ *Department:* A row field
- ◆ *Month:* A column field
- ◆ *Division:* A page field

- ◆ *Budget:* A data field

- ◆ *Actual:* A data field

Next, the procedure uses the Add method of the CalculatedFields collection to create the calculated field Variance, which subtracts the Actual amount from the Budget amount. The code then adds four calculated items to compute the quarterly totals. By default, the calculated items are added to the right side of the pivot table, so additional code is required to move them adjacent to the months to which they refer. (For example, Q1 is placed after March.) Finally, the code changes the captions displayed in the pivot table. For example, Sum of Budget is replaced by Budget ($).

I created this procedure by recording my actions while I created and modi-fied the pivot table. Then I cleaned up the code to make it more readable and efficient.

Creating a Pivot Table from an External Database

In the preceding example, the source data was in a worksheet. As you probably know, Excel also enables you to use an external data source to create a pivot table. The example in this section demonstrates how to write VBA code to create a pivot table based on data stored in an Access database file.

The Access database consists of a single table that is identical to the data used in the previous example.

The code that creates the pivot table is shown in Listing 17-3. It assumes that the budget.mdb database file is stored in the same directory as the workbook.

Listing 17-3: Generating a Pivot Table from an External Database

```
Sub CreatePivotTableFromDB()
    Dim PTCache As PivotCache
    Dim PT As PivotTable
```

Continued

Listing 17-3 *(Continued)*

```
'   Delete PivotSheet if it exists
    On Error Resume Next
    Application.DisplayAlerts = False
    Sheets("PivotSheet").Delete
    On Error GoTo 0

'   Create a Pivot Cache
    Set PTCache = ActiveWorkbook.PivotCaches.Add _
      (SourceType:=xlExternal)

'   Connect to database, and do query
    DBFile = ThisWorkbook.Path & "\budget.mdb"
    ConString = "ODBC;DSN=MS Access Database;DBQ=" & DBFile


     QueryString = "SELECT * FROM BUDGET"
    With PTCache
        .Connection = ConString
        .CommandText = QueryString
    End With

'   Add new worksheet
    Worksheets.Add
    ActiveSheet.Name = "PivotSheet"

'   Create pivot table
    Set PT = PTCache.CreatePivotTable( _
      TableDestination:=Sheets("PivotSheet").Range("A1"), _
      TableName:="BudgetPivot")

'   Add fields
    With PT
'       Add fields
        .PivotFields("DEPARTMENT").Orientation = xlRowField
        .PivotFields("MONTH").Orientation = xlColumnField
        .PivotFields("DIVISION").Orientation = xlPageField
        .PivotFields("BUDGET").Orientation = xlDataField
        .PivotFields("ACTUAL").Orientation = xlDataField
    End With
End Sub
```

Notice that the SourceType argument for the Add method of the PivotCaches collection is specified as xlExternal. In the example in the previous section (which used data in a worksheet database), the SourceType argument was xlDatabase.

The `PivotCache` object needs the following information to retrieve the data from the external file:

◆ *A connection string:* This describes the type of data source and the file-name. In this example, the connection string specifies an Open Database Connectivity (ODBC) data source that is a Microsoft Access file named `budget.mdb`.

◆ *A query string:* This is a Structured Query Language (SQL) statement that determines which records and fields are returned. In this example, the entire `Budget` table is selected.

This information is passed to the `PivotCache` object by setting the `Connection` and `CommandText` properties. After the data is stored in the pivot cache, the pivot table is created by using the `CreatePivotTable` method.

SQL is a standard language for performing database queries. For more information, consult the online help. Better yet, you might want to purchase a book that deals exclusively with SQL.

Creating Multiple Pivot Tables

The final example creates a series of pivot tables that summarize data collected in a customer survey. That data is stored in a worksheet database (see Figure 17-5) and consists of 100 rows. Each row contains the respondent's sex, plus a numerical rating using a 1–5 scale for each of the 14 survey items.

	A	B	C	D	E	F	G	H	I	J	
			Store locations are	Store hours are	Stores are well-	You are easy to reach by	I like your	Employees	Employees	Employee are knowledge	P
1	Name	Sex	convenient	convenient	maintained	phone	web site	are friendly	are helpful	able	co
2	Subject1	Male	1	4	4	4	1	1	2	1	
3	Subject2	Female	2	5	1	1	4	2	4	3	
4	Subject3	Male	1	1	4	2	3	3	2	1	
5	Subject4	Male	2	1	3	5	1	2	3	4	
6	Subject5	Female	2	2	5	5	4	2	1	5	
7	Subject6	Female	2	4	3	3	1	1	4	4	
8	Subject7	Female	2	4	5	4	5	3	2	5	
9	Subject8	Male	3	2	1	2	3	4	3	1	
10	Subject9	Female	3	4	4	4	5	1	4	1	
11	Subject10	Male	2	1	5	5	5	1	4	1	
12	Subject11	Male	4	3	3	2	1	2	4	2	
13	Subject12	Female	2	1	4	5	5	5	3	1	
14	Subject13	Female	4	3	4	3	2	5	3	3	
15	Subject14	Female	2	3	4	2	1	1	4	2	
16	Subject15	Female	1	3	5	1	2	2	4	1	
17	Subject16	Male	1	4	1	3	4	3	4	4	
18	Subject17	Female	3	4	3	5	5	4	4	3	
19	Subject18	Male	1	5	5	3	5	3	4	2	

Figure 17-5: Creating a series of pivot tables will summarize this survey data.

Figure 17-6 shows a few of the resulting pivot tables. Each survey item is summarized in two pivot tables (one showing percentages, and one showing the actual frequencies).

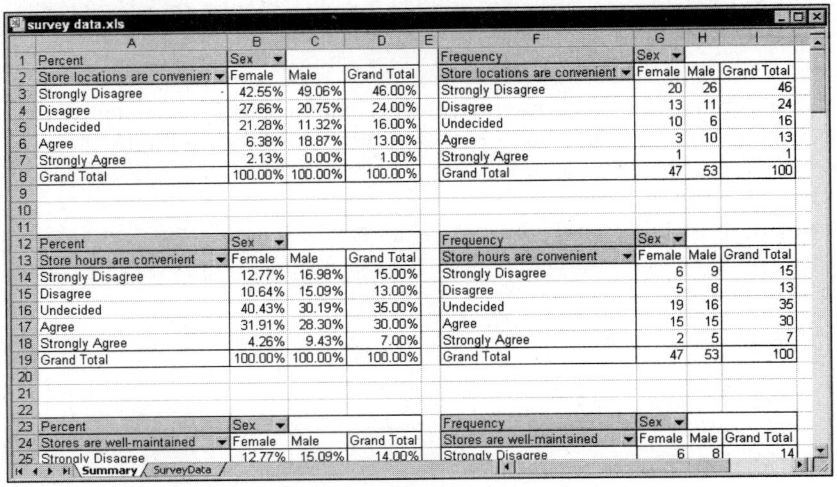

Percent	Sex		
Store locations are convenien	Female	Male	Grand Total
Strongly Disagree	42.55%	49.06%	46.00%
Disagree	27.66%	20.75%	24.00%
Undecided	21.28%	11.32%	16.00%
Agree	6.38%	18.87%	13.00%
Strongly Agree	2.13%	0.00%	1.00%
Grand Total	100.00%	100.00%	100.00%

Frequency	Sex		
Store locations are convenient	Female	Male	Grand Total
Strongly Disagree	20	26	46
Disagree	13	11	24
Undecided	10	6	16
Agree	3	10	13
Strongly Agree	1		1
Grand Total	47	53	100

Percent	Sex		
Store hours are convenient	Female	Male	Grand Total
Strongly Disagree	12.77%	16.98%	15.00%
Disagree	10.64%	15.09%	13.00%
Undecided	40.43%	30.19%	35.00%
Agree	31.91%	28.30%	30.00%
Strongly Agree	4.26%	9.43%	7.00%
Grand Total	100.00%	100.00%	100.00%

Frequency	Sex		
Store hours are convenient	Female	Male	Grand Total
Strongly Disagree	6	9	15
Disagree	5	8	13
Undecided	19	16	35
Agree	15	15	30
Strongly Agree	2	5	7
Grand Total	47	53	100

Percent	Sex		
Stores are well-maintained	Female	Male	Grand Total
Strongly Disagree	12.77%	15.09%	14.00%

Frequency	Sex		
Stores are well-maintained	Female	Male	Grand Total
Strongly Disagree	6	8	14

Figure 17-6: A VBA procedure created these pivot tables.

The VBA code that created the pivot tables is presented in Listing 17-4.

Listing 17-4: Creating Multiple Pivot Tables from a Complex External Database

```
Sub MakePivotTables()
'   This procedure creates 28 pivot tables
    Dim PTCache As PivotCache
    Dim PT As PivotTable
    Dim SummarySheet As Worksheet
    Dim ItemName As String
    Dim Row As Integer, i As Integer

    Application.ScreenUpdating = False

'   Delete Summary sheet if it exists
    On Error Resume Next
    Application.DisplayAlerts = False
    Sheets("Summary").Delete
    On Error GoTo 0

'   Add Summary sheet
    Set SummarySheet = Worksheets.Add
    ActiveSheet.Name = "Summary"
```

```
'   Create Pivot Cache
    Set PTCache = ActiveWorkbook.PivotCaches.Add( _
      SourceType:=xlDatabase, _
      SourceData:=Sheets("SurveyData").Range("A1"). _
      CurrentRegion.Address)

    Row = 1
    For i = 1 To 14
        ItemName = Sheets("SurveyData").Cells(1, i + 2)
'       Create pivot table
        Set PT = PTCache.CreatePivotTable _
            (TableDestination:=SummarySheet.Cells(Row, 6), _
             TableName:=ItemName)
        Row = Row + 11

'       Add the fields
        With PT.PivotFields(ItemName)
            .Orientation = xlDataField
            .Name = "Frequency"
            .Function = xlCount
        End With

        PT.AddFields RowFields:=Array(ItemName, "Data")
        PT.PivotFields("Sex").Orientation = xlColumnField
    Next i

    Row = 1
    For i = 1 To 14
        ItemName = Sheets("SurveyData").Cells(1, i + 2)
'       Create pivot table
        Set PT = PTCache.CreatePivotTable _
            (TableDestination:=SummarySheet.Cells(Row, 1), _
             TableName:=ItemName & "2")
        Row = Row + 11

        With PT.PivotFields(ItemName)
            .Orientation = xlDataField
            .Name = "Percent"
            .Function = xlCount
            .Calculation = xlPercentOfColumn
        End With
```

Continued

Listing 17-4 *(Continued)*

```
        PT.AddFields RowFields:=Array(ItemName, "Data")
        PT.PivotFields("Sex").Orientation = xlColumnField
    Next i

'   Replace numbers with descriptive text
    SummarySheet.Activate
    With Range("A:A,F:F")
        .Replace "1", "Strongly Disagree"
        .Replace "2", "Disagree"
        .Replace "3", "Undecided"
        .Replace "4", "Agree"
        .Replace "5", "Strongly Agree"
    End With

'   Adjust column widths
    Columns("A:I").EntireColumn.AutoFit
End Sub
```

Notice that the pivot tables are created within two loops, and all come from a single `PivotCache` object. The `Row` variable keeps track of the start of each pivot table. After the pivot tables are created, the code replaces the numeric categories in the first column with text. (For example, *1* is replaced with Strongly Agree.) Finally, the column widths are adjusted.

Modifying Pivot Tables

An Excel pivot table is designed to be flexible. For example, users can easily change a row field to a column field and hide certain items in the pivot table that are not relevant to their current needs. You might want to provide your own interface to make it even easier for the user to make certain pivot table changes. The example in this section presents a pivot table that can be controlled by a series of OptionButtons and two `CheckBox` controls, as shown in Figure 17-7.

The pivot table contains four additional calculated items (Q1, Q2, Q3, and Q4), which compute quarterly totals. The VBA code that's executed when `OptionButton1` (Months Only) is selected is shown in Listing 17-5. The procedure is straightforward and similar to the event handler procedures for the other OptionButtons.

Listing 17-5: Responding to a User Request to Adjust a Pivot Table Option

```
Private Sub OptionButton1_Click()
'   Months only
    Application.ScreenUpdating = False
```

```
With ActiveSheet.PivotTables(1).PivotFields("Month")
    .PivotItems("Jan").Visible = True
    .PivotItems("Feb").Visible = True
    .PivotItems("Mar").Visible = True
    .PivotItems("Apr").Visible = True
    .PivotItems("May").Visible = True
    .PivotItems("Jun").Visible = True
    .PivotItems("Jul").Visible = True
    .PivotItems("Aug").Visible = True
    .PivotItems("Sep").Visible = True
    .PivotItems("Oct").Visible = True
    .PivotItems("Nov").Visible = True
    .PivotItems("Dec").Visible = True
    .PivotItems("Q1").Visible = False
    .PivotItems("Q2").Visible = False
    .PivotItems("Q3").Visible = False
    .PivotItems("Q4").Visible = False
End With
End Sub
```

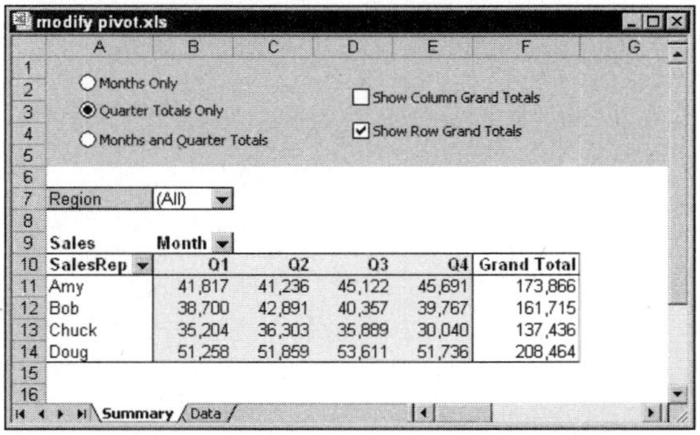

Figure 17-7: The user can use the controls to adjust the pivot table.

The CheckBox controls simply toggle the display of the grand totals. These event handler procedures follow:

```
Private Sub CheckBox1_Click()
'   Column Grand Totals
    Application.ScreenUpdating = False
    ActiveSheet.PivotTables(1).ColumnGrand = CheckBox1.Value
End Sub
```

```
Private Sub CheckBox2_Click()
'    Row Grand Totals
     Application.ScreenUpdating = False
     ActiveSheet.PivotTables(1).RowGrand = CheckBox2.Value
End Sub
```

Pivot tables, of course, can be modified in many other ways. As I mention, the easiest way to create VBA code that modifies pivot tables is to turn on the macro recorder while you make the changes manually. Then adjust the code and copy it to the event handler procedures for your controls.

Chapter 18

Working with Charts

IN THIS CHAPTER

Excel's charting feature lets you create a wide variety of charts using data that's stored in a worksheet. In this chapter, I discuss the following:

◆ Essential background information on Excel charts

◆ The difference between embedded charts and chart sheets

◆ Understanding the `Chart` object model

◆ Using the macro recorder to help you learn about `Chart` objects

◆ Examples of common charting tasks that use VBA

◆ Examples of more complex charting macros

◆ Some interesting (and useful) chart-making tricks

EXCEL SUPPORTS MORE THAN 100 DIFFERENT CHART TYPES, and you have a great deal of control over nearly every aspect of each chart.

About Charts

A chart is simply packed with objects, each of which has its own properties and methods. Because of this, manipulating charts with Visual Basic for Applications (VBA) can be a bit of a challenge. In this chapter, I discuss the key concepts that you need to understand in order to write VBA code that generates or manipulates charts. The secret, as you'll see, is a good understanding of the object hierarchy for charts. First, a bit of background about Excel charts.

Chart locations

In Excel, a chart can be located in either of two places within a workbook:

◆ *As an embedded object on a worksheet:* A worksheet can contain any number of embedded charts.

◆ *In a separate chart sheet:* A chart sheet holds a single chart.

> As I discuss later in this chapter, you can also store embedded charts on a chart sheet. See "Storing multiple charts on a chart sheet."

Most charts are created manually, by using the Chart Wizard. But you can also create charts by using VBA. And, of course, you can use VBA to modify existing charts.

> The fastest way to create a chart on a new sheet is to select your data and then press F11. Excel creates a new chart sheet and uses the default chart type.

A key concept when working with charts is the *active chart* — that is, the chart that's currently selected. When the user clicks an embedded chart or activates a chart sheet, a Chart object is activated. In VBA, the ActiveChart property returns the activated Chart object (if any). You can write code to work with this Chart object, much like you can write code to work with the Workbook object returned by the ActiveWorkbook property.

Here's an example: If a chart is activated, the following statement will display the Name property for the Chart object:

```
MsgBox ActiveChart.Name
```

If a chart is not activated, the preceding statement generates an error.

> As you'll see later in this chapter, it's not necessary to activate a chart in order to manipulate it with VBA.

The Chart object model

To get a feel for the number of objects involved when working with charts, turn on the macro recorder, create a chart, and perform some routine chart-editing tasks. You might be surprised by the amount of code that Excel generates. When you first start exploring the object model for a Chart object, you'll probably be very confused . . . which is not surprising because the object model *is* very confusing. It's also very deep.

For example, assume that you want to change the title displayed in an embedded chart. The top-level object, of course, is the Application object (Excel). The Application object contains a Workbook object, and the Workbook object contains a Worksheet object. The Worksheet object contains a ChartObject object, which contains a Chart object. The Chart object has a ChartTitle object, and the ChartTitle object has a Text property which stores the text that's displayed as the chart's title.

Here's another way to look at this hierarchy for an embedded chart:

Application
  Workbook
   Worksheet
    ChartObject
    Chart
     ChartTitle

Your VBA code must, of course, follow this object model precisely. For example, to set a chart's title to YTD Sales, you can write a VBA instruction like this:

```
WorkSheets("Sheet1").ChartObjects(1).Chart.ChartTitle. _
  .Text = "YTD Sales"
```

This statement assumes the active workbook as the Workbook object. The statement works with the first item in the ChartObjects collection on the worksheet named Sheet1. The Chart property returns the actual Chart object, and the ChartTitle property returns the ChartTitle object. Finally, you get to the Text property.

For a chart sheet, the object hierarchy is a bit different because it doesn't involve the Worksheet object or the ChartObject object. For example, here's the hierarchy for the ChartTitle object for a chart in a chart sheet:

Application
  Workbook
  Chart
   ChartTitle

In terms of VBA, you could use this statement to set the chart title to YTD Sales.

```
Sheets("Chart1").ChartTitle.Text = "YTD Sales"
```

In other words, a chart sheet is actually a `Chart` object, and it has no containing `ChartObject` object. Put another way, the parent object for an embedded chart is a `ChartObject` object, and the parent object for a chart on a separate chart sheet is a `Workbook` object.

Both of the following statements will display a message box with the word `Chart` in it:

```
MsgBox TypeName(Sheets("Sheet1").ChartObjects(1).Chart)
```

```
Msgbox TypeName(Sheets("Chart1"))
```

 When you create a new embedded chart, you're adding to the `ChartObjects` collection contained in a particular worksheet. (There is no `Charts` collection for a worksheet.) When you create a new chart sheet, you're adding to the `Charts` collection and the `Sheets` collection for a particular workbook.

Recording Chart Macros

Perhaps the best way to become familiar with the `Chart` object model is to turn on the macro recorder while you create and manipulate charts. Even though the macro recorder tends to generate lots of extraneous and inefficient code, the recorded code will still give you insights regarding the objects, properties, and methods that you need to know.

Excel's macro recorder always activates a chart and then uses the `ActiveChart` property to return the actual `Chart` object. In Excel, it's not necessary to select an object (or activate a chart) in order to work with it in VBA. And, as I mention, the macro recorder generates lots of extraneous code. Therefore, if efficiency is among your goals, you should *never* actually use unedited recorded macros, especially those that manipulate charts.

Chart creation macro recorder output

I turned on the macro recorder while I created a chart (shown in Figure 18-1) and then performed some simple customizations to it. The chart uses the data in range A1:F2.

Following in Listing 18-1 is the code generated by the macro recorder:

Listing 18-1: Code Generated by the Macro Recorder

```
Sub Macro1()
    Range("A1:F2").Select
    Charts.Add
```

```
     ActiveChart.ChartType = xlColumnClustered
     ActiveChart.SetSourceData _
        Source:=Sheets("Sheet1").Range("A1:F2"), _
        PlotBy:=xlRows
     ActiveChart.Location _
        Where:=xlLocationAsObject, _
        Name:="Sheet1"
     ActiveChart.HasLegend = False
     ActiveChart.ApplyDataLabels _
        Type:=xlDataLabelsShowValue, LegendKey:=False
     ActiveChart.HasDataTable = False
     ActiveChart.Axes(xlCategory).Select
     Selection.TickLabels.Orientation = xlHorizontal
     ActiveChart.ChartTitle.Select
     Selection.Font.Bold = True
     Selection.AutoScaleFont = True
     With Selection.Font
         .Name = "Arial"
         .Size = 12
         .Strikethrough = False
         .Superscript = False
         .Subscript = False
         .OutlineFont = False
         .Shadow = False
         .Underline = xlUnderlineStyleNone
         .ColorIndex = xlAutomatic
         .Background = xlAutomatic
     End With
     ActiveChart.PlotArea.Select
     Selection.Top = 18
     Selection.Height = 162
     ActiveChart.ChartArea.Select
     ActiveChart.Axes(xlValue).Select
     With ActiveChart.Axes(xlValue)
         .MinimumScaleIsAuto = True
         .MaximumScale = 0.6
         .MinorUnitIsAuto = True
         .MajorUnitIsAuto = True
         .Crosses = xlAutomatic
         .ReversePlotOrder = False
         .ScaleType = xlLinear
     End With
  End Sub
```

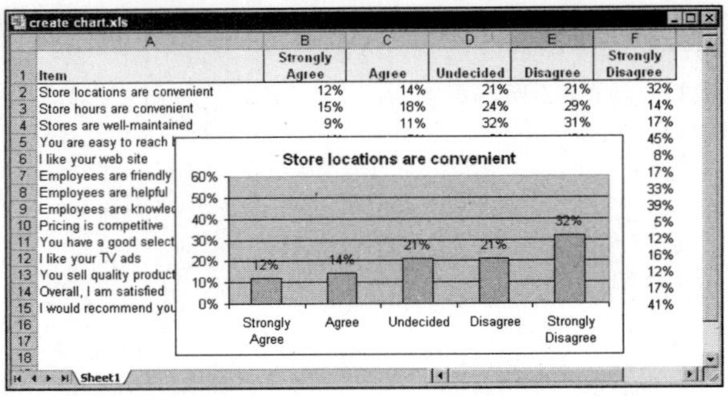

Figure 18-1: This chart was created while Excel's macro recorder was turned on.

Cleaning up the chart creation macro recorder output

Much of the code generated for the macro in the previous section is not necessary; it sets values for properties that really don't need to be set. Following is the listing for my edited macro. This performs exactly like the macro in the previous section, but it's significantly shorter and more efficient. Setting the ScreenUpdating property to False eliminates the screen refreshing.

```
Sub CleanedMacro()
    Application.ScreenUpdating = False
    Charts.Add
    ActiveChart.Location _
      Where:=xlLocationAsObject, Name:="Sheet1"
    With ActiveChart
        .SetSourceData Range("A1:F2")
        .HasTitle = True
        .ChartType = xlColumnClustered
        .HasLegend = False
        .ApplyDataLabels Type:=xlDataLabelsShowValue
        .Axes(xlCategory).TickLabels.Orientation = xlHorizontal
        .ChartTitle.Font.Bold = True
        .ChartTitle.Font.Size = 12
        .PlotArea.Top = 18
        .PlotArea.Height = 162
        .Axes(xlValue).MaximumScale = 0.6
        .Deselect
    End With
    Application.ScreenUpdating = True
End Sub
```

When you create a chart with the Add method of the Charts collection, the created chart is always a chart sheet. In the preceding code, the Location method moves the chart to a worksheet.

A workbook that contains both the recorded macro and the cleaned-up macro is included on the companion CD-ROM, so you can compare the performance.

Common VBA Charting Techniques

In this section, I describe how to perform some common tasks that involve charts.

Using VBA to activate a chart

When a user clicks on an embedded chart, the chart is activated. Your VBA code can activate an embedded chart with the Activate method. Here's an example:

```
ActiveSheet.ChartObjects("Chart 1").Activate
```

If the chart is on a chart sheet, use a statement like this:

```
Sheets("Chart1").Activate
```

After a chart is activated, you can refer to it in your code with ActiveChart. For example, the following instruction displays the name of the active chart. If there is no active chart, the statement generates an error:

```
MsgBox ActiveChart.Name
```

To modify a chart with VBA, it's not necessary to activate it. The two procedures that follow have exactly the same effect: That is, they change the embedded chart named Chart 1 to an area chart. The first procedure activates the chart before performing the manipulations; the second one doesn't.

```
Sub ModifyChart1()
    ActiveSheet.ChartObjects("Chart 1").Activate
    ActiveChart.Type = xlArea
    ActiveChart.Deselect

End Sub
```

```
Sub ModifyChart2()
    ActiveSheet.ChartObjects("Chart 1").Chart.Type = xlArea
End Sub
```

A chart embedded on a worksheet can easily be converted to a chart sheet. To do so manually, just activate the embedded chart and choose Chart → Location. In the Chart Location dialog box, select the As New Sheet option and specify a name. This action essentially copies the Chart object (contained in a ChartObject object) to a chart sheet and then destroys its containing ChartObject object.

You can also convert an embedded chart to a chart sheet with VBA. Here's an example that converts the first ChartObject on a worksheet named Sheet1 to a chart sheet named MyChart:

```
Sub ConvertChart1()
    Sheets("Sheet1").ChartObjects(1).Chart. _
        Location xlLocationAsNewSheet, "MyChart"
End Sub
```

The following example does just the opposite of the preceding procedure: It converts the chart on a chart sheet named MyChart to an embedded chart on the worksheet named Sheet1.

```
Sub ConvertChart2()
    Charts("MyChart") _
        .Location xlLocationAsObject, "Sheet1"
End Sub
```

Using the Location method also activates the relocated chart.

When you activate a chart contained in a ChartObject, the chart is actually contained in a window that is normally invisible. To see an embedded chart in its own window, right-click the ChartObject and select Chart Window from the shortcut menu. The embedded chart will remain on the worksheet, but the chart will also appear in its own floating window (see Figure 18-2). You can move and resize this window, but you can't maximize it. If you move the window, you'll notice that the embedded chart is still displayed in its original location. Activating any other window makes the ChartObject window invisible again.

The following VBA code displays the window for the first ChartObject on the active sheet:

```
ActiveSheet.ChartObjects(1).Activate
ActiveChart.ShowWindow = True
```

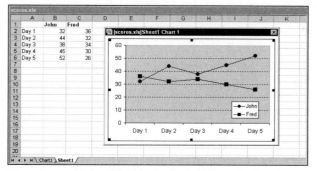

Figure 18-2: Displaying an embedded chart in a window.

 For a practical application of using a window to display an embedded chart, see "Printing embedded charts on a full page," later in this chapter.

Using VBA to deactivate a chart

When you record a macro that deactivates a chart, you'll find that the macro recorder generates a statement such as this:

```
ActiveWindow.Visible = False
```

This statement does indeed deactivate the chart, but it is certainly not very clear as to why the chart is deactivated. When writing macros that work with charts, you might prefer to use the Deselet method to deactivate a chart:

```
ActiveChart.Deselect
```

These two statements have slightly different effects. When an embedded chart is the active chart, executing Deselect method does not select any cells on the worksheet. Setting the Visible property of the ActiveWindow object to False, however, causes the previously selected range to be reselected.

Determining whether a chart is activated

A common type of macro performs some manipulations on the active chart (the chart selected by a user). For example, a macro might change the chart's type, apply colors, or change the font size.

The question is, how can your VBA code determine whether the user has actually selected a chart? By selecting a chart, I mean either activating a chart sheet or activating an embedded chart by clicking it. Your first inclination might be to check the TypeName property of the Selection, as in this expression:

```
TypeName(Selection) = "Chart"
```

This expression above evaluates to True if a chart sheet is active, but it *won't* be True if an embedded *chart* is selected. Rather, when an embedded chart is selected, the actual selection will be an object within the Chart object. For example, the selection might be a Series object, a ChartTitle object, a Legend object, a PlotArea object, and so on.

The solution is to determine whether ActiveChart is Nothing. The ChartIsSelected function, which follows, returns True if a chart sheet is active or if an embedded chart is activated but returns False if a chart is not activated:

```
Private Function ChartIsSelected() As Boolean
    ChartIsSelected = Not ActiveChart Is Nothing
End Function
```

This function determines whether the ActiveChart object is Nothing. If so, a chart is not activated.

Deleting from the ChartObjects or Charts collection

To delete all ChartObject objects on a worksheet, you can simply use the Delete method of the ChartObjects collection:

```
ActiveSheet.ChartObjects.Delete
```

To delete all chart sheets in the active workbook, use the following statement:

```
ActiveWorkbook.Charts.Delete
```

Normally, deleting sheets causes Excel to display a warning like the one shown in Figure 18-3. The user must reply to this prompt in order for the macro to continue. If you are deleting a sheet with a macro, you probably won't want this warning prompt to display. To eliminate the prompt, use the following series of statements:

```
Application.DisplayAlerts = False
ActiveWorkbook.Charts.Delete
Application.DisplayAlerts = True
```

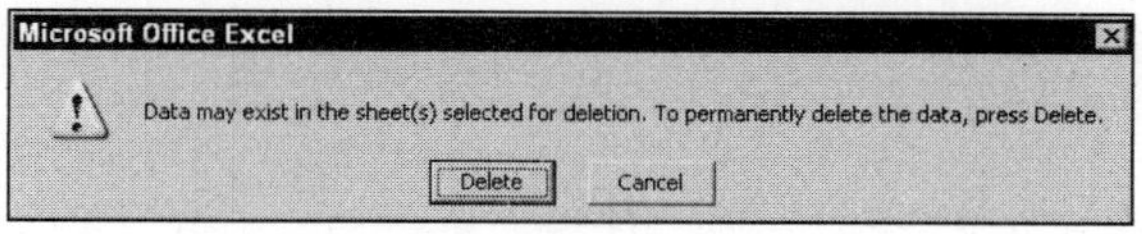

Microsoft Office Excel	✕

⚠ Data may exist in the sheet(s) selected for deletion. To permanently delete the data, press Delete.

[Delete]   Cancel

Figure 18-3: Attempting to delete one or more chart sheets results in this message.

Using VBA to apply chart formatting

A common type of chart macro applies formatting to a chart. The following example applies several different types of formatting to the active chart:

```
Sub ChartMods1()
    If ActiveChart Is Nothing Then
        MsgBox "Select a chart."
        Exit Sub
    End If
    With ActiveChart
        .Type = xlArea
        .ChartArea.Font.Name = "Arial"
        .ChartArea.Font.FontStyle = "Regular"
        .ChartArea.Font.Size = 9
        .PlotArea.Interior.ColorIndex = xlNone
        .Axes(xlValue).TickLabels.Font.Bold = True
        .Axes(xlCategory).TickLabels.Font.Bold = True
        If .HasLegend = True Then .Legend.Position = xlBottom
    End With
End Sub
```

The procedure starts by ensuring that a chart is selected. If not, a message appears, and the procedure ends. Also, notice the use of an `If` statement to determine whether the chart has a legend. This is to avoid an error that would occur when trying to set the `Position` property of the `Legend` object if the chart had no legend.

ON THE CD   A workbook with this example is available on the companion CD-ROM.

Following is another version of the `ChartMods` procedure. In this case, it works on a specific chart: the one contained in a `ChartObject` named `Chart 1`, located on `Sheet1`. Notice that the chart is never activated.

```
Sub ChartMods2()
    With Sheets("Sheet1").ChartObjects("Chart 1").Chart
        .Type = xlArea
        .ChartArea.Font.Name = "Arial"
        .ChartArea.Font.FontStyle = "Regular"
        .ChartArea.Font.Size = 9
        .PlotArea.Interior.ColorIndex = xlNone
        .Axes(xlValue).TickLabels.Font.Bold = True
        .Axes(xlCategory).TickLabels.Font.Bold = True
        If .HasLegend = True Then .Legend.Position = xlBottom
    End With
End Sub
```

Looping through all charts

In some cases, you may need to perform an operation on all charts. This example changes the chart type of every embedded chart on the active sheet. The procedure uses a For-Next loop to cycle through each object in the ChartObjects collection, and then accesses the Chart object in each and changes its ChartType property. An Area chart is specified by using the predefined constant xlArea. Consult the online help for other chart type constants.

```
Sub ChangeChartType()
    Dim chtobj as ChartObject
    For Each chtobj In ActiveSheet.ChartObjects
        chtobj.Chart.ChartType = xlArea
    Next chtobj
End Sub
```

The following macro performs the same operation as the preceding procedure but works on all the chart sheets in the active workbook:

```
Sub ChangeChartType2()
    Dim cht as Chart
    For Each cht In ActiveWorkbook.Charts
        cht.ChartType = xlArea
    Next cht
End Sub
```

The following example changes the legend font for all charts on the active sheet. It uses a For-Next loop to process all ChartObject objects:

```
Sub LegendMod()
    Dim chtobj as ChartObject
    For Each chtobj In ActiveSheet.ChartObjects
```

```
        With chtobj.Chart.Legend.Font
            .Name = "Arial"
            .FontStyle = "Bold"
            .Size = 12
        End With
    Next chtobj
End Sub
```

Sizing and aligning ChartObjects

A ChartObject object has standard positional and sizing properties that you can access with your VBA code. The following example resizes all ChartObject objects on a sheet so that they match the dimensions of the active chart. It also arranges the ChartObject objects so that they appear one after the other along the left side of the worksheet.

```
Sub SizeAndAlignCharts()
    Dim W As Long, H As Long
    Dim TopPosition As Long, LeftPosition As Long
    Dim ChtObj As ChartObject
    If ActiveChart Is Nothing Then Exit Sub
    'Get size of active chart
    W = ActiveChart.Parent.Width
    H = ActiveChart.Parent.Height
    TopPosition = 1
    LeftPosition = 1
    For Each ChtObj In ActiveSheet.ChartObjects
        ChtObj.Width = W
        ChtObj.Height = H
        ChtObj.Top = TopPosition
        ChtObj.Left = LeftPosition
        TopPosition = TopPosition + ChtObj.Height
    Next ChtObj
End Sub
```

The TopPosition variable keeps track of the vertical location for the next chart. Each time through the loop, this variable is incremented by the value of H (which is the height of each ChartObject).

This workbook is available on the companion CD-ROM.

Working with Pivot Charts

Excel 2000 introduced a new facet to charting: pivot charts. This handy feature lets you create a dynamic chart that's attached to a pivot table. The pivot chart displays the current layout of the pivot table graphically. When you create a pivot table, you have an option of creating either a pivot table alone or a pivot chart that also includes an associated pivot table. To create a pivot chart from an existing pivot table, activate the pivot table and click the Chart Wizard button. The chart is created on a new chart sheet. By default, a new pivot chart always appears on a chart sheet (see the accompanying figure). However, you can choose the Chart → Location command to convert it to an embedded chart.

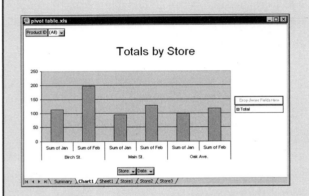

When Microsoft adds a new feature to Excel, it also needs to augment Excel's object model so that the new feature is exposed and can be controlled by VBA. In the case of pivot charts, you'll find a `PivotLayout` object, located in the `Chart` object. The best way to become familiar with this object is to record your actions while you modify a pivot chart and then examine the code produced. Then you can learn more about the objects, properties, and methods by consulting the online help.

More Charting Examples

In this section, I describe some additional charting techniques. I discuss two examples that demonstrate how to use VBA to change the data used by a chart.

Using names in a SERIES formula

As you probably know, a chart can consist of any number of series, and the data used by each series is determined by the range references in its SERIES formula. For more about this topic, see the sidebar, "Understanding a Chart's SERIES Formula."

In some cases, using range names in the SERIES formulas in a chart can greatly simplify things if you need to change the chart's source data using VBA. For example, consider the following SERIES formula:

```
=SERIES(,Sheet1!$A$1:$A$6,Sheet1!$B$1:$B$6,1)
```

You can define range names for the two ranges (for example, `Categories` and `Data`) and then edit the SERIES formula so that it uses the range names instead of the range references. The edited formula would be

```
=SERIES(,Sheet1!Categories,Sheet1!Data,1)
```

After you define the names and edit the SERIES formula, your VBA code can work with the names, and the changes will be reflected in the chart. For example, the following statement redefines the refers-to range as `Data`:

```
Range("B1:B12").Name = "Data"
```

After executing this statement, the chart will update itself and use the new definition of `Data`.

The `Resize` method of the `Range` object is useful for resizing a named range. For example, the following code expands the range named `Data` to include one additional row:

```
With Range("Data")
    .Resize(.Rows.Count + 1, 1).Name = "Data"
End With
```

A new feature in Excel 2003 makes it easier to work with charts that use an expanding range. The trick is to designate your data range as a list by choosing the Data → List → Create List command. After doing so, you can add new data to the bottom of the list, and your chart will update automatically to include the new data.

Understanding a Chart's SERIES Formula

The data used in each series in a chart is determined by its SERIES formula. When you select a data series in a chart, the SERIES formula appears in the formula bar. This is not a real formula: In other words, you can't use it in a cell, and you can't use worksheet functions within the SERIES formula. You can, however, edit the arguments in the SERIES formula.

A SERIES formula has the following syntax:

```
=SERIES(series_name, category_labels, values, order, sizes)
```

The arguments that you can use in the SERIES formula include

- ◆ `series_name`: (Optional) A reference to the cell that contains the series name used in the legend. If the chart has only one series, the name argument is used as the title. This argument can also consist of text in quotation marks. If omitted, Excel creates a default series name (for example, Series 1).

- ◆ `category_labels`: (Optional) A reference to the range that contains the labels for the category axis. If omitted, Excel uses consecutive integers beginning with 1. For XY charts, this argument specifies the X values. A non-contiguous range reference is also valid. The ranges' addresses are separated by a comma and enclosed in parentheses. The argument could also consist of an array of comma-separated values (or text in quotation marks) enclosed in curly brackets.

- ◆ `values`: (Required) A reference to the range that contains the values for the series. For XY charts, this argument specifies the Y values. A noncontiguous range reference is also valid. The ranges addresses are separated by a comma and enclosed in parentheses. The argument could also consist of an array of comma-separated values enclosed in curly brackets.

- ◆ `order`: (Required) An integer that specifies the plotting order of the series. This argument is relevant only if the chart has more than one series. Using a reference to a cell is not allowed.

- ◆ `sizes`: (Only for bubble charts) A reference to the range that contains the values for the size of the bubbles in a bubble chart. A noncontiguous range reference is also valid. The ranges addresses are separated by a comma and enclosed in parentheses. The argument could also consist of an array of values enclosed in curly brackets.

Range references in a SERIES formula are always absolute, and they always include the sheet name. For example:

```
=SERIES(Sheet1!$B$1,,Sheet1!$B$2:$B$7,1)
```

A range reference can consist of a noncontiguous range. If so, each range is separated by a comma, and the argument is enclosed in parentheses. In the following SERIES formula, the values range consists of B2:B3 and B5:B7:

```
=SERIES(,,(Sheet1!$B$2:$B$3,Sheet1!$B$5:$B$7),1)
```

You can substitute range names for the range references. If you do so, Excel changes the reference in the SERIES formula to include the workbook. For example:

```
=SERIES(Sheet1!$B$1,,budget.xls!MyData,1)
```

Using VBA to specify the data used by a chart

The examples in this section describe VBA techniques that enable you to change the data used by a chart.

CHANGING CHART DATA BASED ON THE ACTIVE CELL

Figure 18-4 displays a chart based on the data in the row of the active cell. When the user moves the cell pointer, the chart is updated automatically.

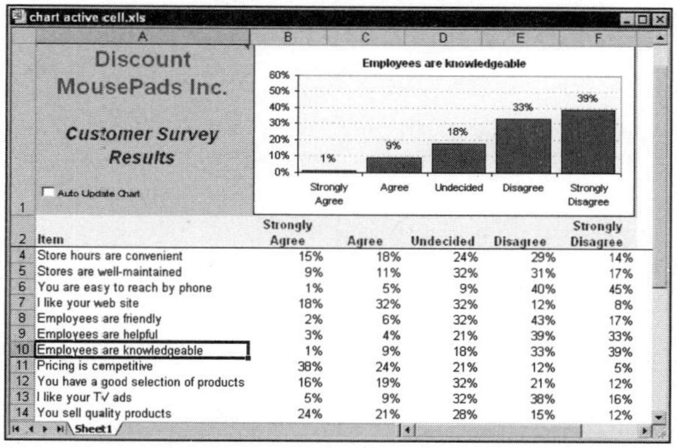

Figure 18-4: This chart always displays the data from the row of the active cell.

This example uses an event handler for the Worksheet object. The SelectionChange event occurs whenever the user changes the selection by moving the cell pointer. The event handler procedure for this event (which is located in the code module for the Sheet1 object) is as follows:

```
Private Sub Worksheet_SelectionChange(ByVal Target _
 As Excel.Range)
    Call UpdateChart
End Sub
```

In other words, every time that the user moves the cell cursor, the Worksheet_ SelectionChange procedure is executed. This procedure calls the UpdateChart procedure, which follows:

```
Sub UpdateChart()
    Dim TheChartObj As ChartObject
    Dim TheChart As Chart
    Dim UserRow As Long
    Dim CatTitles As Range
    Dim SrcRange As Range
    Dim SourceData As Range
    If Sheets("Sheet1").CheckBox1 Then
        Set TheChartObj = ActiveSheet.ChartObjects(1)
        Set TheChart = TheChartObj.Chart
        UserRow = ActiveCell.Row
        If UserRow < 3 Or IsEmpty(Cells(UserRow, 1)) Then
            TheChartObj.Visible = False
        Else
            Set CatTitles = Range("A2:F2")
            Set SrcRange = Range(Cells(UserRow, 1), _
             Cells(UserRow, 6))
            Set SourceData = Union(CatTitles, SrcRange)
            TheChart.SetSourceData _
              Source:=SourceData, PlotBy:=xlRows
            TheChartObj.Visible = True
        End If
    End If
End Sub
```

The first step is to determine whether the Auto Update Chart check box is marked. If this check box is not selected, nothing happens. The UserRow variable contains the row number of the active cell. The If statement checks to make sure that the active cell is in a row that contains data. (The data starts in row 3.) If the cell cursor is in a row that doesn't have data, the ChartObject object is hidden. Otherwise, the code creates a Range object (CatTitle) that holds the category titles and another Range object (SrcRange) that contains the data for the row. These two Range objects are joined by using the VBA Union function and assigned to a Range object named SourceData. Finally, the SourceData range is assigned to the chart by using the SetSourceData method of the Chart object.

CHANGING CHART DATA BY USING A COMBOBOX

The next example uses a `ComboBox` control on a chart sheet to allow the user to select a chart. Figure 18-5 shows how this looks:

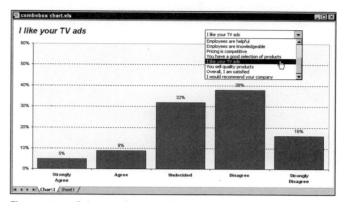

Figure 18-5: Selecting from the ComboBox changes the source data for the chart.

 The ComboBox used in this example is from the Forms toolbar (not the Control Toolbox toolbar). For some reason, Excel does not let you add ActiveX controls to a chart sheet.

 This workbook is available on the companion CD-ROM.

A macro named `DropDown1_Change` is attached to the ComboBox. When the user makes a selection from the ComboBox, the following procedure is executed:

```
Sub DropDown1_Change()
    Dim ListIndex As Integer
    ListIndex = ActiveChart.DropDowns(1).Value
    Call UpdateChart(ListIndex)
End Sub
```

This procedure calls the `UpdateChart` procedure and passes an integer that represents the user's choice. Following is the listing of the `UpdateChart` procedure. This is very similar to the `UpdateChart` procedure in the preceding section.

```
Sub UpdateChart(Item)
'   Updates the chart using the selected dropdown item
    Dim TheChart As Chart
    Dim DataSheet As Worksheet
    Dim CatTitles As Range, SrcRange As Range
    Dim SourceData As Range

    Set TheChart = Sheets("Chart1")
    Set DataSheet = Sheets("Sheet1")

    With DataSheet
        Set CatTitles = .Range("A1:F1")
        Set SrcRange = .Range(.Cells(Item + 2, 1), _
            .Cells(Item + 2, 6))
    End With
    Set SourceData = Union(CatTitles, SrcRange)

    With TheChart
        .SetSourceData Source:=SourceData, PlotBy:=xlRows
        .ChartTitle.Left = TheChart.ChartArea.Left
        .Deselect
    End With
End Sub
```

Using VBA to determine the ranges used in a chart

You might need a VBA macro that must determine the ranges used by each series in chart. For example, you might want to increase the size of each series by adding a new cell. Following is a description of three properties that seem relevant to this task:

◆ `Formula` property: Returns or sets the SERIES formula for the `Series`. When you select a series in a chart, its SERIES formula is displayed in the formula bar. The `Formula` property returns this formula as a string.

◆ `Values` property: Returns or sets a collection of all the values in the series. This can be a range on a worksheet or an array of constant values but not a combination of both.

◆ `XValues` property: Returns or sets an array of X values for a chart series. The `XValues` property can be set to a range on a worksheet or to an array of values, but it can't be a combination of both. The `Xvalues` property can also be empty.

If you create a VBA macro that needs to determine the data range used by a particular chart series, you might think that the `Values` property of the `Series` object is just the ticket. Similarly, the XValues property seems to be the way to get the range that contains the X values (or category labels). In theory, that certainly *seems* correct. But in practice, it doesn't work. When you set the Values property for a Series object, you can specify a Range object or an array. But when you read this property, it is always an array. Unfortunately, the object model provides no way to get a Range object used by a Series object.

One possible solution is to write code to parse the SERIES formula and extract the range addresses. This sounds simple, but it's actually a difficult task because a SERIES formula can be very complex. Following are a few examples of valid SERIES formulas.

```
=SERIES(Sheet1!$B$1,Sheet1!$A$2:$A$4,Sheet1!$B$2:$B$4,1)
=SERIES(,,Sheet1!$B$2:$B$4,1)
=SERIES(,Sheet1!$A$2:$A$4,Sheet1!$B$2:$B$4,1)
=SERIES("Sales Summary",,Sheet1!$B$2:$B$4,1)
=SERIES(,{"Jan","Feb","Mar"},Sheet1!$B$2:$B$4,1)
=SERIES(,(Sheet1!$A$2,Sheet1!$A$4),(Sheet1!$B$2,Sheet1!$B$4),1)
=SERIES(Sheet1!$B$1,Sheet1!$A$2:$A$4,Sheet1!$B$2:$B$4,1,Sheet1!$C$2:$C$4)
```

As you can see, a SERIES formula can have missing arguments, use arrays, and even use noncontiguous range addresses. And to confuse the issue even more, a bubble chart has an additional argument (for example, the last SERIES formula in the preceding list). Attempting to parse out the arguments is certainly not a trivial programming task

I worked on this problem for several years, and I eventually arrived at a solution. The trick involves evaluating the SERIES formula by using a dummy function. This function accepts the arguments in a SERIES formula and returns a 2 x 5 element array that contains all the information in the SERIES formula.

I simplified the solution by creating four custom VBA functions, each of which accepts one argument (a reference to a Series object) and returns a two-element array. These functions are the following:

◆ SERIESNAME_FROM_SERIES: The first array element contains a string that describes the data type of the first SERIES argument (Range, Empty, or String). The second array element contains a range address, an empty string, or a string.

◆ XVALUES_FROM_SERIES: The first array element contains a string that describes the data type of the second SERIES argument (Range, Array, Empty, or String). The second array element contains a range address, an array, an empty string, or a string.

◆ VALUES_FROM_SERIES: The first array element contains a string that describes the data type of the third SERIES argument (Range or Array). The second array element contains a range address or an array.

◆ BUBBLESIZE_FROM_SERIES: The first array element contains a string that describes the data type of the fifth SERIES argument (Range, Array, or Empty). The second array element contains a range address, an array, or an empty string. This function is relevant only for bubble charts.

Note that there is not a function to get the fourth SERIES argument (plot order). This argument can be obtained directly by using the PlotOrder property of the Series object.

The VBA code for these functions is too lengthy to be listed here, but it's available on the companion CD-ROM. It's documented in such a way that it can be easily adapted to other situations.

The following example demonstrates: It displays the address of the values range for the first series in the active chart.

```
Sub ShowValueRange()
    Dim Ser As Series
    Dim x As Variant
    Set Ser = ActiveChart.SeriesCollection(1)
    x = VALUES_FROM_SERIES(Ser)
    If x(1) = "Range" Then
        MsgBox Range(x(2)).Address
    End If
End Sub
```

The variable x is defined as a variant and will hold the two-element array that's returned by the VALUES_FROM_SERIES function. The first element of the x array contains a string that describes the data type. It the string is Range, the message box displays the address of the range contained in the second element of the x array.

Figure 18-6 shows another example. The chart has three data series. Buttons on the sheet execute macros that expand and contract each of the data ranges.

The ContractAllSeries procedure is listed below. This procedure loops through the SeriesCollection collection and uses the XVALUE_FROM_SERIES and VALUES_FROM_SERIES functions to retrieve the current ranges. It then uses the Resize method to decrease the size of the ranges.

```
Sub ContractAllSeries()
    Dim s As Series
    Dim Result As Variant
```

```
    Dim DRange As Range
    For Each s In
ActiveSheet.ChartObjects(1).Chart.SeriesCollection
        Result = XVALUES_FROM_SERIES(s)
        If Result(1) = "Range" Then
            Set DRange = Range(Result(2))
            If DRange.Rows.Count > 1 Then
                Set DRange = DRange.Resize(DRange.Rows.Count - 1)
                s.XValues = DRange
            End If
        End If
        Result = VALUES_FROM_SERIES(s)
        If Result(1) = "Range" Then
            Set DRange = Range(Result(2))
            If DRange.Rows.Count > 1 Then
                Set DRange = DRange.Resize(DRange.Rows.Count - 1)
                s.Values = DRange
            End If
        End If
    Next s
End Sub
```

The ExpandAllSeries procedure is very similar. When executed, it expands each range by one cell.

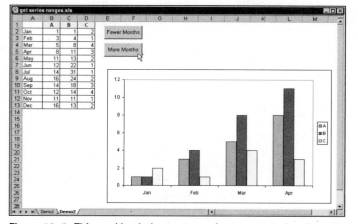

Figure 18-6: This workbook demonstrates how to expand and contract the chart series by using VBA macros.

Using VBA to display arbitrary data labels on a chart

One of the most frequent complaints about Excel's charting is its inflexible data labeling feature. For example, consider the XY chart in Figure 18-7. It might be useful to display the associated name for each data point. However, you can search all day, and you'll never find the Excel command that lets you do this automatically. (*Hint:* Such a command doesn't exist.) Data labels are limited to the values only . . . unless you want to edit each data label manually and replace it with text of your choice.

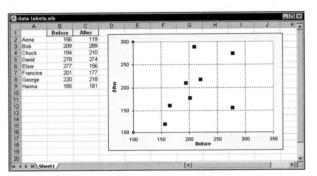

Figure 18-7: An XY chart with no data labels.

Listing 18-2 presents a simple procedure that works with the first chart on the active sheet. It prompts the user for a range and then loops through the Points collection and changes the Text property to the values found in the range.

Listing 18-2: Retrieving Data Point Labels from Field Names in The Worksheet

```
Sub DataLabelsFromRange()
    Dim DLRange As Range
    Dim Cht As Chart
    Dim i As Integer

'   Specify chart
    Set Cht = ActiveSheet.ChartObjects(1).Chart

'   Prompt for a range
    On Error Resume Next
    Set DLRange = Application.InputBox _
      (prompt:="Range for data labels?", Type:=8)
    If DLRange Is Nothing Then Exit Sub
    On Error GoTo 0
```

```
'    Add data labels
     Cht.SeriesCollection(1).ApplyDataLabels _
       Type:=xlDataLabelsShowValue, _
       AutoText:=True, _
       LegendKey:=False

'    Loop through the Points, and set the data labels
     Pts = Cht.SeriesCollection(1).Points.Count
     For i = 1 To Pts
         Cht.SeriesCollection(1). _
           Points(i).DataLabel.Text = DLRange(i)
     Next i
End Sub
```

This example is available on the companion CD-ROM.

Figure 18-8 shows the chart after running the `DataLabelsFromRange` procedure and specifying A2:A9 as the data range.

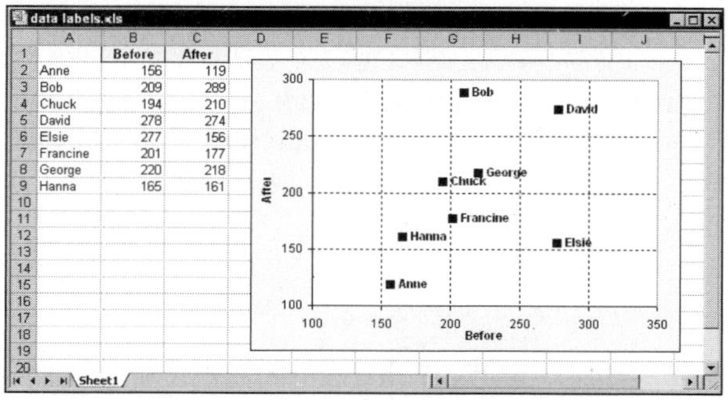

	A	B	C
1		Before	After
2	Anne	156	119
3	Bob	209	289
4	Chuck	194	210
5	David	278	274
6	Elsie	277	156
7	Francine	201	177
8	George	220	218
9	Hanna	165	161

Figure 18-8: This XY chart has data labels, thanks to a VBA procedure.

The preceding procedure is rather crude and does very little error checking. In addition, it only works with the first `Series` object. The Power Utility Pak (which you can obtain by using the coupon in the back of the book) includes a much more sophisticated chart data-labeling utility.

Displaying a chart in a UserForm

In Chapter 15, I describe a way to display a chart in a UserForm. The technique saves the chart as a GIF file and then loads the GIF file into an Image control on the UserForm.

The example in this section uses that same technique but adds a new twist: The chart is created on the fly and uses the data in the row of the active cell. Figure 18-9 shows an example.

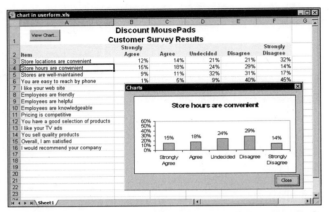

Figure 18-9: The chart in this UserForm is created on-the-fly from the data in the active row.

The UserForm for this example is very simple. It contains an Image control and a CommandButton (Close). The worksheet that contains the data has a button that executes the following procedure:

```
Sub ShowChart()
    Dim UserRow As Long
    UserRow = ActiveCell.Row
    If UserRow < 2 Or IsEmpty(Cells(UserRow, 1)) Then
        MsgBox _
         "Move the cell cursor to a row that contains data."
        Exit Sub
    End If
    CreateChart UserRow
    UserForm1.Show
End Sub
```

Because the chart is based on the data in the row of the active cell, the procedure warns the user if the cell cursor is in an invalid row. If the active cell is appropriate, ShowChart calls the CreateChart procedure to create the chart and then displays the UserForm.

The CreateChart procedure shown in Listing 18-3 accepts one argument, which represents the row of the active cell. This procedure originated from a macro recording that I cleaned up to make more general.

Listing 18-3: Automatically Generating a Chart without User Interaction

```
Sub CreateChart(r)
    Dim TempChart As Chart
    Dim CatTitles As Range
    Dim SrcRange As Range, SourceData As Range

    Application.ScreenUpdating = False

    Set CatTitles = ActiveSheet.Range("A2:F2")
    Set SrcRange = ActiveSheet.Range(Cells(r, 1), Cells(r, 6))
    Set SourceData = Union(CatTitles, SrcRange)

'   Add a chart
    Set TempChart = Charts.Add

'   Fix it up
    With TempChart
        .ChartType = xlColumnClustered
        .SetSourceData Source:=SourceData, PlotBy:=xlRows
        .HasLegend = False
        .PlotArea.Interior.ColorIndex = xlNone
        .Axes(xlValue).MajorGridlines.Delete
        .ApplyDataLabels Type:=xlDataLabelsShowValue, _
         LegendKey:=False
        .ChartTitle.Font.Size = 14
        .ChartTitle.Font.Bold = True
        .Axes(xlValue).MaximumScale = 0.6
        .Axes(xlCategory).TickLabels.Font.Size = 10
        .Axes(xlCategory).TickLabels.Orientation = _
         xlHorizontal
        .Location Where:=xlLocationAsObject, Name:="Sheet1"
    Enc With

'   Adjust the ChartObject's size
    With ActiveSheet.ChartObjects(1)
        .Width = 300
```

Continued

Listing 18-3 *(Continued)*

```
        .Height = 150
        .Visible = False
    End With
End Sub
```

When the `CreateChart` procedure ends, the worksheet contains a `ChartObject` with a chart of the data in the row of the active cell. However, the `ChartObject` is not visible because `ScreenUpdating` was turned off and its `Visible` property was set to `False`.

The final instruction of the `ShowChart` procedure loads the UserForm. Following is a listing of the `UserForm_Initialize` procedure. This procedure saves the chart as a GIF file, deletes the `ChartObject`, and loads the GIF file into the `Image` control.

```
Private Sub UserForm_Initialize()
    Dim CurrentChart As Chart
    Dim Fname As String

    Set CurrentChart = ActiveSheet.ChartObjects(1).Chart

'   Save chart as GIF
    Fname = ThisWorkbook.Path & Application.PathSeparator _
     & "temp.gif"
    CurrentChart.Export FileName:=Fname, FilterName:="GIF"
    ActiveSheet.ChartObjects(1).Delete

'   Show the chart
    Image1.Picture = LoadPicture(Fname)
    Application.ScreenUpdating = True
End Sub
```

ON THE CD   This workbook is available on the companion CD-ROM.

Understanding Chart Events

Excel supports several events associated with charts. For example, when a chart is activated, it generates an `Activate` event. The `Calculate` event occurs after the chart receives new or changed data. You can, of course, write VBA code that gets executed when a particular event occurs.

Refer to Chapter 19 for additional information about events.

Table 18-1 lists all the chart events supported by Excel 97 and later versions.

TABLE 18-1 EVENTS RECOGNIZED BY THE CHART OBJECT

Event	Action That Triggers the Event
Activate	A chart sheet or embedded chart is activated.
BeforeDoubleClick	An embedded chart is double-clicked. This event occurs before the default double-click action.
BeforeRightClick	An embedded chart is right-clicked. The event occurs before the default right-click action.
Calculate	New or changed data is plotted on a chart.
Deactivate	A chart is deactivated.
DragOver	A range of cells is dragged over a chart.
DragPlot	A range of cells is dragged and dropped onto a chart.
MouseDown	A mouse button is pressed while the pointer is over a chart.
MouseMove	The position of the mouse pointer changes over a chart.
MouseUp	A mouse button is released while the pointer is over a chart.
Resize	A chart is resized.
Select	A chart element is selected.
SeriesChange	The value of a chart data point is changed.

An example of using Chart events

To program an event handler for an event taking place on a chart sheet, your VBA code must reside in the code module for the Chart object. To activate this code module, double-click the Chart item in the Project window. Then in the code module, select Chart from the Object drop-down list on the left and then select the event from the Procedure drop-down list on the right (see Figure 18-10).

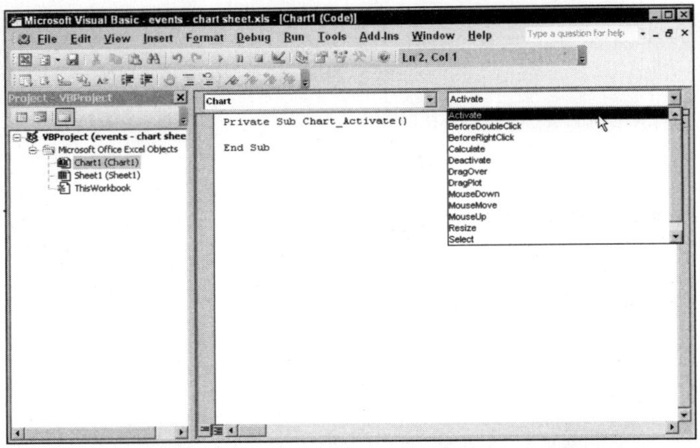

Figure 18-10: Selecting an event in the code module for a `Chart` object.

>
> **NOTE** Because there is not a code module for embedded charts, the procedure that I describe in this section works only for chart sheets. You can also handle events for embedded charts, but you must do some initial set-up work that involves creating a class module. This procedure is described later in "Enabling events for an embedded chart."

The example that follows simply displays a message when the user activates a chart sheet, deactivates a chart sheet, or selects any element on the chart. I created a workbook with a chart sheet; then I wrote three event handler procedures named

◆ `Chart_Activate`: Executed when the chart sheet is activated

◆ `Chart_Deactivate`: Executed when the chart sheet is deactivated

◆ `Chart_Select`: Executed when an element on the chart sheet is selected

The `Chart_Activate` procedure follows:

```
Private Sub Chart_Activate()
    Dim msg As String
    msg = "Hello " & Application.UserName & vbCrLf & vbCrLf
    msg = msg & "You are now viewing the six-month sales "
    msg = msg & "summary for Products 1-3." & vbCrLf & vbCrLf
    msg = msg & _
      "Click an item in the chart to find out what it is."
```

```
        MsgBox msg, vbInformation, ActiveWorkbook.Name
End Sub
```

This procedure simply displays a message whenever the chart is activated. See Figure 18-11.

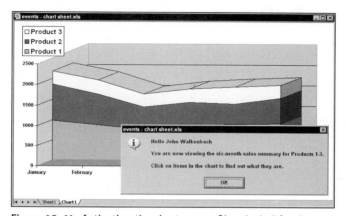

Figure 18-11: Activating the chart causes `Chart_Activate` to display this message.

The `Chart_Deactivate` procedure that follows also displays a message but only when the chart sheet is deactivated:

```
Private Sub Chart_Deactivate()
    Dim msg As String
    msg = "Thanks for viewing the chart."
    MsgBox msg, , ActiveWorkbook.Name
End Sub
```

The `Chart_Select` procedure that follows is executed whenever an item on the chart is selected:

```
Private Sub Chart_Select(ByVal ElementID As Long, _
   ByVal Arg1 As Long, ByVal Arg2 As Long)
    Dim Id As String
    Select Case ElementID
        Case xlAxis: Id = "Axis"
        Case xlAxisTitle: Id = "AxisTitle"
        Case xlChartArea: Id = "ChartArea"
        Case xlChartTitle: Id = "ChartTitle"
        Case xlCorners: Id = "Corners"
        Case xlDataLabel: Id = "DataLabel"
```

```
        Case xlDataTable: Id = "DataTable"
        Case xlDownBars: Id = "DownBars"
        Case xlDropLines: Id = "DropLines"
        Case xlErrorBars: Id = "ErrorBars"
        Case xlFloor: Id = "Floor"
        Case xlHiLoLines: Id = "HiLoLines"
        Case xlLegend: Id = "Legend"
        Case xlLegendEntry: Id = "LegendEntry"
        Case xlLegendKey: Id = "LegendKey"
        Case xlMajorGridlines: Id = "MajorGridlines"
        Case xlMinorGridlines: Id = "MinorGridlines"
        Case xlNothing: Id = "Nothing"
        Case xlPlotArea: Id = "PlotArea"
        Case xlRadarAxisLabels: Id = "RadarAxisLabels"
        Case xlSeries: Id = "Series"
        Case xlSeriesLines: Id = "SeriesLines"
        Case xlShape: Id = "Shape"
        Case xlTrendline: Id = "Trendline"
        Case xlUpBars: Id = "UpBars"
        Case xlWalls: Id = "Walls"
        Case xlXErrorBars: Id = "XErrorBars"
        Case xlYErrorBars: Id = "YErrorBars"
        Case Else:: Id = "Some unknown thing"
    End Select
    MsgBox "Selection type:" & Id
End Sub
```

This procedure displays a message box that contains a description of the selected item. When the `Select` event occurs, the `ElementID` argument contains an integer that corresponds to what was selected. The `Arg1` and `Arg2` arguments provide additional information about the selected item (see the Help system for details). The `Select Case` structure converts the built-in constants to descriptive strings.

 This is not a comprehensive listing of all items that could appear in a `Chart` object. For example, it doesn't include objects specific to a pivot chart. That's why I include the `Case Else` statement.

Enabling events for an embedded chart

As I note in the preceding section, `Chart` events are automatically enabled for chart sheets but not for charts embedded in a worksheet. To use events with an embedded chart, you need to perform the following steps.

CREATE A CLASS MODULE

In the Visual Basic Editor (VBE) window, select your project in the Project window and choose Insert → Class Module. This will add a new (empty) class module to your project. Then use the Properties window to give the class module a more descriptive name (such as `clsChart`). Renaming the class module isn't necessary, but it's a good practice.

DECLARE A PUBLIC CHART OBJECT

The next step is to declare a `Public` variable that will represent the chart. The variable should be of type `Chart`, and it must be declared in the class module by using the `WithEvents` keyword. If you omit the `WithEvents` keyword, the object will not respond to events. Following is an example of such a declaration:

```
Public WithEvents clsChart As Chart
```

CONNECT THE DECLARED OBJECT WITH YOUR CHART

Before your event handler procedures will run, you must connect the declared object in the class module with your embedded chart. You do this by declaring an object of type `clsChart` (or whatever your class module is named). This should be a module-level object variable, declared in a regular VBA module (not in the class module). Here's an example:

```
Dim MyChart As New clsChart
```

Then you must write code to associate the `clsChart` object with a particular chart. The statement below accomplishes this.

```
Set MyChart.clsChart = ActiveSheet.ChartObjects(1).Chart
```

After the preceding statement is executed, the `clsChart` object in the class module points to the first embedded chart on the active sheet. Consequently, the event handler procedures in the class module will execute when the events occur.

WRITE EVENT HANDLER PROCEDURES FOR THE CHART CLASS

In this section, I describe how to write event handler procedures in the class module. Recall that the class module must contain a declaration such as

```
Public WithEvents clsChart As Chart
```

After this new object has been declared with the `WithEvents` keyword, it appears in the Object drop-down list box in the class module. When you select the new object in the Object box, the valid events for that object are listed in the Procedure drop-down box on the right (see Figure 18-12).

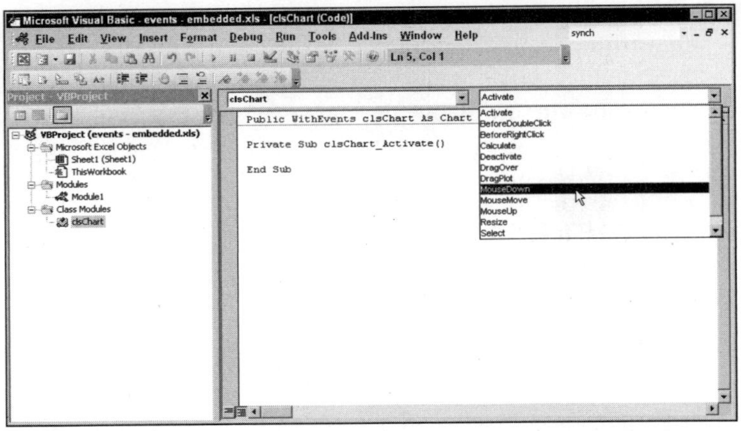

Figure 18-12: The Procedure list displays valid events for the new object.

The following example is a simple event handler procedure that is executed when the embedded chart is activated. This procedure simply pops up a message box that displays the name of the Chart object's parent (which is a ChartObject object).

```
Private Sub clsChart_Activate()
    MsgBox clsChart.Parent.Name & " was activated!"
End Sub
```

ON THE CD   The companion CD-ROM contains a workbook that demonstrates the concepts that I describe in this section.

Example: Using Chart events with an embedded chart

The example in this section provides a practical demonstration of the information presented in the previous section. The example shown in Figure 18-13 consists of an embedded chart that functions as a clickable image map. Clicking one of the chart columns activates a worksheet that shows detailed data for the region.

The workbook is set up with four worksheets. The sheet named Main contains the embedded chart. The other sheets are named North, South, and West. Formulas in B1:B4 sum the data in the respective sheets, and this summary data is plotted in the chart. Clicking a column in the chart triggers an event, and the event handler procedure activates the appropriate sheet so that the user can view the details for the desired region.

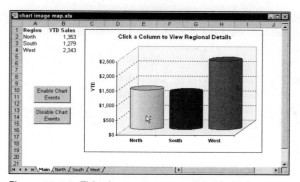

Figure 18-13: This chart serves as a clickable image map.

The workbook contains both a class module named EmbChartClass and a normal VBA module named Module1. For demonstration purposes, the Main worksheet also contains two buttons: One executes a procedure named EnableChartEvents; the other executes a procedure named DisableChartEvents. (Both are located in Module1.) In addition, each of the other worksheets contains a button that executes the ReturntoMain macro that reactivates the Main sheet.

The complete listing of Module1 follows:

```
Dim SummaryChart As New EmbChartClass

Sub EnableChartEvents()
'    Called by worksheet button
     Range("A1").Select
     Set SummaryChart.myChartClass = _
       Worksheets(1).ChartObjects(1).Chart
End Sub

Sub DisableChartEvents()
'    Called by worksheet button
     Set SummaryChart.myChartClass = Nothing
     Range("A1").Select
End Sub

Sub ReturnToMain()
'    Called by worksheet button
     Sheets("Main").Activate
End Sub
```

The first instruction declares a new object variable SummaryChart to be of type EmbChartClass — which, as you recall, is the name of the class module. When the user clicks the Enable Chart Events button, the embedded chart is assigned to the SummaryChart object, which, in effect, enables the events for the chart. Listing 18-4 shows the class module for EmbChartClass.

Clicking the chart generates a MouseDown event, which executes the myChartClass_MouseDown procedure. This procedure uses the GetChartElement method to determine what element of the chart was clicked. The GetChartElement method returns information about the chart element at specified X and Y coordinates (information that is available via the arguments for the myChartClass_ MouseDown procedure).

Listing 18-4: Reacting to Which Column Has Been Clicked

```
Public WithEvents myChartClass As Chart

Private Sub myChartClass_MouseDown(ByVal Button As Long, _
  ByVal Shift As Long, ByVal X As Long, ByVal Y As Long)

    Dim IDnum As Long
    Dim a As Long, b As Long

'   The next statement returns values for
'   IDNum, a, and b
    myChartClass.GetChartElement X, Y, IDnum, a, b

'   Was a series clicked?
    If IDnum = xlSeries Then
        Select Case b
            Case 1
                Sheets("North").Activate
            Case 2
                Sheets("South").Activate
            Case 3
                Sheets("West").Activate
        End Select
    End If
    Range("A1").Select
End Sub
```

 This workbook is available on the companion CD-ROM.

VBA Charting Tricks

This section contains a few charting tricks that I've discovered over the years. Some of these techniques might be useful in your applications, and others are simply for fun. At the very least, studying them could give you some new insights into the object model for charts.

Printing embedded charts on a full page

When an embedded chart is selected, you can print the chart by choosing File → Print. The embedded chart will be printed on a full page by itself (just as if it were on a chart sheet), yet it will remain an embedded chart.

The following macro prints all embedded charts on the active sheet, and each chart is printed on a full page:

```
Sub PrintEmbeddedCharts()
    For Each chtObj In ActiveSheet.ChartObjects
        chtObj.Chart.Print
    Next chtObj
End Sub
```

Creating a "dead" chart

Normally, an Excel chart uses data stored in a range. Change the data in the range, and the chart is updated automatically. In some cases, you might want to unlink the chart from its data ranges and produce a *dead chart* (a chart that never changes). For example, if you plot data generated by various what-if scenarios, you might want to save a chart that represents some baseline so that you can compare it with other scenarios.

The three ways to create such a chart are

◆ *Copy the chart and paste it as a picture.* Activate the chart and choose Edit → Copy. Then press the Shift key and choose Edit → Paste Picture. (The Paste Picture command is available only if you press Shift when you select the Edit menu.) The result will be a picture of the copied chart. Alternatively, you can press Shift and choose Edit → Copy Picture to display the Copy Picture dialog box (this dialog box provides several copy options). Then use Edit → Paste to paste the image.

◆ *Convert the range references to arrays.* Click a chart series and then click the formula bar. Press F9 to convert the ranges to an array. Repeat this for each series in the chart.

◆ *Use VBA to assign an array rather than a range to the* XValues *or* Values *properties of the* Series *object.*

The charts in the x18galry.xls file are dead charts. This file is a special workbook used by Excel to store its custom chart formats. If you open this workbook, you'll find 20 chart sheets. Each chart sheet has dummy data, which uses an array rather than a range as its source.

The procedure below makes a picture of the active chart directly on top of the chart (the original chart is not deleted). It works with both embedded charts and charts on a chart sheet.

```
Sub ConvertChartToPicture()
    Dim TheChart As Chart
    If ActiveChart Is Nothing Then Exit Sub
    Set TheChart = ActiveChart
    Application.ScreenUpdating = False
    TheChart.CopyPicture Appearance:=xlPrinter, _
      Size:=xlScreen, Format:=xlPicture
    If TypeName(ActiveSheet) = "Chart" Then
        ActiveChart.Paste
    Else
        ActiveSheet.Paste
        Selection.Left = TheChart.Parent.Left
        Selection.Top = TheChart.Parent.Top
    End If
    TheChart.Parent.Delete
    Application.ScreenUpdating = True
End Sub
```

 This example is available on the companion CD-ROM.

The procedure below creates a chart (see Figure 18-14) by using arrays. The data is not stored in the worksheet. As you can see, the SERIES formula contains arrays and not range references.

```
Sub CreateADeadChart()
    Charts.Add
    ActiveChart.Location _
      Where:=xlLocationAsObject, Name:="Sheet1"
```

```
With ActiveChart
    .SeriesCollection.NewSeries
    .SeriesCollection(1).XValues = Array("Jan", "Feb", "Mar")
    .SeriesCollection(1).Values = Array(125, 165, 189)
    .SeriesCollection(1).Name = "Sales"
    .ChartType = xlColumnClustered
    .HasLegend = False
    .Deselect
End With
End Sub
```

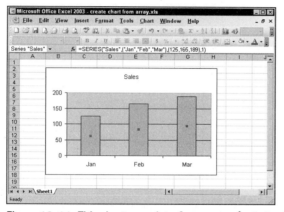

Figure 18-14: This chart uses data from arrays (not stored in a worksheet).

 This example is available on the companion CD-ROM.

Because there's a limit to the length of a chart's SERIES formula, you'll find that this technique works only for relatively small data sets.

Displaying text with the MouseOver event

A common charting question deals with modifying chart tips. A *chart tip* is the small message that appears next to the mouse pointer when you move the mouse over a chart. The chart tip displays the chart element name and (for series) the value of the data point. The Chart object model does not expose these chart tips, so there is no way to modify them.

TIP To turn chart tips on or off, choose Tools → Options. Click the Chart tab and select or unselect the two check boxes in the Chart tips section.

This section describes an alternative to chart tips. Figure 18-15 shows a column chart that uses the `MouseOver` event. When the mouse pointer is positioned over a column, the text box (a `Shape` object) in the upper left displays information about the data point. The information is stored in a range and can consist of anything you like.

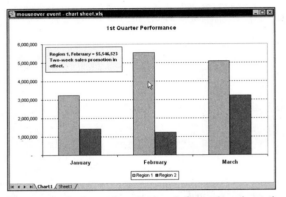

Figure 18-15: A text box displays information about the data point under the mouse pointer.

The event procedure that follows is located in the code module for the Chart sheet that contains the chart.

```
Private Sub Chart_MouseMove(ByVal Button As Long, ByVal Shift As Long, _
  ByVal X As Long, ByVal Y As Long)
    Dim ElementID As Long
    Dim arg1 As Long, arg2 As Long
    Dim NewText As String
    On Error Resume Next
    ActiveChart.GetChartElement X, Y, ElementID, arg1, arg2
    If ElementId = xlSeries Then
        NewText = Sheets("Sheet1").Range("Comments").Offset(arg2, arg1)
    Else
        NewText = ""
        ActiveChart.Shapes(1).Visible = False
    End If
```

```
   If NewText <> ActiveChart.Shapes(1).TextFrame.Text Then
       ActiveChart.Shapes(1).TextFrame.Text = NewText
       ActiveChart.Shapes(1).Visible = True
   End If
End Sub
```

This procedure monitors all mouse movements on the Chart sheet. The mouse coordinates are contained in the X and Y variables, which are passed to the procedure. The Button and Shift arguments are not used in this procedure.

As in the previous example, the key component in this procedure is the GetChartElement method. If ElementId is xlSeries, the mouse pointer is over a series. The NewText variable then is assigned the text in a particular cell. This text contains descriptive information about the data point (see Figure 18-16). If the mouse pointer is not over a series, the text box is hidden. Otherwise, it displays the contents of NewText.

	A	B	C	D
1		Region 1	Region 2	
2	January	3,245,151	1,434,343	
3	February	5,546,523	1,238,709	
4	March	5,083,204	3,224,855	
5				
6	Comments			
7		Region 1, January = $3,245,151	Region 2, January = $1,434,343	
8		Region 1, February = $5,546,523 Two-week sales promotion in effect.	Region 2, February = $1,238,709	
9		Region 1, March = $5,083,204	Region 2, March = $3,224,855 L.A. merger took place in week three.	
10				

mouseover event - chart sheet.xls

◄ ► ►│\ Chart1 \Sheet1 /

Figure 18-16: Range B7:C9 contains data point information that's displayed in the text box on the chart.

ON THE CD   The companion CD-ROM contains this example set up for an embedded chart and for a chart sheet.

Animated charts

Most people don't realize it, but Excel is capable of performing simple animations. For example, you can animate shapes and charts. Consider the XY chart shown in Figure 18-17.

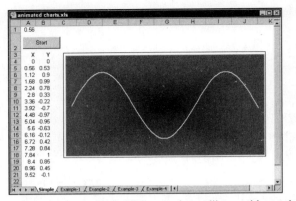

Figure 18-17: A simple VBA procedure will turn this graph into an interesting animation.

The X values (column A) depend on the value in cell A1. The value in each row is the previous row's value, plus the value in A1. Column B contains formulas that calculate the SIN of the corresponding value in column A. The following simple procedure produces an interesting animation. It simply changes the value in cell A1, which causes the values in the X and Y ranges to change.

```
Sub AnimateChart()
    Dim i As Integer
    Range("A1") = 0
    For i = 1 To 150
        Range("A1") = Range("A1") + 0.035
    Next i
    Range("A1") = 0
End Sub
```

ON THE CD   The companion CD-ROM contains a workbook that includes this animated chart, plus several other animation examples.

Creating a hypocycloid chart

Even if you hated your high school trigonometry class, you'll probably like the example in this section – which relies heavily on trigonometric functions. The workbook shown in Figure 18-18 can display an infinite number of dazzling hypocycloid curves. A *hypocycloid* curve is the path formed by a point on a circle that rolls inside of another circle. This, as you might recall from your childhood, is the same technique used in Hasbro's popular Spirograph toy.

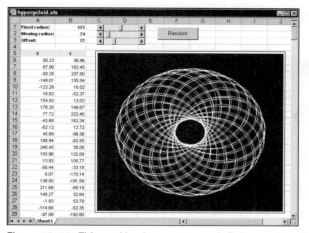

Figure 18-18: This workbook generates an infinite number of hypocycloid curves.

 This workbook is available on the companion CD-ROM. You'll also find a much more sophisticated version that features color change and animation.

The chart is an XY chart. The X and Y data are generated by using formulas stored in columns A and B. The scroll bar controls at the top let you adjust the three parameters that determine the look of the chart. These controls are linked to cells B1, B2, and B3. These are controls from the Forms toolbar and are not ActiveX controls. In addition, the chart has a Random button that generates random values for the three parameters.

The workbook contains only one macro (which follows), which is executed when the Random button is clicked. This macro simply generates three random numbers between 1 and 250 and inserts them into the worksheet.

```
Sub Random_Click()
    Randomize
    Range("B1") = Int(Rnd * 250)
    Range("B2") = Int(Rnd * 250)
    Range("B3") = Int(Rnd * 250)
End Sub
```

Creating a "clock" chart

Figure 18-19 shows an XY chart formatted to look like a clock. It not only looks like a clock, but it also functions as a clock. I can't think of a single reason why anyone would need to display a clock like this on a worksheet, but creating the workbook was challenging, and you might find it instructive.

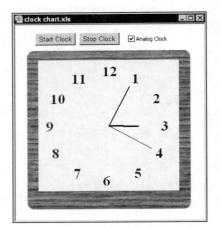

Figure 18-19: This clock is fully functional and is actually an XY chart in disguise.

 This workbook is available on the companion CD-ROM.

Besides the clock chart, the workbook contains a text box that displays the time as a normal string, as shown in Figure 18-20. Normally this is hidden, but it can be displayed by deselecting the Analog Clock check box.

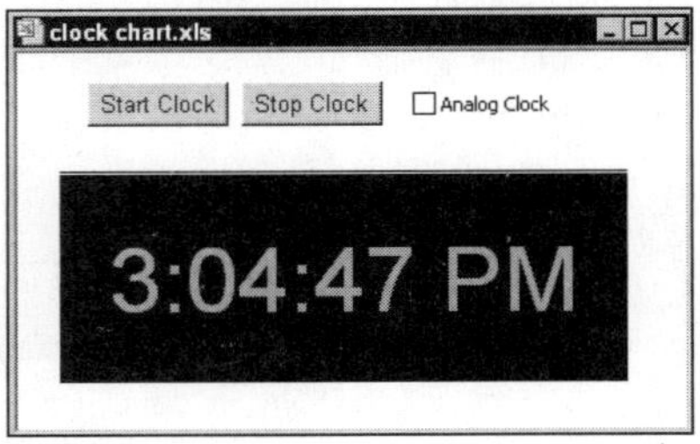

Figure 18-20: Displaying a digital clock in a worksheet is much easier but not as fun to create.

As you explore this workbook from the CD-ROM, here are a few things to keep in mind:

◆ The ChartObject is named ClockChart, and it covers up a range named DigitalClock, which is used to display the time digitally.

◆ The two buttons on the worksheet are from the Forms toolbar, and each has a macro assigned (StartClock and StopClock).

◆ The CheckBox control (named cbClockType) on the worksheet is from the Forms toolbar — not from the Control Toolbox toolbar. Clicking the object executes a procedure named cbClockType_Click, which simply toggles the Visible property of the ChartObject. When it's invisible, the digital clock is revealed.

◆ The chart is an XY chart with four Series objects. These series represent the hour hand, the minute hand, the second hand, and the 12 numbers.

◆ The UpdateClock procedure is executed when the Start Clock button is clicked. This procedure determines which clock is visible and performs the appropriate updating.

◆ The UpdateClock procedure uses the OnTime method of the Application object. This method lets you execute a procedure at a specific time. Before the UpdateClock procedure ends, it sets up a new OnTime event that will occur in one second. In other words, the UpdateClock procedure is called every second.

◆ The UpdateClock procedure uses some basic trigonometry to determine the angles at which to display the hands on the clock.

◆ Unlike most charts, this one does not use any worksheet ranges for its data. Rather, the values are calculated in VBA and transferred directly to the Values and XValues properties of the chart's Series object.

 Although this clock is an interesting demo, it is not feasible to display a continually updating clock in a worksheet. The VBA macro must be running at all times in the background, and this would probably interfere with other macros and reduce the overall performance.

Charting Tricks That Don't Use Macros

This section contains additional chart tricks that don't involve macros. You may be surprised by how much you can accomplish without using VBA.

Controlling a data series by using Autofiltering

Figure 18-21 shows a chart that displays daily data for 365 days. What if you only want to plot, say, the data for February? You could, of course, redefine the chart's data range. Or, you could take advantage of Excel's AutoFilter command.

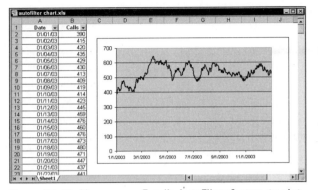

Figure 18-21: You can use Excel's AutoFilter feature to plot only a subset of the data.

By default, a chart does not display data that's hidden. Because Excel's AutoFilter feature works by hiding rows that don't meet your criteria, it's a simple solution. Choose Data → Filter → AutoFilter to turn on the AutoFilter mode. Each row heading in the filtered list displays a drop-down arrow. Click the arrow and select Custom from the list. Then enter filter criteria that will select the dates that you want to plot. The setting shown in Figure 18-22, for example, hides all rows except those that have a date in February.

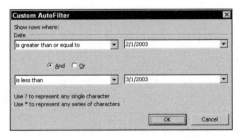

Figure 18-22: Use the Custom AutoFilter dialog box to filter a list.

This workbook is available on the companion CD-ROM.

The resulting chart is shown in Figure 18-23.

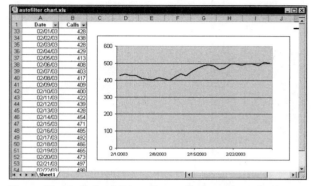

Figure 18-23: Only visible cells are displayed in a chart.

If this technique doesn't seem to be working, you need to change a setting for the chart. Activate the chart and then choose Tools → Options. In the Options dialog box, click the Chart tab and place a check mark next to Plot Visible Cells Only. Also, to ensure that the chart doesn't disappear when its rows are hidden, set its positioning to Don't Move or Size with Cells. Choose the Format → Selected Chart Area command to change this setting.

Storing multiple charts on a chart sheet

Most Excel users who take the time to think about it would agree that a chart sheet holds a single chart. Most of the time, that's a true statement. However, it's certainly possible to store multiple charts on a single chart sheet. In fact, Excel lets you do this directly. If you activate an embedded chart and then choose Chart → Location, Excel displays its Chart Location dialog box. If you select the As New Sheet option and specify an existing chart sheet as the location, the chart will appear on top of the chart in the chart sheet.

Most of the time, you want to add embedded charts to an empty chart sheet. To create an empty chart sheet, select a single blank cell and press F11. Figure 18-24 shows an example of a chart sheet that contains six embedded charts.

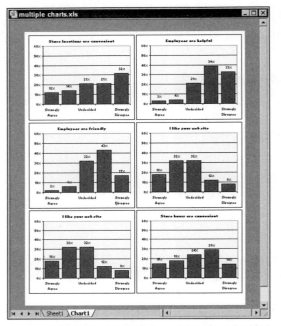

Figure 18–24: This chart sheet contains six embedded charts.

 This workbook is available on the companion CD-ROM. It also contains a simple macro to size and align the charts.

Creating a self-expanding chart

One of the most common questions related to charting is: *How can I create a chart that will expand automatically when I add new data to the worksheet?*

To understand this issue, examine Figure 18-25, which shows a worksheet set up to store sales information that is updated daily. The chart displays all the data in the worksheet. When new data is entered, the chart series must be expanded to include the new data. On the other hand, if data is deleted, the chart series should also be contracted to exclude the deleted cells. It's certainly possible — if you're willing to do a little up-front work.

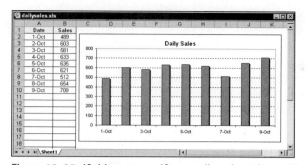

Figure 18-25: If this were a self-expanding chart, it would update automatically when new data is entered.

 If you use Excel 2003, this trick is not necessary. You can choose the Data → List → Create List command to designate your data as a list. When you create a chart from the data, the chart will expand automatically when you add new data to the list.

One option, of course, is to specify a larger-than-required range for the chart data series. The problem with this approach is that the chart plots the empty cells, and the result is a lopsided chart that displays lots of empty space. In the majority of situations, this solution is not satisfactory.

Because this technique can be tricky, this section presents a step-by-step example. I start with a standard chart and then make the changes necessary to make the chart expand automatically when new data is added as well as to contract when data is deleted.

The example makes use of a simple worksheet that has dates in column A and sales amounts in column B. The assumption is that a new date and sales figure are each added daily and that the chart should display all the data.

CREATING THE CHART

The first step is to create a standard chart that uses the data that currently exists. Figure 18-25, in the preceding section, shows the data and a column chart created from the data. The chart contains a single series and its SERIES formula is as follows:

```
=SERIES(Sheet1!$B$1,Sheet1!$A$2:$A$11,Sheet1!$B$2:$B$11,1)
```

This SERIES formula specifies that

◆ The series name is in cell B1.

◆ The category labels are in A2:A11.

◆ The values are in B2:B11.

So far, this is just a common chart. If you add a new date and value, the chart will not display the new data. But that will soon change.

CREATING NAMED FORMULAS

In this step, you create two named formulas. The names will eventually serve as arguments in the SERIES formula. In case you're not familiar with the concept of a named formula, I explain this later in this section. To create the named formulas:

1. Choose Insert → Name → Define to bring up the Define Name dialog box.

2. In the Names in Workbook field, enter **Date**. In the Refers To field, enter this formula:

   ```
   =OFFSET(Sheet1!$A$2,0,0,COUNTA(Sheet1!$A:$A)-1,1)
   ```

3. Click Add to create the formula named *Date*.

   Notice that the OFFSET function refers to the first category label (cell A2) and uses the COUNTA function to determine the number of labels in the column. Because column A has a heading in row 1, the formula subtracts 1 from the number.

4. Type **Sales** in the Names in Workbook field. Enter this formula in the Refers To field:

   ```
   =OFFSET(Sheet1!$B$2,0,0,COUNTA(Sheet1!$B:$B)-1,1)
   ```

   In this case, the OFFSET function refers to the first data point (cell B2). Again, the COUNTA function is used to get the number of data points, and it is adjusted to account for the label in cell B1.

5. Click Add to create the formula named *Sales*.

6. Click Close to close the Define Name dialog box.

After you perform these steps, the workbook contains two new names, *Date* and *Sales*.

MODIFYING THE SERIES

The final step is to modify the chart so that it makes use of the two new names rather than the hard-coded range references.

1. Activate the chart and choose Chart → Source Data to bring up the Source Data dialog box.

2. In the Values field, enter **Sheet1!Sales**.

3. In the Category (x) Axis Labels field, enter **Sheet1!Dates**.

4. Verify that the dialog box looks like Figure 18-26 and then click OK.

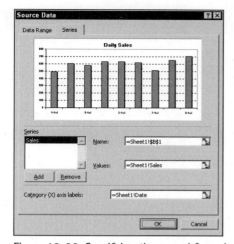

Figure 18-26: Specifying the named formulas in the Source Data dialog box.

In Steps 2 and 3, note that the name was preceded by the worksheet name and an exclamation point. Because named formulas are workbook-level names (as opposed to sheet-level names), you should (technically) enter the *workbook* name, an exclamation point, and the name. However, Excel is very accommodating in this regard and changes it for you. If you access the Source Data dialog box again, you'll discover that Excel substituted the workbook's name for the sheet reference that you entered:

```
=dailysales.xls!Sales
```

Bottom line? When using these named formulas, you can precede the name with either the worksheet name or the workbook name. (I find it easier to use the worksheet name.) But keep in mind that if the sheet name or workbook name includes a space character, you must enclose it in single quotation marks, like this:

```
='daily sales.xls'!Sales
```

or

```
='sales data'!sales
```

For more information about names, refer to the sidebar, "How Excel Handles Names."

How Excel Handles Names

Excel supports two types of names: workbook-level names and worksheet-level names. The scope of a workbook-level name is the entire workbook. Normally, when you create a name for a cell or range, that name can be used in any worksheet.

You can also create sheet-level names. A sheet-level name incorporates the sheet name as part of its name. For example, *Sheet1!Data* is a sheet-level name. When you create this name, you can use it in formulas in Sheet1 without the sheet qualifier. For example:

```
=Data*4
```

But if you enter this formula in a different worksheet, Excel will not recognize the name unless you fully qualify it:

```
=Sheet1!Data*4
```

Sheet-level names are useful because they enable you to use the same name on different worksheets. For example, you might create sheet-level names such as *Sheet1!Interest, Sheet2!Interest,* and *Sheet3!Interest.* Each name refers to a cell on its own sheet. A formula that uses the name *Interest* uses the definition for its own sheet.

The named formulas used in this chapter are workbook-level names because they are not preceded by a sheet name. But when you enter a name in a field in the Source Data dialog box, Excel (for some reason) requires that you qualify the name with either the sheet name or the workbook name.

 An alternative to using the Source Data dialog box is to edit the chart's SERIES formula directly.

TESTING YOUR SELF-EXPANDING CHART

To test the results of your efforts, either enter new data in columns A and B or delete data from the bottom of the columns. If you performed the preceding steps correctly, the chart will update automatically. If you receive an error message or the chart doesn't update itself, review the preceding steps carefully. This method *does* work!

UNDERSTANDING HOW A SELF-EXPANDING CHART WORKS

Many people use this self-expanding chart technique without fully understanding how it works. There's certainly nothing wrong with that. If you go through the hands-on exercise that I previously describe, you should be able to adapt the procedures to your own charts. But understanding *how* it works will make it possible to go beyond the basic concept and create more powerful types of dynamic charts.

ABOUT NAMED FORMULAS IN SELF-EXPANDING CHARTS

The self-expanding chart that I describe in this chapter takes advantage of a powerful feature called *named formulas*. You're probably familiar with the concept of named cells and ranges. But did you know that naming cells and ranges is really a misnomer? When you create a name for a range, you are really creating a named formula.

When you work with the Define Name dialog box, the Refers To field contains the formula, and the Names in Workbook field contains the formula's name. You'll find that the contents of the Refers to field always begin with an equal sign — a sure sign that it's a formula.

Unlike a normal formula, a named formula doesn't exist in a cell. Rather, it exists in Excel's memory and does not have a cell address. But you can access the result of a named formula by referring to its name, either in a standard formula or in a chart's SERIES formula.

After defining the two named formulas, Excel evaluates these formulas every time that the worksheet is calculated. But these named formulas aren't used in any cells, so there is no visible effect of creating these named formulas until you use them to define the chart series.

To get a better handle on named formulas, use the Define Name dialog box to create the following formula, and name it *Sum12Cells*.

```
=SUM($A$1:$A$12)
```

After you create the named formula, enter the following formula into any cell:

```
=Sum12Cells
```

This formula will return the sum of A1:A12.

ABOUT THE OFFSET FUNCTION IN SELF-EXPANDING CHARTS

The key to mastering self-expanding charts is understanding the OFFSET function. This function returns a range that is offset from a specified reference cell. Arguments for the OFFSET function let you specify the distance from the reference cell and the dimensions of the range (the number of rows and columns).

The OFFSET function has five arguments, as follows:

◆ `reference`: The first argument for the OFFSET function is essentially the anchor cell, used by the second and third argument.

◆ `rows`: This argument indicates how many rows to move from the reference address to begin the range.

◆ `cols`: This argument indicates how many columns to move from the reference address to begin the range.

◆ `height`: This argument indicates the number of rows to be included in the range.

◆ `width`: The final argument indicates the number of columns to be included in the range.

If the columns used for the data contain any other entries, COUNTA will return an incorrect value. To keep things simple, don't put any other data in the column. If the column contains additional information, you'll need to adjust the `height` argument in the COUNTA function.

Recall that the named formula *Sales* was defined as

`=OFFSET(Sheet1!$B$2,0,0,COUNTA(Sheet1!$B:$B)-1,1)`

If there are 11 entries in column B, the COUNTA function returns 11. This result is adjusted by one to account for the column heading. Therefore, the named formula can be expressed as

`=OFFSET(Sheet1!$B$2,0,0,10,1)`

This formula uses cell B2 as the anchor cell and returns a reference to the range that is

◆ Offset from cell B2 by 0 rows (second argument, `rows`)

◆ Offset from cell B2 by 0 columns (third argument, `cols`)

◆ Ten cells high (fourth argument, `height`)

◆ One cell wide (fifth argument, `width`)

In other words, the OFFSET function returns a reference to range B2:B11, and this is the range used by the chart series. When a new data point is added, the OFFSET function returns a reference to range B2:B12.

Subsequent examples in this chapter use the same basic concept but vary in the arguments supplied to the OFFSET function.

To keep things simple, this example makes use of a single data series. However, these techniques can be applied to charts with any number of data series. You will, however, have to make the necessary adjustments for each series.

Creating an interactive chart

The final example, shown in Figure 18-27, is a useful application that allows the user to choose two U.S. cities (from a list of 284 cities) and view a chart that compares the cities by month in any of the following categories: average precipitation, average temperature, percent sunshine, and average wind speed.

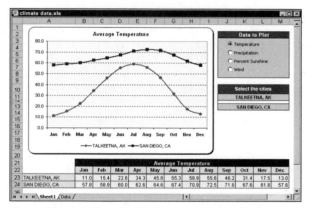

Figure 18-27: This application uses a variety of techniques to plot monthly climate data for two selected U.S. cities.

The interactivity is provided by using Excel's built-in features — no macros are required. The cities are chosen from a drop-down list, using Excel's Data Validation feature, and the data option is selected using four Option Button controls. The pieces are all connected using a few formulas.

This example demonstrates that it is indeed possible to create a user-friendly, interactive application without the assistance of macros.

This workbook is available on the companion CD-ROM.

The following sections describe the steps I took to set up this application.

GETTING THE DATA TO CREATE AN INTERACTIVE CHART

I did a Web search and spent about five minutes locating the data I needed at the National Climatic Data Center. I copied the data from my browser window, pasted it to an Excel worksheet, and did a bit of clean up work. The result was four 13-column tables of data, which I named *PrecipitationData, TemperatureData, SunshineData,* and *WindData.* To keep the interface as clean as possible, I put the data on a separate sheet (named *Data*).

CREATING THE OPTION BUTTON CONTROLS FOR AN INTERACTIVE CHART

I needed a way to allow the user to select the data to plot and decided to use Option Button controls from the Forms toolbar. Because option buttons work as a group, the four Option Button controls are all linked to the same cell (cell O3). Cell O3, therefore, contains a value from 1–4, depending on which option button is selected.

I needed a way to obtain the name of the data table based on the numeric value in cell O3. The solution was to write a formula (in cell O4) that uses Excel's CHOOSE function:

```
=CHOOSE(O3,"TemperatureData","PrecipitationData","SunshineData","WindData")
```

Therefore, cell O4 displays the name of one of the four named data tables. I then did some cell formatting behind the Option Button controls to make them more visible.

CREATING THE CITY LISTS FOR THE INTERACTIVE CHART

The next step is setting up the application: Create drop-down lists to enable the user to choose the cities to be compared in the chart. Excel's Data Validation feature makes creating a drop-down list in a cell very easy. First, I did some cell merging to create a wider field. I merged cells J11:M11 for the first city list and gave them the name *City1.* I merged cells J13:M13 for the second city list and gave them the name *City2.*

To make working with the list of cities easier, I created a named range, *CityList,* which refers to the first column in the *PrecipitationData* table.

Following are the steps that I used to create the drop-down lists:

1. Select J11:M11. (Remember, these are merged cells.)

2. Choose Data → Validation to display Excel's Data Validation dialog box.

3. Select the Settings tab in the Data Validation dialog box.

4. In the Allow field, choose List.

5. In the Source field, enter **=CityList**.

6. Click OK.

7. Copy J11:M11 to J13:M13. This duplicates the Data Validation settings for the second city.

Figure 18-28 shows the result.

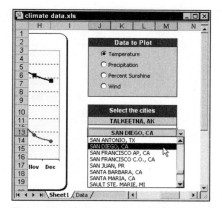

Figure 18-28: Use the Data Validation drop-down to select a city.

CREATING THE INTERACTIVE CHART DATA RANGE

The key to this application is that the chart uses data in a specific range. The data in this range is retrieved from the appropriate data table using formulas that utilize the VLOOKUP function. Figure 18-29 shows the range of data that is used by the chart.

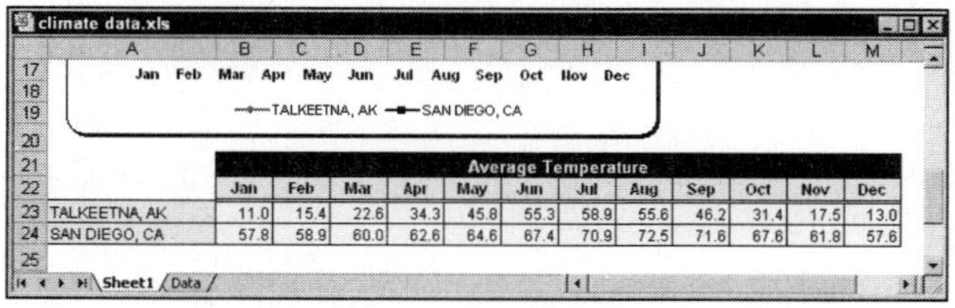

Figure 18-29: The chart uses the data retrieved by formulas in A22:M24.

The formula in cell A23, which looks up data based on the contents of *City1*, is

```
=VLOOKUP(City1,INDIRECT(DataTable),COLUMN(),FALSE)
```

The formula in cell A24 is the same except that it is looking up data based on the contents of *City2:*

```
=VLOOKUP(City2,INDIRECT(DataTable),COLUMN(),FALSE)
```

After entering these formulas, I simply copied them across to the next 12 columns.

 You may be wondering about the use of the COLUMN function for the third argument of the VLOOKUP function. This function returns the column number of the cell that contains the formula. This is a convenient way to avoid hard-coding the column to be retrieved and allows the same formula to be used in each column.

The label above the months is generated by a formula that refers to the DataTable cell and constructs a descriptive title: The formula is

```
="Average " &LEFT(DataTable,LEN(DataTable)-4)
```

CREATING THE INTERACTIVE CHART

After completing the previous tasks, the final step — creating the actual chart — is a breeze. The line chart has two data series and uses the data in A22:M24. The chart title is linked to cell A21. The data in A22:M24 changes, of course, whenever an Option Button control is selected or a new city is selected from either of the Data Validation lists.

Chapter 19

Understanding Excel's Events

IN THIS CHAPTER

This chapter explains the concept of Excel events, and I include many examples that you can adapt to your own needs. As you can see, understanding events can give your Excel applications a powerful edge. Here you will find

- An overview of the types of events that Excel can monitor

- Essential background information for working with events

- Examples of `Workbook` events, `Worksheet` events, `Chart` events, and `UserForm` events

- Using `Application` events to monitor all open workbooks

- Examples of processing time-based events and keystroke events

IN SEVERAL EARLIER CHAPTERS IN THIS BOOK, I present examples of VBA *event handler procedures,* which are specially named procedures that are executed when a specific event occurs. A simple example is the `CommandButton1_Click` procedure that is executed when the user clicks a CommandButton stored on a UserForm or on a worksheet.

Excel is capable of monitoring a wide variety of events, and executing your VBA code when a particular event occurs. Following are just a few examples of the types of events that Excel can recognize:

- A workbook is opened or closed.

- A window is activated.

- A worksheet is activated or deactivated.

- Data is entered into a cell or the cell is edited.

- A workbook is saved.

◆ A worksheet is calculated.

◆ An object is clicked.

◆ The data in a chart is updated.

◆ A particular key or key combination is pressed.

◆ A cell is double-clicked.

◆ A particular time of day occurs.

Event Types That Excel Can Monitor

Excel is programmed to monitor many different events that occur. These events can be classified as the following:

◆ *Workbook events:* Events that occur for a particular workbook. Examples of such events include `Open` (the workbook is opened or created), `BeforeSave` (the workbook is about to be saved), and `NewSheet` (a new sheet is added).

◆ *Worksheet events:* Events that occur for a particular worksheet. Examples include `Change` (a cell on the sheet is changed), `SelectionChange` (the user moves the cell indicator), and `Calculate` (the worksheet is recalculated).

◆ *Chart events:* Events that occur for a particular chart. These events include `Select` (an object in the chart is selected) and `SeriesChange` (a value of a data point in a series is changed). To monitor events for an embedded chart, you use a class module as I demonstrate in Chapter 18.

◆ *Application events:* Events that occur for the application (Excel). Examples include `NewWorkbook` (a new workbook is created), `WorkbookBeforeClose` (any workbook is about to be closed), and `SheetChange` (a cell in any open workbook is altered). To monitor `Application`-level events, you need to use a class module.

◆ *UserForm events:* Events that occur for a particular UserForm or an object contained on the UserForm. For example, a UserForm has an `Initialize` event (occurs before the UserForm is displayed), and a CommandButton on a UserForm has a `Click` event (occurs when the button is clicked).

◆ *Events not associated with objects:* The final category consists of two useful `Application`-level events that I call `On` events: `OnTime` and `OnKey`. These work in a different manner than other events.

This chapter is organized according to the preceding list. Within each section, I provide examples to demonstrate some of the events.

What You Should Know about Events

This section provides some essential information relevant to working with events and writing event handler procedures.

Understanding event sequences

As you can see, some actions trigger multiple events. For example, when you insert a new worksheet into a workbook, this action triggers three Application-level events:

◆ WorkbookNewSheet: Occurs when a new worksheet is added

◆ SheetDeactivate: Occurs when the active worksheet is deactivated

◆ SheetActivate: Occurs when the newly added worksheet is activated

 Event sequencing is a bit more complicated than you might think. The events listed above are Application-level events. When adding a new worksheet, additional events occur at the Workbook level and at the Worksheet level.

At this point, just keep in mind that events fire in a particular sequence, and knowing what the sequence is can be critical when writing event handler procedures. Later in this chapter, I describe how to determine the order of the events that occur for a particular action (see "Monitoring Application-level events").

Where to put event handler procedures

VBA newcomers often wonder why their event handler procedures aren't being executed when the corresponding event occurs. The answer is almost always because these procedures are located in the wrong place.

In the Visual Basic Editor (VBE) window, each project is listed in the Projects window. The project components are arranged in a collapsible list, as shown in Figure 19-1.

Each of the following components has its own code module:

◆ Sheet objects (for example, Sheet1, Sheet2, and so on).

◆ Chart objects (that is, chart sheets).

◆ ThisWorkbook object.

◆ General VBA modules. You never put event handler procedures in a general (that is, nonobject) module.

◆ Class modules.

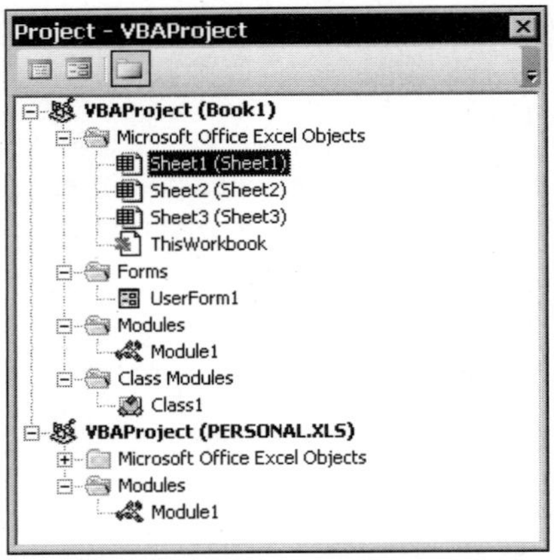

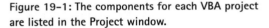

Figure 19-1: The components for each VBA project are listed in the Project window.

Even though the event handler procedure must be located in the correct module, the procedure can call other standard procedures stored in other modules. For example, the following event handler procedure, located in the module for the ThisWorkbook object, calls a procedure named WorkbookSetup, which could be stored in a regular VBA module:

```
Private Sub Workbook_Open()
    Call WorkbookSetup
End Sub
```

Programming Events in Older Versions of Excel

Versions of Excel prior to Office 97 also supported events, but the programming techniques required to take advantage of those were quite different from those that I describe in this chapter.

For example, if you have a procedure named Auto_Open stored in a regular VBA module, this procedure will be executed when the workbook is opened. Beginning with Excel 97, the Auto_Open procedure is supplemented by the Workbook_Open event handler procedure, stored in the code module for the ThisWorkbook object, and executed prior to Auto_Open.

Before Excel 97, it was often necessary to explicitly set up events. For example, if you needed to execute a procedure whenever data was entered into a cell, you would need to execute a statement such as

```
Sheets("Sheet1").OnEntry = "ValidateEntry"
```

This statement instructs Excel to execute the procedure named `ValidateEntry` whenever data is entered into a cell. With Excel 97 and later, you simply create a procedure named `Worksheet_Change` and store it in the code module for the `Sheet1` object.

For compatibility reasons, Excel 97 and later versions still support the older event mechanism (although they are no longer documented in the Help system). If you're developing applications that will be used only with Excel 97 or later, you definitely want to use the techniques that I describe in this chapter.

Disabling events

By default, all events are enabled. To disable all events, execute the following VBA instruction:

```
Application.EnableEvents = False
```

To enable events, use

```
Application.EnableEvents = True
```

Disabling events does *not* apply to events triggered by UserForm controls — for example, the `Click` event generated by clicking a CommandButton control on a UserForm.

Why would you need to disable events? The main reason is to prevent an infinite loop of cascading events.

For example, suppose that cell A1 of your worksheet must always contain a value less than or equal to 12. You can write some code that is executed whenever data is entered into a cell to validate the cell's contents. In this case, you are monitoring the `Change` event for a `Worksheet` with a procedure named `Worksheet_Change`. Your procedure checks the user's entry, and if the entry isn't less than or equal to 12, it displays a message and then clears that entry. The problem is that clearing the entry with your VBA code generates a new `Change` event, so your event handler procedure is executed again. This is not what you want to happen, so you need to disable events before you clear the cell, and then enable events again so that you can monitor the user's next entry.

Another way to prevent an infinite loop of cascading events is to declare a `Static` Boolean variable at the beginning of your event-handler procedure, such as this:

```
Static AbortProc As Boolean
```

Whenever the procedure needs to make its own changes, set the `AbortProc` variable to True (otherwise, make sure that it's set to `False`). Insert the following code at the top of the procedure:

```
If AbortProc Then
    AbortProc = False
    Exit Sub
End if
```

The event procedure is re-entered, but the `True` state of `AbortProc` causes the procedure to end. In addition, `AbortProc` is reset back to `False`.

For a practical example of validating data, see "Validating data entry," later in this chapter.

Disabling events in Excel applies to all workbooks. For example, if you disable events in your procedure and then open another workbook that has, say, a `Workbook_Open` procedure, that procedure will not execute.

Entering event handler code

Every event handler procedure has a predetermined name. Following are some examples of event handler procedure names:

◆ `Worksheet_SelectionChange`

◆ `Workbook_Open`

◆ `Chart_Activate`

◆ `Class_Initialize`

You can declare the procedure by typing it manually, but a much better approach is to let the VBE do it for you.

Figure 19-2 shows the code module for the ThisWorkbook object. To insert a procedure declaration, select Workbook from the objects list on the left. Then select the event from the procedures list on the right. When you do so, you get a procedure "shell" that contains the procedure declaration line and an End Sub statement.

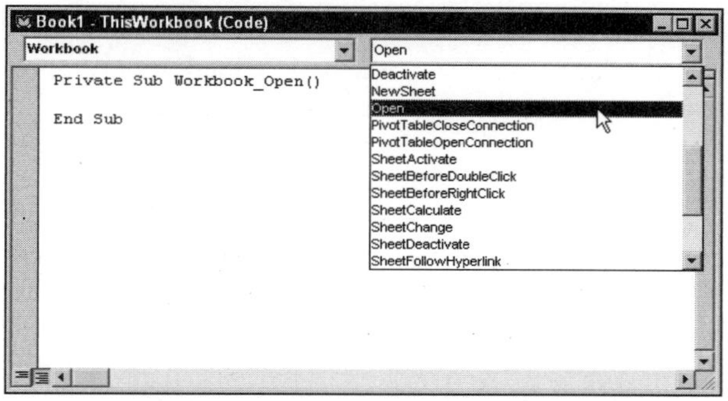

Figure 19-2: The best way to create an event procedure is to let the VBE do it for you.

For example, if you select Workbook from the objects list and Open from the procedures list, the VBE inserts the following (empty) procedure:

```
Private Sub Workbook_Open()

End Sub
```

Your code, of course, goes between these two statements.

Event handler procedures that use arguments

Some event handler procedures use an argument list. For example, you might need to create an event handler procedure to monitor the SheetActivate event for a workbook. If you use the technique described in the previous section, the VBE creates the following procedure:

```
Private Sub Workbook_SheetActivate(ByVal Sh As Object)

End Sub
```

This procedure uses one argument (Sh), which represents the sheet that was activated. In this case, Sh is declared as an Object data type rather than a Worksheet data type. That's because the activated sheet can also be a chart sheet.

Your code, of course, can make use of the data passed as an argument. The following procedure is executed whenever a sheet is activated. It displays the type and name of the activated sheet by using VBA's TypeName function and accessing the Name property of the object passed in the argument:

```
Private Sub Workbook_SheetActivate(ByVal Sh As Object)
    MsgBox TypeName(Sh) & vbCrLf & Sh.Name
End Sub
```

Several event handler procedures use a Boolean argument named Cancel. For example, the declaration for a workbook's BeforePrint event is as follows:

```
Private Sub Workbook_BeforePrint(Cancel As Boolean)
```

The value of Cancel passed to the procedure is False. However, your code can set Cancel to True, which will cancel the printing. The following example demonstrates:

```
Private Sub Workbook_BeforePrint(Cancel As Boolean)
    Msg = "Have you loaded the 5164 label stock?"
    Ans = MsgBox(Msg, vbYesNo, "About to print...")
    If Ans = vbNo Then Cancel = True
End Sub
```

The Workbook_BeforePrint procedure is executed before the workbook is printed. This routine displays the message box shown in Figure 19-3. If the user clicks the No button, Cancel is set to True, and nothing is printed.

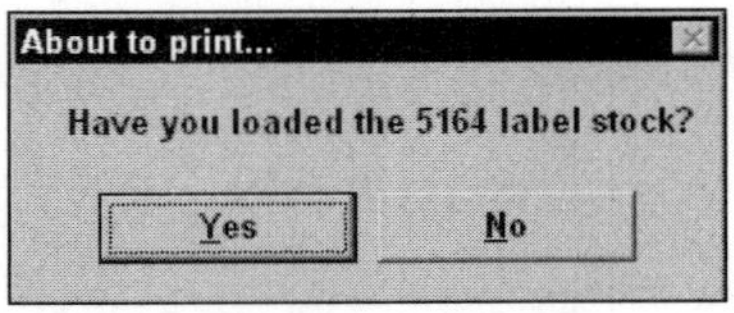

![About to print... dialog box with message "Have you loaded the 5164 label stock?" and Yes and No buttons]

Figure 19-3: You can cancel the print operation by changing the Cancel argument.

The BeforePrint event also occurs when the user previews a worksheet.

Unfortunately, Excel does not provide a sheet-level BeforePrint event. Therefore, your code cannot determine what is about to be printed.

Workbook-Level Events

Workbook-level events occur within a particular workbook. Table 19-1 lists the workbook events, along with a brief description of each. Workbook event handler procedures are stored in the code module for the ThisWorkbook object.

TABLE 19-1 WORKBOOK EVENTS

Event	Action That Triggers the Event
Activate	A workbook is activated.
AddinInstall	A workbook is installed as an add-in.
AddinUninstall	A workbook is uninstalled as an add-in.
AfterXMLExport**	An XML file has been exported.
AfterXMLImport**	An XML file has been imported, or an XML data connection has been refreshed.
BeforeClose	A workbook is about to be closed.
BeforePrint	A workbook (or anything in it) is about to be printed or previewed.
BeforeSave	A workbook is about to be saved.
BeforeXMLExport**	An XML file is about to be exported, or an XML data connection is about to be refreshed.
BeforeXMLImport**	An XML file is about to be imported
Deactivate	A workbook is deactivated.
NewSheet	A new sheet is created in a workbook.
Open	A workbook is opened.
PivotTableCloseConnection*	An external data source connection for a pivot table is closed.
PivotTableOpenConnection*	An external data source connection for a pivot table is opened.
SheetActivate	Any sheet is activated.
SheetBeforeDoubleClick	Any worksheet is double-clicked. This event occurs before the default double-click action.

Continued

TABLE 19-1 WORKBOOK EVENTS *(Continued)*

Event	Action That Triggers the Event
SheetBeforeRightClick	Any worksheet is right-clicked. This event occurs before the default right-click action.
SheetCalculate	Any worksheet is calculated (or recalculated).
SheetChange	Any worksheet is changed by the user or by an external link.
SheetDeactivate	Any sheet is deactivated.
SheetFollowHyperlink	A hyperlink on a sheet is clicked.
SheetPivotTableUpdate*	A pivot table is updated with new data.
SheetSelectionChange	The selection on any worksheet is changed.
Sync**	A workbook that is part of a Document Workspace is synchronized with the copy on the server.
WindowActivate	Any workbook window is activated.
WindowDeactivate	Any workbook window is deactivated.
WindowResize	Any workbook window is resized.

These events occur only in Excel 2002 and are not supported in previous versions.

**These events occur only in Excel 2003 Professional Edition and are not supported in previous versions or in the non-Professional Edition of Excel 2003.

If you need to monitor events for *any* workbook, you need to work with Application-level events (see "Application Events," later in this chapter). The remainder of this section presents examples of using Workbook-level events. All the example procedures that follow must be located in the code module for the ThisWorkbook object. If you put them into any other type of code module, they won't work.

The Open event

One of the most common events that is monitored is the Open event for a workbook. This event is triggered when the workbook (or add-in) is opened and executes the Workbook_Open procedure. A Workbook_Open procedure can do almost anything and often is used for tasks such as

◆ Displaying welcome messages.

◆ Opening other workbooks.

◆ Setting up custom menus or toolbars.

◆ Activating a particular sheet or cell.

◆ Ensuring that certain conditions are met. For example, a workbook may require that a particular add-in is installed.

◆ Setting up certain automatic features. For example, you can define key combinations (see "The OnKey event" later in this chapter).

◆ Setting a worksheet's ScrollArea property (which isn't stored with the workbook).

◆ Setting UserInterfaceOnly protection for worksheets so that your code can operate on protected sheets. This setting is an argument for the Protect method and is not stored with the workbook.

 If the user holds down the Shift key when opening a workbook, the workbook's Workbook_Open procedure will not execute. And, of course, the procedure will not execute if the workbook is opened with macros disabled.

Following is a simple example of a Workbook_Open procedure. It uses VBA's Weekday function to determine the day of the week. If it's Friday, a message box appears, reminding the user to perform a weekly file backup. If it's not Friday, nothing happens.

```
Private Sub Workbook_Open()
   If Weekday(Now) = vbFriday Then
       Msg = "Today is Friday. Make sure that you "
       Msg = Msg & "do your weekly backup!"
       MsgBox Msg, vbInformation
   End If
End Sub
```

The Activate event

The following procedure is executed whenever the workbook is activated. This procedure simply maximizes the active window.

```
Private Sub Workbook_Activate()
    ActiveWindow.WindowState = xlMaximized
End Sub
```

The SheetActivate event

The following procedure is executed whenever the user activates any sheet in the workbook. If the sheet is a worksheet, the code simply selects cell A1. If the sheet is not a worksheet, nothing happens. This procedure uses VBA's TypeName function to ensure that the activated sheet is a worksheet (as opposed to a chart sheet).

```
Private Sub Workbook_SheetActivate(ByVal Sh As Object)
    If TypeName(Sh) = "Worksheet" Then _
        Range("A1").Select
End Sub
```

An alternative method to avoid the error that occurs when you try to select a cell on a chart sheet is to simply ignore the error.

```
Private Sub Workbook_SheetActivate(ByVal Sh As Object)
    On Error Resume Next
    Range("A1").Select
End Sub
```

The NewSheet event

The following procedure is executed whenever a new sheet is added to the workbook. The sheet is passed to the procedure as an argument. Because a new sheet can be either a worksheet or a chart sheet, this procedure determines the sheet type. If it's a worksheet, the code inserts a date and time stamp in cell A1 on the new sheet.

```
Private Sub Workbook_NewSheet(ByVal Sh As Object)
    If TypeName(Sh) = "Worksheet" Then _
        Sh.Range("A1") = "Sheet added " & Now()
End Sub
```

The BeforeSave event

The BeforeSave event occurs before the workbook is actually saved. As you know, choosing the File→Save command sometimes brings up the Save As dialog box. This happens if the workbook has never been saved or if it was opened in read-only mode.

When the Workbook_BeforeSave procedure is executed, it receives an argument (SaveAsUI) that lets you identify whether the Save As dialog box will be displayed. The following example demonstrates:

```
Private Sub Workbook_BeforeSave _
    (ByVal SaveAsUI As Boolean, Cancel As Boolean)
    If SaveAsUI Then
```

```
        MsgBox "Make sure you save this file on drive J."
    End If
End Sub
```

When the user attempts to save the workbook, the `Workbook_BeforeSave` procedure is executed. If the save operation will bring up Excel's Save As dialog box, the `SaveAsUI` variable is `True`. The procedure above checks this variable and displays a message only if the Save As dialog box will be displayed. If the procedure sets the `Cancel` argument to `True`, the file will not be saved.

The Deactivate event

The following example demonstrates the `Deactivate` event. This procedure is executed whenever the workbook is deactivated, and essentially never lets the user deactivate the workbook. When the `Deactivate` event occurs, the code reactivates the workbook and displays a message.

```
Private Sub Workbook_Deactivate()
    Me.Activate
    MsgBox "Sorry, you may not leave this workbook"
End Sub
```

I do not recommend using procedures, such as this one, that attempt to "take over" Excel. It can be very frustrating and confusing for the user. Rather, I would recommend training the user how to use your application correctly.

This simple example illustrates the importance of understanding event sequences. If you try out this procedure, you'll see that it works well if the user attempts to activate another workbook. However, it's important to understand that the workbook `Deactivate` event is also triggered by the following actions:

◆ Closing the workbook

◆ Opening a new workbook

◆ Minimizing the workbook

In other words, this procedure might not perform as it was originally intended. It does prevent the user from activating a different workbook directly, but he or she can close the workbook, open a new one, or minimize the workbook. The message box will still appear, but the actions will occur anyway.

The BeforePrint event

The `BeforePrint` event occurs when the user requests a print or a print preview but before the printing or previewing actually occurs. The event uses a `Cancel` argument, so your code can cancel the printing or previewing by setting the `Cancel` variable to `True`. Unfortunately, there is no way to determine whether the `BeforePrint` event was triggered by a print request or a preview request.

Before Excel 2002, users were often dismayed to discover that it was not possible to print a workbook's full path in the page header or footer. Excel 2002 solved this problem by adding a new option to the Header and Footer dialog boxes (accessed from the Page Setup dialog box).

If you're still using an older version of Excel, the only solution is to write code that inserts the workbook's path into the header or footer. The `Workbook_BeforePrint` event is perfect for this. The following code demonstrates:

```
Private Sub Workbook_BeforePrint(Cancel As Boolean)
    For Each sht In ThisWorkbook.Sheets
        sht.PageSetup.LeftFooter = _
          "&8" & ThisWorkbook.FullName
    Next sht
End Sub
```

This procedure loops through each sheet in the workbook and sets the `LeftFooter` property of the `PageSetup` object to the `FullName` property of the workbook (which is the filename and path). It also sets the font size to 8 points.

This example exposes an inconsistency in Excel's object model. To change the font size of header or footer text, you must use a string that contains a special formatting code. In the example above, &8 is the code for 8-point font. Ideally, there should be a `Font` object available for page headers and footers. To find out the other formatting codes available, consult the online help (or record a macro while you access the Page Setup dialog box).

When testing `BeforePrint` event handlers, you can save time (and paper) by previewing rather than actually printing.

The BeforeClose event

The `BeforeClose` event occurs before a workbook is closed. This event is often used in conjunction with a `Workbook_Open` event handler. For example, you might use the `Workbook_Open` procedure to create a custom menu for your workbook, and then use the `Workbook_BeforeClose` procedure to delete the custom menu when the workbook is closed. That way, the custom menu is available only when the workbook is open.

As you know, if you attempt to close a workbook that hasn't been saved, Excel displays a prompt asking whether you want to save the workbook before closing, as shown in Figure 19-4.

Microsoft Office Excel

Do you want to save the changes you made to 'budget 2004.xls'?

| Yes | No | Cancel |

Figure 19-4: When this message appears, `Workbook_BeforeClose` has already done its thing.

A potential problem can arise because by the time the user sees this message, the `BeforeClose` event has already occurred — which means that your `Workbook_BeforeClose` procedure has already executed.

Consider this scenario: You need to display a custom menu when a particular workbook is open. Therefore, your workbook uses a `Workbook_Open` procedure to create the menu when the workbook is opened, and it uses a `Workbook_BeforeClose` procedure to remove the menu when the workbook is closed. These two event handler procedures follow. Both of these call other procedures, which are not shown here.

```
Private Sub Workbook_Open()
    Call CreateMenu
End Sub

Private Sub Workbook_BeforeClose(Cancel As Boolean)
    Call DeleteMenu
End Sub
```

As I note earlier, Excel's Do you want to save . . . prompt occurs *after* the Workbook_BeforeClose event handler runs. So if the user clicks Cancel, the workbook remains open, but the custom menu item has already been deleted!

One solution to this problem is to bypass Excel's prompt and write your own code in the Workbook_BeforeClose procedure to ask the user to save the workbook. The following code demonstrates:

```
Private Sub Workbook_BeforeClose(Cancel As Boolean)
    Dim Msg As String
    If Me.Saved = False Then
        Msg = "Do you want to save the changes you made to "
        Msg = Msg & Me.Name & "?"
        Ans = MsgBox(Msg, vbQuestion + vbYesNoCancel)
        Select Case Ans
            Case vbYes
                Me.Save
            Case vbCancel
                Cancel = True
                Exit Sub
        End Select
    End If
    Call DeleteMenu
    Me.Saved = True
End Sub
```

This procedure checks the Saved property of the Workbook object to determine whether the workbook has been saved. If so, no problem — the DeleteMenu procedure is executed, and the workbook is closed. But if the workbook has not been saved, the procedure displays a message box that duplicates the one that Excel would normally show. If the user clicks Yes, the workbook is saved, the menu is deleted, and the workbook is closed. If the user clicks No, the code sets the Saved property of the Workbook object to True (but doesn't actually save the file), deletes the menu, and the file is closed. If the user clicks Cancel, the BeforeClose event is canceled, and the procedure ends without deleting the menu.

Worksheet Events

The events for a Worksheet object are some of the most useful. As you can see, monitoring these events can make your applications perform feats that would otherwise be impossible.

Table 19-2 lists the worksheet events, with a brief description of each.

TABLE 19-2 WORKSHEET EVENTS

Event	Action That Triggers the Event
Activate	The worksheet is activated.
BeforeDoubleClick	The worksheet is double-clicked.
BeforeRightClick	The worksheet is right-clicked.
Calculate	The worksheet is calculated (or recalculated).
Change	Cells on the worksheet are changed by the user or by an external link.
Deactivate	The worksheet is deactivated.
FollowHyperlink	A hyperlink on the sheet is clicked.
PivotTableUpdate*	A pivot table on the sheet is updated.
SelectionChange	The selection on the worksheet is changed.

This event was added in Excel 2002 and is not supported in previous versions.

Remember that the code for a worksheet event must be stored in the code module for the specific worksheet.

TIP To quickly activate the code module for a worksheet, right-click the sheet tab and then choose View Code.

The Change event

The Change event is triggered when any cell in a worksheet is changed by the user or by a VBA procedure. The Change event is not triggered when a calculation generates a different value for a formula or when an object is added to the sheet.

When the Worksheet_Change procedure is executed, it receives a Range object as its Target argument. This Range object represents the changed cell or range that triggered the event. The following procedure is executed whenever the worksheet is changed. It displays a message box that shows the address of the Target range:

```
Private Sub Worksheet_Change(ByVal Target As Excel.Range)
    MsgBox "Range " & Target.Address & " was changed."
End Sub
```

To get a better feel for the types of actions that generate a `Change` event for a worksheet, enter the preceding procedure in the code module for a `Worksheet` object. After entering this procedure, activate Excel and make some changes to the worksheet by using various techniques. Every time that the `Change` event occurs, you'll see a message box that displays the address of the range that was changed.

When I ran this procedure, I discovered some interesting quirks. Some actions that should trigger the event don't, and other actions that should not trigger the event do!

◆ Changing the formatting of a cell does not trigger the `Change` event (as expected), but choosing the Edit → Clear → Formats command *does* trigger the event.

◆ Adding, editing, or deleting a cell comment does not trigger the `Change` event.

◆ Pressing Delete generates an event even if the cell is empty to start with.

◆ Cells that are changed by using Excel commands may or may not trigger the `Change` event. For example, the Data → Form command and the Data → Sort command do not trigger the event. But the Tools → Spelling command and the Edit → Replace command do trigger the `Change` event.

◆ If your VBA procedure changes a cell, it *does* trigger the `Change` event.

As you can see from the preceding list, it's not a good idea to rely on the `Change` event to detect cell changes for critical applications.

 To add to the confusion, triggers for the `Change` event vary, depending on the version of Excel. For versions earlier than Excel 2002, filling a range by choosing the Edit → Fill command does not generate a `Change` event — nor does choosing the Edit → Delete command to delete cells.

Monitoring a specific range for changes

The `Change` event occurs when any cell on the worksheet is changed. But in most cases, all you care about are changes made to a specific cell or range. When the `Worksheet_Change` event handler procedure is called, it receives a `Range` object as its argument. This `Range` object represents the cell or cells that were changed.

Assume that your worksheet has a range named `InputRange`, and you would like to monitor changes made only within this range. There is no `Change` event for a `Range` object, but you can perform a quick check within the `Worksheet_Change` procedure. The following procedure demonstrates:

```
Private Sub Worksheet_Change(ByVal Target As Excel.Range)
    Dim VRange As Range
    Set VRange = Range("InputRange")
    If Not Intersect(Target, VRange) Is Nothing Then _
        MsgBox "A changed cell is in the input range."
End Sub
```

This example uses a `Range` object variable named `VRange`, which represents the worksheet range that you are interested in monitoring for changes. The procedure uses VBA's `Intersect` function to determine whether the `Target` range (passed to the procedure in its argument) intersects with `VRange`. The `Intersect` function returns an object that consists of all the cells that are contained in both of its arguments. If the `Intersect` function returns `Nothing`, the ranges have no cells in common. The `Not` operator is used so the expression returns `True` if the ranges *do* have at least one cell in common. Therefore, if the changed range has any cells in common with the range named `InputRange`, a message box is displayed. Otherwise, the procedure ends, and nothing happens.

MONITORING A RANGE TO MAKE FORMULAS BOLD
The following example monitors a worksheet and also makes formula entries bold and non-formula entries not bold.

 This example is available on the companion CD-ROM.

```
Private Sub Worksheet_Change(ByVal Target As Excel.Range)
    Dim cell As Range
    For Each cell In Target
        cell.Font.Bold = cell.HasFormula
    Next cell
End Sub
```

Because the object passed to the `Worksheet_Change` procedure can consist of a multicell range, the procedure loops through each cell in the `Target` range. If the cell has a formula, it is made bold. Otherwise, the `Bold` property is set to `False`.

MONITORING A RANGE TO VALIDATE DATA ENTRY
Excel's Data Validation feature is a useful tool, but it suffers from a potentially serious problem. When you paste data to a cell that uses data validation, the pasted value not only fails to get validated, but it also deletes the validation rules associated

with the cell! This fact makes the Data Validation feature practically worthless for critical applications. In this section, I demonstrate how you can make use of the Change event for a worksheet to create your own data validation procedure.

The companion CD-ROM contains two versions of this example. One uses the EnableEvents property to prevent cascading Change events; the other uses a Static variable (see "Disabling events," earlier in this chapter).

Listing 19-1 presents a procedure that is executed when a cell is changed by the user. The validation is restricted to the range named InputRange. Values entered into this range must be integers between 1 and 12.

Listing 19-1: Determining Whether a Cell Entry is To Be Validated

```
Private Sub Worksheet_Change(ByVal Target As Excel.Range)
    Dim VRange As Range, cell As Range
    Dim Msg As String
    Dim ValidateCode As Variant
    Set VRange = Range("InputRange")
    If Intersect(VRange, Target) Is Nothing Then Exit Sub
    For Each cell In Intersect(VRange, Target)
        ValidateCode = EntryIsValid(cell)
        If TypeName(ValidateCode) = "String" Then
            Msg = "Cell " & cell.Address(False, False) & ":"
            Msg = Msg & vbCrLf & vbCrLf & ValidateCode
            MsgBox Msg, vbCritical, "Invalid Entry"
            Application.EnableEvents = False
            cell.ClearContents
            cell.Activate
            Application.EnableEvents = True
        End If
    Next cell
End Sub
```

The Worksheet_Change procedure creates a Range object (named VRange) that represents the worksheet range that is validated. Then it loops through each cell in the Target argument, which represents the cell or cells that were changed. The code determines whether each cell is contained in the range to be validated. If so, it passes the cell as an argument to a custom function (EntryIsValid), which returns True if the cell is a valid entry.

If the entry is not valid, the EntryIsValid function returns a string that describes the problem, and the user is informed via a message box (see Figure 19-5). When the message box is dismissed, the invalid entry is cleared from the cell, and the cell is activated. Notice that events are disabled before the cell is cleared. If events were not disabled, clearing the cell would produce a Change event that causes an endless loop.

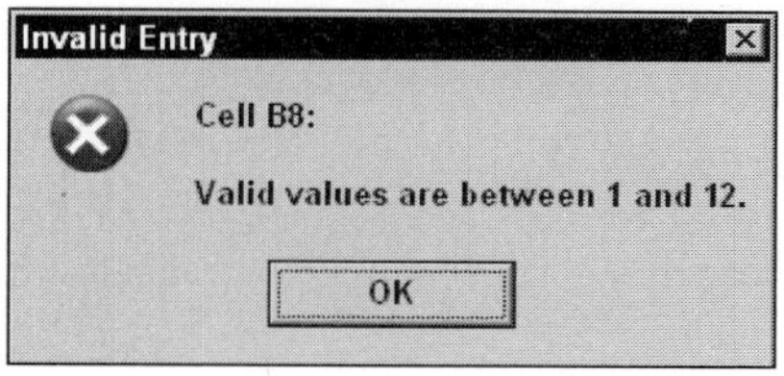

Figure 19-5: This message box describes the problem when the user makes an invalid entry.

The EntryIsValid function procedure is presented in Listing 19-2.

Listing 19-2: Validating an Entry Just Made into a restricted Range

```
Private Function EntryIsValid(cell) As Variant
'    Returns True if cell is an integer between 1 and 12
'    Otherwise it returns a string that describes the problem

'    Numeric?
    If Not WorksheetFunction.IsNumber (cell) Then
        EntryIsValid = "Non-numeric entry."
        Exit Function
    End If
'    Integer?
    If CInt(cell) <> cell Then
        EntryIsValid = "Integer required."
        Exit Function
    End If
'    Between 1 and 12?
    If cell < 1 Or cell > 12 Then
        EntryIsValid = "Valid values are between 1 and 12."
        Exit Function
    End If
'    It passed all the tests
    EntryIsValid = True
End Function
```

The SelectionChange event

The following procedure demonstrates the SelectionChange event. It's executed whenever the user makes a new selection on the worksheet.

```
Private Sub Worksheet_SelectionChange(ByVal Target _
 As Excel.Range)
    Cells.Interior.ColorIndex = xlNone
    With ActiveCell
        .EntireRow.Interior.ColorIndex = 36
        .EntireColumn.Interior.ColorIndex = 36
    End With
End Sub
```

This procedure shades the row and column of the active cell, which makes it very easy to identify the active cell. The first statement removes the background color for all cells in the worksheet. Next, the entire row and column of the active cell is shaded light yellow. Figure 19-6 shows the shading in effect.

	A	B	C	D	E	F	G	H	Pro
1		Project-1	Project-2	Project-3	Project-4	Project-5	Project-6	Project-7	
2	Jan-2002	1812	3003	2633	2988	2010	4094	4474	
3	Feb-2002	4590	944	3125	4319	3925	4668	3188	
4	Mar-2002	2524	2027	4732	978	3803	2223	3075	
5	Apr-2002	3775	1134	3955	3317	4743	1357	3033	
6	May-2002	2357	3470	538	3221	2032	570	4740	
7	Jun-2002	3416	2497	551	2165	3703	411	3258	
8	Jul-2002	548	3346	292	3181	4935	4708	4742	
9	Aug-2002	292	1946	122	2927	2244	4564	1119	
10	Sep-2002	3429	112	4623	3404	2969	367	4749	
11	Oct-2002	4109	3701	1179	3357	2674	3781	4783	
12	Nov-2002	4422	2009	1308	3119	3597	3913	1212	
13	Dec-2002	4873	3128	3785	2739	4956	80	3779	
14	Jan-2003	557	852	3144	2661	2723	364	2005	
15	Feb-2003	2113	3358	4548	4126	1507	3601	186	
16	Mar-2003	3076	1320	675	1217	2267	695	4552	
17	Apr-2003	3531	3212	1766	4843	4086	637	1116	
18	May-2003	4897	3455	72	3335	3875	2789	1467	
19	Jun-2003	200	3093	888	3765	4174	1986	1444	
20	Jul-2003	3011	3867	3559	4976	2631	418	3622	

Figure 19-6: Moving the cell cursor causes the active cell's row and column to be shaded.

 This example is available on the companion CD-ROM.

You won't want to use the procedure if your worksheet contains background shading because it will be wiped out.

The BeforeRightClick event

When the user right-clicks in a worksheet, Excel displays a shortcut menu. If, for some reason, you'd like to prevent the shortcut menu from appearing in a particular sheet, you can trap the RightClick event. The following procedure sets the Cancel argument to True, which cancels the RightClick event and thereby cancels the shortcut menu. Instead, a message box is displayed.

```
Private Sub Worksheet_BeforeRightClick _
   (ByVal Target As Excel.Range, Cancel As Boolean)
      Cancel = True
      MsgBox "The shortcut menu is not available."
End Sub
```

Chapter 24 describes other methods to disable shortcut menus.

Chart Events

By default, events are enabled only for charts that reside on a Chart sheet. To work with events for an embedded chart, you need to create a class module.

Refer to Chapter 18 for examples that deal with Chart events. Chapter 18 also describes how to create a class module to enable events for embedded charts.

Table 19-3 contains a list of the chart events as well as a brief description of each.

TABLE 19-3 EVENTS RECOGNIZED BY A CHART SHEET

Event	Action That Triggers the Event
Activate	The chart sheet or embedded chart is activated.
BeforeDoubleClick	The chart sheet or an embedded chart is double-clicked. This event occurs before the default double-click action.
BeforeRightClick	The chart sheet or an embedded chart is right-clicked. The event occurs before the default right-click action.
Calculate	New or changed data is plotted on a chart.
Deactivate	The chart is deactivated.
DragOver	A range of cells is dragged over a chart.
DragPlot	A range of cells is dragged and dropped onto a chart.
MouseDown	A mouse button is pressed while the pointer is over a chart.
MouseMove	The position of the mouse pointer changes over a chart.
MouseUp	A mouse button is released while the pointer is over a chart.
Resize	The chart is resized.
Select	A chart element is selected.
SeriesChange	The value of a chart data point is changed.

Using the Object Browser to Locate Events

The Object Browser is a useful tool that can help you learn about objects and their properties and methods. It can also help you find out which objects support a particular event. For example, say you'd like to find out which objects support the MouseMove event. Activate the VBE and press F2 to display the Object Browser window. Make sure that <All Libraries> is selected; then type **MouseMove** and click the binoculars icon (see the accompanying figure).

The Object Browser displays a list of matching items. Events are indicated with a small yellow lightning bolt. From this list, you can see which objects support the MouseMove event. Most of the objects located are controls in the MSForms library, home of the UserForm control. But you can also see that Excel's Chart object supports the MouseMove event.

Notice how the list is divided into three columns: Library, Class, and Members. The match for the item that you're searching for might appear in any of these columns. This brings up a crucial point: The name of an event or term belonging to one library or class could be the same as that for another belonging to a different library or class — although they probably don't share the same functionality. So be sure to click each item in the Object Browser list and check the status bar at the bottom of the list for the syntax. You might find, for instance, that one class or library treats an event differently.

Application Events

In earlier sections, I discuss `Workbook` events and `Worksheet` events. Those events are monitored for a particular workbook. If you would like to monitor events for all open workbooks or all worksheets, you use `Application` level events.

> **NOTE** Creating event handler procedures to handle `Application` events always requires a class module and some set-up work.

Table 19-4 lists the `Application` events with a brief description of each.

TABLE 19-4 EVENTS RECOGNIZED BY THE APPLICATION OBJECT

Event	Action That Triggers the Event
NewWorkbook	A new workbook is created.
SheetActivate	Any sheet is activated.
SheetBeforeDoubleClick	Any worksheet is double-clicked. This event occurs before the default double-click action.
SheetBeforeRightClick	Any worksheet is right-clicked. This event occurs before the default right-click action.
SheetCalculate	Any worksheet is calculated (or recalculated).
SheetChange	Cells in any worksheet are changed by the user or by an external link.
SheetDeactivate	Any sheet is deactivated.
SheetFollowHyperlink	A hyperlink is clicked.
SheetPivotTableUpdate*	Any pivot table is updated.
SheetSelectionChange	The selection changes on any worksheet except a chart sheet.
WindowActivate	Any workbook window is activated.
WindowDeactivate	Any workbook window is deactivated.
WindowResize	Any workbook window is resized.
WorkbookActivate	Any workbook is activated.
WorkbookAddinInstall	A workbook is installed as an add-in.
WorkbookAddinUninstall	Any add-in workbook is uninstalled.
WorkbookAfterXMLExport**	An XML file has been exported.
WorkbookAfterXMLImport**	An XML file has been imported, or an XML data connection has been refreshed.
WorkbookBeforeClose	Any open workbook is closed.
WorkbookBeforePrint	Any open workbook is printed.
WorkbookBeforeSave	Any open workbook is saved.
WorkbookBeforeXMLExport**	An XML file is about to be exported, or an XML data connection is about to be refreshed.

Event	Action That Triggers the Event
WorkbookBeforeXMLImport**	An XML file is about to be imported.
WorkbookDeactivate	Any open workbook is deactivated.
WorkbookNewSheet	A new sheet is created in any open workbook.
WorkbookOpen	A workbook is opened.
WorkbookPivotTableCloseConnection*	An external data source connection for any pivot table is closed.
WorkbookPivotTableOpenConnection*	An external data source connection for any pivot table is opened.
WorkbookSync**	A workbook that is part of a Document Workspace is synchronized with the copy on the server.

*These events occur only in Excel 2002 and later and are not supported in previous versions.

**These events occur only in Excel 2003 Professional Edition and are not supported in previous versions or in the non-Professional Edition of Excel 2003.

Enabling Application-level events

To make use of Application-level events, you need to

1. Create a new class module.

2. Set a name for this class module in the Properties window under *Name*.

   By default, VBA gives each new class module a default name such as Class1, Class2, and so on. I strongly recommend that you give your class module a more meaningful name, such as clsApp.

3. In the class module, declare a public Application object by using the WithEvents keyword. For example:

   ```
   Public WithEvents XL As Application
   ```

4. Create a variable that you will use to refer to the declared Application object in the class module. This should be a module-level object variable, declared in a regular VBA module (not in the class module). For example:

   ```
   Dim X As New clsApp
   ```

5. Connect the declared object with the `Application` object. This is often done in a `Workbook_Open` procedure. For example:

```
Set X.XL = Application
```

6. Write event handler procedures for the `XL` object in the class module.

This procedure is virtually identical to that required to use events with an embedded chart. See Chapter 18.

Determining when a workbook is opened

The example in this section keeps track of every workbook that is opened by storing information in a text file. I started by inserting a new class module and naming it `clsApp`. The code in the class module is

```
Public WithEvents AppEvents As Application

Private Sub AppEvents_WorkbookOpen _
  (ByVal Wb As Excel.Workbook)
    Call UpdateLogFile(Wb)
End Sub
```

This declares `AppEvents` as an `Application` object with events. The `AppEvents_WorkbookOpen` procedure will be called whenever a workbook is opened. This event handler procedure calls `UpdateLogFile` and passes the `Wb` variable, which represents the workbook that was opened. I then added a VBA module and inserted the following code:

```
Dim AppObject As New clsApp

Sub Init()
'    Called by Workbook_Open
    Set AppObject.AppEvents = Application
End Sub

Sub UpdateLogFile(Wb)
    txt = Wb.FullName
    txt = txt & "," & Date & "," & Time
    txt = txt & "," & Application.UserName
    Fname = ThisWorkbook.Path & "\logfile.txt"
```

```
        Open Fname For Append As #1
        Write #1, txt
        Close #1
        MsgBox txt
End Sub
```

Notice at the top that the AppObject variable is declared as type clsApp; this is the name of the class module. The call to Init is in the Workbook_Open procedure, which is in the code module for ThisWorkbook. This procedure is as follows:

```
Private Sub Workbook_Open()
    Call Init
End Sub
```

The UpdateLogFile procedure opens a text file — or creates it if it doesn't exist. It then writes key information about the workbook that was opened: The filename and full path, the date, the time, and the username.

The Workbook_Open procedure calls the Init procedure. Therefore, when the workbook opens, the Init procedure creates the object variable.

This example is available on the companion CD-ROM. Make sure that you copy the file to your hard drive before using it. The text file is written to the same directory as the workbook, so the code will fail if the workbook is stored on a CD-ROM drive.

Monitoring Application-level events

To get a feel for the event generation process, you might find it helpful to see a list of events that get generated as you go about your work.

The companion CD-ROM contains a workbook that displays, in a UserForm, each Application-level event as it occurs (see Figure 19-7).

The workbook contains a class module with 21 procedures defined, one for each Application-level event. Here's an example of one of them:

```
Private Sub XL_NewWorkbook(ByVal Wb As Excel.Workbook)
    LogEvent "NewWorkbook: " & Wb.Name
End Sub
```

Each of these procedures calls the LogEvent procedure and passes an argument that consists of the event name and the object. The LogEvent procedure follows:

```
Sub LogEvent(txt)
    EventNum = EventNum + 1
    With UserForm1
        With .lblEvents
            .AutoSize = False
            .Caption = .Caption & vbCrLf & txt
            .Width = UserForm1.FrameEvents.Width - 20
            .AutoSize = True
        . End With
        .FrameEvents.ScrollHeight = .lblEvents.Height + 20
        .FrameEvents.ScrollTop = EventNum * 20
    End With
End Sub
```

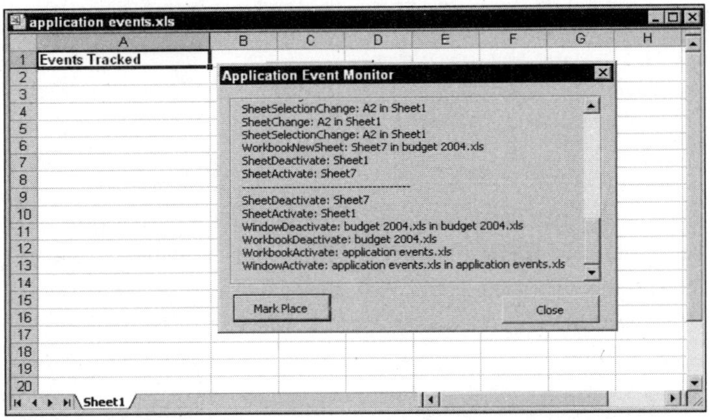

Figure 19-7: This workbook uses a class module to monitor all Application-level events.

The LogEvent procedure updates the UserForm by modifying the Caption property of the Label control named lblEvents. The procedure also adjusts the ScrollHeight and ScrollTop properties of the Frame named FrameEvents, which contains the Label. Adjusting these properties causes the most recently added text to be visible while older text scrolls out of view.

UserForm Events

A UserForm supports quite a few events, and each control placed on a UserForm has its own set of events. Table 19-5 lists the UserForm events that you can trap.

TABLE 19-5 EVENTS RECOGNIZED BY A USERFORM

Event	Action That Triggers the Event
Activate	The UserForm is activated.
AddControl	A control is added at runtime.
BeforeDragOver	A drag-and-drop operation is in progress while the pointer is over the form.
BeforeDropOrPaste	The user is about to drop or paste data: that is, when the user has released the mouse button.
Click	A mouse is clicked while the pointer is over the form.
DblClick	A mouse is double-clicked while the pointer is over the form.
Deactivate	The UserForm is deactivated.
Error	A control detects an error and cannot return the error information to a calling program.
Initialize	The UserForm is about to be shown.
KeyDown	A key is pressed.
KeyPress	The user presses any ANSI key.
KeyUp	A key is released.
Layout	A UserForm changes size.
MouseDown	A mouse button is pressed.
MouseMove	The mouse is moved.
MouseUp	A mouse button is released.
QueryClose	Occurs before a UserForm closes.
RemoveControl	A control is removed from the UserForm at runtime.
Resize	The UserForm is resized.
Scroll	The UserForm is scrolled.
Terminate	The UserForm is terminated.
Zoom	The UserForm is zoomed.

Many of the examples in Chapters 13 through 15 demonstrate event handling for UserForms and UserForm controls.

Events Not Associated with an Object

The events that I discuss earlier in this chapter are all associated with an object (Application, Workbook, Sheet, and so on.). In this section, I discuss two additional rogue events: OnTime and OnKey. These events are not associated with an object. Rather, these events are accessed by using methods of the Application object.

Unlike the other events discussed in this chapter, you program these On events in a general VBA module.

The OnTime event

The OnTime event occurs at a specified time of day. The following example demonstrates how to program Excel so that it beeps and then displays a message at 3 p.m.:

```
Sub SetAlarm()
    Application.OnTime TimeValue("15:00:00"), "DisplayAlarm"
End Sub

Sub DisplayAlarm()
    Beep
    MsgBox "Wake up. It's time for your afternoon break!"
End Sub
```

In this example, the SetAlarm procedure uses the OnTime method of the Application object to set up the OnTime event. This method takes two arguments: the time (3 p.m., in the example) and the procedure to execute when the time occurs (DisplayAlarm in the example). After SetAlarm is executed, the DisplayAlarm procedure will be called at 3 p.m., bringing up the message in Figure 19-8.

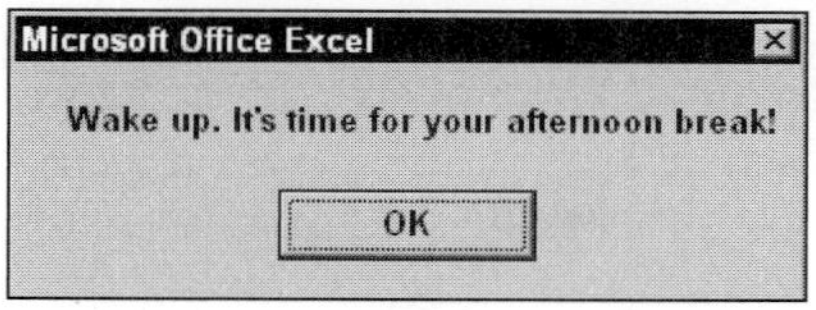

Microsoft Office Excel [×]

Wake up. It's time for your afternoon break!

OK

Figure 19-8: This message box was programmed
to display at a particular time of day.

If you want to schedule an event relative to the current time — for example, 20
minutes from now — you can write an instruction like this:

```
Application.OnTime Now + TimeValue("00:20:00"), "DisplayAlarm"
```

You can also use the OnTime method to schedule a procedure on a particular day.
The following statement runs the DisplayAlarm procedure at 12:01 a.m. on April 1,
2004:

```
Application.OnTime DateSerial(2004, 4, 1) + _
    TimeValue("00:00:01"), "DisplayAlarm"
```

The OnTime method has two additional arguments. If you plan to use this
method, you should refer to the online help for complete details.

The two procedures that follow demonstrate how to program a repeated event. In
this case, cell A1 is updated with the current time every five seconds. Executing the
UpdateClock procedures writes the time to cell A1 and also programs another
event five seconds later. This event re-runs the UpdateClock procedure. To stop the
events, execute the StopClock procedure (which cancels the event). Note that
NextTick is a module-level variable that stores the time for the next event.

```
    Dim NextTick As Date

Sub UpdateClock()
'    Updates cell A1 with the current time
    ThisWorkbook.Sheets(1).Range("A1") = Time
'    Set up the next event five seconds from now
    NextTick = Now + TimeValue("00:00:05")
    Application.OnTime NextTick, "UpdateClock"
End Sub
```

```
Sub StopClock()
'    Cancels the OnTime event (stops the clock)
     On Error Resume Next
     Application.OnTime NextTick, "UpdateClock", , False
End Sub
```

The OnTime event persists even after the workbook is closed. In other words, if you close the workbook without running the StopClock procedure, the workbook will reopen itself in five seconds (assuming that Excel is still running). To prevent this, use a Workbook_BeforeClose event procedure that contains the following statement:

```
Call StopClock
```

To see an example of a repeating OnTime event, see the analog clock example in Chapter 18.

The OnKey event

While you're working, Excel constantly monitors what you type. Because of this, you can set up a keystroke or a key combination that, when pressed, executes a particular procedure. The only time when these keystrokes won't be recognized is when you're entering a formula or working with a dialog box.

The following example uses the OnKey method to set up an OnKey event. This event reassigns the PgDn and PgUp keys. After the Setup_OnKey procedure is executed, pressing PgDn executes the PgDn_Sub procedure, and pressing PgUp executes the PgUp_Sub procedure. The net effect is that pressing PgDn moves the cursor down one row, and pressing PgUp moves the cursor up one row.

```
Sub Setup_OnKey()
    Application.OnKey "{PgDn}", "PgDn_Sub"
    Application.OnKey "{PgUp}", "PgUp_Sub"
End Sub

Sub PgDn_Sub()
    On Error Resume Next
    ActiveCell.Offset(1, 0).Activate
End Sub
```

```
Sub PgUp_Sub()
    On Error Resume Next
    ActiveCell.Offset(-1, 0).Activate
End Sub
```

Notice that the key codes are enclosed in curly brackets — not parentheses. For a complete list of the keyboard codes, consult the online help. Search for *OnKey*.

In the preceding examples, I used `On Error Resume Next` to ignore any errors that were generated. For example, if the active cell is in the first row, trying to move up one row causes an error. Also, if the active sheet is a chart sheet, an error will occur because there is no such thing as an active cell in a chart sheet.

By executing the following procedure, you cancel the `OnKey` events and return these keys to their normal functionality:

```
Sub Cancel_OnKey()
    Application.OnKey "{PgDn}"
    Application.OnKey "{PgUp}"
End Sub
```

Contrary to what you might expect, using an empty string as the second argument for the `OnKey` method does *not* cancel the `OnKey` event. Rather, it causes Excel to simply ignore the keystroke and do nothing at all. For example, the following instruction tells Excel to ignore Alt+F4 (the percent sign represents the Alt key):

```
    Application.OnKey "%{F4}", ""
```

Although you can use the `OnKey` method to assign a shortcut key for executing a macro, it's better to use the Macro Options dialog box for this task. For more details, see Chapter 9.

Chapter 20

Interacting with Other Applications

IN THIS CHAPTER

In this chapter, I outline the ways in which your Excel applications can interact with other applications. Of course, I also provide several examples.

◆ Starting or activating another application from Excel

◆ Displaying Windows Control Panel dialogs

◆ Using Automation to control another application

◆ A simple example of using ADO to retrieve data

◆ Using `SendKeys` as a last resort

IN THE EARLY DAYS OF PERSONAL COMPUTING, interapplication communication was rare. In the pre-multitasking era, users had no choice but to use one program at a time. Interapplication communication was usually limited to importing files; even copying information and pasting it into another application – something that virtually every user now takes for granted – was impossible.

Nowadays, most software is designed to support at least some type of communication with other applications. At the very least, most Windows programs support the Clipboard for copy-and-paste operations between applications. Many Windows products support Dynamic Data Exchange (DDE), and other products also support Automation.

Starting an Application from Excel

Starting up another application from Excel is often useful. For example, you might want to execute another Microsoft Office application or even a DOS batch file from Excel. Or, as an application developer, you might want to make it easy for a user to access the Windows Control Panel.

Using the VBA Shell function

The Visual Basic for Applications (VBA) `Shell` function makes launching other programs relatively easy. Listing 20-1 presents a procedure that starts the Windows Character Map application, which enables the user to insert a special character.

Listing 20-1: Launching a Windows Utility Application

```
Sub CharMap()
    Dim Program As String
    Dim TaskID As Double
    On Error Resume Next
    Program = "charmap.exe"
    TaskID = Shell(Program, 1)
    If Err <> 0 Then
        MsgBox "Cannot start " & Program, vbCritical, "Error"
    End If
End Sub
```

You'll recognize the application that this procedure launches in Figure 20-1.

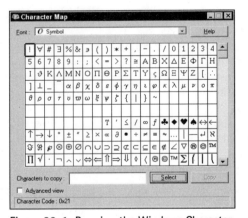

Figure 20-1: Running the Windows Character Map program from Excel.

If you're using Excel 2002 or later, the Windows Character Map program is no longer necessary. You can take advantage of the Excel Insert → Symbol command.

The `Shell` function returns a task identification number for the application. You can use this number later to activate the task. The second argument for the `Shell` function determines how the application is displayed. (1 is the code for a normal-size window, with the focus.) Refer to the Help system for other values for this argument.

If the `Shell` function is not successful, it generates an error. Therefore, this procedure uses an `On Error` statement to display a message if the executable file cannot be found or if some other error occurs.

It's important to understand that your VBA code does not pause while the application that was started with the `Shell` function is running. In other words, the `Shell` function runs the application *asynchronously*. If the procedure has more instructions after the `Shell` function is executed, they are executed concurrently with the newly loaded program. If any instruction requires user intervention (for example, displaying a message box), Excel's title bar flashes while the other application is active.

In some cases, you might want to launch an application with the `Shell` function, but you need your VBA code to pause until the application is closed. For example, the launched application might generate a file that is used later in your code. Although you can't pause the execution of your code, you *can* create a loop that does nothing except monitor the application's status. Listing 20-2 shows an example that displays a message box when the application launched by the `Shell` function has ended.

Listing 20-2: Waiting for an Application to End

```
Declare Function OpenProcess Lib "kernel32" _
    (ByVal dwDesiredAccess As Long, _
    ByVal bInheritHandle As Long, _
    ByVal dwProcessId As Long) As Long

Declare Function GetExitCodeProcess Lib "kernel32" _
    (ByVal hProcess As Long, _
    lpExitCode As Long) As Long

Sub RunCharMap2()
    Dim TaskID As Long
    Dim hProc As Long
    Dim lExitCode As Long
    Dim ACCESS_TYPE As Integer, STILL_ACTIVE As Integer
    Dim Program As String

    ACCESS_TYPE = &H400
    STILL_ACTIVE = &H103

    Program = "Charmap.exe"
    On Error Resume Next

'   Shell the task
    TaskID = Shell(Program, 1)
```

Continued

Listing 20-2 *(Continued)*

```
'   Get the process handle
    hProc = OpenProcess(ACCESS_TYPE, False, TaskID)

    If Err <> 0 Then
        MsgBox "Cannot start " & Program, vbCritical, "Error"
        Exit Sub
    End If

    Do  'Loop continuously
'       Check on the process
        GetExitCodeProcess hProc, lExitCode
'       Allow event processing
        DoEvents
    Loop While lExitCode = STILL_ACTIVE

'   Task is finished, so show message
    MsgBox Program & " is finished"
End Sub
```

While the launched program is running, this procedure continually calls the `GetExitCodeProcess` function from within a `Do-Loop` structure, testing for its returned value (`lExitCode`). When the program is finished, `lExitCode` returns a different value, the loop ends, and the VBA code resumes executing.

 Both of the preceding examples are available on the companion CD-ROM.

Using the Windows ShellExecute API function

`ShellExecute` is a Windows Application Programming Interface (API) function that is useful for starting other applications. Importantly, this function can start an application if only the filename is known (assuming that the file type is registered with Windows). For example, you can use `ShellExecute` to open a Web document by starting the default Web browser. Or, you can use an e-mail address to start the default e-mail client.

The API declaration follows (this code goes at the top of a VBA module):

```
Private Declare Function ShellExecute Lib "shell32.dll" _
    Alias "ShellExecuteA" (ByVal hWnd As Long, _
    ByVal lpOperation As String, ByVal lpFile As String, _
```

```
ByVal lpParameters As String, ByVal lpDirectory As String, _
ByVal nShowCmd As Long) As Long
```

The following procedure demonstrates how to call the `ShellExecute` function. In this example, it opens a graphic file by using the graphics program that's set up to handle GIF files.

```
Sub ShowGraphic()
    Dim FileName As String
    FileName = "c:\face.gif"
    Call ShellExecute(0&, vbNullString, FileName, _
        vbNullString, vbNullString, vbNormalFocus)
End Sub
```

The following example is similar, but it opens a Web URL by using the default browser.

```
Sub OpenURL()
    Dim URL As String
    URL = "http://www.microsoft.com"
    Call ShellExecute(0&, vbNullString, URL, _
        vbNullString, vbNullString, vbNormalFocus)
End Sub
```

This technique can also be used with an e-mail address. The example below opens the default e-mail client and then addresses an e-mail to the recipient.

```
Sub StartEmail()
    Dim Addr As String
    Addr = "mailto:bgates@microsoft.com"
    Call ShellExecute(0&, vbNullString, Addr, _
        vbNullString, vbNullString, vbNormalFocus)
End Sub
```

Activating an Application with Excel

In the previous section, I discuss various ways to start an application. You might find that if an application is already running, using the `ShellExecute` function could start another instance of it. In most cases, you want to *activate* the instance that's running — not start another instance of it.

Using AppActivate

The following `StartCalculator` uses the `AppActivate` statement to activate an application if it's already running (in this case, the Windows Calculator). The argument for AppActivate is the caption of the application's title bar. If the AppActivate statement generates an error, the Calculator is not running. Therefore, the routine starts the application.

```
Sub StartCalculator()
    Dim AppFile As String
    Dim CalcTaskID As Double

    AppFile = "Calc.exe"
    On Error Resume Next
    AppActivate "Calculator"
    If Err <> 0 Then
        Err = 0
        CalcTaskID = Shell(AppFile, 1)
        If Err <> 0 Then MsgBox "Can't start Calculator"
    End If
End Sub
```

 This example is available on the companion CD-ROM.

Activating a Microsoft Office application

If the application that you want to start is one of several Microsoft applications, you can use the ActivateMicrosoftApp method of the Application object. For example, the following procedure starts Word:

```
Sub StartWord()
    Application.ActivateMicrosoftApp xlMicrosoftWord
End Sub
```

If Word is already running when the preceding procedure is executed, it is activated. The other constants available for this method are

- ◆ xlMicrosoftPowerPoint
- ◆ xlMicrosoftMail
- ◆ xlMicrosoftAccess
- ◆ xlMicrosoftFoxPro
- ◆ xlMicrosoftProject
- ◆ xlMicrosoftSchedulePlus

Running Control Panel Dialog Boxes

Windows provides quite a few system dialog boxes and wizards, most of which are accessible from the Windows Control Panel. You might need to display one or more of these from your Excel application. For example, you might want to display the Windows Date and Time Properties dialog box as shown in Figure 20-2.

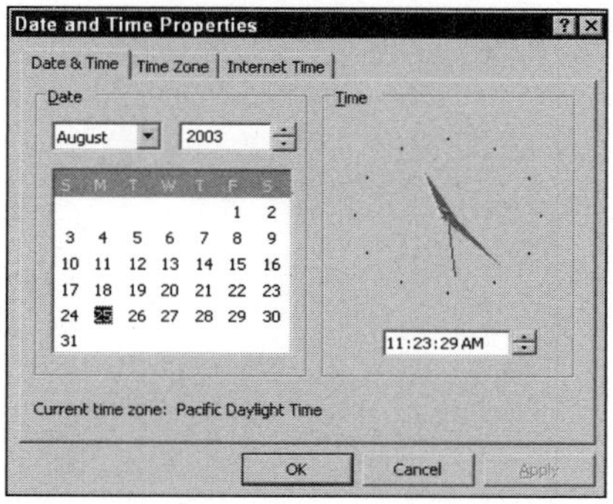

Figure 20-2: Use VBA to display a Control Panel dialog box.

The key to running other system dialog boxes is to execute the rundll32.exe application by using the VBA Shell function.

The following procedure displays the Date and Time dialog box:

```
Sub ShowDateTimeDlg()
    Dim Arg As String
    Dim TaskID As Double
    Arg = "rundll32.exe shell32.dll,Control_RunDLL timedate.cpl"
    On Error Resume Next
    TaskID = Shell(Arg)
    If Err <> 0 Then
        MsgBox ("Cannot start the application.")
    End If
End Sub
```

Following is the general format for the rundll32.exe application:

```
rundll32.exe shell32.dll,Control_RunDLL filename.cpl,@n,t
```

- ◆ filename.cpl: The name of one of the Control Panel *.CPL files
- ◆ n: The zero-based number of the applet within the *.CPL file
- ◆ t: The number of the tab (for multi-tabbed applets)

A workbook that displays12 additional control panel applets, depicted in Figure 20-3, is available on the companion CD-ROM.

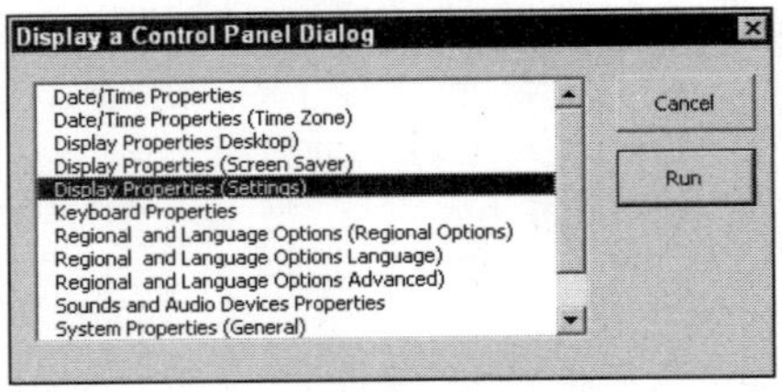

Figure 20–3: The workbook that displays this dialog box demonstrates how to run system dialog boxes from Excel.

Using Automation in Excel

You can write an Excel macro to control other applications, such as Microsoft Word. More accurately, the Excel macro will control Word's automation server. In such circumstances, Excel is the *client application,* and Word is the *server application.* Or you can write a Visual Basic application to control Excel. The process of one application's controlling another is sometimes known as *Object Linking and Embedding (OLE)* or simply *Automation.*

The concept behind Automation is quite appealing. A developer who needs to generate a chart, for example, can just reach into another application's grab bag of objects, fetch a Chart object, and then manipulate its properties and use its methods. Automation, in a sense, blurs the boundaries between applications. An end user might be working with an Access object and not even realize it.

Some applications, such as Excel, can function as either a client application or a server application. Other applications can function only as client applications or only as server applications.

In this section, I demonstrate how to use VBA to access and manipulate the objects exposed by other applications. The examples use Microsoft Word, but the concepts apply to any application that exposes its objects for Automation — which accounts for an increasing number of applications.

Working with foreign objects using Automation

As you might know, you can use Excel's Insert → Object command to embed an object, such as a Word document, in a worksheet. In addition, you can create an object and manipulate it with VBA. (This action is the heart of Automation.) When you do so, you usually have full access to the object. For developers, this technique is generally more beneficial than embedding the object in a worksheet. When an object is embedded, the user must know how to use the Automation object's application. But when you use VBA to work with the object, you can program the object so that the user can manipulate it by an action as simple as a button click.

Early versus late binding

Before you can work with an external object, you must create an instance of the object. This can be done in either of two ways: early binding or late binding. *Binding* refers to matching the function calls written by the programmer to the actual code that implements the function.

EARLY BINDING

To use early binding, you create a reference to the object library by choosing the Tools → References command in the Visual Basic Editor (VBE), which brings up the dialog box shown in Figure 20-4.

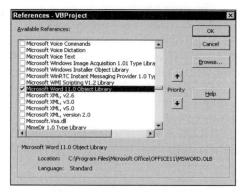

Figure 20-4: Attaching a reference to an object library file.

After the reference to the object library is established, you can use the Object Browser shown in Figure 20-5 to view the object names, methods, and properties. To access the Object Browser, press F2 in the VBE.

When you use early binding, you must establish a reference to a version-specific object library. For example, you can specify Microsoft Word 9.0 Object Library (for Word 2000), Microsoft Word 10.0 Object Library (for Word 2002), or Microsoft Word 11.0 Object Library (for Word 2003). Then you use a statement like the following to create the object:

```
Dim WordApp As New Word.Application
```

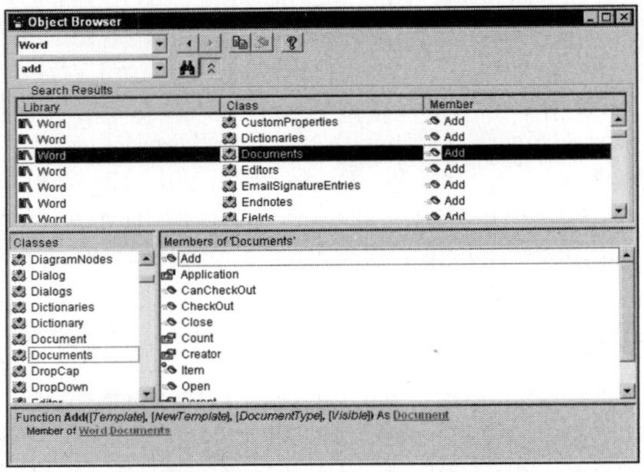

Figure 20-5: Use the Object Browser to learn about the objects in a referenced library.

Using early binding to create the object by setting a reference to the object library usually is more efficient and also often yields better performance. Early binding is an option, however, only if the object that you are controlling has a separate type library or object library file. You also need to ensure that the user of the application actually has a copy of the specific library installed.

Another advantage of early binding is that you can use constants that are defined in the object library. For example, Word (like Excel) contains many predefined constants that you can use in your VBA code. If you use early binding, you can use the constants in your code. If you use late binding, you'll need to use the actual value rather than the constant.

Still another advantage in using early binding is that you can take advantage of the VBE Object Browser and Auto List Members option to make it easier to access properties and methods; this feature doesn't work when you use late binding because the type of the object is known only at runtime.

LATE BINDING

At runtime, you use either the CreateObject function to create the object or the GetObject function to obtain a saved instance of the object. Such an object is declared as a generic Object type, and its object reference is resolved at runtime.

You can use late binding even when you don't know which version of the application is installed on the user's system. For example, the following code, which works with Word 97 and later, creates a Word object:

```
Dim WordApp As Object
Set WordApp = CreateObject("Word.Application")
```

If multiple versions of Word are installed, you can create an object for a specific version. The following statement, for example, uses Word 2003:

```
Set WordApp = CreateObject("Word.Application.11")
```

The Registry key for Word's Automation object and the reference to the `Application` object in VBA just happen to be the same: `Word.Application`. They do not, however, refer to the same thing. When you declare an object `As Word.Application` or `As New Word.Application`, the term refers to the `Application` object in the `Word` library. But when you invoke the function `CreateObject("Word.Application")`, the term refers to the moniker by which the latest version of Word is known in the Windows System Registry. This isn't the case for all Automation objects, although it is true for the main Office 2003 components. If the user replaces Word 2002 with Word 2003, `CreateObject("Word.Application")` will continue to work properly, referring to the new application. If Word 2003 is removed, however, `CreateObject("Word.Application.11")`, which uses the alternate version-specific moniker for Word 2003, will fail to work.

The `CreateObject` function used on an Automation object such as `Word.Application` or `Excel.Application` always creates a new *instance* of that Automation object. That is, it starts up a new and separate copy of the automation part of the program. Even if an instance of the Automation object is already running, a new instance is started, and then an object of the specified type is created.

To use the current instance or to start the application and have it load a file, use the `GetObject` function.

If you need to automate an Office application, it is recommended that you use early binding and reference the earliest version of the product that you expect could be installed on your client's system. For example, if you need to be able to automate Word 97, Word 2000, Word 2002, and Word 2003, you should use the type library for Word 97 to maintain compatibility with all four versions. This, of course, will mean that you can't make use of features found in the later version of Word.

GetObject versus CreateObject

VBA's `GetObject` and `CreateObject` functions both return a reference to an object, but they work in different ways.

The `CreateObject` function is used to create an interface to a new instance of an application. Use this function when the application is not running. If an instance of the application is already running, a new instance is started. For example, the following statement starts Excel, and the object returned in `XLApp` is a reference to the `Excel.Application` object that it created.

```
Set XLApp = CreateObject("Excel.Application")
```

Continued

> ## GetObject versus CreateObject *(Continued)*
>
> The GetObject function is either used with an application that's already running or to start an application with a file already loaded. The following statement, for example, starts Excel with the file Myfile.xls already loaded. The object returned in XLBook is a reference to the Workbook object (the Myfile.xls file).
>
> Set XLBook = GetObject("C:\Myfile.xls")

A simple example of late binding

The following example demonstrates how to create a Word object by using late binding. This procedure creates the object, displays the version number, closes the Word application, and then destroys the object (thus freeing the memory that it used).

```
Sub GetWordVersion()
    Dim WordApp As Object
    Set WordApp = CreateObject("Word.Application")
    MsgBox WordApp.Version
    WordApp.Quit
    Set WordApp = Nothing
End Sub
```

The Word object that's created in this procedure is invisible. If you'd like to see the object while it's being manipulated, set its Visible property to True, as follows:

```
WordApp.Visible = True
```

This example can also be programmed using early binding. Before doing so, choose the Tools → References command to set a reference to the Word object library. Then you can use the following code:

```
Sub GetWordVersion()
    Dim WordApp As New Word.Application
    MsgBox WordApp.Version
    WordApp.Quit
    Set WordApp = Nothing
End Sub
```

Controlling Word from Excel

The example in this section demonstrates an Automation session by using Word. The `MakeMemos` procedure creates three customized memos in Word and then saves each document to a file. The information used to create the memos is stored in a worksheet, as shown in Figure 20-6.

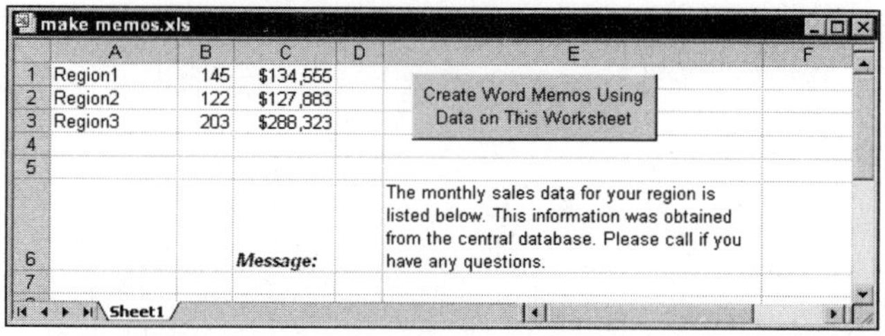

Figure 20-6: Word automatically generates three memos based on this Excel data.

The `MakeMemos` procedure, presented in Listing 20-3, starts by creating an object called `WordApp`. The routine cycles through the three rows of data in `Sheet1` and uses Word's properties and methods to create each memo and save it to disk. A range named `Message` (in cell E6) contains the text used in the memo. All the action occurs behind the scenes: That is, Word is not visible.

Listing 20-3: Generating Word Documents from an Excel VBA Program

```
Sub MakeMemos()
'    Creates memos in word using Automation
     Dim WordApp As Object
     Dim Data As Range, message As String
     Dim Records As Integer, i As Integer
     Dim Region As String, SalesAmt As String, SalesNum As String
     Dim SaveAsName As String

'    Start Word and create an object (late binding)
     Set WordApp = CreateObject("Word.Application")

'    Information from worksheet
     Set Data = Sheets("Sheet1").Range("A1")
     Message = Sheets("Sheet1").Range("Message")
```

Continued

Listing 20-3 *(Continued)*

```
'    Cycle through all records in Sheet1
     Records = Application.CountA(Sheets("Sheet1").Range("A:A"))
     For i = 1 To Records
'        Update status bar progress message
         Application.StatusBar = "Processing Record " & i

'        Assign current data to variables
         Region = Data.Cells(i, 1).Value
         SalesNum = Data.Cells(i, 2).Value
         SalesAmt = Format(Data.Cells(i, 3).Value, "#,000")

'        Determine the file name
         SaveAsName = ThisWorkbook.Path & "\" & Region & ".doc"

'        Send commands to Word
         With WordApp
             .Documents.Add
             With .Selection
                 .Font.Size = 14
                 .Font.Bold = True
                 .ParagraphFormat.Alignment = 1
                 .TypeText Text:="M E M O R A N D U M"
                 .TypeParagraph
                 .TypeParagraph
                 .Font.Size = 12
                 .ParagraphFormat.Alignment = 0
                 .Font.Bold = False
                 .TypeText Text:="Date:" & vbTab & _
                     Format(Date, "mmmm d, yyyy")
                 .TypeParagraph
                 .TypeText Text:="To:" & vbTab & Region & _
                 " Manager"
                 .TypeParagraph
                 .TypeText Text:="From:" & vbTab & _
                     Application.UserName
                 .TypeParagraph
                 .TypeParagraph
                 .TypeText Message
                 .TypeParagraph
                 .TypeParagraph
                 .TypeText Text:="Units Sold:" & vbTab & _
                 SalesNum
```

```
                    .TypeParagraph
                    .TypeText Text:="Amount:" & vbTab & _
                      Format(SalesAmt, "$#,##0")
               End With
                    .ActiveDocument.SaveAs FileName:=SaveAsName
          End With
     Next i

'    Kill the object
     WordApp.Quit
     Set WordApp = Nothing

'    Reset status bar
     Application.StatusBar = ""
     MsgBox Records & " memos were created and saved in " & _
        ThisWorkbook.Path
End Sub
```

Figure 20-7 shows a document created by the `MakeMemos` procedure.

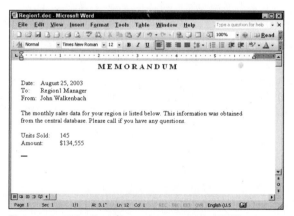

Figure 20-7: An Excel procedure created this Word document.

This workbook is available on the companion CD-ROM. However, do not run this procedure directly from the CD-ROM. The code attempts to write the files to the same directory as the Excel workbook.

Creating this macro involved several steps. I started by recording a macro in Word. I recorded my actions while creating a new document, adding and formatting some text, and saving the file. That Word macro provided the information that I needed about the appropriate properties and methods. I then copied the macro to an Excel module. Notice that I used With-End With. I added a dot before each instruction between With and End With. For example, the original Word macro contained (among others) the following instruction:

```
Documents.Add
```

I modified the macro as follows:

```
With WordApp
    .Documents.Add
'    more instructions here
End With
```

The macro that I recorded in Word used a few of Word's built-in constants. Because this example uses late binding, I had to substitute actual values for those constants. I was able to learn the values by using the Immediate window in Word's VBE.

Controlling Excel from another application

You can, of course, also control Excel from another application (such as another programming language or a Word VBA procedure). For example, you might want to perform some calculations in Excel and return the result to a Word document.

You can create any of the following Excel objects with the adjacent functions:

◆ **Application** object: `CreateObject("Excel.Application")`

◆ **Workbook** object: `CreateObject("Excel.Sheet")`

◆ **Chart** object: `CreateObject("Excel.Chart")`

Listing 20-4 shows a procedure that is located in a VBA module in a Word 2003 document. This procedure creates an Excel Worksheet object — whose moniker is "Excel.Sheet" — from an existing workbook.

Listing 20-4: Producing an Excel Worksheet on a Word Document

```
Sub MakeExcelChart()
    Dim XLSheet As Object
    Dim StartVal, PctChange
    Dim Wbook As String
```

```
'   Create a new document
    Documents.Add

'   Prompt for values
    StartVal = InputBox("Starting Value?")
    PctChange = InputBox("Percent Change?")

'   Create Sheet object
    Wbook = ThisDocument.Path & "\projections.xls"
    Set XLSheet = GetObject(Wbook, "Excel.Sheet").ActiveSheet

'   Put values in sheet
    XLSheet.Range("StartingValue") = StartVal
    XLSheet.Range("PctChange") = PctChange
    XLSheet.Calculate

'   Insert page heading
    Selection.Font.Size = 14
    Selection.Font.Bold = True
    Selection.TypeText "Monthly Increment: " & _
       Format(PctChange, "0.0%")
    Selection.TypeParagraph
    Selection.TypeParagraph

'   Copy data from sheet & paste to document
    XLSheet.Range("data").Copy
    Selection.Paste

'   Copy chart and paste to document
    XLSheet.ChartObjects(1).Copy
    Selection.PasteSpecial _
        Link:=False, _
        DataType:=wdPasteMetafilePicture, _
        Placement:=wdInLine, DisplayAsIcon:=False

'   Kill the object
    Set XLSheet = Nothing
End Sub
```

The initial workbook is shown in Figure 20-8. The MakeExcelChart procedure prompts the user for two values and inserts the values into the worksheet.

Recalculating the worksheet updates a chart. The data and the chart are then copied from the Excel object and pasted into a new document. The results are shown in Figure 20-9.

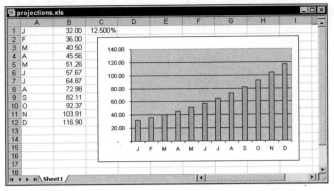

Figure 20-8: A VBA procedure in Word uses this worksheet.

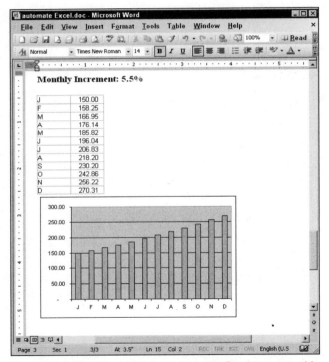

Figure 20-9: The Word VBA procedure uses Excel to create this document.

Sending Personalized E-Mail via Outlook

The example in this section demonstrates automation with Microsoft Outlook.

Figure 20-10 shows a worksheet that contains data used in the e-mail messages: name, e-mail address, and bonus amount. The procedure in Listing 20-5 loops through the rows in the worksheet, retrieves the data, and creates an individualized message (stored in the `Msg` variable).

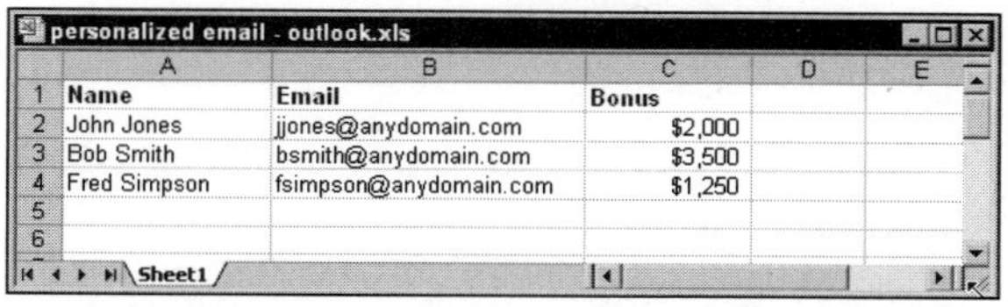

	A	B	C	D	E
1	**Name**	**Email**	**Bonus**		
2	John Jones	jjones@anydomain.com	$2,000		
3	Bob Smith	bsmith@anydomain.com	$3,500		
4	Fred Simpson	fsimpson@anydomain.com	$1,250		
5					
6					

Figure 20-10: This information is used in the Outlook Express e-mail messages.

Listing 20-5: Sending Outlook E-Mail from Excel

```
Sub SendEmail()
  'Uses early binding
  'Requires a reference to the Outlook Object Library
  Dim OutlookApp As Outlook.Application
  Dim MItem As Outlook.MailItem
  Dim cell As Range
  Dim Subj As String
  Dim EmailAddr As String
  Dim Recipient As String
  Dim Bonus As String
  Dim Msg As String

  'Create Outlook object
  Set OutlookApp = New Outlook.Application

  'Loop through the rows
  For Each cell In Columns("B").Cells.SpecialCells(xlCellTypeConstants)
    If cell.Value Like "*@*" Then
      'Get the data
      Subj = "Your Annual Bonus"
```

Continued

Listing 20-5 *(Continued)*

```
        Recipient = cell.Offset(0, -1).Value
        EmailAddr = cell.Value
        Bonus = Format(cell.Offset(0, 1).Value, "$0,000.")

       'Compose message
        Msg = "Dear " & Recipient & vbCrLf & vbCrLf
        Msg = Msg & "I am pleased to inform you that your annual bonus is "
        Msg = Msg & Bonus & vbCrLf & vbCrLf
        Msg = Msg & "William Rose" & vbCrLf
        Msg = Msg & "President"

       'Create Mail Item and send it
        Set MItem = OutlookApp.CreateItem(olMailItem)
        With MItem
          .To = EmailAddr
          .Subject = Subj
          .Body = Msg
          .Send
        End With
      End If
  Next
End Sub
```

This example uses early binding, so it requires a reference to the Outlook Object Library. Notice that two objects are involved: an `Outlook` object, and a `MailItem` object. The `Outlook` object is created with this statement:

```
Set OutlookApp = New Outlook.Application
```

The `MailItem` object is created with this statement:

```
Set MItem = OutlookApp.CreateItem(olMailItem)
```

The code sets the `To`, `Subject`, and `Body` properties, and then uses the `Send` method to send each message.

This example is available on the companion CD-ROM. You must have Microsoft Outlook installed.

Subsequent sections in this chapter describe other ways of sending e-mail through Excel. See "Sending E-Mail Attachments from Excel" and "Using SendKeys."

Working with ADO

ADO (ActiveX Data Objects) is an object model that enables you to access data stored in a variety of database formats. Importantly, this methodology allows you to use a single object model for all your databases. This is currently the preferred data access methodology and should not be confused with DAO (Data Access Objects).

This section presents a simple example that uses ADO to retrieve data from an Access database.

ADO programming is a very complex topic. If you have a need to access external data in your Excel application, you'll probably want to invest in one or more books that cover this topic in detail.

The example in Listing 20-6 retrieves data from an Access database named `budget.mdb`. This database contains one table (named Budget), and the table has seven fields. This example retrieves the data in which the `Item` field contains the text *Lease* and the `Division` field contains the text *N. America*. The qualifying data is stored in a `Recordset` object, and the data is then transferred to a worksheet (see Figure 20-11).

	A	B	C	D	E	F	G
1	DIVISION	DEPARTMENT	CATEGORY	ITEM	MONTH	BUDGET	ACTUAL
2	N. America	Data Processing	Facility	Lease	Jan	3450	2631
3	N. America	Human Resources	Facility	Lease	Jan	4353	3875
4	N. America	Accounting	Facility	Lease	Jan	3898	2979
5	N. America	Training	Facility	Lease	Jan	3185	3545
6	N. America	Security	Facility	Lease	Jan	3368	4120
7	N. America	R&D	Facility	Lease	Jan	3926	3432
8	N. America	Operations	Facility	Lease	Jan	3329	3715
9	N. America	Shipping	Facility	Lease	Jan	4095	2892
10	N. America	Sales	Facility	Lease	Jan	3242	2687
11	N. America	Advertising	Facility	Lease	Jan	3933	3580
12	N. America	Public Relations	Facility	Lease	Jan	4316	4328
13	N. America	Data Processing	Facility	Lease	Feb	4440	4357
14	N. America	Human Resources	Facility	Lease	Feb	4210	3196
15	N. America	Accounting	Facility	Lease	Feb	2860	3658
16	N. America	Training	Facility	Lease	Feb	4468	3759
17	N. America	Security	Facility	Lease	Feb	3499	3568
18	N. America	R&D	Facility	Lease	Feb	3394	4196
19	N. America	Operations	Facility	Lease	Feb	4187	3074

Figure 20-11: This data was retrieved from an Access database.

Listing 20-6: Using ADO to Retrieve Data from an Access File

```vba
Sub ADO_Demo()
'    This demo requires a reference to
'    the Microsoft ActiveX Data Objects 2.x Library

    Dim DBFullName As String
    Dim Cnct As String, Src As String
    Dim Connection As ADODB.Connection
    Dim Recordset As ADODB.Recordset
    Dim Col As Integer

    Cells.Clear

'    Database information
    DBFullName = ThisWorkbook.Path & "\budget.mdb"

'    Open the connection
    Set Connection = New ADODB.Connection
    Cnct = "Provider=Microsoft.Jet.OLEDB.4.0; "
    Cnct = Cnct & "Data Source=" & DBFullName & ";"
    Connection.Open ConnectionString:=Cnct

'    Create RecordSet
    Set Recordset = New ADODB.Recordset
    With Recordset
'        Filter
        Src = "SELECT * FROM Budget WHERE Item = 'Lease' "
        Src = Src & "and Division = 'N. America'"
        .Open Source:=Src, ActiveConnection:=Connection

'        Write the field names
        For Col = 0 To Recordset.Fields.Count - 1
            Range("A1").Offset(0, Col).Value = _
                Recordset.Fields(Col).Name
        Next

'        Write the recordset
        Range("A1").Offset(1, 0).CopyFromRecordset Recordset
    End With
    Set Recordset = Nothing
    Connection.Close
    Set Connection = Nothing
End Sub
```

This example, along with the Access database, is available on the companion CD-ROM.

Sending E-Mail Attachments from Excel

As you probably know, Excel has commands to send worksheets or workbooks via e-mail. And, of course, you can use VBA to automate these types of tasks. The procedure below sends the active workbook (as an attachment) to joeblow@ anydomain.com. The e-mail message has the subject My Workbook.

```
Sub SendWorkbook()
    ActiveWorkbook.SendMail "joeblow@anydomain.com", "My Workbook"
End Sub
```

If you would like to e-mail only a single sheet from a workbook, you need to copy the sheet to a new (temporary) workbook, send that workbook as an attachment, and then close the temporary file. Here's an example that sends Sheet1 from the active workbook.

```
Sub Sendasheet()
    ActiveWorkbook.Worksheets("sheet1").Copy
    ActiveWorkbook.SendMail "joeblow@anydomain.com", "My Sheet"
    ActiveWorkbook.Close False
End Sub
```

In the preceding example, the file will have the default workbook name (for example, Book2.xls). If you would like to give the single-sheet workbook attachment a more meaningfule name, you need to save the temporary workbook and then delete it after it's sent. The following procedure saves Sheet1 to a file named my file.xls. After sending this temporary workbook as an e-mail attachment, the code uses VBA's Kill statement to delete the file.

```
Sub SendOneSheet()
    Dim Filename As String
    Filename = "my file.xls"
    ActiveWorkbook.Worksheets("sheet1").Copy
    ActiveWorkbook.SaveAs Filename
    ActiveWorkbook.SendMail "joeblow@anydomain.com", "My Sheet"
```

```
     ActiveWorkbook.Close False
     Kill Filename
End Sub
```

Using SendKeys

Not all applications support Automation. In some cases, you can still control some aspects of the application even if it doesn't support Automation. You can use Excel's SendKeys method to send keystrokes to an application, simulating actions that a user might perform.

Although using the SendKeys method might seem like a good solution, you'll find that this can be very tricky. A potential problem is that it relies on a specific user interface. If a later version of the program that you're sending keystrokes has a different user interface, your application might no longer work. Consequently, you should use SendKeys only as a last resort.

Following is a very simple example. This procedure runs the Windows Calculator program and sets it up for Scientific mode: That is, it executes the View → Scientific command.

```
Sub TestKeys()
     Shell "calc.Exe", vbNormalFocus
     AppActivate "Calculator"
     Application.SendKeys "%vs", True
End Sub
```

In this example, the code sends out Alt+V (the percent sign represents the Alt key) followed by S. SendKeys is documented in Help system, which describes how to send nonstandard keystrokes, such as Alt and Ctrl key combinations.

Listing 20-7 is a more elaborate procedure that uses SendKeys. This routine is similar to the Outlook example that I present earlier in this chapter. The difference is that it creates e-mail messages for Outlook Express – Microsoft's e-mail client that doesn't support automation.

Listing 20-7: Using SendKeys to Send Personalized E-Mail Via Outlook Express

```
Sub SendEmail()
  Dim cell As Range
  Dim Subj As String
  Dim EmailAddr As String
  Dim Recipient As String
  Dim Bonus As String
  Dim Msg As String
  Dim HLink As String
  For Each cell In Columns("B").Cells.SpecialCells(xlCellTypeConstants)
```

```
        If cell.Value Like "*@*" Then
          'Get the data
          Subj = "Your Annual Bonus"
          Recipient = cell.Offset(0, -1).Value
          EmailAddr = cell.Value
          Bonus = Format(cell.Offset(0, 1).Value, "$0,000.")

         'Compose message
          Msg = "Dear " & Recipient & "%0A"
          Msg = Msg & "%0A" & "I am pleased to inform "
          Msg = Msg & "you that your annual bonus is "
          Msg = Msg & Bonus & "%0A"
          Msg = Msg & "%0A" & "William Rose"
          Msg = Msg & "%0A" & "President"

          'Build hyperlink
          HLink = "mailto:" & EmailAddr & "?"
          HLink = HLink & "subject=" & Subj & "&"
          HLink = HLink & "body=" & Msg

          'Send it
          ActiveWorkbook.FollowHyperlink HLink
          Application.Wait (Now + TimeValue("0:00:02"))
          SendKeys "%s", True
        End If
      Next
    End Sub
```

Figure 20-12 shows a worksheet that contains data used in the e-mail messages: name, e-mail address, and bonus amount.

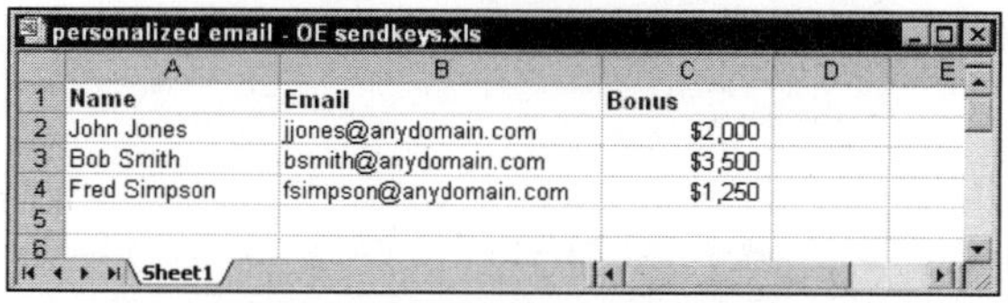

	A	B	C	D	E
1	Name	Email	Bonus		
2	John Jones	jjones@anydomain.com	$2,000		
3	Bob Smith	bsmith@anydomain.com	$3,500		
4	Fred Simpson	fsimpson@anydomain.com	$1,250		
5					
6					

Figure 20-12: This information is used in the Outlook Express e-mail messages.

The `SendEmail` procedure assumes that Outlook Express is the default e-mail client. It loops through the rows in the worksheet and creates a message (stored in the `Msg` variable). It uses the `FollowHyperlink` method to launch Outlook Express' New Message window. For the first record, the hyperlink is

```
mailto:jjones@anydomain.com?subject=Your Annual Bonus
&body=Dear John Jones%0A%0AI am pleased to inform you
that your annual bonus is $2,000.%0A%0AWilliam Rose%0APresident
```

The %0A character sequence represents a line break.

The procedure then pauses for two seconds and then uses SendKeys to issue the Alt+S command, which puts the message in the Outlook Express Outbox. This pause is required to ensure that the e-mail message is onscreen when the keystrokes are sent. You might need to adjust the delay, depending on your system. You might find that a one-second delay is sufficient, but others might need to increase it to two or more seconds.

Although this technique works fine, note the character limit on the length of the hyperlink (around 730 characters). Therefore, this is suitable only for short messages.

Figure 20-13 shows one of the messages in Outlook Express.

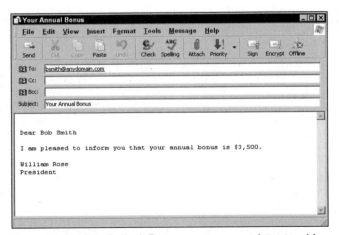

Figure 20-13: This Outlook Express message uses data stored in a worksheet.

Chapter 21

Creating and Using Add-Ins

IN THIS CHAPTER

In this chapter, I explain the benefits of using add-ins, and I show you how to create your own add-ins by using only the tools built into Excel. Read on to discover

- ◆ An overview of add-ins and why this concept is important for developers
- ◆ Details about Excel's Add-In Manager
- ◆ How to create an add-in, including a hands-on example
- ◆ How XLA files differ from XLS files
- ◆ Examples of VBA code that manipulates add-ins
- ◆ How to optimize your add-in for speed and size

ONE OF EXCEL'S MOST USEFUL FEATURES for developers is the capability to create add-ins. Creating add-ins adds a professional touch to your work and, as you'll see, add-ins offer several key advantages over standard workbook files.

What Is an Add-In?

Generally speaking, a *spreadsheet add-in* is something added to a spreadsheet to give it additional functionality. For example, Excel ships with several add-ins. One of the most popular is the *Analysis ToolPak,* which adds statistical and analysis capabilities that are not built into Excel.

Some add-ins (such as the Analysis ToolPak) also provide new worksheet functions that can be used in formulas. The new features usually blend in well with the original interface, so they appear to be part of the program. This is referred to as *seamless integration.*

Comparing an add-in with a standard workbook

Any knowledgeable Excel user can create an add-in from an XLS workbook; no additional software or programming tools are required. Any XLS file can be converted to an add-in, but not all XLS files are appropriate for add-ins. An Excel add-in is basically a normal XLS workbook with the following differences:

◆ The IsAddin property of the ThisWorkbook object is True. By default, this property is False.

◆ The workbook window is hidden in such a way that it can't be unhidden by choosing the Window → Unhide command. This means that you can't display worksheets or chart sheets contained in an add-in unless you write code to copy the sheet to a standard workbook.

◆ An add-in is not a member of the Workbooks collection. Rather, it's a member of the AddIns collection. However, you *can* access an add-in via the Workbooks collection (see "Collection membership," later in this chapter).

◆ Add-ins can be installed and uninstalled by choosing the Tools → Add-Ins command. After it's installed, an add-in remains installed across Excel sessions.

◆ The Macro dialog box (invoked by choosing Tools → Macro → Macros) does not display the names of the macros contained in an add-in.

◆ A custom worksheet function stored within an add-in can be used in formulas without you having to precede its name with the source workbook's filename.

By default, an add-in has an .xla file extension. This is not a requirement, however. An add-in file can have any extension that you like.

Why create add-ins?

You might decide to convert your XLS application into an add-in for any of the following reasons:

◆ *To restrict access to your code and worksheets:* When you distribute an application as an add-in and you protect its VBA project with a password, users can't view or modify the sheets or the Visual Basic for Applications (VBA) code in the workbook. Therefore, if you use proprietary techniques in your application, you can prevent anyone from copying the code – or at least make it more difficult to do so.

♦ *To avoid confusion:* If a user loads your application as an add-in, the file is not visible and is therefore less likely to confuse novice users or get in the way. Unlike a hidden XLS workbook, an add-in can't be unhidden.

♦ *To simplify access to worksheet functions:* Custom worksheet functions stored within an add-in don't require the workbook name qualifier. For example, if you store a custom function named MOVAVG in a workbook named `Newfuncs.xls`, you must use a syntax like the following to use this function in a different workbook:

```
=Newfuncs.xls!MOVAVG(A1:A50)
```

But if this function is stored in an add-in file that's open, you can use a much simpler syntax because you don't need to include the file reference:

```
=MOVAVG(A1:A50)
```

♦ *To provide easier access for users:* After you identify the location of your add-in, it appears in the Add-Ins dialog box with a friendly name and a description of what it does.

♦ *To gain better control over loading:* Add-ins can be opened automatically when Excel starts, regardless of the directory in which they are stored.

♦ *To avoid displaying prompts when unloading:* When an add-in is closed, the user never sees the Save change in *xxx*? prompt.

Every add-in that you create will contain macros. An additional advantage of using an add-in is to avoid the macro warning that appears when a workbook is opened (and the user's security level is Medium). When an add-in is installed, the user will not see the macro warning message as long as the Trust All Installed Add-Ins and Templates setting is in effect. This setting is controlled in the Trusted Publishers tab of the Security dialog box. To access this dialog box, choose Tools → Macro → Security.

About COM Add-Ins

Excel also supports COM (Component Object Model) add-ins. These files have a DLL or EXE file extension. A COM add-in can be written so it works with all Office applications that support add-ins. An additional advantage is that the code is compiled, thereby offering better security. Unlike XLA add-ins, a COM add-in cannot contain Excel sheets or charts. COM add-ins are developed with Visual Basic 5 (or later), Visual Basic .NET, or with the Office Developer Edition. Discussion of creating COM add-in procedures is well beyond the scope of this book.

Understanding Excel's Add-In Manager

The most efficient way to load and unload add-ins is with Excel's Add-Ins dialog box, which you access by choosing Tools → Add-Ins. This command displays the Add-Ins dialog box, as shown in Figure 21-1. The list box contains the names of all add-ins that Excel knows about, and check marks identify add-ins that are open. You can open and close add-ins from this dialog box by clearing or marking the check boxes.

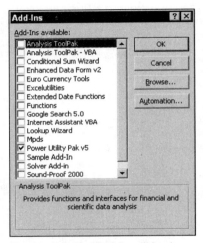

Figure 21-1: The Add-Ins dialog box.

 Beginning with Excel 2002, the Add-Ins dialog box features a new button: Automation. Use this button to install a COM add-in. Although Excel 2000 supports COM add-ins, it doesn't provide a direct way to install them.

 You can also open most add-in files by choosing the File → Open command. Because an add-in is never the active workbook, however, you can't close an add-in by choosing File → Close. You can remove the add-in only by exiting and restarting Excel or by executing VBA code to close the add-in. For example:

```
Workbooks("myaddin.x.a").Close
```

Opening an add-in with the File → Open command opens the file, but the add-in is not officially installed.

When you open an add-in, you might or might not notice anything different about Excel. In almost every case, however, the user interface changes in some way: Excel displays either a new menu, one or more new menu items on an existing menu, or a toolbar. For example, when you open the Analysis ToolPak add-in, this add-in gives you a new menu item on the Tools menu: Data Analysis. When you open Excel's Euro Currency Tools add-in, you'll get a new toolbar named EuroValue. If the add-in contains only custom worksheet functions, the new functions appear in the Insert Function dialog box.

Creating an Add-In

As I note earlier, you can convert any workbook to an add-in, but not all workbooks are appropriate candidates for add-ins. Generally, a workbook that benefits most from being converted to an add-in is one that contains macros — especially general-purpose macro procedures. A workbook that consists only of worksheets would be inaccessible as an add-in because worksheets within add-ins are hidden from the user. You can, however, write code that copies all or part of a sheet from your add-in to a visible workbook.

Creating an add-in from a workbook is simple. The following steps describe how to create an add-in from a normal workbook file:

1. Develop your application and make sure that everything works properly.

   Don't forget to include a way to execute the macro or macros in the add-in. You might want to add a new menu or menu item or to create a custom toolbar. See Chapter 23 for details on customizing menus and Chapter 22 for a discussion of custom toolbars.

2. Test the application by executing it when a different workbook is active.

   This simulates the application's behavior when it's used as an add-in because an add-in is never the active workbook.

3. Activate the Visual Basic Editor (VBE) and select the workbook in the Project window. Choose Tools → *xxx* Properties and then click the Protection tab. Select the Lock Project for Viewing check box and then enter a password (twice). Click OK.

   This step is necessary only if you want to prevent others from viewing or modifying your macros or UserForms.

A Few Words about Security

Microsoft has never promoted Excel as a product that creates applications in which the source code is secure. The password feature provided in Excel is sufficient to prevent casual users from accessing parts of your application that you'd like to keep hidden. Excel 2002 and later includes stronger security than previous versions, but your passwords can be cracked. If you must be absolutely sure that no one ever sees your code or formulas, Excel is not your best choice as a development platform.

4. Reactivate Excel and choose File → Properties, click the Summary tab, and enter a brief descriptive title in the Title field and a longer description in the Comments field.

   This step is not required, but it makes the add-in easier to use by displaying descriptive text in the Add-Ins dialog box.

5. Choose File → Save As.

6. In the Save As dialog box, select Microsoft Excel Add-In (*.xla) from the Save as Type drop-down list.

7. Click Save. A copy of the workbook is saved (with an .xla extension), and the original XLS workbook remains open.

A workbook being converted to an add-in must have at least one worksheet. For example, if your workbook contains only chart sheets or Excel 5/95 dialog sheets, the Microsoft Excel Add-In (*.xla) option does not appear in the Save As dialog box. Also, this option appears only when a worksheet is active when you choose the File → Save As command.

An Add-In Example

In this section, I discuss the steps involved in creating a useful add-in. The example uses the Text Tools utility that I describe in Chapter 16.

The XLS version of the Text Tools utility is available on the companion CD-ROM. You can use this file to create the described add-in.

Setting up the workbook for the example add-in

In this example, you'll be working with a workbook that has already been developed and debugged. The workbook consists of the following items:

- ◆ *A worksheet named* Sheet1*:* This sheet is used to hold pre-processed data, which can be restored if the user chooses to undo the operation.

- ◆ *A UserForm named* UserForm1*:* This dialog box serves as the primary user interface. The code module for this UserForm contains several event handler procedures.

- ◆ *A VBA module named* Module1*:* This contains several procedures, including a procedure that displays the UseForm1 UserForm.

- ◆ ThisWorkbook *code module:* This contains two event handler procedures (Workbook_Open and Workbook_BeforeClose) that contain code to create and delete the menu item on the Tools menu.

 See Chapter 16 for details about how the Text Tools utility works.

Testing the workbook for the example add-in

Before converting this workbook to an add-in, you need to test it. To simulate what happens when the workbook is an add-in, you should test the workbook when a different workbook is active. Remember, an add-in is *never* the active workbook, so testing it when another workbook is active will help you locate potential problems — such as incorrect references to ThisWorkbook.

Open a new workbook to try out the various features in the Text Tools utility. Do everything that you can think of to try to make it fail. Better yet, seek the assistance of someone unfamiliar with the application to give it a crash test.

Adding descriptive information for the example add-in

I recommend entering a description of your add-in, but this step is not required. Choose the File → Properties command, which opens the Properties dialog box. Then click the Summary tab, as shown in Figure 21-2.

Enter a title for the add-in in the Title field. This text appears in the Add-Ins dialog box. In the Comments field, enter a description. This information appears at the bottom of the Add-Ins dialog box when the add-in is selected.

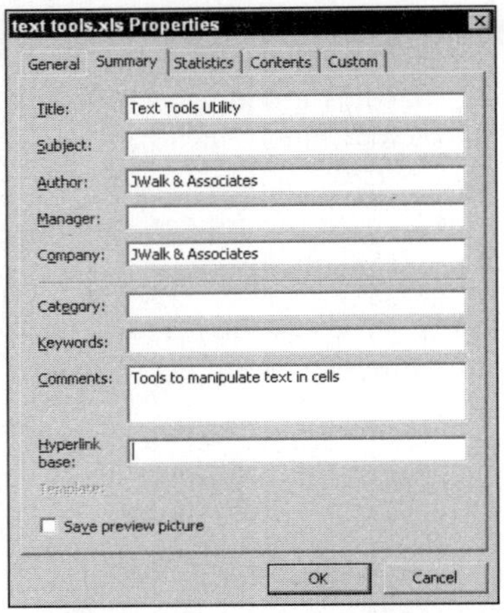

Figure 21-2: Use the Properties dialog box to enter descriptive information about your add-in.

Creating an add-in

To create an add-in, do the following:

1. Activate the VBE and select the future add-in workbook in the Project window.

2. Choose Debug → Compile. This step forces a compilation of the VBA code and also identifies any syntax errors so that you can correct them. When you save a workbook as an add-in, Excel creates the add-in even if it contains syntax errors.

3. Choose Tools → *xxx* Properties to display the Project Properties dialog box (where *xxx* represents the name of the project). Click the General tab and enter a new name for the project. By default, all VB projects are named *VBProject*. In this example, the project name was changed to *TextToolsVBA*. This step is optional but recommended.

4. With the Project Properties dialog box still displayed, click the Protection tab. Select the Lock Project for Viewing check box and enter a password (twice). The code will remain viewable, and the password protection will take effect the next time that the file is opened. Click OK.

   If you don't need to protect the project, you can skip this step.

5. Save the workbook by using its *.XLS name. This step is not really necessary, but it gives you an XLS backup of your XLA file.

6. Choose File → Save As. Excel displays its Save As dialog box.

About Excel's Add-In Manager

You access Excel's Add-In Manager by choosing the Tools → Add-Ins command, which displays the Add-Ins dialog box. This dialog box lists the names of all the available add-ins. Those that are checked are open.

In VBA terms, the Add-In dialog box lists the `Title` property of each `AddIn` object in the `AddIns` collection. Each add-in that appears with a check mark has its `Installed` property set to `True`.

You can install an add-in by marking its check box, and you can clear an installed add-in by removing the check mark from its box. To add an add-in to the list, use the Browse button to locate its file. By default, the Add-In dialog box lists files of the following types:

◆ XLA: An add-in created from an XLS file

◆ XLL: A standalone compiled DLL file

If you click the Automation button (available only in Excel 2002 and later), you can browse for COM add-ins. Note that the Automation Servers dialog box will probably list many files, and the file list is not limited to COM add-ins that work with Excel.

You can enroll an add-in file into the `AddIns` collection with the `Add` method of VBA's `AddIns` collection, but you can't remove one by using VBA. You can also open an add-in using VBA by setting the `AddIn` object's `Installed` property to `True`. Setting it to `False` closes the add-in.

The Add-In Manager stores the installed status of the add-ins in the Windows Registry when you exit Excel. Therefore, all add-ins that are installed when you close Excel are automatically opened the next time that you start Excel.

---

7. In the Save as Type drop-down list, select Microsoft Excel Add-In (*.xla).

8. Click Save. A new add-in file is created, and the original XLS version remains open.

Add-ins can be located in any directory. By default, Excel proposes the following directory:

```
C:\Documents and Settings\<username>\Application Data\Microsoft\AddIns
```

Installing an add-in

To avoid confusion, close the XLS workbook before installing the add-in created from that workbook.

To install an add-in, do the following:

1. Choose the Tools → Add-Ins command. Excel displays the Add-Ins dialog box.

2. Click the Browse button and locate the add-in that you just created. After you find your new add-in, the Add-Ins dialog box displays the add-in in its list. As shown in Figure 21-3, the Add-Ins dialog box also displays the descriptive information that you provided in the Properties dialog box.

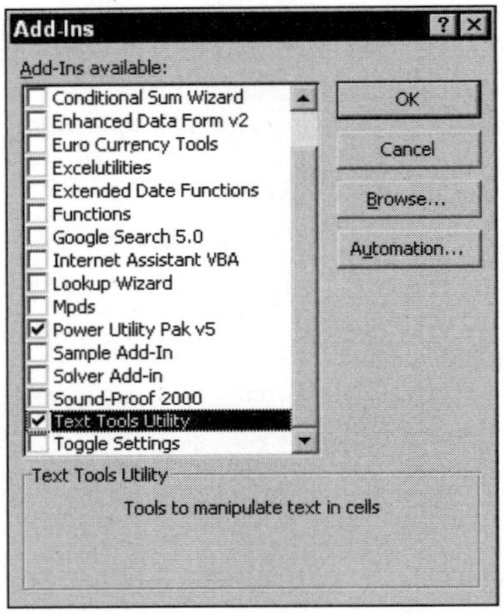

Figure 21-3: The Add-Ins dialog box, with the new add-in selected.

3. Click OK to close the dialog box and open the add-in.

When the Text Tools add-in is opened, the Tools menu displays the new menu item that executes the `StartTextTool` procedure in the add-in.

Distributing an add-in

You can distribute this add-in to other Excel users simply by giving them a copy of the XLA file (they don't need the XLS version) along with instructions on how to install it. After they install the add-in, the new Text Tools Utility command appears on the Tools menu. If you locked the file with a password, your macro code cannot be viewed or modified by others unless they know the password.

Modifying an add-in

If you need to modify an add-in, first open it and then unlock it. To unlock it, activate the VBE and then double-click its project's name in the Project window. You'll be prompted for the password. Make your changes and then save the file from the VBE (choose File → Save).

If you create an add-in that stores its information in a worksheet, you must set its IsAddIn property to False before you can view that workbook in Excel. You do this in the Properties window as shown in Figure 21-4 when the ThisWorkbook object is selected. After you make your changes, set the IsAddIn property back to True before you save the file. If you leave the IsAddIn property set to False, the file is saved as a regular workbook, although it still has the XLA extension. At this point, attempting to install this file by using the Add-Ins dialog box results in an error.

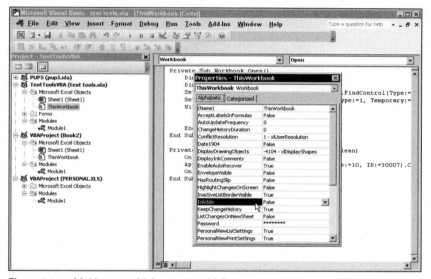

Figure 21-4: Making an add-in not an add-in.

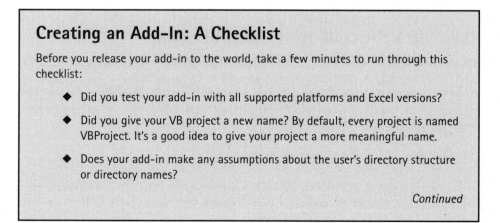

Creating an Add-In: A Checklist

Before you release your add-in to the world, take a few minutes to run through this checklist:

◆ Did you test your add-in with all supported platforms and Excel versions?

◆ Did you give your VB project a new name? By default, every project is named VBProject. It's a good idea to give your project a more meaningful name.

◆ Does your add-in make any assumptions about the user's directory structure or directory names?

Continued

Creating an Add-In: A Checklist *(Continued)*

◆ When you use the Add-Ins dialog box to load your add-in, is its name and description correct and appropriate?

◆ If your add-in uses VBA functions that aren't designed to be used in a work-sheet, have you declared the functions as `Private`? If not, these functions will appear in the Paste Function dialog box.

◆ Did you force a recompile of your add-in to ensure that it contains no syntax errors?

◆ Did you account for any international issues? For example, if your add-in creates a new item on the Tools menu, will it fail if the Tools menu has a non-English name?

◆ Is your add-in file optimized for speed? See "Optimizing the Performance of Add-Ins" later in this chapter.

Comparing XLA and XLS Files

This section begins by comparing an add-in XLA file with its XLS source file. Later in this chapter, I discuss methods that you can use to optimize the performance of your add-in. I describe a technique that might reduce its file size, which makes it load more quickly and use less disk space and memory.

XLS and XLA file size and structure

An add-in based on an XLS source file is exactly the same size as the original. The VBA code in XLA files is not compressed or optimized in any way, so faster performance is not among the benefits of using an add-in.

XLA file VBA collection membership

An add-in is a member of the `AddIns` collection but is not an official member of the `Workbooks` collection. You can refer to an add-in by using the `Workbooks` method of the `Application` object, and supplying the add-in's filename as its index. The following instruction creates an object variable that represents an add-in named `Myaddin.xla`:

```
Set TestAddin = Workbooks("Myaddin.xla")
```

Add-ins cannot be referenced by an index number in the `Workbooks` collection. If you use the following code to loop through the `Workbooks` collection, the `Myaddin.xla` workbook is not displayed:

```
For Each w in Application.Workbooks
    MsgBox w.Name
Next w
```

The following `For-Next` loop, on the other hand, displays `Myaddin.xla` — assuming that Excel "knows" about it — in the Add-Ins dialog box:

```
For Each a in Application.AddIns
    MsgBox a.Name
Next a
```

Visibility of XLS and XLA files

Ordinary XLS workbooks are displayed in one or more windows. For example, the following statement displays the number of windows for the active workbook:

```
MsgBox ActiveWorkbook.Windows.Count
```

You can manipulate the visibility of each window for an XLS workbook by choosing the Window → Hide command or by changing the `Visible` property. The following code hides all windows for the active workbook:

```
For Each Win In ActiveWorkbook.Windows
    Win.Visible = False
Next Win
```

Add-in files are never visible, and they don't officially have windows, even though they have unseen worksheets. Consequently, they don't appear in the windows list when you select the Window command. If `Myaddin.xla` is open, the following statement returns 0:

```
MsgBox Workbooks("Myaddin.xla").Windows.Count
```

Worksheets and chart sheets in XLS and XLA files

Add-in XLA files, like XLS files, can have any number of worksheets or chart sheets. But, as I note earlier in this chapter, an XLS file must have at least one worksheet in order for it to be converted to an add-in.

When an add-in is open, your VBA code can access its contained sheets as if it were an ordinary workbook. Because add-in files aren't part of the `Workbooks` collection, though, you must always reference an add-in by its name and not by an index number. The following example displays the value in cell A1 of the first worksheet in `Myaddin.xla`, which is assumed to be open:

```
MsgBox Workbooks("Myaddin.xla").Worksheets(1).Range("A1").Value
```

If your add-in contains a worksheet that you would like the user to see, you can either copy it to an open workbook or create a new workbook from the sheet.

The following code, for example, copies the first worksheet from an add-in and places it in the active workbook (as the last sheet):

```
Sub CopySheetFromAddin()
    Dim AddinSheet As Worksheet
    Dim NumSheets As Long
    Set AddinSheet = Workbooks("Myaddin.xla").Sheets(1)
    NumSheets = ActiveWorkbook.Sheets.Count
    AddinSheet.Copy After:=ActiveWorkbook.Sheets(NumSheets)
End Sub
```

Creating a new workbook from a sheet within an add-in is even simpler:

```
Sub CreateNewWorkbook()
    Workbooks("Myaddin.xla").Sheets(1).Copy
End Sub
```

The preceding examples assume that the code is in a file other than the add-in file. VBA code within an add-in should always use `ThisWorkbook` to qualify references to sheets or ranges within the add-in. For example, the following statement is assumed to be in a VBA module in an add-in file. This statement displays the value in cell A1 on Sheet 1:

```
MsgBox ThisWorkbook.Sheets("Sheet1").Range("A1").Value
```

Accessing VBA procedures in an add-in

Accessing the VBA procedures in an add-in is a bit different from accessing procedures in a normal XLS workbook. First of all, when you choose the Tools → Macro → Macros command, the Macro dialog box does not display the names of macros that are in open add-ins. It's almost as if Excel is trying to prevent you from accessing them.

If you know the name of the procedure in the add-in, you can enter it directly into the Macro dialog box and click Run to execute it. The Sub procedure must be in a general VBA module and not in a code module for an object.

Because procedures contained in an add-in aren't listed in the Macro dialog box, you must provide other means to access them. Your choices include direct methods (such as shortcut keys, custom menus, and custom toolbars) as well as indirect methods (such as event handlers). One such candidate, for example, may be the `OnTime` method, which executes a procedure at a specific time of day.

You can use the `Run` method of the `Application` object to execute a procedure in an add-in. For example:

```
Application.Run "Myaddin.xla!DisplayNames"
```

Another option is to use the Tools → References command in the VBE to enable a reference to the add-in. Then you can refer directly to one of its procedures in your VBA code without the filename qualifier. In fact, you don't need to use the `Run` method; you can call the procedure directly as long as it's not declared as `Private`. The following statement executes a procedure named `DisplayNames` in an add-in that has been added as a reference:

```
Call DisplayNames
```

Even when a reference to the add-in has been established, its macro names do not appear in the Macro dialog box.

Function procedures defined in an add-in work just like those defined in an XLS workbook. They're easy to access because Excel displays their names in the Insert Function dialog box, under the User Defined category (by default). The only exception is if the `Function` procedure was declared with the `Private` keyword; then the function does not appear there. That's why it's a good idea to declare custom functions as `Private` if they will be used only by other VBA procedures and are not designed to be used in worksheet formulas.

An example of an add-in that does *not* declare its functions as `Private` is Microsoft's Lookup Wizard add-in (included with Excel). After installing this add-in, click the Insert Function button. You'll find more than three-dozen non-worksheet functions listed in the User Defined category of the Insert Function dialog box. These functions are not intended to be used in a worksheet formula.

Sleuthing a Protected Add-In

The Macro dialog box does not display the names of procedures contained in add-ins. But what if you'd like to run such a procedure, but the add-in is protected so that you can't view the code to determine the name of the procedure? Use the Object Browser!

To illustrate, choose the Tools → Add-Ins command to install the Lookup Wizard add-in. This add-in is distributed with Excel and is protected, so you can't view the code.

1. Activate the VBE and then select the Lookup.xla project in the Project window.

2. Press F2 to activate the Object Browser.

3. In the Libraries drop-down list, select Lookup. This displays all the classes in the Lookup.xla add-in, as depicted in the following figure.

4. Select various items in the Classes list to see what class they are and the members that they contain.

In the example above, the Lookup_Common class is a module, and its members consist of a number of variables, constants, procedures, and functions. One of these procedures, DoLookupCommand, sounds like it might be the main procedure that starts the wizard. To test this theory, activate Excel and then choose Tools → Macro → Macros. Type **DoLookupCommand** in the Macro Name box and then click Run. Sure enough! You'll see the first dialog box of the Lookup Wizard.

Armed with this information, you can write VBA code to start the Lookup Wizard.

As I discuss earlier, you can use worksheet functions contained in add-ins without the workbook name qualifier. For example, if you have a custom function named MOVAVG stored in the file `Newfuncs.xls`, you would use the following instruction to address the function from a worksheet belonging to a different workbook:

```
=Newfuncs.xls!MOVAVG(A1:A50)
```

But if this function is stored in an add-in file that's open, you can omit the file reference and write the following instead:

```
=MOVAVG(A1:A50)
```

Manipulating Add-Ins with VBA

In this section, I present information that will help you write VBA procedures that manipulate add-ins.

Understanding the AddIns collection

The `AddIns` collection consists of all add-ins that Excel knows about. These add-ins can either be installed or not. Choosing the Tools → Add-Ins command displays the Add-Ins dialog box, which lists all members of the `AddIns` collection. Those entries accompanied by a check mark are installed.

ADDING AN ITEM TO THE ADDINS COLLECTION

The add-in files that make up the `AddIns` collection can be stored anywhere. Excel maintains a partial list of these files and their locations in the Windows Registry. For Excel 2003, this list is stored at

```
HKEY_CURRENT_USER\Software\Microsoft\Office\11.0\Excel\Add-in Manager
```

You can use the Windows Registry Editor (`regedit.exe`) to view this Registry key. Note that the standard add-ins that are shipped with Excel do not appear in this Registry key. In addition, add-in files stored in the following directory will also appear in the list but will not be listed in the Registry:

```
C:\Documents and Settings\<username>\Application Data\Microsoft\AddIns
```

You can add a new `AddIn` object to the `AddIns` collection either manually or programmatically by using VBA. To add a new add-in to the collection manually, choose Tools → Add-Ins, click the Browse button, and locate the add-in.

To enroll a new member of the `AddIns` collection with VBA, use the collection's `Add` method. Here's an example:

```
Application.AddIns.Add "c:\files\newaddin.xla"
```

After the preceding instruction is executed, the `AddIns` collection has a new member, and the Add-Ins dialog box shows a new item in its list. If the add-in already exists in the collection, nothing happens, and an error is not generated.

If the add-in that you're enrolling is on removable media (for example, a floppy disk or CD-ROM), you can also copy the file to Excel's library directory with the `Add` method. The following example copies `Myaddin.xla` from drive A and adds it to the `AddIns` collection. The second argument (`True`, in this case) specifies whether the add-in should be copied. If the add-in resides on a hard drive, the second argument can be ignored.

```
Application.AddIns.Add "a:\Myaddin.xla", True
```

Enrolling a new workbook into the `AddIns` collection does not install it. To install the add-in, set its `Installed` property to `True`.

The Windows Registry does not actually get updated until Excel closes normally. Therefore, if Excel ends abnormally (that is, if it crashes), the add-in's name will not get added to the Registry, and the add-in will not be part of the `AddIns` collection when Excel restarts.

REMOVING AN ITEM FROM THE ADDINS COLLECTION

Oddly, there is no direct way to remove an add-in from the `AddIns` collection. The `AddIns` collection does not have a `Delete` or `Remove` method. One way to remove an add-in from the Add-Ins dialog box is to edit the Windows Registry database (using `regedit.exe`). After you do this, the add-in will not appear in the Add-Ins dialog box the next time that you start Excel. Note that this method is not guaranteed to work with all add-in files.

Another way to remove an add-in from the `AddIns` collection is to delete, move, or rename its XLA file. You'll get a warning like the one in Figure 21-5 the next time that you try to install or uninstall the add-in, along with an opportunity to remove it from the `AddIns` collection.

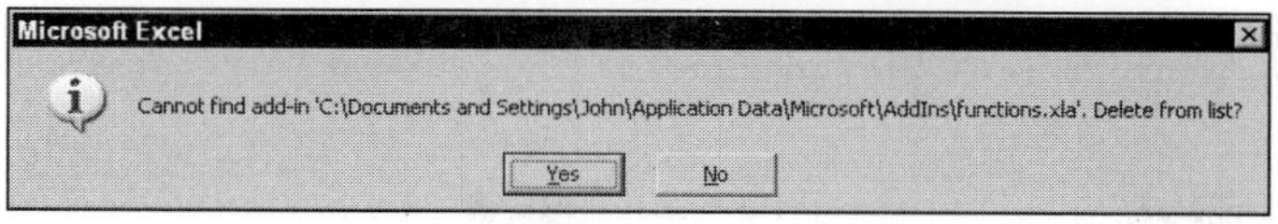

Figure 21-5: One very direct way to remove a member of the AddIns collection.

AddIn object properties

An AddIn object is a single member of the AddIns collection. For example, to display the filename of the first member of the AddIns collection, use the following:

```
Msgbox AddIns(1).Name
```

An AddIn object has 14 properties, which you can read about in the Help system. Five of these properties are hidden properties. Some of the terminology is a bit confusing, so I'll discuss a few of the more important properties.

THE NAME PROPERTY OF AN ADDIN OBJECT

This property holds the filename of the add-in. Name is a read-only property, so you can't change the name of the file by changing the Name property.

THE PATH PROPERTY OF AN ADDIN OBJECT

This property holds the drive and path where the add-in file is stored. It does not include a final backslash or the filename.

THE FULLNAME PROPERTY OF AN ADDIN OBJECT

This property holds the add-in's drive, path, and filename. This property is a bit redundant because this information is also available from the Name and Path properties. The following instructions produce exactly the same message:

```
MsgBox AddIns(1).Path & "\" & AddIns(1).Name
MsgBox AddIns(1).FullName
```

THE TITLE PROPERTY OF AN ADDIN OBJECT

This hidden property holds a descriptive name for the add-in. The Title property is what appears in the Add-Ins dialog box. This property is read-only, and the only way to add or change the Title property of an add-in is to use the File→Properties command (click the Summary tab, and enter text into the Title field). You must use this menu command with the XLS version of the file before converting it to an add-in.

Typically, a member of a collection is addressed by way of its Name property setting. The AddIns collection is different; it uses the Title property instead. The following example displays the filename for the Analysis ToolPak add-in (that is, analys32.xll), whose Title property is "Analysis ToolPak".

```
Sub ShowName()
    MsgBox AddIns("Analysis Toolpak").Name
End Sub
```

You can, of course, also reference a particular add-in with its index number if you happen to know it. But in the vast majority of cases, you will want to refer to an add-in by using its Name property.

THE COMMENTS PROPERTY OF AN ADDIN OBJECT

This hidden property stores text that is displayed in the Add-Ins dialog box when a particular add-in is selected. Comments is a read-only property. The only way to change it is to use the Properties dialog box before you convert the workbook to an add-in. Comments can be as long as 255 characters, but the Add-Ins dialog box can display only about 100 characters.

THE INSTALLED PROPERTY OF AN ADDIN OBJECT

The Installed property is True if the add-in is currently installed — that is, if it is checked in the Add-Ins dialog box. Setting the Installed property to True opens the add-in. Setting it to False unloads it. Here's an example of how to install (that is, open) the Analysis ToolPak add-in with VBA:

```
Sub InstallATP()
    AddIns("Analysis ToolPak").Installed = True
End Sub
```

After this procedure is executed, the Add-Ins dialog box displays a check mark next to Analysis ToolPak. If the add-in is already installed, setting its Installed property to True has no effect. To remove this add-in (uninstall it), simply set the Installed property to False.

If an add-in was opened with the File → Open command, it is not considered to be officially installed. Consequently, its Installed property is False.

The following procedure displays the number of add-ins in the AddIns collection and the number of those that are installed. You'll find that the count does not include add-ins that were opened with the File → Open command.

```
Sub CountInstalledAddIns()
    Dim Count As Integer
    Dim Item As AddIn
```

```
    Dim Msg As String
    Count = 0
    For Each Item In AddIns
        If Item.Installed Then Count = Count + 1
    Next Item
    Msg = "Add-ins: " & AddIns.Count & vbCrLf
    Msg = Msg & "Installed: " & Count
    MsgBox Msg
End Sub
```

The next procedure loops through all add-ins in the AddIns collection and uninstalls any add-in that's installed. This procedure does not affect add-ins that were opened with the File → Open command.

```
Sub UninstallAll()
    Dim Count As Integer
    Dim Item As AddIn
    Count = 0
    For Each Item In AddIns
        If Item.Installed Then
            Item.Installed = False
            Count = Count + 1
        End If
    Next Item
    MsgBox Count & " Add-Ins Uninstalled."
End Sub
```

You can determine whether a particular workbook is an add-in by accessing its IsAddIn property. This is not a read-only property, so you can also convert a workbook to an add-in by setting the IsAddIn property to True.

And, conversely, you can convert an add-in to a workbook by setting the IsAddIn property to False. After doing so, the add-in's worksheets will be visible in Excel — even if the add-in's VBA project is protected.

ACCESSING AN ADD-IN AS A WORKBOOK

As I mention earlier, there are two ways to open an add-in file: with the File → Open command and with the Tools → Add-Ins command. The latter method is the preferred method for the following reason: When you open an add-in with the File → Open command, its Installed property is *not* set to True. Therefore, you cannot close the file by using the Add-Ins dialog box. In fact, the only way to close such an add-in is with a VBA statement such as the following:

```
Workbooks("Myaddin.xla").Close
```

Using the `Close` method on an installed add-in removes the add-in from memory, but it does *not* set its `Installed` property to `False`. Therefore, the Add-Ins dialog box still lists the add-in as installed, which can be very confusing. The proper way to remove an installed add-in is to set its `Installed` property to `False`.

As you might have surmised, Excel's add-in capability is a bit quirky, and this component has not been improved in many years. Therefore, as a developer, you need to pay particular attention to issues involving installing and uninstalling add-ins.

AddIn object events

An `AddIn` object has two events: `AddInInstall` (raised when it is installed) and `AddInUninstall` (raised when it is uninstalled). You can write event handler procedures for these events in the `ThisWorkbook` object for the add-in.

The following example is displayed as a message when the add-in is installed:

```
Private Sub Workbook_AddinInstall()
    MsgBox ThisWorkbook.Name & _
       " add-in in has been installed."
End Sub
```

Don't confuse the `AddInInstall` event with the `Open` event. The `AddInInstall` event occurs only when the add-in is first installed — not every time that it is opened. If you need to execute code every time that the add-in is opened, use a `Workbook_Open` procedure.

For additional information about events, see Chapter 19.

Optimizing the Performance of Add-Ins

It should be obvious that you want your add-in to be as fast and efficient as possible. In this section, I describe some techniques that you might find helpful.

Maximizing code speed in add-ins

If you ask a dozen Excel programmers to automate a particular task, chances are that you'll get a dozen different approaches. Most likely, not all these approaches will perform equally well.

Following are a few tips that you can use to ensure that your code runs as quickly as possible:

◆ *Set the `Application.ScreenUpdating` property to `False`* when writing data to a worksheet or performing any other actions that cause changes to the display.

◆ *Declare the data type for all variables used and avoid variants whenever possible.* Use an `Option Explicit` statement at the top of each module to force yourself to declare all variables.

◆ *Create object variables to avoid lengthy object references.* For example, if you're working with a `Series` object for a chart, create an object variable by using code like this:

```
Dim S1 As Series
Set S1 = ActiveWorkbook.Sheets(1).ChartObjects(1). _
    Chart.SeriesCollection(1)
```

◆ *Whenever possible, declare object variables as a specific object type* — not `As Object`.

◆ *Use the `With-End With` construct,* when appropriate, to set multiple properties or call multiple methods for a single object.

◆ *Remove all extraneous code.* This is especially important if you've used the macro recorder to create procedures.

◆ If possible, *manipulate data with VBA arrays rather than worksheet ranges.* Reading and writing to a worksheet takes much longer than manipulating data in memory. This is not a firm rule, however. For best results, test both options.

◆ *Avoid linking UserForm controls to worksheet cells.* Doing so may trigger a recalculation whenever the user changes the UserForm control.

◆ *Compile your code before creating the add-in.* This could increase the file size, but it eliminates the need for Excel to compile the code before executing the procedures.

Controlling an add-in's file size

Excel workbooks (including add-ins) have always suffered from a serious problem: *bloat*. You might have noticed that the size of your files tends to increase over time, even if you don't add any new content. This is especially true if you delete a lot of code and then replace it with other code. Making lots of changes to worksheets also seems to add to file bloat.

If you want to make your add-in — or any workbook, for that matter — as small as possible, you need to re-create your workbook. Here's how.

1. Make a backup of your application and keep it in a safe place.

2. Activate the VBE and then export all the components for your project that contain VBA code (modules, code modules, UserForms, and possibly ThisWorkbook, worksheet, and chart modules). Make a note of the filenames and the location.

3. Create a new workbook.

4. Copy the contents of all the worksheets from your original application to worksheets in the new workbook. Be especially careful if you used named ranges in your workbook — they must be re-created.

5. Import the components that you exported in Step 2.

6. Compile the code.

7. If applicable, reattach any toolbars that were attached to your original workbook.

8. Save the new workbook.

9. Test the new workbook thoroughly to ensure that nothing was lost in the process.

There's an excellent chance that the newly created file will be much smaller than your original. The size reduction depends on many factors, but I've been able to reduce the size of my XLA files by as much as 55 percent with this process.

 TIP Another method that might reduce the size of your file is to save it in HyperText Markup Language (HTML) format. Then open the HTML file and save it back to the XLS format. I've had mixed success with this. Sometimes it reduces the size of the file, but in other cases, the new file size is actually larger than the original.

Special Problems with Add-Ins

Add-ins are great, but you should realize by now that there's no free lunch. Add-ins present their share of problems — or should I say *challenges?* In this section, I discuss some issues that you need to know about if you'll be developing add-ins for widespread user distribution.

Ensuring that an add-in is installed

In some cases, you might need to ensure that your add-in is installed properly: that is, opened via the Tools → Add-Ins command and not the File → Open command. This section describes a technique that determines just that. If the add-in isn't properly installed, the code displays a message (see Figure 21-6), and the file is closed. In other words, the add-in remains open only if it is properly installed.

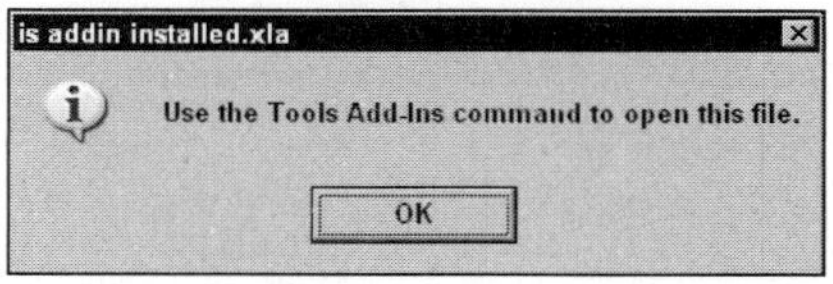

Figure 21-6: When attempting to open the add-in incorrectly, the user sees this message.

Listing 21-1 presents the code module for this example's ThisWorkbook object. This technique relies on the fact that the AddInInstall event occurs before the Open event for the workbook.

Listing 21-1: Ensuring That an Accessible Add-In Is Properly Installed and Workable

```
Dim InstalledProperly As Boolean

Private Sub Workbook_AddinInstall()
    InstalledProperly = True
End Sub

Private Sub Workbook_Open()
    Dim Msg As String
    If InstalledProperly Then Exit Sub
```

Continued

Listing 21–1 *(Continued)*

```
        Msg = "Use the Tools Add-Ins command to open this file."
        MsgBox Msg, vbInformation, ThisWorkbook.Name
        ThisWorkbook.Close
    End Sub
```

If the add-in is installed properly, the `Workbook_AddinInstall` procedure is executed. This procedure sets the Boolean variable `InstalledProperly` to `True`. If the add-in was opened by choosing the File → Open command, the `Workbook_AddinInstall` procedure is not executed, so the `InstalledProperly` variable has its default value (`False`).

When the `Workbook_Open` procedure is executed, it checks the value of `InstalledProperly`. If this variable is `True`, the procedure ends. If not, the code displays instructions for proper installation, and the file is closed.

    This add-in is available on the companion CD-ROM. Try opening it by choosing File → Open and then choose the Tools → Add-In command to install it properly.

Referencing other files from an add-in

If your add-in uses other files, you need to be especially careful when distributing the application. You can't assume anything about the storage structure of the system that users will run the application on. The easiest approach is to insist that all files for the application be copied to a single directory. Then you can use the `Path` property of your application's workbook to build path references to all other files.

For example, if your application uses a custom help file, be sure that the help file is copied to the same directory as the application itself. Then you can use a procedure like the following to make sure that the help file can be located:

```
Sub GetHelp()
    Dim Path As String
    Path = ThisWorkbook.Path
    Application.Help Path & "\USER.CHM"
End Sub
```

If your application uses Application Programming Interface (API) calls to standard Windows DLLs, you can assume that these can be found by Windows. But if you use custom DLLs, the best practice is to make sure that they're installed in the `Windows\System` directory (which might or might not be named `Windows\System`). You'll need to use the `GetSystemDirectory` Windows API function to determine the exact path of the System directory.

Detecting the proper Excel version for your add-in

If your add-in makes use of any features unique to Excel 2003, you'll want to warn users who attempt to open the add-in with an earlier version. The following code does the trick:

```
Sub CheckVersion()
    If Val(Application.Version) < 11 Then
        MsgBox "This works only with Excel 2003 or later"
        ThisWorkbook.Close
    End If
End Sub
```

The Version property of the Application object returns a string. For example, this might return 11.0a. This procedure uses VBA's Val function, which ignores everything after the first alphabetic character.

See Chapter 26 for additional information about compatibility.

Part VI

Developing Applications

Chapter 22

Creating Custom Toolbars

IN THIS CHAPTER

Toolbars, of course, are a pervasive user interface element found in virtually all software these days. In this chapter, I describe how to create and modify toolbars.

◆ An overview of command bars, which include toolbars

◆ Understanding how Excel keeps track of toolbars

◆ Customizing toolbars manually

◆ Lots of examples that demonstrate how to use VBA to manipulate toolbars

EXCEL IS DEFINITELY NOT A TOOLBAR-DEFICIENT PRODUCT. Excel 2003 comes with more than 60 built-in toolbars, and it's easy to construct new toolbars or customize existing ones either manually or by using Visual Basic for Applications (VBA).

About Command Bars

Beginning with Excel 97, Microsoft introduced a completely new way of handling toolbars. Technically, a toolbar is known as a `CommandBar` object. In fact, what's commonly called a toolbar is actually one of three types of command bars:

◆ *Toolbar:* This is a bar with one or more clickable controls. This chapter focuses on this type of command bar.

◆ *Menu bar:* The two built-in menu bars are Worksheet Menu Bar and Chart Menu Bar (see Chapter 23).

◆ *Shortcut menu:* This is the menu that pops up when you right-click an object (see Chapter 23).

Because a menu bar is also a command bar, virtually all the information in this chapter also applies to menu bars. In Chapter 23, I discuss the nuances of dealing with custom menus.

Toolbar Manipulations

The following list summarizes the ways in which you can customize toolbars in Excel:

♦ *Remove controls from built-in toolbars:* You can get rid of controls that you never use and free up a few pixels of screen space.

♦ *Add controls to built-in toolbars:* You can add as many controls as you want to any toolbar. These controls can be custom buttons or buttons from other toolbars, or they can come from the stock of controls that Excel provides.

♦ *Create new toolbars:* You can create as many new toolbars as you like, with toolbar controls from any source.

♦ *Change the functionality of built-in toolbar controls:* You do this by attaching your own macro to a built-in control.

♦ *Change the image that appears on any toolbar control:* Excel includes a rudimentary but functional toolbar button editor although several other image-changing techniques exist.

You can perform these customizations manually by using the Customize dialog box. This dialog box can be displayed using a number of different commands: Choose View → Toolbars → Customize, choose the Tools → Customize command, or right-click any toolbar and choose Customize. In addition, you can customize toolbars by writing VBA code.

Don't be afraid to experiment with toolbars. If you mess up a built-in toolbar, you can easily reset it to its default state. Just access the Customize dialog box and click the Toolbars tab. Then select the toolbar in the list and click the Reset button.

How Excel Handles Toolbars

Before you start working with custom toolbars, it's important to understand how Excel deals with toolbars in general. You might be surprised.

Storing toolbars

Toolbars can be attached to Excel worksheet or add-in files, which makes it easy to distribute custom toolbars with your applications (see "Distributing toolbars" later in this chapter). You can attach any number of toolbars to a workbook or add-in. When the user opens your file, the attached toolbars automatically appear. An exception is when a toolbar with the same name already exists. In such a case, the new toolbar does not replace the existing one (and the user is not told that a newer toolbar is available). For more information, see "When toolbars don't work correctly," later in this chapter.

Excel stores toolbar information in an XLB file. Excel 2003, running under Windows XP, stores its XLB file here:

```
\Documents and Settings\<user name>\Application Data\Microsoft\Excel
```

The exact filename and location will vary depending on the Excel version and the Windows version. For Excel 2003, the file is named `excel11.xlb`; for Excel 2002, the file is named `excel10.xlb`.

If you upgrade to Excel 2003 from a previous version, the information in your old XLB file will not be migrated to Excel 2003. In other words, you will lose any toolbar customizations that you've made.

Why is this XLB file important? Assume that a colleague gives you an Excel workbook that has a custom toolbar stored in it. When you open the workbook, the toolbar appears. You examine the workbook but decide that you're not interested in it. Nonetheless, when you exit Excel, the custom toolbar is added to your XLB file. If you make *any* toolbar changes — from the minor adjustment of a built-in toolbar to the introduction of a custom toolbar — the XLB file is resaved when you exit Excel. Because the entire XLB file is loaded every time that you start Excel, the time that it takes to start and exit Excel increases significantly as the XLB file grows in size. Plus, all those toolbars eat up memory and system resources. Therefore, it's in your best interest to delete custom toolbars that you never use. Choose the View → Toolbars → Customize command to do this.

A common cause of Excel crashes at start-up is a corrupt XLB file. If you find that Excel crashes immediately when it is started, try renaming your `*.xlb` file.

When toolbars don't work correctly

Excel's approach to storing toolbars can cause problems. Suppose you develop an application that uses a custom toolbar, and you attach that toolbar to the application's workbook. The first time that an end user opens the workbook, the toolbar is displayed. When the user closes Excel, your toolbar is saved in the user's XLB file. If the user alters the toolbar in any way — for example, if he or she accidentally removes a button — the next time your application is opened, the correct toolbar does *not* appear. Rather, the user sees the altered toolbar, which now lacks an important button. In other words, a toolbar attached to a workbook is not displayed if the user already has a toolbar with the same name. In many cases, this is *not* what you want to happen.

Fortunately, you can write VBA code to prevent this scenario. The trick is to never allow your custom toolbar to be added to the user's toolbar collection. One way to do this is to create the toolbar on the fly every time that the workbook is opened and then delete it when your application closes. With this process, the toolbar is never stored in the user's XLB file. You might think that creating a toolbar on the fly would be a slow process. As you'll see later in this chapter, creating toolbars with VBA is amazingly fast.

Another option is to attach the toolbar to your workbook and write VBA code that deletes the toolbar when the workbook is closed (using a `Workbook_BeforeClose` event procedure).

Manipulating Toolbars and Buttons Manually

Excel makes it easy for you to create new toolbars and modify existing toolbars. In fact, you might not even have to use VBA to work with toolbars because you can do just about all your toolbar customization without it.

 Understand that any customizations that you make to a toolbar, either built-in or custom, are permanent. In other words, the changes remain in effect even when you restart Excel. These toolbar changes are not associated with a particular workbook. To restore a toolbar to its original state, you must reset it.

About command bar customization mode

To perform any type of manual toolbar (or menu) customization, Excel needs to be in what I call *command bar customization mode*. You can put Excel into this mode by using any of these techniques:

◆ Choose View → Toolbars → Customize.

◆ Choose Tools → Customize.

 ◆ Right-click any toolbar or menu and select Customize from the shortcut
   menu.

When Excel is in command bar customization mode, the Customize dialog box is
displayed, and you can manipulate toolbars and menus any way that you like.
You'll find that you can right-click menus and toolbars to get a handy shortcut
menu (see Figure 22-1). After you make your customization, click the Close button
in the Customize dialog box.

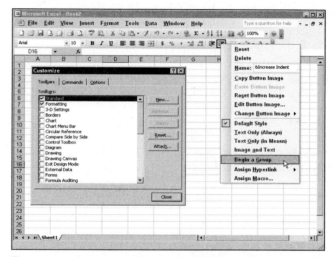

Figure 22-1: In command bar customization mode, you can alter
all toolbars and menus.

The Customize dialog box includes three tabs:

 ◆ *Toolbars:* Lists all the available toolbars, including custom toolbars that
   you have created. The list box also includes the two menu bars (Worksheet
   Menu Bar and Chart Menu Bar) plus any other custom menu bars.

 ◆ *Commands:* Lists by category all the available built-in commands. Use this
   tab to add new items to a toolbar or menu bar.

 ◆ *Options:* Lets you select various options that relate to toolbars and menus.
   These include icon size, screen tips, and menu animations.

The Options tab of the Customize dialog box contains an option called Always Show Full Menus. I strongly recommend that you turn on this option. When this option is off, incomplete menus are displayed. Apparently, Microsoft thought this option would lessen confusion for beginners. In fact, it usually has the opposite effect.

In the sections that follow, I briefly describe how to perform some common toolbar modifications manually via the Customize dialog box.

HIDING OR DISPLAYING A TOOLBAR

The Toolbars tab in the Customize dialog box displays every toolbar (built-in toolbars and custom toolbars). Add a check mark to display a toolbar; remove the check mark to hide it. The changes take effect immediately.

CREATING A NEW TOOLBAR

To create a new toolbar, click the New button of the Customize dialog box and then enter a name in the New Toolbar dialog box that appears. Excel creates and displays an empty toolbar. You can then add buttons (or menu commands) to the new toolbar.

Figure 22-2 shows a custom toolbar that I created manually. This toolbar, called Custom Formatting, contains the formatting tools that I use most frequently. Notice that this toolbar includes drop-down menus as well as standard toolbar buttons.

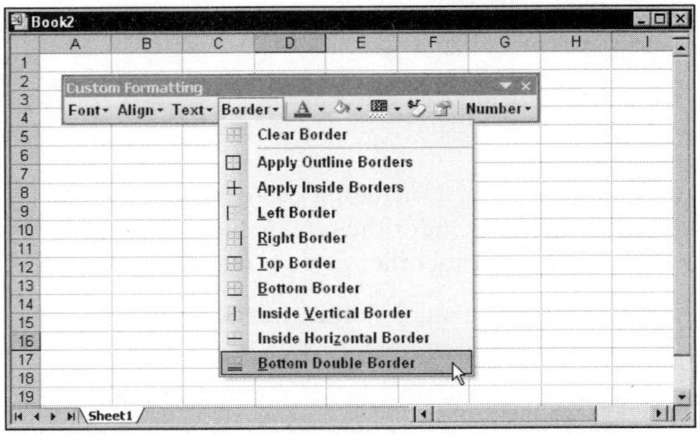

Figure 22-2: A custom toolbar that contains formatting tools.

RENAMING A CUSTOM TOOLBAR

To rename a custom toolbar, select it from the Toolbars list and then click the Rename button. Enter a new name in the Rename Toolbar dialog box. You cannot rename a built-in toolbar.

DELETING A CUSTOM TOOLBAR

To delete a custom toolbar, select it from the Toolbars list and then click the Delete button. You cannot delete a built-in toolbar.

RESETTING A BUILT-IN TOOLBAR

If you've customized a built-in toolbar, you might wish to restore it to its uncustomized state. To do so, select it from the Toolbars list and then click the Reset button. The toolbar is restored to its default state. If you've added any custom tools to the toolbar, they are removed. If you've removed any of the default tools, they are restored. The Reset button is disabled when a custom toolbar is selected.

MOVING AND COPYING CONTROLS ON A TOOLBAR

When Excel is in command bar customization mode (that is, the Customize dialog box is displayed), you can copy and move toolbar controls freely among any visible toolbars. To move a control, drag it to its new location, either within the current toolbar or on a different toolbar. To copy a control, press Ctrl while you drag that control to another toolbar. You can also copy a control within the same toolbar.

INSERTING A NEW CONTROL IN A TOOLBAR

To add a new control to a toolbar, use the Commands tab of the Customize dialog box, as shown in Figure 22-3.

Figure 22-3: The Commands tab contains
a list of every available built-in control.

Here, the controls are arranged in 17 categories. When you select a category, the controls in that category appear to the right. To add a control to a toolbar, locate it in the Commands list; then click and drag it to the toolbar.

ADDING A TOOLBAR BUTTON THAT EXECUTES A MACRO

To create a new toolbar button to which you will attach a macro, activate the Commands tab of the Customize dialog box, and then choose Macros from the

Categories list. Drag the command labeled Custom Button to your toolbar; by default, this button has a smiley face image.

After adding the button, right-click it and select your options from the menu shown in Figure 22-4. You'll want to change the name, assign a macro, and (I hope) change the image.

Figure 22–4: Customizing a toolbar button.

 Selecting Change Button Image from the shortcut menu displays a list of 42 images. This is a tiny subset of all of the available images you can use. See "Adjusting a toolbar button image" later in this chapter.

Distributing custom toolbars

In this section, I describe how to distribute custom toolbars to others, and I outline what you need to be aware of to prevent problems.

ATTACHING A TOOLBAR TO A WORKBOOK

To store a toolbar in a workbook file, choose View → Toolbars → Customize to display the Customize dialog box. Click the Attach button to bring up the Attach Toolbars dialog box, as shown in Figure 22-5. This dialog box lists all the custom toolbars in the Toolbars collection in the list box on the left. Toolbars already stored in the workbook are shown in the list box on the right.

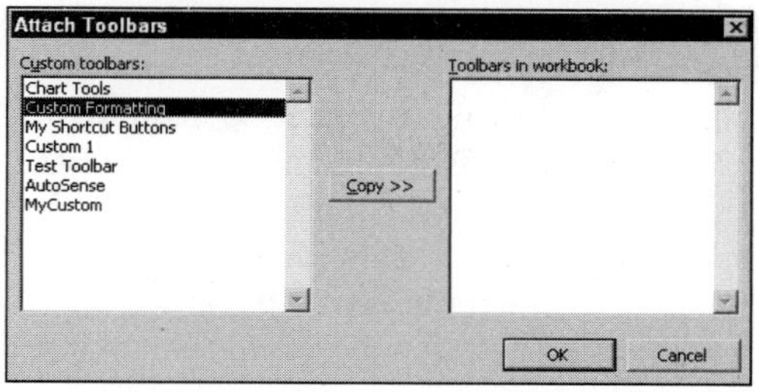

Attach Toolbars

Custom toolbars: Toolbars in workbook:

Chart Tools
Custom Formatting
My Shortcut Buttons
Custom 1
Test Toolbar   Copy >>
AutoSense
MyCustom

OK   Cancel

Figure 22-5: The Attach Toolbars dialog box.

To attach a toolbar, select it and click the Copy button. When a toolbar in the right list box is selected, the Copy button toggles to Delete, which you can click to remove a selected toolbar from a workbook.

 Oddly, there is no way to attach or detach toolbars from a workbook with VBA. These operations must be performed manually.

 The copy of the toolbar stored in the workbook always reflects its contents at the time that you attach it. If you modify the toolbar after attaching it, the changed version is not automatically stored in the workbook. You must manually remove the old toolbar and then attach the edited toolbar.

A toolbar that's attached to a workbook automatically appears when the workbook is opened unless the workspace already has a toolbar by the same name. See "How Excel Handles Toolbars" earlier in this chapter.

DISTRIBUTING A TOOLBAR WITH AN ADD-IN

As I mention in Chapter 21, distributing an application as an add-in is often the preferred method for end users. Not surprisingly, an add-in can also include one or more custom toolbars. But you need to be aware of a potential glitch.

Here's a typical scenario: You create an application that uses a custom toolbar. The buttons on that toolbar execute VBA procedures in the application's workbook. You attach the toolbar to the workbook and save the workbook. You create an add-in from the workbook. You close the XLS version of the application. You install the add-in. You click a button on the custom toolbar, *and the XLS file opens!*

Your intent, of course, is to have the toolbar buttons execute procedures in the add-in—not the XLS file. But the version of the toolbar in the add-in does not replace the version in the XLS file. Consequently, clicking a button opens the XLS file so that the macro can be executed. You can avoid this problem by deleting the toolbar that's attached to the XLS file. After doing so, the version in the add-in file will be displayed. The approach I prefer is to write code to create the toolbar on the fly when the add-in is opened. I discuss this topic in detail later in the chapter (see "Creating a command bar").

Manipulating the CommandBars Collection

The `CommandBars` collection, contained in the `Application` object, is a collection of all `CommandBar` objects. Each `CommandBar` object has a collection of `Controls`. All these objects have properties and methods that enable you to control toolbars with VBA procedures.

In this section, I provide some key background information that you should know about before you start writing code to manipulate toolbars. As always, a thorough understanding of the object model will make your task much easier.

You manipulate Excel command bars (including toolbars) by using objects located within the `CommandBars` collection. This collection consists of the following items:

◆ All of Excel 2003's built-in toolbars (63 of them).

◆ Any other custom toolbars that you create.

◆ A built-in menu bar named Worksheet Menu Bar. This appears when a worksheet is active.

◆ A built-in menu bar named Chart Menu Bar. This appears when a chart sheet is active.

◆ Any other custom menu bars that you create.

◆ All of Excel 2003's built-in shortcut menus (61 of them).

Command bar types

As I mention at the beginning of this chapter, there are actually three types of command bars, each of which is distinguished by its `Type` property. Possible settings for the `Type` property of the `CommandBars` collection are shown in the following table. VBA provides built-in constants for the command bar types.

Type	Description	Constant
0	Toolbar	`msoBarTypeNormal`
1	Menu Bar	`msoBarTypeMenuBar`
2	Shortcut Menu	`msoBarTypePopUp`

Listing all CommandBar objects

If you're curious about the objects in the `CommandBars` collection, the following procedure should be enlightening. Executing this procedure generates a list (as shown in Figure 22-6) of all `CommandBar` objects in the `CommandBars` collection. For Excel 2003, it lists a total of 126 built-in command bars, plus any custom menu bars or toolbars. For each command bar, the procedure lists its `Index`, `Name`, and `Type` property settings (displayed as Toolbar, Menu Bar, or Shortcut) as well as whether it's a built-in command bar.

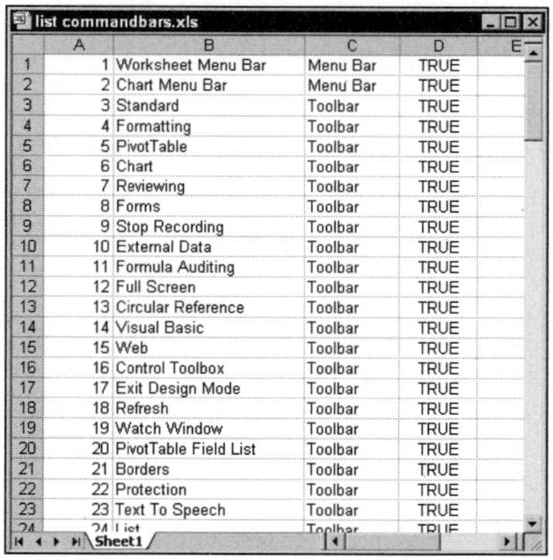

	A	B	C	D
1	1	Worksheet Menu Bar	Menu Bar	TRUE
2	2	Chart Menu Bar	Menu Bar	TRUE
3	3	Standard	Toolbar	TRUE
4	4	Formatting	Toolbar	TRUE
5	5	PivotTable	Toolbar	TRUE
6	6	Chart	Toolbar	TRUE
7	7	Reviewing	Toolbar	TRUE
8	8	Forms	Toolbar	TRUE
9	9	Stop Recording	Toolbar	TRUE
10	10	External Data	Toolbar	TRUE
11	11	Formula Auditing	Toolbar	TRUE
12	12	Full Screen	Toolbar	TRUE
13	13	Circular Reference	Toolbar	TRUE
14	14	Visual Basic	Toolbar	TRUE
15	15	Web	Toolbar	TRUE
16	16	Control Toolbox	Toolbar	TRUE
17	17	Exit Design Mode	Toolbar	TRUE
18	18	Refresh	Toolbar	TRUE
19	19	Watch Window	Toolbar	TRUE
20	20	PivotTable Field List	Toolbar	TRUE
21	21	Borders	Toolbar	TRUE
22	22	Protection	Toolbar	TRUE
23	23	Text To Speech	Toolbar	TRUE
24	24	List	Toolbar	TRUE

Figure 22-6: VBA code produced this list of all `CommandBar` objects.

```
Sub ShowCommandBarNames()
    Dim Row As Integer
    Dim cbar As CommandBar
```

```
        Cells.Clear
        Row = 1
        For Each cbar In CommandBars
            Cells(Row, 1) = cbar.Index
            Cells(Row, 2) = cbar.Name
            Select Case cbar.Type
                Case msoBarTypeNormal
                    Cells(Row, 3) = "Toolbar"
                Case msoBarTypeMenuBar
                    Cells(Row, 3) = "Menu Bar"
                Case msoBarTypePopUp
                    Cells(Row, 3) = "Shortcut"
            End Select
            Cells(Row, 4) = cbar.BuiltIn
            Row = Row + 1
        Next cbar
End Sub
```

When you work with toolbars, you can turn on the macro recorder to see what's happening in terms of VBA code. Most (but not all) of the steps that you take while customizing toolbars generate VBA code. By examining this code, you can discover how the object model for toolbars is put together. The object model actually is fairly simple and straightforward (for a change).

Creating a command bar

In VBA, you create a new toolbar by using the Add method of the CommandBars collection. The following instruction creates a new toolbar with a default name, such as Custom 1. The created toolbar is initially empty (has no controls) and is not visible (its Visible property is False).

```
CommandBars.Add
```

More often, you'll want to set some properties when you create a new toolbar. The following example demonstrates one way to do this:

```
Sub CreateAToolbar()
    Dim TBar As CommandBar
    Set TBar = CommandBars.Add
    With TBar
        .Name = "MyToolbar"
        .Top = 0
```

```
      .Left = 0
      .Visible = True
   End With
End Sub
```

The CreateAToolbar procedure uses the Add method of the CommandBars collection to add a new toolbar and create an object variable, Tbar, that represents this new toolbar. Subsequent instructions provide a name for the toolbar, set its position to the extreme upper-left corner of the screen, and make it visible. The Top and Left properties specify the position of the toolbar, and these settings represent screen coordinates — not Excel's window coordinates.

When you access the CommandBars collection in a code module for ThisWorkbook, you must precede the references with the Application object. For example:

```
Application.CommandBars.Add
```

You need to qualify the reference because the ThisWorkbook object has a CommandBars property. If your code is in a standard VBA module or in a code module for a UserForm, Sheet, or Chart, this is not necessary.

You might expect the ThisWorkbook.CommandBars property to return a list of command bars attached to the workbook — but it doesn't. In other words, the CommandBars property of a Workbook object is completely useless.

Referring to command bars in VBA

You can refer to a particular CommandBar object by its Index or its Name property. For example, the Standard toolbar has an Index property setting of 3, so you can refer to this toolbar in either of the following ways:

```
CommandBars(3)
CommandBars("Standard")
```

If you use a name, be aware that it is case-insensitive. In other words, you can use Standard, STANDARD, standard, and so on.

Index numbering for command bars is not at all consistent across versions of Excel! For example, in Excel 2002, the Chart Type toolbar has an Index of 74. In Excel 2003, the Organization Chart toolbar has an Index of 74. If your application must work in different versions of Excel, you should always use the `Name` property instead of the `Index` property.

Deleting a command bar using VBA

To delete a custom toolbar, use the `Delete` method of the `CommandBar` object. The following instruction deletes the toolbar named `MyToolbar`:

```
CommandBars("MyToolbar").Delete
```

If the toolbar doesn't exist, the instruction generates an error. To avoid the error message when you attempt to delete a toolbar that might or might not exist, the simplest solution is to ignore the error. The following code deletes `MyToolbar` if it exists. If it doesn't exist, no error message is displayed.

```
On Error Resume Next
CommandBars("MyToolbar").Delete
On Error GoTo 0
```

Another approach is to create a custom function that determines whether a particular toolbar is in the `CommandBars` collection. The following function accepts a single argument (a potential `CommandBar` object name) and returns `True` if the command bar exists. This function loops through the `CommandBars` collection and exits if it finds a command bar with a name that matches the argument.

```
Function CommandBarExists(n) As Boolean
    Dim cb As CommandBar
    For Each cb In CommandBars
        If UCase(cb.Name) = UCase(n) Then
            CommandBarExists = True
            Exit Function
        End If
    Next cb
    CommandBarExists = False
End Function
```

Properties of command bars

The following are some of the more useful properties of a `CommandBar` object:

◆ `BuiltIn`: Read-only. `True` if the object is one of Excel's built-in command bars.

◆ `Enabled`: If `False`, the command bar is hidden and does not appear in the list of available command bars.

◆ `Left`: The command bar's left position in pixels.

◆ `Name`: The command bar's display name.

◆ `Position`: An integer that specifies the position of the command bar. Possible values are as follows:

- `msoBarLeft`: The command bar is docked on the left.

- `msoBarTop`: The command bar is docked on the top.

- `msoBarRight`: The command bar is docked on the right.

- `msoBarBottom`: The command bar is docked on the bottom.

- `msoBarFloating`: The command bar isn't docked.

- `msoBarPopup`: The command bar is a shortcut menu.

◆ `Protection`: An integer that specifies the type of protection for the command bar. Possible values are as follows:

- `msoBarNoProtection`: (Default) Not protected. The command bar can be customized by the user.

- `msoBarNoCustomize`: The command bar cannot be customized.

- `msoBarNoResize`: The command bar cannot be resized.

- `msoBarNoMove`: The command bar cannot be moved.

- `msoBarNoChangeVisible`: The command bar's visibility state cannot be changed by the user.

- `msoBarNoChangeDock`: The command bar cannot be docked to a different position.

- `msoBarNoVerticalDock`: The command bar cannot be docked along the left or right edge of the window.

- `msoBarNoHorizontalDock`: The command bar cannot be docked along the top or bottom edge of the window.

◆ `Top`: The command bar's top position in pixels.

◆ `Type`: Returns an integer that represents the type of command bar. Possible values are as follows:

- `msoBarTypeNormal`: Toolbar.

- ■ msoBarTypeMenuBar: Menu bar.

- ■ msoBarTypePopUp: Shortcut menu.

◆ Visible: True if the command bar is visible.

The VBA examples in the following sections demonstrate the use of some of the command bar properties.

COUNTING CUSTOM TOOLBARS
The following function returns the number of custom toolbars. It loops through the CommandBars collection and increments a counter if the command bar represented by cb is a toolbar and if its BuiltIn property is False.

```
Function CustomToolbars()
    Dim cb As CommandBar
    Dim Count As Integer
    Count = 0
    For Each cb In CommandBars
        If cb.Type = msoBarTypeNormal Then
            If Not cb.BuiltIn Then
                Count = Count + 1
            End If
        End If
    Next cb
    CustomToolbars = Count
End Function
```

PREVENTING A TOOLBAR FROM BEING MODIFIED
The Protection property of a CommandBar object provides you with many options for protecting a CommandBar. The following instruction sets the Protection property for a toolbar named MyToolbar:

```
CommandBars("MyToolbar").Protection = msoBarNoCustomize
```

After this instruction is executed, the user is unable to customize the toolbar.

The Protection constants are *additive,* which means that you can apply different types of protection with a single command. For example, the following instructions adjust the MyToolbar toolbar so that it cannot be customized or moved:

```
Set cb = CommandBars("MyToolbar")
cb.Protection = msoBarNoCustomize + msoBarNoMove
```

All the constants for this property are listed in the Help system.

CREATING AN AUTOSENSE TOOLBAR

Many of Excel's built-in toolbars seem to have some intelligence; that is, they appear when you're working in a specific context and disappear when you stop working in that context. For example, the Chart toolbar normally appears when you activate a chart, and it disappears when you deactivate the chart. At one time, Microsoft referred to this feature as *toolbar autosensing,* but Microsoft stopped using that term in later versions. For lack of a better name, I'll continue to use *autosensing* to refer to this automatic toolbar behavior.

To disable autosensing for a particular toolbar, just close the toolbar while you're working in the context in which it normally appears. To re-enable autosensing for that toolbar, make the toolbar visible again while you're working in its context.

You might want to program toolbar autosensing for your application. For example, you might want to make a toolbar visible only when a certain worksheet is activated or when a cell in a particular range is activated. Thanks to Excel's support for events, this sort of programming is relatively easy.

The procedure in Listing 22-1 creates a toolbar when the workbook is opened and uses the SelectionChange events of one of its worksheets to determine whether the active cell is contained in a range named ToolbarRange. If so, the toolbar is made visible; if not, the toolbar is hidden. In other words, the toolbar is visible only when the active cell is within a specific range of the worksheet.

This procedure, which is called by the Workbook_Open procedure, creates a simple toolbar named AutoSense. The four toolbar buttons are set up to execute procedures named Button1, Button2, Button3, and Button4. Note that, before creating the toolbar, the code deletes the existing toolbar of the same name (if it exists).

Listing 22-1: Toolbar Visible Only When Cell Pointer Falls within Given Range

```
Sub CreateToolbar()
'    Creates a demo toolbar named "AutoSense"
     Dim AutoSense As CommandBar
     Dim Button As CommandBarButton
     Dim i As Integer

'    Delete the existing toolbar if it exists
     On Error Resume Next
     CommandBars("AutoSense").Delete
     On Error GoTo 0
```

Continued

Listing 22-1 *(Continued)*

```
'   Create the toolbar
    Set AutoSense = CommandBars.Add
    For i = 1 To 4
        Set Button = AutoSense.Controls.Add(msoControlButton)
        With Button
            .OnAction = "Button" & i
            .FaceId = i + 37
        End With
    Next i
    AutoSense.Name = "AutoSense"
End Sub
```

The event handler procedure for the SelectionChange event (which is located in the code module for Sheet1) is as follows:

```
Private Sub Worksheet_SelectionChange(ByVal Target As _
  Excel.Range)
    If Union(Target, Me.Range("ToolbarRange")).Address = _
      Me.Range("ToolbarRange").Address Then
        CommandBars("AutoSense").Visible = True
    Else
        CommandBars("AutoSense").Visible = False
    End If
End Sub
```

This procedure checks the selected cells. If the selected range is contained within a range named ToolbarRange, the AutoSense toolbar's Visible property is set to True; otherwise, it is set to False.

The workbook also contains a Workbook_BeforeClose procedure that deletes the AutoSense toolbar when the workbook is closed. This technique, of course, can be adapted to provide other types of autosensing capability for a toolbar.

 For a comprehensive discussion of the types of events that Excel recognizes, see Chapter 19.

HIDING (AND LATER RESTORING) ALL TOOLBARS

Some developers like to "take over" Excel when their application is loaded. For example, they like to hide all toolbars, the status bar, and the formula bar. It's only proper, however, for them to clean up when their application is closed. This includes restoring the toolbars that were originally visible.

The example in this section describes a way to hide all toolbars and then restore them when the application is closed. The HideAllToolbars procedure is called from the Workbook_Open event handler, and the RestoreToolbars procedure is called by the Workbook_BeforeClose event handler.

The code keeps track of which toolbars were visible by storing their names in a worksheet named TBSheet. When the workbook closes, the RestoreToolbars subroutine reads these cells and displays the toolbars. Using a worksheet to store the toolbar names is safer than using a VBA array (which can lose its values). Both procedures are shown in Listing 22-2.

Listing 22-2: Removing All Toolbars and Then Restoring Them

```
Sub HideAllToolbars()
    Dim TB As CommandBar
    Dim TBNum As Integer
    Dim TBSheet As Worksheet
    Set TBSheet = Sheets("TBSheet")
    Application.ScreenUpdating = False

'   Clear the sheet
    TBSheet.Cells.Clear

'   Hide all visible toolbars and store
'   their names
    TBNum = 0
    For Each TB In CommandBars
        If TB.Type = msoBarTypeNormal Then
            If TB.Visible Then
                TBNum = TBNum + 1
                TB.Visible = False
                TBSheet.Cells(TBNum, 1) = TB.Name
            End If
        End If
    Next TB
    Application.ScreenUpdating = True
End Sub

Sub RestoreToolbars()
    Dim TBSheet As Worksheet
        Dim cell As Range

    Set TBSheet = Sheets("TBSheet")
    Application.ScreenUpdating = False
```

Continued

Listing 22-2 *(Continued)*

```
'   Unhide the previously displayed the toolbars
    On Error Resume Next
    For Each cell In TBSheet.Range("A:A") _
      .SpecialCells(xlCellTypeConstants)
        CommandBars(cell.Value).Visible = True
    Next cell
    Application.ScreenUpdating = True
End Sub
```

In some cases, you might find that hiding the visible toolbars is insufficient. For example, the autosensing toolbars will still appear in their appropriate context. One solution is to set the Enabled property to False for all the toolbars that you don't want to appear.

Referring to controls in a command bar

A CommandBar object such as a toolbar contains CommandBarControl objects. These objects are accessed via the Controls property of the CommandBar object.

Three types of controls are available:

◆ Button: A CommandBarButton object

◆ ComboBox: A CommandBarComboBox object

◆ Menu: A CommandBarPopup object

The following Test procedure displays the Caption property for the first CommandBarControl object contained in the Standard toolbar which has an index of 3.

```
Sub Test()
    MsgBox CommandBars(3).Controls(1).Caption
End Sub
```

When you execute this procedure, you'll see the message box shown in Figure 22-7 (assuming that your Standard toolbar has not been modified).

Using index numbers for command bar controls works regardless of the user's setting of the Always Show Full Menus option (located in the Options tab of the Customize dialog box).

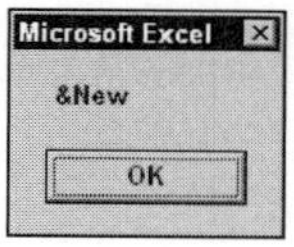

Figure 22-7: Displaying the Caption
property for a control.

Rather than use an index number to refer to a control, you can use its Caption
property setting. The following procedure produces the same result as the previous
one:

```
Sub Test2()
    MsgBox CommandBars("Standard").Controls("New").Caption
End Sub
```

Referring to a control by using its caption is language-dependent. Therefore,
the example above will not work in non-English language versions of Excel.
The solution is to use the FindControl method to locate the control by
using its Id property. I describe this in Chapter 23.

If you display the Caption property for a control, you'll see that it probably
includes an ampersand (&). The letter following the ampersand is the underlined hot
key in the displayed text (for example, &New). When you refer to a command bar
control by using its Caption property, there is no need to include the ampersand.

In some cases, Control objects may contain other Control objects. For
example, the first control on the Drawing toolbar contains other controls.
(This also demonstrates that you can include menu items on a toolbar.) The
concept of Controls within Controls will become clearer in Chapter 23,
where I discuss menus.

Listing the controls on a command bar

The following procedure displays the Caption property for each Control object
within a CommandBar object. This example uses the Standard toolbar.

```
Sub ShowControlCaptions()
    Dim Cbar as CommandBar
```

```
    Set CBar = CommandBars("Standard")
    Cells.Clear
    Row = 1
    For Each ctl In CBar.Controls
        Cells(Row, 1) = ctl.Caption
        Row = Row + 1
    Next ctl
End Sub
```

The output of the ShowControlCaptions procedure is shown in Figure 22-8.

Figure 22–8: A list of the captions for each control on the Standard toolbar.

Listing all controls on all toolbars

The following procedure loops through all command bars in the collection. If the command bar is a toolbar — that is, if its Type property is set to msoBarTypeNormal — another loop displays the Caption for each toolbar button. msoBarTypeNormal is a built-in constant that has the value of 0.

```
Sub ShowAllToolbarControls()
    Dim row As Integer
    Dim Cbar As CommandBar
    Dim ctl As CommandBarControl

    Cells.Clear
    row = 1
```

```
    For Each Cbar In CommandBars
        If Cbar.Type = msoBarTypeNormal Then
            Cells(row, 1) = Cbar.Name
            For Each ctl In Cbar.Controls
                Cells(row, 2) = ctl.Caption
                row = row + 1
            Next ctl
        End If
    Next Cbar
End Sub
```

Partial output of the `ShowAllToolbarControls` procedure is shown in Figure 22-9.

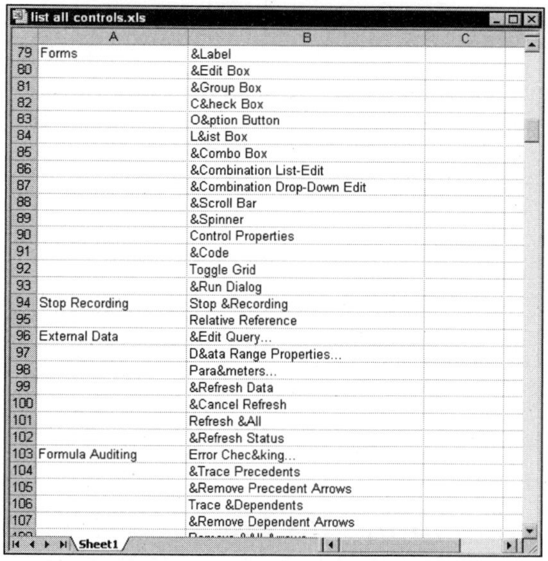

Figure 22-9: A list of the captions for each control on all toolbars.

Adding a control to a command bar

To add a new control to a `CommandBar` object, use the `Add` method of the `Controls` collection object. The following instruction adds a new control to a toolbar named `MyToolbar`. Its `Type` property is set to the `msoControlButton` constant, which creates a standard button.

```
CommandBars("MyToolbar").Controls.Add Type:=msoControlButton
```

The toolbar button added in the preceding instruction is just a blank button; clicking it has no effect. Most of the time, you'll want to set some properties when you add a new button to a toolbar. The following code adds a new control, gives it an image through the FaceId property, assigns a macro by way of the OnAction property, and specifies a caption:

```
Sub AddButton()
    Dim NewBtn As CommandBarButton
    Set NewBtn = CommandBars("MyToolbar").Controls.Add _
      (Type:=msoControlButton)
    With NewBtn
      .FaceId = 300
      .OnAction = "MyMacro"
      .Caption = "Tooltip goes here"
    End With
End Sub
```

The AddButton procedure creates an object variable (NewBtn) that represents the added control. The With-End With construct then sets the properties for the object.

You can perform the same action without using an object variable, as shown in the code that follows.

```
Sub AddButton()
    With CommandBars("MyToolbar").Controls.Add _
        (Type:=msoControlButton)
      .FaceId = 300
      .OnAction = "MyMacro"
      .Caption = "Tooltip goes here"
    End With
End Sub
```

Deleting a control from a command bar

To delete a control from a CommandBar object, use the Delete method of the CommandBarControl object. The following instruction deletes the first control on a toolbar named MyToolbar:

```
CommandBars("MyToolbar").Controls(1).Delete
```

You can also specify the control by referring to its caption. The following instruction deletes a control that has a caption of SortButton:

```
CommandBars("MyToolbar").Controls("SortButton").Delete
```

Properties of command bar controls

Command bar controls have a number of properties that determine how the controls look and work. Following is a list of a few of the more useful properties for command bar controls:

◆ `BeginGroup`: If `True`, a separator bar appears before the control.

◆ `BuiltIn`: Read-only. `True` if the control is one of Excel's built-in controls.

◆ `Caption`: The text that is displayed for the control. If the control shows only an image, the caption appears when you move the mouse pointer over the control.

◆ `Enabled`: If `True`, the control can be clicked.

◆ `FaceID`: A number that represents a graphic image displayed next to the control's text, or on the button if the control is a toolbar button.

◆ `Id`: Read-only. A code number for a built-in control.

◆ `OnAction`: The name of a VBA procedure to be executed when the user clicks the control.

◆ `State`: Determines whether a control appears pressed. This property is available only for a `CommandBarButton` control.

◆ `Style`: Determines whether the control appears with a caption and/or image. This property is available only for `CommandBarButton` and `CommandBarComboBox` controls.

◆ `ToolTipText`: Text that appears when the user moves the mouse pointer over the control.

◆ `Type`: An integer that determines the type of the control.

SETTING A CONTROL'S STYLE PROPERTY

The `Style` property of a control determines its appearance; this property applies only to `CommandBarButton` and `CommandBarComboBox` controls. This property is usually specified by using a built-in constant. For example, to display a button with an image and text, set the `Style` property to `msoButtonIconAndCaption`. Following are valid style settings for a `CommandBarButton`:

◆ `msoButtonAutomatic`

◆ `msoButtonCaption`

◆ `msoButtonIcon`

◆ `msoButtonIconAndCaption`

◆ `msoButtonIconAndCaptionBelow`

◆ msoButtonIconAndWrapCaption

◆ msoButtonIconAndWrapCaptionBelow

◆ msoButtonWrapCaption

For a CommandBarComboBox, the valid settings are msoComboLabel or msoCombo Normal.

Figure 22-10 shows a toolbar with seven command button controls, each demonstrating a different style.

Figure 22-10: The seven values of the Style property for a command button control.

A workbook that creates this toolbar is available on the companion CD-ROM.

The text displayed on a control is the control's Caption property, and its image is determined by the value of the FaceID property.

ADJUSTING A TOOLBAR BUTTON IMAGE

When you're in Excel's command bar customization mode, you can right-click any toolbar button and select Change Button Image. (Refer to Figure 22-4.) Doing so displays a list of 42 images from which you can select. Most of the time, none of these images is exactly what you need. Therefore, you must specify the image with VBA.

The image (if any) displayed on a toolbar control is determined by its FaceId property. For an image to be displayed, the control's Style property can be set to any value *except* msoButtonCaption.

The following instruction sets the FaceId property of the first button on the MyToolbar toolbar image to 45, which is the code number for a mailbox icon:

```
CommandBars("MyToolbar").Controls(1).FaceId = 45
```

How do you determine the code number for a particular image? Well, you could use trial and error. . . . But a better way is to use a VBA procedure that displays all the possible toolbar button images. This code, shown in Listing 22-3, creates a toolbar with 200 buttons. In addition, the toolbar contains a combo box that you can use to specify which set of buttons to show. Initially, the toolbar shows FaceIds 1–200. The second set shows 201–400, and so on.

For more information about using a drop-down control, see "Using other types of command bar controls," later in this chapter.

Listing 22-3: Creating a Toolbar to Display All Button Images

```
Dim ButtonGroup As Long

Sub ShowFaceIDs()
    Dim NewToolbar As CommandBar
    Dim NewButton As CommandBarButton
    Dim SetNum As CommandBarComboBox
    Dim i As Integer

'   Delete existing FaceIds toolbar if it exists
    On Error Resume Next
    Application.CommandBars("FaceIds").Delete
    On Error GoTo 0
    ButtonGroup = 1

'   Add an empty toolbar
    Set NewToolbar = Application.CommandBars.Add _
        (Name:="FaceIds", temporary:=True)
    NewToolbar.Visible = True

'   Add 200 buttons
    For i = 1 To 200
        Set NewButton = NewToolbar.Controls.Add _
            (Type:=msoControlButton, ID:=2950)
    Next i

'   Add a drop-down
    Set SetNum = NewToolbar.Controls.Add(Type:=msoControlDropdown)
    For i = 1 To 18
        SetNum.AddItem "Set " & i
    Next i
    With SetNum
        .ListIndex = ButtonGroup
        .Caption = "Button Set Number"
        .OnAction = "NewButtons"
```

Continued

Listing 22-3 *(Continued)*

```
    End With
    NewToolbar.Width = 400

'   Set up the buttons
    Call NewButtons
End Sub

Sub NewButtons()
'   Adjusts the buttons, based on the selected set in the drop-down
    Dim i As Long
    ButtonGroup = CommandBars("FaceIds").Controls
      ("Button Set Number").ListIndex
    For i = 1 To 200
        With CommandBars("FaceIds").Controls(i)
            .FaceId = (ButtonGroup - 1) * 200 + i
            .Caption = "FaceID = " & (ButtonGroup - 1) * 200 + i
            .OnAction = "EmptySub"
        End With
    Next i
End Sub
```

Figure 22-11 shows the toolbar that's created by the ShowFaceIDs procedure.

Figure 22-11: This toolbar shows all built-in
toolbar button images, in groups of 200.

The ShowFaceIDs procedure creates the toolbar and adds the buttons. It calls the
NewButtons procedure, sets the FaceID property, and adds a caption. (The caption
appears when the mouse pointer is moved over a button.) Selecting a different item
in the drop-down control also runs the NewButtons procedure. The button set is
determined by the module-level variable ButtonGroup.

This workbook is available on the companion CD-ROM.

USING CUSTOM TOOLBAR IMAGES

Although Excel provides a huge variety of toolbar images, you might prefer to create a custom image for a toolbar button. You can use the Button Editor, as shown in Figure 22-12, to edit the pixels in a 16 x 16 button image. To access the Button Editor, choose View → Toolbars → Customize. Then, while the Customize dialog box is displayed, right-click a toolbar button and choose Edit Button Image.

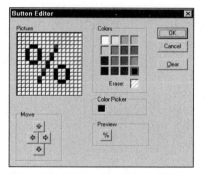

Figure 22-12: Use the Button Editor to modify a toolbar button image.

 The toolbar buttons in Excel 2003 use more colors than in previous versions.

If you're using VBA to create a toolbar on-the-fly, you can use the PasteFace method to paste an image from the Clipboard. The code below assumes that Sheet1 contains a picture object named CustomIcon. This picture is copied to the Clipboard, a toolbar button is added, and the PasteFace method pastes the copied image to the toolbar.

```
ThisWorkbook.Sheets("Sheet1").Pictures("CustomIcon").Copy
Set MyButton = CommandBars("MyCustom").Controls.Add (Type:=msoControlButton)
MyButton.PasteFace
```

CHANGING A CONTROL'S CAPTION DYNAMICALLY

The procedure in Listing 22-4 creates a toolbar that contains a single button. The caption on this button displays the number format string for the active cell (see Figure 22-13). The procedure uses Worksheet events to monitor when the selection is changed. When a SelectionChange event occurs, a procedure is executed that changes the caption in the button.

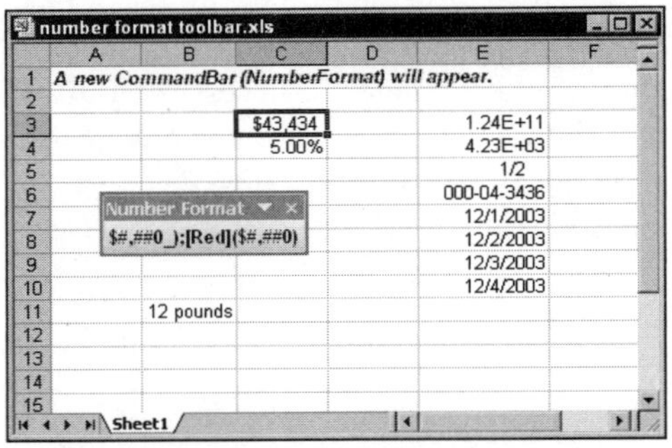

Figure 22–13: This toolbar button displays the number format for the active cell.

Listing 22–4: Showing the User the Current Cell's Number Format

```
Sub MakeNumberFormatDisplay()
    Dim TBar As CommandBar
    Dim NewBtn As CommandBarButton

'    Delete existing toolbar if it exists
    On Error Resume Next
    CommandBars("Number Format").Delete
    On Error GoTo 0

'    Create a new toolbar
    Set TBar = CommandBars.Add
    With TBar
        .Name = "Number Format"
        .Visible = True
    End With

'    Add a button control
    Set NewBtn = CommandBars("Number Format").Controls.Add _
        (Type:=msoControlButton)
    With NewBtn
        .Caption = ""
        .OnAction = "ChangeNumFormat"
```

```
      .TooltipText = "Click to change the number format"
      .Style = msoButtonCaption
    End With
    Call UpdateToolbar
End Sub
```

 For more information about events, see Chapter 19.

The `UpdateToolbar` procedure, which follows, simply copies the `NumberFormat` property of the `ActiveCell` to the `Caption` property of the button control:

```
Sub UpdateToolbar()
'    Sets caption to active cell's number format string
    On Error Resume Next
    CommandBars("Number Format"). _
      Controls(1).Caption = ActiveCell.NumberFormat
    If Err <> 0 Then CommandBars("Number Format"). _
      Controls(1).Caption = ""
End Sub
```

The button's `OnAction` property is set to a procedure named `ChangeNumFormat`, which follows. The following procedure displays the Number tab of Excel's Format Cells dialog box (see Figure 22-14).

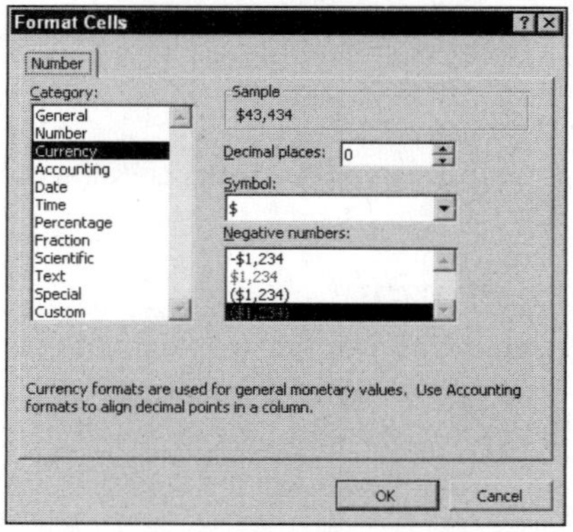

Figure 22-14: Clicking the dynamic toolbar button created
in Listing 22-3 displays the Format Cells dialog box.

```
Sub ChangeNumFormat()
    Application.Dialogs(xlDialogFormatNumber).Show
    Call UpdateToolbar
End Sub
```

This technique works quite well, but it does have a flaw: If the user changes the number format with a button on the Formatting toolbar, the display in the Number Format is not changed because changing the number format of a cell does not trigger a trappable event.

ASSIGNING A CUSTOM MACRO TO A BUILT-IN BUTTON

Each of Excel's built-in toolbar buttons executes a specific internal procedure. You can assign your own macro to a built-in button. To do so, just use the OnAction property. The following instruction assigns a macro to the Sort Ascending toolbar button.

```
CommandBars("Standard").Controls("Sort Ascending").OnAction = "ShowMsg"
```

After executing the instruction, clicking the Sort Ascending button will no longer work. Rather, it will execute the ShowMsg VBA procedure.

To return the button to its normal functionality, assign an empty string to its OnAction property:

```
CommandBars("Standard").Controls("Sort Ascending").OnAction = ""
```

EXECUTING A COMMAND BAR BUTTON

Command bar controls have an Execute method. When invoked, this method runs the internal procedure assigned to a built-in control. For example, executing the following instruction is equivalent to clicking the Sort Ascending button on the Standard toolbar:

```
CommandBars("Standard").Controls("Sort Ascending").Execute
```

Using the Execute method with a custom command bar button runs the macro assigned to its OnAction property.

USING OTHER TYPES OF COMMAND BAR CONTROLS

A standard toolbar button is just one type of five control types that you can add to a toolbar. The control type is determined by the Type property of the control.

The built-in constants for the control types that you can add to a command bar are as follows:

◆ msoControlButton: A standard button.

◆ msoControlEdit: An edit box.

◆ `msoControlComboBox`: A combo box.

◆ `msoControlDropdown`: A drop-down list.

◆ `msoControlButtonPopup`: A button that, when clicked, displays other controls. Use this control to create a menu with menu items.

> The `Type` property for a `Control` object is a read-only property that's set when the control is created. In other words, you can't change a control's type after it has been created.

The `MakeMonthList` procedure in Listing 22-5 creates a new toolbar, adds a drop-down list control, and fills that control with the names of each month. It also sets the `OnAction` property so that clicking the control executes a procedure named `PasteMonth`, which pastes the selected month into the active cell. The resulting toolbar is shown in Figure 22-15.

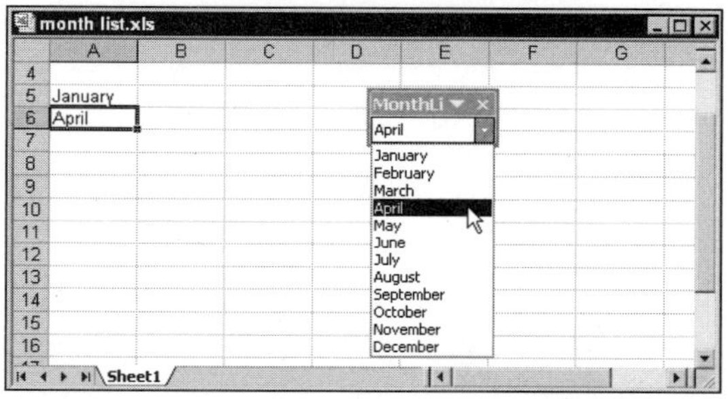

Figure 22-15: This toolbar contains a drop–down list control, with an attached macro.

Listing 22-5: Attaching a Drop-down List to a Command Bar

```
Sub MakeMonthList()
    Dim TBar As CommandBar
    Dim NewDD As CommandBarControl

'   Delete existing toolbar if it exists
    On Error Resume Next
    CommandBars("MonthList").Delete
    On Error GoTo 0
```

Continued

Listing 22-5 *(Continued)*

```
'    Create a new toolbar
    Set TBar = CommandBars.Add
    With TBar
        .Name = "MonthList"
        .Visible = True
    End With

'    Add a DropDown control
    Set NewDD = CommandBars("MonthList").Controls.Add _
      (Type:=msoControlDropdown)
    With NewDD
        .Caption = "DateDD"
        .OnAction = "PasteMonth"
        .Style = msoButtonAutomatic

'        Fill it with month name
        For i = 1 To 12
            .AddItem Format(DateSerial(1, i, 1), "mmmm")
        Next i
        .ListIndex = 1
    End With
End Sub
```

The `PasteMonth` procedure follows:

```
Sub PasteMonth()
'    Puts the selected month in the active cell
    On Error Resume Next
    With CommandBars("MonthList").Controls("DateDD")
        ActiveCell.Value = .List(.ListIndex)
    End With
End Sub
```

The workbook has an additional twist: It uses a `Worksheet_SelectionChange` event handler. This procedure, which follows, is executed whenever the user makes a new selection on the worksheet. The procedure determines whether the active cell contains a month name. If so, it sets the `ListIndex` property of the drop-down list control in the toolbar.

```
Private Sub Worksheet_SelectionChange(ByVal Target _
  As Excel.Range)
    For i = 1 To 12
```

```
      Set ActCell = Target.Range("A1")
      If ActCell.Value = Format(DateSerial(1, i, 1), _
       "mmmm") Then
          CommandBars("MonthList").Controls("DateDD") _
           .ListIndex = i
          Exit Sub
      End If
    Next i
End Sub
```

Chapter 23

Creating Custom Menus

IN THIS CHAPTER

Virtually every Windows program has a menu system, which usually serves as the primary user interface element. The Windows standard places the menu bar directly beneath the application's title bar. In addition, most programs now implement another type of menu: shortcut menus. Typically, right-clicking an item displays a context-sensitive shortcut menu containing relevant commands. In this chapter, I cover the following:

◆ An overview of Excel's menu system

◆ Types of menu modifications that you can make

◆ How to manipulate menus with VBA

◆ Various menu programming techniques used with events

◆ A useful (and very easy) technique for creating custom menus

◆ A procedure for replacing standard menu conventions with your own

◆ How to customize the shortcut menus

EXCEL USES A TRADITIONAL WINDOW MENU BAR AND SHORTCUT MENUS. Developers have almost complete control over Excel's entire menu system, including shortcut menus. This chapter tells you everything you need to know about working with Excel's menus.

A Few Words about Excel's Menu Bar

If you've read Chapter 22, you already know that a menu bar (like a toolbar) is a `CommandBar` object. In fact, the techniques that I describe in Chapter 22 also apply to menu bars.

So how does a menu bar differ from a toolbar? In general, a menu bar is displayed at the top of the Excel window, directly below the title bar. When clicked, the top-level controls on a menu bar display a drop-down list of menu items. A menu bar can also contain three window control buttons (Minimize, Restore, and

Close) that are displayed only when a workbook window is maximized. Toolbars, on the other hand, usually consist of graphical icons and do not display any control buttons.

These rules are definitely not cast in stone. You can, if desired, add traditional toolbar buttons to a menu bar or add traditional menu items to a toolbar. You can even move a menu bar from its traditional location and make it free-floating. Although Excel supports multiple menu bars, only one can be visible at any time.

Beginning with Excel 2002, Excel's menu bar displays a "Type a question for help" box, which is a quick way to search the Help system. If you would prefer not to see this box, you can hide it by using the following VBA statement:

```
Application.CommandBars.
    DisableAskAQuestionDropDown = False
```

What You Can Do with Excel's Menus

Typical Excel users get by just fine with the standard menus. Because you're reading this book, however, you're probably not the typical Excel user. You might want to modify menus to make your life easier and to make life easier for the folks who use the spreadsheets that you develop.

To modify Excel menus, you can remove elements, add elements, and change elements. In addition, you can temporarily replace Excel's standard menu bar with one of your own creation. You can change Excel's menus two ways: manually, or with Visual Basic for Applications (VBA) code.

When you close Excel, it saves any changes that you've made to the menu system, and these changes appear the next time that you open Excel. The information about menu modifications is stored in your XLB file.

See Chapter 22 for more information about the XLB file.

In many situations, *you won't want your menu modifications to be saved between sessions.* Generally, you'll need to write VBA code to change the menus while a particular workbook is open and then change them back when the workbook closes. Therefore, you'll need VBA code to modify the

menu when the workbook is opened and more VBA code to return the
menus to normal when the workbook is closed.

Understanding Excel menu terminology

Menu terminology is often a bit confusing at first because many of the terms are
similar. The following list presents the official Excel menu terminology that I refer
to in this chapter:

◆ *Command bar:* An object that can function as a menu bar, a shortcut
   menu, or a toolbar. It is represented by the `CommandBar` object in the
   Microsoft Office Object Library.

◆ *Menu bar:* The row of words that appears directly below the application's
   title bar. Excel has two menu bars: One is displayed when a worksheet is
   active, and the other is displayed when a chart sheet is active or when an
   embedded chart is activated.

◆ *Menu:* A single, top-level element of a menu bar. For example, both of
   Excel's menu bars have a File menu.

◆ *Menu item:* An element that appears in the drop-down list when you
   select a menu. For example, the first menu item under the File menu is
   New. Menu items also appear in submenus and shortcut menus.

◆ *Separator bar:* A horizontal line that appears between two menu items.
   The separator bar is used to group similar menu items.

◆ *Submenu:* A second-level menu that is under some menus. For example,
   the Edit menu has a submenu called Clear.

◆ *Submenu item:* A menu item that appears in the list when you select a
   submenu. For example, the Edit → Clear submenu contains the following
   submenu items: All, Formats, Contents, and Comments.

◆ *Shortcut menu:* The floating list of menu items that appears when you
   right-click a selection or an object. The shortcut menu that appears
   depends on the current context.

◆ *Enabled:* A menu or a menu item that can be used. If a menu or a menu
   item isn't enabled, its text appears grayed, and it can't be used.

◆ *Checked:* The status of a menu item that represents an on/off or True/False
   state. A menu item can display a graphical box that is checked or
   unchecked. The View → Status Bar menu item is an example.

◆ *Image:* A small, graphical icon that appears next to some menu items. In
   VBA terms, the code associated with each image is known as a `FaceID`.
   See Chapter 22 for more information about the `FaceID` property.

◆ *Shortcut key combination:* A keystroke combination that serves as an alternative method to execute a menu item. The shortcut key combination is displayed at the right side of the menu item. For example, Ctrl+S is the shortcut key combination for the File → Save command.

Removing Excel menu elements

You can remove any part of the Excel menu system: menu items, menus, and entire menu bars. For example, if you don't want the end users of your application fiddling with the display, you can remove the View menu from the Worksheet Menu Bar. You can also remove one or more menu items from a menu. If you remove the New menu item from the File menu, for example, users can't use the menu to create a new workbook. Finally, you can eliminate Excel's menu bar and replace it with one that you've created. You might do this if you want your application to be completely under the control of your macros.

 Simply removing menu bars, menus, or menu items does not affect the alternative method of accomplishing some actions. Specifically, if corresponding shortcut keys, toolbar buttons, or shortcut menus perform the same action as a menu command, those alternative methods still work. For example, if you remove the New menu item from the File menu, the user can still use the New Workbook toolbar button, the Ctrl+N shortcut, the Task Pane, or the desktop shortcut menu to create a new workbook.

Adding Excel menu elements

You can add custom menus to built-in menu bars, and you can add custom menu items to a built-in menu. In fact, you can create an entirely new menu bar if you like. For example, you might develop an application that doesn't require any of Excel's built-in menus. A simple solution is to create a new menu bar that consists of custom menus and custom menu items that execute your macros. You can hide Excel's normal menu bar and replace it with your own.

Changing Excel menu elements

If you get bored with Excel's standard menu text, you can change it to something else — for instance, you can change the Tools menu to the Miscellaneous menu. You can also assign your own macros to built-in menu items. You have many other options for changing menu elements, including rearranging the order of the menus on a menu bar (for example, to make the Help menu appear first instead of last).

Moving Up from Excel 5/95?

If you've customized menus in Excel 5 or Excel 95, you can pretty much forget everything that you ever learned. Beginning with Excel 97, menu customization has changed significantly in the following respects:

◆ *A menu bar is actually a toolbar in disguise.* If you don't believe me, grab the vertical bars at the very left of the menu bar and drag the bar away. You'll end up with a floating toolbar. The official (VBA) term for both menus and toolbars is *command bar.*

◆ *The Excel 5/95 Menu Editor is gone.* To edit a menu manually, you choose the View → Toolbars → Customize command. Understand, however, that Excel 5/95 workbooks that contain menus customized by using the old Menu Editor still work in Excel 97 and later. However, to make any changes to these modified menus, you must do so in Excel 5/95. Better yet, just remove the menu edits (using Excel 5/95) if you plan to use your workbook with a later version of Excel.

◆ *There is no direct way to assign a VBA macro to a new menu item on the Tools menu.* This was a piece of cake with Excel 5/95. Later in this chapter, however, I provide VBA code that you can use to add a new menu item to the Tools menu.

◆ *Excel 2000 and later, by default, displays only the most recently used menu items.* In my opinion, this is one of the worst ideas that Microsoft has come up with. I can't imagine why anyone would want the order of his or her menu items to be shifting around. Fortunately, this feature can be disabled in the Options tab of the Customize dialog box.

Be careful if you change the captions for Excel's menus. Some Excel developers rely on the standard menu captions when they create new menus — and their code will fail if you've modified your menu captions. As you'll see in the later section, "Adding a menu: Take 2," using the `FindControl` method in your code will eliminate these problems.

The remainder of this chapter focuses on writing VBA code to modify menus.

Chapter 22 provides background information about the Customize dialog box.

Using VBA to Customize Excel Menus

In this section, I present some practical examples of VBA code that manipulates Excel's menus.

Listing Excel menu information

The ListMenuInfo procedure, which follows, might be instructive for those who will be customizing Excel menus. It displays the caption for each item (menu, menu item, and submenu item) on the Worksheet Menu Bar.

```
Sub ListMenuInfo()
    Dim row As Integer
    Dim Menu As CommandBarControl
    Dim MenuItem As CommandBarControl
    Dim SubMenuItem As CommandBarControl
    row = 1
    On Error Resume Next
    For Each Menu In CommandBars(1).Controls
        For Each MenuItem In Menu.Controls
            For Each SubMenuItem In MenuItem.Controls
                Cells(row, 1) = Menu.Caption
                Cells(row, 2) = MenuItem.Caption
                Cells(row, 3) = SubMenuItem.Caption
                row = row + 1
            Next SubMenuItem
        Next MenuItem
    Next Menu
End Sub
```

Notice that this code uses On Error Resume Next to avoid the error message that appears when the procedure attempts to access a submenu item that doesn't exist.

Figure 23-1 shows a portion of the ListMenuInfo procedure's output.

Referencing the CommandBars Collection

The `CommandBars` collection is a member of the `Application` object. When you reference this collection in a regular VBA module, you can omit the reference to the `Application` object because it is assumed. For example, the following statement (contained in a standard VBA module) displays the name of the first element of the `CommandBars` collection:

```
MsgBox CommandBars(1).Name
```

When you reference the `CommandBars` collection from a code module for a `ThisWorkbook` object, you must precede it with a reference to the `Application` object, like this:

```
MsgBox Application.CommandBars(1).Name
```

	A	B	C	D	E	F
153	&Insert	&Name	&Create...			
154	&Insert	&Name	&Apply...			
155	&Insert	&Name	&Label...			
156	&Insert	Co&mment				
157	&Insert	Ink &Annotations				
158	&Insert	&Picture	&Clip Art...			
159	&Insert	&Picture	&From File...			
160	&Insert	&Picture	From &Scanner or Camera...			
161	&Insert	&Picture	Ink &Drawing and Writing			
162	&Insert	&Picture	&AutoShapes			
163	&Insert	&Picture	&WordArt...			
164	&Insert	&Picture	&Organization Chart			
165	&Insert	Dia&gram...				
166	&Insert	&Object...				
167	&Insert	Hyperl&ink...				
168	F&ormat	C&ells...				
169	F&ormat	&Row	H&eight...			
170	F&ormat	&Row	&AutoFit			
171	F&ormat	&Row	&Hide			
172	F&ormat	&Row	&Unhide			
173	F&ormat	&Column	&Width...			
174	F&ormat	&Column	&AutoFit Selection			
175	F&ormat	&Column	&Hide			
176	F&ormat	&Column	&Unhide			
177	F&ormat	&Column	&Standard Width...			
178	F&ormat	S&heet	&Rename			

Figure 23-1: A portion of the output from the `ListMenuInfo` procedure.

A workbook that contains this procedure is available on the companion CD-ROM.

Menu-Making Conventions

You might have noticed that menus in Windows programs typically adhere to some established conventions. No one knows where these conventions came from, but you should follow them if you want to give the impression that you know what you're doing. When you modify menus, keep the following points in mind:

◆ Tradition dictates that the File menu is always first and that the Help menu is always last.

◆ Menu text is always proper (or title) case: That is, the first letter of each word is uppercase except for minor words such as *the, a,* and *and.*

◆ A top-level menu does not cause any action. In other words, each menu must have at least one menu item.

◆ Menu items are usually limited to three or fewer words.

◆ Every menu item should have a hot key (an underlined letter) that's unique within the menu.

◆ A menu item that displays a dialog box is followed by an ellipsis (...).

◆ Menu item lists should be kept relatively short. Sometimes, submenus provide a good alternative to long lists. If you must have a lengthy list of menu items, use separator bars to separate items into logical groups.

◆ If possible, disable menu items that are not appropriate in the current context. In VBA terminology, to disable a menu item, set its `Enabled` property to `False`.

◆ Some menu items serve as toggles. When the option is on, the menu item is preceded by a check mark.

Adding a new menu to a menu bar

In this section, I describe how to use VBA to add a new menu to the Worksheet Menu Bar. The Worksheet Menu Bar is the first item in the `CommandBars` collection, so you can reference it one of two ways:

◆ *By its name:* `CommandBars("Worksheet Menu Bar")`

◆ *By its index:* `CommandBars(1)`

In VBA terms, you use the `Add` method to append a new control to the `Controls` collection. The new control is a pop-up control of type `msoControlPopup`. You can specify the new control's position; if you don't, the new menu is added to the end of the menu bar.

Adding a new menu is a two-step process:

1. Use the `Add` method to create an object variable that refers to the new control. Arguments for the `Add` method enable you to specify the control's type, its ID (useful only if you're adding a built-in menu), its position, and whether it's a temporary control that will be deleted when Excel closes.

2. Adjust the properties of the new control. For example, you'll probably want to specify a `Caption` property and an `OnAction` property.

ADDING A MENU: TAKE 1

In this example, the objective is to add a new Budgeting menu to the Worksheet Menu Bar and to position this new menu to the left of the Help menu.

```
Sub AddNewMenu()
    Dim HelpIndex As Integer
    Dim NewMenu As CommandBarPopup

'   Get Index of Help menu
    HelpIndex = CommandBars(1).Controls("Help").Index

'   Create the menu
    Set NewMenu = CommandBars(1).Controls.Add _
      (Type:=msoControlPopup, _
       Before:=HelpIndex, _
       Temporary:=True)

'   Add a caption
    NewMenu.Caption = "&Budgeting"
End Sub
```

The preceding code is *not* a good example of how to add a menu, and it might or might not insert the menu at the proper position. It suffers from two problems:

◆ *It assumes that the Help menu exists.* The user might have removed the Help menu.

◆ *It assumes that the Help menu has* Help *as its caption.* Non-English versions of Excel could have a different caption for their menus.

ADDING A MENU: TAKE 2

Listing 23-1 presents a better demonstration. It uses the `FindControl` method to attempt to locate the Help menu. If the Help menu is not found, the code adds the new menu item to the end of the Worksheet Menu Bar.

Listing 23-1: Adding the Budgeting Menu to Excel's Main Menu Bar

```
Sub AddNewMenu()
    Dim HelpMenu As CommandBarControl
    Dim NewMenu As CommandBarPopup

'   Find the Help Menu
    Set HelpMenu = CommandBars(1).FindControl(Id:=30010)

    If HelpMenu Is Nothing Then
'       Add the menu to the end
        Set NewMenu = CommandBars(1).Controls _
         .Add(Type:=msoControlPopup, Temporary:=True)
    Else
'       Add the menu before Help
        Set NewMenu = CommandBars(1).Controls _
         .Add(Type:=msoControlPopup, Before:=HelpMenu.Index, _
         Temporary:=True)
    End If

'   Add a caption
    NewMenu.Caption = "&Budgeting"
End Sub
```

 The procedure in Listing 23-1 creates an essentially useless menu — it has no menu items. See "Adding a menu item to the Tools menu" later in this chapter for an example of how to add a menu item to a menu.

To use the FindControl method, you must know the ID property of the control that you're looking for. Each of Excel's built-in CommandBar controls has a unique ID property. For this example, I determined the ID property of the Help menu by executing the following statement:

```
MsgBox CommandBars(1).Controls("Help").ID
```

The message box displayed 30010, which is the value that I used as the ID argument for the FindControl method. Table 23-1 shows the ID property settings for the top-level controls in Excel's menu bars.

TABLE 23-1 ID PROPERTY SETTINGS FOR EXCEL'S TOP-LEVEL MENUS

Menu	ID Setting
File	30002
Edit	30003
View	30004
Insert	30005
Format	30006
Tools	30007
Data	30011
Chart	30022
Window	30009
Help	30010

Deleting a menu from a menu bar

To delete a menu, use the `Delete` method. The following example deletes the menu in the Worksheet Menu Bar whose caption is `Budgeting`. Notice that I use `On Error Resume Next` to avoid the error message that appears if the menu does not exist.

```
Sub DeleteMenu()
    On Error Resume Next
    CommandBars(1).Controls("Budgeting").Delete
End Sub
```

Recall that the Budgeting menu was given a caption by using this instruction:

```
NewMenu.Caption = "&Budgeting"
```

When you reference a menu by using its caption, the ampersand is optional.

Adding menu items to a menu

In the previous example under "Adding a new menu to a menu bar," I demonstrate how to add a menu to a menu bar. Listing 23-2 adds to the original procedure and in doing so, demonstrates how to add menu items to the new menu.

Listing 23-2: Adding Selections and Submenu Items to the Budgeting Menu

```
Sub CreateMenu()
    Dim HelpMenu As CommandBarControl
    Dim NewMenu As CommandBarPopup
    Dim MenuItem As CommandBarControl
    Dim Submenuitem As CommandBarButton

'   Delete the menu if it already exists
    Call DeleteMenu

'   Find the Help Menu
    Set HelpMenu = CommandBars(1).FindControl(Id:=30010)

    If HelpMenu Is Nothing Then
'       Add the menu to the end
        Set NewMenu = CommandBars(1).Controls _
          .Add(Type:=msoControlPopup, temporary:=True)
    Else
'       Add the menu before Help
        Set NewMenu = CommandBars(1).Controls _
          .Add(Type:=msoControlPopup, Before:=HelpMenu.Index, _
          temporary:=True)
    End If

'   Add a caption for the menu
    NewMenu.Caption = "&Budgeting"

'   FIRST MENU ITEM
    Set MenuItem = NewMenu.Controls.Add _
      (Type:=msoControlButton)
    With MenuItem
        .Caption = "&Data Entry..."
        .FaceId = 162
        .OnAction = "Macro1"
    End With

'   SECOND MENU ITEM
    Set MenuItem = NewMenu.Controls.Add _
      (Type:=msoControlButton)
    With MenuItem
        .Caption = "&Generate Reports..."
        .FaceId = 590
```

```
          .OnAction = "Macro2"
      End With

'    THIRD MENU ITEM
      Set MenuItem = NewMenu.Controls.Add _
        (Type:=msoControlPopup)
      With MenuItem
          .Caption = "View &Charts"
          .BeginGroup = True
      End With

'    FIRST SUBMENU ITEM
      Set SubMenuItem = MenuItem.Controls.Add _
        (Type:=msoControlButton)
      With SubMenuItem
          .Caption = "Monthly &Variance"
          .FaceId = 420
          .OnAction = "Macro3"
      End With

'    SECOND SUBMENU ITEM
      Set SubMenuItem = MenuItem.Controls.Add _
        (Type:=msoControlButton)
      With SubMenuItem
          .Caption = "Year-To-Date &Summary"
          .FaceId = 422
          .OnAction = "Macro4"
      End With
End Sub
```

Specifically, the `CreateMenu` procedure builds the menu shown in Figure 23-2. This menu has three menu items, and the last menu item is a submenu with two submenu items.

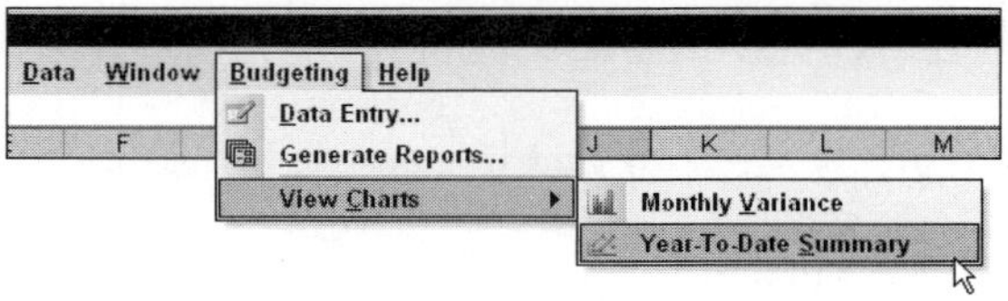

Figure 23-2: A VBA procedure created this menu and its associated menu items.

This example is available on the companion CD-ROM.

You might be wondering why the code in the preceding example deletes the menu (if it already exists) and doesn't simply exit the procedure. Rebuilding the menu ensures that the latest version is added to the menu bar. This also makes it much easier on you while you're developing the code because you don't have to delete the menu manually before testing your procedure. As you might have noticed, creating menus is very fast, so the additional time required to rebuild a menu is negligible.

When you examine the CreateMenu procedure, keep the following points in mind:

◆ The control type for the first two menu items is msoControlButton. The type of the third menu item, however, is msoControlPopup because the third menu item has submenu items. Therefore, the MenuItem variable was declared as a generic CommandBarControl.

◆ The BeginGroup property of the third menu item is True, which causes a separator bar to appear before the item. The separator bar is purely cosmetic, grouping similar menu items together.

◆ The FaceID property determines which image (if any) appears next to the menu text. The FaceID number represents a built-in image.

◆ The text for the Caption properties uses an ampersand (&) to indicate the hot key (or accelerator key) for the menu item. The hot key is the underlined letter that provides keyboard access to the menu item.

ADDING A MENU ITEM TO THE TOOLS MENU

The example in Listing 23-2 adds several menu items to a custom menu on the Worksheet Menu Bar. Often, you'll simply want to add a menu item to one of Excel's built-in menus, such as the Tools menu.

With Excel 5 and Excel 95, assigning a macro to a new menu item on the Tools menu was easy. For some reason, this feature was removed, beginning with Excel 97. This section demonstrates how to write VBA code to add a menu item to Excel's Tools menu.

Listing 23-3 adds the menu item Clear All But Formulas to the Tools menu. Clicking this menu item executes a procedure named ClearAllButFormulas.

Listing 23-3: Adding a Selection to Excel's Tools Menu

```
Sub AddMenuItem()
    Dim ToolsMenu As CommandBarPopup
    Dim NewMenuItem As CommandBarButton

'   Delete the menu if it already exists
    Call DeleteMenuItem

'   Find the Tools Menu
    Set ToolsMenu = CommandBars(1).FindControl(Id:=30007)
    If ToolsMenu Is Nothing Then
        MsgBox "Cannot add menu item."
        Exit Sub
    Else
        Set NewMenuItem = ToolsMenu.Controls.Add _
          (Type:=msoControlButton)
        With NewMenuItem
            .Caption = "&Clear All But Formulas"
            .FaceId = 348
            .OnAction = "ClearAllButFormulas"
            .BeginGroup = True
        End With
    End If
End Sub
```

Figure 23-3 shows the Tools menu with the new menu item. Note that the code does not refer to the Tools menu by its caption. Rather, it identifies the menu by using its ID property (which is 30007).

 This example is available on the companion CD-ROM.

DELETING A MENU ITEM FROM THE TOOLS MENU

To delete a menu item, use the Delete method of the Controls collection. The following example deletes the Clear All But Formulas menu item on the Tools menu. Note that it uses the FindControl method to handle the situation when the Tools menu has a different caption.

```
Sub DeleteMenuItem()
    On Error Resume Next
    CommandBars(1).FindControl(Id:=30007). _
```

```
        Controls("&Clear All But Formulas").Delete
End Sub
```

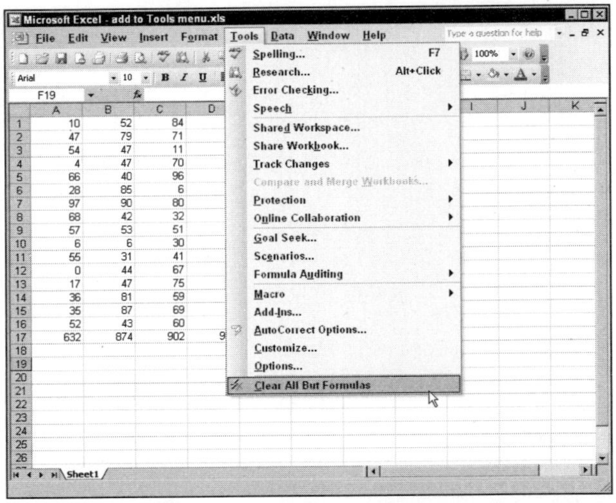

Figure 23-3: A new menu item has been added to the Tools menu.

Displaying a shortcut key with a menu item

Some of Excel's built-in menu items also display a shortcut key combination that when pressed, has the same effect as the menu command. For example, Excel's Edit menu lists several shortcut keys.

To display a shortcut key combination as part of your menu item, use the ShortcutText property. It's important to understand that setting the ShortcutText property does not actually assign the shortcut key — it simply affects the display in the menu. You must write additional code to set up the shortcut key.

Like the earlier Listing 23-3, Listing 23-4 creates a menu item Clear All But Formulas on the Tools menu. However, the following procedure sets the Shortcut Text property to the string Ctrl+Shift+C and also uses the MacroOptions method to set up the shortcut key.

Listing 23-4: Adding a Menu Selection That Features a Shortcut Key

```
Sub AddMenuItem()
    Dim ToolsMenu As CommandBarPopup
    Dim NewMenuItem As CommandBarButton

'   Delete the menu if it already exists
    Call DeleteMenuItem

'   Find the Tools Menu
```

```
Set ToolsMenu = CommandBars(1).FindControl(Id:=30007)
If ToolsMenu Is Nothing Then
    MsgBox "Cannot add a menu item - use Ctrl+Shift+C."
    Exit Sub
Else
    Set NewMenuItem = ToolsMenu.Controls.Add _
     (Type:=msoControlButton)
    With NewMenuItem
        .Caption = "&Clear All But Formulas"
        .FaceId = 348
        .ShortcutText = "Ctrl+Shift+C"
        .OnAction = "ClearAllButFormulas"
        .BeginGroup = True
    End With
End If

' Create the shortcut key
Application.MacroOptions _
  Macro:="ClearAllButFormulas", _
  HasShortcutKey:=True, _
  ShortcutKey:="C"
End Sub
```

After this procedure is executed, the menu item is displayed as shown in Figure 23-4.

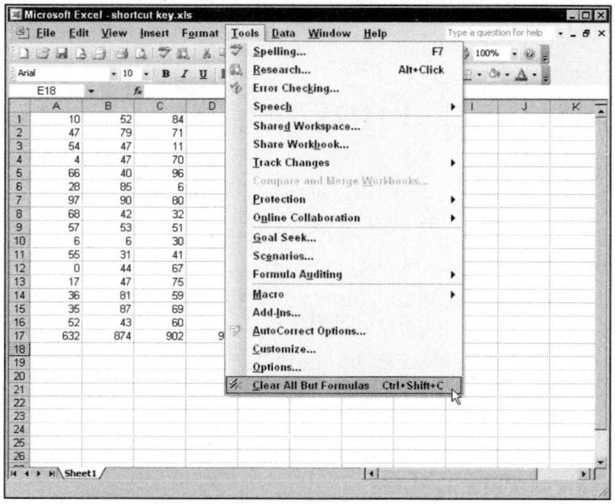

Figure 23-4: The Clear All But Formulas menu item also displays a shortcut key combination.

This example is available on the companion CD-ROM.

Fixing a menu that has been reset

Consider this scenario: You write VBA code that creates a new menu when your workbook application is opened. The user opens another workbook containing a macro that resets Excel's menu bar. Or consider this: The user plays around with the Customize dialog box, selects the Workbook Menu Bar from the list of that dialog box, and then clicks the Reset button. In both cases, your custom menu is destroyed.

Your menu-making code is probably triggered by the Workbook_Open event, so the only way that the user can get your menu back is to close and reopen the workbook. To provide another way, create a key combination that executes the procedure that builds your menu.

Apparently, applications that reset Excel's menu bar are not uncommon. Users of my Power Utility Pak add-in sometimes tell me that the PUP v5 menu has disappeared for no apparent reason. This is always caused by some other application that feels it must reset the Worksheet Menu Bar. Therefore, I added a key combination (Ctrl+Shift+U) that when pressed, rebuilds the PUP v5 menu. The following statement, when executed, associates the CreateMenu procedure with the Ctrl+Shift+U key combination.

```
Application.MacroOptions _Macro:="CreateMenu", _
    HasShortcutKey:=True, ShortcutKey:="U"
```

Menu Programming That Works with Events

Suppose that you want to create a menu when a workbook opens. You'll also want to delete the menu when the workbook closes because menu modifications remain in effect between Excel sessions. Or suppose that you want a menu to be available only when a particular workbook or worksheet is active. These sorts of things are relatively easy to program, thanks to Excel's event handlers.

The examples in this section demonstrate various menu-programming techniques used in conjunction with events.

I discuss event programming in depth in Chapter 19.

Adding and deleting menus automatically

If you need a menu to be created when a workbook is opened, use the Workbook_Open event. The following code, stored in the code module for the ThisWorkbook object, executes the CreateMenu procedure (not shown here):

```
Private Sub Workbook_Open()
    Call CreateMenu
End Sub
```

To delete the menu when the workbook is closed, use a procedure such as the following. This procedure is executed before the workbook closes, and it executes the DeleteMenu procedure (not shown here).

```
Private Sub Workbook_BeforeClose(Cancel As Boolean)
    Call DeleteMenu
End Sub
```

A problem could arise, however, if the workbook is not saved when the user closes it. Excel's Save Workbook before Closing prompt occurs *after* the Workbook_BeforeClose event handler runs. So if the user clicks Cancel, the workbook remains open, but your custom menu has already been deleted!

One solution to this problem is to bypass Excel's prompt and write your own code in the Workbook_BeforeClose procedure to ask the user to save the workbook. The following code demonstrates how:

```
Private Sub Workbook_BeforeClose(Cancel As Boolean)
    If Not Me.Saved Then
        Msg = "Do you want to save the changes you made to "
        Msg = Msg & Me.Name & "?"
        Ans = MsgBox(Msg, vbQuestion + vbYesNoCancel)
        Select Case Ans
            Case vbYes
                Me.Save
            Case vbNo
                Me.Saved = True
```

```
                    Case vbCancel
                        Cancel = True
                        Exit Sub
                End Select
            End If
            Call DeleteMenu
    End Sub
```

This procedure determines whether the workbook has been saved. If it has, no problem; the DeleteMenu procedure is executed, and the workbook is closed. But if the workbook has not been saved, the procedure displays a message box that duplicates the one Excel normally shows. If the user clicks Yes, the workbook is saved, the menu is deleted, and the workbook is closed. If the user clicks No, the code sets the Saved property of the Workbook object to True (without actually saving the file) and deletes the menu. If the user clicks Cancel, the BeforeClose event is canceled, and the procedure ends without deleting the menu.

Disabling or hiding menus

When a menu or menu item is disabled, its text appears in a faint shade of gray, and clicking it has no effect. Excel disables its menu items when they are out of context. For example, the Links menu item on the Edit menu is disabled when the active workbook does not contain any links.

You can write VBA code to enable or disable both built-in and custom menus or menu items. Similarly, you can write code to hide menus or menu items. The key, of course, is tapping into the correct event.

The following procedures are stored in the code module for the ThisWorkbook object:

```
Private Sub Workbook_Open()
    Call AddMenu
End Sub

Private Sub Workbook_BeforeClose(Cancel As Boolean)
    Call DeleteMenu
End Sub

Private Sub Workbook_Activate()
    Call UnhideMenu
End Sub

Private Sub Workbook_Deactivate()
    Call HideMenu
End Sub
```

When the workbook is opened, the AddMenu procedure is called. When the workbook is closed, the DeleteMenu workbook is called. Two additional event handler procedures are executed when the workbook is activated or deactivated. The UnhideMenu procedure is called when the workbook is activated, and the HideMenu procedure is called when the workbook is deactivated.

The HideMenu procedure sets the Visible property of the menu to False, which effectively removes it from the menu bar. The UnhideMenu procedure does just the opposite. The net effect is that the menu is visible only when the workbook is active. These procedures, which assume that the Caption for the menu is "Budgeting", are as follows:

```
Sub UnhideMenu()
    CommandBars(1).Controls("Budgeting").Visible = True
End Sub

Sub HideMenu()
    CommandBars(1).Controls("Budgeting").Visible = False
End Sub
```

To disable the menu rather than hide it, simply access the Enabled property instead of the Visible property.

 This example is available on the companion CD-ROM.

Working with checked menu items

Several of Excel's menu items appear with or without a check mark. For example, the View → Formula Bar menu item displays a check mark if the formula bar is visible and does not display a check mark if the formula bar is hidden. When you select this menu item, the formula bar's visibility is toggled, and the check mark is either displayed or not.

You can add this type of functionality to your custom menu items. Figure 23-5 shows a menu item that displays a check mark only when the active sheet is displaying grid lines. Selecting this item toggles the grid-line display and also adjusts the check mark. The check mark display is determined by the State property of the menu item control.

The trick here is keeping the check mark in sync with the active sheet. To do so, it's necessary to update the menu item whenever a new sheet, a new workbook, or a new window is activated. This is done by setting up application-level events.

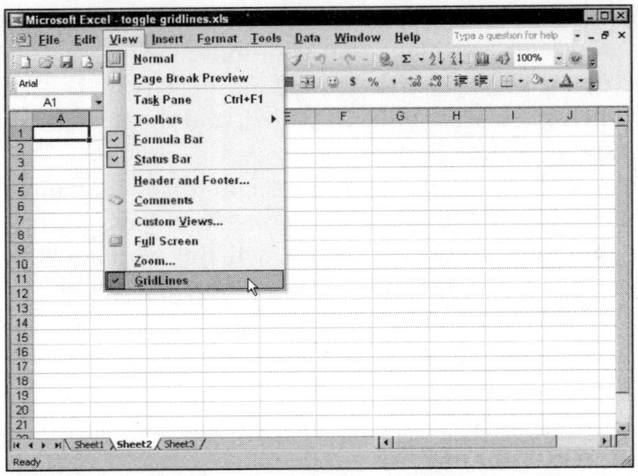

Figure 23-5: The GridLines menu item displays a check mark
if the active sheet displays grid lines.

ADDING THE MENU ITEM

The `AddMenuItem` procedure shown in Listing 23-5 is executed when the workbook
is opened. It creates a new `GridLines` menu item on the View menu.

Listing 23-5: Augmenting a Built-in Excel Menu

```
Dim AppObject As New XLHandler

Sub AddMenuItem()
    Dim ViewMenu As CommandBarPopup
    Dim NewMenuItem As CommandBarButton

'   Delete the menu if it already exists
    Call DeleteMenuItem

'   Find the View Menu
    Set ViewMenu = CommandBars(1).FindControl(ID:=30004)
    If ViewMenu Is Nothing Then
        MsgBox "Cannot add menu item."
        Exit Sub
    Else
        Set NewMenuItem = ViewMenu.Controls.Add _
          (Type:=msoControlButton)
        With NewMenuItem
            .Caption = "&GridLines"
            .OnAction = "ToggleGridlines"
        End With
    End If
```

```
'   Set up application event handler
    Set AppObject.AppEvents = Application
End Sub
```

The `AddMenuItem` procedure adds the new menu item to the Worksheet Menu Bar and not the Chart Menu Bar. Therefore, the new menu item isn't displayed when a chart sheet is active (which is just what you want).

Notice that the final statement in the `AddMenuItem` procedure sets up the application-level events that will be monitored. These event procedures, which are stored in a class module named `XLHandler`, are as follows:

```
Public WithEvents AppEvents As Excel.Application

Private Sub AppEvents_SheetActivate(ByVal Sh As Object)
    Call CheckGridlines
End Sub

Private Sub AppEvents_WorkbookActivate _
  (ByVal Wb As Excel.Workbook)
    Call CheckGridlines
End Sub

Private Sub AppEvents_WindowActivate _
  (ByVal Wb As Workbook, ByVal Wn As Window)
    Call CheckGridlines
End Sub
```

This procedure has one flaw: Changing the gridline setting from the Options dialog box is not detected.

TOGGLING THE GRIDLINE DISPLAY

The net effect is that when the user changes worksheets or workbooks, the following `CheckGridlines` procedure is executed. This procedure ensures that the check mark displayed on the GridLines menu option is in sync with the sheet.

```
Sub CheckGridlines()
    Dim TG As CommandBarButton
    On Error Resume Next
    Set TG = CommandBars(1).FindControl(Id:=30004). _
      Controls("&GridLines")
    If ActiveWindow.DisplayGridlines Then
```

```
        TG.State = msoButtonDown
    Else
        TG.State = msoButtonUp
    End If
End Sub
```

This procedure checks the active window and sets the State property of the menu item. If grid lines are displayed, it adds a check mark to the GridLines menu item. If grid lines are not displayed, it removes the check mark from the menu item.

KEEPING THE MENU IN SYNC WITH THE SHEET

When the menu item is selected, the OnAction property of that menu item triggers the ToggleGridlines procedure, as follows:

```
Sub ToggleGridlines()
    If TypeName(ActiveSheet) = "Worksheet" Then
        ActiveWindow.DisplayGridlines = _
            Not ActiveWindow.DisplayGridlines
        Call CheckGridlines
    End If
End Sub
```

This procedure simply toggles the gridline display of the active window. I use an If-Then construct to ensure that the active sheet is a worksheet

Creating Custom Menus the Easy Way

When Excel 97 was released, I was a bit frustrated with the amount of code required to create a custom menu, so I developed a technique that simplifies the process considerably. My technique uses a worksheet, shown in Figure 23-6, to store information about the new menu. A VBA procedure reads the data in the workbook and creates the menu, menu items, and submenu items.

The worksheet consists of a table with five columns:

◆ *Level:* This is the location of the particular item relative to the hierarchy of the menu system. Valid values are 1, 2, and 3. Level 1 is for a menu; 2 is for a menu item; and 3 is for a submenu item. Normally, you'll have one level 1 item, with level 2 items below it. A level 2 item might or might not have level 3 (submenu) items.

◆ *Caption:* This is the text that appears in the menu, menu item, or submenu. To underline a character, place an ampersand (&) before it.

- *Position/Macro:* For level 1 items, this should be an integer that represents the position in the menu bar. For level 2 or level 3 items, this is the macro that executes when the item is selected. If a level 2 item has one or more level 3 items, the level 2 item might not have a macro associated with it.
- *Divider:* Enter **True** if a separator bar should be placed before the menu item or submenu item.
- *FaceID:* This optional entry is a code number that represents the built-in graphic images displayed next to an item.

Figure 23-7 shows the menu that was created from the worksheet data.

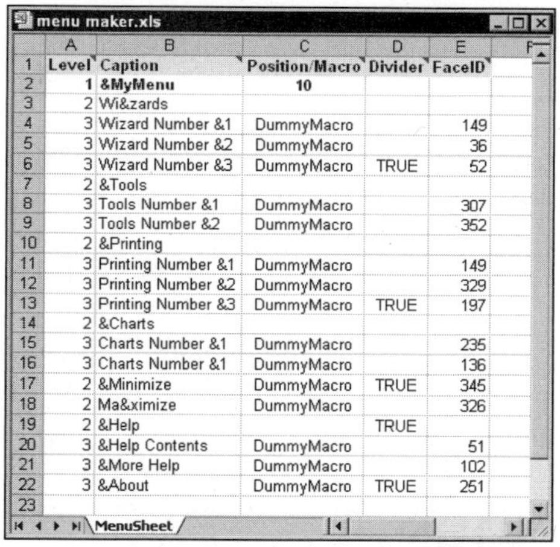

	A	B	C	D	E
1	Level	Caption	Position/Macro	Divider	FaceID
2	1	&MyMenu	10		
3	2	Wi&zards			
4	3	Wizard Number &1	DummyMacro		149
5	3	Wizard Number &2	DummyMacro		36
6	3	Wizard Number &3	DummyMacro	TRUE	52
7	2	&Tools			
8	3	Tools Number &1	DummyMacro		307
9	3	Tools Number &2	DummyMacro		352
10	2	&Printing			
11	3	Printing Number &1	DummyMacro		149
12	3	Printing Number &2	DummyMacro		329
13	3	Printing Number &3	DummyMacro	TRUE	197
14	2	&Charts			
15	3	Charts Number &1	DummyMacro		235
16	3	Charts Number &1	DummyMacro		136
17	2	&Minimize	DummyMacro	TRUE	345
18	2	Ma&ximize	DummyMacro		326
19	2	&Help		TRUE	
20	3	&Help Contents	DummyMacro		51
21	3	&More Help	DummyMacro		102
22	3	&About	DummyMacro	TRUE	251
23					

Figure 23-6: The information in this worksheet is used to create a custom menu.

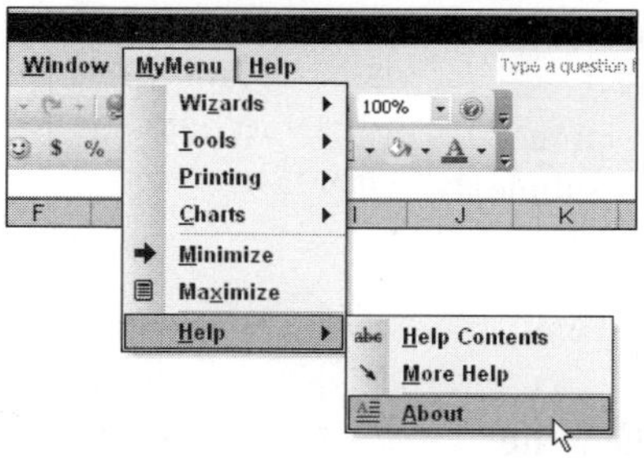

Figure 23-7: This menu was created from the data stored in a worksheet.

This workbook is available on the companion CD-ROM.

To use this technique in your workbook or add-in, follow the steps described next.

1. Open the example workbook from the CD-ROM.

2. Copy all the code in Module1 to a module in your project.

3. Add procedures such as the following to the code module for the ThisWorkbook object:

```
Private Sub Workbook_Open()
    Call CreateMenu
End Sub
Private Sub Workbook_BeforeClose(Cancel As Boolean)
    Call DeleteMenu
End Sub
```

4. Insert a new worksheet and name it MenuSheet. Better yet, copy the MenuSheet from the example file.

5. Customize the MenuSheet to correspond to your custom menu.

 There is no error handling in the example workbook, so it's up to you to make sure that the menu is created properly.

Creating a Substitute Worksheet Menu Bar

In some cases, you might want to hide Excel's standard Worksheet Menu Bar and replace it with a completely customized menu bar.

The MakeMenuBar procedure in Listing 23-6 creates a new menu bar named MyMenuBar. This menu bar consists of two menus. The first menu is the standard File menu, copied from the Worksheet Menu Bar. The second menu contains two items: Restore Normal Menu and Help.

Listing 23-6: Replacing Excel's Built-in Menu with Your Own

```
Sub MakeMenuBar()
    Dim NewMenuBar As CommandBar
    Dim NewMenu As CommandBarControl
    Dim NewItem As CommandBarControl

    '   Delete menu bar if it exists
    Call DeleteMenuBar

    '   Add a menu bar
    Set NewMenuBar = CommandBars.Add(MenuBar:=True)
    With NewMenuBar
        .Name = "MyMenuBar"
        .Visible = True
    End With

    '   Copy the File menu (ID=30002) from Worksheet Menu Bar

    CommandBars("Worksheet Menu Bar").FindControl(ID:=30002).Copy _
       Bar:=CommandBars("MyMenuBar")

    '   Add a new menu
    Set NewMenu = NewMenuBar.Controls.Add _
       (Type:=msoControlPopup)
    NewMenu.Caption = "&Commands"

    '   Add a new menu item
    Set NewItem = NewMenu.Controls.Add(Type:=msoControlButton)
    With NewItem
        .Caption = "&Restore Normal Menu"
        .OnAction = "DeleteMenuBar"
    End With

    '   Add a new menu item
    Set NewItem = NewMenu.Controls.Add(Type:=msoControlButton)
    With NewItem
        .Caption = "&Help"
        .OnAction = "ShowHelp"
    End With
End Sub
```

Figure 23-8 shows the new menu bar.

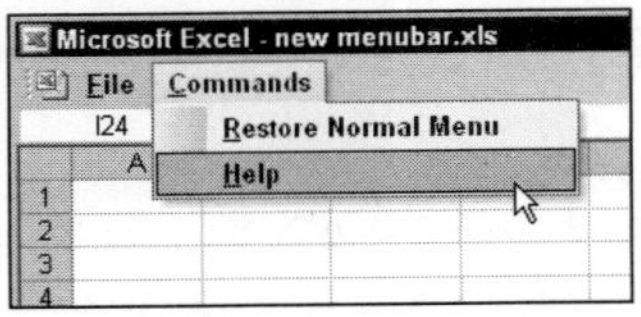

```
Microsoft Excel - new menubar.xls
File  Commands
I24        Restore Normal Menu
     A     Help
1
2
3
4
```

Figure 23-8: A custom menu bar replaces
the standard Worksheet Menu Bar.

Notice that nothing in this procedure hides the Worksheet Menu Bar. The instruction Set NewMenuBar = CommandBars.Add(MenuBar:=True) adds the new command bar. When the Visible property of this new command bar is set to True, it then takes over as the worksheet menu bar. Only one menu bar can be active at a time.

 A standard toolbar (as I discuss in Chapter 22) has a Type property of msoBarTypeNormal. A menu bar, as created in the preceding code, has a Type property of msoBarTypeMenuBar.

Deleting the custom menu bar displays the Worksheet Menu Bar and makes it the active menu bar. The following DeleteMenuBar procedure returns things to normal:

```
Sub DeleteMenuBar()
    On Error Resume Next
    CommandBars("MyMenuBar").Delete
    On Error GoTo 0
End Sub
```

The preceding code locates the File menu command bar control by using the FindControl method. This menu is then copied from the Worksheet Menu Bar to the new menu bar by using the Copy method:

```
CommandBars("Worksheet Menu Bar").FindControl(ID:=30002).Copy _
    Bar:=CommandBars("MyMenuBar")
```

When this instruction is executed, the File menu (along with all of its menu items and submenu items) appears on the new menu bar. Be aware that the menu and submenu items are not true copies of the corresponding items on the Worksheet Menu Bar. For example, change the Caption property for the New menu item on MyMenuBar (change it from *New* to *New Workbook*). That change will also be reflected in the New menu item in the Worksheet Menu Bar. So when you restore the Worksheet Menu Bar, the modified caption will be displayed.

Working with Shortcut Menus

A *shortcut menu* is a pop-up menu that appears when you right-click virtually anything in Excel. Excel 2003 has 61 shortcut menus. You can't use Excel's Customize dialog box to remove or modify shortcut menus. The only way to customize shortcut menus is through VBA.

A shortcut menu is a command bar, with a `Type` setting of `msoBarTypePopup`. To work with a shortcut menu, you need to know its `Index` or `Name` property setting. You can use the following procedure to generate a list of all shortcut menus. This list displays information about each shortcut menu in one row of a worksheet: the `Index`, `Name`, and a list of all menu items.

```
Sub ListShortCutMenus()
    Row = 1
    For Each cbar In CommandBars
        If cbar.Type = msoBarTypePopup Then
            Cells(Row, 1) = cbar.Index
            Cells(Row, 2) = cbar.Name
            For col = 1 To cbar.Controls.Count
                Cells(Row, col + 2) = _
                 cbar.Controls(col).Caption
            Next col
            Row = Row + 1
        End If
    Next cbar
End Sub
```

Figure 23-9 shows a portion of the output. This procedure will also help you identify the names of various shortcut menus. For example, who would guess that the shortcut menu that appears when you right-click a sheet tab is named *Ply*?

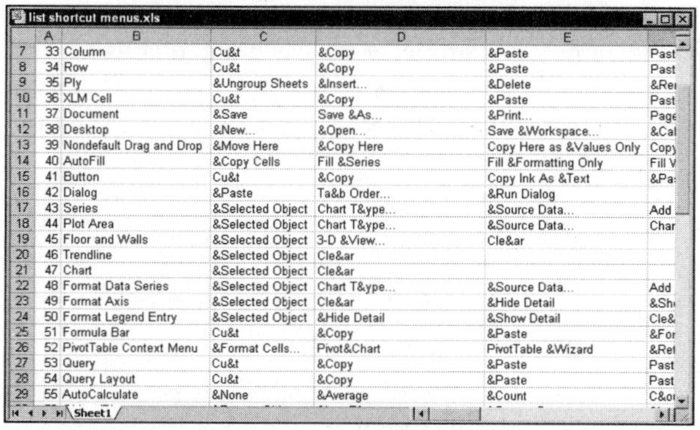

list shortcut menus.xls

	A	B	C	D	E	
7	33	Column	Cu&t	&Copy	&Paste	Past
8	34	Row	Cu&t	&Copy	&Paste	Past
9	35	Ply	&Ungroup Sheets	&Insert...	&Delete	&Re
10	36	XLM Cell	Cu&t	&Copy	&Paste	Past
11	37	Document	&Save	Save &As...	&Print...	Page
12	38	Desktop	&New...	&Open...	Save &Workspace...	&Cal
13	39	Nondefault Drag and Drop	&Move Here	&Copy Here	Copy Here as &Values Only	Copy
14	40	AutoFill	&Copy Cells	Fill &Series	Fill &Formatting Only	Fill V
15	41	Button	Cu&t	&Copy	Copy Ink As &Text	&Pa
16	42	Dialog	&Paste	Ta&b Order...	&Run Dialog	
17	43	Series	&Selected Object	Chart T&ype...	&Source Data...	Add
18	44	Plot Area	&Selected Object	Chart T&ype...	&Source Data...	Char
19	45	Floor and Walls	&Selected Object	3-D &View...	Cle&ar	
20	46	Trendline	&Selected Object	Cle&ar		
21	47	Chart	&Selected Object	Cle&ar		
22	48	Format Data Series	&Selected Object	Chart T&ype...	&Source Data...	Add
23	49	Format Axis	&Selected Object	Cle&ar	&Hide Detail	&Sh
24	50	Format Legend Entry	&Selected Object	&Hide Detail	&Show Detail	Cle&
25	51	Formula Bar	Cu&t	&Copy	&Paste	&For
26	52	PivotTable Context Menu	&Format Cells...	Pivot&Chart	PivotTable &Wizard	&Re
27	53	Query	Cu&t	&Copy	&Paste	Past
28	54	Query Layout	Cu&t	&Copy	&Paste	Past
29	55	AutoCalculate	&None	&Average	&Count	C&o

Sheet1

Figure 23-9: A listing of all shortcut menus, plus the menu items in each.

This workbook is available on the companion CD-ROM.

Although you can refer to a shortcut menu by its Index property, this is not recommended. For some reason, Index values have not remained consistent between Excel versions. Rather, you should use the Name property to refer to a shortcut menu.

Adding menu items to shortcut menus

Adding a menu item to a shortcut menu works just like adding a menu item to a regular menu. The following example demonstrates how to add a menu item to the Cell shortcut menu that appears when you right-click a cell. This menu item is added to the end of the shortcut menu, with a separator bar above it.

```
Sub AddItemToShortcut()
    Dim NewItem As CommandBarControl
    Set NewItem = CommandBars("Cell").Controls.Add
    With NewItem
        .Caption = "Toggle Word Wrap"
        .OnAction = "ToggleWordWrap"
        .BeginGroup = True
    End With
End Sub
```

Selecting the new menu item executes a procedure named ToggleWordWrap (not shown here). Figure 23-10 shows the new shortcut menu in action.

The previous example used the OnAction property to assign a macro to the shortcut menu item. The following example doesn't use OnAction. Rather, it adds a built-in command (Hide) to the shortcut menu that appears when you click the title bar of a workbook window.

```
Sub AddItemToShortcut()
    Dim NewItem As CommandBarControl
    Set NewItem = CommandBars("Document").Controls.Add(ID:=865)
    NewItem.Caption = "Hide Window"
End Sub
```

Selecting this shortcut menu item is equivalent to choosing the Window → Hide command. This command has an ID of 865, which I discovered by executing this instruction:

```
MsgBox CommandBars("Worksheet Menu Bar"). _
    Controls("Window").Controls("Hide").ID
```

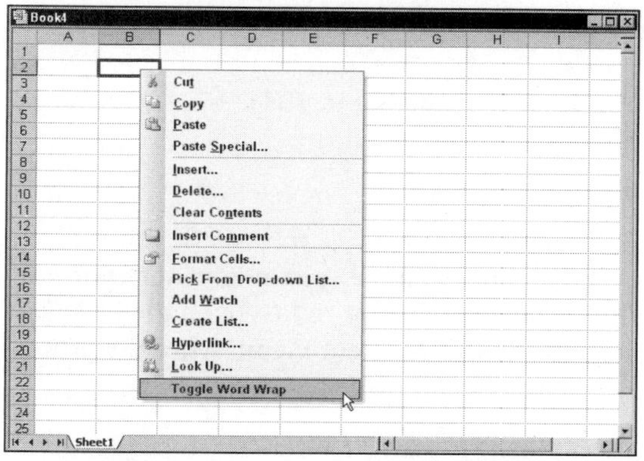

Figure 23-10: This shortcut menu has a new menu item.

Deleting menu items from shortcut menus

The following procedure uses the Delete method to remove the menu item added by the procedure in the preceding section:

```
Sub RemoveItemFromShortcut()
    On Error Resume Next
    CommandBars("Cell").Controls("Toggle Word Wrap").Delete
End Sub
```

The On Error Resume Next statement avoids the error message that appears if the menu item is not on the shortcut menu.

The following procedure removes the Hide menu item from two shortcut menus: the one that appears when you right-click a row header and the one that appears for a column header:

```
Sub RemoveHideMenuItems()
    CommandBars("Column").Controls("Hide").Delete
    CommandBars("Row").Controls("Hide").Delete
End Sub
```

Disabling shortcut menu items

As an alternative to removing menu items, you might want to disable one or more items on certain shortcut menus while your application is running. When an item is disabled, it appears in a light gray color, and clicking it has no effect. The following procedure disables the Hide menu item from the Row and Column shortcut menus:

```
Sub DisableHideMenuItems()
    CommandBars("Column").Controls("Hide").Enabled = False
    CommandBars("Row").Controls("Hide").Enabled = False
End Sub
```

Disabling shortcut menus

You can also disable entire shortcut menus. For example, you might not want the user to access the commands generally made available by right-clicking a cell. The following DisableCell procedure disables the Cell shortcut menu. After the procedure is executed, right-clicking a cell has no effect.

```
Sub DisableCell()
    CommandBars("Cell").Enabled = False
End Sub
```

If you want to disable *all* shortcut menus, use the following procedure:

```
Sub DisableAllShortcutMenus()
    Dim cb As CommandBar
    For Each cb In CommandBars
        If cb.Type = msoBarTypePopup Then _
           cb.Enabled = False
    Next cb
End Sub
```

You'll find that after running this procedure, the Toolbar List shortcut menu will still appear. (This is the shortcut menu that appears when you right-click any toolbar.) I'm not aware of any way to prevent this shortcut menu from being displayed.

Disabling the shortcut menus "sticks" between sessions. Therefore, you'll probably want to restore the shortcut menus before closing Excel. To restore the shortcut menus, modify the preceding procedure to set the Enabled property to True.

Resetting shortcut menus

The Reset method restores a shortcut menu to its original, default condition. If your application adds items to a shortcut menu, it's better to remove the items individually when your application closes. Otherwise, you might delete customizations made by other applications.

The following procedure resets the Cell shortcut menu to its normal state:

```
Sub ResetCellMenu()
    CommandBars("Cell").Reset
End Sub
```

Creating new shortcut menus

You can create an entirely new shortcut menu. Listing 23-7 creates a shortcut menu named MyShortcut and adds six menu items to it. These menu items have their OnAction property set to execute a simple procedure that displays one of the tabs in the Format Cells dialog box. For example, the ShowNumberFormat procedure is

```
Sub ShowFormatNumber()
    Application.Dialogs(xlDialogFormatNumber).Show
End Sub
```

Listing 23-7: Creating an Entirely New and Separate Shortcut Menu

```
Sub CreateShortcut()
    Set myBar = CommandBars.Add _
      (Name:="MyShortcut", Position:=msoBarPopup, _
       Temporary:=True)

'   Add a menu item
    Set myItem = myBar.Controls.Add(Type:=msoControlButton)
    With myItem
        .Caption = "&Number Format..."
        .OnAction = "ShowFormatNumber"
        .FaceId = 1554
    End With

'   Add a menu item
    Set myItem = myBar.Controls.Add(Type:=msoControlButton)
    With myItem
        .Caption = "&Alignment..."
        .OnAction = "ShowFormatAlignment"
```

Continued

Listing 23-7 *(Continued)*

```
            .FaceId = 217
        End With

    '   Add a menu item
        Set myItem = myBar.Controls.Add(Type:=msoControlButton)
        With myItem
            .Caption = "&Font..."
            .OnAction = "ShowFormatFont"
            .FaceId = 291
        End With

    '   Add a menu item
        Set myItem = myBar.Controls.Add(Type:=msoControlButton)
        With myItem
            .Caption = "&Borders..."
            .OnAction = "ShowFormatBorder"
            .FaceId = 149
            .BeginGroup = True
        End With

    '   Add a menu item
        Set myItem = myBar.Controls.Add(Type:=msoControlButton)
        With myItem
            .Caption = "&Patterns..."
            .OnAction = "ShowFormatPatterns"
            .FaceId = 1550
        End With

    '   Add a menu item
        Set myItem = myBar.Controls.Add(Type:=msoControlButton)
        With myItem
            .Caption = "Pr&otection..."
            .OnAction = "ShowFormatProtection"
            .FaceId = 2654
        End With
End Sub
```

Figure 23-11 shows how this new shortcut menu looks.

After the shortcut menu is created, you can display it by using the ShowPopup method. The following procedure, located in the code module for a Worksheet object, is executed when the user right-clicks a cell:

```
Private Sub Worksheet_BeforeRightClick _
  (ByVal Target As Excel.Range, Cancel As Boolean)
    If Union(Target.Range("A1"), Range("data")).Address = _
      Range("data").Address Then
        CommandBars("MyShortcut").ShowPopup
        Cancel = True
    End If
End Sub
```

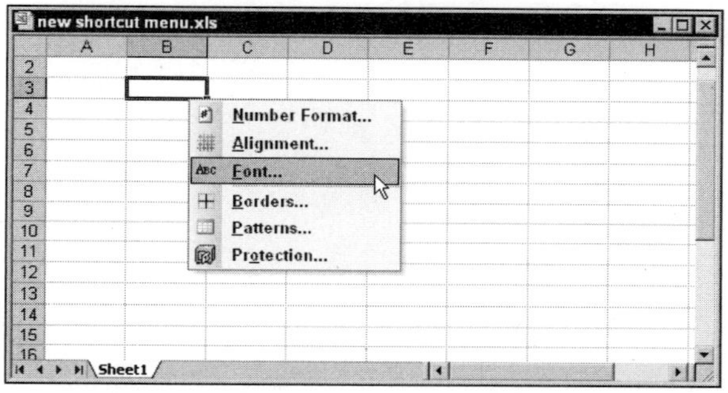

Figure 23-11: This new shortcut menu was created with VBA.

If the cell the user right-clicks is within a range named data, the MyShortcut menu appears. Setting the Cancel argument to True ensures that the normal shortcut menu is not displayed.

ON THE CD   The companion CD-ROM contains an example that creates a new shortcut menu and displays it in place of the normal Cell shortcut menu.

Chapter 24

Providing Help for Your Applications

COMPUTER USERS HAVE BECOME RATHER SPOILED over the years. In the early days of personal computers, software companies rarely provided onscreen help. And the "help" provided often proved less than helpful. Now, just about all commercial software provides help; and more often than not, the help serves as the primary documentation. Thick software manuals are an endangered species (good riddance!).

Help for Your Excel Applications

If you develop a nontrivial application in Excel, you might want to consider building in some sort of help for end users. Doing so makes the users feel more comfortable with the application and could eliminate many of those time-wasting phone calls from users with basic questions. Another advantage is that help is always available: That is, the instructions can't be misplaced or buried under a pile of books.

You can add user help to your applications in a number of ways, ranging from simple to complex. The method that you choose depends on your application's scope and complexity and how much effort you're willing to put into this phase of development. Some applications might require only a brief set of instructions on how to start them. Others could benefit from a full-blown, searchable Help system. Most often, applications need something in between.

Online Help?

In the past, I've always referred to Excel's onscreen assistance as *online help.* In fact, that's the common name for this type of assistance. But in recent years, the term *online* has come to refer to information available via the Internet. Some people were confused by the expression *online help* because the help information is actually stored on their local drive.

Therefore, I now use the expression *Help system* to refer to assistance provided by an application. But, with Excel 2003, things have come full circle. For the first time, you can access help information that truly is online. Excel 2003's Help system enables you to view locally stored help information or (with an Internet connection) search for more up-to-date information at the Microsoft Web site.

This chapter classifies user help into two categories:

◆ *Unofficial Help system:* This method of displaying help uses standard Excel components (such as a UserForm).

◆ *Official Help system:* This Help system uses a compiled CHM file produced by Microsoft's HyperText Markup Language (HTML) Help System.

Creating a compiled help file is not a trivial task, but it is worth the effort if your application is complex or if it will be used by a large number of people.

All the examples in this chapter are available on the companion CD-ROM.

About the Examples in This Chapter

Many of the examples in this chapter use a simple workbook application to demonstrate various ways of providing help. The application uses data stored in a worksheet to generate and print form letters.

As you can see in the following figure, cells display the total number of records in the database (C2, calculated by a formula), the current record number (C3), the first record to print (C4), and the last record to print (C5). To display a particular record, the user enters a value into cell C3. To print a series of form letters, the user specifies the first and last record numbers in cells C4 and C5.

The application is simple, but it does consist of several discrete components that demonstrate various ways of displaying context-sensitive help.

The form letter workbook consists of the following components:

Form	A worksheet that contains the text of the form letter.
Data	A worksheet that contains a seven-field database.
HelpSheet	A worksheet present only in the examples that store help text on a worksheet.
PrintMod	A Visual Basic for Applications (VBA) module that contains macros to print the form letters.
HelpMod	A VBA module that contains macros that control the help display. The content of this module varies, depending on the type of help being demonstrated.
UserForm1	A UserForm present only if the help technique involves a UserForm.

Help Systems That Use Excel Components

Perhaps the most straightforward method of providing help to your users is to use the features contained in Excel itself. The primary advantage of this method is that you don't need to learn how to create HTML Help files – which can be a major undertaking and might take longer to develop than your application.

In this section, I provide an overview of some help techniques that use the following built-in Excel components:

◆ *Cell comments:* This is about as simple as it gets.

◆ *A text box control:* A simple macro is all it takes to toggle the display of a text box that shows help information.

◆ *A worksheet:* A simple way to add help is to insert a worksheet, enter your help information, and name its tab *Help*. When the user clicks the tab, the worksheet is activated.

◆ *A custom UserForm:* A number of techniques involve displaying help text in a UserForm.

Using cell comments for help

Perhaps the simplest way to provide user help is to use cell comments. This technique is most appropriate for describing the type of input that's expected in a cell. When the user moves the mouse pointer over a cell that contains a comment, that comment appears in a small window, like a ToolTip. Another advantage is that this technique does not require any macros.

Automatic display of cell comments is an option. The following VBA instruction ensures that cell comment indicators are displayed for cells that contain comments:

```
Application.DisplayCommentIndicator = xlCommentIndicatorOnly
```

 Another option is to use Excel's Data → Validation command, which displays a dialog box that lets you specify valid validation criteria for a cell or range. The Input Message tab of the Data Validation dialog box lets you specify a message that is displayed when the cell is activated. This text is limited to approximately 250 characters.

Using a text box for help

Using a text box to display help information is also easy to implement. Simply create a text box by using the Text Box button on the Drawing toolbar, enter the help text, and format it to your liking. Figure 24-1 shows an example of a text box set up to display help information.

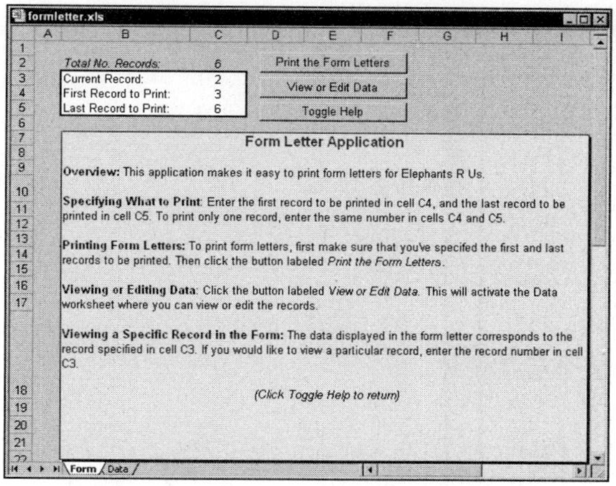

Figure 24-1: Use a text box to display help for the user.

Using the Text Box button from the Drawing toolbar is preferable to using an ActiveX `TextBox` control from the Control Toolbox toolbar because it allows *rich text formatting*. In other words, creating a text box from the Drawing toolbar enables you to apply formatting to individual characters within the text box.

Most of the time, you won't want the text box to be visible. Therefore, you can add a button to your application to execute a macro that toggles the `Visible` property of the text box. An example of such a macro follows. In this case, the TextBox is named `HelpText`.

```
Sub ToggleHelp()
    ActiveSheet.TextBoxes("HelpText").Visible = _
      Not ActiveSheet.TextBoxes("HelpText").Visible
End Sub
```

Using a worksheet to display help text

Another easy way to add help to your application is to create a macro that activates a separate worksheet that holds the help information. Just attach the macro to a button control, toolbar button, or menu item, and voilà! . . . quick-and-dirty help.

Figure 24-2 shows a sample help worksheet. I designed the range that contains the help text to simulate a page from a yellow notebook pad — a fancy touch that you might or might not like.

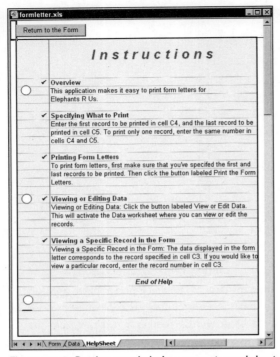

Figure 24-2: Putting user help in a separate worksheet is an easy way to go.

To keep the user from scrolling around the HelpSheet worksheet, the macro sets the ScrollArea property of the worksheet. Because this property is not stored with the workbook, it's necessary to set it when the worksheet is activated. I also protected the worksheet to prevent the user from changing the text, and I "froze" the first row so that the Return button is always visible, regardless of how far down the sheet the user scrolls.

The main disadvantage of using this technique is that the help text isn't visible along with the main work area. One possible solution is to write a macro that opens a new window to display the sheet.

Displaying help in a UserForm

Another way to provide help to the user is to display the text in a UserForm. In this section, I describe several techniques that involve UserForms.

USING LABEL CONTROLS TO DISPLAY HELP TEXT

Figure 24-3 shows a UserForm that contains two Label controls: one for the title, and one for the actual text. A SpinButton control enables the user to navigate among the topics. The text itself is stored in a worksheet, with topics in column A and text in column B.

Figure 24-3: Clicking the SpinButton determines
the text displayed in the Labels.

Clicking the SpinButton executes the following procedure. This procedure simply
sets the Caption property of the two Label controls to the text in the appropriate
row of the worksheet (named HelpSheet).

```
Private Sub SpinButton1_Change()
    HelpTopic = SpinButton1.Value
    LabelTopic.Caption = Sheets("HelpSheet"). _
      Cells(HelpTopic, 1)
    LabelText.Caption = Sheets("HelpSheet").Cells(HelpTopic, 2)

    Me.Caption = APPNAME & " (Help Topic " & HelpTopic & " of " _
      & SpinButton1.Max & ")"
End Sub
```

Here, APPNAME is a global constant that contains the application's name.

USING A SCROLLING LABEL TO DISPLAY HELP TEXT

This technique displays help text in a single Label control. Because a Label control cannot contain a vertical scrollbar, the Label is placed inside a Frame control, which *can* contain a scrollbar. Figure 24-4 shows an example of a UserForm set up in this manner. The user can scroll through the text by using the Frame's scrollbar.

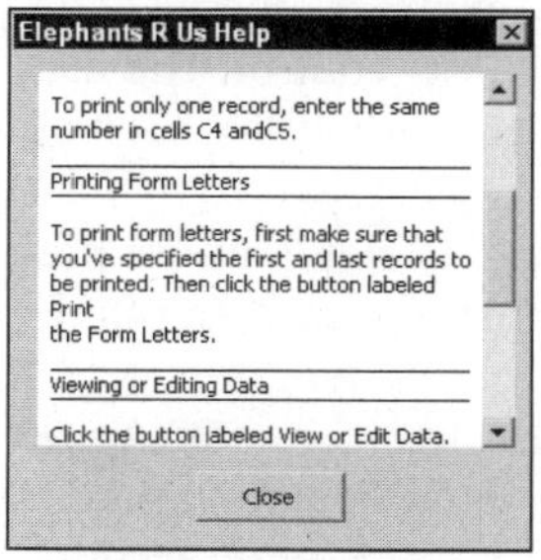

Figure 24-4: Inserting a Label control inside
a Frame control adds scrolling to the Label.

The text displayed in the Label is read from a worksheet named HelpSheet when the UserForm is initialized. Listing 24-1 presents the UserForm_Initialize procedure for this worksheet. Notice that the code adjusts the Frame's ScrollHeight property to ensure that the scrolling covers the complete height of the Label. Again, APPNAME is a global constant that contains the application's name.

Listing 24-1: Making the Label Control Display Scrollable Text from the Worksheet

```
Private Sub UserForm_Initialize()
    Me.Caption = APPNAME & " Help"
    LastRow = Sheets("HelpSheet").Range("A65536") _
     .End(xlUp).Row
    txt = ""
    For r = 1 To LastRow
      txt = txt & Sheets("HelpSheet").Cells(r, 1) _
        .Text & vbCrLf
    Next r
    With Label1
        .Top = 0
        .Caption = txt
        .Width = 160
        .AutoSize = True
    End With
    With Frame1
        .ScrollHeight = Label1.Height
        .ScrollTop = 0
    End With
End Sub
```

Because a Label cannot display formatted text, I used underscore characters in the HelpSheet worksheet to delineate the Help topic titles.

USING A DROPDOWN CONTROL TO SELECT A HELP TOPIC

The example in this section improves upon the previous example. Figure 24-5 shows a UserForm that contains a DropDown control and a Label control. The user can select a topic from the DropDown or view the topics sequentially by clicking the Previous or Next button.

This example (Listing 24-2) is a bit more complex than the example in the previous section, but it's also a lot more flexible. It uses the Label-within-a-scrolling-Frame technique (described previously) to support help text of any length.

The help text is stored in a worksheet named HelpSheet in two columns (A and B). The first column contains the topic headings, and the second column contains the text. The ComboBox items are added in the UserForm_Initialize procedure. The CurrentTopic variable is a module-level variable that stores an integer that represents the Help topic.

Figure 24-5: Designate the topic of the Label
text with a drop-down list control.

Listing 24-2: Label-within-a-Scrolling-Frame Technique

```
Private Sub UpdateForm()
    ComboBoxTopics.ListIndex = CurrentTopic - 1
    Me.Caption = HelpFormCaption & _
      " (" & CurrentTopic & " of " & TopicCount & ")"

    With LabelText
        .Caption = HelpSheet.Cells(CurrentTopic, 2)
        .AutoSize = False
        .Width = 212
        .AutoSize = True
    End With
    With Frame1
        .ScrollHeight = LabelText.Height + 5
        .ScrollTop = 1
    End With

    If CurrentTopic = 1 Then
        NextButton.SetFocus
    ElseIf CurrentTopic = TopicCount Then
        PreviousButton.SetFocus
    End If
    PreviousButton.Enabled = CurrentTopic <> 1
    NextButton.Enabled = CurrentTopic <> TopicCount
End Sub
```

Using the Office Assistant to display help

You're probably familiar with the *Office Assistant* — the cutesy screen character
that's always ready to help out. In my experience, most people hate this feature.

In Office 2003, the Office Assistant is not installed by default. Therefore, this method of providing help is probably not your best choice.

The Office Assistant is quite programmable, and (if you're so inclined) you can even use it to display help for the user. Figure 24-6 shows the Office Assistant displaying some help text.

Figure 24-6: Use the Office Assistant to deliver custom help.

The main procedure for using the Office Assistant to display help is shown in Listing 24-3. The help text is stored in two columns on a worksheet named HelpSheet. Column A contains the topics, and column B contains the help text.

Listing 24-3: Calling Up the Office Assistant to Display Custom Help

```
Public Const APPNAME As String = "Elephants R Us"
Dim Topic As Integer
Dim HelpSheet As Worksheet

Sub ShowHelp()
    Set HelpSheet = ThisWorkbook.Worksheets("HelpSheet")
    On Error Resume Next
    Application.Assistant.On = True
    If Err.Number <> 0 Then
        MsgBox "The Office Assistant is not installed.", vbCritical
        Exit Sub
    End If
    On Error GoTo 0
    Topic = 1
    With Assistant.NewBalloon
        .Heading = "Help Topic " & Topic & ": " & _
```

```
            vbCrLf & HelpSheet.Cells(Topic, 1)
        .Text = HelpSheet.Cells(Topic, 2)
        .Button = msoButtonSetNextClose
        .BalloonType = msoBalloonTypeButtons
        .Mode = msoModeModeless
        .Callback = "ProcessRequest"
        .Show
    End With
End Sub
```

The procedure begins by making sure that the Office Assistant is turned on. If setting the On property generates an error, the Office Assistant is not installed. The user sees a message, and the procedure ends.

If the Office Assistant is installed, the procedure creates a new Balloon object (you'll recall that the Office Assistant's help text is displayed in a balloon) and uses the first help topic in the HelpSheet worksheet to set the Heading and Text properties. It sets the Button property, so it displays Next and Close buttons like a wizard. The procedure then sets the Mode property to msoModeModeless so that the user can continue working while the help is displayed. The Callback property contains the procedure name that's executed when a button is clicked. Finally, the Assistant balloon is displayed by using the Show method.

The ProcessRequest procedure, shown in Listing 24-4, is called when any of the buttons are clicked.

Listing 24-4: Engaging the Customized Help through the Office Assistant

```
Sub ProcessRequest(bln As Balloon, lbtn As Long, lPriv _
  As Long)
    NumTopics = _
        WorksheetFunction.CountA(HelpSheet.Range("A:A"))
    Assistant.Animation = msoAnimationCharacterSuccessMajor
    Select Case lbtn
        Case msoBalloonButtonBack
            If Topic <> 1 Then Topic = Topic - 1
        Case msoBalloonButtonNext
            If Topic <> NumTopics Then Topic = Topic + 1
        Case msoBalloonButtonClose
            bln.Close
            Exit Sub
    End Select
    With bln
        .Close
        Select Case Topic
            Case 1
```

Continued

Listing 24-4 *(Continued)*

```
                .Button = msoButtonSetNextClose
            Case NumTopics
                .Button = msoButtonSetBackClose
            Case Else
                .Button = msoButtonSetBackNextClose
        End Select
        .Heading = "Help Topic " & Topic & ": " & _
            vbCrLf & HelpSheet.Cells(Topic, 1)
        .Text = HelpSheet.Cells(Topic, 2)
        .Show
    End With
End Sub
```

The `ProcessRequest` procedure displays one of several animations and then uses a `Select Case` construct to take action depending on which button was clicked. The button clicked is passed to this procedure through the `lbtn` variable. The procedure also specifies which buttons to display based on the current topic.

If you have an interest in programming the Office Assistant, I refer you to the Help system for the details.

Simulating What's This? Help in a UserForm

Some of Excel's dialog boxes display a small question mark button in the title bar, next to the Close button. In Excel 2003, clicking this question mark displays help for the dialog box. In previous versions of Excel, clicking the question mark displayed What's This? help. The user could click on a dialog box control and see a small pop-up explanation of that control. I don't know why What's This? help was removed from Excel 2003.

Custom UserForms have all the infrastructure to provide What's This? help, but there's one problem: It simply doesn't work. For example, a UserForm has a `WhatsThisButton` property and a `WhatsThisHelp` property. However, this technique does not display the pop-up help text in an HTML Help file. See the next section for more information about HTML Help files.

Each `UserForm` control has a `ControlTipText` property. If you specify text for this property, that text will display in a pop-up window when the user moves the mouse over the control.

Another way to display help for a UserForm is to use a control, taking advantage of the `MouseMove` property to display the text based on the position of the mouse pointer. Figure 24-7 shows a UserForm that uses a `Label` control to display help text for each control. In addition, it uses a ToggleButton to allow the user to turn this help mode on and off. When help mode is turned off, the UserForm is made smaller to hide the Label.

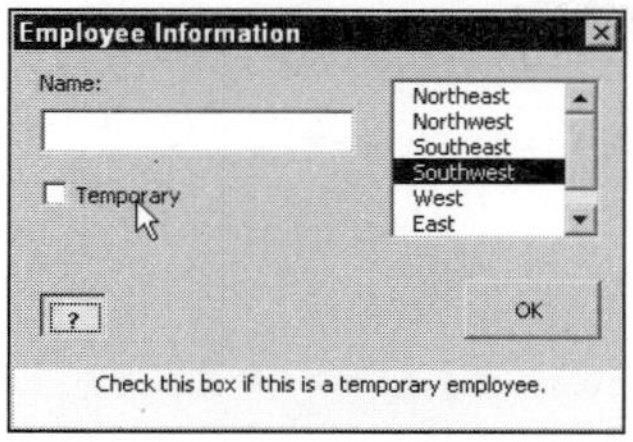

Employee Information

Name:

☐ Temporary

Northeast
Northwest
Southeast
Southwest
West
East

? OK

Check this box if this is a temporary employee.

Figure 24–7: Displaying help in a `Label` control.

Using the HTML Help System

Currently, the most common Help system used in Windows applications is HTML Help, which uses CHM files. This system has pretty much replaced the old Windows Help System (WinHelp), which used HLP files. Both of these Help systems enable the developer to associate a context ID with a particular help topic. This makes it possible to display a particular help topic in a context-sensitive manner.

In this section, I briefly describe the HTML help-authoring systems. Details on creating such Help systems are well beyond the scope of this book. However, you'll find lots of information and examples online.

 If you plan to develop a large-scale Help system, I strongly recommend that you purchase a help-authoring software product to make your job easier. Help-authoring software makes it much easier to develop Help files because the software takes care of lots of the tedious details for you. Many products are available, including freeware, shareware, and commercial offerings. Perhaps the most popular help-authoring product is RoboHelp, from eHelp Corporation. RoboHelp creates both WinHelp and HTML Help Systems. For more information, visit the company's Web site at this address: `www. ehelp.com`.

Microsoft has designated HTML Help as the Windows standard for providing user help. This system essentially compiles a series of HTML files into a compact Help system. Additionally, you can create a combined table of contents and index as well as use keywords for advanced hyperlinking capability. HTML Help can also make use of additional tools such as graphics files, ActiveX controls, scripting, and DHTML (Dynamic HTML). Figure 24-8 shows an example of an HTML Help System.

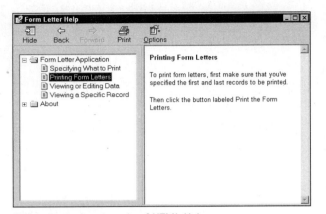

Figure 24–8: An example of HTML Help.

HTML Help is displayed by the HTML Help Viewer, which uses the layout engine of Internet Explorer. The information is displayed in a window, and the table of contents, index, and search tools are displayed in a separate pane. In addition, the help text can contain standard hyperlinks that display another topic or even a document on the Internet. Importantly, HTML Help can also access files stored on a Web site. This is ideal for directing users to a source of up-to-date information that might not have been available when the Help system was created.

You might have noticed that Office 2003 implements help differently than in previous versions. For some reason, the designers chose to use the task bar to display help topics, and the help is displayed in a separate window. So, accessing help in Office 2003 essentially requires two windows. To me, this is a giant step backward in terms of usability. Sometimes, Microsoft's decisions simply defy logic and common sense.

Like WinHelp, you need a special compiler to create an HTML Help System. The HTML Help Workshop, along with lots of additional information, is available free from from the Microsoft Web site at this address:

http://msdn.microsoft.com/library/tools/htmlhelp/chm/HH1Start.htm

To get a feel for how HTML files are created, display any topic in Excel's Help system. Then right-click the document and choose View Source. You'll be able to view the original HTML source document.

Associating a Help File with Your Application

You can associate a particular HTML Help file with your Excel application in one of two ways: by using the Project Properties dialog box or by writing VBA code.

In the Visual Basic Editor (VBE), choose Tools → *xxx* Properties (where *xxx* corresponds to your project's name). In the Project Properties dialog box, click the General tab and specify a compiled HTML Help file for the project. This file should have a CHM extension.

It's a good practice to keep your application's Help file in the same directory as the application. The following instruction sets up an association to `Myfuncs.chm`, which is assumed to be in the same directory as the workbook:

```
ThisWorkbook.VBProject.HelpFile = ThisWorkbook.Path & "\Myfuncs.chm"
```

After a Help file is associated with your application, you can call up a particular Help topic in the following situations:

◆ When the user presses F1 while a custom worksheet function is selected in the Insert Function dialog box.

◆ When the user presses F1 while a UserForm is displayed. The Help topic associated with the control that has the focus is displayed.

Associating a Help Topic with a VBA Function

If you create custom worksheet functions with VBA, you might want to associate a Help file and context ID with each function. After these items are assigned to a function, the Help topic can be displayed from the Insert Function dialog box by pressing F1.

To specify a context ID for a custom worksheet function, follow these steps:

1. Create the function as usual.

2. Make sure that your project has an associated Help file (refer to the preceding section).

3. In the VBE, press F2 to activate the Object Browser.

4. Select your project from the Project/Library drop-down list.

5. In the Classes window, select the module that contains your function.

6. In the Members Of window, select the function.

7. Right-click the function and then select Properties from the shortcut menu. This displays the Member Options dialog box, as shown in Figure 24-9.

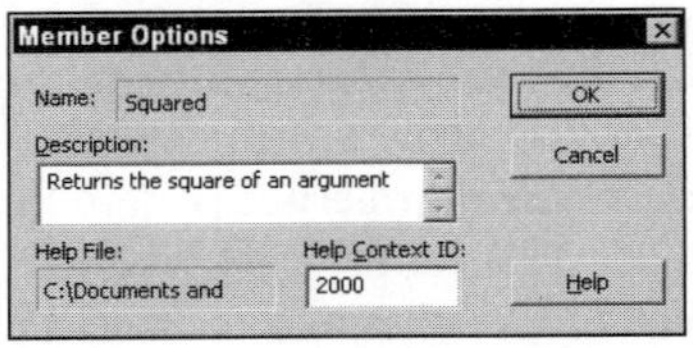

Figure 24-9: Specify a context ID for a custom function in the Member Options dialog box.

8. Enter the context ID of the Help topic for the function. You can also enter a description of the function.

> The Member Options dialog box does not let you specify the Help file. It always uses the Help file associated with the project.

You might prefer to write VBA code that sets up the context ID and Help file for your custom functions. You can do this by using the MacroOptions method. The following procedure uses the MacroOptions method to specify a description, Help file, and context ID for two custom functions (AddTwo and Squared):

```
Sub SetOptions()
'    Set options for the AddTwo function
    Application.MacroOptions Macro:="AddTwo", _
        Description:="Returns the sum of two numbers", _
        HelpFile:=ThisWorkbook.Path & "\myfuncs.chm", _
        HelpContextID:=1000

'    Set options for the Squared function
    Application.MacroOptions Macro:="Squared", _
        Description:="Returns the square of an argument", _
        HelpFile:=ThisWorkbook.Path & "\myfuncs.chm", _
        HelpContextID:=2000
End Sub
```

Other Ways to Display HTML Help

VBA provides several different ways to display specific Help topics. I describe these in the following sections.

Using the Help method

Use the `Help` method of the `Application` object to display a Help file — either a WinHelp HLP file or an HTML Help CHM file. This method works even if the Help file doesn't have any context IDs defined.

The syntax for the `Help` method is as follows:

```
Application.Help(helpFile, helpContextID)
```

Both arguments are optional. If the name of the Help file is omitted, Excel's Help file is displayed. If the context ID argument is omitted, the specified Help file is displayed with the default topic.

The following example displays the default topic of `Myapp.chm`, which is assumed to be in the same directory as the workbook that it's called from. Note that the second argument is omitted.

```
Sub ShowHelpContents()
    Application.Help ThisWorkbook.Path & "\Myapp.chm"
End Sub
```

The following instruction displays the Help topic with a context ID of `1002` from an HTML Help file named `Myapp.chm`:

```
Application.Help ThisWorkbook.Path & "\Myapp.chm", 1002
```

Displaying Help from a message box

When you use VBA's `MsgBox` function to display a message box, you include a Help button by adding the `vbMsgBoxHelpButton` constant to the function's second argument. You'll also need to include the Help filename as its fourth argument. The context ID (optional) is its fifth argument. The following code, for example, generates the message box shown in Figure 24-10:

```
Sub MsgBoxHelp()
    Msg = "Do you like using Excel?"
    Buttons = vbQuestion + vbYesNo + vbMsgBoxHelpButton
    HelpFile = ThisWorkbook.Path & "\AppHelp.chm"
```

```
        ContextID = 1002
        Ans = MsgBox(Msg, Buttons, , HelpFile, ContextID)
        If Ans = vbYes Then Call CloseDown
End Sub
```

Figure 24-10: A message box with a Help button.

Displaying Help from an input box

VBA's InputBox function can also display a Help button if its sixth argument contains the Help filename. The following example produces the InputBox shown in Figure 24-11:

```
Sub ShowInputBox()
    Msg = "Enter a value"
    DefaultVal = 0
    HFile = ThisWorkbook.Path & "\AppHelp.chm"
    ContextID = 1002
    x = InputBox( _
        Prompt:=Msg, _
        Default:=DefaultVal, _
        HelpFile:=HFile, _
        Context:=ContextID)
End Sub
```

Figure 24-11: An InputBox with a Help button.

Chapter 25

Developing User-Oriented Applications

IN THIS CHAPTER

In this chapter, I attempt to pull together some of the information presented in the previous chapters.

◆ A description of a user-oriented application

◆ A close look at the Loan Amortization Wizard, which generates a worksheet with an amortization schedule for a fixed-rate loan

◆ A demonstration of application development concepts and techniques by the Loan Amortization Wizard

◆ An application development checklist

THIS DISCUSSION CENTERS ON A USER-ORIENTED APPLICATION called the Loan Amortization Wizard. Useful in its own right, this workbook demonstrates quite a few important application development techniques.

What Is a User-Oriented Application?

I reserve the term *user-oriented application* for an Excel application that can be used by someone with minimal training. These applications produce useful results even for users who know virtually nothing about Excel.

The Loan Amortization Wizard discussed in this chapter qualifies as a user-oriented application because it's designed in such a way that the end user doesn't need to know the intimate details of Excel to use it. Replying to a few simple prompts produces a useful and flexible worksheet complete with formulas.

The Loan Amortization Wizard

The Loan Amortization Wizard generates a worksheet that contains an amortization schedule for a fixed-rate loan. An amortization schedule projects month-by-month details for a loan. The details include the monthly payment amount, the amount of the payment that goes toward interest, the amount that goes toward reducing the principal, and the new loan balance.

An alternative, of course, is to create a template file (*.XLT). As you'll see, this wizard approach offers several advantages.

Figure 25-1 shows an amortization schedule generated by the Loan Amortization Wizard.

Book1								
	A	B	C	D	E	F	G	H
1	**Amortization Schedule**							
2	**Prepared by Tina Blackwell**							
3	*Generated Tuesday, September 02, 2003*							
4								
5	Purchase Price:		$425,000.00					
6	Down Pmt Pct:		20.00%					
7	Down Pmt:		$85,000.00					
8	Loan Amount:		$340,000.00					
9	Term (Months):		360					
10	Interest Rate:		7.10%					
11	First Payment:		1/1/2004					
12								
13	Pmt No.	Year	Month	Payment	Interest	Principal	Balance	
14	1	2004	1	$2,284.91	$2,011.67	$273.24	$339,726.76	
15	2	2004	2	$2,284.91	$2,010.05	$274.86	$339,451.90	
16	3	2004	3	$2,284.91	$2,008.42	$276.48	$339,175.41	
17	4	2004	4	$2,284.91	$2,006.79	$278.12	$338,897.29	
18	5	2004	5	$2,284.91	$2,005.14	$279.77	$338,617.53	
19	6	2004	6	$2,284.91	$2,003.49	$281.42	$338,336.11	
20	7	2004	7	$2,284.91	$2,001.82	$283.09	$338,053.02	
21	8	2004	8	$2,284.91	$2,000.15	$284.76	$337,768.26	
22	9	2004	9	$2,284.91	$1,998.46	$286.45	$337,481.81	
23	10	2004	10	$2,284.91	$1,996.77	$288.14	$337,193.67	
24	11	2004	11	$2,284.91	$1,995.06	$289.85	$336,903.82	
25	12	2004	12	$2,284.91	$1,993.35	$291.56	$336,612.26	
26	*2004 Total*			*$27,418.90*	*$24,031.17*	*$3,387.74*	*$336,612.26*	
27	13	2005	1	$2,284.91	$1,991.62	$293.29	$336,318.98	
28	14	2005	2	$2,284.91	$1,989.89	$295.02	$336,023.95	

Sheet2 / Sheet1

Figure 25–1: This amortization schedule shows details for a 30–year mortgage loan.

ON THE CD

The Loan Amortization Wizard is available on the CD-ROM that accompanies this book. It's an unprotected add-in.

Using the Loan Amortization Wizard application

The Loan Amortization Wizard consists of a five-step dialog box sequence that collects information from the user. Typical of a wizard, this enables the user to go forward and backward through the steps. Clicking the Finish button creates the new worksheet. If all the steps haven't been completed when the user clicks Finish, default values are used. Clicking the Cancel button closes the UserForm, and no action is taken.

This application uses a single UserForm with a `MultiPage` control to display the five steps, shown in Figures 25-2 through 25-6.

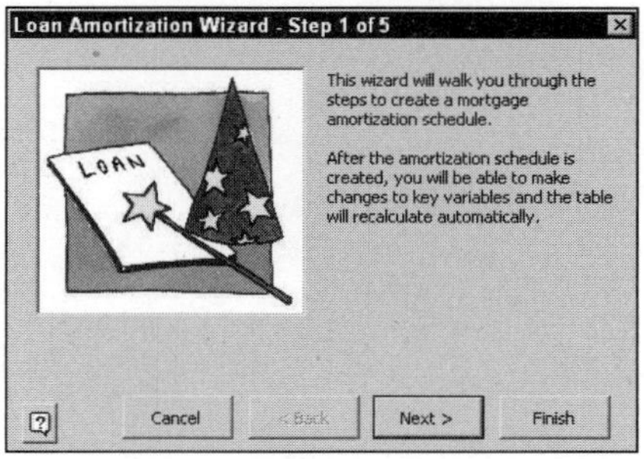

Figure 25-2: Step 1 of the Loan Amortization Wizard.

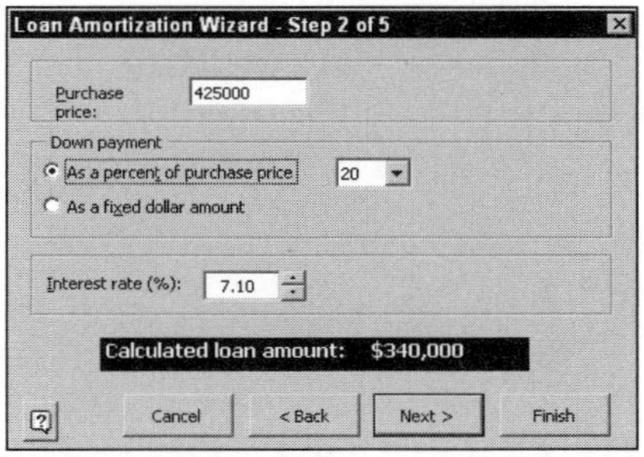

Figure 25-3: Step 2 of the Loan Amortization Wizard.

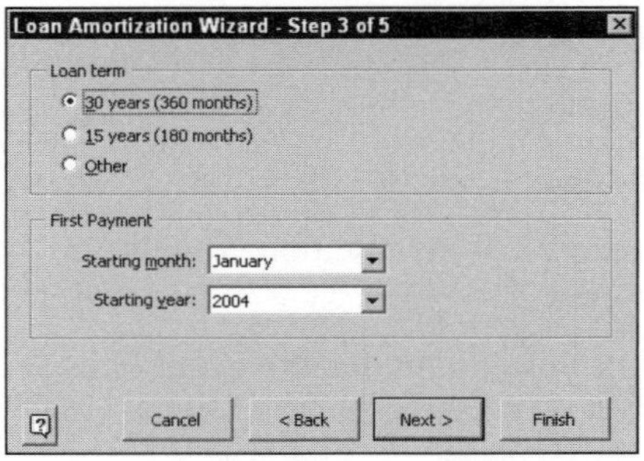

Figure 25-4: Step 3 of the Loan Amortization Wizard.

Figure 25-5: Step 4 of the Loan Amortization Wizard.

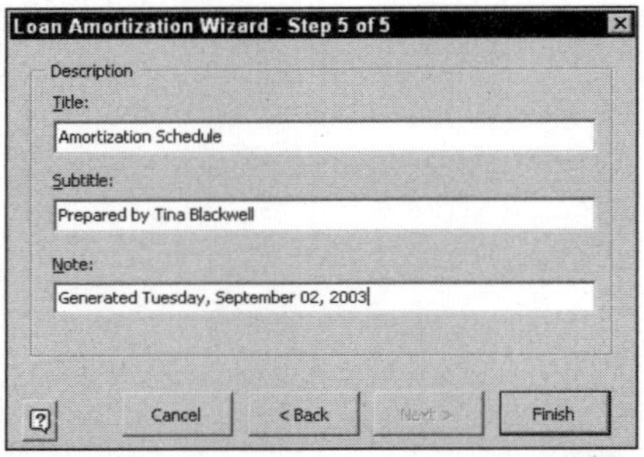

Figure 25-6: Step 5 of the Loan Amortization Wizard.

The Loan Amortization Wizard workbook structure

The Loan Amortization Wizard consists of the following components:

◆ `FormMain`: A UserForm that serves as the primary user interface.

◆ `FormHelp`: A UserForm that displays online help.

◆ `HelpSheet`: A worksheet that contains the text used in the online help.

◆ `ModMain`: A Visual Basic for Applications (VBA) module that contains a procedure that displays the main UserForm.

◆ `ThisWorkbook`: The code module for this object contains the event handler procedures `Workbook_Open` and `Workbook_BeforeClose`, which create and delete a menu item, respectively.

How the Loan Amortization Wizard works

The Loan Amortization Wizard is an add-in, so it should be installed by choosing the Tools → Add-Ins command. It works equally well, however, if it's opened with the File → Open command.

Creating the Loan Amortization Wizard

The Loan Amortization Wizard application started out as a simple concept and evolved into a relatively complex project. My primary goal was to demonstrate as many development concepts as possible and still have a useful end product. I would like to say that I clearly envisioned the end result before I began developing the application, but I'd be lying.

My basic idea was much less ambitious. I simply wanted to create an application that gathered user input and created a worksheet. But after I got started, I began thinking of ways to enhance my simple program. I eventually stumbled down several blind alleys. Some folks could consider my wanderings time-wasting, but those false starts became a vital part of the development process.

I completed the entire project in one (long) day, and I spent a few more hours fine-tuning and testing it.

ADDING THE MENU ITEM TO THE TOOLS MENU

When the workbook is opened, the `Workbook_Open` procedure adds a new Loan Amortization Wizard menu item to the Tools menu. Clicking this menu item executes the `StartAmortizationWizard` procedure, which simply displays the `FormMain` UserForm.

 Refer to Chapter 23 for information about creating new menu items.

INITIALIZING FORMMAIN FOR THE WIZARD

The `UserForm_Initialize` procedure for `FormMain` does quite a bit of work:

◆ It sets the `MultiPage` control's `Value` property to 0. This ensures that it displays the first page, regardless of its value when the workbook was last saved.

◆ It adds items to three `ComboBox` controls used on the form.

◆ It calls the `GetDefaults` procedure, which retrieves the most recently used setting from the Windows Registry (see the upcoming "Saving and retrieving default settings").

◆ It checks whether a workbook is active. If not, the code disables the OptionButton that enables the user to create the new worksheet in the active workbook.

◆ If a workbook is active, an additional check determines whether the workbook's structure is protected. If so, the procedure disables the OptionButton that enables the user to create the worksheet in the active workbook.

PROCESSING EVENTS WHILE THE USERFORM IS DISPLAYED

The code module for the `FormMain` UserForm contains several event handler procedures that respond to the `Click` and `Change` events for the controls on the UserForm.

Clicking the Back and Next buttons determines which page of the `MultiPage` control is displayed. The `MultiPage1_Change` procedure adjusts the UserForm's caption and enables and disables the Back and Next buttons as appropriate. See Chapter 15 for more information about programming a wizard.

DISPLAYING HELP IN THE WIZARD

You have several options when it comes to displaying online help. I chose a simple technique that employs the UserForm shown in Figure 25-7 to display text stored in a worksheet. You'll notice that this help is context-sensitive. When the user clicks the Help button, the Help topic displayed is relevant to the current page of the `MultiPage` control.

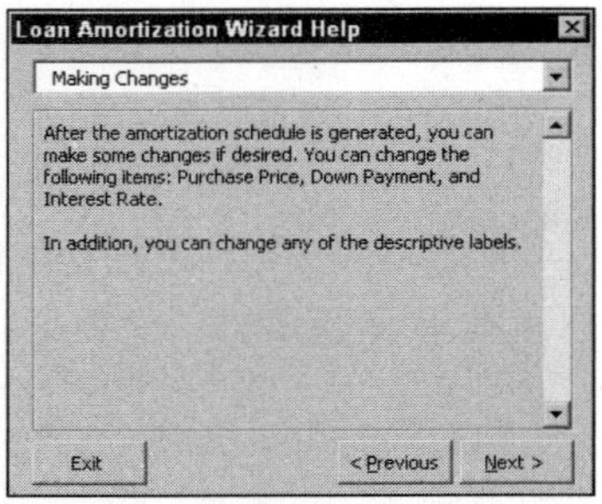

Figure 25-7: User help is presented in a UserForm that copies text stored in a worksheet.

For more information about the technique of transferring worksheet text to a UserForm, consult Chapter 24.

CREATING THE NEW WORKSHEET

When the user clicks the Finish button, the action begins. The `Click` event handler procedure for this button performs the following actions:

◆ It calls a function named `DataIsValid`, which checks the user's input to ensure that it's valid. If all the entries are valid, the function returns `True`, and the procedure continues. If an invalid entry is encountered, `DataIsValid` sets the focus to the control that needs to be corrected and returns a descriptive error message (see Figure 25-8).

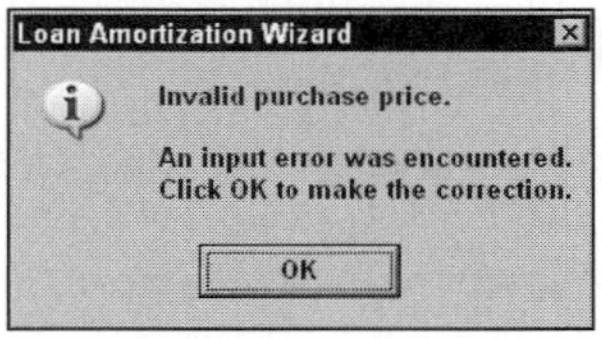

Figure 25-8: If an invalid entry is made, the focus is set back to the control that contains the error.

◆ If the user's responses are valid, the procedure creates a new worksheet either in the active workbook or in a new workbook, per the user's request.

◆ The loan *parameters* (purchase price, down payment information, loan amount, term, and interest rate) are written to the worksheet. This requires the use of some `If` statements because the down payment can be expressed as a percentage of the purchase price or as a fixed amount.

◆ The column headers are written to the worksheet.

◆ The first row of formulas is written below the column headers. The first row is different from the remaining rows because its formulas refer to data in the loan parameters section. The other formulas all refer to the previous row. Notice that I use named ranges in the formulas. These are sheet-level names, so the user can store more than one amortization schedule in the same workbook.

♦ For unnamed references, I use row number and column number notation, which is much easier than trying to determine actual cell addresses.

♦ The second row of formulas is written to the worksheet and then copied down one row for each month.

♦ If the user requested annual totals as opposed to simply monthly data, the procedure uses the Subtotal method to create subtotals. This, by the way, is an example of how using a native feature in Excel can save *lots* of coding.

♦ Because subtotaling the Balance column isn't appropriate, the procedure replaces formulas in the balance column with a formula that returns the year-end balance.

♦ When Excel adds subtotals, it also creates an outline. If the user didn't request an outline, the procedure uses the ClearOutline method to remove it. If an outline was requested, the procedure hides the outline symbols.

♦ Next, the procedure applies formatting to the cells: number formatting, plus an AutoFormat if the user requested color output.

♦ The procedure then adjusts the column widths, freezes the titles just below the header row, and protects the formulas and a few other key cells that can't be changed. The sheet is protected but not with a password.

♦ Finally, the SaveDefaults procedure writes the current values of the UserForm's controls to the Windows Registry. These values will be the new default settings the next time that the user creates an amortization schedule. (See "Saving and retrieving default settings," next.)

SAVING AND RETRIEVING DEFAULT SETTINGS

If you run this application, you'll notice that the FormMain UserForm always displays the setting that you most recently used. In other words, it remembers your last choices and uses them as the new default values. This step makes it very easy to generate multiple *what-if* amortization schedules that vary in only a single parameter. This is accomplished by storing the values in the Windows Registry and then retrieving them when the UserForm is initialized. When the application is used for the first time, the Registry doesn't have any values, so it uses the default values stored in the UserForm controls.

The following GetDefaults procedure loops through each control on the UserForm. If the control is a TextBox, ComboBox, OptionButton, CheckBox, or SpinButton, it calls VBA's GetSetting function and reads the value to the Registry. Note that the third argument for GetSetting is the value to use if the setting is not found. In this case, it uses the value of the control specified at design time. APPNAME is a global constant that contains the name of the application.

```
Sub GetDefaults()
'   Reads default settings from the registry
    Dim ctl As Control
    Dim CtrlType As String

    For Each ctl In Me.Controls
        CtrlType = TypeName(ctl)
        If CtrlType = "TextBox" Or _
            CtrlType = "ComboBox" Or _
            CtrlType = "OptionButton" Or _
            CtrlType = "CheckBox" Or _
            CtrlType = "SpinButton" Then
            ctl.Value = GetSetting _
                (APPNAME, "Defaults", ctl.Name, ctl.Value)
        End If
    Next ctl
End Sub
```

Figure 25-9 shows how these values appear in the Registry, from the perspective of the Windows Registry Editor program.

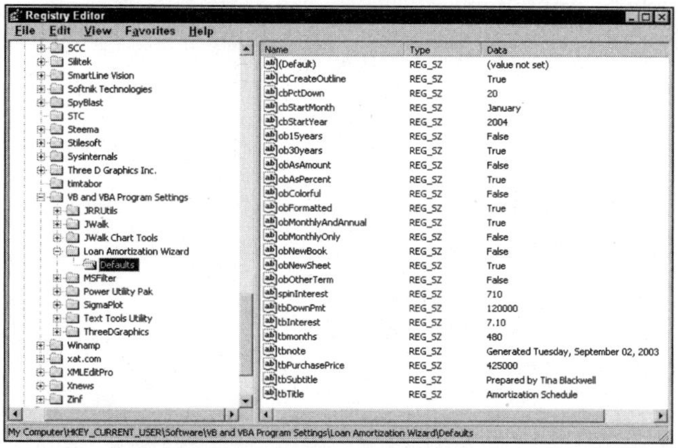

Figure 25-9: The Windows Registry stores the default values for the wizard.

The following SaveDefaults procedure is similar. It uses VBA's SaveSetting statement to write the current values to the Registry.

```
Sub SaveDefaults()
'   Writes current settings to the registry
    Dim ctl As Control
    Dim CtrlType As String

    For Each ctl In Me.Controls
        CtrlType = TypeName(ctl)
        If CtrlType = "TextBox" Or _
            CtrlType = "ComboBox" Or _
            CtrlType = "OptionButton" Or _
            CtrlType = "CheckBox" Or _
            CtrlType = "SpinButton" Then
            SaveSetting APPNAME, "Defaults", ctl.Name, CStr(ctl.Value)
        End If
    Next ctl
End Sub
```

Notice that the code uses the CStr function to convert each setting to a string. This is to avoid problems for those who use non-English regional settings. Without the string conversion, True and False are translated to the user's language before they are stored in the Registry. But they are *not* translated back to English when the setting is retrieved — which causes an error.

The SaveSetting statement and the GetSetting function always use the following Registry key:

HKEY_CURRENT_USER\Software\VB and VBA Program Settings\

Potential enhancements for the Loan Amortization Wizard

It's been said that you never finish writing an application — you just stop working on it. Without even thinking too much about it, I can come up with several enhancements for the Loan Amortization Wizard:

◆ An option to display cumulative totals for interest and principal

◆ An option to work with adjustable rate loans and make projections based on certain interest rate scenarios

◆ More formatting options (for example, no decimal places, no dollar signs, and so on)

◆ Options to enable the user to specify page headers or footers

Application Development Concepts

It's often difficult to follow the logic in an application developed by someone other than yourself. To help you understand my work, I included lots of comments in the code and described the general program flow in the preceding sections. But if you really want to understand this application, I suggest that you use the Debugger to step through the code.

Application Development Checklist

When developing user-oriented applications, you need to keep in mind many things. Let the following checklist serve as a reminder:

◆ *Did you clean up after yourself?* Make sure that you restore toolbars and menus to their original state when the application ends.

◆ *Do the dialog boxes all work from the keyboard?* Don't forget to add hot keys and check the tab order carefully.

◆ *Did you make any assumptions about directories?* If your application reads or writes files, you can't assume that a particular directory exists or that it's the current directory.

◆ *Did you make provisions for canceling all dialog boxes?* You can't assume that the user will end a dialog box by clicking the OK button.

◆ *Did you assume that no other worksheets are open?* If your application is the only workbook open during testing, you could overlook something that happens when other workbooks are open.

◆ *Did you assume that a workbook is visible?* It's possible, of course, to use Excel with no workbooks visible.

◆ *Did you attempt to optimize the speed of your application?* For example, you often can speed up your application by declaring variable types and defining object variables.

◆ *Are your procedures adequately documented?* Will you understand your code if you revisit it in six months?

◆ *Did you include appropriate end-user documentation?* Doing so often eliminates (or at least reduces) the number of follow-up questions.

◆ *Did you allow time to revise your application?* Chances are that the application won't be perfect the first time out. Build in some time to fix it.

At the very least, the Loan Amortization Wizard demonstrates some useful techniques and concepts that are important for Excel developers:

◆ Creating a custom menu item that's displayed only when a particular workbook (or add-in) is open

◆ Using a wizard-like UserForm to gather information

◆ Setting the `Enabled` property of a control dynamically

◆ Linking a `TextBox` and a `SpinButton` control

◆ Displaying online help to a user

◆ Naming cells with VBA

◆ Writing and copying formulas with VBA

◆ Reading from and writing to the Windows Registry

Developing user-oriented applications in Excel is not easy. You must be keenly aware of how people will use (and abuse) the application in real life. Although I tried to make this application completely bulletproof, I did not do extensive real-world testing, so I wouldn't be surprised if it fails under some conditions.

Part VII

Other Topics

Chapter 26

Compatibility Issues

IN THIS CHAPTER

If your application also needs to run on earlier versions of Excel, Excel for Macintosh, or international versions of Excel, you must know about some potential issues. These issues are the topic of this chapter:

◆ How to make sure that your Excel 2003 applications will also work with previous versions of Excel

◆ Issues to be aware of if you're developing Excel applications for international use

IF THE APPLICATIONS THAT YOU'VE DEVELOPED WITH EXCEL 2003 will be used only by others who also use the same version of Excel, you can skip this chapter.

What Is Compatibility?

Compatibility is an often-used term among computer people. In general, it refers to how well software performs under various conditions. These conditions might be defined in terms of hardware, software, or a combination of the two. For example, software that is written specifically for a 32-bit operating system such as Windows XP will not run under the older 16-bit versions of Windows 3.*x*. In other words, 32-bit applications are not compatible with Windows 3.*x*. And, as I'm sure you realize, software written for Windows will not run directly on other operating systems, such as Macintosh or Linux.

In this chapter, I discuss a more specific compatibility issue, involving how your Excel 2003 applications will work with earlier versions of Excel for Windows and Excel for Macintosh. The fact that two versions of Excel might use the same file format isn't always enough to ensure complete compatibility between the contents of their files. For example, Excel 97, Excel 2000, Excel 2002, Excel 2003, and Excel 2002 for Macintosh all use the same file format, but compatibility issues are rampant. Just because a particular version of Excel can open a worksheet file or an add-in doesn't guarantee that that version of Excel can carry out the Visual Basic for Applications (VBA) macro instructions contained in it.

The compatibility problem is more serious than you might think. You can run into compatibility problems even within the same major version of Excel. For example, Excel 2002 exists in at least three different sub-versions: the original release; the first service pak known as SP-1; plus another service release, SP-2. Although these service paks were intended primarily to fix security problems, it's possible that other bugs were also fixed. (Microsoft rarely provides specific details.) Therefore, you can't be guaranteed that an application developed with the original release of Excel 2002 will perform flawlessly with Excel 2002 SP-1. And the reverse is also true: You can't be assured that an application developed with Excel 2002 SP-1 will work correctly with the original Excel 2002.

And with Office 2003, things get even more confusing. The version of Excel that's contained in the Pro version of Office has additional features compared with the other editions of Office 2003. For example, the Pro version has some new eXtensible Markup Language (XML) features and also supports "information rights management." Therefore, if your application depends on these features, simply checking for Excel 2003 is not sufficient. You also need to determine whether these features are actually available.

The point here is that Excel is a moving target, and there is really no way that you can guarantee complete compatibility. Unfortunately, cross-version compatibility doesn't happen automatically. In most cases, you need to do quite a bit of additional work to achieve compatibility.

Types of Compatibility Problems

You need to be aware of five categories of potential compatibility problems. These are listed here and discussed further in this chapter:

- *File format issues:* Workbooks can be saved in several different Excel file formats. Earlier versions of Excel might not be able to open workbooks that were saved in a later version file format.

- *New feature issues:* It should be obvious that a feature introduced in a particular version of Excel cannot be used in previous versions of Excel.

- *32-bit versus 16-bit issues:* If you use Windows Application Programming Interface (API) calls, you need to pay attention to this issue if your application must work with 16-bit versions of Excel (such as Excel 5).

- *Windows versus Macintosh issues:* If your application must work on both platforms, plan to spend lots of time ironing out various compatibility problems.

- *International issues:* If your application will be used by those who speak another language, you must address a number of additional issues.

After reading this chapter, it should be clear that there is only one way to ensure compatibility: You must test your application on every target platform and with every target version of Excel. Often, this is simply not feasible. However, there are measures that you, as a developer, can take to help ensure that your application works with different versions of Excel.

If you're reading this chapter in search of a complete list of specific compatibility issues among the various versions of Excel, you will be disappointed. As far as I know, no such list exists, and it would be virtually impossible to compile one. These types of issues are far too numerous and complex.

A good source for information about potential compatibility problems is Microsoft's online Knowledge Base. The URL is

`http://search.support.microsoft.com`

This will often help you identify bugs that appear in a particular version of Excel.

Excel File Formats Supported

As you probably know, Excel allows you to save a workbook in a format for earlier versions. In addition, you can save a workbook in a dual-version format that combines two file formats in a single file. These dual-version formats result in a larger file, but unfortunately, these dual-version formats sometimes introduce problems of their own.

If your application must work with earlier versions of Excel, you need to make sure that your file is saved in the appropriate file format. The various Excel file formats that can be saved by Excel 2002 are

◆ *Microsoft Excel Workbook (*.xls):* The standard Excel 2003 file format. Can be opened by Excel 97, Excel 2000, Excel 2002, and Excel 2003.

◆ *Microsoft Excel 5.0/95 Workbook:* A format that can be opened by Excel 5.0 and later versions.

◆ *Microsoft Excel 97-2000 & 5.0/95 Workbook:* A dual format that can be opened by Excel 5 and later versions.

◆ *Microsoft Excel 4.0 Worksheet (*.xls):* Can be opened by Excel 4 and later versions. This format saves a single sheet only.

◆ *Microsoft Excel 3.0 Worksheet (*.xls):* Can be opened by Excel 3 and later versions. This format saves a single sheet only.

◆ *Microsoft Excel 2.1 Worksheet (*.xls):* Can be opened by Excel 2.1 and later versions. This format saves a single sheet only.

◆ *Microsoft Excel 4.0 Workbook (*.xlw):* Can be opened by Excel 4.0 and later versions. This format saves multisheet files, but they are not the same format as Excel 5 workbooks.

You can use VBA to access the `FileFormat` property of the `Workbook` object to determine the file format for a particular workbook. The instruction that follows, for example, displays a value that represents the file format for the active workbook:

```
MsgBox ActiveWorkbook.FileFormat
```

Predefined constants are available for the `FileFormat` property. For example, the statement that follows displays `True` if the active workbook is an Excel 5 file:

```
MsgBox ActiveWorkbook.FileFormat = xlExcel5
```

Table 26-1 lists the constants and values for various Excel file formats.

TABLE 26-1 CONSTANTS AND VALUES FOR VARIOUS EXCEL FILE FORMATS

Excel Version	Constant	Value
Excel 2.1	xlExcel2	16
Excel 3.0	xlExcel3	29
Excel 4.0	xlExcel4Workbook	35
Excel 5	xlExcel5	39
Excel 95/97	xlExcel9795	43
Excel in HTML format	xlHtml	44
Excel add-in	xlAddIn	18
Excel 97/2000/2002/2003	xlWorkbookNormal	-4143

Determining Excel's Version Number

The `Version` property of the `Application` object returns the version of Excel. The returned value is a string, so you might need to convert it to a value. VBA's `Val` function is perfect for this. The following function, for example, returns `True` if the user is running Excel 2003 or later (note: Excel 2003 is version 11):

```
Function XL11OrLater()
    XL11OrLater = Val(Application.Version) >= 11

End Function
```

Avoid Using New Features

If your application must work with Excel 2003 and earlier versions, you need to avoid any features that were added after the earliest Excel version that you will support. Another alternative is to incorporate the new features selectively. In other words, your code can determine which version of Excel is being used, and then take advantage of the new features or not.

VBA programmers must be careful not to use any objects, properties, or methods that aren't available in earlier versions. In general, the safest approach is to develop your application with the lowest common denominator. For compatibility with Excel 97 and later, you should use Excel 97 for development; then test thoroughly by using the other versions.

But Will It Work on a Mac?

One of the most prevalent problems that I hear about concerns Macintosh compatibility. Excel for Macintosh represents a very small proportion of the total Excel market, and many developers choose to simply ignore it. The good news is that Excel files are compatible across both platforms. The bad news is that the features supported are not identical, and VBA macro compatibility is far from perfect.

You can write VBA code to determine which platform your application is running. The following function accesses the `OperatingSystem` property of the `Application` object and returns `True` if the operating system is any version of Windows (that is, if the returned string contains the text `"Win"`):

```
Function WindowsOS() As Boolean
    If Application.OperatingSystem like "*Win*" Then
```

```
        WindowsOS = True
    Else
        WindowsOS = False
    End If
End Function
```

Many subtle (and not so subtle) differences exist between the Windows versions and the Mac versions of Excel. Many of those differences are cosmetic (for example, different default fonts), but others are much more serious. For example, Excel for Macintosh doesn't include ActiveX controls. Also, it uses the 1904 date system as the default, so workbooks that use dates could be off by four years. Excel for Windows, by default, uses the 1900 date system. On the Macintosh, a date serial number of 1 refers to January 1, 1904; in Excel for Windows, that same serial number represents January 1, 1900.

Another limitation concerns Windows API functions: They won't work with Excel for Macintosh. If your application depends on such functions, you need to develop a workaround.

If your code deals with paths and filenames, you need to construct your path with the appropriate path separator (a colon for the Macintosh; a backslash for Windows). A better approach is to avoid hard-coding the path separator character and use VBA to determine it. The following statement assigns the path separator character to a variable named PathSep:

```
PathSep = Application.PathSeparator
```

After this statement is executed, your code can use the PathSep variable in place of a hard-coded colon or backslash.

Rather than try to make a single file compatible with both platforms, most developers choose to develop on one platform (typically Excel for Windows) and then modify the application so that it works on the Mac platform. In other words, you'll probably need to maintain two separate versions of your application.

There is only one way to make sure that your application is compatible with the Macintosh version of Excel: You must test it thoroughly on a Macintosh, and be prepared to develop some workarounds for routines that don't work correctly.

Creating an International Application

The final compatibility issue deals with language issues and international settings. Excel is available in many different language versions. The following statement displays the country code for the version of Excel:

```
MsgBox Application.International(xlCountryCode)
```

The United States/English version of Excel has a country code of 1. Other country codes are listed in Table 26-2.

TABLE 26–2 **EXCEL COUNTRY CODES**

Country	Country Code
English	1
Russian	7
Greek	30
Dutch	31
French	33
Spanish	34
Hungarian	36
Italian	39
Czech	42
Danish	45
Swedish	46
Norwegian	47
Polish	48
German	49
Portuguese (Brazil)	55
Thai	66
Japanese	81
Korean	82
Vietnamese	84
Simplified Chinese	86
Turkish	90
Indian	91
Urdu	92

Continued

TABLE 26-2 EXCEL COUNTRY CODES *(Continued)*

Country	Country Code
Portuguese	351
Finnish	358
Traditional Chinese	886
Arabic	966
Hebrew	972
Farsi	982

If your application will be used by those who speak another language, you need to ensure that the proper language is used in your dialog boxes. Also, you need to identify the user's decimal and thousands separator characters. In the United States, these are almost always a period and a comma, respectively. However, users in other countries might have their systems set up to use other characters. Yet another issue is date and time formats: The United States is one of the few countries that use the (illogical) month/date/year format.

If you're developing an application that will be used only by people with your company, you probably won't need to be concerned with international compatibility. But if your company has offices throughout the world, or if you plan to distribute your application outside your country, you need to address a number of issues to ensure that your application will work properly. I discuss these issues in this section.

Multilanguage applications

An obvious consideration involves the language that is used in your application. For example, if you use one or more dialog boxes, you probably want the text to appear in the language of the user. Fortunately, this is not too difficult (assuming, of course, that you can translate your text or know someone who can).

The companion CD-ROM contains a dialog box wizard that is set up to use any of three languages: English, Spanish, or German. This example is based on a dialog box example that I present in Chapter 14.

The first step of the dialog box language wizard (found on the CD) contains three OptionButtons that enable the user to select a language. The text for the three languages is stored in a worksheet.

Figures 26-1 through 26-3 show the UserForm displaying text in all three languages.

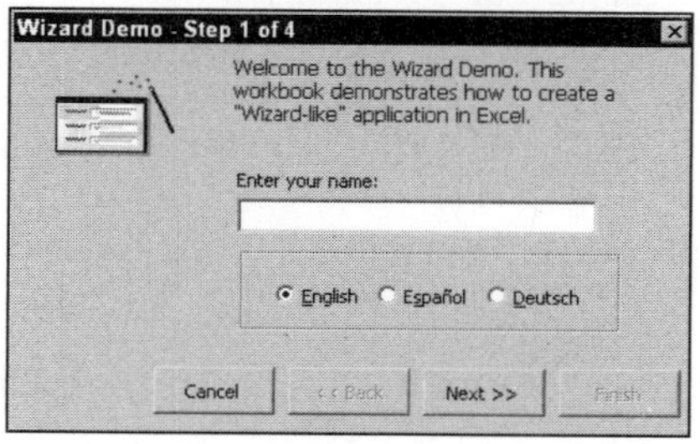

Figure 26–1: The Wizard Demo, in English.

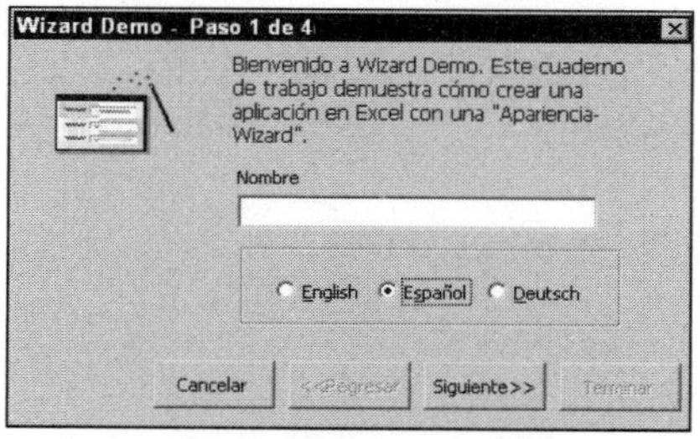

Figure 26–2: The Wizard Demo, in Spanish.

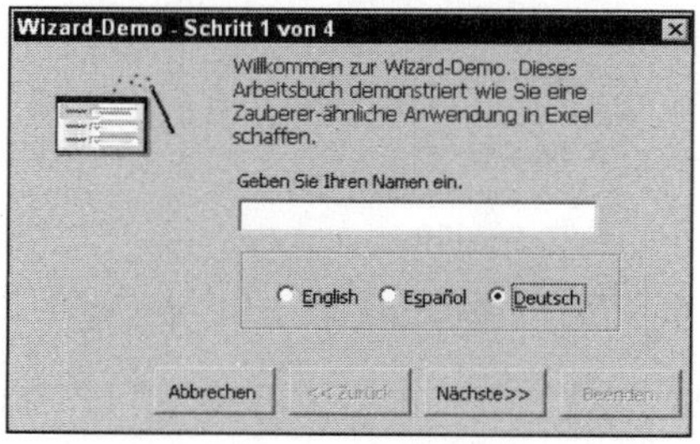

Figure 26–3: The Wizard Demo, in German.

VBA language considerations

In general, you need not be concerned with the language in which you write your VBA code. Excel uses two object libraries: the Excel object library and the VBA object library. When you install Excel, it registers the English language version of these object libraries as the default libraries. (This is true regardless of the language version of Excel.)

Using local properties

If your code will display worksheet information such as a formula or a range address, you probably want to use the local language. For example, the following statement displays the formula in cell A1:

```
MsgBox Range("A1").Formula
```

For international applications, a better approach is to use the FormulaLocal property rather than the Formula property:

```
MsgBox Range("A1").FormulaLocal
```

Several other properties also have local versions. These are shown in Table 26-3 (refer to Help system for specific details).

TABLE 26-3 PROPERTIES THAT HAVE LOCAL VERSIONS

Property	Local Version	Return Contents
Address	AddressLocal	An address
Category	CategoryLocal	A function category
Formula	FormulaLocal	A formula
FormulaR1C1	FormulaR1C1Local	A formula, using R1C1 notation
Name	NameLocal	A name
NumberFormat	NumberFormatLocal	A number format
RefersTo	RefersToLocal	A reference
RefersToR1C1	RefersToR1C1Local	A reference, using R1C1 notation

Identifying system settings

Generally, you cannot assume that the end user's system is set up like the system on which you develop your application. For international applications, you need to be aware of the following settings:

◆ *Decimal separator:* The character used to separate the decimal portion of a value

◆ *Thousands separator:* The character used to delineate every three digits in a value

◆ *List separator:* The character used to separate items in a list

You can determine the current separator settings by accessing the `International` property of the `Application` object. For example, the following statement displays the decimal separator, which won't always be a period:

```
MsgBox Application.International(xlDecimalSeparator)
```

The 45 international settings that you can access with the `International` property are listed in Table 26-4.

TABLE 26–4 CONSTANTS FOR THE INTERNATIONAL PROPERTY

Constant	What It Returns
xlCountryCode	Country version of Microsoft Excel.
xlCountrySetting	Current country setting in the Windows Control Panel.
xlDecimalSeparator	Decimal separator.
xlThousandsSeparator	Thousands separator.
xlListSeparator	List separator.
xlUpperCaseRowLetter	Uppercase row letter (for R1C1-style references).
xlUpperCaseColumnLetter	Uppercase column letter.
xlLowerCaseRowLetter	Lowercase row letter.
xlLowerCaseColumnLetter	Lowercase column letter.
xlLeftBracket	Character used instead of the left bracket ([) in R1C1-style relative references.
xlRightBracket	Character used instead of the right bracket ([) in R1C1-style references.
xlLeftBrace	Character used instead of the left brace ({) in array literals.
xlRightBrace	Character used instead of the right brace (}) in array literals.

Continued

TABLE 26-4 CONSTANTS FOR THE INTERNATIONAL PROPERTY *(Continued)*

Constant	What It Returns
xlColumnSeparator	Character used to separate columns in array literals.
xlRowSeparator	Character used to separate rows in array literals.
xlAlternateArraySeparator	Alternate array item separator to be used if the current array separator is the same as the decimal separator.
xlDateSeparator	Date separator (/).
xlTimeSeparator	Time separator (:).
xlYearCode	Year symbol in number formats (y).
xlMonthCode	Month symbol (m).
xlDayCode	Day symbol (d).
xlHourCode	Hour symbol (h).
xlMinuteCode	Minute symbol (m).
xlSecondCode	Second symbol (s).
xlCurrencyCode	Currency symbol.
xlGeneralFormatName	Name of the General number format.
xlCurrencyDigits	Number of decimal digits to be used in currency formats.
xlCurrencyNegative	A value that represents the currency format for negative currency values.
xlNoncurrencyDigits	Number of decimal digits to be used in noncurrency formats.
xlMonthNameChars	Always returns three characters for backward-compatibility. Abbreviated month names are read from Microsoft Windows and can be any length.
xlWeekdayNameChars	Always returns three characters for backward-compatibility. Abbreviated weekday names are read from Microsoft Windows and can be any length.
xlDateOrder	An integer that represents the order of date elements.

Constant	What It Returns
xl24HourClock	True if the system is using 24-hour time; False if the system is using 12-hour time.
xlNonEnglishFunctions	True if the system is not displaying functions in English.
xlMetric	True if the system is using the metric system; False if the system is using the English measurement system.
xlCurrencySpaceBefore	True if a space is added before the currency symbol.
xlCurrencyBefore	True if the currency symbol precedes the currency values; False if it follows them.
xlCurrencyMinusSign	True if the system is using a minus sign for negative numbers; False if the system is using parentheses.
xlCurrencyTrailingZeros	True if trailing zeros are displayed for zero currency values.
xlCurrencyLeadingZeros	True if leading zeros are displayed for zero currency values.
xlMonthLeadingZero	True if a leading zero is displayed in months (when months are displayed as numbers).
xlDayLeadingZero	True if a leading zero is displayed in days.
xl4DigitYears	True if the system is using four-digit years; False if the system is using two-digit years.
xlMDY	True if the date order is month-day-year for dates displayed in the long form; False if the date order is day/month/year.
xlTimeLeadingZero	True if a leading zero is displayed in times.

Date and time settings

If your application writes formatted dates and will be used in other countries, you might want to make sure that the date is in a format familiar to the user. The best approach is to specify a date by using VBA's DateSerial function and let Excel take care of the formatting details (it will use the user's short date format).

The following procedure uses the `DateSerial` function to assign a date to the `StartDate` variable. This date is then written to cell A1 with the local short date format.

```
Sub WriteDate()
    Dim StartDate As Date
    StartDate = DateSerial(2003, 4, 15)
    Range("A1") = StartDate
End Sub
```

If you need to do any other formatting for the date, you can write code to do so after the date has been entered into the cell. Excel provides several named date and time formats, plus quite a few named number formats. These are all described in the online help (search for *named date/time formats* or *named numeric formats*).

Chapter 27

Manipulating Files with VBA

IN THIS CHAPTER
In this chapter, I describe how to use Visual Basic for Applications (VBA) to perform common file operations and work directly with text files.

- ◆ A basic overview of VBA text file manipulation features

- ◆ Performing common file operations with both traditional techniques and the `FileSearch` object

- ◆ Various ways to open a text file

- ◆ Examples of reading and writing a text file with VBA

- ◆ Code to import more than 256 columns of data into a workbook

- ◆ Sample code for exporting a range to HTML format

MANY APPLICATIONS THAT YOU DEVELOP FOR EXCEL require working with external files. For example, you might need to get a listing of files in a directory, delete files, rename files, and so on. Excel, of course, can import and export several types of text files. In many cases, however, Excel's built-in text file handling isn't sufficient. For example, you might need to import a text file that contains more than 256 columns of data. Or you might want to export a range of cells to a simple HyperText Markup Language (HTML) or eXtensible Markup Language (XML) file.

Performing Common File Operations

Excel provides you with a number of ways to perform common file operations:

- ◆ Use traditional VBA statements and functions. This method works for all versions of Excel.

- ◆ Use the `FileSearch` object, which is easier to use and offers some distinct advantages. This method works for Excel 97 and later.

◆ Use the `FileSystemObject`, which makes use of the Microsoft Scripting Library. This method works for Excel 2000 and later.

In the sections that follow, I discuss these three methods and present examples.

Using VBA file-related commands

The VBA commands that you can use to work with files are summarized in Table 27-1.

TABLE 27-1 VBA FILE-RELATED COMMANDS

Command	What It Does
ChDir	Changes the current directory
ChDrive	Changes the current drive
Dir	Returns a filename or directory that matches a specified pattern or file attribute
FileCopy	Copies a file
FileDateTime	Returns the date and time when a file was last modified
FileLen	Returns the size of a file, in bytes
GetAttr	Returns a value that represents an attribute of a file
Kill	Deletes a file
MkDir	Creates a new directory
Name	Renames a file or directory
RmDir	Removes an empty directory
SetAttr	Changes an attribute for a file

The remainder of this section consists of examples that demonstrate some of the file manipulation commands.

CREATING A VBA FUNCTION TO DETERMINE WHETHER A FILE EXISTS

The following function returns True if a particular file exists and False if it does not exist. If the Dir function returns an empty string, the file could not be found, so the function returns False.

```
Function FileExists(fname) As Boolean
    FileExists = Dir(fname) <> ""
End Function
```

The argument for the FileExists function consists of a full path and filename. The function can either be used in a worksheet or called from a VBA procedure.

CREATING A VBA FUNCTION TO DETERMINE WHETHER A PATH EXISTS

The following function returns True if a specified path exists and False otherwise:

```
Function PathExists(pname) As Boolean
'    Returns TRUE if the path exists
    On Error Resume Next

    PathExists = (GetAttr(pname) And vbDirectory) = vbDirectory
End Function
```

CREATING A VBA PROCEDURE TO DISPLAY A LIST OF FILES IN A DIRECTORY

The following procedure displays (in the active worksheet) a list of files contained in a particular directory, along with the file size and date:

```
Sub ListFiles()
    Directory = "c:\windows\desktop\"
    r = 1
'   Insert headers
    Cells(r, 1) = "FileName"
    Cells(r, 2) = "Size"
    Cells(r, 3) = "Date/Time"
    Range("A1:C1").Font.Bold = True
'   Get first file
    f = Dir(Directory, 7)
    Do While f <> ""
        r = r + 1
        Cells(r, 1) = f
        Cells(r, 2) = FileLen(Directory & f)
        Cells(r, 3) = FileDateTime(Directory & f)
'       Get next file
        f = Dir()
    Loop
End Sub
```

Figure 27-1 shows an example of the output of the ListFiles subroutine.

	A	B	C	D
1	FileName	Size	Date/Time	
2	233238-0800[1].wav	778486	2/27/2003 9:10	
3	Akufen_My Way_10_My Way.mp3	6234001	3/6/2003 16:42	
4	All_Of_Me.mp3	2173947	7/13/2002 8:10	
5	Alone.mp3	5736631	8/14/2002 9:47	
6	AloneBut_Never_Alone.mp3	3488114	7/28/2002 16:40	
7	Alpha_School.mp3	3367627	7/13/2002 8:24	
8	Always.mp3	5345843	8/2/2002 11:30	
9	Always_a_Part.mp3	7729669	9/9/2002 11:14	
10	Amor_Perdido_Lost_Love.mp3	4226561	9/5/2002 11:03	
11	Am_I_the_Same_Girl_Soulful_Strut.mp3	5062094	7/29/2002 17:43	
12	And_I_Got_Left_Behind.mp3	7568754	9/9/2002 10:57	
13	And_I_Love_Him.mp3	2395537	7/13/2002 8:36	
14	Anja.mp3	5918415	7/20/2002 8:42	
15	Anythings_Possible_Fattburger_With_Evan_Marks.mp3	6227844	7/28/2002 16:59	
16	Anything_And_Everything_Chieli_Minucci.mp3	4739483	7/28/2002 16:57	
17	Anything_Goes.mp3	2906694	8/2/2002 11:40	
18	Any_Place_I_Hang_My_Hat_Is_Home.mp3	5208826	8/1/2002 11:35	
19	Arlo Guthrie_Alice's Restaurant_01_Alice's Restaurant	30323597	5/1/2003 17:51	
20	Arms_Of_Mary_Leo_Kottke.mp3	3014144	8/2/2002 11:33	
21	Art Pepper_Arthur's Blues_04_But Beautiful.mp3	7943055	11/10/2002 20:42	
22	Art Pepper_Arthur's Blues_04_But Beautiful.wav	87561260	3/11/2003 6:51	
23	Ashok Pathak_Ancient Court Raga Traditions -The Path	50746043	5/7/2003 15:44	
24	Ashok Pathak_Ancient Court Raga Traditions -The Path	51348618	5/7/2003 15:48	

Figure 27-1: Output from the ListFiles procedure.

Notice that the procedure uses the Dir function twice. The first time, it retrieves the first filename found. Subsequent calls retrieve additional filenames. When no more files are found, the function returns an empty string.

The companion CD-ROM contains a more sophisticated version of this procedure that allows you to select a directory from a dialog box.

The Dir function also accepts wildcard file specifications in its first argument. To get a list of Excel files, for example, you could use a statement such as

```
f = Dir(Directory & "*.xl?", 7)
```

This statement retrieves the name of the first *.xl? file in the specified directory. (It could have an XLS, XLT, or XLA extension.) The second argument for the Dir function lets you specify the attributes of the files. An argument of 7 retrieves filenames that have no attributes, read-only files, hidden files, and system files. Consult the Help system for specifics.

If you need to display a list of files to allow a user to select one, this is not the most efficient approach. Rather, you'll want to use the GetOpenFilename method, which I discuss in Chapter 12.

Using the FileSearch object

The FileSearch object is a member of the Microsoft Office object library. This object essentially gives your VBA code all the functionality of the Windows Find File dialog box. For example, you can use this object to locate files that match a file specification (such as *.xls) and even search for files that contain specific text. You can use this object with Excel 97 and later versions.

Table 27-2 summarizes some of the key methods and properties of the FileSearch object. For a complete list and details, consult the online help.

TABLE 27-2 PROPERTIES AND METHODS OF THE FILESEARCH OBJECT

Property or Method	What It Does
FileName	The name of the file to be located. (Wildcard characters are acceptable.)
FoundFiles	Returns an object that contains the names of the files found.
LookIn	The directory to be searched.
SearchSubfolders	True if subdirectories are to be searched.
Execute	Performs the search.
NewSearch	Resets the FileSearch object.

The remainder of this section consists of examples that demonstrate use of the FileSearch object.

USING FILESEARCH TO DETERMINE WHETHER A FILE EXISTS

The following function takes two arguments (the path and the filename) and returns True if the file exists in the specified directory. After the Execute method is run, the Count property of the FoundFiles object will be 1 if the file is found.

```
Function FileExists2(path, fname) As Boolean
    With Application.FileSearch
        .NewSearch
        .Filename = fname
        .LookIn = path
        .Execute
        FileExists2 = .FoundFiles.Count = 1
    End With
End Function
```

As far as I can tell, you cannot use the `FileSearch` object to determine whether a path exists.

USING FILESEARCH TO DISPLAY A LIST OF FILES IN A DIRECTORY

The following procedure in Listing 27-1 displays (in the active worksheet) a list of files contained in a particular directory, along with the file size and date:

Listing 27-1: Using FileSearch to Display a List of Files in a Directory

```
Sub ListFiles2()
    Directory = "c:\windows\desktop\"
'   Insert headers
    r = 1
    Cells(r, 1) = "FileName"
    Cells(r, 2) = "Size"
    Cells(r, 3) = "Date/Time"
    Range("A1:C1").Font.Bold = True
    r = r + 1
    With Application.FileSearch
        .NewSearch
        .LookIn = Directory
        .Filename = "*.*"
        .SearchSubFolders = False
        .Execute
        For i = 1 To .FoundFiles.Count
            Cells(r, 1) = .FoundFiles(i)
            Cells(r, 2) = FileLen(.FoundFiles(i))
            Cells(r, 3) = FileDateTime(.FoundFiles(i))
            r = r + 1
        Next i
    End With
End Sub
```

The `FileSearch` object essentially ignores all Windows shortcut files (files with a `*.lnk` extension).

The companion CD-ROM contains a more sophisticated version of this procedure that allows you to select a directory.

Using the FileSystemObject object

The FileSystemObject object is a member of the Windows Scripting Host and provides access to a computer's file system. This object is often used in script-oriented Web pages (for example, VBScript and JavaScript) and can be used with Excel 2000 and later versions.

The Windows Scripting Host is often used as a way to spread computer viruses. Consequently, the Windows Scripting Host is disabled on many systems. Therefore, use caution if you are designing an application that will be used on many different systems.

Documentation for the FileSystemObject object is available online at

http://msdn.microsoft.com/scripting

USING FILESYSTEMOBJECT TO DETERMINE WHETHER A FILE EXISTS

The Function procedure that follows accepts one argument (the path and filename) and returns True if the file exists:

```
Function FileExists3(fname) As Boolean
    Dim FileSys As Object
    Set FileSys = CreateObject("Scripting.FileSystemObject")
    FileExists3 = FileSys.FileExists(fname)
End Function
```

The function creates a new FileSystemObject object named FileSys and then accesses the FileExists property for that object.

The companion CD-ROM contains an example that demonstrates all three methods (VBA commands, FileSearch, and FileSystemObject) of determining whether a file exists.

USING FILESYSTEMOBJECT TO DETERMINE WHETHER A PATH EXISTS

The Function procedure that follows accepts one argument (the path) and returns True if the file exists:

```
Function PathExists2(path) As Boolean
    Dim FileSys As Object
    Dim FolderObj As Object
    Set FileSys = CreateObject("Scripting.FileSystemObject")
    On Error Resume Next
    Set FolderObj = FileSys.getfolder(path)
    PathExists2 = Err = 0
End Function
```

The function attempts to create a new Folder object named FolderObj. If this operation is successful, the directory exists. If an error occurs, the directory does not exist.

USING FILESYSTEMOBJECT TO LIST INFORMATION ABOUT ALL AVAILABLE DISK DRIVES

The procedure shown in Listing 27-2 uses FileSystemObject to retrieve and display various information about all disk drives. The procedure loops through the Drives collection and writes various property values to a worksheet. Figure 27-2 shows the results run on a system with a floppy disk drive, a hard drive, and two CD-ROM drives. The data shown is the drive letter, whether the drive is "ready," the drive type, the volume name, the total size, and the available space.

	A	B	C	D	E	F	G
1	A	FALSE	Removable				
2	C	TRUE	Fixed		40015953920	12227559424	
3	D	FALSE	CD-ROM				
4	E	TRUE	CD-ROM	OFFICE11	420077568	0	
5							
6							
7							

show drive info.xls — Sheet1

Figure 27-2: Output from the ShowDriveInfo procedure.

On some versions of Windows, the TotalSize and AvailableSpace properties might return incorrect results for drives that exceed two gigabytes in size. Figure 27-2 shows an example of this error. This problem doesn't occur with Windows NT or with Windows 2000 or later.

This workbook is available on the companion CD-ROM.

Listing 27-2: Using FileSystemObject to Retrieve and Display Disk Drive Information

```
Sub ShowDriveInfo()
    Dim FileSys, Drv
    Dim Row As Integer

    Set FileSys = CreateObject("Scripting.FileSystemObject")
    Cells.Clear
    Row = 0
    On Error Resume Next
    For Each Drv In FileSys.Drives
        Row = Row + 1
        Cells(Row, 1) = Drv.DriveLetter
        Cells(Row, 2) = Drv.IsReady
        Select Case Drv.DriveType
            Case 0: Cells(Row, 3) = "Unknown"
            Case 1: Cells(Row, 3) = "Removable"
            Case 2: Cells(Row, 3) = "Fixed"
            Case 3: Cells(Row, 3) = "Network"
            Case 4: Cells(Row, 3) = "CD-ROM"
            Case 5: Cells(Row, 3) = "RAM Disk"
        End Select
        Cells(Row, 4) = Drv.VolumeName
        Cells(Row, 5) = Drv.TotalSize
        Cells(Row, 6) = Drv.AvailableSpace
    Next Drv
End Sub
```

Locating files that contain specific text

The following procedure searches the My Documents directory (and its subdirectories) for all *.xls files that contain the text *budget*. The found filenames are then added to a ListBox on a UserForm.

```
Sub FindFiles()
    With Application.FileSearch
        .NewSearch
        .LookIn = "C:\My Documents"
```

```
            .SearchSubFolders = True
            .TextOrProperty = "budget"
            .MatchTextExactly = False
            .Filename = "*.xls"
            .Execute
            For i = 1 To .FoundFiles.Count
                UserForm1.ListBox1.AddItem .FoundFiles(i)
            Next i
        End With
        UserForm1.Show
End Sub
```

Working with Text Files

VBA contains a number of statements that allow low-level manipulation of files. These Input/Output (I/O) statements give you much more control over files than Excel's normal text file import and export options.

A file can be accessed in any of three ways:

◆ *Sequential access:* By far the most common method. This allows reading and writing individual characters or entire lines of data.

◆ *Random access:* Used only if you're programming a database application, which you shouldn't be doing in VBA because better techniques do exist.

◆ *Binary access:* Used to read or write to any byte position in a file, such as storing or displaying a bitmap image. Rarely (if ever) used in VBA.

Because random and binary access files are rarely used with VBA, this chapter focuses on sequential access files, which are accessed in a sequential manner. In other words, your code starts reading from the beginning of the file and reads each line sequentially. For output, your code writes data to the end of the file.

The method of reading and writing text files discussed in this book is the traditional data-channel approach. Another option is to use the object approach. The FileSystemObject object contains a TextStream object that can be used to read and write text files. The FileSystemObject object is part of the Windows Scripting Host. As I mention earlier, this scripting service is disabled on many systems because of the strong possibility of transferring a virus.

Opening a text file

VBA's Open statement (not to be confused with the Open method of the Workbooks object) is used to open a file for reading or writing. Before you can read from or write to a file, you must open it.

The Open statement is quite versatile and has a rather complex syntax:

```
Open pathname For mode [Access access] [lock]  _
  As [#]filenumber [Len=reclength]
```

- ◆ pathname: (Required) The pathname part of the Open statement is quite straightforward. It simply contains the name and path (optional) of the file to be opened.

- ◆ mode: (Required) The file mode must be one of the following:

  - ■ Append: A sequential access mode that either allows the file to be read, or data to be appended to the end of the file.

  - ■ Input: A sequential access mode that allows the file to be read but not written to.

  - ■ Output: A sequential access mode that allows the file to be read or written to. In this mode, a new file is always created. (An existing file with the same name is deleted.)

  - ■ Binary: A random access mode that allows data to be read or written to on a byte-by-byte basis.

  - ■ Random: A random access mode that allows data to be read or written in units determined by the reclength argument of the Open statement.

- ◆ access: (Optional) The access argument determines what can be done with the file. It can be Read, Write, or Read Write.

- ◆ lock: (Optional) The lock argument is useful for multiuser situations. The options are Shared, Lock Read, Lock Write, and Lock Read Write.

- ◆ filenumber: (Required) A file number ranging from 1 to 511. You can use the FreeFile function to get the next available file number. (Read about FreeFile in the upcoming section, "Getting a file number.")

- ◆ reclength: (Optional) The record length (for random access files) or the buffer size (for sequential access files).

Reading a text file

The basic procedure for reading a text file with VBA consists of the following steps:

1. Open the file by using the `Open` statement.

2. Specify the position in the file by using the `Seek` function (optional).

3. Read data from the file (by using the `Input`, `Input #`, or `Line Input #` statements).

4. Close the file by using the `Close` statement.

Writing a text file

The basic procedure for writing a text file is

1. Open or create the file by using the `Open` statement.

2. Specify the position in the file by using the `Seek` function (optional).

3. Write data to the file by using the `Write #` or `Print #` statements.

4. Close the file by using the `Close` statement.

Getting a file number

Most VBA programmers simply designate a file number in their `Open` statement. For example:

```
Open "myfile.txt" For Input As #1
```

Then you can refer to the file in subsequent statements as #1.

If a second file is opened while the first is still open, you would designate the second file as #2:

```
Open "another.txt" For Input As #2
```

Another approach is to use VBA's `FreeFile` function to get a file handle. Then you can refer to the file by using a variable. Here's an example:

```
FileHandle = FreeFile
Open "myfile.txt" For Input As FileHandle
```

Determining or setting the file position

For sequential file access, it's rarely necessary to know the current location in the file. If for some reason you need to know this, you can use the `Seek` function.

> ## Excel's Text File Import and Export Features
>
> Excel supports three types of text files:
>
> ◆ *CSV (Comma-Separated Value) files:* Columns of data are separated by a comma, and each row of data ends in a carriage return. For some non-English versions of Excel, a semi-colon rather than a comma is used.
>
> ◆ *PRN:* Columns of data are aligned by character position, and each row of data ends in a carriage return.
>
> ◆ *TXT (Tab-delimited) files:* Columns of data are separated by Tab characters, and each row of data ends in a carriage return.
>
> When you attempt to open a text file with the File → Open command, the Text Import Wizard might appear to help you delineate the columns. If the text file is tab-delimited or comma-delimited, Excel usually opens the file without displaying the Text Import Wizard. The Text to Columns Wizard (accessed by choosing Data → Text to Columns) is identical to the Text Import Wizard but works with data stored in a single column.

Statements for reading and writing

VBA provides several statements to read and write data to a file.

Three statements are used for reading data from a sequential access file:

◆ Input: Reads a specified number of characters from a file

◆ Input #: Reads data as a series of variables, with variables separated by a comma

◆ Line Input #: Reads a complete line of data (delineated by a carriage return and/or linefeed character)

Two statements are used for writing data to a sequential access file:

◆ Write #: Writes a series of values, with each value separated by a comma and enclosed in quotes. If you end the statement with a semicolon, a carriage return/linefeed sequence is not inserted after each value. Data written with Write # is usually read from a file with an Input # statement.

◆ Print #: Writes a series of values, with each value separated by a Tab character. If you end the statement with a semicolon, a carriage return/linefeed sequence is not inserted after each value. Data written with Print # is usually read from a file with a Line Input # or an Input statement.

Text File Manipulation Examples

This section contains a number of examples that demonstrate various techniques that manipulate text files.

Importing data in a text file

The following example reads a text file and then places each line of data in a single cell (beginning with the active cell):

```
Sub ImportData()
    Open "c:\windows\desktop\textfile.txt" For Input As #1
    r = 0
    Do Until EOF(1)
        Line Input #1, data
        ActiveCell.Offset(r, 0) = data
        r = r + 1
    Loop
    Close #1
End Sub
```

In most cases, this procedure won't be very useful because each line of data is simply dumped into a single cell. You can, however, choose the Data→Text to Columns command to parse the data to columns.

Exporting a range to a text file

The following example (Listing 27-3) is a simple example that writes the data in a selected worksheet range to a CSV text file.

Notice that the procedure uses two `Write #` statements. The first statement ends with a semicolon so a carriage return/linefeed sequence is not written. For the last cell in a row, however, the second `Write #` statement does not use a semicolon, which causes the next output to appear on a new line.

I use a variable named `Data` to store the contents of each cell. If the cell is numeric, the variable is converted to a value. This step ensures that numeric data will not be stored with quotation marks. If a cell is empty, its `Value` property returns 0. Therefore, the code also checks for a blank cell (by using the `IsEmpty` function) and substitutes an empty string instead of a zero.

Listing 27-3: Writing Data in a Selected Worksheet Range to a CSV Text File

```
Sub ExportRange()
    Dim Filename As String
    Dim NumRows As Long, NumCols As Integer
```

```
    Dim r As Long, c As Integer
    Dim Data
    Dim ExpRng As Range
    Set ExpRng = Selection
    NumCols = ExpRng.Columns.Count
    NumRows = ExpRng.Rows.Count
    Filename = "c:\windows\desktop\textfile.txt"
    Open Filename For Output As #1
        For r = 1 To NumRows
            For c = 1 To NumCols
                Data = ExpRng.Cells(r, c).Value
                If IsNumeric(Data) Then Data = Val(Data)
                If IsEmpty(ExpRng.Cells(r, c)) Then Data = ""
                If c <> NumCols Then
                    Write #1, Data;
                Else
                    Write #1, Data
                End If
            Next c
        Next r
    Close #1
End Sub
```

This example is available on the companion CD-ROM.

Figure 27-3 shows the contents of the resulting file.

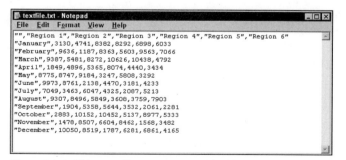

Figure 27-3: This text file was generated by VBA.

Importing a text file to a range

The following subroutine in Listing 27-4 reads the text file created in the previous example and then stores the values beginning at the active cell. The code reads each character and essentially parses the line of data, ignoring quote characters and looking for commas to delineate the columns.

Listing 27-4: Reading the Text File from Listing 27-3 and Storing the Values Beginning at the Active Cell

```
Sub ImportRange()
    Dim ImpRng As Range
    Dim Filename As String
    Dim r As Long, c As Integer
    Dim txt As String, Char As String * 1
    Dim Data
    Dim i As Integer

    Set ImpRng = ActiveCell
    On Error Resume Next
    Filename = "c:\windows\desktop\textfile.txt"
    Open Filename For Input As #1
    If Err <> 0 Then
        MsgBox "Not found: " & Filename, vbCritical, "ERROR"
        Exit Sub
    End If
    r = 0
    c = 0
    txt = ""
    Application.ScreenUpdating = False
    Do Until EOF(1)
        Line Input #1, Data
        For i = 1 To Len(Data)
            Char = Mid(Data, i, 1)
            If Char = "," Then 'comma
                ActiveCell.Offset(r, c) = txt
                c = c + 1
                txt = ""
            ElseIf i = Len(Data) Then 'end of line
                If Char <> Chr(34) Then txt = txt & Char
                ActiveCell.Offset(r, c) = txt
                txt = ""
            ElseIf Char <> Chr(34) Then
                txt = txt & Char
            End If
        Next i
```

```
        c = 0
        r = r + 1
    Loop
    Close #1
    Application.ScreenUpdating = True
End Sub
```

The procedure above has a flaw: It doesn't handle data that contains a comma or a quote character. In addition, an imported date will be surrounded by number signs: for example, #2001-05-12#.

This example is available on the companion CD-ROM.

Logging Excel usage

The example in this section writes data to a text file every time that Excel is opened and closed. In order for this to work reliably, the procedure must be located in a workbook that's opened every time you start Excel. The Personal Macro Workbook is an excellent choice.

The following procedure, stored in the code module for the ThisWorkbook object, is executed when the file is opened:

```
Private Sub Workbook_Open()
    Open Application.Path & "\excelusage.txt" _
      For Append As #1
    Print #1, "Started " & Now
    Close #1
End Sub
```

The procedure appends a new line to a file named excelusage.txt. The new line contains the current date and time and might look something like this:

```
Started 09/16/03 9:27:43 PM
```

The following procedure is executed when the workbook is closed. It appends a new line that contains the word Stopped, along with the current date and time.

```
Private Sub Workbook_BeforeClose(Cancel As Boolean)
    Open Application.Path & "\excelusage.txt" _
      For Append As #1
    Print #1, "Stopped " & Now
    Close #1
End Sub
```

Filtering a text file

The example in this section demonstrates how to work with two text files at once. The FilterFile procedure that follows reads a text file (infile.txt) and copies only the rows that contain a specific text string to a second text file (output.txt).

```
Sub FilterFile()
    Open "infile.txt" For Input As #1
    Open "output.txt" For Output As #2
    TextToFind = "January"
    Do Until EOF(1)
        Line Input #1, data
        If InStr(1, data, TextToFind) Then
            Print #2, data
        End If
    Loop
    Close
End Sub
```

 This example is available on the companion CD-ROM.

Importing more than 256 columns of data

It's not uncommon to need to import a text file that exceeds Excel's 256-column capacity. If you attempt to open such a file with the File → Open command, Excel simply ignores any data past column 256 (and doesn't even warn you about it).

Listing 27-5 is a variation of the ImportRange procedure presented earlier in this chapter. It reads a text file and then imports the data into a new workbook. If the data contains more than 256 columns of data, additional sheets are added to the workbook.

Listing 27-5: Reading a Text File and Importing the Data into a New Workbook

```
Sub ImportLongLines()
'   Imports a text file with >256 columns of data
```

```
Dim ImpRange As Range
Dim r As Long, c As Integer
Dim CurrLine As Long
Dim Data As String, Char As String, Txt As String
Dim i As Integer
Dim CurrSheet As Worksheet

' Create a new workbook with one sheet
Workbooks.Add xlWorksheet


Open ThisWorkbook.Path & "\longfile.txt" For Input As #1
r = 0
c = 0
Set ImpRange = ActiveWorkbook.Sheets(1).Range("A1")
Application.ScreenUpdating = False

' Read the first line, and insert new sheets if necessary
CurrLine = CurrLine + 1
Line Input #1, Data
For i = 1 To Len(Data)
    Char = Mid(Data, i, 1)
'   Are we out of columns?
    If c <> 0 And c Mod 256 = 0 Then
        With ActiveWorkbook.Sheets
            Set CurrSheet = .Add(after:=.Sheets(.Count))
        End With
        Set ImpRange = CurrSheet.Range("A1")
        c = 0
    End If
'   End of the field?
    If Char = "," Then
        ImpRange.Offset(r, c) = Txt
        c = c + 1
        Txt = ""
    Else
'       Skip quote characters
        If Char <> Chr(34) Then _
            Txt = Txt & Mid(Data, i, 1)

'       End of the line?
        If i = Len(Data) Then
            ImpRange.Offset(r, c) = Txt
```

Continued

Listing 27-5 *(Continued)*

```
                c = c + 1
                Txt = ""
            End If
        End If
    Next i


'   Read the remaining data
    c = 0
    CurrLine = 1
    Set ImpRange = ActiveWorkbook.Sheets(1).Range("A1")
    r = r + 1

    Do Until EOF(1)
        Set ImpRange = ActiveWorkbook.Sheets(1).Range("A1")
        CurrLine = CurrLine + 1
        Line Input #1, Data
        Application.StatusBar = "Processing line " & CurrLine
        For i = 1 To Len(Data)
            Char = Mid(Data, i, 1)
'           Are we out of columns?
            If c <> 0 And c Mod 256 = 0 Then
                c = 0
                Set ImpRange = ImpRange.Parent.Next.Range("A1")
            End If

'           End of the field
            If Char = "," Then
                ImpRange.Offset(r, c) = Txt
                c = c + 1
                Txt = ""
            Else
'               Skip quote characters
                If Char <> Chr(34) Then _
                    Txt = Txt & Mid(Data, i, 1)

'               End of the line?
                If i = Len(Data) Then
                    ImpRange.Offset(r, c) = Txt
                    c = c + 1
```

```
                Txt = ""
            End If
        End If
    Next i
    c = 0
    Set ImpRange = ActiveWorkbook.Sheets(1).Range("A1")
    r = r + 1
 Loop

'   Tidy up
    Close #1
    Application.ScreenUpdating = True
    Application.StatusBar = False
End Sub
```

This procedure consists of two parts. The first part reads the first row of data and adds new sheets, if necessary. The second part reads the remaining data in the text file. The code assumes that the first row is typical of the remaining data and that it has the maximum number of columns.

This example is available on the companion CD-ROM, along with a text file that contains 100 rows, each with 600 columns of data.

Exporting a range to HTML format

The example in this section demonstrates how to export a range of cells to an HTML file. An *HTML file,* as you might know, is simply a text file that contains special formatting tags that describe how the information will be presented in a browser.

Why not use Excel's File → Save as Web Page command? The procedure listed here has a distinct advantage: It does not produce bloated HTML code. For example, I used the ExportToHTML procedure to export a range of 70 cells. The file size was 2.6KB. Then I used Excel's File → Save as Web Page command to export the sheet. The result was 15.8KB — more than six times larger. But, on the other hand, the ExportToHTML procedure does not maintain all the cell formatting. In fact, the only formatting information that it produces is bold and italic. You'll find that this procedure has another serious limitation: It cannot handle merged cells.

You might want to use the ExportToHTML procedure, here in Listing 27-6, as the basis for additional customizations.

Listing 27-6: Exporting a Range of Cells to an HTML File

```
Sub ExportToHTML()
'    Dim ws As Worksheet
    Dim Filename As Variant
    Dim TDOpenTag As String, TDCloseTag As String
    Dim CellContents As String
    Dim Rng As Range
    Dim r As Long, c As Integer

'   Use the selected range of cells
    Set Rng = Application.Intersect(ActiveSheet.UsedRange,
Selection)

'   Get a file name
    Filename = Application.GetSaveAsFilename( _
        InitialFileName:="myrange.htm", _
        fileFilter:="HTML Files(*.htm), *.htm")
    If Filename = False Then Exit Sub

'   Open the text file
    Open Filename For Output As #1

'   Write the <TABLE> tag
    Print #1, "<TABLE BORDER=1 CELLPADDING=3>"

'   Loop through the cells
    For r = 1 To Rng.Rows.Count
        Print #1, "<TR>"
        For c = 1 To Rng.Columns.Count
            TDOpenTag = "<TD ALIGN=RIGHT>"
            TDCloseTag = "</TD>"
            If Rng.Cells(r, c).Font.Bold Then
                TDOpenTag = TDOpenTag & "<B>"
                TDCloseTag = "</B>" & TDCloseTag
            End If
            If Rng.Cells(r, c).Font.Italic Then
                TDOpenTag = TDOpenTag & "<I>"
                TDCloseTag = "</I>" & TDCloseTag
            End If
            CellContents = Rng.Cells(r, c).Text
            Print #1, TDOpenTag & CellContents & TDCloseTag
        Next c
        Print #1, "</TR>"
```

```
    Next r
'   Close the table
    Print #1, "</TABLE>"

'   Close the file
    Close #1

'   Tell the user
    MsgBox Rng.Count & " cells exported to " & Filename
End Sub
```

 This example is available on the companion CD-ROM.

The procedure starts by determining the range to export. This is based on the intersection of the selected range and the used area of the worksheet. This ensures that entire rows or columns are not processed. Next, the user is prompted for a file-name, and the text file is opened. The bulk of the work is done within two For-Next loops. The code generates the appropriate HTML tags and writes the information to the text file. Finally, the file is closed, and the user sees a summary message.

Figure 27-4 shows a range in a worksheet, and Figure 27-5 shows how it looks in a browser after being converted to HTML.

export to HTML.xls

	A	B	C	D	E	F	G
1							
2			New York	Los Angeles	Chicago	Total	
3		January	$3,813.00	$8,874.00	$15,174.00	$27,861.00	
4		February	$21,161.00	$611.00	$7,786.00	$29,558.00	
5		March	$21,097.00	$963.00	$10,357.00	$32,417.00	
6		April	$15,392.00	$19,794.00	$9,850.00	$45,036.00	
7		May	$12,858.00	$22,693.00	$8,698.00	$44,249.00	
8		June	$14,336.00	$1,819.00	$111.00	$16,266.00	
9		July	$19,842.00	$354.00	$11,558.00	$31,754.00	
10		August	$15,716.00	$2,003.00	$20,739.00	$38,458.00	
11		September	$4,219.00	$2,976.00	$8,080.00	$15,275.00	
12		October	$12,338.00	$20,490.00	$15,769.00	$48,597.00	
13		November	$18,693.00	$5,389.00	$14,664.00	$38,746.00	
14		December	$17,141.00	$13,602.00	$12,920.00	$43,663.00	
15		Total	$176,606.00	$99,568.00	$135,706.00	$411,880.00	
16							
17							

Sheet1

Figure 27-4: A worksheet range, ready to be converted to HTML.

C:\Documents and Settings\John\Desktop\myrange.htm - Microsoft Internet E... _□×

File   Edit   View   Favorites   Tools   Help

Back   Forward   Stop   Refresh   Home   Favorites   Print   Edit   Size   »

Address   C:\Documents and Settings\John\Desktop\myrange.htm   ▼

	New York	Los Angeles	Chicago	Total
January	$3,813.00	$8,874.00	$15,174.00	$27,861.00
February	$21,161.00	$611.00	$7,786.00	$29,558.00
March	$21,097.00	$963.00	$10,357.00	$32,417.00
April	$15,392.00	$19,794.00	$9,850.00	$45,036.00
May	$12,858.00	$22,693.00	$8,698.00	$44,249.00
June	$14,336.00	$1,819.00	$111.00	$16,266.00
July	$19,842.00	$354.00	$11,558.00	$31,754.00
August	$15,716.00	$2,003.00	$20,739.00	$38,458.00
September	$4,219.00	$2,976.00	$8,080.00	$15,275.00
October	$12,338.00	$20,490.00	$15,769.00	$48,597.00
November	$18,693.00	$5,389.00	$14,664.00	$38,746.00
December	$17,141.00	$13,602.00	$12,920.00	$43,663.00
Total	$176,606.00	$99,568.00	$135,706.00	$411,880.00

Done   My Computer

Figure 27-5: The worksheet data after being converted to HTML.

Exporting a range to an XML file

This example exports an Excel range to a simple XML data file. As you might know, an *XML file* uses tags to wrap each data item. The procedure in this section uses the labels in the first row as the XML tags. Figure 27-6 shows the range in a worksheet, and Figure 27-7 shows the XML file displayed in Internet Explorer.

Although Excel 2003 has improved support for XML files, it surprisingly can't create an XML file from an arbitrary range of data unless you have a map file (schema) for the data.

export to XML.xls   _□×

	A	B	C	D	E	F	G	H
1	EmployeeID	LastName	FirstName	Title	BirthDate	HireDate	Address	City
2	9001	Davolio	Nancy	Sales Representative	12/8/68	5/1/01	507 - 20th Ave. E. Apt. 2A	Seattle
3	9002	Fuller	Andrew	Vice President, Sales	2/19/52	8/14/02	908 W. Capital Way	Tacom
4	9003	Leverling	Janet	Sales Representative	8/30/63	4/1/00	722 Moss Bay Blvd.	Kirklar
5	9004	Peacock	Margaret	Sales Representative	9/19/58	5/3/99	4110 Old Redmond Rd.	Redmc
6	9005	Buchanan	Steven	Sales Manager	3/4/55	10/17/93	14 Garrett Hill	Londo
7	9006	Suyama	Michael	Sales Representative	7/2/63	10/17/97	Coventry House□Miner Rd.	Londo
8	9007	King	Robert	Sales Representative	5/29/60	1/2/98	Edgeham Hollow Winchest	Londo
9	9008	Callahan	Laura	Inside Sales Coordinator	1/9/58	3/5/94	4726 - 11th Ave. N.E.	Seattle
10	9009	Dodsworth	Anne	Sales Representative	7/2/69	11/15/99	7 Houndstooth Rd.	Londo
11	9102	Jackson	Raymond	Sales Representative	2/16/52	3/4/00	11 Franklin Way	Portlar

Sheet1

Figure 27-6: The data in this range will be converted to XML.

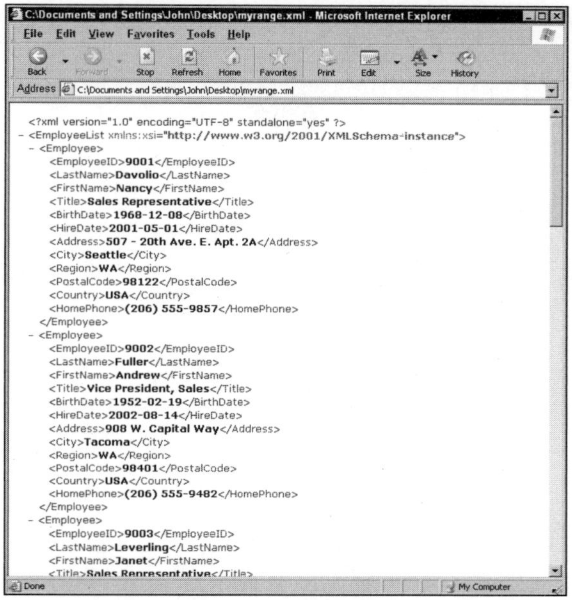

Figure 27-7: The worksheet data after being converted to XML.

The `ExportToXML` procedure is in Listing 27-7. You'll notice that it has a lot in common with the `ExportToHTML` procedure in the previous section.

Listing 27-7: Exporting an Excel Range to a Simple XML Data File

```
Sub ExportToXML()
'    Dim ws As Worksheet
     Dim Filename As Variant
     Dim TDOpenTag As String, TDCloseTag As String
     Dim CellContents As String
     Dim Rng As Range
     Dim r As Long, c As Integer

'    Set the range
     Set Rng = Range("A1:L11")

'    Get a file name
     Filename = Application.GetSaveAsFilename( _
         InitialFileName:="myrange.xml", _
         fileFilter:="XML Files(*.xml), *.xml")
```

Continued

Listing 27-7 *(Continued)*

```
    If Filename = False Then Exit Sub

'   Open the text file
    Open Filename For Output As #1

'   Write the <xml> tag
    Print #1, "<?xml version=""1.0"" encoding=""UTF-8"" standalone=""yes""?>"
    Print #1, _
    "<EmployeeList xmlns:xsi=""http://www.w3.org/2001/XMLSchema-instance"">"

'   Loop through the cells
    For r = 2 To Rng.Rows.Count
        Print #1, "<Employee>"
        For c = 1 To Rng.Columns.Count
            Print #1, "<" & Rng.Cells(1, c) & ">";
            If IsDate(Rng.Cells(r, c)) Then
                Print #1, Format(Rng.Cells(r, c), "yyyy-mm-dd");
            Else
                Print #1, Rng.Cells(r, c).Text;
            End If
            Print #1, "</" & Rng.Cells(1, c) & ">"
        Next c
        Print #1, "</Employee>"
    Next r
'   Close the table
    Print #1, "</EmployeeList>"

'   Close the file
    Close #1

'   Tell the user
    MsgBox Rng.Rows.Count - 1 & " records were exported to " & Filename
End Sub
```

Chapter 28

Manipulating Visual Basic Components

IN THIS CHAPTER
This chapter discusses a topic that some readers might find extremely useful: writing Visual Basic for Applications (VBA) code that manipulates components in a VBA project. Read on to discover the following:

◆ An overview of the VBA Integrated Development Environment (IDE) and its object model

◆ Important information for Excel 2002 and Excel 2003 users

◆ How to use VBA to add and remove modules from a project

◆ How to write VBA code that creates more VBA code

◆ How to use VBA to help create UserForms

◆ A useful function that creates a UserForm on-the-fly

THE VBA IDE CONTAINS AN OBJECT MODEL that exposes key elements of your VBA projects, including the Visual Basic Editor (VBE) itself. You can write VBA code that adds or removes modules, generates other VBA code, or even creates a UserForm on-the-fly.

Introducing the IDE

The *IDE* is essentially an Object Linking and Embedding (OLE) Automation interface for the Visual Basic Editor. After you establish a reference to the Visual Basic for Applications Extensibility Library (use the VBE's Tools → References command), you have access to all the VBE's objects, properties, and methods, and you can also declare objects from the IDE's member classes.

In the References dialog box, you can add a reference to Microsoft Visual Basic for Applications Extensibility. This gives you access to an object called VBIDE. Creating a reference to VBIDE enables you to declare object variables contained in the VBIDE and also gives you access to a number of predefined constants that relate to the IDE. Actually, you can access the objects in the IDE *without* creating a reference, but you won't be able to use the constants in your code nor will you be able to declare specific objects that refer to IDE components.

Refer to Chapter 20 for background information about OLE Automation.

After you understand how the IDE object model works, you can write code to perform a variety of operations, including the following:

◆ Adding and removing VBA modules

◆ Inserting VBA code

◆ Creating UserForms

◆ Adding controls to a UserForm

Important Note for Excel 2002 and 2003 Users

If you're using Excel to develop applications for others to use, be aware that things have changed, beginning with Excel 2002. To reduce the possibility of macro viruses, Microsoft made it much more difficult for a VBA macro to modify components in a VBA project. If you attempt to execute any of the procedures in this chapter, you will probably see an error message like the one that follows:

```
Microsoft Visual Basic

Run-time error '1004':

Programmatic access to Visual Basic Project is not trusted



  Continue       End         Debug         Help
```

Whether you see this error message depends on a setting in Excel's Security dialog box (accessed by choosing Tools → Macro → Security). This setting, called *Trust Access to Visual Basic Project,* is turned off by default. Even if the user chooses to trust the macros contained in the workbook, the macros cannot modify the VBA project if this setting is turned off. Note that this setting applies to all workbooks and cannot be changed only for a particular workbook.

You can't access the value of this particular setting directly. The only way to detect this setting is to attempt to access the VBProject object and then check for an error. The following code demonstrates:

```
On Error Resume Next
Set x = ActiveWorkbook.VBProject
If Err <> 0 Then
  MsgBox "Your security settings do not allow this macro to run."
  Exit Sub
End If
```

Not all the examples in this chapter are intended to be used by end users. Many of them are designed to assist developers create projects. For these projects, you'll want to turn off the Trust Access to Visual Basic Project setting.

The IDE Object Model

Programming the IDE requires an understanding of its object model. The top object in the object hierarchy is the VBE (Visual Basic Environment). As with Excel's object model, the VBE contains other objects. A simplified version of the IDE object hierarchy is as follows:

```
VBE
  VBProject
   VBComponent
      CodeModule
      Designer
      Property
   Reference
  Window
  CommandBar
```

This chapter ignores the Extensibility Library's `Windows` collection and `CommandBars` collection, which aren't all that useful for Excel developers. Rather, the chapter focuses on the `VBProject` object, which can be *very* useful for developers — but make sure that you read the "Important Note for Excel 2002 and 2003 Users" sidebar.

The VBProjects collection

Every open workbook or add-in is represented by a `VBProject` object. To access the `VBProject` object for a workbook, use the `VBProject` property of the `Workbook` object. The following instructions, for example, create an object variable that represents the `VBProject` object for the active workbook:

```
Dim VBP As VBProject
Set VBP = ActiveWorkbook.VBProject
```

If you get an error message when VBA encounters the `Dim` statement, make sure that you've added a reference to Microsoft Visual Basic for Applications Extensibility.

Each `VBProject` object contains a collection of the VBA component objects in the project (UserForms, modules, class modules, or document modules). Not surprisingly, this collection is called `VBComponents`. A `VBProject` object also contains a `References` collection for the project, representing the libraries being referenced currently by the project.

You cannot directly add a new member to the `VBProjects` collection. Rather, you do so indirectly by opening or creating a new workbook in Excel. Doing so automatically adds a new member to the `VBProjects` collection. Similarly, you can't remove a `VBProject` object directly; closing a workbook removes the `VBProject` object from the collection.

THE VBCOMPONENTS COLLECTION

To access a member of the `VBComponents` collection, use the `VBComponents` property with an index number or name. The following instructions demonstrate the two ways to access a VBA component and create an object variable:

```
Set VBC = ThisWorkbook.VBProject.VBComponents(1)
Set VBC = ThisWorkbook.VBProject.VBComponents("Module1")
```

THE REFERENCES COLLECTION

Every VBA project in Excel contains a number of references. You can view, add, or delete the references for a project by choosing the Tools → References command (see Figure 28-1). Every project contains some references (such as VBA itself, Excel, OLE Automation, and the Office object library), and you can add additional references to a project as needed.

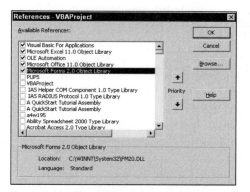

Figure 28-1: The References dialog box shows the references for each project.

You can also manipulate the references for a project using VBA. The References collection contains Reference objects, and the Reference class for these objects has properties and methods. The following procedure, for example, displays a message box that lists the Name, Description, and FullPath property for each Reference object in the active workbook's project:

```
Sub ListReferences()
    Dim Ref As Reference
    Msg = ""
    For Each Ref In ActiveWorkbook.VBProject.References
        Msg = Msg & Ref.Name & vbCrLf
        Msg = Msg & Ref.Description & vbCrLf
        Msg = Msg & Ref.FullPath & vbCrLf & vbCrLf
    Next Ref
    MsgBox Msg
End Sub
```

Figure 28-2 shows the result of running this procedure when a workbook that contains five references is active.

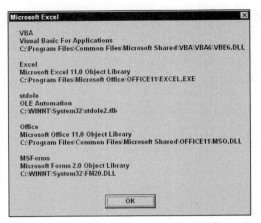

Figure 28-2: This message box displays information about
the references for a project.

NOTE   Because it declares an object variable of type `Reference`, the `List`
`References` procedure requires a reference to the VBA Extensibility
Library. If you declare `Ref` as a generic `Object`, the VBA Extensibility Library
reference is not needed.

You can also add a reference programmatically using either of two methods of
the `Reference` class. The `AddFromFile` method adds a reference if you know its
filename and storage path. `AddFromGuid` adds a reference if you know the reference's *globally unique identifier*, or GUID. Refer to the Help system for complete
details.

Displaying All Components in a VBA Project

The `ShowComponents` procedure, shown in Listing 28-1, loops through each VBA
component in the active workbook and writes the following information to a
worksheet:

◆ The component's name

◆ The component's type

◆ The number of lines of code in the code module for the component

Listing 28-1: Displaying Each Active VBA Component in a Worksheet

```vba
Sub ShowComponents()
    Dim VBP As VBProject
    Set VBP = ActiveWorkbook.VBProject
    NumComponents = VBP.VBComponents.Count
    Cells.ClearContents
    For i = 1 To NumComponents
'       Name
        Cells(i, 1) = VBP.VBComponents(i).Name

'       Type
        Select Case VBP.VBComponents(i).Type
            Case 1
                Cells(i, 2) = "Module"
            Case 2
                Cells(i, 2) = "Class Module"
            Case 3
                Cells(i, 2) = "UserForm"
            Case 100
                Cells(i, 2) = "Document Module"
        End Select
'   Lines of code
        Cells(i, 3) = _
            VBP.VBComponents(i).CodeModule.CountOfLines
    Next i
End Sub
```

Figure 28-3 shows the result of running the ShowComponents procedure. In this case, the VBA project contained five components, and only one of them had a non-empty code module.

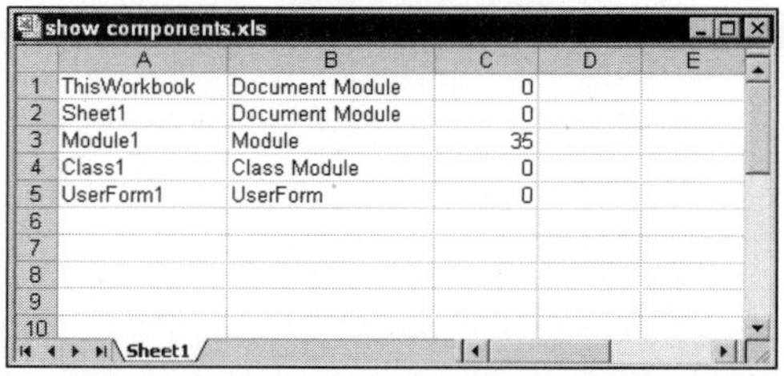

	A	B	C	D	E
1	ThisWorkbook	Document Module	0		
2	Sheet1	Document Module	0		
3	Module1	Module	35		
4	Class1	Class Module	0		
5	UserForm1	UserForm	0		
6					
7					
8					
9					
10					

Figure 28-3: The result of executing the ShowComponents procedure.

This workbook is available on the companion CD-ROM. Notice that it contains a reference to the VBA Extensibility Library.

Replacing a Module with an Updated Version

The example in this section demonstrates how to replace a VBA module with a different VBA module. Besides demonstrating three VBComponent methods (Export, Remove, and Import), the procedure also has a practical use. For example, you might distribute a workbook to a group of users and then later discover that a macro contains an error or needs to be updated. Because the users could have added data to the workbook, it's not practical to replace the entire workbook. The solution, then, is to distribute another workbook that contains a macro that replaces the VBA module with an updated version stored in a file.

This example consists of two workbooks:

* *UserBook.xls: Contains a module (Module1) that needs to be replaced

* *UpdateUserBook.xls: Contains VBA procedures to replace Module1 in UserBook.xls with a later version of Module1 stored in UpdateUserBook.xls

The BeginUpdate procedure shown in Listing 28-2 is contained in the UpdateUserBook workbook, which would be distributed to users of UserBook.xls. This procedure ensures that UserBook.xls is open. It then informs the user of what is about to happen with the message shown in Figure 28-4.

Microsoft Excel	☒
ⓘ This macro will replace Module1 in UserBook.XLS with an updated Module. Click OK to continue.	
[OK] [Cancel]	

Figure 28-4: This message box informs the user that a module will be replaced.

Listing 28-2: Preparing the User for Some Changes That Are Afoot

```
Sub BeginUpdate()
    Filename = "UserBook.xls"
```

```
'   Activate workbook
    On Error Resume Next
    Workbooks(Filename).Activate
    If Err <> 0 Then
        MsgBox Filename & " must be open!", vbCritical
        Exit Sub
    End If

    Msg = "This macro will replace Module1 in UserBook.XLS "
    Msg = Msg & "with an updated Module." & vbCrLf & vbCrLf
    Msg = Msg & "Click OK to continue."
    If MsgBox(Msg, vbInformation + vbOKCancel) = vbOK Then
        Call ReplaceModule
    Else
        MsgBox "Module not replaced!", vbCritical
    End If
End Sub
```

When the user clicks OK, the `ReplaceModule` procedure is called. This procedure, shown in Listing 28-3, replaces the existing `Module1` in `UserBook.xls` with an updated version stored in the `UpdateUserBook` workbook.

Listing 28-3: Updating the Existing Code Module with a Revised One

```
Sub ReplaceModule()
'   Export Module1 from this workbook
    Filename = ThisWorkbook.Path & "\tempmodxxx.bas"
    ThisWorkbook.VBProject.VBComponents("Module1") _
      .Export Filename

'   Replace Module1 in UserBook
    Set VBP = ActiveWorkbook.VBProject
    On Error GoTo ErrHandle
    With VBP.VBComponents
        .Remove VBP.VBComponents("Module1")
        .Import Filename
    End With

'   Delete the temporary module file
    Kill Filename
    MsgBox "The module has been replaced.", vbInformation
    Exit Sub
```

Continued

Listing 28-3 *(Continued)*

```
ErrHandle:
'   Did an error occur?
    MsgBox "ERROR. The module may not have been replaced.", _
      vbCritical
End Sub
```

The procedure in Listing 28-3 performs the following steps:

1. It exports `Module1` (the updated module) to a file. The file has an unusual name to reduce the likelihood of overwriting an existing file.

2. It removes `Module1` (the old module) from `UserBook.xls`, using the `Remove` method of the `VBComponents` collection.

3. It imports the module (saved in Step 1) to `UserBook.xls`.

4. It deletes the file saved in Step 1.

5. It reports the action to the user. General error handling is used to inform the user that an error occurred.

 This example (which uses two files) is available on the companion CD-ROM. Because the macro writes to the active directory, make sure that you copy the files to your hard drive before running the example.

Using VBA to Write VBA Code

The example in this section demonstrates how you can write VBA code that writes more VBA code. The `AddSheetAndButton` procedure does the following:

1. Inserts a new worksheet.

2. Adds a CommandButton to the worksheet.

3. Adjusts the position, size, and caption of the CommandButton.

4. Inserts an event handler procedure for the CommandButton named `CommandButton1_Click` in the sheet's code module. This procedure simply activates `Sheet1`.

Listing 28-4 provides the `AddSheetAndButton` procedure.

Listing 28-4: Generating a New Worksheet, Built-in Button, and Event Handler

```
Sub AddSheetAndButton()
    Dim NewSheet As Worksheet
    Dim NewButton As OLEObject

'   Add the sheet
    Set NewSheet = Sheets.Add

'   Add a CommandButton
    Set NewButton = NewSheet.OLEObjects.Add _
      ("Forms.CommandButton.1")
    With NewButton
        .Left = 4
        .Top = 4
        .Width = 100
        .Height = 24
        .Object.Caption = "Return to Sheet1"
    End With

'   Add the event handler code
    Code = "Sub CommandButton1_Click()" & vbCrLf
    Code = Code & "    On Error Resume Next" & vbCrLf
    Code = Code & "    Sheets(""Sheet1"").Activate" & vbCrLf
    Code = Code & "    If Err <> 0 Then" & vbCrLf
    Code = Code & "        MsgBox ""Cannot activate Sheet1.""" _
      & vbCrLf
    Code = Code & "    End If" & vbCrLf
    Code = Code & "End Sub"

    With ActiveWorkbook.VBProject. _
      VBComponents(NewSheet.Name).CodeModule
        NextLine = .CountOfLines + 1
        .InsertLines NextLine, Code
    End With
End Sub
```

Figure 28-5 shows a worksheet and CommandButton that were added by the AddSheetAndButton procedure.

The tricky part of this procedure is inserting the VBA code into the code module for the new worksheet. The code is stored in a variable named Code, with each instruction separated by a carriage return and linefeed sequence. The InsertLines method adds the code to the code module for the inserted worksheet.

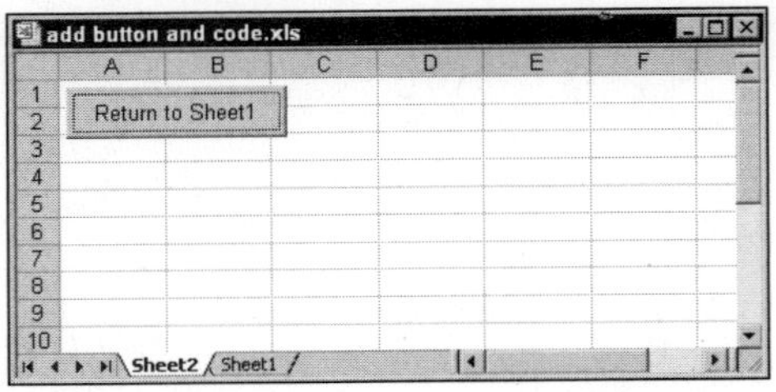

Figure 28-5: This sheet, the CommandButton, and its
event handler were added by using VBA.

The NextLine variable stores the number of existing lines in the module incremented by one. This ensures that the procedure is added to the end of the module.
If you simply insert the code beginning at line 1, it causes an error if the user's system is set up to add an Option Explicit statement to each module automatically.

Figure 28-6 shows the procedure that is created by the AddSheetAndButton procedure in its new home in the code window.

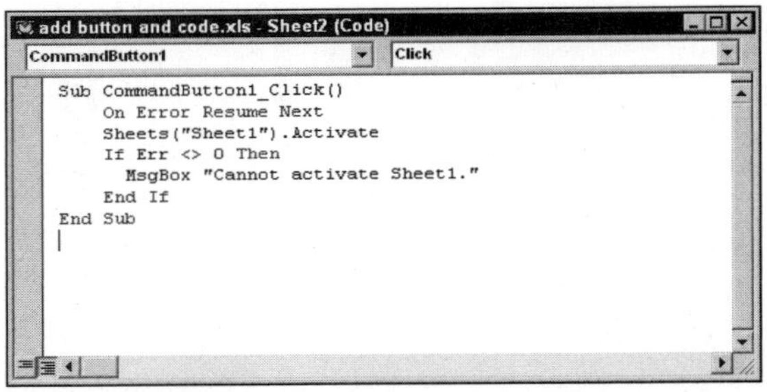

Figure 28-6: VBA generated this event handler procedure.

Adding Controls to a UserForm at Design Time

If you've spent any time developing UserForms, you probably know that it can be
quite tedious to add and adjust the controls so that they're aligned and sized con-
sistently. Even if you take full advantage of the VBE formatting commands, it can
still take a considerable amount of time to get the controls to look just right.

The UserForm shown in Figure 28-7 contains 100 CommandButtons, all of
which are identical in size and positioned precisely on the form. Furthermore, each
CommandButton has its own event handler procedure. Adding these buttons manually and creating their event handlers would take some time — lots of time. Adding
them automatically at design time by using a VBA procedure takes about three
seconds.

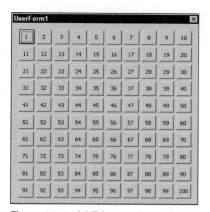

Figure 28-7: A VBA procedure added the
CommandButtons on this UserForm.

Design-time versus runtime UserForm manipulations

It's important to understand the distinction between manipulating UserForms or controls at design time and manipulating these objects at runtime. Runtime manipulations are apparent when the UserForm is shown, but the changes made are not permanent. For example, you might write code that changes the Caption property of the UserForm before the form is displayed. The new caption appears when the UserForm is shown, but when you return to the VBE, the UserForm displays its original caption. Part IV of this book contains many examples of code that perform runtime manipulation of UserForms and controls.

Design-time manipulations, on the other hand, are permanent — just as if you made the changes manually by using the tools in the VBE. Normally, you perform design-time manipulations as a way to automate some of the tedious chores in designing a UserForm. To make design-time manipulations, you access the Designer object for the UserForm.

To demonstrate the difference between design-time and runtime manipulations, I developed two simple procedures that add a CommandButton to a UserForm. One procedure adds the button at runtime; the other adds it at design time.

The following RunTimeButton procedure is very straightforward. When used in a general (non-UserForm) module, it simply adds a CommandButton, changes a few of its properties, and then displays the UserForm. The CommandButton appears on the form when the form is shown, but when you view the form in the VBE, the CommandButton is not there.

```
Sub RunTimeButton()
'    Adds a button at runtime
     Dim Butn As CommandButton
     Set Butn = UserForm1.Controls.Add("Forms.CommandButton.1")
```

```
    With Butn
        .Caption = "Added at runtime"
        .Width = 100
        .Top = 10
    End With
    UserForm1.Show
End Sub
```

Following is the `DesignTimeButton` procedure. What's different here is that this procedure uses the `Designer` object, which is contained in the `VBComponent` object. Specifically, it uses the `Add` method to add the CommandButton. Because the `Designer` object was addressed, the CommandButton is added to the UserForm just as if you did it manually in the VBE.

```
Sub DesignTimeButton()
'   Adds a button at design time
    Dim Butn As CommandButton
    Set Butn = ThisWorkbook.VBProject. _
      VBComponents("UserForm1") _
      .Designer.Controls.Add("Forms.CommandButton.1")
    With Butn
        .Caption = "Added at design time"
        .Width = 120
        .Top = 40
    End With
End Sub
```

Adding 100 CommandButtons at design time

The example in this section demonstrates how to take advantage of the `Designer` object to help you design a UserForm. In this case, the code adds 100 CommandButtons (perfectly spaced and aligned), sets the `Caption` property for each CommandButton, and also creates 100 event handler procedures (one for each CommandButton).

Listing 28-5 shows the complete code for the `Add100Buttons` procedure.

Listing 28-5: Generating an Instant 100-Button UserForm

```
Sub Add100Buttons()
    Dim UFvbc As Object 'VBComponent
    Dim CMod As Object 'CodeModule
    Dim ctl As Control
    Dim cb As CommandButton
    Dim n As Integer, c As Integer, r As Integer
    Dim code As String
```

```
    Set UFvbc = ThisWorkbook.VBProject.VBComponents("UserForm1")

' Delete all controls, if any
    For Each ctl In UFvbc.Designer.Controls
      UFvbc.Designer.Controls.Remove ctl.Name
    Next ctl

' Delete all VBA code
    UFvbc.CodeModule.DeleteLines 1, UFvbc.CodeModule.CountOfLines

' Add 100 CommandButtons
    n = 1
    For r = 1 To 10
      For c = 1 To 10
        Set cb = _
          UFvbc.Designer.Controls.Add("Forms.CommandButton.1")
        With cb
          .Width = 22
          .Height = 22
          .Left = (c * 26) - 16
          .Top = (r * 26) - 16
          .Caption = n
        End With

'        Add the event handler code
        With UFvbc.CodeModule
          code = ""
          code = code & "Private Sub CommandButton" & n & _
           "_Click" & vbCr
          code = code & "Msgbox ""This is CommandButton" & n & _
            """" & vbCr
          code = code & "End Sub"
          .InsertLines .CountOfLines + 1, code
        End With
        n = n + 1
      Next c
    Next r
End Sub
```

The Add100Buttons procedure requires a UserForm named UserForm1. You'll
need to make the UserForm a bit larger than its default size so that the buttons will
fit. The procedure starts by deleting all controls on the form using the Remove
method of the Controls collection, and then deleting all the code in the code
module by using the DeleteLines method of the CodeModule object. Next, the
CommandButtons are added and the event handler procedures are created within

two For-Next loops. These event handlers are very simple. Here's an example of such a procedure for CommandButton1:

```
Private Sub CommandButton1_Click()
  MsgBox "This is CommandButton1"
End Sub
```

If you remember to clear the form and its attached code each time before you have the Add100Buttons procedure generate the controls, it'll be easier for you to test various parameters such as button width and spacing. Just change a few values, rerun the procedure, and see how it looks. There's no need to delete the old controls manually before rerunning the procedure.

If you'd like to show the form after adding the controls at design time, you need to add the following instruction right before the End Sub statement:

```
VBA.UserForms.Add("UserForm1").Show
```

It took me quite a while to figure out how to actually display the UserForm. When the VBA interpreter generates the 100-button UserForm, it indeed exists in VBA's memory, but it isn't officially part of the project yet. So you need the Add method to formally enroll UserForm1 into the collection of UserForms. The return value of this method (yes, it has one) is a reference to the form itself, which is why the Show method can be appended to the end of the Add method. So as a rule, the UserForm must be added to the UserForms collection before it can be used.

Creating UserForms Programmatically

The final topic in this chapter demonstrates how to use VBA code to create UserForms at runtime. I present two examples: One is relatively simple and the other is quite a bit more complex.

A simple runtime UserForm example

The example in this section isn't all that useful — in fact, it's completely useless. But it does demonstrate some useful concepts. The MakeForm procedure performs several tasks:

1. It creates a temporary UserForm in the active workbook by using the Add method of the VBComponents collection.

2. It adds a CommandButton control to the UserForm by using the Designer object.

3. It adds an event handler procedure to the UserForm's code module (CommandButton1_Click). This procedure, when executed, simply displays a message box and then unloads the form.

4. It displays the UserForm.

5. It deletes the UserForm.

The net result is a UserForm that's created on-the-fly, put to use, and then deleted. This example and the one in the next section both blur the distinction between modifying forms at design time and modifying forms at runtime. The form is created by using design-time techniques, but it all happens at runtime.

 The Help system documentation for topics dealing with creating UserForms is quite poor. Consequently, I relied heavily on trial and error when I developed this procedure.

Listing 28-6 shows complete listing for the MakeForm procedure:

Listing 28-6: Generating a UserForm on-the-Fly

```
Sub MakeForm()
    Dim TempForm As Object
    Dim NewButton As Msforms.CommandButton
    Dim Line As Integer

    Application.VBE.MainWindow.Visible = False

'   Create the UserForm
    Set TempForm = ThisWorkbook.VBProject. _
      VBComponents.Add(3) 'vbext_ct_MSForm
    With TempForm
        .Properties("Caption") = "Temporary Form"
        .Properties("Width") = 200
        .Properties("Height") = 100
    End With

'   Add a CommandButton
    Set NewButton = TempForm.Designer.Controls _
      .Add("forms.CommandButton.1")
    With NewButton
        .Caption = "Click Me"
```

Continued

Listing 28-6 *(Continued)*

```
            .Left = 60
            .Top = 40
        End With

    '   Add an event-hander sub for the CommandButton
        With TempForm.CodeModule
            Line = .CountOfLines
            .InsertLines Line + 1, "Sub CommandButton1_Click()"
            .InsertLines Line + 2, "   MsgBox ""Hello!"""
            .InsertLines Line + 3, "   Unload Me"
            .InsertLines Line + 4, "End Sub"
        End With

    '   Show the form
        VBA.UserForms.Add(TempForm.Name).Show
    '
    '   Delete the form
        ThisWorkbook.VBProject.VBComponents.Remove TempForm
    End Sub
```

This procedure creates and shows the simple UserForm shown in Figure 28-8.

Figure 28-8: This UserForm and its underlying
code were generated on-the-fly.

The workbook that contains the MakeForm procedure does not need a reference to the VBA Extensibility Library because it declares TempForm as a generic Object (not specifically as a VBComponent object). Moreover, it doesn't use any built-in constants.

Notice that one of the first instructions hides the VBE window by setting its Visible property to False. This eliminates the onscreen flashing that might occur while the form and code are being generated.

A useful (but not so simple)
dynamic UserForm example

The example in this section is both instructive and useful. It consists of a function named GetOption that displays a UserForm. Within this UserForm are a number of OptionButtons, whose captions are specified as arguments to the function. The function returns a value that corresponds to the OptionButton selected by the user. Listing 28-7 shows the complete function.

Listing 28-7: A Dynamically Generated Option Button Form

```
Function GetOption(OpArray, Default, Title)
    Dim TempForm As Object
    Dim NewOptionButton As Msforms.OptionButton
    Dim NewCommandButton1 As Msforms.CommandButton
    Dim NewCommandButton2 As Msforms.CommandButton
    Dim i As Integer, TopPos As Integer
    Dim MaxWidth As Long
    Dim Code As String

'   Hide VBE window to prevent screen flashing
    Application.VBE.MainWindow.Visible = False

'   Create the UserForm
    Set TempForm = _
      ThisWorkbook.VBProject.VBComponents.Add(3)
    TempForm.Properties("Width") = 800

'   Add the OptionButtons
    TopPos = 4
    MaxWidth = 0 'Stores width of widest OptionButton
    For i = LBound(OpArray) To UBound(OpArray)
        Set NewOptionButton = TempForm.Designer.Controls. _
          Add("forms.OptionButton.1")
        With NewOptionButton
            .Width = 800
            .Caption = OpArray(i)
            .Height = 15
            .Left = 8
            .Top = TopPos
            .Tag = i
            .AutoSize = True
            If Default = i Then .Value = True
            If .Width > MaxWidth Then MaxWidth = .Width
```

Continued

Listing 28-7 *(Continued)*

```
        End With
        TopPos = TopPos + 15
    Next i

'   Add the Cancel button
    Set NewCommandButton1 = TempForm.Designer.Controls. _
        Add("forms.CommandButton.1")
    With NewCommandButton1
        .Caption = "Cancel"
        .Height = 18
        .Width = 44
        .Left = MaxWidth + 12
        .Top = 6
    End With

'   Add the OK button
    Set NewCommandButton2 = TempForm.Designer.Controls. _
        Add("forms.CommandButton.1")
    With NewCommandButton2
        .Caption = "OK"
        .Height = 18
        .Width = 44
        .Left = MaxWidth + 12
        .Top = 28
    End With

'   Add event-hander subs for the CommandButtons
    Code = ""
    Code = Code & "Sub CommandButton1_Click()" & vbCrLf
    Code = Code & "   GETOPTION_RET_VAL=False" & vbCrLf
    Code = Code & "   Unload Me" & vbCrLf
    Code = Code & "End Sub" & vbCrLf
    Code = Code & "Sub CommandButton2_Click()" & vbCrLf
    Code = Code & "   Dim ctl" & vbCrLf
    Code = Code & "   GETOPTION_RET_VAL = False" & vbCrLf
    Code = Code & "   For Each ctl In Me.Controls" & vbCrLf
    Code = Code & "      If TypeName(ctl) = ""OptionButton""" _
        & " Then" & vbCrLf
    Code = Code & "         If ctl Then GETOPTION_RET_VAL = " _
        & "ctl.Tag" & vbCrLf
    Code = Code & "      End If" & vbCrLf
    Code = Code & "   Next ctl" & vbCrLf
```

```
Code = Code & "  Unload Me" & vbCrLf
Code = Code & "End Sub"

With TempForm.CodeModule
    .InsertLines .CountOfLines + 1, Code
End With

'   Adjust the form
    With TempForm
        .Properties("Caption") = Title
        .Properties("Width") = NewCommandButton1.Left + _
          NewCommandButton1.Width + 10
        If .Properties("Width") < 160 Then
            .Properties("Width") = 160
            NewCommandButton1.Left = 106
            NewCommandButton2.Left = 106
        End If
        .Properties("Height") = TopPos + 24
    End With

'   Show the form
    VBA.UserForms.Add(TempForm.Name).Show

'   Delete the form
    ThisWorkbook.VBProject.VBComponents.Remove VBComponent:=TempForm

'   Pass the selected option back to the calling procedure
    GetOption = GETOPTION_RET_VAL
End Function
```

The GetOption function is remarkably fast, considering all that's going on behind the scenes. On my system, the form appears almost instantaneously. The UserForm is deleted after it has served its purpose.

USING THE GETOPTION FUNCTION

The GetOption function takes three arguments:

◆ OpArray: A string array that holds the items to be displayed in the form as OptionButtons.

◆ Default: An integer that specifies the default OptionButton that is selected when the UserForm is displayed. If 0, none of the OptionButtons are selected.

◆ Title: The text to display in the title bar of the UserForm.

HOW GETOPTION WORKS

The GetOption function performs the following operations:

1. Hides the VBE window to prevent any flashing that could occur when the UserForm is created or the code is added.

2. Creates a UserForm and assigns it to an object variable named TempForm.

3. Adds the OptionButton controls by using the array passed to the function via the OpArray argument. It uses the Tag property of the control to store the index number. The Tag setting of the chosen option is the value that's eventually returned by the function.

4. Adds two CommandButtons: the OK button and the Cancel button.

5. Creates an event handler procedure for each of the CommandButtons.

6. Does some final cleanup work. It adjusts the position of the CommandButtons as well as the overall size of the UserForm.

7. Displays the UserForm. When the user clicks OK, the CommandButton1_ Click procedure is executed. This procedure determines which OptionButton is selected and also assigns a number to the GETOPTION_ RET_VAL variable (a Public variable).

8. Deletes the UserForm after it's dismissed.

9. Returns the value of GETOPTION_RET_VAL as the function's result.

A significant advantage of creating the UserForm on-the-fly is that the function is self-contained in a single module and doesn't even require a reference to the VBA Extensibility Library. Therefore, you can simply export this module (which is named modOptionsForm) and then import it into any of your workbooks, thus giving you access to the GetOption function.

The following procedure demonstrates how to use the GetOption function. In this case, the UserForm presents five options (contained in the Ops array).

```
Sub TestGetOption()
    Dim Ops(1 To 5)
    Dim UserOption
    Ops(1) = "North"
    Ops(2) = "South"
    Ops(3) = "West"
    Ops(4) = "East"
    Ops(5) = "All Regions"
```

```
   UserOption = GetOption(Ops, 5, "Select a region")
   Debug.Print UserOption
   MsgBox Ops(UserOption)
End Sub
```

The UserOption variable contains the index number of the option selected by the user. If the user clicks Cancel, the UserOption variable is set to False.

Figure 28-9 shows the UserForm that this function generated.

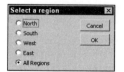

Figure 28-9: The GetOption function
generated this UserForm.

 The UserForm adjusts its size to accommodate the number of elements in the array passed to it. Theoretically, the UserOption function can accept an array of any size. Practically speaking, however, you'll want to limit the number of options to keep the UserForm at a reasonable size.

WHAT GETOPTION MAKES

Following are the event handler procedures for the two CommandButtons. This is the code generated within the GetOption function and placed in the code module for the temporary UserForm.

```
Sub CommandButton1_Click()
   GETOPTION_RET_VAL = False
   Unload Me
End Sub

Sub CommandButton2_Click()
   Dim ctl
   GETOPTION_RET_VAL = False
   For Each ctl In Me.Controls
     If TypeName(ctl) = "OptionButton" Then
       If ctl Then GETOPTION_RET_VAL = ctl.Tag
     End If
   Next ctl
   Unload Me
End Sub
```

NOTE   Because the UserForm is deleted after it's used, you can't see what it looks like in the VBE. So if you'd like to view the UserForm, convert the following instruction to a comment by typing an apostrophe (') in front of it:

```
ThisWorkbook.VBProject.VBComponents.Remove _
    VBComponent:=TempForm
```

Chapter 29

Understanding Class Modules

IN THIS CHAPTER

This chapter presents an introduction to class modules and includes several examples that might help you better understand this feature and give you ideas for using class modules in your own projects.

- ◆ An introduction to class modules

- ◆ A list of some typical uses for class modules

- ◆ Examples that demonstrate some key concepts related to class modules

FOR MANY VBA PROGRAMMERS, THE CONCEPT OF A CLASS MODULE is a mystery. This feature has been available in Visual Basic for several years and was added to Excel beginning with Excel 97.

What Is a Class Module?

A *class module* is a special type of Visual Basic for Applications (VBA) module that you can insert into a VBA project. Basically, a class module enables the programmer (you) to create a new object class. As you should know by now, programming Excel really boils down to manipulating objects. A class module allows you to create new objects, along with corresponding properties, methods, and events.

Examples in previous chapters in this book have used class modules. See Chapters 15, 18, 19, and 23.

At this point, you might be asking, "Do I really need to create new objects?" The answer is no. You don't *need* to, but you might want to after you understand some of the benefits of doing so. In many cases, a class module simply serves as a substitute for functions or procedures, but it could be a more convenient and manageable alternative. In other cases, however, you'll find that a class module is the only way to accomplish a particular task.

Following is a list of some typical uses for class modules:

◆ *To handle events associated with embedded charts.* (See Chapter 18 for an example.)

◆ *To monitor application-level events,* such as activating any worksheet. (See Chapters 19 and 23 for examples.)

◆ *To encapsulate a Windows Application Programming Interface (API) function to make it easier to use in your code.* For example, you can create a class that makes it easy to detect or set the state of the Num Lock or Caps Lock key. Or you can create a class that simplifies access to the Windows Registry.

◆ *To enable multiple objects in a UserForm to execute a single procedure.* Normally, each object has its own event handler. The example in Chapter 15 demonstrates how to use a class module so that multiple CommandButtons have a single `Click` event handler procedure.

◆ *To create reusable components that can be imported into other projects.* After you create a general-purpose class module, you can import it into other projects to reduce your development time.

Example: Creating a NumLock Class

In this section, I provide step-by-step instructions for creating a useful, albeit simple, class module. This class module creates a `NumLock` class that has one property (`Value`) and one method (`Toggle`).

Detecting or changing the state of the Num Lock key requires several Windows API functions, and the procedure varies depending on the version of Windows. In other words, it's fairly complicated. The purpose of this class module is to simplify things. All the API declarations and code are contained in a class module (not in your normal VBA modules). The benefits? Your code will be much easier to work with, and you can use this class module in your other projects.

After the class is created, your VBA code can determine the current state of the Num Lock key by using an instruction such as the following, which displays the `Value` property:

```
MsgBox NumLock.Value
```

Or, your code can change the state of the Num Lock key by changing the `Value` property. The following instruction, for example, turns on the Num Lock key:

```
NumLock.Value = True
```

In addition, your code can toggle the Num Lock key by using the `Toggle` method:

```
NumLock.Toggle
```

It's important to understand that a class module contains the code that *defines* the object, including its properties and methods. You can then create an instance of this object in your VBA general code modules and manipulate its properties and methods.

To better understand the process of creating a class module, you might want to follow the instructions in the sections that follow. Start with an empty workbook.

Inserting a class module

Activate the Visual Basic Editor (VBE) and choose Insert → Class Module. This adds an empty class module named `Class1`. If the Properties window isn't displayed, press F4 to display it. Then change the name of the class module to `NumLockClass` (see Figure 29-1).

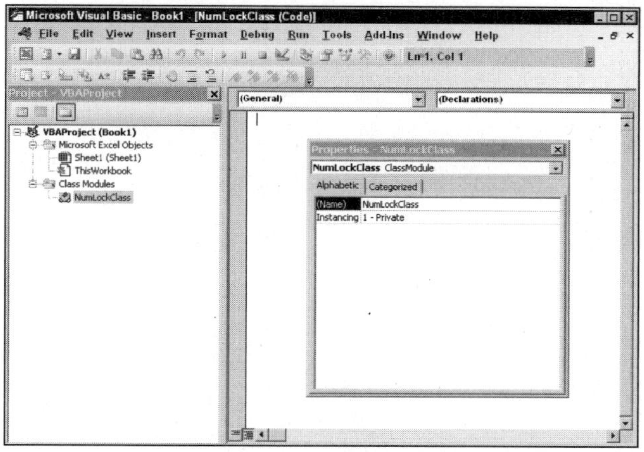

![Screenshot of Microsoft Visual Basic editor showing the Project window with NumLockClass under Class Modules and the Properties window for NumLockClass.]

Figure 29-1: An empty class module named `NumLockClass`.

Adding VBA code to the class module

In this step, you create the code for the `Value` property. To detect or change the state of the Num Lock key, the class module needs the required Windows API declarations that are used to detect and set the Num Lock key. That code follows in Listing 29-1.

The VBA code for this example was adapted from an example at the Microsoft Web site.

Listing 29-1: Detecting and Setting the Num Lock Key

```
' Type declaration
Private Type OSVERSIONINFO
    dwOSVersionInfoSize As Long
    dwMajorVersion As Long
    dwMinorVersion As Long
    dwBuildNumber As Long
    dwPlatformId As Long
    szCSDVersion As String * 128
End Type


' API declarations
Private Declare Function GetVersionEx Lib "Kernel32" _
    Alias "GetVersionExA" _
    (lpVersionInformation As OSVERSIONINFO) As Long

Private Declare Sub keybd_event Lib "user32" _
    (ByVal bVk As Byte, _
    ByVal bScan As Byte, _
    ByVal dwflags As Long, ByVal dwExtraInfo As Long)

Private Declare Function GetKeyboardState Lib "user32" _
    (pbKeyState As Byte) As Long

Private Declare Function SetKeyboardState Lib "user32" _
    (lppbKeyState As Byte) As Long

'Constant declarations
Const VK_NUMLOCK = &H90
Const VK_SCROLL = &H91
Const VK_CAPITAL = &H14
Const KEYEVENTF_EXTENDEDKEY = &H1
Const KEYEVENTF_KEYUP = &H2
Const VER_PLATFORM_WIN32_NT = 2
Const VER_PLATFORM_WIN32_WINDOWS = 1
```

Next, you need a procedure that retrieves the current state of the Num Lock key. I'll call this the `Value` property of the object. You can use any name for the property; `Value` seems like a good choice. To retrieve the state, insert the following `Property Get` procedure:

```
Property Get Value() As Boolean
'    Get the current state
    Dim keys(0 To 255) As Byte
```

```
    GetKeyboardState keys(0)
    Value = keys(VK_NUMLOCK)
End Property
```

 The details of `Property` procedures are described later in this chapter. See "Programming properties of objects."

This procedure, which uses the `GetKeyboardState` Windows API function to determine the current state of the Num Lock key, is called whenever VBA code reads the `Value` property of the object. For example, a VBA statement such as this executes the `Property Get` procedure:

```
MsgBox NumLock.Value
```

You now need a procedure that sets the Num Lock key to a particular state: either on or off. You can do this with the following `Property Let` procedure in Listing 29-2:

Listing 29-2: Setting the Num Lock Key to a Particular State

```
Property Let Value(boolVal As Boolean)
    Dim o As OSVERSIONINFO
    Dim keys(0 To 255) As Byte
    o.dwOSVersionInfoSize = Len(o)
    GetVersionEx o
    GetKeyboardState keys(0)
'   Is it already in that state?
    If boolVal = True And keys(VK_NUMLOCK) = 1 Then Exit Property
    If boolVal = False And keys(VK_NUMLOCK) = 0 Then Exit Property
'   Toggle it
    If o.dwPlatformId = VER_PLATFORM_WIN32_WINDOWS Then '(Win95)
        'Toggle numlock
       keys(VK_NUMLOCK) = IIf(keys(VK_NUMLOCK) = 0, 1, 0)
        SetKeyboardState keys(0)
    ElseIf o.dwPlatformId = VER_PLATFORM_WIN32_NT Then ' (WinNT)
        'Simulate Key Press
        keybd_event VK_NUMLOCK, &H45, KEYEVENTF_EXTENDEDKEY Or 0, 0
        'Simulate Key Release
        keybd_event VK_NUMLOCK, &H45, KEYEVENTF_EXTENDEDKEY Or _
          KEYEVENTF_KEYUP, 0
    End If
End Property
```

The `Property Let` procedure takes one argument, which is either `True` or `False`. A VBA statement such as the following sets the `Value` property of the `NumLock` object to `True` by executing the `Property Let` procedure:

```
NumLock.Value = True
```

Finally, you need a procedure to toggle the `NumLock` state, as shown in Listing 29-3:

Listing 29-3: Toggling the NumLock State

```
Sub Toggle()
'    Toggles the state
     Dim o As OSVERSIONINFO
     o.dwOSVersionInfoSize = Len(o)
     GetVersionEx o
     Dim keys(0 To 255) As Byte
     GetKeyboardState keys(0)
     If o.dwPlatformId = VER_PLATFORM_WIN32_WINDOWS Then '(Win95)
         'Toggle numlock
         keys(VK_NUMLOCK) = IIf(keys(VK_NUMLOCK) = 0, 1, 0)
         SetKeyboardState keys(0)
     ElseIf o.dwPlatformId = VER_PLATFORM_WIN32_NT Then ' (WinNT)
         'Simulate Key Press
         keybd_event VK_NUMLOCK, &H45, KEYEVENTF_EXTENDEDKEY Or 0, 0
         'Simulate Key Release
         keybd_event VK_NUMLOCK, &H45, KEYEVENTF_EXTENDEDKEY Or _
            KEYEVENTF_KEYUP, 0
     End If
End Sub
```

Notice that `Toggle` is a standard `Sub` procedure (not a `Property Let` or `Property Get` procedure). A VBA statement such as the following toggles the state of the `NumLock` object by executing the `Toggle` procedure.

Using the NumLock class

Before you can use the `NumLockClass` class module, you must create an instance of the object. The following statement, which resides in a regular VBA module (not the class module), does just that:

```
Dim NumLock As New NumLockClass
```

Notice that the object type is `NumLockClass` (that is, the name of the class module). The object variable itself can have any name, but `NumLock` certainly seems like a logical name for this.

The following procedure sets the Value property of the NumLock object to True, which results in the Num Lock key being turned on:

```
Sub NumLockOn()
    Dim NumLock As New NumLockClass
    NumLock.Value = True
End Sub
```

The next procedure displays a message box that indicates the current state of the Num Lock key (True is on; False is off):

```
Sub GetNumLockState()
    Dim NumLock As New NumLockClass
    MsgBox NumLock.Value
End Sub
```

The following procedure toggles the Num Lock key:

```
Sub ToggleNumLock()
    Dim NumLock As New NumLockClass
    NumLock.Toggle
End Sub
```

Notice that there's another way to toggle the Num Lock key without using the Toggle method:

```
Sub ToggleNumLock2()
    Dim NumLock As New NumLockClass
    NumLock.Value = Not NumLock.Value
End Sub
```

 The completed class module for this example is available on the companion CD-ROM. The workbook also contains a class module to detect and set the state of the Caps Lock key and the Scroll Lock key.

More about Class Modules

The example in the preceding section demonstrates how to create a new object class with a single property named Value and a single method named Toggle. An object class can contain any number of properties, method, and events.

Naming the object class

The name that you use for the class module in which you define the object class is also the name of the object class. By default, class modules are named `Class1`, `Class2`, and so on. Usually, you'll want to provide a more meaningful name for your object class.

Programming properties of objects

Most objects have at least one property, and you can give them as many as you need. After a property is defined, you can use it in your code, using the standard "dot" syntax:

```
object.property
```

The VBE Auto List Members option works with objects defined in a class module. This makes it easier to select properties or methods when writing code.

Properties for the object that you define can be read-only, write-only, or read/write. You define a read-only property with a single procedure – using the `Property Get` keyword. Here's an example of a `Property Get` procedure:

```
Property Get FileNameOnly() As String
    FileNameOnly = ""
    For i = Len(FullName) To 1 Step -1
        Char = Mid(FullName, i, 1)
        If Char = "\" Then
            Exit Function
        Else
            FileNameOnly = Char & FileNameOnly
        End If
    Next i
End Property
```

You might have noticed that a `Property Get` procedure works like a `Function` procedure. The code performs calculations and then returns a property value that corresponds to the procedure's name. In this example, the procedure's name is `FileNameOnly`. The property value returned is the filename part of a path string (contained in a `Public` variable named `FullName`). For example, if `FullName` is `c:\windows\myfile.txt`, the procedure returns a property value of `myfile.txt`. The `FileNameOnly` procedure is called when VBA code references the object and property.

For read/write properties, you create two procedures: a `Property Get` procedure (which reads a property value) and a `Property Let` procedure (which writes a property value). The value being assigned to the property is treated as the final argument (or the only argument) of a `Property Get` procedure.

Two example procedures follow:

```
Dim XLFile As Boolean
Property Get SaveAsExcelFile() As Boolean
    SaveAsExcelFile = XLFile
End Property

Property Let SaveAsExcelFile(boolVal As Boolean)
    XLFile = boolVal
End Property
```

 Use Property Set in place of Property Let when the property is an object data type.

A Public variable in a class module can also be used as a property of the object. In the preceding example, the Property Get and Property Let procedures could be eliminated and replaced with this module level declaration:

```
Public SaveAsExcelFile As Boolean
```

In the unlikely event that you need to create a write-only property, you create a single Property Let procedure with no corresponding Property Get procedure.

The preceding examples use a Boolean module-level variable named XLFile. The Property Get procedure simply returns the value of this variable as the property value. If the object were named FileSys, for example, the following statement would display the current value of the SaveAsExcelFile property:

```
MsgBox FileSys.SaveAsExcel=ile
```

The Property Let statement, on the other hand, accepts an argument and uses the argument to change the value of a property. For example, you could write a statement such as the following to set the SaveAsExcelFile property to True:

```
FileSys.SaveAsExcelFile = True
```

In this case, the value True is passed to the Property Let statement, thus changing the property's value.

The preceding examples use a module-level variable named XLFile that actually stores the property value. You'll need to create a variable that represents the value for each property that you define within your class module.

Normal procedure-naming rules apply to property procedures, and you'll find that VBA won't let you use some names if they are reserved words. So if you get a syntax error when creating a property procedure, try changing the name of the procedure.

Programming methods for objects

A method for an object class is programmed by using a standard Sub or Function procedure placed in the class module. An object might or might not use methods. Your code executes a method using standard notation:

```
object.method
```

Like any other VBA method, a method that you write for an object class will perform some type of action. The following procedure is an example of a method that saves a workbook in one of two file formats, depending on the value of the XLFile variable. As you can see, there is nothing special about this procedure.

```
Sub SaveFile()
    If XLFile Then
        ActiveWorkbook.SaveAs FileName:=FName, _
          FileFormat:=xlWorkbookNormal
    Else
        ActiveWorkbook.SaveAs FileName:=FName, _
          FileFormat:=xlCSV
    End If
End Sub
```

The CSVFileClass example in the next section should clarify the concepts of properties and methods for object classes defined in a class module.

Class module events

Every class module has two events: Initialize and Terminate. The Initialize event is triggered when a new instance of the object is created; the Terminate event is triggered when the object is destroyed. You might want to use the Initialize event to set default property values.

The frameworks for these event handler procedures are as follows:

```
Private Sub Class_Initialize()
'    Initialization code goes here
End Sub
```

```
Private Sub Class_Terminate()
'    Termination code goes here
End Sub
```

An object is *destroyed* (and its memory is freed) when the procedure or module in which it is declared finishes executing. You can destroy an object at any time by setting it to `Nothing`. The following statement, for example, destroys the object named `MyObject`:

```
Set MyObject = Nothing
```

Example: A CSV File Class

The example presented in this section defines an object class called `CSVFileClass`. This class has two properties and two methods:

- *Properties*

  - `ExportRange`: (Read/write) A worksheet range to be exported as a CSV file

  - `ImportRange`: (Read/write) The range into which a CSV file will be imported

- *Methods*

  - `Import`: Imports the CSV file represented by the `CSVFileName` argument into the range represented by the `ImportRange` property

  - `Export`: Exports the range represented by the `ExportRange` property to a CSV file represented by the `CSVFileName` argument

Class module-level variables for the CSVFileClass

A class module must maintain its own private variables that mirror the property settings for the class. The `CSVFileClass` class module uses two variables to keep track of the two property settings. These variables are declared at the top of the class module:

```
Private RangeToExport As Range
Private ImportToCell As Range
```

`RangeToExport` is a `Range` object that represents the range to be exported. `ImportToCell` is a `Range` object that represents the upper-left cell of the range into which the file will be imported. These variables are assigned values by the `Property Get` and `Property Let` procedures listed in the next section.

Property procedures for the CSVFileClass

The property procedures for the `CSVFileClass` class module are shown in Listing 29-4. The `Property Get` procedures return the value of a variable, and the `Property Let` procedures set the value of a variable.

Listing 29-4: Property Procedures for the CSVFileClass Module

```
Property Get ExportRange() As Range
    Set ExportRange = RangeToExport
End Property

Property Let ExportRange(rng As Range)
    Set RangeToExport = rng
End Property

Property Get ImportRange() As Range
    Set ImportRange = ImportToCell
End Property

Property Let ImportRange(rng As Range)
    Set ImportToCell = rng
End Property
```

Method procedures for the CSVFileClass

The `CSVFileClass` class module contains two procedures that represent the two methods. These are listed and discussed in the sections that follow.

THE EXPORT PROCEDURE

The `Export` procedure in Listing 29-5 is called when the `Export` method is executed. It takes one argument: the full name of the file receiving the exported range. The procedure provides some basic error handling. For example, it ensures that the `ExportRange` property has been set by checking the `RangeToExport` variable. The procedure sets up an error handler to trap other errors.

Listing 29-5: Exporting a Worksheet Range with a Class Module Method

```
Sub Export(CSVFileName)
'   Exports a range to CSV file
    If RangeToExport Is Nothing Then
        MsgBox "ExportRange not specified"
        Exit Sub
    End If

    On Error GoTo ErrHandle
    Application.ScreenUpdating = False
```

```
    Set ExpBook = Workbooks.Add(xlWorksheet)
    RangeToExport.Copy
    Application.DisplayAlerts = False

    With ExpBook
        .Sheets(1).Paste
        .SaveAs FileName:=CSVFileName, FileFormat:=xlCSV
        .Close SaveChanges:=False
    End With
    Application.CutCopyMode = False
    Application.ScreenUpdating = True
    Application.DisplayAlerts = True
    Exit Sub
ErrHandle:
    ExpBook.Close SaveChanges:=False
    Application.CutCopyMode = False
    Application.ScreenUpdating = True
    Application.DisplayAlerts = True
    MsgBox "Error " & Err & vbCrLf & vbCrLf & Error(Err), _
        vbCritical, "Export Method Error"
End Sub
```

The `Export` procedure works by copying the range specified by the `RangeToExport` variable to a new temporary workbook, saving the workbook as a CSV text file, and closing the file. Because screen updating is turned off, the user does not see this happening. If an error occurs — for example, an invalid filename is specified — the procedure jumps to the `ErrHandle` section and displays a message box that contains the error number and description.

THE IMPORT PROCEDURE

The `Import` procedure in Listing 29-6 imports a CSV file specified by the `CSV FileName` argument and copies its contents to a range specified by the `ImportToCell` variable, which maintains the `ImportRange` property. The file is then closed. Again, screen updating is turned off, so the user does not see the file being opened. Like the `Export` procedure, the `Import` procedure incorporates some basic error handling.

Listing 29-6: Importing Text File Contents into a Range with a Class Module Method

```
Sub Import(CSVFileName)
'   Imports a CSV file to a range
    If ImportToCell Is Nothing Then
        MsgBox "ImportRange not specified"
        Exit Sub
    End If
```

Continued

Listing 29-6 *(Continued)*

```
    If CSVFileName = "" Then
        MsgBox "Import FileName not specified"
        Exit Sub
    End If

    On Error GoTo ErrHandle
    Application.ScreenUpdating = False
    Application.DisplayAlerts = False
    Workbooks.Open CSVFileName
    Set CSVFile = ActiveWorkbook
    ActiveSheet.UsedRange.Copy Destination:=ImportToCell
    CSVFile.Close SaveChanges:=False
    Application.ScreenUpdating = True
    Application.DisplayAlerts = True
    Exit Sub
ErrHandle:
    CSVFile.Close SaveChanges:=False
    Application.ScreenUpdating = True
    Application.DisplayAlerts = True
    MsgBox "Error " & Err & vbCrLf & vbCrLf & Error(Err), _
        vbCritical, "Import Method Error"
End Sub
```

Using the CSVFileClass object

To create an instance of a CSVFileClass object in your code, start by declaring a variable as type CSVFileClass. Here's an example:

```
Dim CSVFile As New CSVFileClass
```

You might prefer to declare the object variable first and then create the object when needed. This requires a Dim statement and a Set statement:

```
Dim CSVFile As CSVFileClass
' other code may go here
Set CSVFile = New CSVFileClass
```

The advantage of using both a Dim and a Set statement is that the object isn't actually created until the Set statement is executed. You might want to use this technique to save memory by not creating an object if it's not needed. For example, your code might contain logic that determines whether the object is actually created. In addition, using the Set command enables you to create multiple instances of an object.

After creating an instance of the object, you can write other instructions to access the properties and methods defined in the class module.

As you can see in Figure 29-2, the VBE Auto List Members feature works just like any other object. After you type the variable name, followed by a dot, you'll see a list of properties and methods for the object.

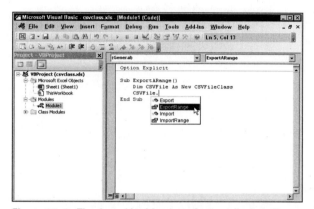

Figure 29-2: The Auto List Members feature displays the available properties and methods.

The following procedure demonstrates how to save the current range selection to a CSV file named `temp.csv`, which is stored in the same directory as the current workbook:

```
Sub ExportARange()
    Dim CSVFile As New CSVFileClass
    With CSVFile
        .ExportRange = ActiveWindow.RangeSelection
        .Export CSVFileName:=ThisWorkbook.Path & "\temp.csv"
    End With
End Sub
```

Using the `With-End With` structure isn't mandatory. For example, the procedure could be written as follows:

```
Sub ExportARange()
    Dim CSVFile As New CSVFileClass
    CSVFile.ExportRange = ActiveWindow.RangeSelection
    CSVFile.Export CSVFileName:=ThisWorkbook.Path & "\temp.csv"
End Sub
```

The following procedure demonstrates how to import a CSV file, beginning at the active cell:

```
Sub ImportAFile()
    Dim CSVFile As New CSVFileClass
    With CSVFile
    On Error Resume Next
        .ImportRange = ActiveCell
        .Import CSVFileName:=ThisWorkbook.Path & "\temp.csv"
    End With
    If Err <> 0 Then _
      MsgBox "Cannot import " & ThisWorkbook.Path & "\temp.csv"
End Sub
```

Your code can work with more than one instance of an object. The following code, for example, creates an array of three CSVFileClass objects:

```
Sub Export3Files()
    Dim CSVFile(1 To 3) As New CSVFileClass
    CSVFile(1).ExportRange = Range("A1:A20")
    CSVFile(2).ExportRange = Range("B1:B20")
    CSVFile(3).ExportRange = Range("C1:C20")

    For i = 1 To 3
        CSVFile(i).Export CSVFileName:="File" & i & ".csv"
    Next i
End Sub
```

Chapter 30

Frequently Asked Questions about Excel Programming

IN THIS CHAPTER

If you like to cruise the Internet, you're undoubtedly familiar with *FAQs* — lists of *frequently asked questions* (and their answers) about a particular topic. FAQs are prevalent in the Usenet discussion groups and are posted in an attempt to reduce the number of messages that ask the same questions over and over again. They rarely serve their intended purpose, however, because the same questions keep appearing despite the FAQs.

I've found that people tend to ask the same questions about Excel programming, so I put together a list of FAQs that cover programming topics for Excel 97 and later versions.

- ◆ Lists of frequently asked questions about Excel programming

- ◆ Where to go if your question isn't answered here

Although this FAQ list certainly won't answer all your questions, it covers many common questions and might set you straight about a thing or two. The questions (and many of the answers) came from the following sources:

- ◆ `microsoft.public.excel.*` newsgroups

- ◆ Microsoft Knowledge Base

- ◆ E-mail sent to me in an attempt to get some free consulting

I organized this list of questions by assigning each question to one of these categories:

- ◆ General Excel

- ◆ The Visual Basic Editor (VBE)

- ◆ `Sub` procedures and `Function` procedures

- ◆ Objects, properties, methods, and events

> ## What If My Question Isn't Answered Here?
>
> If this chapter doesn't provide an answer to your question, start by checking the index of this book. This book includes lots of information that doesn't qualify as a frequently asked question. If you come up empty-handed, check out the resources listed in Appendix A.

- ◆ UserForms
- ◆ Add-ins
- ◆ CommandBars

In some cases, my classifications are rather arbitrary; a question could justifiably be assigned to other categories. Moreover, questions within each category are listed in no particular order.

By the way, most of the information in this chapter is discussed in greater detail in other chapters in this book.

General Excel Questions

Why does Excel have two macro languages?

Early versions of Excel used a macro language called *XLM*. The VBA language was introduced in Excel 5 and is vastly superior in every way. XLM has been phased out, so you should use VBA for new macro development.

I need to distribute a workbook to someone who still uses Excel 4. Is there a way to record my actions to an XLM macro?

No. Beginning with Excel 97, the macro recorder can generate only VBA macro code. Generally speaking, it's not a good idea to develop a workbook with a version of Excel that's newer than the Excel version that it will be used with.

Do XLM macros written for previous versions of Excel work in Excel 97 and later versions?

In most cases, they will work perfectly.

I'm looking for a third-party utility that will convert my Excel 4 macros to VBA. Am I out of luck?

Yes, you are. No such utility exists, and it is extremely unlikely that one will be written. Such conversions must be done manually. Because all versions of Excel can execute XLM macros, however, there is really no reason to convert these macros unless you'd like to update them to incorporate new features found in later versions of Excel.

Can I call a VBA procedure from an Excel 4.0 XLM macro?

Yes, you can do so by using XLM's RUN function. For example, the following macro runs the `Test` procedure contained in `Module1` in workbook `Book1.xls`:

```
=RUN(Book1.xls!Module1.Test)
```

Can I automatically convert Lotus 1-2-3 or Quattro Pro macros to VBA macros?

No. You must rewrite the macros for Excel.

Where can I find examples of VBA code?

The Internet has thousands of VBA examples. A good starting point is my Web site:

```
www.j-walk.com/ss/
```

Or, do a search at

```
www.google.com
```

Is there a utility that will convert my Excel application into a standalone EXE file?

No.

How can I add a drop-down list to a cell so that the user can choose a value from the list?

Type the list of valid entries in a single column. You can hide this column from the user if you wish. Select the cell or cells that will display the list of entries, choose Data → Validation, and then select the Settings tab. From the Allow drop-down list, select List. In the Source box, enter a range address or a reference to the items in your sheet. Make sure that the In-Cell Dropdown check box is selected. If the list is short, you can simply type the items, each separated by a comma. This technique does not require any macros.

Can I use this drop-down list method if my list is stored on a different worksheet in the workbook?

Yes. You need to create a name for the list (for example, `ListEntries`). Then, in the Data Validation dialog box, enter **=ListEntries** in the Source box. Make sure that you include the initial equal sign; otherwise, it won't work.

I use Application.Calculation to set the calculation mode to manual. However, this seems to affect all workbooks and not just the active workbook.

The `Calculation` property is a member of the `Application` object. Therefore, the calculation mode affects all workbooks. You cannot set the calculation mode for only one workbook. Excel 2000 and later provides a new `Worksheet` object property: `EnableCalculation`. When this property is `False`, the worksheet will not be calculated, even if the user requests a calculation. Setting the property to `True` will cause the sheet to be calculated.

How can I increase the number of columns in a worksheet?

You can't. This number is fixed and cannot be changed. Microsoft continues to ignore what must amount to thousands of requests for more worksheet columns.

How can I increase the number of rows in a worksheet?

See the answer to the previous question.

Can I change the color of the sheet tabs?

If you use Excel 2002 or later, right-click the sheet tab and select Tab Color. Previous versions of Excel do not allow you to change the tab color.

Can I change the font of the sheet tabs?

Yes, but you must go outside of Excel to do so. If you use Windows XP, access the Windows Control Panel and select Display. In the Display Properties dialog box, click the Appearance tab, and then click the Advanced button. In the Advanced Appearance dialog box, access the Item list and then select Scrollbar. Use the spinner to increase or decrease the size. This setting will affect other programs. The procedure varies slightly with other versions of Windows.

Can I change the default font and color of cell comments?

Yes. See the answer to the previous question – but select ToolTip in the Item list. Use the controls to change the settings. This setting will affect other programs.

Can I play sounds in Excel?

Yes, you can play WAV and MIDI files, but it requires Windows Application Programming Interface (API) functions (see Chapter 11). If you're using Excel 2002 or later, you can take advantage of the new Speech object. The following statement, when executed, greets the user by name:

```
Application.Speech.Speak ("Hello" & Application.UserName)
```

When I open a workbook, Excel asks whether I want to update the links. I've searched all my formulas, and I cannot find any links in this workbook. Is this a bug?

Probably not. If you use Excel 2002 or later, try using the Edit → Links → Break Link command. Links can occur in places other than formulas. If you have a chart in your workbook, click each data series in the chart and examine the SERIES formula in the formula bar. If the formula refers to another workbook, you've identified the link. To eliminate it, move the chart's data into the current workbook and re-create your chart.

If your workbook contains any Excel 5/95 dialog sheets, select each object in each dialog box and examine the formula bar. If any object contains a reference to another workbook, edit or delete that reference.

Choose Insert → Name → Define. Scroll down the list in the Define Name dialog box and examine the Refers To box. Delete names that refer to another workbook or that contain an erroneous reference (such as #REF!). This is the most common cause of "phantom links."

Excel crashes every time I start it.

When Excel is started, it opens an *.xlb file, which contains your menu and toolbar customizations. If this file is damaged, it might cause Excel to crash when it is started. Also, this file might (for some reason) be very large. In such a case, this could also cause Excel to crash. Typically, your *.xlb file should be 500K or smaller.

If Excel crashes when it is started, try deleting your *.xlb file. To do so, close Excel. Then search your hard drive for *.xlb. (The filename and location will vary.) Create a backup copy of this file, delete the file, and then try restarting Excel. Hopefully, Excel will now start up normally.

Deleting your *.xlb file will also delete any toolbar or menu customizations.

How can I print the workbook's full path and filename in a page header?

If you use Excel 2002 or later, you can take advantage of a new feature in the Page Setup dialog box. When this dialog is displayed, click the Header/Footer tab and click Custom Header. You'll find a new icon that inserts the code to print the full path and filename of the workbook. Note, however, that if the workbook has not been saved, the path name might be incorrect. (It uses the default workbook path.)

For older versions of Excel, you need to use a VBA macro and take advantage of the WorkbookBeforePrint event. For example, place the following procedure in the code module for the ThisWorkbook object to print the workbook's full path and filename in the left header of each sheet:

```
Private Sub Workbook_BeforePrint(Cancel As Boolean)
    For Each sht In ThisWorkbook.Sheets
        sht.PageSetup.LeftHeader = ThisWorkbook.FullName
    Next sht
End Sub
```

The Visual Basic Editor

In Excel 95, my VBA modules were located in my workbook. I can't see them when I open the file with Excel 97 or later.

The modules are still there, but you view and edit them in the Visual Basic Editor. Press Alt+F11 to toggle between the VBE and Excel.

Can I use the VBA macro recorder to record all my macros?

No. Recording is useful for very simple macros only. Macros that use variables, looping, or any other type of program flow changes cannot be recorded. You can, however, often take advantage of the macro recorder to write some parts of your code or to discover the relevant properties or methods.

Excel 95 had a "record at mark" feature that enabled you to record a macro beginning at a particular location within an existing macro. Is that feature still available?

No, it was removed beginning with Excel 97. To add new, recorded code to an existing macro, you need to record it and then cut and paste the code to your existing macro.

I have some macros that are general in nature. I would like to have these available all the time. What's the best way to do this?

Consider storing those general-purpose macros in your Personal Macro Workbook. This is a (normally) hidden workbook that is loaded automatically by Excel. When you record a macro, you have the option of recording it to your Personal Macro Workbook. The file, `Personal.xls`, is stored in your `\XLStart` directory.

I can't find my Personal Macro Workbook. Where is it?

The `Personal.xls` file doesn't exist until you record a macro to it.

I locked my VBA project with a password, and I forget what it was. Is there any way to unlock it?

Several third-party password-cracking products exist. Use a Web search engine, and search for *Excel password*. The existence of these products should tell you that Excel passwords are not very secure.

How can I write a macro to change the password of my project?

You can't. The protection elements of a VBA project are not exposed in the object model. Most likely, this was done to make it more difficult for password-cracking software.

When I insert a new module, it always starts with an Option Explicit line. What does this mean?

If `Option Explicit` is included at the top of a module, it means that you must declare every variable before you use it (which is a good idea). If you don't want this line to appear in new modules, activate the VBE, choose the Tools → Options command, click the Editor tab, and clear the Require Variable Declaration check box. Then you can either declare your variables or let VBA handle the data typing automatically.

Why does my VBA code appear in different colors? Can I change these colors?

VBA uses color to differentiate various types of text: comments, keywords, identifiers, statements with a syntax error, and so on. You can adjust these colors and the font used by choosing the Tools → Options command (Editor Format tab) in the VBE.

I want to delete a VBA module by using VBA code. Can I do this?

Yes. The following code deletes Module1 from the active workbook:

```
With ActiveWorkbook.VBProject
    .VBComponents.Remove .VBComponents("Module1")
End With
```

This might not work with Excel 2002 and later. See the next question.

I wrote a macro in Excel 2000 that adds VBA code to the VB project. When I run it in Excel 2003, I get an error message. What's wrong?

Excel 2002 introduced a new setting: Trust Access to Visual Basic Project. By default, this setting is turned off. To change it, choose Tools → Macro → Security and click the Trusted Sources tab in the Security dialog box.

How can I write a macro to change the user's macro security setting? I want to avoid the "this workbook contains macros" message when my application is opened.

The ability to change the security level using VBA would pretty much render the entire macro security system worthless. Think about it.

When I open a workbook, I get the standard macro warning message. However, I deleted all the macros in this workbook! Is there a virus?

Probably not. In addition to deleting your macros, make sure that you also delete the VBA module in which they were stored.

I don't understand how the UserInterfaceOnly option works when protecting a worksheet.

When protecting a worksheet, you can use a statement such as

```
ActiveSheet.Protect UserInterfaceOnly:=True
```

This causes the sheet to be protected, but your macros can still make changes to the sheet. It's important to understand that this setting is not saved with the workbook. When the workbook is reopened, you'll need to re-execute the statement in order to reapply the UserInterfaceOnly protection.

How can I tell whether a workbook has a macro virus?

In the VBE, activate the project that corresponds to the workbook. Examine all the code modules (including the ThisWorkbook code module) and look for VBA code that is not familiar to you. Usually, virus code will not be formatted well and will contain lots of unusual variable names. Another option is to use a commercial virus-scanning program.

I'm having trouble with the concatenation operator (&) in VBA. When I try to concatenate two strings, I get an error message.

VBA is probably interpreting the ampersand as a type-declaration character. Make sure that you insert a space before and after the concatenation operator.

I can't seem to get the VBA line continuation character (underscore) to work.

The line continuation sequence is actually two characters: a space followed by an underscore.

After deleting a major amount of VBA code, I've noticed that the XLS file size is not reduced accordingly. Why is this?

Excel doesn't always do a good job of cleaning up after itself. This sometimes causes some subtle problems with variables that you no longer use. One way to fix it is to export your module to a file, delete the module, and then import it again. Or, try saving your workbook as a HyperText Markup Language (HTML) file. Then open the HTML file and save it back to an XLS file. In many cases, this will reduce the size of your file.

I distributed an XLS application to many users. On some machines, my VBA error-handling procedures don't work. Why not?

The error-handling procedures won't work if the user has the Break on All Errors option set. This option is available in the Options dialog box (General tab) in the VBE. Unfortunately, you can't change this setting with VBA.

Procedures

What's the difference between a VBA procedure and a macro?

Nothing, really. The term *macro* is a carry-over from the old days of spreadsheets. These terms are now used interchangeably.

What's a procedure?

A *procedure* is a grouping of VBA instructions that can be called by name. If these instructions are to give an explicit result (such as a value) back to the instruction that called them, they most likely belong to a Function procedure. Otherwise, they probably belong to a Sub procedure.

What is a variant data type?

Variables that aren't specifically declared are assigned the variant type by default, and VBA automatically converts the data to the proper type when it's used. This is particularly useful for retrieving values from a worksheet cell when you don't know in advance what the cell contains. Generally, it's a good idea to specifically declare your variables with the Dim, Public, or Private statement because using variants is a bit slower and is not the most efficient use of memory.

What's the difference between a variant array and an array of variants?

A *variant* is a unit of memory with a special data type that can contain any kind of data: a single value or an array of values (that is, a *variant array*). The following code creates a variant that contains an array:

```
Dim X As Variant
X = Array(30, 40, 50)
```

A normal array can contain items of a specified data type, including nontyped variants. The following statement creates an array that consists of 12 variants:

```
Dim X (0 To 2) As Variant
```

Although a variant containing an array is conceptually different from an array whose elements are of type variant, the array elements are accessed in the same way.

What's a type-definition character?

VBA lets you append a character to a variable's name to indicate the data type. For example, you can declare the MyVar variable as an integer by tacking % onto the name, as follows:

```
Dim MyVar%
```

Here's a list of the type-declaration characters supported by VBA:

- ◆ Integer: %
- ◆ Long: &
- ◆ Single: !
- ◆ Double: #
- ◆ Currency: @
- ◆ String: $

I wrote a VBA function that works perfectly when I call it from another procedure. But it doesn't work when I use it in a worksheet formula. What's wrong?

VBA functions called from a worksheet formula have some limitations. In general, they must be strictly "passive." That is, they can't change the active cell, apply formatting, open workbooks, or change the active sheet. If the function attempts to do any of these things, the formula will return an error.

Functions can only perform calculations and return a value. An exception to this rule is the VBA MsgBox function. A custom function can display a message box whenever it is recalculated. This is very handy for debugging a custom function.

I would like to create a procedure that automatically changes the formatting of a cell based on the data that I enter. For example, if I enter a value greater than 0, the cell's background color should be red. Is this possible?

It's certainly possible, and you don't need any programming. Use Excel's Conditional Formatting feature, accessed with the Format → Conditional Formatting command.

The Conditional Formatting feature is useful, but I'd like to perform other types of operations when data is entered into a cell.

In that case, you can take advantage of the `Change` event for a worksheet object. Whenever a cell is changed, the `Change` event is triggered. If the code module for the `Sheet` object contains a procedure named `Worksheet_Change`, this procedure will be executed automatically.

What other types of events can be monitored?

Lots! Search the Help system for *events* to get a complete listing.

I tried entering an event procedure (Sub Workbook_ Open), but the procedure isn't executed when the workbook is opened. What's wrong?

You probably put the procedure in the wrong place. Workbook event procedures must be in the code module for the `ThisWorkbook` object. Worksheet event procedures must be in the code module for the appropriate `Sheet` object, as shown in the VBE Project window.

I can write an event procedure for a particular workbook, but can I write an event procedure that will work for any workbook that's open?

Yes, but you need to use a class module. Details are in Chapter 19.

I'm very familiar with creating formulas in Excel. Does VBA use the same mathematical and logical operators?

Yes. And it includes some additional operators that aren't valid in worksheet formulas. These additional VBA operators are listed in the following table:

Operator	Function
\	Division with an integer result
Eqv	Returns True if both expressions are true or both are false
Imp	Logical implication on two expressions
Is	Compares two object variables
Like	Compares two strings by using wildcard characters
Xor	Returns True if only one expression is true

How can I execute a procedure that's in a different workbook?

Use the Run method of the Application object. The following instruction executes a procedure named Macro1 located in the Personal.xls workbook:

```
Run "Personal.xls!Macro1"
```

Another option is to add a reference to the workbook. Do this by choosing the Tools → References command in the VBE. After you've added a reference, you can then run the procedures in the referenced workbook.

I've used VBA to create several custom functions. I like to use these functions in my worksheet formulas, but I find it inconvenient to precede the function name with the workbook name. Is there any way around this?

Yes. Convert the workbook that holds the function definitions to an XLA add-in. When the add-in is open, you can use the functions in any other worksheet without referencing the function's filename.

In addition, if you set up a reference to the workbook that contains the custom functions, you can use the function without preceding it with the workbook name. To create a reference, choose the Tools → References command in the VBE.

I would like a particular workbook to be loaded every time that I start Excel. I would also like a macro in this workbook to execute automatically. Am I asking too much?

Not at all. To open the workbook automatically, just store it in your \XLStart directory. To have the macro execute automatically, create a Workbook_Open macro in the code module for the workbook's ThisWorkbook object.

I have a workbook that uses a Workbook_Open procedure. Is there a way to prevent this from executing when I open the workbook?

Yes. Hold down Shift when you issue the File→Open command. To prevent a Workbook_BeforeClose procedure from executing, press Shift when you close the workbook. Using the Shift key will not prevent these procedures from executing when you're opening an add-in.

Can a VBA procedure access a cell's value in a workbook that is not open?

VBA can't do it, but Excel's old XLM language can. Fortunately, you can execute XLM from VBA. Here's a simple example that retrieves the value from cell A1 on Sheet1 in a workbook named myfile.xls in the c:\files directory:

```
MsgBox ExecuteExcel4Macro("'c:\files\[myfile.xls]Sheet1'!R1C1")
```

Note that the cell address must be in RC notation.

How can I prevent the "save file" prompt from being displayed when I close a workbook from VBA?

You can use this statement:

```
ActiveWorkbook.Close SaveChanges:=False
```

Or, you can set the workbook's Saved property to True by using a statement like this:

```
ActiveWorkbook.Saved = True
```

This statement, when executed, does not actually save the file, so any unsaved changes will be lost when the workbook is closed.

A more general solution to avoid Excel prompts is to insert the following instruction:

```
Application.DisplayAlerts = False
```

Normally, you'll want to set the DisplayAlerts property back to True after the file is closed.

How can I set things up so that my macro runs once every hour?

You need to use the OnTime method of the Application object. This enables you to specify a procedure to execute at a particular time of day. When the procedure ends, use the OnTime method again to schedule another event in one hour.

How do I prevent a macro from showing in the macro list?

Declare the procedure by using the Private keyword:

```
Private Sub MyMacro()
```

Or you can add a dummy optional argument, declared as a specific data type:

```
Sub MyMacro (Optional FakeArg as Integer)
```

Can I save a chart as a GIF file?

Yes. The following code saves the first embedded chart on Sheet1 as a GIF file named Mychart.gif:

```
Set CurrentChart = Sheets("Sheet1").ChartObjects(1).Chart
Fname = ThisWorkbook.Path & "\Mychart.gif"
CurrentChart.Export Filename:=Fname, FilterName:="GIF"
```

Are variables in a VBA procedure available to other VBA procedures? What if the procedure is in a different module? Or in a different workbook?

You're talking about a variable's *scope*. There are three levels of scope: local, module, and public. Local variables have the narrowest scope and are declared within a procedure. A local variable is visible only to the procedure in which it was declared. Module-level variables are declared at the top of a module, prior to the first procedure. Module-level variables are visible to all procedures in the module.

Public variables have the broadest scope, and they are declared by using the `Public` keyword.

Functions

I created a custom worksheet function. When I access this function with the Insert Function dialog, it reads "No help available." How can I get the Insert Function dialog box to display a description of my function?

To add a description for your custom function, activate the workbook that contains the Function procedure. Then choose Tools → Macro → Macros to display the Macro dialog box. Your function won't be listed, so you must type it into the Macro name box. After typing the function's name, click Options to display the Macro Options dialog box. Enter the descriptive text in the Description box.

Can I also display help for the arguments for my custom function in the Insert Function dialog box?

Unfortunately, no.

My custom worksheet function appears in the User Defined category in the Insert Function dialog box. How can I make my function appear in a different function category?

You need to use VBA to do this. The following instruction assigns the function named `MyFunc` to `Category` 1 (Financial):

```
Application.MacroOptions Macro:="MyFunc", Category:=1
```

The following table lists the valid function category numbers.

Number	Category
0	No category (appears only in All)
1	Financial

Number	Category
2	Date & Time
3	Math & Trig
4	Statistical
5	Lookup & Reference
6	Database
7	Text
8	Logical
9	Information
10	Commands (normally hidden)
11	Customizing (normally hidden)
12	Macro Control (normally hidden)
13	DDE/External (normally hidden)
14	User Defined (default)
15	Engineering (valid only if the Analysis ToolPak add-in is installed)

How can I create a new function category?

You can create a new function category by using an XLM macro. However, this method is not reliable and is not recommended.

I have a custom function that will be used in a worksheet formula. If the user enters arguments that are not appropriate, how can I make the function return a true error value (#VALUE!)?

If your function is named MyFunction, you can use the following instruction to return an error value to the cell that contains the function:

```
MyFunction =  CVErr(xlErrValue)
```

In this example, xlErrValue is a predefined constant. Constants for the other error values are listed in the Help system.

How can I force a recalculation of formulas that use my custom worksheet function?

Press Ctrl+Alt+F9.

Can I use Excel's built-in worksheet functions in my VBA code?

In most cases, yes. Excel's worksheet functions are accessed via the `WorksheetFunction` method of the `Application` object. For example, you could access the SUM worksheet functions with a statement such as the following:

```
Ans = Application.WorksheetFunction.Sum(Range("A1:A3"))
```

This example assigns the sum of the values in A1:A3 (on the active sheet) to the `Ans` variable.

Generally, if VBA includes an equivalent function, you cannot use Excel's worksheet version. For example, because VBA has a function to compute square roots (`Sqr`), you cannot use the SQRT worksheet function in your VBA code.

Excel 95 doesn't support the WorksheetFunction method. Does that mean I can't make my Excel 2002 application compatible with Excel 95?

No. Actually, using the `WorksheetFunction` method is superfluous. The following statements have exactly the same result:

```
ans = Application.WorksheetFunction.Sum(Range("A1:A3"))
ans = Application.Sum(Range("A1:A3"))
```

Can I use Analysis ToolPak functions in my VBA code?

Yes, but it takes a few extra steps. In Excel, choose Tools → Add-Ins, and place a check mark next to the Analysis ToolPak - VBA add-in. Then activate your VB project and choose Tools → References. Place a check mark next to `atpvbaen.xls` to create a reference. Then you can use any of the Analysis ToolPak functions in your code. For example, the following statement uses the Analysis ToolPak CONVERT function to convert 5,000 meters to miles:

```
MsgBox CONVERT(5000, "m", "mi")
```

Is there any way to force a line break in the text of a message box?

Use a carriage return or a linefeed character to force a new line. The following statement displays the message box text on two lines. vbCrLf is a built-in constant that represents a carriage return.

```
MsgBox "Hello" & vbCr & Application.UserName
```

Objects, Properties, Methods, and Events

I don't understand the concept of objects. Is there a listing of the Excel objects I can use?

Yes. The Help system has the information in a graphical format.

I'm overwhelmed with all the properties and methods available. How can I find out which methods and properties are available for a particular object?

There are several ways. You can use the Object Browser available in the VBE. Press F2 to access the Object Browser and then choose Excel from the Libraries/ Workbooks drop-down list. The Classes list (on the left) shows all the Excel objects. When you select an object, its corresponding properties and methods appear in the Member of list on the right.

You can also get a list of properties and methods as you type. For example, enter the following:

```
Range("A1").
```

When you type the dot, you'll see a list of all properties and methods for a Range object. If this doesn't work, choose Tools → Options, click the Editor tab, and place a check mark next to Auto List Members.

And, of course, the Help system for VBA is very extensive; it lists the properties and methods available for most objects of importance. The easiest way to access these lists is to type the object name into the Immediate window at the bottom of the VBE and move the cursor anywhere within the object name. Press F1, and you'll get the help topic appropriate for the object.

What's the story with collections? Is a collection an object? What are collections?

A *collection,* which is an object that contains a group of related objects, is designated by a plural noun. For example, the Worksheets collection is an object that contains all the Worksheet objects in a workbook. You can think of this as an array: Worksheets(1) refers to the first Worksheet object in the Workbook. Rather than use index numbers, you can also use the actual worksheet name, such as Worksheets("Sheet1"). The concept of a collection makes it easy to work with all related objects at once and to loop through all objects in a collection by using the For Each-Next construct.

When I refer to a worksheet in my VBA code, I get a "subscript out of range" error. I'm not using any subscripts. What gives?

This error occurs when you attempt to access an element in a collection that doesn't exist. For example, the following instruction generates the error if the active workbook does not contain a worksheet named MySheet:

```
Set X = ActiveWorkbook.Worksheets("MySheet")
```

How can I prevent the user from scrolling around the worksheet?

You can either hide the unused rows and columns or use a VBA instruction to set the scroll area for the worksheet. The following instruction, for example, sets the scroll area on Sheet1 so that the user cannot activate any cells outside of B2:D50:

```
Worksheets("Sheet1").ScrollArea = "B2:D50"
```

To set scrolling back to normal, use a statement like this:

```
Worksheets("Sheet1").ScrollArea = ""
```

Keep in mind that the ScrollArea setting is not saved with the workbook. Therefore, you need to execute the ScrollArea assignment instruction whenever the workbook is opened. This instruction can go in the Workbook_Open event handler procedure.

What's the difference between using Select and Application.Goto?

The Select method of the Range object selects a range on the *active* worksheet only. Use Application.Goto to select a range on any worksheet in a workbook.

`Application.Goto` might or might not make another sheet the active sheet. The `Goto` method also lets you scroll the sheet so that the range is in the upper-left corner.

What's the difference between activating a range and selecting a range?

In some cases, the `Activate` method and the `Select` method have exactly the same effect. But in other cases, they produce quite different results. Assume that range A1:C3 is selected. The following statement activates cell C3. The original range remains selected, but C3 becomes the active cell — that is, the cell that contains the cell pointer.

```
Range("C3").Activate
```

Again, assuming that range A1:C3 is selected, the following statement selects a single cell, which also becomes the active cell.

```
Range("C3").Select
```

Is there a quick way to delete all values from a worksheet yet keep the formulas intact?

Yes. The following code works on the active sheet and deletes all nonformula cells. (The cell formatting is not affected.)

```
On Error Resume Next
Cells.SpecialCells(xlCellTypeConstants, 23).ClearContents
```

Using `On Error Resume Next` prevents the error message that occurs if no cells qualify.

I know how to write a VBA instruction to select a range by using a cell address, but how can I write one to select a range if I know only its row and column number?

Use the `Cells` method. The following instruction, for example, selects the cell in the 5th row and the 12th column (that is, cell L5):

```
Cells(5, 12).Select
```

Is there a VBA command to quit Excel? When I try to record the File → Exit command, Excel closes down before I can see what code it generates.

Use the following instruction to end Excel:

```
Application.Quit
```

How can I turn off the screen updating while a macro is running?

The following instruction turns off screen updating and speeds up macros that modify the display:

```
Application.ScreenUpdating = False
```

What's the easiest way to create a range name in VBA?

If you turn on the macro recorder while you name a range, you'll get code something like this:

```
Range("D14:G20").Select
ActiveWorkbook.Names.Add Name:="InputArea", _
    RefersToR1C1:="=Sheet1!R14C4:R20C7"
```

A much simpler method is to use a statement like this:

```
Sheets("Sheet1").Range("D14:G20").Name = "InputArea"
```

How can I determine whether a particular cell or range has a name?

You need to check the Name property of the Name object contained in the Range object. The following function accepts a range as an argument and returns the name of the range (if it has one). If the range has no name, the function returns False.

```
Function RangeName(rng) As Variant
    On Error Resume Next
    RangeName = rng.Name.Name
    If Err <> 0 Then RangeName = False
End Function
```

Can I disable the Setup and Margins buttons that are displayed in Excel's Print Preview window?

Yes, use a statement like this:

```
ActiveSheet.PrintPreview EnableChanges:=False
```

The `EnableChanges` argument for the `PrintPreview` method is not documented in the Help system, but this argument does appear in the Object Browser.

Can I display messages in the status bar while a macro is running? I have a lengthy macro, and it would be nice to display its progress in the status bar.

Yes. Assign the text to the `StatusBar` property of the `Application` object. Here's an example:

```
Application.StatusBar = "Now processing File " & FileNum
```

When your routine finishes, return the status bar back to normal with the following instruction:

```
Application.StatusBar = False
```

I recorded a VBA macro that copies a range and pastes it to another area. The macro uses the Select method. Is there a more efficient way to copy and paste?

Yes. Although the macro recorder generally selects cells before doing anything with them, selecting is not necessary and can actually slow down your macro. Recording a very simple copy-and-paste operation generates four lines of VBA code, two of which use the `Select` method. Here's an example:

```
Range("A1").Select
Selection.Copy
Range("B1").Select
ActiveSheet.Paste
```

These four lines can be replaced with a single instruction, such as the following:

```
Range("A1").Copy Range("B1")
```

Notice that this instruction does not use the `Select` method.

I have not been able to find a method to sort a VBA array. Does this mean that I have to copy the values to a worksheet and then use the Range.Sort method?

There is no built-in way to sort an array in VBA. Copying the array to a worksheet is one method, but you'll probably be better off if you write your own sorting procedure. Many sorting algorithms are available, and some are quite easy to code in VBA. This book contains VBA code for several sorting techniques.

My macro works with the selected cells, but it fails if something else (like a chart) is selected. How can I make sure that a range is selected?

You can use VBA's `TypeName` function to check the `Selection` object. Here's an example:

```
If TypeName(Selection) <> "Range" Then
    MsgBox "Select a range!"
    Exit Sub
End If
```

Another approach is to use the `RangeSelection` property, which returns a `Range` object that represents the selected cells on the worksheet in the specified window, even if a graphic object is active or selected. This property applies to a `Window` object — not a `Workbook` object. The following instruction, for example, displays the address of the selected range:

```
MsgBox ActiveWindow.RangeSelection.Address
```

How can I determine whether a chart is activated?

Use a statement like this:

```
If ActiveChart Is Nothing Then MsgBox "Select a chart"
```

The message box will be displayed only if a chart is not activated. (This includes embedded charts and a chart on a chart sheet.)

My VBA macro needs to count the number of rows selected by the user. Using Selection.Rows.Count doesn't work when nonadjacent rows are selected. Is this a bug?

Actually, this is the way it's supposed to work. The Count method returns the number of elements in only the *first* area of the selection (a noncontiguous selection has multiple areas). To get an accurate row count, your VBA code must first determine the number of areas in the selection and then count the number of rows in each area. Use Selection.Areas.Count to count the number of areas. Here's an example that stores the total number of selected rows in the NumRows variable:

```
NumRows = 0
For Each areaCounter In Selection.Areas
    NumRows = NumRows + areaCounter.Rows.Count
Next areaCounter
```

By the way, this process is also relevant to counting columns and cells.

I use Excel to create invoices. Can I generate a unique invoice number?

One way to do this is to use the Windows Registry. The following code demonstrates:

```
Counter = GetSetting("XYZ Corp", "InvoiceNum", "Count", 0)
Counter = Counter + 1
SaveSetting "XYZ Corp", "InvoiceNum", "Count", Counter
```

When these statements are executed, the current value is retrieved from the Registry, incremented by one, and assigned to the Counter variable. Then this updated value is stored back to the Registry. You can use the value of Counter as your unique invoice number.

Is there a workbook property that forces an Excel workbook to always remain visible so it won't be hidden by another application's window?

No.

How can I stop Excel from displaying messages while my macro is running? For example, I'd like to eliminate the message that appears when my macro deletes a worksheet.

The following statement turns off most of Excel's warning messages:

```
Application.DisplayAlerts = False
```

Then use the following statement after the operation is completed.

```
Application.DisplayAlerts = True
```

Is there a VBA instruction to select the last entry in a column or row? Normally, I can use Ctrl+Shift+↓ or Ctrl+Shift+→ to do this, but how can I do it with a macro?

The VBA equivalent for Ctrl+Shift+↓ is the following:

```
Selection.End(xlDown).Select
```

The constants used for the other directions are xlToLeft, xlToRight, and xlUp.

How can I determine the last nonempty cell in a particular column?

The following instruction displays the address of the last nonempty cell in column A:

```
MsgBox ActiveSheet.Range("A65536").End(xlUp).Address
```

The following instruction is a bit more forward-looking. It will work even if Excel worksheets ever have more than 65,536 rows:

```
MsgBox ActiveSheet.Cells(Rows.Count, 1).End(xlUp).Address
```

But that instruction won't work if cell A65536 is not empty!

To handle that unlikely occurrence, use this code:

```
With ActiveSheet.Cells(Rows.Count, 1)
    If IsEmpty(.Value) Then
        MsgBox .End(xlUp).Address
    Else
        MsgBox .Address
    End If
End With
```

VBA references can become very lengthy, especially when you need to fully qualify an object by referencing its sheet and workbook. Can I reduce the length of these references?

Yes. Use the Set statement to create an object variable. Here's an example:

```
Dim MyRange as Range
Set MyRange = ThisWorkbook.Worksheets("Sheet1").Range("A1")
```

After the Set statement is executed, you can refer to this single-cell Range object simply as MyRange. For example, you can assign a value to the cell with the following:

```
MyRange.Value = 10
```

Besides making it easier to refer to objects, using object variables can also help your code execute more quickly.

Can I declare an array if I don't know how many elements it will have?

Yes. You can declare a dynamic array with the Dim statement, using empty parentheses, and then allocate storage for that array later with the ReDim statement when you know how many elements the array should have. Use ReDim Preserve if you don't want to lose the current array contents when reallocating it.

Can I let the user undo my macro?

Yes, but it's not something that can be done automatically. To enable the user to undo the effects of your macro, your VBA code module must keep track of what was changed by the macro and then be capable of restoring the original state if the user chooses Edit → Undo.

To enable the Edit → Undo command, use the OnUndo method as the last action in your macro. This method enables you to specify text that will appear on the

Undo menu item and also to specify a procedure to run if the user chooses Edit→ Undo. Here's an example:

```
Application.OnUndo "The Last Macro", "MyUndoMacro"
```

I have a 1-2-3 macro that pauses so the user can enter data into a certain cell. How can I get the same effect in a VBA macro?

Excel can't duplicate that type of behavior, but you can use Excel's InputBox statement to get a value from a user and place it in a particular cell. The first instruction that follows, for example, displays an input box. When the user enters a value, that value is placed in cell A1.

```
UserVal = Application.InputBox(prompt:="Value?", Type:=1)
If TypeName(UserVal)<>"Boolean" Then Range("A1") = UserVal
```

VBA has an InputBox function, but there's also an InputBox method for the Application object. Are these the same?

No. Excel's InputBox method is more versatile because it allows validation of the user's entry. The preceding example uses 1 (which represents a numeric value) for the Type argument of the InputBox method. This ensures that the user enters a value into the input box.

When I use the RGB function to assign a color, the color sometimes isn't correct. What am I doing wrong?

Probably nothing. An Excel workbook can use only 56 different colors (the color palette). If a specified RGB color isn't in the palette, Excel uses the closest match it can find.

I'm trying to write a VBA instruction that creates a formula. To do so, I need to insert a quote character (") within quoted text. How can I do that?

Assume that you want to enter the following formula into cell B1 with VBA:

```
=IF(A1="Yes",TRUE,FALSE)
```

The following instruction generates a syntax error:

```
Range("B1").Formula = "=IF(A1="Yes",TRUE,FALSE)"    'erroneous
```

The solution is to use two double quotes side by side. The following instruction produces the desired result:

```
Range("B1").Formula = "=IF(A1=""Yes"",TRUE,FALSE)"
```

Another approach is to use VBA's Chr function with an argument of 34, which returns a quotation mark. The following example demonstrates:

```
Range("B1").Formula = _
  "=IF(A1=" & Chr(34) & "Yes" & Chr(34) & ",TRUE,FALSE)"
```

I created an array, but the first element in that array is being treated as the second element. What's wrong?

Unless you tell it otherwise, VBA uses 0 as the first index number for an array. If you want all your arrays to always start with 1, insert the following statement at the top of your VBA module:

```
Option Base 1
```

Or you can specify the upper and lower bounds of an array when you declare it. Here's an example:

```
Dim Months(1 To 12) As String
```

I would like my VBA code to run as quickly as possible. Any suggestions?

Here are a few general tips: Make sure that you declare all your variables. Use Option Explicit at the top of your modules to force yourself to do this. If you reference an Excel object more than once, create an object variable for it. Use the With-End With construct whenever possible. If your macro writes information to a worksheet, turn off screen updating by using Application.ScreenUpdating = False. If your application enters data into cells that are referenced by one or more formulas, set the calculation mode to manual to avoid unnecessary calculations.

UserForms

I need to get just a few pieces of information, and a UserForm seems like overkill. Are there any alternatives?

Yes, check out VBA's `MsgBox` function and its `InputBox` function. Alternatively, you might want to use Excel's `InputBox` method.

I have 12 CommandButtons on a UserForm. How can I assign a single macro to be executed when any of the buttons is clicked?

There is no easy way to do this because each CommandButton has its own `Click` event procedure. One solution is to call another procedure from each of the `CommandButton_Click` procedures. Another solution is to use a class module to create a new class. This technique is described in Chapter 15.

How can I display a chart in a UserForm?

There is no direct way to do this. One solution is to write a macro that saves the chart to a GIF file and then loads the GIF file into an `Image` control on the UserForm.

How can I remove the "X" from the title bar of my UserForm? I don't want the user to click that button to close the form.

Removing the Close button on a UserForm's title bar requires some complex API functions. A simpler approach is to intercept all attempts to close the UserForm by using a `UserForm_QueryClose` event procedure in the code module for the UserForm. The following example does not allow the user to close the form by clicking the Close button:

```
Private Sub UserForm_QueryClose _
  (Cancel As Integer, CloseMode As Integer)
    If CloseMode = vbFormControlMenu Then
        MsgBox "You can't close the form like that."
        Cancel = True
    End If
End Sub
```

I've created a UserForm whose controls are linked to cells on the worksheet with the ControlSource property. Is this the best way to do this?

In general, you should avoid using links to worksheet cells unless you absolutely must. Doing so can slow your application down because the worksheet is recalculated every time that a control changes the cell. In addition, if your UserForm has a Cancel button, the cells might have already been changed when the user clicks Cancel.

Can I create a control array for a UserForm? It's possible with Visual Basic, but I can't figure out how to do it with Excel VBA.

You can't create a control array, but you can create an array of Control objects. The following code creates an array consisting of all CommandButton controls:

```
Private Sub UserForm_Initialize()
    Dim Buttons() As CommandButton
    Cnt = 0
    For Each Ctl In UserForm1.Controls
        If TypeName(Ctl) = "CommandButton" Then
            Cnt = Cnt + 1
            ReDim Preserve Buttons(1 To Cnt)
            Set Buttons(Cnt) = Ctl
        End If
    Next Ctl
End Sub
```

Is there any difference between hiding a UserForm and unloading a UserForm?

Yes, the Hide method keeps the UserForm in memory but makes it invisible. The Unload statement unloads the UserForm, beginning the "termination" process (invoking the Terminate event for the UserForm) and removing the UserForm from memory.

How can I make my UserForm stay open while I do other things?

By default, each UserForm is *modal,* which means that it must be dismissed before you can do anything else. Beginning with Excel 2000, however, you can make a

UserForm modeless by writing `vbModeless` as the argument for the `Show` method. Here's an example:

```
UserForm1.Show vbModeless
```

Excel 97 gives me a compile error when I write UserForm1.Show vbModeless. How can I make the form modeless in Excel 2000 and later, while allowing it to remain modal in Excel 97?

Test for the version of Excel that the user is running and then execute a separate procedure if the version is Excel 2000 or later. The following code demonstrates how:

```
Sub ShowUserForm()
    If Val(Application.Version) >= 9 Then
      ShowModelessForm
    Else
      UserForm1.Show
    End If
End Sub

Sub ShowModelessForm()
    Dim frm As Object
    Set frm = UserForm1
    frm.Show 0  ' vbModeless
End Sub
```

Because the `ShowModelessForm` procedure is not executed in Excel 97, it will not cause a compile error.

I need to display a progress indicator like those you see when you're installing software while a lengthy process is being executed. How can I do this?

You can do this with a UserForm. Chapter 15 describes several different techniques, including one where I gradually stretch a shape inside a frame while the lengthy process is running.

How can I use Excel's drawing tools to create simple drawings on my UserForm?

You can't use the drawing tools directly with a UserForm, but you can do so indirectly. Start by creating the drawing on a worksheet. Then select the drawing and choose Edit → Copy. Activate your UserForm and insert an `Image` object. Press F4 to display the Properties window. Select the `Picture` property and press Ctrl+V to paste the Clipboard contents to the `Image` control. You might also need to set the `AutoSize` property to `True`.

How can I generate a list of files and directories into my UserForm so the user can select a file from the list?

There's no need to do that. Use VBA's `GetOpenFilename` method. This displays an Open dialog box in which the user can select a drive, directory, and file.

I need to concatenate strings and display them in a ListBox control. But when I do so, they aren't aligned properly. How can I get them to display equal spacing between strings?

You can use a monospaced font such as Courier New for the ListBox. A better approach, however, is to set up your ListBox to use two columns. (See Chapter 14 for details.)

Is there an easy way to fill a ListBox or ComboBox control with items?

Yes, you can use an array. The statement below adds three items to `ListBox1`.

```
ListBox1.List = Array("Jan", "Feb", "Mar")
```

Can I display a built-in Excel dialog box from VBA?

Most, but not all, of Excel's dialog boxes can be displayed by using the `Application.Dialogs` method. For example, the following instruction displays the dialog box that enables you to format numbers in cells:

```
Application.Dialogs(xlDialogFormatNumber).Show
```

Use the Object Browser to display a list of the constants for the built-in dialog boxes. Press F2 from the VBE, select the `Excel` library, and search for *xlDialog*. You'll probably need to use some trial and error to locate the constant that corresponds to the dialog box that you want to display.

I tried the technique described in the preceding question and received an error message. Why is that?

The Dialogs method will fail if the context isn't appropriate. For example, if you attempt to display the Chart Type dialog box (xlDialogChartType) when a chart is not activated, you'll get an error message.

Every time I create a UserForm, I go through the steps of adding an OK button and a Cancel button. Is there a way to get these controls to appear automatically?

Yes. Set up a UserForm with the controls that you use most often. Then choose File → Export File to save the UserForm. When you want to add a new form to another project, choose File → Import File.

Can I create a UserForm without a title bar?

No. The closest you can get is to make the dialog box's caption blank by setting the Caption property to an empty string.

I recorded a VBA macro that prints to a file. However, there seems to be no way to supply the filename in my code. No matter what I try, I keep getting the prompt to supply a filename.

This common problem was corrected in Excel 2000. In Excel 2000 and later, you can provide a PrToFileName argument for the PrintOut method. Here's an example:

```
ActiveSheet.PrintOut PrintToFile:=True, _
  PrToFileName:="test.prn"
```

When I click a button on my UserForm, nothing happens. What am I doing wrong?

Controls added to a UserForm do nothing unless you write event handler procedures for them. These procedures must be located in the code module for the UserForm, and they must have the correct name.

Can I create a UserForm whose size is always the same, regardless of the video display resolution?

You can, but it's probably not worth the effort. You can write code to determine the video resolution and then make use of the `Zoom` property of a UserForm to change its size. The normal way to deal with this matter is simply to design your UserForm for the lowest resolution that will be used – probably an 800 x 600 display.

Can I create a UserForm box that lets the user select a range in a worksheet by pointing?

Yes. Use the `RefEdit` control for this. See Chapter 14 for an example.

Can I change the startup position of a UserForm?

Yes, you can set the UserForm's `Left` and `Top` properties. But for these to be effective, you need to set the UserForm's `StartUpPosition` property to 0.

Can I add an Excel 5/95 dialog sheet to my workbook?

Yes. Right-click any sheet tab in a workbook and then select Insert from the short-cut menu. In the Insert dialog box, select MS Excel 5.0 Dialog. Be aware that none of the information in this book applies to Excel 5/95 dialog sheets.

Add-Ins

Where can I get Excel add-ins?

You can get Excel add-ins from a number of places:

- ◆ Excel includes several add-ins that you can use whenever you need them. Use the Tools → Add-Ins command to install them.

- ◆ You can download more add-ins from the Microsoft Office Update Web site.

- ◆ Third-party developers distribute and sell add-ins for special purposes.

- ◆ Many developers create free add-ins and distribute them via their Internet sites.

- ◆ You can create your own add-ins.

How do I install an add-in?

You can load an add-in by choosing either the Tools → Add-Ins command or the File → Open command. Using Tools → Add-Ins is the preferred method. An add-in opened with File → Open cannot be closed without using VBA.

When I install my add-in from Excel's Add-Ins dialog box, it shows up without a name or description. How can I give my add-in a description?

Before creating the add-in, use the File → Properties command to bring up the Properties dialog box. Click the Summary tab. In the Title box, enter the text that you want to appear in the Add-Ins dialog box. In the Comments field, enter the description for the add-in. Then create the add-in as usual.

I have several add-ins that I no longer use, yet I can't figure out how to remove them from the Add-Ins Available list in the Add-Ins dialog box. What's the story?

Oddly, there is no way to remove unwanted add-ins from the list directly from Excel. You must edit the Windows Registry and remove the references to the add-in files that you don't want listed. Another way to do this is to move or delete the add-in files. Then when you attempt to open the add-in from the Add-Ins dialog box, Excel will ask whether you want to remove the add-in from the list.

How do I create an add-in?

Activate any worksheet and then choose File → Save As. Then select Microsoft Excel Add-in (*.xla) from the Save as Type drop-down list.

I try to create an add-in, but the Save as Type drop-down box doesn't provide Add-in as an option.

The most likely reason is that the active sheet is not a worksheet.

Should I convert all my essential workbooks to add-ins?

No! Although you *can* create an add-in from any workbook, not all workbooks are suitable. When a workbook is converted to an add-in, it is essentially invisible. For most workbooks, being invisible isn't a good thing.

Do I need to keep two copies of my workbook: the XLS version and the XLA version?

With versions prior to Excel 97, maintaining an XLS and an XLA version was necessary. Beginning with Excel 97, however, this is no longer necessary. An add-in can be converted back to a normal workbook.

How do I modify an add-in after it's been created?

Activate the VBE (press Alt+F11) and then set the `IsAddIn` property of the `ThisWorkbook` object to `False`. Make your changes, set the `IsAddIn` property to `True`, and resave the file.

What's the difference between an XLS file and an XLA file created from an XLS file? Is the XLA version compiled? Does it run faster?

There isn't a great deal of difference between the files, and you generally won't notice any speed differences. VBA code is always compiled before it is executed. This is true whether it's in an XLS file or an XLA file. However, XLA files contain the actual VBA code — not compiled code. Another difference is that the workbook is never visible in an XLA file.

How do I protect the code in my add-in from being viewed by others?

Activate the VBE and choose Tools → *xxxx* Properties (where *xxxx* is the name of your project). Click the Protection tab, select Lock project for viewing, and enter a password.

Are my XLA add-ins safe? In other words, if I distribute an XLA file, can I be assured that no one else will be able to view my code?

Protect your add-in by locking it with a password. This prevents most users from being able to access your code. Recent versions of Excel have improved the security features, but the password still might be broken by using any of a number of utilities. Bottom line? Don't think of an XLA as being a secure file.

CommandBars

Excel 95 had a handy menu editor, but it's missing in Excel 97 and later versions. What gives?

Beginning with Excel 97, the toolbars and menus in Excel are entirely different. Both are called CommandBars. The menu editor is gone, but users can edit CommandBars by using the Customize dialog box (choose Tools → Customize).

Can I edit menus created by Excel 95's menu editor?

Yes, but you need to do so in Excel 95.

When I change a menu with the Customize dialog box, the menu is changed permanently. How can I make the menu change apply to only one workbook?

You'll need to perform your menu changes with VBA code when the workbook is opened, and then restore the menu to normal when the workbook is closed.

I know you can use the FaceId property to add an image to a toolbar control. But how do I figure out which FaceId value goes with a particular image?

Microsoft didn't provide any way to do this, but several utilities exist that make it easy to identify the `FaceId` values. See Chapter 22 for a procedure that you might find helpful.

I attached a new version of my toolbar to a workbook, but Excel continues to use the older version. How do I get it to use the new version of my toolbar?

When Excel opens a workbook that has an attached toolbar, it displays the toolbar only if one with the same name does not already exist on the user's system. The best solution is to write VBA code to create the toolbar on the fly when the workbook is opened and to delete it when the workbook is closed. Alternatively, you can attach the toolbar to the workbook and then write code to delete the toolbar when the workbook is closed.

I've made lots of changes to Excel's toolbars. How can I restore all these toolbars to their original state?

You can use the Customize dialog box and reset each one manually. Or run the following procedure:

```
Sub ResetAllToolbars()
    For Each tb In CommandBars
        If tb.Type = msoBarTypeNormal Then
            If tb.BuiltIn Then tb.Reset
        End If
    Next tb
End Sub
```

Be aware that this procedure will also remove any toolbar customizations performed by add-ins.

Another option is to close Excel and then delete your *.xlb file. Your menus and toolbars will revert to their defaults, and Excel will create a new *.xlb file.

How can I set things up so my custom menu is displayed only when a particular workbook is active?

You need to make use of the WorkbookActivate and WorkbookDeactivate events. In other words, write procedures in the code module for the ThisWorkbook object that hide the custom menu when the workbook is deactivated and unhide the custom menu when the workbook is activated.

How can I add a "spacer" between two buttons on a toolbar?

Set the BeginGroup property of the control after the spacer to True.

How do you display a check mark next to a menu item?

A check mark on a menu item is controlled by the menu item's State property. The following instruction, for example, displays a check mark next to the menu item called My Item:

```
CommandBars(1).Commands("MyMenu"). _
   Commands("My Item").State = msoButtonDown
```

To clear (uncheck) the menu item, set the State property to msoButtonUp.

I accidentally deleted some items from the Worksheet menu and can't get them back. Restarting Excel doesn't fix it.

Choose Tools → Customize, and select the Toolbars tab in the Customize dialog box. Select the Worksheet Menu Bar item, and click the Reset button.

How can I disable all the right-click shortcut menus?

The following procedure will do the job:

```
Sub DisableAllShortcutMenus()
    Dim cb As CommandBar
    For Each cb In CommandBars
        If cb.Type = msoBarTypePopup Then _
           cb.Enabled = False
    Next cb
End Sub
```

Can I disable the toolbar list that appears when the user right-clicks on a toolbar?

Yes, the following instruction will do the job:

```
CommandBars("Toolbar List").Enabled = False
```

Part VIII

Appendixes

Appendix A

Excel Resources Online

If I've done my job, the information provided in this book will be useful to you. It is, however, by no means comprehensive. In addition, new issues tend to crop up, so you'll want to make sure that you're up-to-date. Therefore, I've compiled a list of additional resources that could help you become more proficient in Excel application development. I've classified these resources into three categories:

- ◆ Microsoft technical support
- ◆ Internet newsgroups
- ◆ Internet Web sites

Microsoft Technical Support

Technical support is the common term for assistance provided by a software vendor. In this case, I'm talking about assistance that comes directly from Microsoft. Microsoft's technical support is available in several different forms.

Support options

To find out your support options, choose the Help → About Microsoft Excel command, which displays the About Microsoft Excel dialog box. Then click the Tech Support button. This opens a help file that lists all the support options offered by Microsoft, including both free and fee-based support

My experience is that you should use vendor standard telephone support only as a last resort. Chances are that you'll run up a big phone bill (assuming that you can even get through) and spend lots of time on hold, and you might or might not find an answer to your question.

The truth is that the people who answer the phone are equipped to answer only the most basic questions. And the answers to these basic questions are usually readily available elsewhere.

Microsoft Knowledge Base

Your best bet for solving a problem could be the Microsoft Knowledge Base. This is the primary Microsoft product information source — an extensive, searchable database that consists of tens of thousands of detailed articles containing technical information, bug lists, fix lists, and more.

About the URLs Listed Here

As you know, the Internet is a dynamic entity that tends to change rapidly. Web sites are often reorganized (especially those at the `microsoft.com` domain). Therefore, a particular URL listed in this Appendix might not be available when you try to access it. Each URL was accurate at the time of this writing, but it's possible that a URL could have changed by the time that you read this.

You have free and unlimited access to the Knowledge Base via the Internet. To access the Knowledge Base, use the URL below, and then click the Search the Knowledge Base link.

`http://support.microsoft.com`

Microsoft Excel home page

The official home page of Excel is at

`www.microsoft.com/office/excel/`

Microsoft Office tools on the Web

For information about Office 2003 (including Excel), try this site:

`http://office.microsoft.com`

You'll find product updates, add-ins, examples, and lots of other useful information.

Internet Newsgroups

Usenet is an Internet service that provides access to several thousand special interest groups that enable you to communicate with people who share common interests. There are thousands of newsgroups covering virtually every topic that you can think of (and many that you haven't). Typically, questions posed on a newsgroup are answered within 24 hours — assuming, of course, that the questions are asked in a manner that makes others want to reply.

Besides an Internet connection, you need special newsreader software to access newsgroups. Microsoft Outlook Express (free) is a good choice. This product is part of Internet Explorer.

Spreadsheet newsgroups

The primary Usenet newsgroup for general spreadsheet users is

```
comp.apps.spreadsheets
```

This newsgroup is intended for users of any spreadsheet brand, but about 90 percent of the postings deal with Excel. My advice? Skip this one and head directly for the Microsoft newsgroups.

Microsoft newsgroups

Microsoft has an extensive list of newsgroups, including quite a few devoted to Excel. If your Internet service provider doesn't carry the Microsoft newsgroups, you can access them directly from Microsoft's news server. You'll need to configure your newsreader software or Web browser to access Microsoft's news server, which is at this address:

```
msnews.microsoft.com
```

Table A-1 lists the key newsgroups that you'll find on Microsoft's news server.

TABLE A-1 MICROSOFT.COM'S EXCEL-RELATED NEWSGROUPS

Newsgroup	Topic
microsoft.public.excel.123quattro	Converting 1-2-3 or Quattro Pro sheets into Excel sheets
microsoft.public.excel.charting	Building charts with Excel
microsoft.public.excel.crashesGPFs	Help with General Protection Faults or system failures

Continued

TABLE **A-1** *(Continued)*

Newsgroup	Topic
microsoft.public.excel.interopoledde	Object Linking and Embedding (OLE), Dynamic Data Exchange (DDE), and other cross-application issues
microsoft.public.excel.links	Using links in Excel
microsoft.public.excel.macintosh	Excel issues on the Macintosh operating system
microsoft.public.excel.misc	General topics that do not fit one of the other categories
microsoft.public.excel.newusers	Help for newcomers to Excel
microsoft.public.excel.printing	Printing with Excel
microsoft.public.excel.programming	Programming Excel with VBA or XLM macros
microsoft.public.excel.queryDAO	Using Microsoft Query and Data Access Objects (DAO) in Excel
microsoft.public.excel.sdk	Issues regarding the Excel Software Development Kit
microsoft.public.excel.setup	Setting up and installing Excel
microsoft.public.excel.templates	Spreadsheet Solutions templates and other XLT files
microsoft.public.excel.worksheet.functions	Worksheet functions

Searching newsgroups

Many people don't realize that you can perform a keyword search on past newsgroup postings. Often, this is an excellent alternative to posting a question to the newsgroup because you can get the answer immediately. The best source for searching newsgroup postings is Google, at the following Web address:

http://groups.google.com

A Dozen Tips for Posting to a Newsgroup

1. Make sure that your question has not already been answered. Check the newsgroup's FAQ (if one exists) and also perform a Google search. (See the "Searching newsgroups" section in this Appendix.)

2. Make the subject line descriptive. Postings with a subject line such as "Help me!" and "Another Question" are less likely to be answered than postings with a more specific subject, such as "Sizing a Chart's Plot Area."

3. Specify the spreadsheet product and version that you use. In many cases, the answer to your question depends on your version of Excel.

4. For best results, ask only one question per message, and make your question as specific as possible.

5. Never post advertisements of any kind, even if you think that they're relevant to the group.

6. Keep your question brief and to the point — but provide enough information that someone can answer it adequately.

7. Indicate what you've done to try to answer your own question.

8. Post in the appropriate newsgroup; don't cross-post to other groups unless the question applies to multiple groups.

9. Don't type in all uppercase or all lowercase; check your grammar and spelling.

10. Don't include a file attachment unless it's absolutely necessary. And if it is necessary, make the file as small as possible by removing all extraneous information.

11. Avoid posting in HTML format. Plain text is the preferred format.

12. If you request an e-mail reply in addition to a newsgroup reply, don't use an anti-spam e-mail address that requires the responder to modify your address. (Why cause extra work for someone doing you a favor?)

 Formerly, newsgroup searches were performed at the Deja.com Web site. That site has closed down, and the newsgroup archives were purchased by Google.

How does searching work? Assume that you're having a problem with the ListBox control on a UserForm. You can perform a search using the following keywords:

Excel, ListBox, and UserForm. The Google search engine will probably find dozens of newsgroup postings that deal with these topics. It might take a while to sift through the messages, but there's an excellent chance that you'll find an answer to your question.

Internet Web Sites

The Web has hundreds of sites that deal with Excel. I list a few of my favorites here.

The Spreadsheet Page

This is my own Web site. All humility aside, this is one of best sites on the Web for developer information. It contains files to download, developer tips, instructions for accessing Excel Easter Eggs, an extensive list of links to other spreadsheet sites, information about my books, and even spreadsheet jokes. The URL is

```
http://j-walk.com/ss
```

 This site also contains a list of errors that I've found in each of my books, including the book that you're reading now. (Yes, a few errors have been known to creep into these pages.)

Pearson Software Consulting

This site, maintained by Chip Pearson, contains dozens of useful examples of VBA and clever formula techniques. The URL is

```
www.cpearson.com/excel.htm
```

Stephen Bullen's Excel Page

Stephen's Web site contains some fascinating examples of Excel code, including a section titled "They Said It Couldn't Be Done." The URL is

```
www.bmsltd.co.uk/excel
```

David McRitchie's Excel Pages

David's site is jam-packed with useful Excel information and is updated frequently. The URL is

```
www.mvps.org/dmcritchie/excel/excel.htm
```

Jon Peltier's Excel Page

Those who frequent the `microsoft.public.excel.charting` newsgroup are familiar with Jon Peltier. Jon has an uncanny ability to solve practically any chart-related problem. His Web site contains many Excel tips and an extensive collection of charting examples. The URL is

`www.geocities.com/jonpeltier/Excel/`

Mr. Excel

Mr. Excel (also know as Bill Jelen) has an extensive Web site packed with Excel tips and examples. He even has a discussion board, so you can ask questions and hang out with other Excel users.

`www.mrexcel.com`

Spreadsheet FAQ

Many newsgroups have an *FAQ* — a list of frequently asked questions. The purpose of providing a list of FAQs is to prevent the same questions from being asked over and over. The FAQ for the `comp.apps.spreadsheets` newsgroup is available at

`www.faqs.org/faqs/spreadsheets/faq`

Appendix B

VBA Statements and Functions Reference

This Appendix contains a complete listing of all Visual Basic for Applications (VBA) statements and built-in functions. For details, consult Excel's online help.

 There are no new VBA statements in Excel 2002 or Excel 2003.

TABLE B-1 SUMMARY OF VBA STATEMENTS

Statement	Action
AppActivate	Activates an application window
Beep	Sounds a tone via the computer's speaker
Call	Transfers control to another procedure
ChDir	Changes the current directory
ChDrive	Changes the current drive
Close	Closes a text file
Const	Declares a constant value
Date	Sets the current system date
Declare	Declares a reference to an external procedure in a Dynamic Link Library (DLL)
DefBool	Sets the default data type to Boolean for variables that begin with specified letters

Continued

TABLE B-1 *(Continued)*

Statement	Action
DefByte	Sets the default data type to byte for variables that begin with specified letters
DefCur	Sets the default data type to currency for variables that begin with specified letters
DefDate	Sets the default data type to date for variables that begin with specified letters
DefDec	Sets the default data type to decimal for variables that begin with specified letters
DefDbl	Sets the default data type to double for variables that begin with specified letters
DefInt	Sets the default data type to integer for variables that begin with specified letters
DefLng	Sets the default data type to long for variables that begin with specified letters
DefObj	Sets the default data type to object for variables that begin with specified letters
DefSng	Sets the default data type to single for variables that begin with specified letters
DefStr	Sets the default data type to string for variables that begin with specified letters
DefVar	Sets the default data type to variant for variables that begin with specified letters
DeleteSetting	Deletes a section or key setting from an application's entry in the Windows Registry
Dim	Declares variables and (optionally) their data types
Do-Loop	Loops
End	Used by itself, exits the program; also used to end a block of statements that begin with If, With, Sub, Function, Property, Type, and Select
Enum*	Declares a type for enumeration
Erase	Re-initializes an array

Statement	Action
Error	Simulates a specific error condition
Event*	Declares a user-defined event
Exit Do	Exits a block of Do-Loop code
Exit For	Exits a block of Do-For code
Exit Function	Exits a Function procedure
Exit Property	Exits a property procedure
Exit Sub	Exits a subroutine procedure
FileCopy	Copies a file
For Each-Next	Loops
For-Next	Loops
Function	Declares the name and arguments for a Function procedure
Get	Reads data from a text file
GoSub...Return	Branches
GoTo	Branches
If-Then-Else	Processes statements conditionally
Implements*	Specifies an interface or class that will be implemented in a class module
Input #	Reads data from a sequential text file
Kill	Deletes a file from a disk
Let	Assigns the value of an expression to a variable or property
Line Input #	Reads a line of data from a sequential text file
Load	Loads an object but doesn't show it
Lock...Unlock	Controls access to a text file
Lset	Left-aligns a string within a string variable
Mid	Replaces characters in a string with other characters
MkDir	Creates a new directory
Name	Renames a file or directory

Continued

TABLE B-1 *(Continued)*

Statement	Action
On Error	Branches on an error
On...GoSub	Branches on a condition
On...GoTo	Branches on a condition
Open	Opens a text file
Option Base	Changes default lower limit
Option Compare	Declares the default comparison mode when comparing strings
Option Explicit	Forces declaration of all variables in a module
Option Private	Indicates that an entire module is Private
Print #	Writes data to a sequential file
Private	Declares a local array or variable
Property Get	Declares the name and arguments of a Property Get procedure
Property Let	Declares the name and arguments of a Property Let procedure
Property Set	Declares the name and arguments of a Property Set procedure
Public	Declares a public array or variable
Put	Writes a variable to a text file
RaiseEvent	Fires a user-defined event
Randomize	Initializes the random number generator
ReDim	Changes the dimensions of an array
Rem	Specifies a line of comments (same as an apostrophe ['])
Reset	Closes all open text files
Resume	Resumes execution when an error-handling routine finishes
RmDir	Removes an empty directory
RSet	Right-aligns a string within a string variable
SaveSetting	Saves or creates an application entry in the Windows Registry
Seek	Sets the position for the next access in a text file

Statement	Action
Select Case	Processes statements conditionally
SendKeys	Sends keystrokes to the active window
Set	Assigns an object reference to a variable or property
SetAttr	Changes attribute information for a file
Static	Declares variables at the procedure level, such that the variables retain their value as long as the code is running
Stop	Pauses the program
Sub	Declares the name and arguments of a Sub procedure
Time	Sets the system time
Type	Defines a custom data type
Unload	Removes an object from memory
While...Wend	Loops
Width #	Sets the output line width of a text file
With	Sets a series of properties for an object
Write #	Writes data to a sequential text file

Not available in Excel 97 and earlier editions

Invoking Excel Functions in VBA Instructions

If a VBA function that's equivalent to one you use in Excel is not available, you can use Excel's worksheet functions directly in your VBA code. Just precede the function with a reference to the WorksheetFunction object. For example, VBA does not have a function to convert radians to degrees. Because Excel has a worksheet function for this procedure, you can use a VBA instruction such as the following:

```
Deg = Application.WorksheetFunction.Degrees(3.14)
```

The WorksheetFunction object was introduced in Excel 97. For compatibility with earlier versions of Excel, you can omit the reference to the WorksheetFunction object and write an instruction such as the following:

```
Deg = Application.Degrees(3.14)
```

There are no new VBA functions in Excel 2002 or Excel 2003.

TABLE B-2 SUMMARY OF VBA FUNCTIONS

Function	Action
Abs	Returns the absolute value of a number
Array	Returns a variant containing an array
Asc	Converts the first character of string to its ASCII value
Atn	Returns the arctangent of a number
CallByName*	Executes a method, or sets or returns a property of an object
CBool	Converts an expression to a Boolean data type
CByte	Converts an expression to a byte data type
CCur	Converts an expression to a currency data type
CDate	Converts an expression to a date data type
CDbl	Converts an expression to a double data type
CDec	Converts an expression to a decimal data type
Choose	Selects and returns a value from a list of arguments
Chr	Converts a character code to a string
CInt	Converts an expression to an integer data type
CLng	Converts an expression to a long data type
Cos	Returns the cosine of a number
CreateObject	Creates an Object Linking and Embedding (OLE) Automation object
CSng	Converts an expression to a single data type
CStr	Converts an expression to a string data type
CurDir	Returns the current path
CVar	Converts an expression to a variant data type

Function	Action
CVDate	Converts an expression to a date data type (for compatibility, not recommended)
CVErr	Returns a user-defined error value that corresponds to an error number
Date	Returns the current system date
DateAdd	Adds a time interval to a date
DateDiff	Returns the time interval between two dates
DatePart	Returns a specified part of a date
DateSerial	Converts a date to a serial number
DateValue	Converts a string to a date
Day	Returns the day of the month of a date
DDB	Returns the depreciation of an asset
Dir	Returns the name of a file or directory that matches a pattern
DoEvents	Yields execution so the operating system can process other events
Environ	Returns an operating environment string
EOF	Returns True if the end of a text file has been reached
Err	Returns the error message that corresponds to an error number
Error	Returns the error message that corresponds to an error number
Exp	Returns the base of natural logarithms (e) raised to a power
FileAttr	Returns the file mode for a text file
FileDateTime	Returns the date and time when a file was last modified
FileLen	Returns the number of bytes in a file
Filter	Returns a subset of a string array, filtered
Fix	Returns the integer portion of a number
Format	Displays an expression in a particular format
FormatCurrency*	Returns an expression formatted with the system currency symbol

Continued

TABLE B-2 *(Continued)*

Function	Action
FormatDateTime*	Returns an expression formatted as a date or time
FormatNumber*	Returns an expression formatted as a number
FormatPercent*	Returns an expression formatted as a percentage
FreeFile	Returns the next available file number when working with text files
FV	Returns the future value of an annuity
GetAllSettings	Returns a list of settings and values from the Windows Registry
GetAttr	Returns a code representing a file attribute
GetObject	Retrieves an OLE Automation object from a file
GetSetting	Returns a specific setting from the application's entry in the Windows Registry
Hex	Converts from decimal to hexadecimal
Hour	Returns the hour of a time
IIf	Evaluates an expression and returns one of two parts
Input	Returns characters from a sequential text file
InputBox	Displays a box to prompt a user for input
InStr	Returns the position of a string within another string
InStrRev*	Returns the position of a string within another string, from the end of the string
Int	Returns the integer portion of a number
IPmt	Returns the interest payment for a given period of an annuity
IRR	Returns the internal rate of return for a series of cash flows
IsArray	Returns True if a variable is an array
IsDate	Returns True if a variable is a date
IsEmpty	Returns True if a variable has not been initialized
IsError	Returns True if an expression is an error value
IsMissing	Returns True if an optional argument was not passed to a procedure

Function	Action
IsNull	Returns True if an expression contains a Null value
IsNumeric	Returns True if an expression can be evaluated as a number
IsObject	Returns True if an expression references an OLE Automation object
Join*	Combines strings contained in an array
LBound	Returns the smallest subscript for a dimension of an array
LCase	Returns a string converted to lowercase
Left	Returns a specified number of characters from the left of a string
Len	Returns the number of characters in a string
Loc	Returns the current read or write position of a text file
LOF	Returns the number of bytes in an open text file
Log	Returns the natural logarithm of a number
LTrim	Returns a copy of a string with no leading spaces
Mid	Returns a specified number of characters from a string
Minute	Returns the minute of a time
MIRR	Returns the modified internal rate of return for a series of periodic cash flows
Month	Returns the month of a date
MonthName	Returns the month, as a string
MsgBox	Displays a modal message box
Now	Returns the current system date and time
NPer	Returns the number of periods for an annuity
NPV	Returns the net present value of an investment
Oct	Converts from decimal to octal
Partition	Returns a string representing a range in which a value falls
Pmt	Returns a payment amount for an annuity
Ppmt	Returns the principal payment amount for an annuity

Continued

TABLE **B-2** *(Continued)*

Function	Action
PV	Returns the present value of an annuity
QBColor	Returns a red/green/blue (RGB) color code
Rate	Returns the interest rate per period for an annuity
Replace*	Returns a string in which a substring is replaced with another string
RGB	Returns a number representing an RGB color value
Right	Returns a specified number of characters from the right of a string
Rnd	Returns a random number between 0 and 1
Round	Returns a rounded number
RTrim	Returns a copy of a string with no trailing spaces
Second	Returns the seconds portion of a specified time
Seek	Returns the current position in a text file
Sgn	Returns an integer that indicates the sign of a number
Shell	Runs an executable program
Sin	Returns the sine of a number
SLN	Returns the straight-line depreciation for an asset for a period
Space	Returns a string with a specified number of spaces
Spc	Positions output when printing to a file
Split*	Returns a one-dimensional array containing a number of substrings
Sqr	Returns the square root of a number
Str	Returns a string representation of a number
StrComp	Returns a value indicating the result of a string comparison
StrConv	Returns a converted string
String	Returns a repeating character or string
StrReverse*	Returns a string, reversed

Function	Action
Switch	Evaluates a list of Boolean expressions and returns a value associated with the first True expression
SYD	Returns the sum-of-years' digits depreciation of an asset for a period
Tab	Positions output when printing to a file
Tan	Returns the tangent of a number
Time	Returns the current system time
Timer	Returns the number of seconds since midnight
TimeSerial	Returns the time for a specified hour, minute, and second
TimeValue	Converts a string to a time serial number
Trim	Returns a string without leading spaces and/or trailing spaces
TypeName	Returns a string that describes the data type of a variable
UBound	Returns the largest available subscript for a dimension of an array
UCase	Converts a string to uppercase
Val	Returns the number formed from any initial numeric characters of a string
VarType	Returns a value indicating the subtype of a variable
Weekday	Returns a number indicating a day of the week
WeekdayName*	Returns a string indicating a day of the week
Weekday	Returns a number representing a day of the week
Year	Returns the year of a date

*Not available in Excel 97 and earlier editions

Appendix C

VBA Error Codes

This Appendix contains a complete listing of the error codes for all trappable errors in Visual Basic for Applications (VBA). This information is useful for error trapping. For complete details, consult Excel's online help.

Error Code	Message
3	Return without `GoSub`.
5	Invalid procedure call or argument.
6	Overflow (for example, value too large for an integer).
7	Out of memory. This error rarely refers to the amount of physical memory installed on your system. Rather, it usually refers to a fixed-size area of memory used by Excel or Windows (for example, the area used for graphics or custom formats).
9	Subscript out of range. You will also get this error message if a named item is not found in a collection of objects: For example, if your code refers to `Sheets("Sheet2")`, and `Sheet2` does not exist.
10	This array is fixed or temporarily locked.
11	Division by zero.
13	Type mismatch.
14	Out of string space.
16	Expression too complex.
17	Can't perform requested operation.
18	User interrupt occurred. This error occurs if the user interrupts a macro by pressing the Cancel key.
20	Resume without error. This error probably indicates that you forgot the `Exit Sub` statement before your error handler code.
28	Out of stack space.
35	`Sub` or `Function` not defined.

Continued

Error Code	Message
47	Too many Dynamic Link Library (DLL) application clients.
48	Error in loading DLL.
49	Bad DLL calling convention.
51	Internal error.
52	Bad filename or number.
53	File not found.
54	Bad file mode.
55	File already open.
57	Device Input/Output (I/O) error.
58	File already exists.
59	Bad record length.
61	Disk full.
62	Input past end of file.
63	Bad record number.
67	Too many files.
68	Device unavailable.
70	Permission denied.
71	Disk not ready.
74	Can't rename with different drive.
75	Path/File access error.
76	Path not found.
91	Object variable or `With` block variable not set. This error occurs if you don't use `Set` at the beginning of a statement that creates an object variable. Or, it occurs if you refer to a worksheet object (such as `ActiveCell`) when a chart sheet is active.
92	`For` loop not initialized.
93	Invalid pattern string.
94	Invalid use of `Null`.

Error Code	Message
96	Unable to sink events of object because the object is already firing events to the maximum number of event receivers that it supports.
97	Cannot call friend function on object that is not an instance of defining class.
98	A property or method call cannot include a reference to a private object, either as an argument or as a return value.
321	Invalid file format.
322	Can't create necessary temporary file.
325	Invalid format in resource file.
380	Invalid property value.
381	Invalid property array index.
382	Set not supported at runtime.
383	Set not supported (read-only property).
385	Need property array index.
387	Set not permitted.
393	Get not supported at runtime.
394	Get not supported (write-only property).
422	Property not found.
423	Property or method not found.
424	Object required. This error occurs if text preceding a dot is not recognized as an object.
429	ActiveX component can't create object (might be a registration problem with a library that you've referenced).
430	Class doesn't support Automation or doesn't support expected interface.
432	Filename or class name not found during Automation operation.
438	Object doesn't support this property or method.
440	Automation error.
442	Connection to type library or object library for remote process has been lost. Press OK for dialog box to remove reference.

Continued

Error Code	Message
443	Automation object does not have a default value.
445	Object doesn't support this action.
446	Object doesn't support named arguments.
447	Object doesn't support current locale setting.
448	Named argument not found.
449	Argument not optional.
450	Wrong number of arguments or invalid property assignment.
451	`Property Let` procedure not defined, and `Property Get` procedure did not return an object.
452	Invalid ordinal.
453	Specified DLL function not found.
454	Code resource not found.
455	Code resource lock error.
457	Key is already associated with an element of this collection.
458	Variable uses an Automation type not supported in Visual Basic.
459	Object or class does not support the set of events.
460	Invalid Clipboard format.
461	Method or data member not found.
462	Remote server machine doesn't exist or is unavailable.
463	Class not registered on local machine.
481	Invalid picture.
482	Printer error.
735	Can't save file to TEMP.
744	Search text not found.
746	Replacements too long.
1004	Application-defined or object-defined error. This is a very common catch-all error message. This error occurs when an error doesn't correspond to an error defined by VBA. In other words, the error is defined by Excel (or some other object) and is propagated back to VBA.

Appendix D

What's on the CD-ROM

THIS APPENDIX PROVIDES YOU with information on the contents of the CD that accompanies this book. For the latest and greatest information, please refer to the ReadMe file located at the root of the CD. Here is what you will find:

◆ System requirements

◆ Using the CD with Windows

◆ What's on the CD

◆ Troubleshooting

System Requirements

Make sure that your computer meets the minimum system requirements listed in this section. If your computer doesn't match up to most of these requirements, you could have a problem using the contents of the CD.

For Windows 9.x, Windows 2000, Windows NT4 (with SP 4 or later), Windows Me, or Windows XP:

◆ PC with a Pentium processor running at 120 MHz or faster.

◆ At least 32 MB of total RAM installed on your computer. For best performance, I recommend at least 64MB.

◆ A CD-ROM drive.

Using the CD with Windows

To install the items from the CD to your hard drive, follow these steps:

1. Insert the CD into your computer's CD-ROM drive.

2. A window appears with the following options:

    Install: Gives you the option to install the supplied software and/or the author-created samples on the CD-ROM

Explore: Enables you to view the contents of the CD-ROM in its directory structure

eBook: Enables you to view an electronic version of the book

Exit: Closes the autorun window

If you don't have autorun enabled or if the autorun window doesn't appear, follow these steps to access the CD:

1. Choose Start → Run.

2. In the dialog box that appears, type *d*:\setup.exe, where *d* is the letter of your CD-ROM drive. This brings up the autorun window described in the preceding set of steps.

3. Choose the desired option from the menu. (See Step 2 in the preceding list for a description of these options.)

What's on the CD

The following sections provide a summary of the software and other materials that you'll find on the CD.

Author-created materials

All author-created material from the book, including code listings and samples, are on the CD in the Author folder.

Each chapter of this book that contains example workbooks has its own subdirectory on the CD-ROM. For example, the example files for Chapter 3 are found in the following directory:

```
Author\chap03\
```

Following is a list of the chapter examples, with a brief description of each.

◆ **Chapter 3**

`array examples.xls`: Examples of array formulas.

`count and sum.xls`: Examples of formulas for counting and summing.

`megaformula-1.xls`: The "remove middle name" formula example that uses intermediate formulas.

`megaformula-2.xls`: The "remove middle name" formula example that uses a megaformula.

`megaformula-3.xls`: The "remove middle name" formula example that uses a custom VBA function.

`named formulas.xls`: Examples that use named formulas.

`xdate.exe`: The author's Extended Date Functions add-in for working with dates prior to 1900.

`xdate.txt`: Instructions for installing the Extended Date Functions add-in.

◆ **Chapter 4**

`\amortization`: This subdirectory contains the files used in the loan amortization example.

`employee list.xml`: A simple eXtensible Markup Language (XML) file that contains employee data.

`message.xml`: A simple XML file that contains data for an e-mail message.

◆ **Chapter 6**

`controls on sheet.xls`: A file that uses controls on a worksheet.

◆ **Chapter 7**

`comment object.xls`: Examples of VBA code that manipulates `Comment` objects.

`hello world.xls`: A simple VBA example that says hello to you.

◆ **Chapter 8**

`timing test.xls`: A VBA procedure to demonstrate execution time differences for `Variant` data types.

◆ **Chapter 9**

`sheet sorter.xls`: The sheet-sorting application.

◆ **Chapter 10**

`commission.xls`: Contains various versions of the `Commission` function used to calculate a sales commission.

`draw.xls`: Contains the `Draw` function, which randomly chooses one cell from a range.

`key press.xls`: Demonstrates how to use an Application Programming Interface (API) function to determine whether the Shift, Ctrl, or Alt key is pressed.

`month names.xls`: Demonstrates the `MonthNames` function, which returns an array.

`mysum.xls`: Demonstrates the `MySum` function, which emulates Excel's SUM function.

`reverse.xls`: Demonstrates the `Reverse` function, which returns an error value if its argument is not a string.

`uppercase.xls`: Contains the `UpCase` function that emulates Excel's UPPER function.

`win32api.txt`: Contains Windows API declarations and constants.

`windows directory.xls`: Demonstrates the `ShowWindowsDir` function, which uses an API function to display the Windows directory name.

◆ **Chapter 11**

`about selection.xls`: Contains a procedure that describes the current range selection.

`auto average.xls`: Demonstrates how to insert an AVERAGE function in a manner similar to the Excel AutoSum feature. When this workbook is open, you have access to a new menu command: Tools → Enter Average Formula.

`batch processing.xls`: Demonstrates how to process a series of files. The example uses three additional files: `text01.txt`, `text02.txt`, and `text03.txt`.

`cell type.xls`: Uses the `CellType` function to determine the type of data in a cell.

`date and time.xls`: Contains a procedure that displays the current date and time.

`delete empty rows.xls`: Contains a procedure that deletes all empty rows in a worksheet.

`disk info.xls`: Demonstrates various API functions that return information about disk drives.

`extract element.xls`: Demonstrates the `ExtractElement` function.

`file association.xls`: Demonstrates an API function that returns the full path to the application associated with a particular file.

`fill range.xls`: Contains two procedures that demonstrate how to fill a range with data from an array.

`find by format.xls`: Contains a procedure that selects cells based on formatting.

`in range.xls`: Contains a function that returns `True` if a range is contained inside another range.

inputbox.xls: Contains examples using VBA's InputBox function to prompt for a value.

last saved and printed.xls: Contains the LastSaved and LastPrinted functions, which access a workbook's built-in document properties.

list fonts.xls: Creates a list of all installed fonts.

max all sheets.xls: Contains the MaxAllSheets function, which returns the maximum value across all worksheets in a workbook.

next empty cell.xls: Demonstrates how to insert data into the next empty cell of a worksheet.

page count.xls: Contains a procedure that counts the number of pages to be printed.

play sound.xls: Contains the Alarm function, which plays a sound when a cell meets a certain condition. Uses the sound.wav file.

printer info.xls: Demonstrates an API function that returns information about the default printer.

random functions.xls: Contains the RandomIntegers function (which returns an array of nonduplicated random integers) and the RangeRandomize function (which randomizes a range).

range selections.xls: Demonstrates several common types of range selections relative to the active cell. After opening this file, use the Selection Demo menu.

registry.xls: Demonstrates API functions that enable you to read from and write to the Windows Registry.

select max.xls: Contains a procedure that selects the cell that contains the maximum value.

selective color.xls: Contains a procedure that colors cells based on their contents.

sheet offset.xls: Demonstrates two versions of the SheetOffset function.

sorting demo.xls: Demonstrates three VBA array-sorting procedures.

sound.wav: A sound file used by sound.xls.

sound.xls: Demonstrates API functions that play sound files.

stat functions.xls: Demonstrates the StatFunction function.

synchronize sheets.xls: Contains a procedure that synchronizes worksheets.

`TEXT01.TXT`: Used by the `batch processing.xls` workbook.

`TEXT02.TXT`: Used by the `batch processing.xls` workbook.

`TEXT03.TXT`: Used by the `batch processing.xls` workbook.

`toggles.xls`: Contains procedures that toggle various settings.

`utility functions.xls`: Contains the following functions: `FileExists`, `FileNameOnly`, `PathExists`, `RangeNameExists`, `SheetExists`, and `WorkbookIsOpen`.

`variant transfer.xls`: Demonstrates how to transfer a range of cells to a variant array and transfer a variant array to a range of cells.

`video mode.xls`: Demonstrates an API function that returns the current video resolution.

`worksheet functions.xls`: Contains the following worksheet functions: `SheetName`, `WorkbookName`, `AppName`, `CountBetween`, `LastInColumn`, `LastInRow`, and `IsLike`.

`write and read range.xls`: Contains procedures that write data to a range and read data from a range.

◆ Chapter 12

`erase a range.xls`: Demonstrates how to use an `InputBox` to specify a range to erase.

`get a filename.xls`: Demonstrates how to use the `GetOpenFilename` method.

`get directory.xls`: Demonstrates API functions that display a dialog box that enables the user to select a directory.

`get user name.xls`: Demonstrates how to use an `InputBox` to get a user's name.

◆ Chapter 13

`controls on sheet.xls`: An example of using controls (from the Control Toolbox toolbar) on a worksheet.

`controls on sheet2.xls`: Another example that demonstrates using controls on worksheets.

`get name and sex.xls`: The end result of the hands-on example described in Chapter 13.

`newcontrols.pag`: Contains customized controls for your Toolbox. To import this file as a new page, right-click a Toolbox tab and select Import Page.

`spinbutton events.xls`: Demonstrates the sequence of events pertaining to `SpinButton` controls.

`spinbutton textbox.xls`: Demonstrates how to pair a `SpinButton` control with a `TextBox` control.

`userform events.xls`: Demonstrates the sequence of events pertaining to UserForms.

◆ **Chapter 14**

`change size.xls`: Demonstrates a UserForm that changes sizes.

`fill listbox.xls`: Demonstrates two ways to add items to a `ListBox` control.

`listbox activate sheet.xls`: Demonstrates how to display a list of sheet names in a `ListBox` control.

`listbox item transfer.xls`: Demonstrates how to let the user transfer items between two `ListBox` controls.

`listbox move items.xls`: Demonstrates how to enable the user to move items up and down within a `ListBox` control.

`listbox select rows.xls`: Demonstrates how to use a multicolumn `ListBox` control to enable the user to select rows in a worksheet.

`multicolumn listbox1.xls`: Demonstrates how to create a multicolumn `ListBox` control using data stored in a worksheet.

`multicolumn listbox2.xls`: Demonstrates how to create a multicolumn `ListBox` control using data stored in an array.

`multiple lists.xls`: Demonstrates how to display multiple lists in a single `ListBox` control.

`queryclose.xls`: Demonstrates a technique that ensures that the user can't close a UserForm by clicking its Close button.

`refedit.xls`: Demonstrates the `RefEdit` control.

`selected items.xls`: Demonstrates how to identify selected items in a `ListBox` control.

`splash.xls`: Demonstrates a splash screen that is displayed when the workbook is opened.

`unique1.xls`: Demonstrates how to fill a `ListBox` control with nonduplicated items.

`unique2.xls`: Demonstrates how to fill a `ListBox` control with nonduplicated items.

`userform menus.xls`: Demonstrates two simple menu systems using `CommandButton` controls and a `ListBox` control.

`zoom and scroll sheets.xls`: Demonstrates how to use dialog box controls to zoom and scroll a worksheet.

`zoom.xls`: Demonstrates the use of the `Zoom` property to zoom a dialog box.

◆ **Chapter 15**

`\dataform`: This subdirectory contains the files for the J-Walk Enhanced DataForm add-in. The VB project for this add-in is protected.

`chart in userform.xls`: Demonstrates how to display a chart on a UserForm.

`color picker.xls`: Demonstrates a function that enables the user to select a color from a dialog box.

`modeless userform.xls`: Demonstrates a modeless UserForm that displays information about the active cell.

`modeless userform2.xls`: Demonstrates a more sophisticated modeless UserForm that displays information about the active cell.

`multiple buttons.xls`: Demonstrates how to use a single event handler procedure for multiple controls.

`my msgbox.xls`: Contains the `MyMsgBox` function, which emulates the VBA `MsgBox` function.

`owc chart - advanced.xls`: Creates a chart in a UserForm, using the Office Web Components.

`owc chart - simple.xls`: Creates a chart in a UserForm, using the Office Web Components.

`owc spreadsheet.xls`: Demonstrates the Office Web Components Spreadsheet control.

`progress-1.xls`: Demonstrates how to display a progress indicator while a macro is running. (The progress indicator is not initiated by a UserForm.)

`progress-2.xls`: Demonstrates another way to display a progress indicator while a macro is running. (The progress indicator is initiated by a UserForm.)

`progress-3.xls`: Demonstrates another way to display a progress indicator while a macro is running. (The progress indicator is initiated by a UserForm.)

`wizard.xls`: Demonstrates how to create a multistep wizard.

◆ **Chapter 16**

\helpsource: This directory contains the HyperText Markup Language (HTML) Help source files for the Text Tools add-in.

text tools.xla: The text manipulation utility (unprotected add-in).

text tools.chm: The compiled help file for the text manipulation utility.

undo.xls: Demonstrates one way to undo the effects of a VBA procedure.

◆ **Chapter 17**

budget.mdb: An Access file with budgeting data (used by external db.xls).

budget.xls: Demonstrates how to create a pivot table from a worksheet database with VBA.

external db.xls: Demonstrates how to create a pivot table from an external database table with VBA. This workbook uses the budget.mdb database file.

modify pivot.xls: Demonstrates how to write VBA code to modify a pivot table.

simple db.xls: A very simple worksheet database, used to demonstrate how to create a pivot table. Contains a recorded macro, plus a "cleaned-up" version of the macro.

survey data.xls: Demonstrates how to create multiple pivot tables to analyze survey data.

◆ **Chapter 18**

animated chart.xls: Animated chart example.

autofilter chart.xls: Demonstrates the use of AutoFiltering with a chart.

chart active cell.xls: Demonstrates how to change a chart's data series based on the active cell.

chart formatting.xls: Demonstrates how to format a chart using a macro.

chart image map.xls: Demonstrates how to create a chart that serves as a type of image map.

chart in userform.xls: Demonstrates how to create a chart on-the-fly and display it in a UserForm.

climate data.xls: An interactive chart that uses no macros.

clock chart.xls: An example of a chart formatted to look like an analog clock.

`combobox chart.xls`: Demonstrates how to use a `ComboBox` control to change a chart's data series.

`convert chart to picture.xls`: Demonstrates how to convert a chart to a picture.

`create chart from array.xls`: Demonstrates how to create a chart using data stored in a VBA array.

`create chart.xls`: Contains a recorded macro to create a chart, plus a "cleaned-up" version of the macro.

`dailysales.xls`: Demonstrates how to create a self-expanding chart.

`data labels.xls`: Demonstrates how to use a range for data labels in a chart.

`events - chart sheet.xls`: Demonstrates chart events, with a chart sheet.

`events - embedded.xls`: Demonstrates chart events, with an embedded chart.

`get chart range.xls`: Contains a custom function that returns a `Range` object that represents the data used in a chart.

`hypocycloid - animated.xls`: Contains a chart that plots hypocycloid curves, animated and in color.

`hypocycloid.xls`: Contains a chart that plots hypocycloid curves.

`mouseover event - chart sheet.xls`: Demonstrates how to display text about the chart data (in a chart sheet) under the mouse pointer.

`mouseover event - embedded.xls`: Demonstrates how to display text about the chart data (in an embedded chart) under the mouse pointer.

`multiple charts.xls`: Demonstrates how to display multiple charts on a single chart sheet.

`print embedded charts.xls`: Demonstrates how to print embedded charts on a full sheet of paper.

`size and align charts.xls`: Demonstrates how to size and align a group of charts.

◆ **Chapter 19**

`application events.xls`: Demonstrates how to monitor application-level events (requires Excel 2000 or later version).

`log workbook open.xls`: Demonstrates how to keep track of every workbook that is opened by storing information in a text file.

`make formulas bold.xls`: Demonstrates monitoring cell changes to make each formula cell bold.

`onkey demo.xls`: Demonstrates the use of the `OnKey` method to remap keyboard keys.

`selection change.xls`: Demonstrates monitoring the worksheet selection `Change` event to highlight the active row and column.

`track changes in comment.xls`: Demonstrates a procedure that uses comments to track changes made to cells.

`validate entry1.xls`: Demonstrates how to validate data entered into a cell; uses the `EnableEvents` property.

`validate entry2.xls`: Demonstrates how to validate data entered into a cell; does not use the `EnableEvents` property.

◆ **Chapter 20**

`automate Excel.doc`: A Microsoft Word file that contains a procedure to automate Excel. It uses the `projections.xls` workbook file.

`budget.mdb`: An Access database file, used by the `simple ado example.xls` file.

`control panel dialogs.xls`: Demonstrates how to display any of 50 system dialog boxes.

`make memos.xls`: Demonstrates automation of Microsoft Word to generate memos using data stored in a worksheet.

`personalized email- OE sendkeys.xls`: Demonstrates how to send personalized e-mail from Excel by using Outlook Express and `Sendkeys`.

`personalized email- outlook.xls`: Demonstrates how to send personalized e-mail from Excel by using Outlook.

`projections.xls`: Used in the `automate Excel.doc` example.

`simple ado example.xls`: Demonstrates how to retrieve data from a Microsoft Access file (uses `budget.mdb`).

`start calculator.xls`: Demonstrates how to execute (or activate) the Windows Calculator program.

`start charmap.xls`: Demonstrates two ways to execute the Windows Character Map program.

◆ **Chapter 21**

`is addin installed.xls`: Contains code that determines whether an add-in is properly installed.

`text tools.xls`: The text manipulation utility described in Chapter 16.

◆ **Chapter 22**

`autosense.xls`: Contains a procedure that creates an "autosense" toolbar that is displayed only when the active cell is in a particular range.

`button styles.xls`: Shows the various ways that a CommandBarButton can be displayed.

`hide and restore.xls`: Contains procedures that hide and then later restore toolbars.

`list all controls.xls`: Contains a procedure that displays the `Caption` property for each control on every toolbar.

`list commandbars.xls`: Contains a procedure that lists each CommandBar's name, index number, and type.

`month list.xls`: Demonstrates the use of a drop-down list control on a CommandBar.

`number format toolbar.xls`: Creates a toolbar button that displays the number format string for the active cell.

`show face ids.xls`: Creates a toolbar that makes it easy to determine the `FaceID` properties.

◆ **Chapter 23**

`add new menu.xls`: Contains a procedure that adds a new menu with menu items.

`add to Tools menu.xls`: Contains a procedure that adds a new menu item to the Tools menu on the Worksheet Menu Bar.

`hide menu.xls`: Demonstrates how to display a menu only when a particular workbook is active.

`list menu info.xls`: Contains a procedure that displays the caption for each item (menu, menu item, and submenu item) on the Worksheet Menu Bar.

`list shortcut menus.xls`: Contains a procedure that lists all shortcut menus.

`menu maker.xls`: Demonstrates an easy way to create a menu with information contained in a worksheet.

`new menubar.xls`: Demonstrates how to replace the Excel menu bar with one of your own.

`new shortcut menu.xls`: Contains a procedure that creates a new shortcut menu.

`shortcut key.xls`: Contains a procedure that adds new menu items with a shortcut key.

`toggle gridlines.xls`: Demonstrates how to display a toggle menu with a check mark.

◆ **Chapter 24**

`\assistant`: Files in this subdirectory demonstrate how to display help by using the Office Assistant.

`\comments`: Files in this subdirectory demonstrate how to display help by using cell comments.

`\function`: Files in this subdirectory demonstrate how to display help for custom functions.

`\htmlhelp`: Files in this subdirectory demonstrate a simple HTML Help system (includes the source files).

`\other`: Files in this subdirectory demonstrate other ways to display help: with the Help method, from a message box, and from an input box.

`\textbox`: Files in this subdirectory demonstrate how to display help by using a `TextBox` control on a worksheet.

`\userform controls help`: Files in this subdirectory demonstrate how to display help for controls on a UserForm.

`\userform1`: Files in this subdirectory demonstrate how to display help by using `Label` controls in a UserForm.

`\userform2`: Files in this subdirectory demonstrate how to display help by using a scrolling `Label` control in a UserForm.

`\userform3`: Files in this subdirectory demonstrate how to display help by using a `DropDown` control and a `Label` control in a UserForm.

`\worksheet`: Files in this subdirectory demonstrate how to display help by activating a worksheet.

Note: Some of the examples in Chapter 24 use multiple files, and many use the same filename. Therefore, each example is contained in a separate subdirectory.

◆ **Chapter 25**

`loan amortization wizard.xla`: An add-in wizard that creates an amortization schedule for a fixed-rate loan. This add-in is not protected. When the add-in is installed, access the wizard from the Tools menu.

◆ **Chapter 26**

`multilingual wizard.xls`: A simple wizard that lets the user choose from three languages.

◆ **Chapter 27**

`does file exist.xls`: Contains code to check for the existence of a file, using three different techniques.

`does path exist.xls`: Contains code to check for the existence of a path, using two different techniques.

`export import.xls`: Contains procedures to export a range to a Comma-Separated Value (CSV) file and to import a CSV file at the active cell position.

`export to HTML.xls`: Contains code to export a range of cells to an HTML file.

`export to XML.xls`: Contains code export a range of cells to a simple XML file.

`filter text file.xls`: Contains a procedure that reads a text file (`infile.txt`) and copies only the rows that contain a specific text string to a second text file (`output.txt`).

`import more than 256.xls`: Contains a procedure that reads a text file and stores the data in Sheet1. If the line contains more than 256 columns of data, the additional data is stored in additional sheets. Uses `longfile.txt`, which has 600 columns of data.

`infile.txt`: A text file used by the `filter txt file.xls` example.

`list files1.xls`: Contains a procedure that displays a list of files contained in a particular directory, along with the file size and date.

`list files2.xls`: Contains a procedure that displays a list of files contained in a particular directory, along with the file size and date; uses the `FileSearch` object.

`longfile.txt`: A text file used by the `import more than 256.xls` example.

`show drive info.xls`: Contains a procedure that uses the `FileSystemObject` to retrieve and display various information about all disk drives.

◆ **Chapter 28**

`add 100 buttons.xls`: Contains a procedure that adds 100 CommandButtons and that creates an event handler procedure for each.

`add button and code.xls`: Contains a procedure that adds a CommandButton and a VBA procedure.

`add controls.xls`: Demonstrates how to add controls to a UserForm at design time and at runtime.

add userform.xls: Contains a procedure that creates a UserForm on-the-fly.

options form.xls: Contains a function that creates a UserForm (with OptionButtons) on-the-fly and that returns an integer corresponding to the user's choice.

replace module.xls: Contains a procedure that replaces a module with another module. This example uses the UserBook.xls file.

show components.xls: Contains a procedure that displays information about each Visual Basic (VB) component in the active workbook.

UserBook.xls: Used by the replace module.xls example.

◆ **Chapter 29**

csvclass.xls: Contains a class module that makes it easy to import and export a CSV file.

keyboard.xls: Contains a class module that defines a NumLock, a CapsLock, and a ScrollLock class.

Applications

Power Utility Pak is a collection of Excel add-ins that I developed. The companion CD-ROM contains a copy of the trial version of this product. The trial version can be used for 30 days.

REGISTERING POWER UTILITY PAK
The normal registration fee for Power Utility Pak is $39.95. You can use the coupon in this book, however, to get a free copy of the latest version of Power Utility Pak (you pay shipping and handling only). In addition, you can purchase the complete VBA source code for only $20.

INSTALLING THE TRIAL VERSION
To install the trial version of Power Utility Pak, follow these steps:

1. Make sure that Excel is not running.

2. Locate the PUP5.EXE file on the CD-ROM. This file is located in the PUP\ directory.

3. Double-click PUP5.EXE. This expands the files to a directory that you specify on your hard drive.

4. Start Excel.

5. Choose Tools → Add-Ins and click the Browse button. Locate the PUP5.XLA file in the directory that you specify in Step 3.

6. Make sure that Power Utility Pak v5 is checked in the add-ins list.

7. Click OK to close the Add-Ins dialog box.

After you install Power Utility Pak, it will be available whenever you start Excel, and Excel will have a new menu: PUP v5. Access Power Utility Pak features from the PUP v5menu or choose the Create a PUP toolbar command to generate a toolbar.

Power Utility Pak includes extensive help. Choose PUP v5→Help to view the Help file.

UNINSTALLING POWER UTILITY PAK

If you decide that you don't want Power Utility Pak, follow these instructions to remove it from Excel's list of add-ins:

1. In Excel, choose Tools→Add-Ins.

2. In the Add-Ins dialog box, remove the check mark from Power Utility Pak v5.

3. Click OK to close the Add-Ins dialog box.

To remove Power Utility Pak from your system after you've followed the preceding steps to uninstall it from Excel, delete the directory into which you originally installed it.

Shareware programs are fully functional, trial versions of copyrighted programs. If you like particular programs, register with their authors for a nominal fee and receive licenses, enhanced versions, and technical support. *Freeware programs* are copyrighted games, applications, and utilities that are free for personal use. Unlike shareware, these programs do not require a fee or provide technical support. *GNU software* is governed by its own license, which is included inside the folder of the GNU product. See the GNU license for more details.

Trial, demo, or evaluation versions are usually limited either by time or functionality (such as being unable to save projects). Some trial versions are very sensitive to system date changes. If you alter your computer's date, the programs will "time out" and will no longer be functional.

eBook version of Excel 2003 Power Programming with VBA

The complete (and searchable) text of this book is on the CD-ROM in the Adobe Portable Document Format (PDF), readable with the Adobe Acrobat Reader (also included). (For more information on Adobe Acrobat Reader, go to www.adobe.com.) To install and run Adobe Acrobat Reader, follow these steps:

1. Start Windows Explorer or Windows NT Explorer and then open the Acrobat folder on the CD-ROM.

2. In the Reader folder, double-click the EXE file and follow the instructions presented onscreen for installing Adobe Acrobat Reader.

Troubleshooting

If you have difficulty installing or using any of the materials on the companion CD, try the following solutions:

◆ **Turn off any antivirus software that you might have running.** Installers sometimes mimic virus activity and can make your computer incorrectly believe that it is being infected by a virus. (Be sure to turn the antivirus software back on later.)

◆ **Close all running programs.** The more programs you're running, the less memory is available to other programs. Installers also typically update files and programs; if you keep other programs running, installation might not work properly.

◆ **Reference the ReadMe:** Please refer to the ReadMe file located at the root of the CD-ROM for the latest product information at the time of publication.

If you still have trouble with the CD-ROM, please call the Wiley Product Technical Support phone number: 1 (800) 762-2974. Outside the United States, call 1 (317) 572-3994. You can also contact Wiley Product Technical Support at www.wiley.com/techsupport. Wiley Publishing will provide technical support only for installation and other general quality control items; for technical support on the applications themselves, consult the program's vendor or author.

To place additional orders or to request information about other Wiley products, please call 1 (800) 225-5945.

Index

Symbols and Numerics

continued

continued

continued

continued

continued

continued

continued

continued

continued

continued

continued

continued

continued

Yours Free!

Power Utility Pak v5

"The Excel tools Microsoft forgot"

A $39.95 value: Yours for only $9.95.

PRO-QUALITY TOOLS

The PUP v5 add-in is a dynamite collection of 60 general-purpose Excel utilities, plus 50 new worksheet functions. Install the trial version from the companion CD-ROM. If you like it, use this coupon to receive a free copy of the licensed version.

VBA SOURCE CODE IS AVAILABLE

You can also get the complete VBA source files for only $20.00. Learn how the utilities and functions were written and pick up useful tips and programming techniques in the process. This is a must for all VBA programmers!

YES! Please send Power Utility Pak v5 to...

Name: _____

Company: _____

Address: _____

City: _____ State: _____ ZIP: _____

Daytime Phone: _____ E-mail: _____

Check one:
- ❏ PUP v5 Licensed Version (Free, $6.00 s/h) . ...$ 6.00
- ❏ Developer's Pak: Licensed Version (Free, $6.00 s/h) + VBA Source ($20.00) $26.00

Delivery method (check one):
- ❏ Send me the disk
- ❏ Send download instructions to my e-mail address (shipping/handling fee still applies)

Credit Card No: _____ Expires:_____

Make check or money order (U.S. funds only) payable to

JWalk & Associates Inc.
P.O. Box 12861
La Jolla, CA 92039-2861

Before mailing this coupon, please check the Web site
below to verify the address (it may have changed)

`http://j-walk.com/ss/`

Wiley Publishing, Inc.
End-User License Agreement

READ THIS. You should carefully read these terms and conditions before opening the software packet(s) included with this book "Book". This is a license agreement "Agreement" between you and Wiley Publishing, Inc. "WPI". By opening the accompanying software packet(s), you acknowledge that you have read and accept the following terms and conditions. If you do not agree and do not want to be bound by such terms and conditions, promptly return the Book and the unopened software packet(s) to the place you obtained them for a full refund.

2. **License Grant**. WPI grants to you (either an individual or entity) a nonexclusive license to use one copy of the enclosed software program(s) (collectively, the "Software") solely for your own personal or business purposes on a single computer (whether a standard computer or a workstation component of a multi-user network). The Software is in use on a computer when it is loaded into temporary memory (RAM) or installed into permanent memory (hard disk, CD-ROM, or other storage device). WPI reserves all rights not expressly granted herein.

2. **Ownership**. Ownership. WPI is the owner of all right, title, and interest, including copyright, in and to the compilation of the Software recorded on the disk(s) or CD-ROM "Software Media". Copyright to the individual programs recorded on the Software Media is owned by the author or other authorized copyright owner of each program. Ownership of the Software and all proprietary rights relating thereto remain with WPI and its licensers.

3. **Restrictions on Use and Transfer.**

   (a) You may only (i) make one copy of the Software for backup or archival purposes, or (ii) transfer the Software to a single hard disk, provided that you keep the original for backup or archival purposes. You may not (i) rent or lease the Software, (ii) copy or reproduce the Software through a LAN or other network system or through any computer subscriber system or bulletin-board system, or (iii) modify, adapt, or create derivative works based on the Software.

   (b) You may not reverse engineer, decompile, or disassemble the Software. You may transfer the Software and user documentation on a permanent basis, provided that the transferee agrees to accept the terms and conditions of this Agreement and you retain no copies. If the Software is an update or has been updated, any transfer must include the most recent update and all prior versions.

4. **Restrictions on Use of Individual Programs**. You must follow the individual requirements and restrictions detailed for each individual program in the About the CD-ROM appendix of this Book. These limitations are also contained in the individual license agreements recorded on the Software Media. These limitations may include a requirement that after using the program for a specified period of time, the user must pay a registration fee or discontinue use. By opening the Software packet(s), you will be agreeing to abide by the licenses and restrictions for these individual programs that are detailed in the About the CD-ROM appendix and on the Software Media. None of the material on this Software Media or listed in this Book may ever be redistributed, in original or modified form, for commercial purposes.